jumping

JavaScript™

THE SUNSOFT PRESS

JAVA SERIES

- ***Core Java 1.1*** ***Volume 1: Fundamentals***
  Cay S. Horstmann & Gary Cornell

- ***Graphic Java 1.1,*** ***Second Edition***
  David M. Geary

- ***Inside Java WorkShop***
  Lynn Weaver & Bob Jervis

- ***Instant Java,*** ***Second Edition***
  John A. Pew

- ***Java by Example,*** ***Second Edition***
  Jerry R. Jackson & Alan L. McClellan

- ***Jumping JavaScript***
  Janice Winsor & Brian Freeman

- ***Just Java,*** ***Second Edition***
  Peter van der Linden

- ***Not Just Java***
  Peter van der Linden

jumping JavaScript™

Janice Winsor • Brian Freeman

Sun Microsystems Press
A Prentice Hall Title

The publisher offers discounts on this book when ordered in bulk quantities.
For more information, contact Corporate Sales Department, Prentice Hall PTR,
One Lake Street, Upper Saddle River, NJ 07458. Phone: 800-382-3419; FAX: 201- 236-7141.
E-mail: corpsales@prenhall.com.

Editorial/production supervision: *Eileen Clark*
Cover design director: *Jerry Votta*
Cover designer: *Anthony Gemmellaro*
Cover illustration: *Karen Strelecki*
Manufacturing manager: *Alexis R. Heydt*
Marketing manager: *Stephen Solomon*
Acquisitions editor: *Gregory G. Doench*
Sun Microsystems Press publisher: *Rachel Borden*

10 9 8 7 6 5 4 3 2 1

ISBN 0-13-841941-8

Sun Microsystems Press
A Prentice Hall Title

Contents at a Glance

Part 2 Creating HTML Pages, 85

Part 3 Navigating on the Web, 425

Part 4 Getting User Input, 523

Part 5 Controlling Your Scripts, 761

Part 6 Using System Objects, 793

ix

Contents

Chapter 3
Introducing General Scripting Concepts, 39

Chapter 4
Debugging Scripts, 57

XV

xvii

xix

xxi

Preface

This book is your comprehensive guide to client-side JavaScript™ as implemented in Netscape® Navigator™ 3.x. It contains hundreds of complete script examples along with screen shots that illustrate the results of loading each script. The scripts are included on the CD-ROM.

Audience

This book is for Web authors who are interested in using client-side JavaScript language in their HTML pages.

JavaScript Version

This book describes both the Navigator 2.*x* and 3.*x* version of the JavaScript language, with emphasis on Navigator 3.x functionality. Features that are new with the Navigator 3.0 release are clearly marked with an icon in the margin. Although we make occasional references to JScript, Microsoft's implementation of the JavaScript language, none of the scripts in this book were tested on the Internet Explorer browser.

xxxiii

Because Netscape first implemented the JavaScript language in its Navigator 2.01 release, it's common to refer to the JavaScript version by Navigator release number. The JavaScript language does, however, have its own version numbering system, which is shown in Table P-1.

Table P-1 **JavaScript Version Numbers**

Browser	JavaScript Version Number
Navigator 2.x	1.0
Navigator 3.x	1.1
Internet Explorer 3.x	1.0

Internet Sources of Information

You can find lots of information about the JavaScript language on the Web. This section provides a list of URLs to some sites that we have found to contain useful reference information about the JavaScript language.

Netscape release notes:
`http://home.netscape.com/eng/mozilla/3.0/relnotes`

JavaScript 2.0 Authoring Guide:
`http://home.netscape.com/eng/mozilla/2.0/handbook/javascript`

JavaScript 3.0 Authoring Guide:
`http://home.netscape.com/eng/mozilla/3.0/handbook/javascript`

Reporting new Netscape bugs:
`http://cgi.netscape.com/cgi-bin/auto-bug.cgi`

JavaScript FAQ:
`http://www.freqgrafx.com/411/jsfaq.html`

Netscape product information:
`http://www.netscape.com/comprod/products/navigator/`
`version_2.0/script/`

Cookie property specification:
`http://home.netscape.com/newsref/std/cookie_spec.html`

Netscape JavaScript press release:
`http://home.netscape.com/newsref/pr/newsrelease67.html`

Microsoft JScript product information:
`http://microsoft.com/devonly/prodinfo/jscript/`

Conventions Used in This Book

Table P-2 shows the typographic conventions used in this book.

Table P-2 Typographic Conventions

Typeface or Symbol	Description
NEW IN 3.0	Indicates that the information in the marked paragraphs describes functionality that is new with the Navigator 3.0 release.
`courier`	Indicates a command, file name, object name, method, argument, JavaScript keyword, HTML tag, file content, or code excerpt.
`courier italics`	Indicates a variable that you should replace with a valid value.
italics	Indicates definitions, emphasis, or a book title.

How This Book is Organized

This book is divided into eight parts and 36 chapters.

Part 1, "Getting Started," introduces the JavaScript language, the scripting environment, general scripting concepts, and provides some tips for debugging your scripts.

Part 2, "Creating HTML Pages," introduces JavaScript objects and provides detailed information on how to create windows and documents, control history, work with images, and embed Java applets and plug-ins into your Web pages.

Part 3, "Navigating on the Web," describes how to control location, create active image areas, and work with links.

Part 4, "Getting User Input," contains information about forms objects and the form elements that you use to get input from users: text fields, password fields, text areas, buttons, check boxes, radio buttons, hidden objects, selection lists, and how to include files in an upload.

Part 5, "Controlling Your Scripts," describes JavaScript operators, testing for conditions, and creating loops.

Part 6, "Using System Objects," describes how to work with strings; arrays; the Date, Math, and navigator objects; and how to specify MIME types.

Part 7, "Advanced JavaScript," describes how to create your own JavaScript objects, use the cookie property, and control data tainting.

Part 8, "Appendixes," contains information on creating HTML frames, a list of the JavaScript predefined colors, and a JavaScript quick reference.

A Glossary contains a list of terms.

Jumping JavaScript CD Contents

The CD-ROM accompanying this book includes all of the JavaScript examples referred to in this book formatted for X11, Macintosh®, and Windows™ 95 platforms. To run files off the CD-ROM, mount the CD-ROM in the way specified by your platform and double-click on the `index.html` file at the top level. This `index.html` file is then loaded into your Web browser and provides links to the entire script hierarchy on the CD-ROM.

The CD-ROM was created by using Creative Digital Research's CDR Publisher® HyCD™, which integrates PC, Macintosh, and UNIX® formats onto a single CD-ROM. HyCD is compliant with all of the existing CD-ROM standards:

- PC CD-ROM Format: ISO 9660
- Macintosh CD-ROM Format: HFS
- UNIX CD-ROM Format: ISO 9660 with Rock Ridge Extension
- PC Windows 95 / NT 4.0 Format: Joliet File System

For more information about HyCD and the CDR Publisher, visit Creative Digital Research's Web site at `http://www.hycd.com`.

Note – If you are using a Macintosh computer, the first time you load the CD-ROM, you may be asked to rebuild the CD desktop. After that, you can simply double-click on any file with an `.html` extension to run it in the browser.

Acknowledgments

The authors would like to thank the following people for their contributions to this book:

Greg Doench of Prentice Hall for his patience, help, and support on this project.

Lisa Iarkowski of Prentice Hall for help with templates, art files, and production.

Gail Cocker at Prentice Hall for great jumping frogs for our animation script.

Rachel Borden and John Bortner of SunSoft Press for their patience and unfailing diligence in helping with this project.

Karen Ellison of SunSoft Press for the occasional loan of her system and ongoing support.

Mary Lou Nohr for editing this manuscript with her usual skill and tact.

Mary E. S. Morris for graciously permitting us to include and adapt information from her book, *HTML for Fun and Profit*, SunSoft Press/Prentice Hall, 1996, for use in Appendix A, "HTML Frames," and for technical review comments.

Doug Young for permission to use the `Music.html` script from *Netscape Developer's Guide to Plug-Ins*, published by Prentice Hall Professional Technical Reference, 1996, and for providing us with the accompanying image and audio files.

Danny Goodman for information posted at `http://developer.netscape.com/news/viewsource/archive/ goodman_liveconnect.html` about

LiveConnect and for information posted at http://developer.netscape.com/news/viewsource/archive/ goodman_cookies.html about document cookies.

Gordon McComb of JavaWorld for information posted at http://www.javaworld.com about how the button object click() method can be a security loophole.

Bill Dortch of hIdaho, bdortch@hidaho.com, for providing public-domain cookie functions at http://www.hidaho.com/cookies/cookie.txt and http://www.hidaho.com/cookies/cookie.html.

Janice would like to thank the following people for their contributions to this book:

Mike Blake for his Herculean efforts and flexibility in quickly and efficiently creating a mini-network with a Macintosh, a SPARCstation™, and a NeXTSTEP® Canon™ object.station while the authors watched the 49ers lose to Dallas, and for technical review comments.

Rick Huebsch and Leslie Schwarzbach of Sun Educational Services for providing the opportunity for me to attend the Beta class on *Web Publishing with Java* and for permitting me to keep the course notes to use as resource material for the Java Applets chapter.

John Pew for teaching the Beta class on *Web Publishing with Java* and giving us permission to use applets from his book, *Instant Java*, published by Sun Microsystems Press/Prentice Hall, 1996.

Michael King, Director of Design, Documentation, and Training of The Filoli Information Systems for his ongoing support and friendship.

Ken and Cherie Hesky for information about the origin of the first computer bug.

Dave Barry for unwittingly providing me a quote from *Dave Barry in Cyberspace* for the opening chapter of this book.

My three cats for lap sitting, keyboard walking, and general company keeping while this book was in progress.

Brian would like to thank the following people for their contributions to this book:

David Bryant, Engineering Manager, CDE Application Builder of SunSoft, Inc., for his friendship, support, and the loan of the PowerBook™.

Joe Ushana, Engineering Manager, Silicon Surf of Silicon Graphics, Inc., for his friendship and support in this endeavor.

Matt Goff, Fred Malone, David Moles, and Kinney Wong for their technical review comments.

Debbie Goff for her courier services.

Monica Gaines, Lori Reid, and Terry Haynes for listening and for offering their suggestions.

Mom and Dad for their love and support.

Judy Foddrill for all her love, patience, understanding, and support on this project. Most of all, for putting up with me through the rough times.

PART ONE

Getting Started

CHAPTER 1

- The JavaScript Language
- JavaScript-Enabled Browsers
- The Internet
- The World Wide Web
- How the World Wide Web Works
- Summary of New Terms and Concepts

Introducing the JavaScript Language

This book, *Jumping JavaScript*, is your comprehensive reference guide for learning and using the JavaScript™ language. We've chosen this title for our book to represent the great leap forward that you can make in controlling and creating your own lively, interesting, and dynamic Web pages. The symbol we've used on the cover and throughout this book is the frog. Frogs represent transformation because they start out life as tadpoles, then they gradually shed their tails, grow legs, and start breathing air. Just as the tadpole transforms itself, so you can start transforming your Web pages by using the JavaScript language.

The JavaScript Language

What is the JavaScript language? JavaScript is an *object-based interpreted* scripting language that is embedded in HTML pages. With it you can control and program elements of your own Web pages on the client side without depending on CGI scripts on a server. You can design your own windows, create forms to capture input from users of your Web page, perform mathematical and statistical calculations, and connect to existing Java™ applets and plug-ins. You can also create your own JavaScript custom objects.

We call the JavaScript language object-based because, although it uses objects, it does not contain the complete functionality of *object-oriented* compiled programming languages such as C++ or Java. For more information about JavaScript objects, see Chapter 5, "Introducing Objects."

JavaScript is an interpreted language. You do not need a suite of support tools, such as compilers and debuggers, to write scripts and debug them. All you need is a simple text editor and a JavaScript-enabled browser. As the HTML file is loaded into the browser, the JavaScript code is interpreted and executed.

The JavaScript language was originally developed by Netscape and was first called LiveScript. LiveScript was designed to enable administrators to do server side processing. On the client side, the script was designed to enhance HTML documents and to provide the user with some HTML-level interaction. It was also designed to enable users to communicate with Java applets.

In December 1995, Netscape and Sun Microsystems jointly announced that LiveScript's name would change to JavaScript and that Sun would become part of the development team to take the language into the future. The headline of the press release announcing JavaScript read:

> Netscape and Sun Announce JavaScript, the open, cross-platform object scripting language for enterprise Networks and the Internet
>
> 28 industry-leading companies to endorse JavaScript as a complement to Java for easy online application development

The press release goes on to describe the JavaScript language:

> JavaScript is an easy-to-use object scripting language designed for creating live online applications that link together objects and resources of both clients and servers. While Java is used by programmers to create new objects and applets, JavaScript is designed for use by HTML page authors and enterprise application developers to dynamically script the behavior of objects running on either the client or the server. JavaScript is analogous to Visual Basic in that it can be used by people with little or no programming experience to quickly construct complex applications. JavaScript's design represents the next generation of software designed specifically for the Internet and is:
>
> - designed for creating network-centric applications
> - complementary to and integrated with Java
> - complementary to and integrated with HTML
> - open and cross-platform

You can find the complete text of the press release at
`http://home/netscape.com/newsref/pr/newsrelease67.html.`

According to the Netscape's press release, JavaScript is "an open, freely licensed proposed standard available to the entire Internet community."

The JavaScript language borrows much of its syntax from the Java language (which, in turn, was borrowed from the C and C++ programming languages). It also uses elements from the Awk and Perl scripting languages and was influenced indirectly by the object prototype system used in the Self language.

JavaScript-Enabled Browsers

When you include JavaScript code in an HTML file, it can only be interpreted and displayed on a browser that is JavaScript-enabled. Any browser that does not know how to interpret the JavaScript language will not execute the JavaScript code. To make sure that your HTML file loads on all browsers, you need to add appropriate comments so that the JavaScript code is ignored if it cannot be interpreted. For information on how to include these comments, see Chapter 2, "Introducing the Scripting Environment."

Navigator™ 2.0 was Netscape's first JavaScript-enabled browser. This release contained many bugs. The Navigator 3.0 release fixes many of the 2.0 bugs, introduces some new ones, and provides some new functionality. This book clearly identifies functionality that is new with the Navigator 3.0 release. Major sections containing information about new 3.0 functionality have the frog icon you see in the margin at the beginning of each section. We've also done our best to include information about known bugs. Some of the functionality worked on some platforms but not on others, which made the discovery process rather challenging.

Microsoft has implemented a JScript interpreter of its own for use in Internet Explorer 3.0. According to Microsoft:

> Microsoft® JScript is an open implementation of JavaScript. JScript is a high-performance scripting language designed to create active online content on the World Wide Web. JScript allows developers to link and automate a wide variety of objects in Web pages, including ActiveX™ Controls and "applets" created using the Java language from Sun Microsystems Inc.

For more information on JScript, see:

```
http://microsoft.com/devonly/prodinfo/jscript/
```

Client-Side JavaScript

You embed client-side JavaScript language in HTML Web pages, which is interpreted by a browser. In fact, you might think of the JavaScript language as a complex set of HTML extensions. The JavaScript language provides you with the standard programming language functionality that enables you to test for conditions, create loops, and perform string manipulation and mathematical calculations. In addition, you get a set of powerful properties, methods, and event handlers that enable you to programmatically access all of the interesting aspects of the HTML code: the forms elements, the links, the window, the document, and so on. Mastering the use of these built-in objects is the key to effectively using the JavaScript language in your Web pages.

Server-Side JavaScript

Netscape's server-side JavaScript technology is called LiveWire™. LiveWire contains server-side Java as well as additional functionality that extends the core JavaScript language for use in Web browsers. At this time, no other vendors are providing any server-side JavaScript products. LiveWire provides an exciting alternative to CGI scripts.

LiveWire scripts are embedded directly in HTML pages. They enable you to directly intermix executable server-side scripts with client-side content. When a client computer requests a document that has LiveWire code in it, the server executes the scripts contained in the document and sends the document to the requester. The page that is downloaded to the client can be a mixture of static HTML code and data that is generated dynamically by the LiveWire script.

LiveWire can be either interpreted or compiled. Netscape has a special compiler that provides the ability to precompile LiveWire programs into a binary form that enhances performance.

The Internet

If you're looking at a copy of this book, you probably are already connected to the Internet and familiar with some of the jargon and terminology associated with it. In the following sections we'll review some of the major concepts of the Internet and the World Wide Web.

A *network* is a group of computers that are connected electronically so that they can share information with one another. The *Internet* is a network of networks that enables individuals on a computer on one network to share information with individuals on another network. That network may be right next door or halfway around the world. The most popular use of the Internet is to exchange electronic

mail (called *e-mail*) messages. You can also use the Internet to do research and to access and download files. The Internet relies on network protocols, domains, and IP addresses to communicate between computers.

Network Protocols

The software that enables different types of computers to communicate with one another involves a series of protocols. A *protocol* is a formal set of conventions that defines the format and control of input and output between devices and programs. One commonly used Internet protocol is *TCP/IP*, which stands for transmission control protocol/internet protocol. Other protocols are *ftp*, *gopher*, *http* (the World Wide Web), and simple mail transport protocol (*SMTP*), the most common e-mail protocol used in open systems today.

IP Addresses

Another part of the Internet picture is Internet protocol (IP) addresses. The IP address is a unique Internet address number that identifies each system in a network. An IP address consists of four numbers, each less than 256, separated by a dot. The rightmost number specifies the actual computer, while those to the left usually identify the network and subnetwork.

An example of an IP address is:

```
199.182.120.203
```

Domains

Computers on the Internet are constantly sending messages to other computers. To be able to reach the right computer, the Internet needs to have some kind of addressing scheme. When you send a letter to the President at 1600 Pennsylvania Avenue, Washington, D.C., you expect that letter to arrive at the White House and be delivered to the President (or one of his direct representatives). Instead of street number, name, city, and state, the Internet has its own addressing scheme that involves *domains*.

A domain is a hierarchical structure that is used for network and e-mail naming. Just as an address has a name, a number, a street name, a city, a state, and a zip code, so a domain address has a local address, and a multipart domain address. When you address a letter, you include all of this information along with the name of the person you want to receive the letter. When the Post Office receives that letter, it looks first at the zip code. The zip code tells the Post Office which city and state to deliver the letter to. Then they sort the mail by street name and subsequently by house number. When the mail arrives at the right house, somebody inside the house sorts through the incoming mail and retrieves the letters that have that person's name on them.

Top-level Internet domains are like zip codes. Within the United States, top-level Internet domains include `com` for commercial organizations, `edu` for educational organizations, `gov` for governments, `mil` for the military, `net` for networking organizations, and `org` for other organizations. Because of the rapid growth of the Web, proposals are under consideration for creating a broader set of top-level Internet domains. Outside of the United States, top-level Internet domains designate the country. Subdomains designate the organization and the individual system.

An e-mail domain address has this format:

```
mailbox@subdomain.subdomain2.subdomain1.top-level-domain
```

The part of the address to the left of the @ sign is the local address. The part of the address to the right of the @ sign shows the domain address where the local address is located. A dot (`.`) separates each part of the domain address. The domain can be an organization, a physical area, or a geographic region. Domain addresses are case insensitive. It makes no difference whether you use upper, lower, or mixed case in the domain part of the address. The order of the domain information is hierarchical, with the locations more specific and local the closer they are to the @ sign (although certain British and New Zealand networks reverse the order).

The World Wide Web

The *World Wide Web* (WWW or the Web) and the Internet are not synonymous, although many people use the terms interchangeably. The Web simply is the part of the Internet that uses the `http` protocol to deliver information. `http` stands for hypertext transfer protocol.

All Web pages and information are provided as hypertext markup language (*HTML*) files. HTML is a platform-independent, hypermedia document description language. This means that if you create an HTML page on any kind of computer, that page can be interpreted and displayed on any other kind of computer anywhere on the Internet.

HTML is a set of tags and attributes that you put into a plain text file. These tags and their associated information define how the elements of the page are displayed. With HTML, you can:

- Create platform-independent documents
- Create hypertext links within your document or to other documents on the Internet
- Include graphics and multimedia files

HTML files depend on a *browser* to interpret the HTML tags and attributes, format the information, and display it. Browsers are applications called *clients*. They get most of their information from *servers*. Servers are the applications that enable HTML files to be linked across the network. A *Web server* is a program that waits for requests for documents. When the server receives a request, it gets the appropriate document and sends it over the network to the browser that made the request. Requests can come from the same computer or from a different computer. Figure 1–1 shows a diagram of the process.

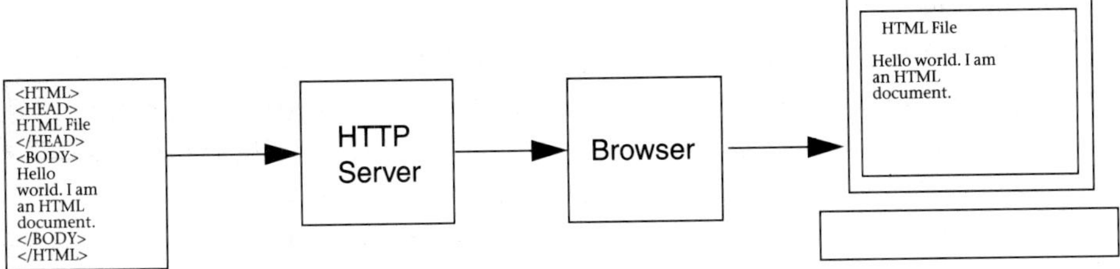

Figure 1–1 Web server and browser

How the World Wide Web Works

The Web uses the concept of a *client-server model*. Special computers or software known as Web servers make linked HTML documents available to the public. Individual client computers request access to this material, using a Web browser. The interaction between server and client is dynamically changing as the Web evolves. In the early days, the Web server maintained access to all of the HTML files and links. When a Web client requested access to a document, the server downloaded text files to the client. Although the network traffic goes in both directions, with requests to the server and files downloaded to the client, most users considered the traffic essentially one-way, as illustrated in Figure 1–2.

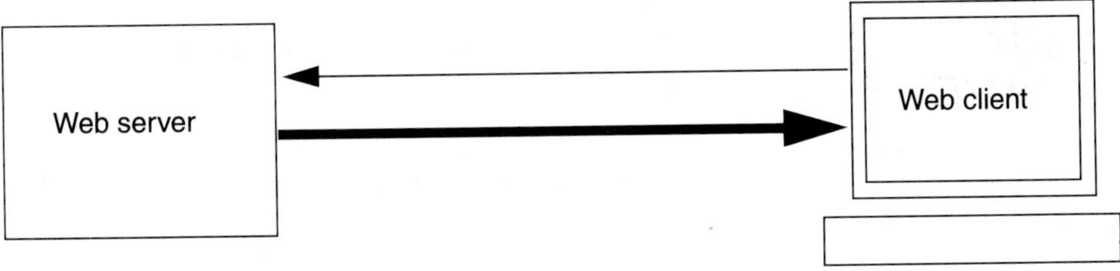

Figure 1–2 Client-server interaction

Or, in the immortal words of Dave Barry (Page 150-151 of *Dave Barry in Cyberspace*, ™®©, 1996):

> As you can see, it takes quite a while for a Web page to appear on your screen. The reason for the delay is that, when you type in a Web address, your computer passes it along to another computer, which in turn passes it along to another computer, and so on through as many as five computers before it finally reaches the workstation of a disgruntled U.S. Postal Service employee, who throws it in the trash. So when browsing the Web, you will almost certainly encounter lengthy delays, which means that it's a good idea to have something else to do while you're waiting, such as reroofing your house.

In this basic scenario, any processing or interesting scripting work is done on the server side, using programs known as common gateway interface (*CGI*) scripts. Writing customized CGI scripts, which are typically programmed using the *Perl* scripting language, requires considerable programming skill. CGI scripts serve as the interface between HTML pages and the Web server. The Web page author must be in control of the server and know how to interact with needed *back-end programs* such as databases. CGI scripts also perform additional services such as processing forms and generating HTML pages. The Web client is essentially a dumb terminal, depending on the server for access to the information and for any processing that is required.

Helper Applications

Many browsers depend on *helper applications* to enhance their capabilities. For example, if you click on a TIFF image and have a helper application for it, the browser launches the helper application to view the image. The window that is opened to display the image is not integrated into the browser window, and you need to close the window when you are through viewing the image.

Plug-ins

To expand the capability of basic browsers to handle embedded information such as audio and video, browsers have added *plug-ins* to enhance their capabilities. You still need to have the plug-in available on your hard disk. Unlike a helper application, however, the plug-in is displayed within the browser window and interacts with the browser in a way that technical people call *transparent* to the user. What this term means is that you don't know that the browser is starting up another application to handle display of the information.

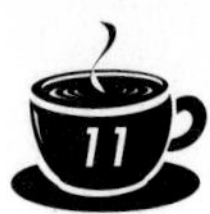

Java Applets

As the Web has evolved, programmers wanted to be able to write their own programs to handle special needs not provided in existing plug-ins. The Java programming language developed by Sun Microsystems enables programmers to build small applications, called *applets*, that the server can download to the browser. These applets cannot be run without a browser or an applet viewer. They are downloaded into the client computer memory as separate files and run as the user needs them. When the user moves to another Web page, the applets are automatically discarded.

To run a Java applet, the browser company must have licensed Sun's technology and incorporated it into the browser. Netscape Navigator 2.0 and later browsers are Java-enabled. Sun provides its own Java-enabled browser called Hot Java™. Other browser makers have also adopted Java as a part of their products. The advent of Java applets provides more interesting capabilities on the client system. However, the interaction is still primarily one-way from the server to the client, as shown in Figure 1–3.

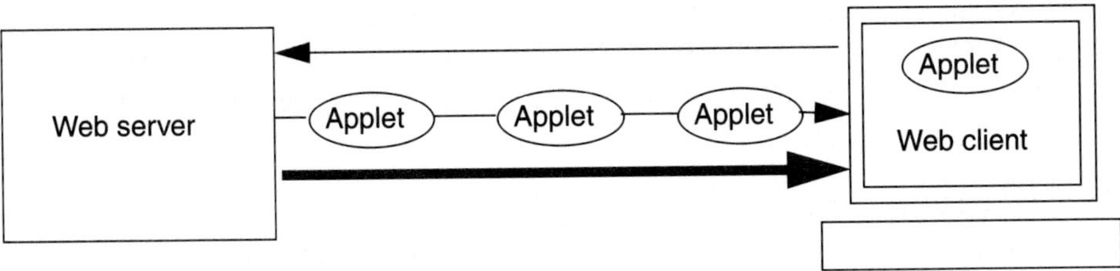

Figure 1–3 Client-server interaction with Java applets

Looming on the horizon is the scenario illustrated in Figure 1–4, where both the client and server send applets back and forth to each other. Some of these applets may live partly on the Net. For example, the client might send the server an applet that initiates a custom database search. An applet that is sent to the server from the client is called a *servlet*. New Java Servlet APIs will enable developers to create customized server applications and "servlets," or small executable programs that users can upload to run on networks or servers.

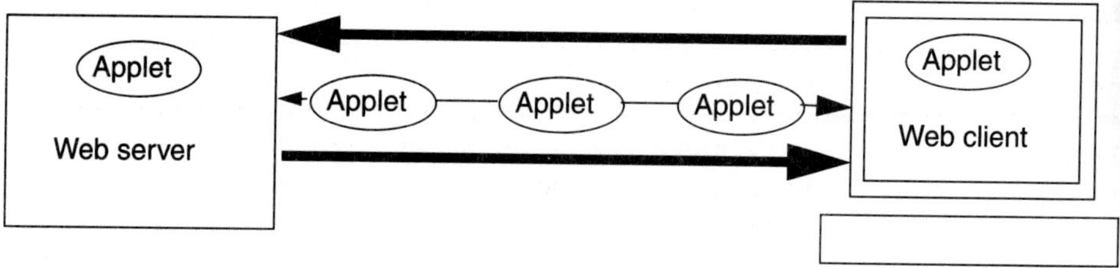

Figure 1–4 Client-server interaction with Java applets moving in both directions

Summary of New Terms and Concepts

The new terms and concepts introduced in this chapter are listed in alphabetical order in Table 1-1. The terms and concepts are also included in the glossary at the end of the book.

Table 1-1 Summary of New Terms and Concepts

Term/Concept	Description
applet	A small application written in the Java language that requires a browser to execute.
back-end programs	The programs, such as databases, on the server that provide information to CGI scripts.
browser	An application that downloads HTML files from a Web server and displays the formatted file. Also called a *client*.
CGI script	Common gateway interface scripts serve as the interface between HTML pages and the Web server.
client	A computer on the World Wide Web that receives data and information from a server which handles requests for information and locates the files.
client-server model	The arrangement of computers on the World Wide Web in which some computers (the clients) receive data and information from another computer (the server) that handles requests for information and locates the files.

Table 1-1 Summary of New Terms and Concepts (Continued)

Term/Concept	Description
domain	A directory structure used for network and e-mail naming. Within the United States, top-level Internet domains include `com` for commercial organizations, `edu` for educational organizations, `gov` for government, `mil` for the military, `net` for networking organizations, and `org` for other organizations. Outside of the United States, top-level Internet domains designate the country. Subdomains designate the organization and the individual computer.
e-mail	Electronic mail
ftp	A file transfer protocol used to transfer text or binary files from one computer to another over a network.
gopher	A file transfer protocol used to transfer text or binary files from one computer to another over a network. The name originated because you ask the program to "go for" it.
helper applications	An application that can display special formats; opened when the user clicks on an item in the browser that contains special formatting. Although the helper application is started from a browser, it is not integrated into the browser.
HTML	Hypertext Markup Language is the platform-independent hypermedia markup language used in the World Wide Web.
http	Hypertext transfer protocol is used to transfer HTML files over the Internet.
Internet	A network of networks that enables individuals on a computer on one network to share information with individuals on another network that may be next door or halfway around the world.
interpreted code	Any script or program that is read line-by-line at the time it is run.
network	A group of computers that are connected electronically so that they can share information with one another.
object-based	A programming style that uses the concepts of objects, methods, and events but does not provide all of the complexity of a true object-oriented programming style.

Table 1-1 Summary of New Terms and Concepts (Continued)

Term/Concept	Description
object-oriented	A programming style in which programs are organized as cooperative collections of objects, each of which represents an instance of some class, and whose classes are all members of a hierarchy of classes that are united by inheritance relationships.
Perl	The scripting language that is used to write most CGI scripts.
plug-in	An application that enhances and expands the capability of another application and is completely integrated within it so that the user is not aware that a plug-in is being used.
protocol	A formal set of conventions that define the format and control of input and output between devices and programs. Common protocols are TCP/IP, ftp, gopher, http, and e-mail.
route-independent address	An e-mail address that uses domain information to locate the recipient without needing to know the specific route that the message takes.
server	A computer on the World Wide Web that handles requests for information and locates files requested by a client computer.
servlet	An applet that is sent to the server from the client.
SMTP	Simple mail transport protocol is the most common e-mail protocol used in open systems today.
transparent	Any application or process that is started automatically so that no user action is required. Also describes a system that passes through all data exactly as it is received.
Web client	The recipient of downloaded information from a server.
Web server	A device that is dedicated to serving other nodes attached to the network. Also, an application that enables HTML files to be linked across the network.
World Wide Web	The part of the Internet that uses the http protocol to deliver information. Abbreviated as WWW or the Web. Some anonymous pundit claims that the acronym WWW actually stands for world wide wait.

This chapter introduces the JavaScript language and provides an overview of the Internet and World Wide Web. In the next chapter you'll learn some scripting terminology, look at the steps involved in writing a script, and create your first script.

CHAPTER 2

- Hello World Tradition
- Scripting Terminology
- Understanding the Elements of the Hello World Script
- Using the Basic Template
- Recommended Programming Style Guide
- Looking at the Script-Writing Process
- Creating the Hello World Script
- Summary of New Terms and Concepts

ntroducing the Scripting Environment

This chapter describes how to create a simple JavaScript program that displays the message "Hello World." It provides a basic template you can use for most of your JavaScript programs, describes the elements used in the Hello World script, and shows you how to create and run the script.

Hello World Tradition

In the programming world, it's a long-standing tradition that the first words a new program displays are the words "Hello World." This message shows that the program is up and running and can display text.

We continue the tradition by showing you how to write a simple JavaScript program that displays the message "Hello World!" The left column below contains the script. The right column contains a line-by-line explanation of this script.

Script	Explanation
<HTML>	Start of HTML document
<HEAD>	Start of HTML document head
<TITLE>Hello World!</TITLE>	Specify window title text
<SCRIPT LANGUAGE="JavaScript">	Start JavaScript
document.write("Hello World!")	Display the words between quotes in the HTML document
</SCRIPT>	End JavaScript
</HEAD>	End of HTML head

<BODY>	Start HTML body
</BODY>	End HTML body
</HTML>	End HTML document

Scripting Terminology

As we describe some of the fundamentals of scripting, you will gradually be introduced to some terms that are traditionally used to describe how you create and use the components of the scripting or programming language. Each time a new term is introduced, it is shown in *italics*. Any term that is displayed in italics has an entry in the glossary at the back of the book. In addition, we provide a summary table at the end of each chapter containing new terms that were introduced.

Understanding the Elements of the Hello World Script

To write JavaScript Programs, you must know how to:

- Integrate JavaScript code into your HTML documents
- Use the syntax and general structure of the JavaScript language

Sounds pretty simple, doesn't it. This chapter does not explain all of the syntax and structure of the JavaScript language. Instead, we tell you only the information that you need to accomplish a specific task. For a quick-reference summary of JavaScript syntax and structure, see Appendix C, "JavaScript Quick Reference."

The JavaScript language is similar to written languages, in that it has a *syntax*, an order of presentation, and a structure. Just as there are rules of grammar in the English language, so there are rules of grammar in JavaScript. The JavaScript code may look cryptic and difficult to understand at the beginning because it is a programming language, not a spoken language. The computer requires information to be presented in a particular order and structure so that it can understand what you are asking it to do.

To create the simplest Hello World JavaScript program, you need to know how to:

- Create a simple HTML file
- Embed a JavaScript program in HTML
- Display text

Although the Hello World script used in this chapter does not use the following capabilities, we introduce them here to provide you with the basic structural elements you need for writing a script. These additional capabilities show you how to:

- Load a script file
- Add JavaScript comments
- Add HTML comments

JavaScript and HTML

The JavaScript language is *interpreted* from HTML files that are loaded into JavaScript-enabled browsers. As the HTML file is loaded, the computer interprets the code line-by-line, performing the actions in sequence. Most scripting languages are interpreted in this way, in contrast to more structured programming languages such as C and Java, which are *compiled* before they can be run.

You can include JavaScript code in an HTML document in two ways:

- By embedding the JavaScript code in the HTML document
- By loading the JavaScript code from a separate file

Although this book is not about using HTML, we plan to help you along by reminding you of some of the HTML basics as they occur in the examples. For more complete information about how to write HTML code, see Mary E. S. Morris's book, *HTML for Fun and Profit, Gold Signature Edition* published by Prentice-Hall and SunSoft Press, or any other HTML reference book.

Embedding a Script

To embed a JavaScript program in an HTML file, use the HTML tag `<SCRIPT>` to start the script, and the HTML tag `</SCRIPT>` to end the script.

Every JavaScript program has these two tags:

```
<SCRIPT>
Put your JavaScript code here.
</SCRIPT>
```

The `<SCRIPT>` tag can also have *attributes*, which are included as part of the tag. The attribute you want to define is called `LANGUAGE`. Available languages are JavaScript, JScript (Microsoft's version of JavaScript), and VBscript (Visual Basic script). Always define the `LANGUAGE` attribute in your scripts by using the following syntax:

```
<SCRIPT LANGUAGE = "JavaScript">
Put your JavaScript code here.
</SCRIPT>
```

JScript also uses the `JavaScript` language name as its value.

You can specify the JavaScript version of the language as part of the attribute value. Table 2-1 shows JavaScript version numbers for Navigator and Internet Explorer.

Table 2-1 **JavaScript Version Numbers**

Browser	JavaScript Version Number
Navigator 2.x	1.0
Navigator 3.x	1.1
Internet Explorer 3.x	1.0

If you write a script that is using features for a specific version of the language, consider specifying that version as part of your `LANGUAGE` attribute. You include the JavaScript version number immediately after the JavaScript value without a space, as shown below:

```
<SCRIPT LANGUAGE = "JavaScript1.1">
Put your JavaScript code here.
</SCRIPT>
```

At times it can work to your advantage to divide code into language-specific blocks. For example, JavaScript 1.1 has an `image` object and JavaScript 1.0 does not. You can include the `image` object code in a `<SCRIPT>` block that specifies `JavaScript1.1` as the value for the `LANGUAGE` attribute. A JavaScript 1.0 browser simply ignores that block of code.

As you can see from the example, the proper syntax for the attribute is the name of the attribute followed by an equal sign and then the value for the attribute, which is enclosed in double-quotation marks:

```
AttributeName = "AttributeValue"
```

This syntax is similar to the one you use to assign a value to a variable. If you are at all familiar with HTML, you already know about creating variables and assigning values. You will be learning about variables, their syntax, and use in Chapter 3, "Introducing General Scripting Concepts."

Adding Text for Non-JavaScript Browsers

The Navigator 3.0 release provides a set of `<NOSCRIPT></NOSCRIPT>` tags that enable you to provide alternative information to be displayed in browsers that are not JavaScript enabled or in browsers that have turned off JavaScript. Although it is a good idea to provide information for those browsers that do not display JavaScript, the behavior of these tags is not consistent.

Loading a Script File

If you have a JavaScript program that you use more than once, you may find it useful to create the program in a separate file and, in your HTML code, put a URL reference that identifies the location of the file. That way you can reuse a program that you've written and run successfully in more than one HTML file without needing to copy the script into each HTML file. If you make modifications to the JavaScript program file to add new features, you need only make the changes in one place and they are automatically used in each HTML file that contains a pointer to that JavaScript file. JScript may not support loading scripts from a file.

When you create a separate file for your JavaScript program, you must name it with a `.js` suffix, which tells the computer that your file is a JavaScript. The complete syntax is:

```
ProgramName.js
```

It's a good idea to use a descriptive name for your file that reminds you what the script does. For example, if you write a JavaScript counter program, you could name the file `Counter.js`.

The `<SCRIPT>` tag has another attribute name, `SRC`, that tells the HTML interpreter to look for the file.

The syntax for loading a script file is:

```
<SCRIPT LANGUAGE = "JavaScript" SRC = "JavaScriptCode.js">
Put your JavaScript code here.
</SCRIPT>
```

If the JavaScript file is on your local system, you use just the file name, as shown in the previous example. If the JavaScript file is on a server somewhere, you can use the complete URL as the value for the `SRC` attribute.

You can include more than one external script in a file by including multiple references in your HTML file. You cannot, however, reference one `.js` file from within another one.

For an example of loading and using a function from a separate file, see Chapter 4, "Debugging Scripts."

Adding JavaScript Comments

Good programming practice recommends that you annotate each script that you write. You probably will find that the script makes complete sense to you when you're immersed in creating and debugging it. However, if you return to the program after even a brief time away from it, you may not remember your thinking processes. You annotate a script by adding *comments.*

Comments help you in the following ways:

- You can maintain and debug the script more easily.
- Other people who look at your script can understand what you did.
- After some time has elapsed, comments can help you to understand or modify an existing script without having to carefully analyze the code.

The JavaScript program needs to know what information is part of the script to be executed and what information it should skip over. To make sure your comments are skipped, you must use special characters that instruct the JavaScript interpreter to skip over the information.

JavaScript enables you to enter comments in two ways:

- One-line comments: start the line with a double slash (//), which is C++ language commenting style.
- Multiline comments: start the comment with `/*` and end the comment with `*/`, which is C language commenting style.

The `//` tells the HTML interpreter to ignore everything on the line following the double slash. The `/*` and `*/` tell the HTML interpreter to ignore everything between the `/*` and the `*/`.

Some companies and groups have style guidelines for comments and for presentation of code. The following examples show commenting styles as well as indentation styles. See "Recommended Programming Style Guide" on page 28 for more information about code presentation style.

The following example uses a mixed commenting style and tabs to indent the statements.

```
/*
** function description
*/

function foo(variable, variable) {
   var a;
```

```
        statement;      // comment

        //
        // description of next block of code
        //
        if (expression) {
            statement;
        }
        then {
            statement;
        }
    }
```

The following example uses double slashes (//) consistently and spaces to indent the statements.

```
//
// function description
//

function foo(variable, variable)
{
  var a;
  statement;    // comment
  statement;

  //
  // description of next block of code
  //
  if (expression)
  {
    statement;
  }
  then
  {
    statement;
  }
}
```

Adding HTML Comments

Because not all browsers support scripts, you may want to add HTML comments that hide any JavaScript that is embedded in an HTML file from any old-version browsers. With the addition of the HTML comments, any browsers that do not understand JavaScript do not display it.

To add the HTML comment, start the line just after the `<SCRIPT>` tag with the characters `<!--`. Just before the ending `</SCRIPT>` tag, add the line:

```
// End the hiding here -->
```

The // at the beginning of the line is a JavaScript one-line comment. The --> at the end of the line marks the end of the HTML comment. Because these are comment lines, you can add comments text. The comments are not shown when the page is displayed. Be sure, however, that your comments are brief enough that they fit on just one line.

So, the complete syntax with attributes and an HTML comment looks like this:

```
<SCRIPT LANGUAGE = "JavaScript">
<!-- Hide JavaScript code from older browsers
   document.write("Hello, World!")
// End the hiding here -->
</SCRIPT>
```

Displaying Text

You can display text in many different ways in JavaScript. In the Hello World script in this chapter, you use a one-line construction that appears very simple but requires some understanding of the underlying concepts of JavaScript.

The line of code is:

```
document.write("Hello World!")
```

The English equivalent of this statement is:

Write the characters `Hello World!` in the HTML document window.

Let's look at the elements of this line of code:

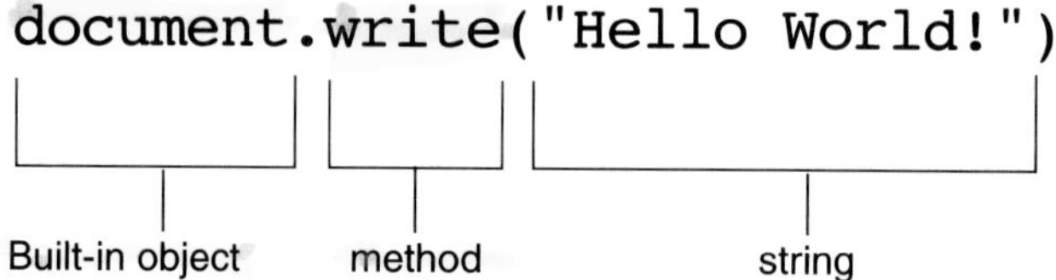

If this were an English sentence, we could diagram it. The *built-in object* is the subject of the sentence. The *method* and the *string* (and its surrounding parentheses and quotes) are the predicate. The predicate describes the circumstances and actions that are to be performed on the subject. In other words, the method and the instructions in the parentheses following the method describe what action is done on the object.

document is one of the built-in objects that JavaScript provides. You'll learn much more about JavaScript built-in objects, methods, and properties in subsequent chapters. For now, all you need to know is that JavaScript provides a set of built-in objects that give you a flexible and easy way to write scripts. An object is always a thing, like a document, a window, a button, or a piece of text. To continue the grammar analogy, an object is like a noun.

Objects have methods, which are simply ways to tell the object to do something. Methods are written with parentheses after the name: `write()`. Other methods for the `document` object are `clear()`, `close()`, `open()`, and `writeln()`. The `writeln()` method is the same as the `write()` method except that it puts the string on a separate line. Methods are always actions, and you can think of them as being like verbs.

So, the object says what *thing* you want to operate on. The method says what *action* to take on that object. And the information inside the parentheses says *how to* use that method.

The `document.write()` method tells the computer to write the information between the parentheses into the first line of the document object.

The `write()` method can display different types of formats: characters, HTML text, images, or plug-ins. If we wanted to get fancy with the Hello World script, we could display a GIF or JPEG file containing an image of the world. But, for now, we're just showing you how to write characters.

The information between the parentheses and the quotation mark is called a string. A string is simply a series of alphanumeric characters. The contents of a string are usually treated as text, even if the string contains numbers.

You now have all the basic pieces you need to put together your first JavaScript program and say hello to the world.

Using the Basic Template

Before we write the script itself, let's look at the framework in which to put the script. It's a good idea for you to use a consistent format for all of your JavaScript files. Client-side JavaScript programs are always embedded in an HTML file. You can either include the script directly in the file, or you can provide a URL that describes the location of the file. Both the location and structure of the JavaScript program in an HTML file are important.

Where you put the JavaScript code in the HTML file depends on when you want the code to be activated:

- Immediately
- Deferred

We have provided two templates that you can use as a model for determining where to put your JavaScript code in the HTML file. The structure of the template is like the structure of a business letter. The information between the `<HEAD>` and `</HEAD>` HTML tags is similar to the date, recipient address, other information, such as order number, and salutation that go before the body of the letter. This information sets the context for the information that is presented in the body.

The HTML tags `<BODY>` and `</BODY>` surround the body of the HTML file, which is similar to the body paragraphs of a business letter.

In the same way, the `</BODY>` and `</HTML>` tags that must be included at the end of the HTML file are similar to the closing remark, name of the sender, attachments, and carbon copy recipients at the end of the letter.

Figure 2–1 illustrates the analogy.

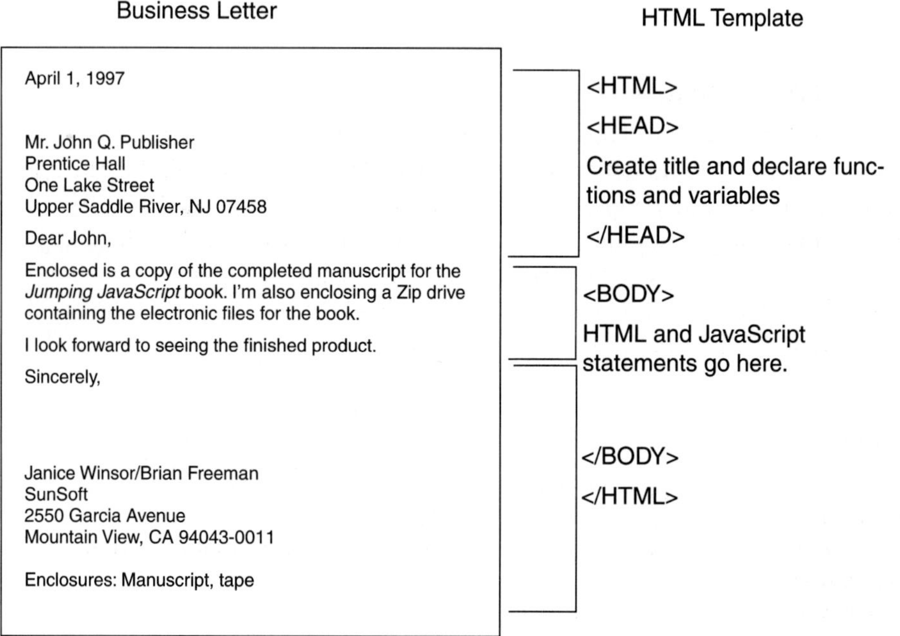

Figure 2–1 Structure of JavaScript template compared to business letter

mmediate Activation Template

f you want your code to be activated immediately, you can put your complete avaScript code either between the HTML `<HEAD>` and `</HEAD>` tags or between he `<BODY>` and `</BODY>` tags. The Hello World script in this chapter puts the ode between the `<HEAD>` and `</HEAD>` tags.

```
<HTML>                                  Start of HTML document
<HEAD>                                  Start of HTML document head
<TITLE>Your Title Here</TITLE>          Provide an HTML title for the window
<SCRIPT LANGUAGE="JavaScript">          Start JavaScript
Put your script statements here         Your JavaScript statements
</SCRIPT>                               End JavaScript
</HEAD>                                 End of HTML head
<BODY>                                  Start HTML body
Put your script statements and          Your JavaScript and HTML statements
HTML display statements here
</BODY>                                 End HTML body
</HTML>                                 End HTML document
```

Deferred Activation

A common programming practice is to declare functions and variables in the `<HEAD>` of the HTML document and embed the statements that call the functions and reference the variables in the `<BODY>` of the HTML document. The variables and functions that you declare in the head of the HTML document are loaded and initialized so that they are available to rest of the script. You'll learn more about functions and variables in Chapter 3, "Introducing General Scripting Concepts." The template for deferred activation is shown below.

```
<HTML>                                  Start of HTML document
<HEAD>                                  Start of HTML document head
<TITLE>Your Title Here</TITLE>          Provide an HTML title for the window
<SCRIPT LANGUAGE="JavaScript">          Start JavaScript
Declare your functions and              Your JavaScript functions and variables
variables here
</SCRIPT>                               End JavaScript
</HEAD>                                 End of HTML head
<BODY>                                  Start HTML body
Put your HTML display statements        Your HTML statements
here
<SCRIPT LANGUAGE="JavaScript")          Start JavaScript
```

```
Put your JavaScript statements      Your JavaScript statements
here
</SCRIPT>                           End JavaScript
</BODY>                             End HTML body
</HTML>                             End HTML document
```

Recommended Programming Style Guide

If you have not written any computer scripts or programs before, here are some suggestions about *programming style* you can follow to make your code easier to read, maintain, and troubleshoot. Troubleshooting problems with computer programs is called debugging because you are searching for pesky bugs that prevent the program from running successfully. For information on how to debug scripts, see Chapter 4, "Debugging Scripts." These guidelines contain references to information that has not yet been introduced. As you become more familiar with writing scripts, refer back to these guidelines.

We provide you with style guidelines for the following topics:

- General comments and rules
- Comments
- Code indentation
- White space
- Statements
- Comparisons
- Identifier style
- Variables
- Functions
- Objects
- Source files

General Comments and Rules

- Write your code so that it is easy to read and maintain. Typically, when you write a script, you spend about 10 percent of the time on the initial coding. Maintaining the script can take 50 percent and more of your time.
- Don't use global variables to store data. The better practice is to encapsulate all of the data associated with an object with the object.

- Don't use the Boolean negation operator (`!`) with non-Boolean expressions.
- Use the semicolon consistently. Use it or don't, but stick with the original style you choose.

Comments

- In general, avoid including information in your comments that is likely to become out-of-date.
- Avoid the assembly language style of commenting every line of code.
- Use C++ style comments (`//`) instead of C style comments (`/* */`), even though both are permitted.
- If you need to leave reminders in the code about uncompleted work, use the following format:

```
// REMIND: mm/dd/yy programmer's_initials Synopsis
// text of the reminder
```

- Use block comments at the beginning of each file and before each function.
- Visually separate block comments from the rest of the code.
- Use internal comments to describe algorithmic details, notes, and related documentation that spans more than a few code statements.
- You can position very short comments on the same line as the code they describe. Tab over to separate the comments from the statements and to line them up with other nearby comments.

Code Indentation

It's a good idea to set up your editor with tabs every two to four spaces across the line. You can use either tabs or spaces to create your indents. Keep the hierarchy of statements clear. Use tabs to add your comments at the end of a line or to align equal signs.

- Move in one indentation level after each { and out one for each }.

```
function foo() {
  if (condition) {
    statements
  } else {
    statements
  }
```

- Use tabs to align information at the end of a line and to add comments.

```
function foo() {
  var longVariableName    = 0
  var shortName           = 0

  shortName = longVariableName   // comment
```

White Space

- Put a space between keywords and the following parenthesis.

```
  with (window.document.submitForm) {
  ...statements...
}
```

- Do not use spaces between function names and their argument lists.

```
windowOpen("", "myWin", "scrollbars=yes")
```

- Do not use a space after an open parenthesis or before a close parenthesis.
- Use spaces after the commas in argument lists.

Statements

- Always use braces around statements that are part of a control statement.
- The generic form of a control statement (`if`, `for`, `while`) is:

```
<<control statement>> {
    ...statements...
}
```

Comparisons

- You can use implicit testing only for Booleans. For all other comparisons (string, number, object, and so on) you must explicitly compare against a value of the appropriate type.
- Always imply a Boolean value for a stand-alone variable:

```
if (boolean_variable)
if (!boolean_variable)
if (string_variable != "")
if (numeric_variable == 0)
if (numeric_variable != 0)
if (floating_point_variable > 0.0)
if (object != null)          // Always use an explicit
                             // test vs. null
if (object)                  // Bad Style - not allowed
```

Identifier Style {variable, function, and object name choices}

- Try to choose identifier names that are meaningful enough that you do not need to use additional comments to explain them.
- Avoid abbreviations.
- Avoid single character variable names, except for loop variables. Loop variables classically are named with the letters `i`, `j`, `k`, `...`

  ```
  for (var i=0; i < max; i++)
    for (var j=0; j < max; j++)
      ...
  ```

- Avoid trailing underscores.
- Construct the identifier for conversion methods that return an object X by using "to" and the object name.

  ```
  toX()
  ```

- Construct the identifier for a method reporting a property X of an object by using "get" and the property name.

  ```
  getX()
  ```

- Construct the identifier for a method changing a property X of an object by using "set" and the property name.

  ```
  setX(value)
  ```

Variables

- For constant variables, use upper case with underscores separating the words.

  ```
  CONSTANT_VARIABLE = 12345
  ```

- For variable names, use lower case with underscores separating the words.

  ```
  variable_name = "This is a variable"
  ```

- Group variable definitions near their use.

  ```
  Define one variable per line.
  ```

Functions

- Begin function names with a lowercase letter, capitalizing the initial letter of each additional "word."
- If the function takes no parameters, keep both parentheses on the same line.

```
function getChar();          // correct
function getChar(
            null
            );               // Not allowed
```

Objects

- Begin object names with an uppercase letter, capitalizing the initial letter of each additional "word." Do not use underscores.

```
function CapWithInternalAlsoCap(argument) {
...statements...
}
```

- Indent and define the function on the next line, followed by the opening brace ({).
- Add the statements for the function.
- Put the closing brace on a new line, lined up with the word object.

```
function MyObject(argument) {
...statements...
}
```

- Put method function declarations after the object declaration in the source file.

Source Files (.js Files to be Included in a Script)

- Put each object in a separate file.
- Begin each file with a comment including:
  - The file name and/or related identifying information including, if applicable, copyright information.
  - A history table listing dates, authors, and summaries of changes.

- If the file contains more than one object, list the objects, along with a very brief description of each.

```
// File:     Example.js
// Date      Author              Changes
// Nov 22 95 Brian Freeman       Created
// Nov 23 95 Brian Freeman       Added new doc conventions
//
```

Looking at the Script-Writing Process

The following checklist describes the process to follow when writing any JavaScript program:

1. Decide what you want the script to do. Come up with a list of objects, functions, and variables that will accomplish the desired task.
2. Decide what editor you are going to use to create your script. You should use a simple editor that does not provide you with WYSIWYG formatting or an HTML editor if you have one available on your computer. On a UNIX® system, use an editor such as `vi`, `emacs`, or a simple text editor. On a Windows™ system, use an editor such as Note Pad. On a Macintosh®, use an editor such as SimpleText, TeachText, BBEdit, or Alpha.
3. Decide whether you are going to embed your script in an HTML document or whether it contains reusable functions that you store as a stand-alone script in its own file.
4. Decide what to name your file. This step may seem simple or obvious, but it is important to give your HTML document or your script a name that clearly indicates what the file does. Obvious names today may not seem so obvious a few months down the line.
5. Use the appropriate suffix for the file name: `.html` for a HTML file, or `.js` for a JavaScript program.
6. Write the script.
7. Include comments at the beginning of the script to describe its purpose, and annotate each section of the script. These comments can be useful when you debug the script, and they help you interpret a script that may be used only occasionally. Comments are also invaluable in helping others to interpret scripts you have written.
8. Save the file often.
9. If you have created a stand-alone script, create an HTML document that contains a pointer to your script file.

10. Open a Web Browser and run the HTML file.
11. From the Navigator browser, you can load the file in two ways: 1) Choose Open from the File menu; 2) If you know the path to the file, click on the Open button and type the name of the file. If the file is local, type `file:///`*`path/filename`*. The separators for file name paths differ depending on your platform: On UNIX, the separator is a slash (/). On Windows system, the separator is a backslash (\). On Macintosh systems the separator is a slash (/) and spaces are represented by `%20`, which is the ASCII equivalent of the space character.
12. If errors occur, debug your script. Edit the file, fix the problem, and reload the script. In Navigator, hold down the Shift key and click on the Reload button. For detailed instructions on how to debug your scripts, see Chapter 4, "Debugging Scripts."

Creating the Hello World Script

Use the following steps to create your first JavaScript program.

1. Open a text editor program and create a document named `hello.html`.
2. Type the following information in the document:

```
<HTML>
<HEAD>
<TITLE>Hello World!</TITLE>
<SCRIPT LANGUAGE="JavaScript">
document.write("Hello World!")
</SCRIPT>
</HEAD>
<BODY>
</BODY>
</HTML>
```

3. Read the information over to make sure you have spelled everything correctly and have matching angle brackets (<>), matching open and close parentheses, and matching HTML and JavaScript open and close tags.

   One of the most common problems with scripts that don't run properly is mismatched elements. You can look and look at a script with a missing `"`, `>`, or `(` and swear that everything is perfect. It's well worth your time to be a careful proofreader.
4. Save the changes.

Running the Hello World Script

To run your JavaScript program, simply load the HTML document into your Web browser. If you have created a script file on the same system as the browser, you load a "local file." You do this by choosing an option from the File menu named something like Open File or Open Local File.

From the Macintosh version of Netscape Navigator, the option from the File menu is Open File, as shown in Figure 2–2.

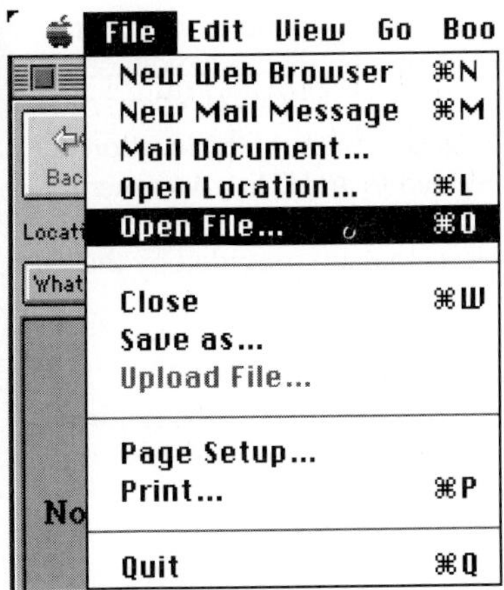

Figure 2–2 Macintosh Navigator File menu

Figure 2–3 shows the result of loading the `hello.html` script in the Macintosh version of Navigator.

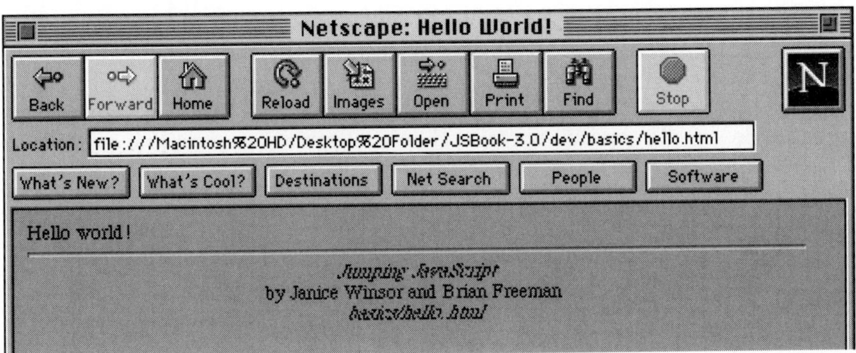

Figure 2–3 Result of loading the Hello World script

Summary of New Terms and Concepts

The new terms and concepts introduced in this chapter are listed in alphabetical order in Table 2-2. The terms and concepts are also included in the glossary at the end of the book.

Table 2-2 **Summary of New Terms and Concepts**

Term/Concept	Description
attribute	An HTML structure that sets a particular parameter value for a specific HTML tag. Examples of attributes are the `LANGUAGE` and `SRC` properties that you can assign to the HTML `<SCRIPT>` tag to define the scripting language and identify the location of a JavaScript file that is not embedded in an HTML document.
built-in objects	The collection of predefined objects that are provided by the JavaScript program.
comments	Any annotation in a script that is marked with special characters either at the beginning of a line or at the beginning and end of the annotation. The interpreter skips over any characters marked as comments.
compiled code	Any script or program that must be checked and verified by a compiler before it can be run.
method	An attribute of an object that instructs the object to perform specific tasks. A method is a function that is attached to an object.
object	A special kind of a variable that provides a way to organize and present data, specify attributes, and provide methods for performing specific tasks.
programming style	The specific way you choose to format your scripting code so that it is easy for a person (as opposed to the computer) to read and interpret.
`<SCRIPT></SCRIPT> tags`	The HTML tags that you use to define the beginning and end of a portion of JavaScript code.

Table 2-2 Summary of New Terms and Concepts (Continued)

Term/Concept	Description
string	A series of alphanumeric characters enclosed in quotation marks.
syntax	The correct way of writing a statement.
template	A structured model used to determine where to locate pieces of JavaScript code within an HTML file.

CHAPTER 3

- Data Types
- Variables
- Functions
- Operators
- Expressions
- Statements
- Summary of New Terms and Concepts

Introducing General Scripting Concepts

Now that you have created and run your first JavaScript, let's take a look at some of the basic elements of the JavaScript language:

- Data types
- Variables
- Functions
- Operators
- Expressions
- Statements

Let's think of writing a script in terms of organizing a potluck party at the beach. Before you get to the party, you perform a set of activities involved in planning the party.

First, you determine the subject of your script, which is to hold a beach party. Then you determine the elements that will make up the script. These elements are the variables or objects that you use within the script to work with all of the aspects of holding a party: type of party, when, where, whom to invite, what to bring, activities.

You determine the time and place to have the party. Usually the time and place are not going to change after you've made your choice, so you can use the specific date and time as values in your party script. These values are called *literals* because they are the real values and you do not expect them to change.

Then, you put together your invitation list. In a script you are likely to create an array, which is simply an ordered list of related data items, to contain your invitation list.

When you have your list of acceptances, you tell each person what you would like brought to the potluck. Next to the list of names, you write down the dish that each person has been assigned to bring. This activity is like assigning values to each variable.

You coordinate activities for the party, so you create a list of possible activities, such as beach volleyball, surfing, football, baseball, kite flying, and frisbee throwing. These activities can be like creating functions to manipulate the variables that are used at a certain place in your script. You set up the basics ahead of time by finding out who can bring the necessary equipment. You can also use methods to manipulate the variables or perform actions such as sending invitations or starting and stopping an activity. You create an agenda that describes the order of events, which is like setting up flow control in a script.

Just as you combine the different elements with actions involved in planning a party, so you combine the different script elements. Figure 3–1 shows the basic building blocks of script writing.

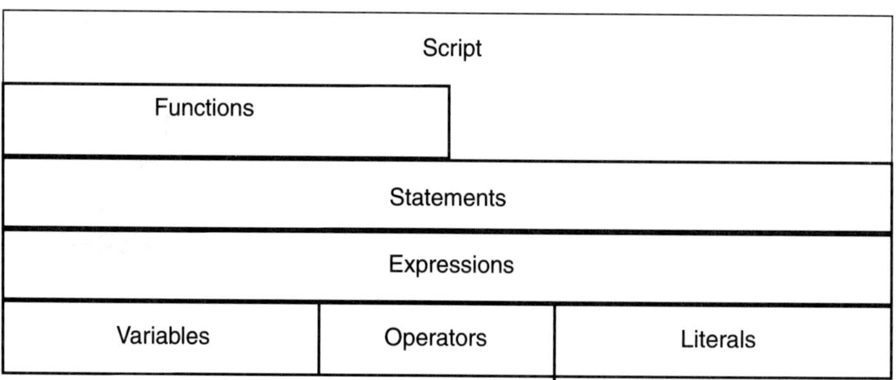

Figure 3–1 Script building blocks

Starting at the bottom of Figure 3–1, the basic script elements are the variables, operators, and literal values that you assign to those variables. Variables and literals are combined into expressions when you join them together with operators like the equal sign. Expressions are combined to form statements.

Statements are combined to form functions. The combination of expressions, statements, and functions form scripts or programs. You can, however, have scripts that are composed only of statements, which is why the Functions block does not go all the way across the diagram. This chapter introduces these basic building blocks.

Data Types

When you write scripts, you almost always work with a chunk of information. This information is often referred to as *data*. You can use several different *types* of data in your scripts:

- Numbers, such as 76 or 3.14159.
- Strings, such as "Hello, World!"
- Logical values (either `true` or `false`). Logical values are also called Boolean values: a statement can be either true or false.
- No value, assigned by using the special keyword `null`. The `null` keyword initializes a variable with no value.

So, the term *data type*, simply refers to whether the data is a number, a string, true or false, or null.

You can assign these data types to variables and also use them with functions. A function is a self-contained mini-program that performs a specific task. You'll learn more about variables in the next section and about functions in "Functions" on page 48.

Variables

The *variable* is one of the fundamentals of every programming language. A variable is a storage location for data. In the beginning of this chapter, we describe determining what each party guest will bring as being similar to assigning variables. When you write your script to manage the organization of your beach party, the first thing you would do would be to decide on the list of party guests. When you have your list of acceptances, the values that you would assign to those variables would be the food and recreational equipment that you ask each guest to bring.

A variable is a convenient way to store data so that it can be used later in the program. It might seem simpler to just use the value wherever it shows up in the script. There are, however, good reasons why you assign values to variables instead of using the *literal value* or expression in your script:

- If you use literal values in your script, you cannot change or operate on them later in the script. You may need to preserve the literal value for use later in the script.
- You can make variable names shorter and more descriptive.

Variables use the following syntax:

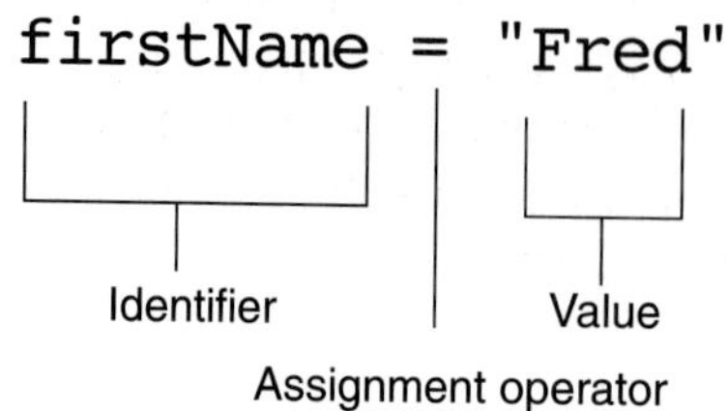

- The *identifier* is the name of the variable.
- The *assignment operator* (in this case, an equal sign) assigns the value on the right of the equal sign to the identifier on the left of the equal sign.
- The *value* specifies the contents of the variable. In this example, the value is a string, so it is enclosed in double quotes.

When you declare a variable, the variable also has a fourth piece:

- The `var` statement, which goes before the identifiers, tells the JavaScript program that the next thing following the space is an identifier for a variable.

Identifiers

An identifier is simply a name that either you or the JavaScript language gives to a variable, function, or object when you declare it.

Use the following rules to create identifiers in your JavaScript code:

- Use any combination of upper- and lowercase letters, and the digits from 0–9 in the rest of the identifier. You can also use the underscore character (_) in the body of the identifier.
- Do not use spaces within the identifier.
- Do not use JavaScript keywords.
- Make sure the identifier is descriptive enough that it helps you remember what part it plays in the script.

- Identifiers can be any length you want.
- Use a mix of upper- and lowercase letters to make your identifiers easier to read. For example, the variable identifier `firstName` is easier to read than `firstname`.

Keywords. *Keywords* are the words that make up the JavaScript language. Keywords are sometimes called *reserved words* because the JavaScript language holds these words in reserve and uses them in a very specific way when a script is executed. You cannot change the usage of a keyword or use one as an identifier. Table 3-1 contains a list of reserved JavaScript keywords. Because it's easy to forget the keywords, you can also find them in Appendix C.

Table 3-1 Reserved JavaScript Keywords

abstract	else	int	switch
boolean	extends	interface	synchronized
break	false	long	this
byte	final	native	throw
case	finally	new	throws
catch	float	null	transient
char	for	package	true
class	function	private	try
const	goto	protected	typeof
continue	if	public	var
default	implements	return	void
delete	import	short	volatile
do	in	static	while
double	instanceof	super	with

Some of the reserved words in this table are not currently used by the JavaScript language. Technically, `true` and `false` are Boolean literals and `null` is an object literal.

White Space

The spaces, tabs, and new lines (line breaks) that you put in your scripts are known as *white space*. You can add extra spaces, tabs, form feeds, and new lines to make your code easier to read. The extra spaces, tabs, form feeds, and new lines are removed by the interpreter. It's up to you whether you put an extra space on either side of the equal sign of any variables you declare or leave the spaces out. The expressions:

```
var firstName="Fred"
```

and

```
var firstName = "Fred"
```

are identical to the JavaScript program.

Tip – Don't put new lines within multiple-line quoted strings or you will get an error message. Instead, put each quoted string on a separate line. For example, instead of:

```
"abcdef
ghijk" + "def"
```

use

```
"abcdefghijk" +
"def"
```

Literal Values

At times you may want to use a literal value instead of assigning the value to a variable. A literal value can be an:

- Integer
- Floating-point number
- Boolean value
- String
- Null

For example, if you're using 76 trombones in your script, and the numeric value of trombones is always 76, and the musical instrument is always a trombone, instead of creating two variables to contain these values, as shown below:

```
var numberOfTrombones = 76
var musicalInstrument = "trombone"
```

ou can simply use the literal value `76` wherever you would have used the ariable `numberOfTrombones` and use the literal value `"trombone"` wherever ou would have used the variable `musicalInstrument`.

literal value is the same whether it stands alone or is assigned as the right-hand art of an expression.

Ve recommend, however, that you create variables for literal values because it nakes future maintenance of a script easier. If the literal value should change, you eed to change it in only one place. And, because you are following good rogramming practice and initializing your variables in the `<HEAD>` of the ocument, the literal is also easier to find.

eclaring a Variable

he action of creating a variable is called *declaring a variable*. It is good rogramming practice to group all of your variables declarations and functions ogether at the beginning of your program. This practice can help you maintain nd debug your program and make it easier for somebody else to understand it.

ou can declare a variable without assigning it a value by using the syntax:

```
var variableName
```

or example, to declare a new variable called `partyLocation`, the JavaScript tatement is:

```
var partyLocation
```

ssigning a Value to a Variable

You can assign a value to a variable you have declared, using one of the ssignment operators. The equal sign (=) is the most common assignment operator. When you assign a value to a variable that has already been declared, you do not use the `var` keyword. Instead, you use the syntax:

```
variableName = value
```

The JavaScript language is *dynamically typed*. What that means is that when you declare a variable, you do not need to specify its data type. The JavaScript language determines the data type at runtime, depending on the context.

In *strongly typed* languages, you cannot create a variable and assign it a numeric data type in one place and a string data type in another part of the program. The program would not compile or interpret properly.

However, in JavaScript, you can define a variable as follows:

```
example = 76
```

The JavaScript language does not give you an error message if, later in the same program, you assign the same variable a string value. For example:

```
example = "trombones"
```

The syntax you use for the value depends on its data type. The data types you car use are:

- Numeric
- String
- Logical or Boolean (true/false)
- Null

Numeric Values. When you assign numeric values, you do not use quotation marks.

For example:

```
day = 25
month = 5
year = 1996
price = 19.95
```

String Values. When you assign a string value, you must put the string within either single or double quotation marks.

```
emptyString = ""
name = "Fred"
message = 'Hello World!'
partyLocation = "Half Moon Bay"
combinedStrings = "abc" + "def"
```

If you do not use quotation marks, the JavaScript language thinks you are assigning the value of one variable to another variable. For example, if you assign the value `Fred` to the variable `name`:

```
name = Fred
```

the JavaScript program thinks you are assigning the value of one variable (`Fred`) to another variable (`name`). If you have not declared a variable named `Fred`, your program will give a runtime error.

you want the string to display either single or double quotation marks as part of s text, put a backslash before each of the quotation marks. This syntax is called *caping a character*. The collection of characters is called an *escape sequence*. To have ıe message variable display "Hello World!" with the quotation marks, the ariable assignment looks like this:

```
message = "\"Hello World!\""
```

ee "Escape Characters for String Formatting" on page 1130 for a complete list of ring literal escape sequences.

ogical Values (Boolean). Some variables can have only a true or false alue. In these cases, you use the Boolean literals `true` and `false` as the value or the variable assignment. For example:

```
married = true
dead = false
```

Null Values. At times you may want to create a variable and not give it any alue at all. This is called assigning a null value. You can assign null values as hown below:

```
variableName = null
```

he following variables produce the same result in a JavaScript program:

```
total = null
middleName = null
```

nitializing a Variable

ou can assign a value to a variable at the time you declare it. This process is nown as *initializing* the variable. You use the following syntax to initialize a ariable:

```
var variableName = value
```

Whether you initialize your variables or just declare them depends on how you ıse the variables and calculate the values in your script.

n general, if an initial value is not required for the code to work properly, you can omit the initial value. For example:

```
var result
var a = 1
var b = 2
result = a + b
```

The variables a and b require an initial value, otherwise `result` could be anything. However, it's good programming practice to initialize each variable. To use good practice, you would rewrite the previous example in the following way:

```
var result = null
var a = 1
var b = 2
result = a + b
```

Functions

Functions are self-contained mini-scripts that you can use to organize blocks of code that recur several times within a script. By creating a function, you can use a single command to trigger complex actions without needing to repeat the code a number of times within the script. You can also develop generic functions that you can reuse in any script.

First, you define the function by using the `function` keyword in the following syntax:

```
function functionName(arguments) {
...
}
```

We suggest that you always define your functions between the HTML `<HEAD>` and `</HEAD>` tags. In this way, the function code is loaded and ready to use when the interpreter comes to the call.

After you have created the function, you *call* it, using the following syntax, from the place in the script where you want the function code to execute:

```
functionName()
```

Calling a function can *return a value*. In other words, the script extracts the value from the function that you defined and uses that value at the place in the script where you called the function.

In the following example, the function `sayHi()` defines an alert window that contains the message `Hi there` and returns a value of `true`. You'll learn more about alert windows in Chapter 6, "Creating Windows."

```
function sayHi() {
  alert("Hi there")
  return true
}
```

In this script, the following statement calls the `sayHi()` function:

```
<BODY onLoad="sayHi()">
```

his function is called from the onLoad event handler, so that the first thing that appens after the window loads is that the alert window is displayed. You'll see is script in its entirety in Chapter 6, "Creating Windows."

'hen you call a function from a script, it executes the function and returns to the lace in the script immediately after the statement that called the function. If a alue is returned from the function, you must assign it to a variable or use it in an xpression. If you do not use the value returned from the function, it is lost.

or example:

```
result = 1 + 2
```

the same as:

```
function add(a,b){
   return a + b
}

result = add(1,2)
```

perators

he JavaScript language provides many *operators* that you can use on values to ompare, contrast, and calculate other values. An operator is a symbol that dicates an action to be performed on one or two values. The values that perators use to compute the result are called *operands*. We've divided these perators into five groups, described in Table 3-2:

able 3-2 Groups of JavaScript Operators

roup	Description
lathematical	Performs mathematical calculations on two or more operands, adding, subtracting, multiplying, or dividing.
ssignment	Assigns the value of the right-hand operand into the variable name on the left side of the assignment operator.
oolean	Performs Boolean arithmetic on one or two Boolean operands.
omparison	Compares the value of two operands and determines if the operands are the same or different. If the same, it returns a value of `true`; if different, it returns a value of `false`.

Table 3-2 Groups of JavaScript Operators (Continued)

Group	Description
Bitwise	Performs arithmetic or column-shifting actions on the binary (base-2) representations of two operands.

Precedence

When the interpreter evaluates operators, the JavaScript language evaluates thos expressions in a specific order. This operator *precedence* determines which operators precede which other operators. Because the interpreter cannot evaluat all of the expressions at the same time, it needs to know where to start. See "Operator Precedence" on page 770 for more information on operator precedenc and a table of operator precedence.

We'll defer the discussion of assignment, comparison, Boolean, and bitwise operators until Chapter 25, "Understanding Operators."

Mathematical Operators

You're probably already familiar with the *mathematical operators* listed in Table 3-

Table 3-3 Mathematical Operators

Operator	Operation
+	Addition
-	Subtraction
*	Multiplication
/	Division
%	Modulus (returns the remainder of a division)

When you use any of these operators, the values that these operators use to compute the result are called operands. In the following statement:

```
2 + 4
```

The 2 and 4 are operands, and the + is the operator. This example uses literal numbers for values. In scripts, it's much more common to use operands that are variables. For example,

```
total = price * discount
```

/hen the values are numeric, the JavaScript language adds the numbers together. [owever, you can use the plus sign (+) to join together (or *concatenate*) two or nore strings. The plus sign, which acts as a *string concatenation operator*, combines ne exact value of the strings. It does not know about words and spaces. When ou join phrases by using this operator, be sure to add a space character, either as art of the individual string or as a separate space. You can add the space as a teral string, as shown in the following example:

```
firstName = "Fred"
lastName = "Spirit"
fullName = firstName + " " + LastName
```

he `fullName` variable returns the value:

```
Fred Spirit
```

ou can also use a similar construction to include values returned by a script in a nore user-friendly output format.

:xpressions

ou combine variables, operators, and values, to create *expressions*. An expression : a combination of variables, literals, functions, objects, and operators that valuates to a single value.

he following examples show some expressions:

```
1 + 1
isBlue
total = price * discount
(1 + (1 * 2)) == ((4 / 2) + 1)
```

tatements

.n individual self-contained chunk of code that performs an action and controls ne sequence of execution is called a *statement*. Statements can contain other tatements.

'he following list describes the types of JavaScript statements:

Empty statement

`if ... then` statement

`while` statement

`for` statement

`break` statement

- `continue` statement
- `return` statement
- `with` statement
- `for` statement

For information on the syntax and use of these statements, see the chapters in Part 5, "Controlling Your Scripts."

Summary of New Terms and Concepts

The new terms and concepts introduced in this chapter are listed in alphabetical order in Table 3-4. The terms and concepts are also included in the glossary at the end of the book

Table 3-4 **Summary of New Terms and Concepts**

Term/Concept	Definition
assign	To change the value of an existing variable.
assignment operator	A symbol that indictes an action to be performed on one or two values. An assignment operator is one of the following symbols: =, +=, =+, *=, /=, %=, <<=, >>=, >>>=, &=, ^=, or |=. The equal sign is the most common assignment operator. The equal sign assigns the value on the right side of the equal sign to the variable on the left side of the equal sign.
call	A programming term that represents a temporary branch in a script to use a different routine, such as a function. After the routine is executed, the main script continues at the next instruction.
code	The complete set of statements that make up a script.
concatenate	To combine two or more similar elements, such as character strings, to form a new, larger element.
data	The information that you use as values in a script.
data type	The numeric, string, Boolean, or null category assigned to a piece of data.
declare a variable	To assign an identifier to a variable. When you declare a variable, you can also assign an initial value it.

Table 3-4 Summary of New Terms and Concepts (Continued)

Term/Concept	Definition
dynamically typed language	A programming language in which you do not need to specify the type of data when you declare a variable. Instead, the data type is determined at runtime and depends on its context.
escape a character	To put a backslash (\) in front of a special character such as a quotation mark (") so that the character is displayed as a part of the output of a script.
escape sequence	A backslash (\) and the character that follows it.
event handler	A JavaScript structure that responds to a specific event such as a mouse click in a certain location. The response is that the script performs an action defined by specific event handler attributes. Event handlers have the same name as the event, preceded by the word on. For example, the event handler for `Click` is `onClick`.
expression	A combination of variables, literals, functions, objects, and operators that evaluates to a single value.
function	A self-contained script or portion of a script designed to do a specific task and, optionally, to return a value.
identifier	The name you assign to a variable, function, or object.
initialize	To assign a value to a variable or object at the time you declare it.
keyword	Any of the terms reserved for a special purpose in the JavaScript language. You cannot use keywords as variable names.
literal	An actual numeric, string, Boolean, or null value; for example, 76 or "trombones". You must enclose string literals in single or double quotes.
mathematical operators	The +, -, *, /, and % symbols that you use to perform the add, subtract, multiply, divide, and modulus operations in a script.
method	A function that is a property of an object.
operand	The variable values that operators act on.

Table 3-4 Summary of New Terms and Concepts (Continued)

Term/Concept	Definition
operator	A symbol that indicates an action to be performed on one or two values. You can have mathematical operators (addition, subtraction, multiplication, division), logical operators (AND, OR, and NOT) and relational operators (equals, less than, and greater than).
pass	To send data or values to a function or applet.
precedence	The sequence that determines which operators precede, or come before, which other operators when an expression is evaluated.
return a value	A value retrieved from memory. When you assign a value to a variable, the value is stored in computer memory. When the script asks for the value for a particular variable, the value is retrieved from memory.
statement	A single unit of programming code that defines and controls the flow of the program.
string concatenation operator	The plus sign (+) that you can use to combine separate strings to form longer phrases.
strongly typed language	A programming language in which variables must be assigned a specific data type.
value	Data, either numeric or alphanumeric.
variable	An identifier that you use to name specific data elements that you plan to use in a script. The contents of a variable are stored in computer memory during the execution of a script.
white space	The spaces, tabs, form feeds, and new lines between characters in a script.

55

CHAPTER 4

- Syntax Errors
- Design or Logic Errors
- JavaScript Error Messages
- Some Debugging Tips and Tricks
- Debugging Checklist
- Summary of New Terms and Concepts

Debugging Scripts

This chapter provides some techniques and tips you can use in debugging your scripts. A *bug* is any error in either hardware or software that results in an unexpected result or a computer malfunction. Such problems have been called bugs since the early days of computing when Grace Hopper found a moth in one of the computer switches used to set the 0s and 1s in the first UNIVAC, or so I'm told. Although this was clearly a hardware bug, the term is used to refer to both hardware and software glitches. And, by extension, when you find those pesky problems and solve them, you *debug* your scripts.

We'd like to suggest that you take a quick browse through this chapter before you start experimenting with scripts and writing your own. Come back to this chapter and use it as a reference when you need to do some real debugging. One way to understand what's happening inside a script, especially one that was written by someone else, is to pick it apart and break it intentionally or to add debugging statements using alerts. Comment out pieces that you don't understand and see what happens. If you think you have a better way of implementing the script, make a copy of the script and try your way to see if it works.

Programming styles are unique. You can write a successful script in many different ways. You may very well have useful and creative ideas on how to script that are not shown in our examples. Be adventuresome and creative in your approach to scripting. Writing faulty scripts and then fixing them is one of the best ways to improve your understanding of the JavaScript language. Once you have that "aha" of understanding, believe me, you'll remember what you've learned.

Compiled programming languages typically provide a suite of debugging tools that you can use to determine where problems are in your program. Interpreted languages usually do not provide debugging tools, although Microsoft now provides a debugger for JScript. The only way you can debug your script without a debugger is by running it and seeing whether the script does what you expect.

You can, however, use some of the elements of the JavaScript language itself to help you debug your scripts. We'll provide some suggestions and examples later in this chapter.

Bugs fall into two broad categories:

- Syntax errors, such as mismatched quotes, braces, or parentheses.
- Design or logic errors, such as undeclared variables, mismatched data types, or failed connections between function calls and their functions.

Note – The distinction between interpreted and compiled JavaScript is getting blurred. Although JavaScript can always be run as an interpreted language, compilers are being added to enhance scripting performance, especially for server-side JavaScript.

Syntax Errors

Interpreted languages are more difficult to debug because of the lack of a formal set of debugging tools. Some smart editors, such as emacs, track pairs of quotes, braces, and parentheses for you. If you don't have access to a smart editor to help you, be very careful to check your syntax before you run the script. Even when you copy someone else's script to try, it's very easy to introduce syntax errors.

Use the following checklist to debug common scripting problems:

- Do all of your HTML tags have matching angle brackets (<>)?
- Do your HTML tags have the proper closing entry tag such as `</BODY>`, `</HTML>`, `</FORM>`, and so on?
- Do you have any missing single or double quotation marks?

- Do you have any missing parentheses or curly braces?
- Are there any typographical errors?
- Are there any spelling errors?
- Do you have any capitalization errors? The JavaScript language is case sensitive. For example, you create a new `Date` object by using the statement `new Date()`. If you type `new date()` instead, you'll get an error message when you run the script saying: `date is not defined`.

When the interpreter encounters a syntax error, it displays a large error window with information about the problem, as shown in Figure 4–1.

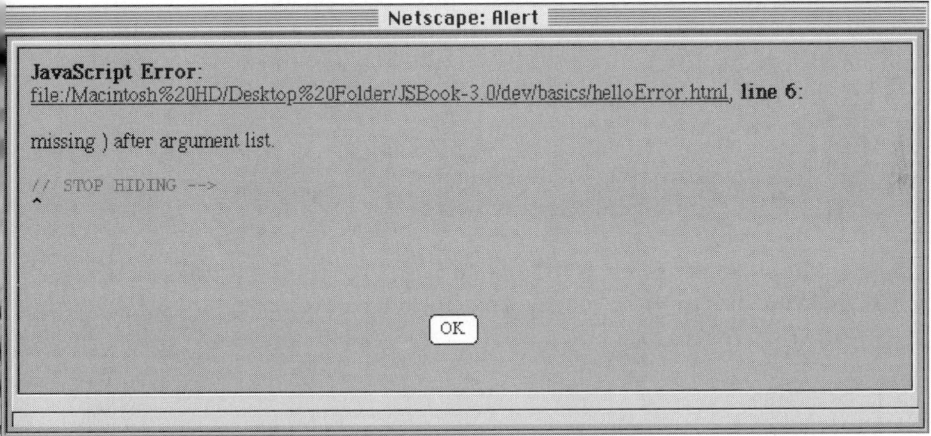

Figure 4–1 JavaScript error window

The error window provides you with the following information:

- The URL or path to the offending file, followed by a line number

  The line number is the interpreter's best guess about the actual line of code (excluding any comments) where the error occurs.
- An error message (in this case, `missing ) after argument list`)
- A line of code with a caret (^) showing the location of the problem
- An OK button

The JavaScript language does its best to provide you with helpful information and is best at detecting syntax errors and showing you the location of the problem. You'll also see error windows for the more complex and devious design or logic errors in your script.

Sometimes the error windows stack on top of each other, with the latest error on the top. When this happens, start with the bottom error message first.

Note – Be aware that the line number in the error message window does not always pinpoint the proper line in the script, although it gets you close to the error.

The error message in Figure 4–1 results from a missing parentheses in the following `helloError.html` script. Can you find the problem? The line numbers below are not in the script itself. We have add them to this example to help you understand how the interpreter counts lines.

```
<!--
        JavaScript Book Example
          debugHelloError.html

    This script is a classic "Hello World" done with
    JavaScript. It contains a syntax error.
-->

1. <HTML>
2. <HEAD>
3. <TITLE>Hello World with Error</TITLE>
4. <SCRIPT LANGUAGE="JavaScript">
<!-- HIDE FROM OLD BROWSERS

5. document.write("Hello there."

// STOP HIDING -->
</SCRIPT>
</HEAD>

<BODY>
<HR>
<CENTER>
<H1>Hello World</H1>
</CENTER>
</BODY>
</HTML>
```

The problem is actually on the fifth line of JavaScript code, not counting the comments which the interpreter skips over (although the error window shows you the error is on line six). The error message tells you that the problem is a missing parenthesis. Because the statements in the error messages do not always point directly to the problem, you need to be a bit of a detective to figure out the specific location of the problem. You can, however, be sure that something's wrong that you must fix before you can run your script successfully.

Design or Logic Errors

Diagnosing and fixing design and logic errors is the most difficult kind of debugging. This section provides information to help you with those thorny problems.

HTML Layout and Script Parsing Order

A common problem when writing scripts is that the interpreter does not interpret the command in exactly the way that you expect. To help you debug your scripts, you need to know the way the interpreter builds a page, called *layout*, and how it substitutes variables with values and *parses* (divides up) statements into recognizable parts. The layout and parsing order can have a definite impact on how your scripts run and whether they produce the results you expect.

When Navigator loads an HTML document, it transforms the HTML tags and values into a graphical display on your computer screen. Layout generally is sequential; Navigator starts from the first line of the HTML file and works its way down, interpreting how to display elements on the screen as it goes. It begins with the `<HEAD>` of an HTML document, then begins at the top of the `<BODY>` and works its way down the file line by line.

When an HTML element is interpreted, the corresponding JavaScript object is created. You cannot use any properties, methods, or event handlers for an object in the script until after you have written the HTML code that creates the object.

In other words, JavaScript can create no object before its time. It can only reflect and operate on the HTML that it has already encountered. Because of this "top-down" behavior, the JavaScript language can only reflect any HTML that it has already encountered.

For example, suppose you define a form with a set of radio buttons:

```
<FORM NAME="genderForm">
<B>Gender:</B>
<INPUT
 TYPE="hidden"
 NAME="answer"
```

```
 VALUE="gender-m">
<INPUT
 TYPE="radio"
 NAME="genderRadio"
 VALUE="sex-m"
 CHECKED
 onClick="genderForm.answer.value='gender-m';
         alert(genderForm.answer.value)"
> Male
<INPUT
 TYPE="radio"
 NAME="genderRadio"
 VALUE="gender-f"
 onClick="genderForm.answer.value='gender-f';
         alert(genderForm.answer.value)"
> Female
</FORM>
```

These radio button elements have corresponding JavaScript objects. You can refer to a form with the name of `genderForm` and to a `radio` object with the name of `genderRadio`.

You can use these objects and their properties anywhere after you have defined the form. You cannot, however, use these objects before you define the form.

So, for example, you could display the value of these objects in a script after the form definition:

```
alert(genderForm.answer.value)
```

However, if you put this statement above the form definition in the HTML page, you would get an error because the objects have not yet been created in the Navigator.

In the same way, once the element has been created by Navigator, the property value is created as part of the form, and setting it in the script does not affect its value or appearance.

For example, suppose you have defined a document title as follows:

```
<TITLE>Select Object</TITLE>
```

This title is reflected in JavaScript as the value of `document.title`. Once the Navigator has displayed this layout in the title bar of the Navigator window, you cannot change the value in JavaScript. If later in the page, you include the following statement:

```
document.title = "Select Object with 3.0 Features"
```

either the value of `document.title` nor the title bar is changed, This statement oes not generate an error; it is simply ignored.

he script parsing order follows the same top-down sequence. It's why you efine your variables and functions as part of the <HEAD></HEAD> HTML tags. ecause the lines of code between these tags are interpreted first, they are loaded nd ready for you when you call them in the body of your script.

perator Precedence

n addition, to make sure that your scripts are accurate, you need to be aware of *perator precedence*. The JavaScript language assigns different priorities to the ifferent types of operators, so that some expressions are evaluated before other xpressions.

ll math and string concatenation is done before comparison operators are valuated. The operators are evaluated according to their precedence level.

you're not getting the answers that you expect from your scripts, you probably eed to test your operator statements to make sure that the statements are being valuated in the proper order.

or more information about operator precedence and a table of operator recedence, see Chapter 25, "Understanding Operators."

avaScript Error Messages

Vhen your script contains information that the interpreter cannot handle, an rror window is displayed containing an error message and some information hat may not always be as helpful as you'd like) about where the error occurred the script. This section describes some of the most common error messages. The rror messages are sort of in alphabetical order. It's tough to alphabetize error nessages that have variable information at the beginning of the line. We've used *omething* as a place holder for the variable information provided by the nterpreter to indicate the source of the problem.

unction does not always return a value

ou are not being consistent in what is being returned from your function. At least ne return statement in the function returns a value and at least one return tatement does not return a value. When you define a function, all of your return tatements within that function should be consistent: they should all return a alue or all not return a value.

he following `debugReturnValueErr.html` script has an improperly defined unction that does not return values for all of the return statements.

```
<!--
        debugReturnValueErr.html

    This example generates the "function does not
    always return a value" error message.
-->

<HTML>
<HEAD>
<TITLE>Fcn Does Not Always Return a Value</TITLE>
<SCRIPT LANGUAGE="JavaScript">
<!-- HIDE FROM OLD BROWSERS

//
// This function generates the "function
// does not always return a value" error
// message.
//
// To correct the error, make the second return
// statement return a value. For example,
//
//   return false
//
function returnValueErr(obj)
{
  if (obj == null)
  {
    return true
  }
  return         // this line generates the error
}
// STOP HIDING -->
</SCRIPT>


<BODY>
<P>When you load this file, it generates the "function does
not always return a value" error message.</P>

<P>To correct the problem, make the second return
statement in returnValueErr() return "false.".</P>

</BODY>
</HTML>
```

igure 4–2 shows the error message that is displayed when you load the ebugReturnValueErr.html script.

Netscape: Alert

JavaScript Error: file:/Macintosh%20HD/Desktop%20Folder/JSBook-3.0/dev/debug/debugReturnValueErr.html, **line 20:**

function does not always return a value.

```
return          // this line generates the error
.................................................^
```

OK

igure 4–2 Error message from debugReturnValueErr.html script

dentifier is a reserved word

'ou used a reserved word as a name for a variable, function, or object. JavaScript eserved words (also called keywords) are used as names for statements, unctions, methods, or objects. Some words are reserved for future use. For xample, `true` is a reserved word. If you use the word true to define a variable, 'ou'll see the `identifier is a reserved word` error message:

```
true = "This statement is true."
```

'or a complete list of JavaScript reserved words, see "Reserved JavaScript Keywords" on page 1129.

nissing) after argument list

)ne of the arguments in your script is missing a closing parenthesis.

nissing } after function body

'ou'll see this error message when you're missing the curly brace at the end of a unction. When the function has nested items such as conditional statements and oops, you'll have multiple pairs of curly braces. In more complex cases, the avaScript interpreter does not always pinpoint the exact spot where the brace is nissing. When you get this error message, you can be sure that there's a missing race within the function specified, although it may not necessarily be at the end.)o a careful check for left and right braces to find the missing culprit.

For a brushup on functions, see Chapter 3, "Introducing General Scripting Concepts."

missing ; after for-loop condition

missing ; after for-loop initializer

You'll see one of these messages if your `for` statement is missing one or more semicolons to separate its arguments. It's easy to make this error because the JavaScript language uses commas everywhere else to separate arguments. The `for` loop syntax comes from the C language.

nested comment

You have nested /* multiline comments. When you use the /* */ comment format, your comment marks must match, in the same way that quotes, parentheses, and brackets always come in pairs.

out of memory

The system is out of memory and cannot perform any more actions. You may see this error message in a script that creates a lot of string objects or that has a runaway loop in it.

something cannot be indexed as an array

You have incorrectly used an array reference for something that is not an array.

something has no properties

You'll see this error message when you've made an incorrect reference to an object. It's most likely you'll encounter this message when you're referencing an object stored as an array. For example, the following `debugNoPropertiesErr.html` file tries to obtain the `name` property of subobjects without first determining their type.

Note – This script uses the `typeof` statement introduced in the Navigator 3.0 release.

```
<!--
        debugNoPropertiesErr.html
    This example generates the "has no property"
    error message.
-->
```

```
<HTML>
<HEAD>
<TITLE>Has No Property</TITLE>
<SCRIPT LANGUAGE="JavaScript">
<!-- HIDE FROM OLD BROWSERS

//
// This function generates the "has no
// property" error message if given certain
// objects.
//
// It's trying to programmatically obtain the name
// of subobjects without testing their type
// first.
//
function displayProperties(obj)
{
  var rvalue = ""

  for (var i in obj) {
    rvalue += "type " + (typeof obj[i]) + ": "
    rvalue += obj[i].name + " = " + obj[i]
    rvalue += "\n"
  }
  return rvalue
}

// STOP HIDING -->
</SCRIPT>

<BODY>
<P>This example generates the "xxx has no
property" error message when you click on the
Display Properties button.</P>

<CENTER>
<FORM NAME="btnForm">
<INPUT TYPE="button" NAME="displayBtn"
  VALUE="Display Properties"
  onClick="alert(displayProperties(window))">
</FORM>
</CENTER>
</BODY>
</HTML>
```

Figure 4–3 shows the error message that is displayed when you load the `debugNoPropertiesErr.html` script.

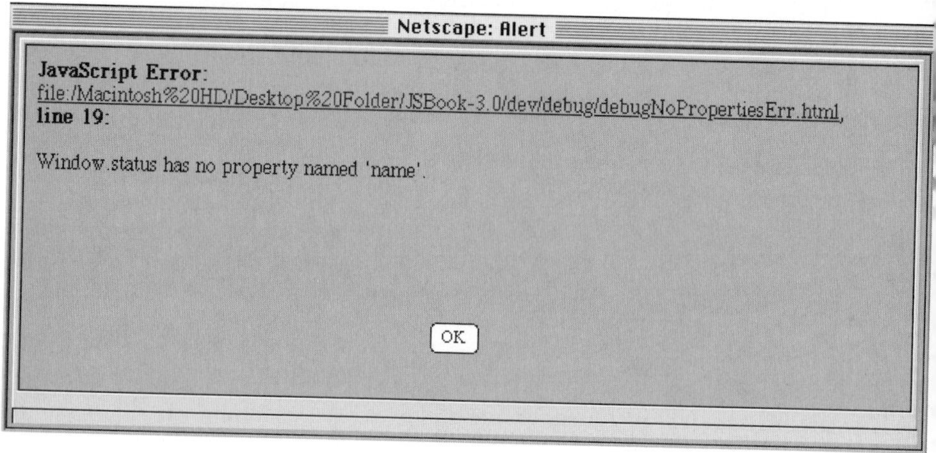

Figure 4–3 Error message from `debugNoPropertiesErr.html` script

something is not defined

If you see this error message, it's likely that you have a mismatch (typo or spelling error) between a function that you call and the function definition. Remember that the JavaScript language is case sensitive, and function calls and function identifiers must match exactly to work properly. For example, if you define a function named `myWin` and call it as `mywin` (without the capital `W`), you'll get this error message.

It could also mean that you forgot to declare a variable.

Another possible reason for this error message is that you forgot to enclose a string literal in quotes. If you create the assignment statement:

```
instrument = trombones
```

the variable `instrument` is assigned the value of the variable `trombones`. If `trombones` hasn't been defined, you will get the error. If, however, you intend to assign the value of `"trombones"` to the variable `instrument`, your statement should be:

```
instrument = "trombones"
```

For a brushup on variables, see Chapter 3, "Introducing General Scripting Concepts."

omething is not a function

'ou've called a function that does not exist or you have used an identifier as a unction when it is not one. To track down this problem, check the following hings:

- Make sure you've defined the function.
- If the function is in a separate `.js` file, make sure you've included the reference to the file and that your function call matches the function definition in the `.js` file.
- Check the spelling and capitalization of function definitions and calls to make sure they match.
- Check the function definition for missing quotes, braces, and parentheses.

omething is not a numeric literal

'ou are trying to perform a numeric operation on a string value instead of a umber. You can use the `parseInt` or `parseFloat` functions to convert strings o numbers. For information on performing numeric calculations, see Chapter 31, Doing Math."

yntax error

This JavaScript generic error message is displayed when the interpreter ncounters a syntax problem with the script but cannot determine exactly what it s.

nterminated string literal

'ou'll see this message when you've forgotten the ending quotation mark for a tring. You're likely to see this message when you concatenate strings or nest uoted strings. If you forget the beginning quotation mark, you'll see the `syntax error` message.

n the following code extract, one of the strings for concatenation is missing its nding quotation mark.

```
// BODY content starts here
 docStr += "<P>This is some text.</P>"
 docStr += "<P>...and some more...</P>"
 docStr += "<P>...and more...</P>
 docStr += "<P>...and more.</P>"
 docStr += "<A HREF=\"http://home.mcom.com\">"
 docStr += "A link to Netscape</A>"

 // the document ends here
 docStr += "</BODY>"
```

Loading this file results in the error window shown in Figure 4–4.

Netscape: Alert

JavaScript Error:
file:/Macintosh%20HD/Desktop%20Folder/JSBook-3.0/dev/objects/document/doc_color.html, **line 51:**

unterminated string literal.

```
  docStr += "<P>...and more...</P>
............^
```

OK

Figure 4–4 Unterminated string literal error message

Notice that the caret is pointing to the first quotation mark because the interpreter does not know where you wanted to end the string. You can see the complete `doc_color.html` script that contains this extract in Chapter 7, "Creating Documents."

Some Debugging Tips and Tricks

Although the JavaScript language does not provide debugging tools, you can use some of the elements of the language to create your own tools to check design or logic errors. This section describes several JavaScript debugging tips and tricks.

Using Netscape JavaScript Protocol to Debug Statements

Netscape Navigator provides you with a way to check single-line statements in the browser. If you're having trouble with a script returning an inappropriate value, you might find this feature helpful.

To access the appropriate Navigator page, from the File menu, choose Open Location, as shown in Figure 4–5.

File Edit View Go Boo
New Web Browser ⌘N
New Mail Message ⌘M
Mail Document...
Open Location... ⌘L
Open File... ⌘O
Close ⌘W
Save as...
Upload File...
Page Setup...
Print... ⌘P
Quit ⌘Q

Figure 4–5 Open Location in the File menu

An Open Location dialog window is displayed. Figure 4–6 shows the Macintosh version.

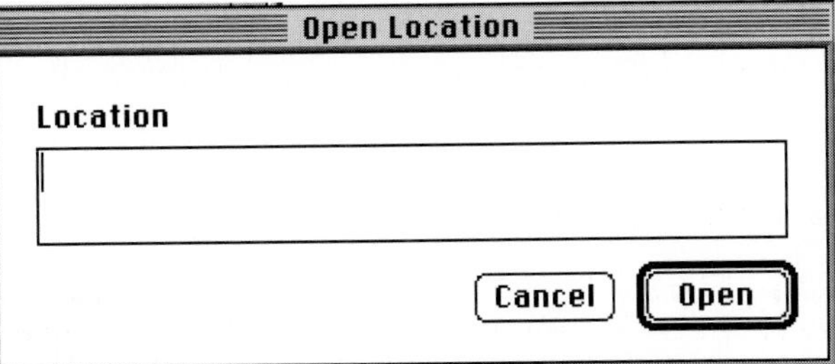

Figure 4–6 Open Location window

Type `javascript:` and click on the Open button. A window with two frames is opened in the browser, as shown in Figure 4–7.

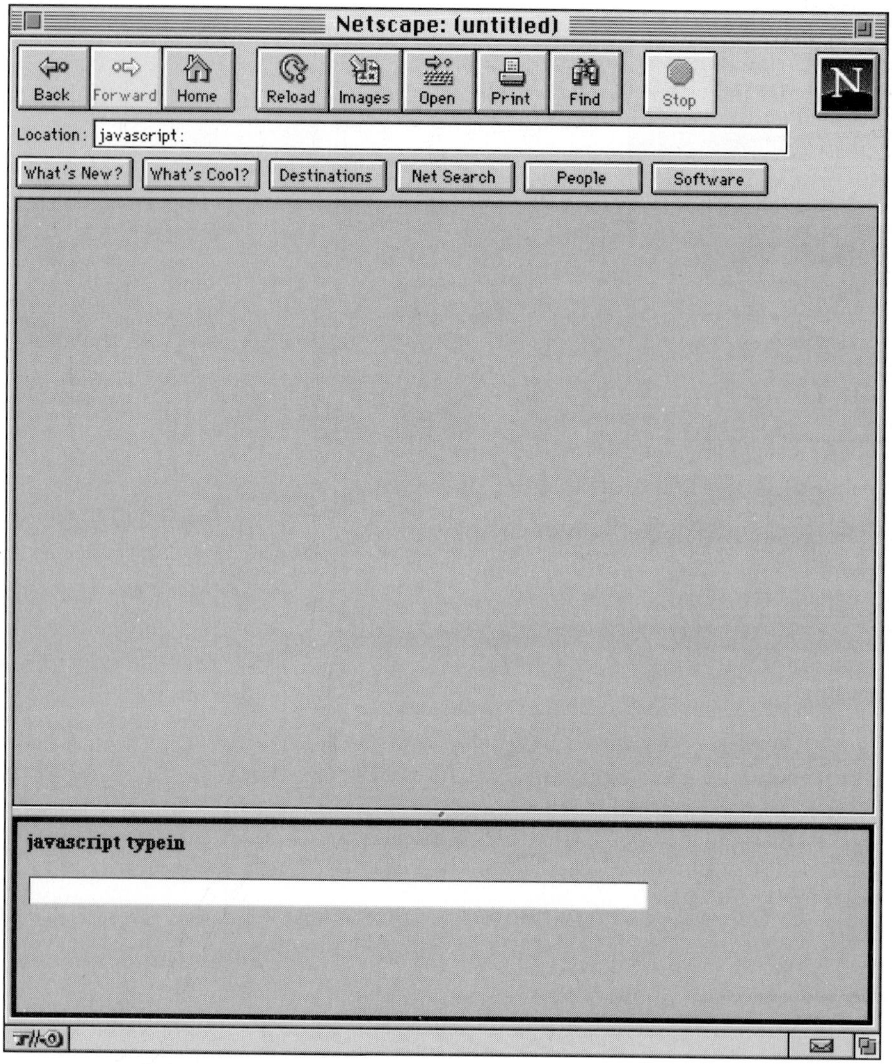

Figure 4–7 JavaScript frames in browser

Once you have this location loaded, you can type a single-line statement in the text field in the bottom frame, and the results are displayed in the top frame.

You can use the text field to assign values to variables, test comparison operators, and even do math. Some statements containing methods may not display a result in the upper frame.

Let's look at a few examples.

You can type in properties and see what results are returned.

For example, typing:

```
parent.frames[0].document.title
```

returns a value of:

```
(Untitled)
```

as long as it's the first statement you type into the window. Otherwise, the statement returns the last string you typed into the text field.

Typing:

```
document.bgColor='blue'
```

turns the background blue and also returns the hexadecimal value for the color, in this case:

```
#0000ff
```

Using Alerts to Set Breakpoints

One of the traditional programming debugging techniques is to set *breakpoints* in a script. A breakpoint is a predefined address in a program where execution is stopped and control is passed to debugging software. Because the `alert()` method of the `window` object displays a modal window that stops operation of a script until the user dismisses it, you can use the `alert()` method as a way to set breakpoints in your script.

In addition, because the `alert()` method of the window object accepts values of any data type as a parameter, you can use the `alert()` method to monitor the value of an expression. Simply use the expression you want to monitor as the parameter to an `alert()` method. The script runs to that point, then stops and displays a window that shows the current value for the expression.

The following `debugNoPropertiesErrAlert.html` script adds an alert to the `debugNoPropertiesErr.html` script from "something has no properties" on page 66. The alert progressively steps through the list of properties and one-by-one builds a complete list of properties. After the last alert is closed, the error message "*xxx* is not a property" is displayed.

```
<!--
        debugNoPropertiesErrAlert.html

    This example generates the "has no property"
    error message and contains an alert() to aid
    the debugging.
-->

<HTML>
```

```
<HEAD>
<TITLE>Has No Property W/Alert</TITLE>
<SCRIPT LANGUAGE="JavaScript">
<!-- HIDE FROM OLD BROWSERS

//
// This function generates the "xxx has no
// property" error message if given certain
// objects.
//
// It's trying to programatically obtain the name
// of subobjects without first testing their type.
//
function displayProperties(obj)
{
  var rvalue = ""

  for (var i in obj) {
    rvalue += "type " + (typeof obj[i]) + ": "
    alert(rvalue)
    rvalue += obj[i].name + " = " + obj[i]
    rvalue += "\n"
  }
  return rvalue
}

// STOP HIDING -->
</SCRIPT>

<BODY>
<P>This example generates the "xxx has no
property" error message when you click on the
Display Properties button.</P>

<CENTER>
<FORM NAME="btnForm">
<INPUT TYPE="button" NAME="displayBtn"
  VALUE="Display Properties"
  onClick="alert(displayProperties(window))">
</FORM>
</CENTER>

</BODY>
</HTML>
```

Figure 4–8 shows the first alert window that is displayed when you click on the Display Properties button.

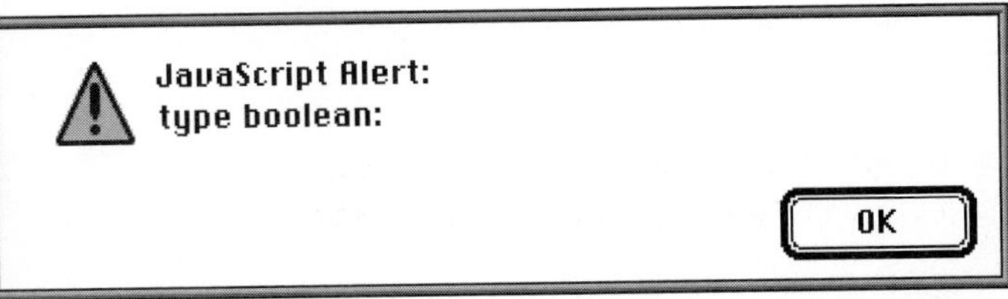

Figure 4–8 First alert from `debugNoPropertiesErrAlert.html` script

String Formatting Tip

If you put a line break in the middle of a string, the interpreter displays error messages. The following code example was split to enable the lines to fit the width of the page:

```
<CENTER><FORM>
<INPUT TYPE="button" VALUE="Nuke the Window"
onClick="confirmClose ('Are you sure you want to
close this window?')">
</FORM></CENTER>
```

When the file containing this code was loaded, the alert windows shown in Figure 4–9 were displayed, one on top of the other.

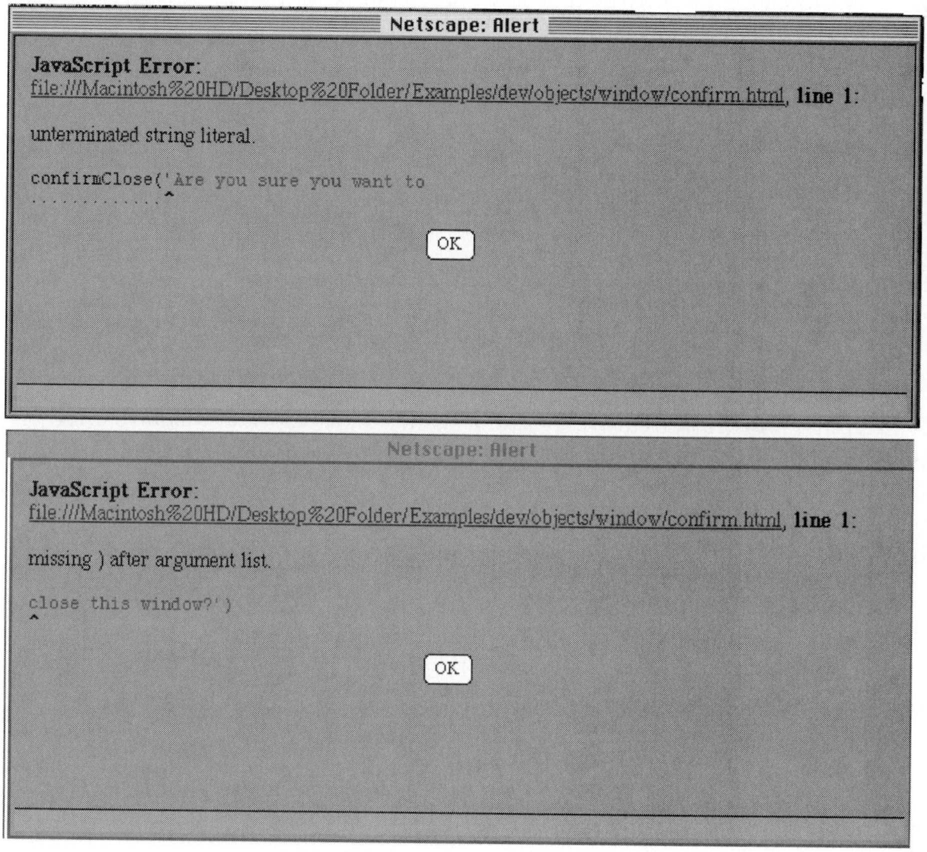

Netscape: Alert

JavaScript Error:
file:///Macintosh%20HD/Desktop%20Folder/Examples/dev/objects/window/confirm.html, **line 1:**

unterminated string literal.

```
confirmClose('Are you sure you want to
.............^
```

OK

Netscape: Alert

JavaScript Error:
file:///Macintosh%20HD/Desktop%20Folder/Examples/dev/objects/window/confirm.html, **line 1:**

missing) after argument list.

```
close this window?')
^
```

OK

Figure 4–9 Alert windows with interpreter error messages

The interpreter thought that the single quotes were not matched because they were not on the same line.

One solution to this problem is to remove the line break completely. Another solution is to put the line break immediately following the `confirmClose()` method, as shown below:

```
<CENTER><FORM>
<INPUT TYPE="button" VALUE="Nuke the Window"
onClick="confirmClose
('Are you sure you want to close this window?')">
</FORM></CENTER>
```

Another solution is to add the two strings together, as shown below:

```
<CENTER><FORM>
<INPUT TYPE="button" VALUE="Nuke the Window"
onClick="confirmClose
('Are you sure you want ' + 'to close this window?')">
</FORM></CENTER>
```

Looking at Object Properties

If you are having problems referencing an object's properties correctly, you can use `getProps()`, which is defined in the `getProps.js` file shown below, and provided on the CD-ROM. If you don't get the proper object references, you need to rework your script to make sure you're referring to the right objects.

The following example is made up of three scripts: `getProps.js` and `displayPropsWin.js` are included in `debugScriptSrc.html`, which displays the properties for a given object in a new window.

```
//
//        getProps.js
//
//  This file contains getProps() and its
//  supporting functions. It can be used to
//  display the properties of an object in either
//  an HTML page or an alert dialog.
//
//  getProps() takes three arguments and returns
//  a string for display in either an HTML
//  page or an alert dialog. How it is formatted
//  is controlled by the third argument. Passing
//  in 'true' formats the string for
//  HTML. 'false' formats for an alert
//  dialog. The first argument is the object you
//  want the properties on. The second argument
//  is a string you want to represent the object
//  name in the output.

/*
** Utility functions
*/

// Generate a new line
//
// Arguments:
//   html - if true, generate an HTML new line
```

```
//
// Return value:
//   A string representing a new line either in
//   HTML or simply a string suitable for display
//   in an alert dialog.
//
function newline(html) {
  var rvalue = ""

  if (html) {
    rvalue += "<BR>"
  }
  else {
    // The Mac requires a carriage return
    if (navigator.appVersion.indexOf("(Mac") != -1)
    {
      rvalue += "\n\r"
    } else {
      rvalue += "\n"
    }
  }
  return rvalue
}

// Generate an indent
//
// Arguments:
//   html - if true, generate an HTML indentation
//
// Return value:
//   A string representing an indentation either in
//   HTML or simply a string suitable for display
//   in an alert dialog.
function indent(html) {
  var rvalue = ""

  if (html) {
    rvalue += "<DD>"
  } else {
    // The Mac seems to have problems with tab
    if (navigator.appVersion.indexOf("(Mac") != -1)
    {
      rvalue += "      "
    } else {
```

```
      rvalue += "\t"
    }
  }
  return rvalue
}

/*
** getProps
*/

// Get the properties for the given object
//
// Arguments:
//    obj      - obtain properties from this
//               object
//    obj_name - a string representing the
//               object name
//    html     - generate html output?
//
// Return Value
//    string of the form:
//      object_name.property = "value"
//      object_name.property = "value"
//      ...
//
//
function getProps(obj, obj_name, html) {
  var rvalue = ""

  rvalue += newline(html)
  rvalue += "The properties of the object "
  rvalue += obj_name + " are:"
  rvalue += newline(html)

  for (var i in obj) {
    rvalue += indent(html)
    rvalue += obj_name + "." + i
    rvalue += " = " + obj[i]
    rvalue += newline(html)
  }
  rvalue += newline(html)

  return unescape(rvalue)
}
```

The `getProps.js` file contains `getProps()` and some formatting functions that you can use to obtain a string containing the properties and values of an object. The function accepts three arguments: a reference to the object you want the properties from, a string representation of the object name, and a Boolean that determines if you want HTML formatting of the returned strings. If `true`, HTML is returned; if `false`, formatted ASCII is returned.

The `displayPropsWin.js` script defines the function `displayPropsWin` which creates a separate window that you can use if you want to display the output from `getProps()` in a separate window. `displayPropsWin()` uses the `getProps` function to do its work.

```
//
//          displayPropsWin.js
//
//   This file defines displayPropsWin().
//
//   displayPropsWin() creates a new window and
//   displays the values of an object's properties
//   in it. It relies on getProps(), which is
//   defined in getProps.js. You need to include:
//
//     <SCRIPT SRC="getProps.js"></SCRIPT>
//
//   in your HTML document for this function to
//   work.
//

//   global variable to hold the properties
//   window—useful if you want to create a
//   button to close the window.
var props_win = null

//   Display the properties of the given object in
//   a new window.
//
//   Arguments:
//     obj      - obtain properties from this
//                object
//     obj_name - a string representing the
//                object name
function displayPropsWin(obj, obj_name) {
  var msg_str   = ""
```

```
    // build up the contents for the window
    msg_str += "<HTML>"
    msg_str += "<HEAD>"
    msg_str += "<TITLE>"
    msg_str += obj_name + "'s Properties"
    msg_str += "</TITLE>"
    msg_str += "</HEAD>"
    msg_str += "<BODY>"
    msg_str += getProps(obj, obj_name, true)
    msg_str += "</BODY>"
    msg_str += "</HTML>"

    // create the window
    props_win = open("", "propsWindow",
      "width=500,height=550,scrollbars=1,resizable=1")

    // write the contents into the window
    props_win.document.open()
    props_win.document.write(msg_str)
    props_win.document.close()
}
```

The following `debugScriptSrc.html` script shows how to include the source from both the `getProps.js` and `displayPropsWin.js` files to call the function `displayPropsWin()`.

```
<!--
          debugScriptSrc.html

    This example show how to use the SRC
    attribute of the SCRIPT tag.
-->

<HTML>
<HEAD>
<TITLE>SCRIPT SRC Attribute</TITLE>

<!--
    Include getProps() for displayPropsWin()
-->
<SCRIPT SRC="getProps.js"></SCRIPT>

<!--
    Include displayPropsWin(), which displays
    the properties of a given object in a new
```

```
    window.
-->
<SCRIPT SRC="displayPropsWin.js"></SCRIPT>
</HEAD>

<BODY>
<P>Click on the button below to display the
document properties of this page.
</P>

<CENTER><FORM>
<INPUT TYPE="button" NAME="props"
VALUE="Display Document Properties"
onClick="displayPropsWin(document,'document')">
</FORM></CENTER>
</BODY>
</HTML>
```

Note – You cannot include one `.js` file within another. If one `.js` file depends on code that is defined in another, you must include both in your HTML file as shown in the previous example.

Figure 4–10 shows the result of loading the `scriptSrc.html` file.

Figure 4–10 Result of `scriptSrc.html` file

Clicking on the Display Document Properties button displays a window with the properties for the document, as shown in Figure 4–11.

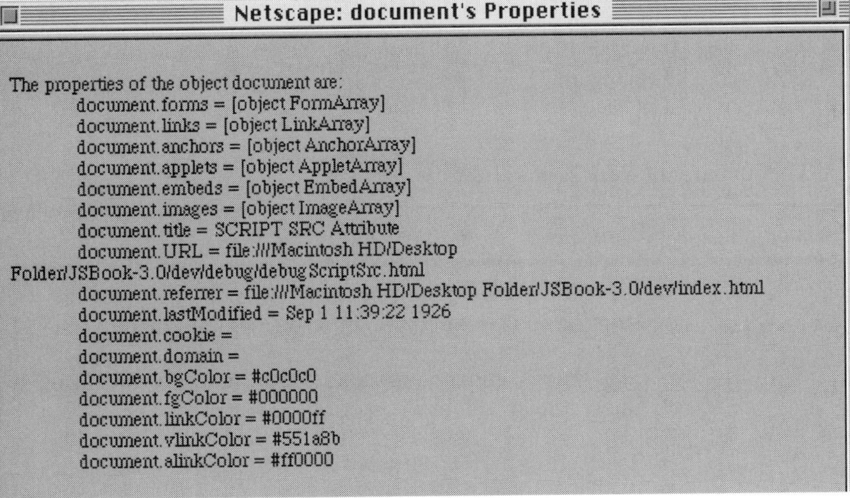

Figure 4–11 Document properties window

Debugging Checklist

This section contains a summary list of things to try when you're debugging a script:

- Do all of your HTML tags have matching angle brackets (<>)?
- Do your HTML tags have the proper closing entry tag such as `</BODY>`, `</HTML>`, `</FORM>`, and so on?
- Do you have any missing single or double quotation marks?
- Do you have any missing parentheses or curly braces?
- Are there any typographical errors?
- Are there any spelling errors?
- Do you have any capitalization errors?
- Have you pressed Shift and clicked on the Reload button in the browser to force a reload of the script.
- Have you tried reopening the file instead of simply reloading it?
- Have you inserted alerts to use as breakpoints in the script?
- Have you commented parts of the script to isolate the pieces that work?
- Have you checked your expression evaluation to make sure your expressions are evaluating correctly? You can use alerts to check your values.

Summary of New Terms and Concepts

The new terms and concepts introduced in this chapter are listed in alphabetical order in Table 4-1. The terms and concepts are also included in the glossary at the end of the book

Table 4-1 Summary of New Terms and Concepts

Term/Concept	Definition
breakpoint	A predefined address in a program at which execution is stopped and control is passed to debugging software.
bug	Any error in either hardware or software that results in an unexpected result or a computer malfunction.
debug	To diagnose and fix software and hardware problems.
layout	The way the interpreter transforms the HTML tags and values into a graphical display on your computer screen.
operator precedence	The hierarchy assigned to JavaScript operators that determines the sequence in which expressions are evaluated.
parse	To analyze a series of words and statements to determine their collective meaning.

PART TWO

Creating HTML Pages

CHAPTER 5

- Object Properties
- Object Methods
- Referencing Object Properties and Methods
- Events
- Object-Manipulation Statements
- Built-in Objects
- Summary of New Terms and Concepts

Introducing Objects

This chapter introduces the concept of JavaScript objects. An object is a self-contained chunk of computer code that you can use and manipulate without needing to understand how the object itself is programmed. In his book *Object Oriented Design with Applications*, published by Benjamin/Cummings Publication Company (1991), Grady Booch describes an object as:

> Something you can do things to. An object has state, behavior, and identity.

When you have a language based on objects, you use it to do object-oriented programming. Object-oriented programming is not easy to define. Of it, Grady Booch says:

> Unfortunately, object-oriented programming means different things to different people. As Rentsch correctly predicted, "My guess is that object-oriented programming will be in the 1980s what structured programming was in the 1970s. Everyone will be in favor of it. Every manufacturer will promote his products as supporting it. Every manager will pay lip service to it. Every programmer will practice it (differently). And no one will know just what it is."

Describing object-oriented programming in depth is beyond the scope of this book. If you are interested in reading more about object-oriented programming, we suggest you refer to Grady Booch's book or to David Taylor's *Object-Oriented Information Systems*, published by Wiley Professional Computing (1992).

The JavaScript language is based on objects. The basic object is a window. Everything that you do in JavaScript takes place in that window object. Within that window you define documents. You can divide the document space by using frames. Inside the document, you can display text and images. You can define forms with user interface (UI) elements such as text fields, text areas, buttons, radio buttons, and selection lists and use the information from those forms to submit data to a script on a server. Each of these elements is a JavaScript object.

In other words, everything in JavaScript is a document, contained in a window, that lives at a specific location (URL) contained within the browser. You can divide the document with frames, and you can put in text fields, buttons, check boxes, and selection lists. When you define HTML tags to create these elements, the corresponding objects for each element are automatically created and ready for you to use.

Because scripts are an integral part of an HTML document, the relationship between the JavaScript and HTML languages is very close. In some cases, it's difficult to separate the two, whereas in other cases, the distinction between the JavaScript language and HTML language is clear. Any time you use HTML tags to create documents, windows, and the user interface elements that are part of the `<FORM></FORM>` HTML tags, the JavaScript language automatically creates a corresponding object for that element.

Each object has its own set of *properties* that you can use to get and (sometimes) set the values defined in the HTML tags. It also has *methods* that enable you to perform actions on the object, and *event handlers* that enable you to delay performing action until some event occurs. The objects that are automatically created from HTML tag definitions are called *built-in objects*.

Because objects are contained within other objects, you can think of the structure as a hierarchy. The Navigator object is at the top of the hierarchy. Below that, windows have location and history. Within the window object is a document object. And within that document object you can use the other built-in objects. Figure 5–1 shows the object hierarchy.

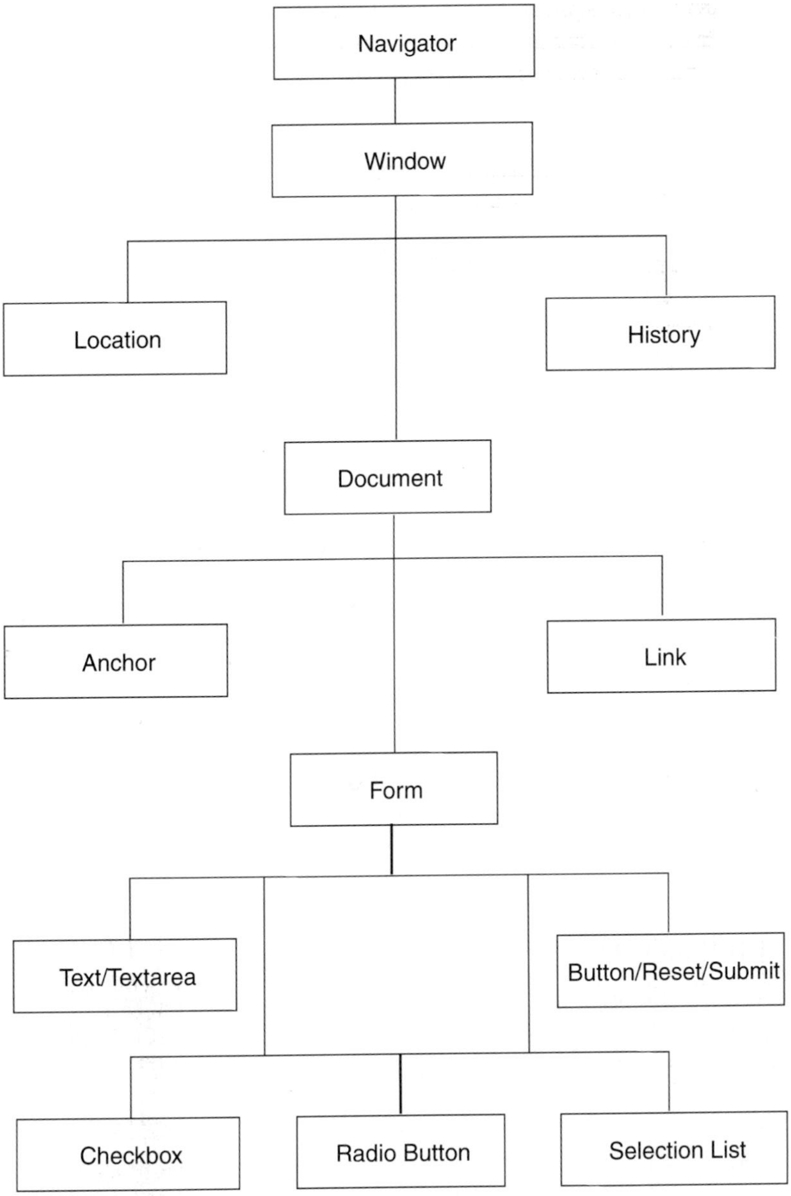

Navigator

Window

Location

History

Document

Anchor

Link

Form

Text/Textarea

Button/Reset/Submit

Checkbox

Radio Button

Selection List

igure 5–1 Built-in object hierarchy (Navigator 2.x release)

The Navigator 3.0 release adds `plugin`, `mimeType`, `applet`, `area`, and `image` objects to the document hierarchy, and `fileUpload` to the form hierarchy, as illustrated in Figure 5–2. Existing objects have a dashed border. New objects have a solid border.

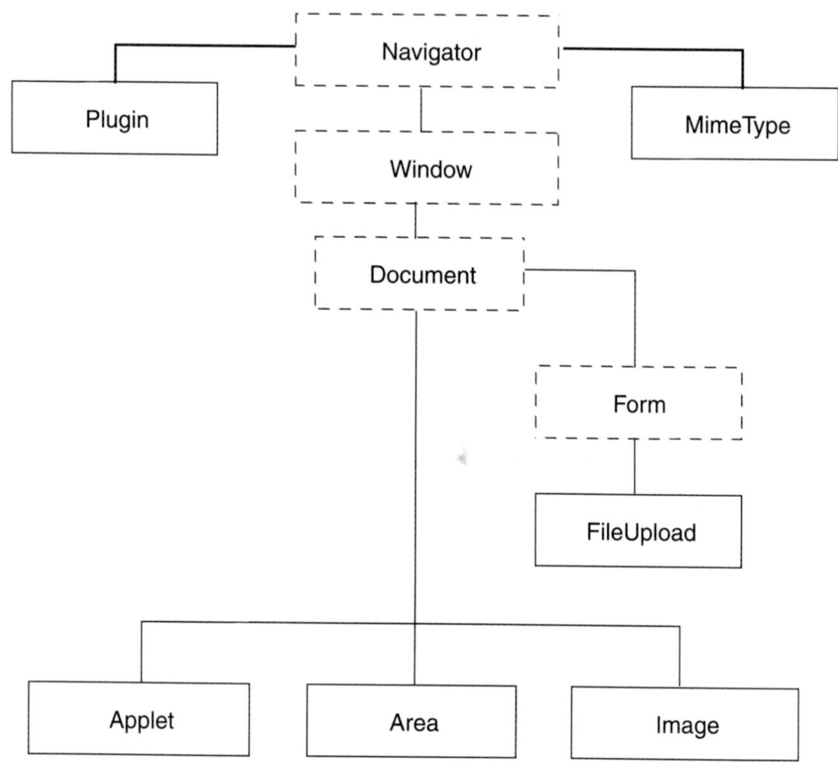

Figure 5–2 New objects in Navigator 3.0

The JavaScript language also provides a set of *system objects*, shown in Figure 5–3, which are not a part of the object hierarchy. The `Array` object is new in the Navigator 3.0 release. System objects are described in Part 6.

Figure 5–3 System objects

Objects can have the following characteristics:

- State, which is defined by the properties of the object.
- Behavior, which is defined by the methods you use to communicate with the object. Note that methods are attached to event handlers. Objects can support events through event handlers.
- Identity, which is the thing that makes each object unique; a document object, for example, is different from a window object.

Let's look at these key concepts in more detail.

Object Properties

The current values of the collection of properties defined by an object give it a state. Properties are the data elements/variables/characteristics stored by an object. They are the things about the object that can change, and so you must define the values for the particular object you are interested in. In the JavaScript language, you reference object properties by using the following syntax:

```
object.property = value
```

Let's use the `document` object as an example. You already know that documents have a title, a location, and a background color. These are properties of the `document` object. The `document` object has other properties that are described in detail in Chapter 7, "Creating Documents."

So, if you see a line of JavaScript code that looks like this:

```
document.bgColor = "blue"
```

it's easy to understand that the `document` object's background color is blue.

Object properties always have a value. That value is something that is either retrievable (*gettable*) or is something that you can set yourself (*settable*). To help you easily determine if a property is gettable or settable, each time we introduce new properties, we present the information about those properties in the following format:

Property	Value	Gettable	Settable
status	string	Yes	Yes
top	window object	Yes	No

The box above shows two of the properties for the `window` object.

Object Methods

A method of an object describes what an object can do. Methods are always verbs such as `write()` or `open()`. In the JavaScript language, you reference object methods by using the following syntax:

```
object.method()
```

So, if you see a JavaScript statement that looks like this:

```
document.write("Hello World!")
```

you know that this statement is saying "Write the string within the parentheses into the document."

And, if you see a statement that looks like this:

```
document.clear()
```

you, by now, can make a well-informed guess that the `clear()` method tells the `document` object to remove anything that is already displayed in the document.

You may notice a distinct similarity between methods and functions. That's because methods are actually functions that are attached to an object. Methods embody the behavior of the object.

Object methods usually return a value. That value is retrieved from somewhere else in the script, usually from a function. To help you easily find the value that is returned by an object method, we present the information about that method in the following format:

Method	Returns
confirm(*message*)	true or false
alert(*message*)	Nothing

The box above shows two of the methods for the `window` object.

Referencing Object Properties and Methods

Objects are linked in a hierarchical order, separated by dots (.). The syntax for objects is similar to the UNIX file system hierarchy. The first item in the string is the object. The object sets the context for everything that comes after it in the

quence. To reference a property or method of an object, you need to follow the erarchy of objects shown in Figure 5–1 on page 89. You reference the property method by using the syntax:

```
object.property
object.method
```

r example, to reference the title property of the `window` object, use:

```
window.title
```

reference the `close()` method of the `window` object, use:

```
window.close()
```

cause an object can be a property of another object, a hierarchy forms. The llowing examples show a hierarchy of forms. The first statement below refers to indow, document, form, elements array, and value. The second statement refers document, form, text field by name, and value.

```
onBlur="required(window.document.myForm.elements[0].
value)"

onChange="verify(document.myForm.firstName.value)"
```

vents

hen you write JavaScript code, some of the code is activated as the HTML is terpreted. At other times, you want the code to be activated when an *event* appens, for example, when a user clicks a mouse button on a link.

ou want events to be handled when the event occurs. Objects support certain ents. For example, you want the `onMouseOver` event handler to be activated nly when the pointer is over a link. The events and the objects that support them e listed in Table 5-1.

able 5-1 JavaScript Events

vent	Description	Object
`oort*`	The loading of an image was stopped.	Images
`lur`	Input focus was removed from the object.	Text, textarea, select, window*, frameset*, button*, checkbox*, fileUpload*, password*, radio*, reset*, submit*

Table 5-1 JavaScript Events (Continued)

Event	Description	Object
`change`	The value of the object was modified.	Text, text area, select, fileUpload*
`click`	The object was clicked on.	Button, radio, checkbox, submit, reset, link
`error*`	The loading of a document or image resulted in an error.	Image, window*
`focus`	Input focus was set to the object.	Text, textarea, select, window*, frameset*, button*, checkbox*, fileUpload*, password*, radio*, reset*, submit*
`load*`	The image or window was loaded	Image, window
`reset*`	The form was reset.	Form
`select`	The value of the object was selected.	Text, textarea
`mouseOut*`	The pointer was moved off an area or link.	Link, area
`mouseOver`	The pointer was moved over a link.	Link, area*
`unload*`	The window was unloaded.	window

* New in Navigator 3.0.
The new `area` object also has a `mouseOver` event.
Windows and framesets now have `blur` and `focus` events.

You define *event handlers* to catch the event you are interested in. Event handlers always are the name of the event preceded by the word on. So, the event handler for a `click` event (when users click on an object) is called `onClick`. If you have set up an `onClick` event handler, then, when a user clicks on a button, the event handler is called.

on't be concerned if these concepts are not clear to you yet. You'll see in detail ɔw to use each of the built-in objects, their properties, and methods in the next ·w chapters when you create your own window object and start filling it with ocuments and other objects.

bject-Manipulation Statements

he JavaScript language provides four statement keywords that you can use ɔecifically with objects to help manipulate their properties:

```
this

for...in

with

new
```

Ve'll take a brief look at these keywords in this chapter. Because they are used rimarily when you create your own objects, you'll see more extensive examples f these keywords in Chapter 34, "Creating Your Own JavaScript Objects."

he this Keyword

complex HTML document can have many forms objects. Each form is ɔntained within the `<FORM></FORM>` tags. In addition, you can create forms ıat have multiple items, such as a set of radio buttons or a selection list. When ou define a form or form element that contains an event handler that calls a ınction defined elsewhere in the document, the JavaScript language provides ou with a shortcut way to refer to the form or form element — the `this` eyword.

he `this` keyword always refers to the current object.

he following code extract defines a form with multiple text fields. Each text field as three event handlers that define what happens:

When the user clicks somewhere else to leave the text field (`onBlur`)

When the user changes the contents of the text field and then clicks somewhere else in the document (`onChange`)

When the user clicks in the text field (`onFocus`)

n each case, the script uses the `this` keyword to refer to the current text field.

```
<FORM NAME = "myForm">
<B>First Name: </B><BR>
<INPUT
 TYPE="text"
```

```
  NAME="firstName"
  VALUE=""
  SIZE=25
  onBlur="required(this.value)"
  onChange="verify(this.value)"
  onFocus="this.select()"
>
</FORM>
```

If you did not use the `this` keyword, you would have to customize each of the event handlers and use the name of each text field. For example, instead of:

```
onBlur="required(this.value)"
onChange="verify(this.value)"
onFocus="this.select()"
```

for the `firstName` text field, you would have to use:

```
onBlur="required(window.document.myForm.firstName.value)
onChange="verify(window.document.myForm.firstName.value)
onFocus="window.document.myForm.firstName.select()"
```

and you would have to refer to any other text fields by their specific names. Instead, it's much easier and cleaner to use the `this` keyword. For more information about creating text fields, see Chapter 16, "Adding Text Fields to a Document."

The for...in Statement

The `for...in` statement is a special form of loop that loops through the properties of a particular object from first to last. You create the loop by using the following syntax:

```
for (counter in objectname)
  {statements}
```

Note that you can use the `this` keyword in place of *`objectname`* to refer to the object, as shown below:

```
for (counter in this)
  {statements}
```

The following code extract defines an object's method that cycles through all of its properties and extracts the value for each.

```
function getProps(obj, obj_name, html) {
  var rvalue = ""

  rvalue += newline(html)
  rvalue += "The properties of the object "
```

```
  rvalue += obj_name + " are:"
  rvalue += newline(html)

  for (var i in obj) {
    rvalue += indent(html)
    rvalue += obj_name + "." + i
    rvalue += " = " + obj[i]
    rvalue += newline(html)
  }
  rvalue += newline(html)

  return unescape(rvalue)
}
```

The with Statement

The `with` statement enables you to tell the JavaScript language which object you are referring to when calling methods and getting properties. You create the `with` statement by using the following syntax:

```
with (object) {statements}
```

When you use this statement, you can call several properties and methods without needing to specifically identify the object for each method.

The following `with.html` script encloses a series of document method calls in a `with` statement.

```
<!--
           with.html

     This example shows how to use the with
     statement.
-->

<HTML>
<HEAD>
<TITLE>with example</TITLE>
</HEAD>

<BODY>
<SCRIPT LANGUAGE="JavaScript">
<!-- HIDE FROM OLD BROWSERS

with( window.document ) {
  open()
  writeln("This is a test of the with statement")
```

```
    writeln("...")
    writeln("this is ONLY a test.<BR>")
    writeln("In the case of a real use, put")
    writeln("a different message here!")
    close()
  }

  // STOP HIDING -->
  </SCRIPT>

  </BODY>
  </HTML>
```

Figure 5–4 shows the result of loading the `with.html` script.

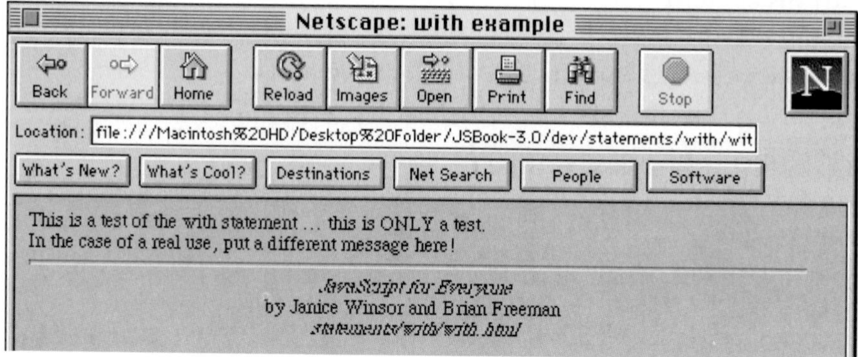

Figure 5–4 Result of loading the `with.html` script

For examples of how to use the `with` statement with the `Math` object, see Chapter 31, "Doing Math."

The new Statement

You use the `new` statement to create a new instance of an object. When you write your own JavaScript objects, first you write a function to define the new object type. Writing the function is like creating a template. To actually create an instance of the object, you use the `new` statement with the function name to create the object. You create the `new` statement by using the following syntax:

```
objectName = new objectType ( param1 [,param2]
...[,paramN] )
```

where *`objectName`* is the name of the new object instance, *`objectType`* is the type of the object, and *`param1...paramN`* are the property values for the object.

ɔr more information about creating your own JavaScript objects, see Chapter 34, Creating Your Own JavaScript Objects."

uilt-in Objects

ou can use any of the built-in objects listed in alphabetical order in Table 5-2. The Navigator 3.0 Update Information column describes whether the object is new or revised in the 3.0 release. The properties and methods for these objects are described in detail in subsequent chapters.

able 5-2 Built-in and System Objects

bject	Navigator 3.0 Update Information
nchor	Unchanged
pplet	New in 3.0
rea	New in 3.0
rray*	New in 3.0
utton	Modified in 3.0
heckbox	Modified in 3.0
ate*	Modified in 3.0
ocument	Modified in 3.0
ileUpload	New in 3.0
orm	Modified in 3.0
idden	Unchanged
istory	Unchanged
mage	New in 3.0
ink	Modified in 3.0
ocation	Modified in 3.0
ath*	Unchanged
imeType	New in 3.0

Table 5-2 Built-in and System Objects (Continued)

Object	Navigator 3.0 Update Information
`navigator`	Modified in 3.0
`password`	Modified in 3.0
`plugin`	New in 3.0
`radio`	Modified in 3.0
`reset`	Modified in 3.0
`select`	Modified in 3.0
`String*`	Modified in 3.0
`submit`	Modified in 3.0
`text`	Modified in 3.0
`textarea`	Modified in 3.0
`window`	Modified in 3.0

* System objects that are not part of the object hierarchy. System objects are described in Part 6.

Summary of New Terms and Concepts

The new terms and concepts introduced in this chapter are listed in alphabetical order in Table 5-3. The terms and concepts are also included in the glossary at the end of the book.

Table 5-3 Summary of New Terms and Concepts

Term/Concept	Description
built-in object	An object that the JavaScript language automatically creates and that corresponds to HTML definitions for window, document, frame, and form elements. Each built-in object has its own predefined set of properties, methods, and event handlers.
event	A specific user action, such as Click or MouseOver, that is recognized by the JavaScript language.
event handler	A JavaScript function that responds to a specific event, such as a mouse click in a certain location.

Table 5-3 Summary of New Terms and Concepts (Continued)

Term/Concept	Description
gettable	A JavaScript property that can be obtained.
object-based language	A programming language that uses the concepts of objects, methods, and events but does not provide all of the complexity of a true object-oriented programming style.
object-oriented language	A programming language in which programs are organized as cooperative collections of objects, each of which represents an instance of some class, and whose classes are all members of a hierarchy of classes that are united by inheritance relationships.
property	A variable of an object. An object has a set of related variables known as properties, and each property is a variable or function. You refer to a property by using the syntax *`object.property`*, for example, `document.bgColor`.
settable	A JavaScript property that can be changed.
system object	An object provided by the JavaScript language that is not created automatically by an HTML tag definition and is not part of the object hierarchy.

CHAPTER 6

- Displaying a Status Message
- Controlling the Structure of a Window
- Referring to a Window
- Referencing document, history, and location Objects in a Window
- Opening a New Window
- Finding Which Window Is the Opener
- Determining the State of a Newly Opened Window
- Displaying Informational Messages in an Alert Window
- Closing a Window
- Displaying a Confirmation Message
- Prompting Users for Input
- Controlling the Input Focus in Windows
- Using Event Handlers to Control Window Focus
- Using Timeouts
- Using Event Handlers on Load and Unload
- Using an Event Handler to Capture Interpreter Error Messages
- Summary of New Terms and Concepts

Creating Windows

Everything that you do with HTML and JavaScript programs takes place within a window. And, logically enough, the `window` object is at the top level of the JavaScript object hierarchy.

Note – Actually, the `navigator` object is at the top level of the JavaScript object hierarchy, but you can safely consider the `window` object to be at the top.

Because the JavaScript program assumes that everything is presented within the context of a `window` object, you do not always need to specify `window` as the object. You can, however, do specific things with the `window` object itself. We start our exploration of the built-in objects with the `window` object.

Each window has, as a minimum, the following elements:

- Title bar — The place where the title of the window is displayed
- Control area — The place where the buttons and controls you use to work within the browser are located

- Window — The place where the HTML document is displayed
- Status bar — The place where system and JavaScript messages to the user of the window are displayed

These parts of the window are shown in Figure 6–1.

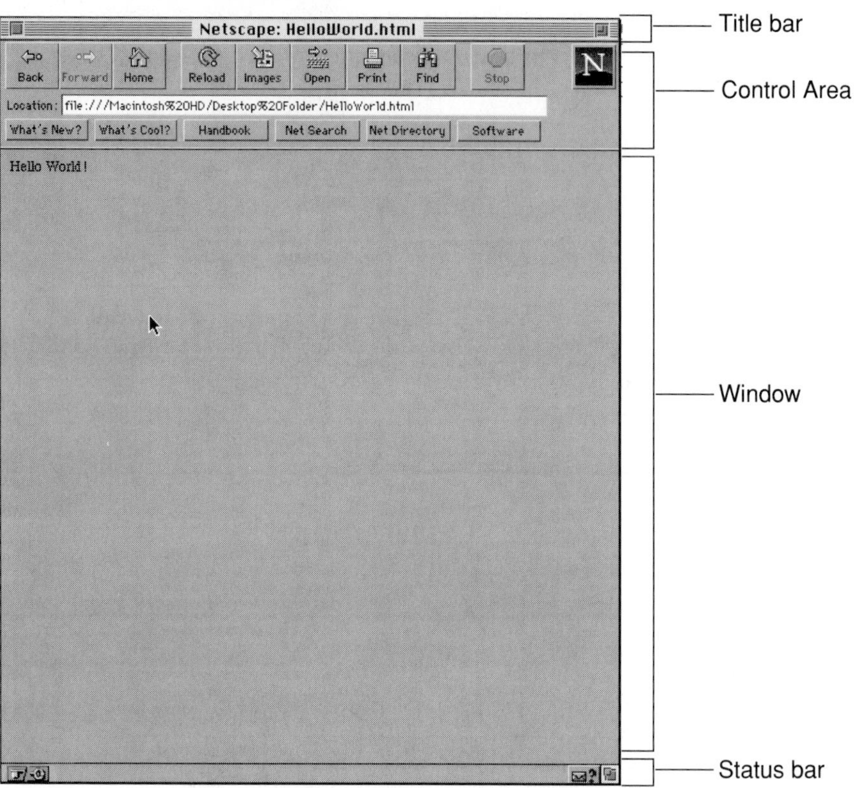

Figure 6–1 Parts of a window

You can control the status bar only of a window that is already opened. However, when you open a new window (using `window.open()`), you can control everything about the window.

You can create your own windows to provide flexibility for your Web page. For example, if you want a larger area to work with in a document, you could create a separate control window with the navigation buttons that help users move around within your site. If you provide a complex service, you could create a separate window that contains the table of contents for the Web site. We'll show you some examples later in this book of how to use separate windows.

The properties, methods, and event handlers for the `window` object are listed in alphabetical order in Table 6-1.

Table 6-1 Properties, Methods, and Event Handlers for the window Object

Properties	Methods	Event Handlers
`closed*`	`alert()`	`onBlur*`
`defaultStatus`	`blur()*`	`onerror*`
`document`	`clearTimeout()`	`onFocus*`
`frames`	`close()`	`onLoad`
`history`	`confirm()`	`onUnload`
`length`	`eval()*`	
`location`	`focus()*`	
`name`	`open()`	
`opener*`	`prompt()`	
`parent`	`scroll()*`	
`self`	`setTimeout()`	
`status`	`toString()*`	
`top`	`valueOf()*`	
`window`		

* New in Navigator 3.0.

Netscape Navigator 2.0 and later releases provide additional HTML tags that you can use to divide the window into *frames*. Each frame within a window has its own `window` object. For more information on HTML frames, see Appendix A, "HTML Frames."

The rest of the chapter explains and provides examples of how to use each of the properties, methods, and event handlers for the `window` object.

Note – This chapter introduces some new scripting concepts. As you work with the examples in this chapter, you will learn some additional scripting techniques that are explained in more detail in later chapters of this book.

Displaying a Status Message

You can use two window properties, `status` and `defaultStatus`, to control the information displayed in the status bar at the bottom of the current window.

Property	Value	Gettable	Settable
status	string	Yes	Yes
defaultStatus	string	Yes	Yes

The `status` property writes a priority or transient message in the status bar at the bottom of the window.

Use the `status` property only for messages that have a temporary effect. For example, when you create a link, you can use the `onMouseOver` event handler for the `link` object to instruct your script to display a status message when the user moves the mouse pointer onto the link. You can set the `status` property at any time. You must always include `return true` as the last statement in the event handler or the status message is never displayed.

Once a document is loaded into a window or a frame, you can use the `defaultStatus` property to write a string in the status bar at the bottom of the window. The `defaultStatus` string is visible any time the mouse pointer is not over an object that displays a status property message. If you do not specify a string, the `defaultStatus` property is an empty string. Usually, you would set the `window.defaultStatus` property in response to an `onLoad` event when a document is loaded into a window.

xample of status and defaultStatus Properties

he following `windowStatus.html` script uses both the `status` and `efaultStatus` properties so you can see how they differ.

```
<!--
       windowStatus.html

    This example uses the window object's status
    and defaultStatus properties. Changing either
    of these properties affects what is displayed
    in the status bar at the bottom of a
    Navigator window.

    To show how status and defaultStatus can be
    changed, event handlers are set up to call
    functions. The window object's onLoad event
    handler is used to set defaultStatus, and
    onMouseOver is used to set status.
    onMouseOver is an event handler of the link
    object. When the events occur, the functions
    setDefaultStatus() and setStatus() actually
    set the properties.
-->
<HTML>
<HEAD>
<TITLE>status and defaultStatus</TITLE>
<SCRIPT LANGUAGE="JavaScript">
<!-- HIDE FROM OLD BROWSERS

//
//   Change the window object's defaultStatus
//   property.
//
function setDefaultStatus(win, msg_str) {
  win.defaultStatus = msg_str
  return true
}

//
//   Change the window object's status property
//
function setStatus(win, msg_str) {
  win.status = msg_str
  return true
```

```
}

//
//   Change the status messages
//
function homeStatus(win) {
  var default_str = "Click on the link to go home."
  var status_str  = "Hey, this isn't our home page!"

  if (!setDefaultStatus(win, default_str))
    return false
  if (!setStatus(win, status_str))
    return false
  return true
}

// STOP HIDING -->
</SCRIPT>
</HEAD>

<!--
    Set up the onLoad event handler. When the
    document is loaded, this event handler is
    called. It in turn calls the
    setDefaultStatus() function above.
-->
<BODY
 onLoad="return setDefaultStatus(self.window,
         'Click on the link to go home.')"
 onUnload="return setDefaultStatus(self.window,'')">

<P>The <CODE>defaultStatus</CODE> message is
displayed when nothing else is in the status bar
at the bottom of the window. The
<CODE>status</CODE> message is displayed in
response to a <CODE>mouseOver</CODE> event.</P>

<P>Move your mouse pointer over "Go Home" and look
at the status bar to see what it is all about.</P>

<!--
    Define the Go Home reference and provide
    URL. When the mouse is moved over the link,
    the onMouseOver event handler is called
```

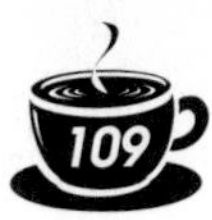


```
     and in turn calls the homeStatus()
     function.
-->
<CENTER>
<A HREF="http://home.netscape.com"
   onMouseOver="return homeStatus(self.window)">
   Go Home</A>
</CENTER>

</BODY>
</HTML>
```

Figure 6–2 shows the window with the `defaultStatus` message displayed in the status bar.

Note – On some Navigator 2.0 platforms, the `status` and `defaultStatus` properties did not work properly unless you set a timeout in the script to delay the activation of the `defaultStatus` until after the document loaded. This bug has been fixed in the Navigator 3.0 release. If the `windowStatus.html` script does not work on your platform, try the `windowStatusTimeout.html` script described in "Ending the Document" on page 117.

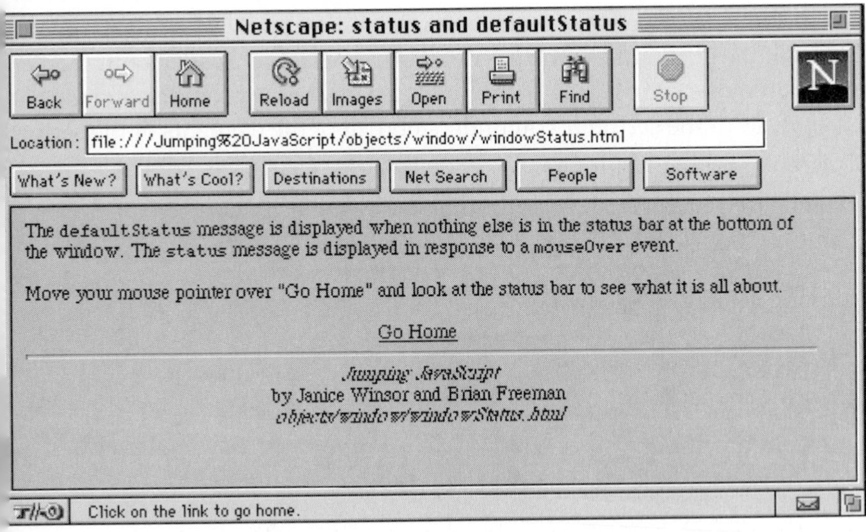

Figure 6–2 Window with `defaultStatus` message in status bar

When you move the pointer onto the Go Home link, the `status` message is displayed in the status bar, as shown in Figure 6–3.

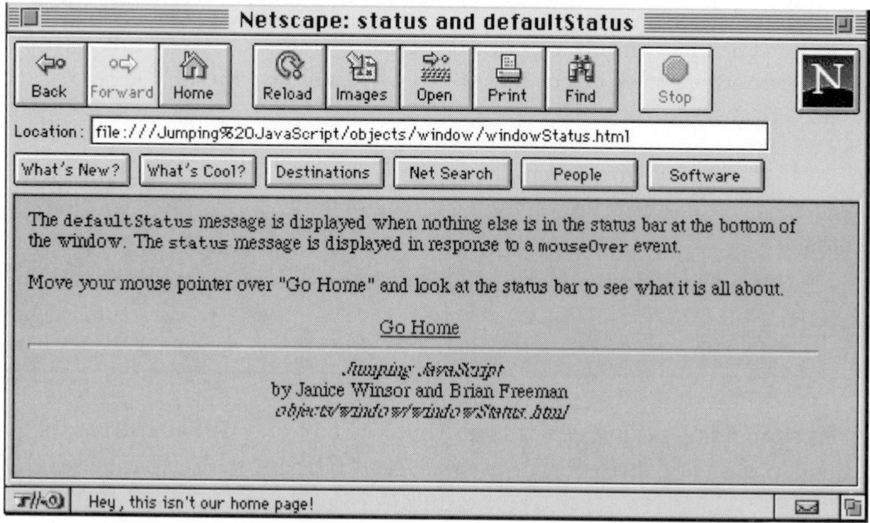

Figure 6–3 Window with `status` message in status bar

Explanation of Example Script

This simple script contains a lot of basic scripting elements that were introduced in Chapter 3, "Introducing General Scripting Concepts." Because this script is the first one that combines all of these elements in a single script, we'll take a look at the script in some detail to make sure you understand exactly what's happening and why all of the elements are included. If you are at all confused about the comments within the script itself, the following paragraphs provide a more detailed analysis of the script. If you understood all of the elements of the script, you can skip over this section.

The elements used in this script perform the following actions:

- Declaring a variable
- Assigning a value to a variable
- Defining functions
- Calling functions
- Using object methods
- Using window properties
- Using event handlers

ou have already learned something about each of these elements. Now we'll take detailed look at how they come together in this script.

you need to refresh your memory about the HTML tags, refer to the HTML ushup box.

HTML Brushup

The following list describes the HTML tags that are used in this script, in alphabetical order.

<!-- -->	Comment
<A></A>	Anchor for hypertext link
<B></B>	Bold
<BODY></BODY>	Document body
<CENTER></CENTER>	Center
<CODE></CODE>	Use code font
<HEAD></HEAD>	Document head
HREF	Point to destination of link
<HR>	Horizontal line
<HTML></HTML>	HTML document indicator
<P></P>	Paragraph
<TITLE></TITLE>	Title
<SCRIPT></SCRIPT>	JavaScript

---

tarting the HTML Document. The first block of text contains commented formation that identifies the name of the script and describes the script. The TML tags define the document as HTML, start the head, and create the title for e window:

```
<!--
      windowStatus.html

    This example uses the window object's status
    and defaultStatus properties. Changing either
    of these properties affects what is displayed
    in the status bar at the bottom of a
    Navigator window.
```

```
      To see how status and defaultStatus can be
      changed, event handlers are set up to call
      functions. The window object's onLoad event
      handler is used to set defaultStatus, and
      onMouseOver is used to set status.
      onMouseOver is an event handler of the link
      object. When the events occur, the functions
      setDefaultStatus() and setStatus() actually
      set the properties.
-->

<HTML>
<HEAD>
<TITLE>status and defaultStatus</TITLE>
```

Starting the JavaScript Code. The `<SCRIPT>` tag and HTML comment begin the JavaScript code. For more information about using the `<SCRIPT>` and `</SCRIPT>` tags, see Chapter 2, "Introducing the Scripting Environment."

```
<SCRIPT LANGUAGE="JavaScript">
<!-- HIDE FROM OLD BROWSERS
```

Defining the Functions. We define three functions in this script:

- `setDefaultStatus()`
- `setStatus()`
- `homeStatus()`

You were introduced to the structure and syntax of functions in Chapter 3, "Introducing General Scripting Concepts."

elow is a line-by-line explanation of the `setDefaultStatus()` function. This ınction is defined first because the following function calls it. This function ıanges the `defaultStatus` property for the `window` object to display the ›propriate message string when the pointer is not over the link.

```
function setDefaultStatus(win,
msg_string) {
```

Define the function with an identifier name of `setDefaultStatus` and two arguments: `win` and `msg_string`. `win` is a reference to a window object and `msg_string` is a reference to a string that is used to set the window `defaultStatus` property. Provide the opening curly brace.

```
win.defaultStatus = msg_string
```

Set the `window` object's `win` `defaultStatus` property to the value of the `msg_string` argument.

```
return true
```

Return a value of `true`, telling the JavaScript interpreter that this event handler completed successfully. If `false` or no value is returned, the `defaultStatus` property does not change to the value contained in `msg_string`.

```
}
```

Closing curly brace marks the end of the function.

elow is a line-by-line explanation of the `setStatus()` function. This function hanges the `status` property for the `window` object to display the appropriate ıessage string when the pointer is over the link.

```
function setStatus(win, msg_str)
{
```

Define the function with an identifier of `setStatus` and two arguments: `win` and `msg_str`. `win` is a reference to the window object that displays the status property and `msg_str` is a reference to the string you want to set the property to. Provide the opening curly brace.

```
win.status = msg_str
```

Set the `window` object's `win` status property to the value of the string referenced by `msg_str`.

`return true`	Return a value of `true`.
`}`	Closing curly brace.

Below is a line-by-line explanation of the `homeStatus()` function, which is used to test the condition of the `setDefaultStatus()` and `setStatus()` function.

`function homeStatus(win) {`	Define the function with an identifier name of `homeStatus` and the argument `win`. `win` is a reference to the `window` object you want to act on. Provide the opening curly brace.
`var default_str = "Click on the link to go home."`	Declare the variable `default_str` and assign it a value.
`var status_str = "Hey, this isn't our home page!"`	Declare the variable `status_str` and assign it a value.
`if (!setDefaultStatus(win, default_str)) return false`	If the value returned by the call to `setDefaultStatus()` is not `true`, return a value of `false`. That is, if `setDefaultStatus()` fails, return `false`.
`if(!setStatus(win, status_str)) return false`	If value returned by the call to `setStatus()` is not true, return a value of false.
`return true`	If both `setdefaultStatus` and `setStatus` worked, return a value of `true`.
`}`	Closing curly brace.

Ending Head. The following three statements end the HTML comment, the JavaScript code, and the head of the document.

```
// STOP HIDING -->
</SCRIPT>
</HEAD>
```

Loading and Clearing the setDefaultStatus message. The following statements, which are embedded in the HTML `<BODY>` tag, use the `onLoad` event handler to return the value returned by the call to `setDefaultStatus()`.

ecause the Navigator 3.0 release does not clear any `defaultStatus` messages om the status bar, it's good practice to clean up after yourself if you have a script ıat displays a `defaultStatus` message. To clear the script, use the `onUnload` vent handler to call the `setDefaultStatus` function with an empty string for ıe message. The event handler definitions are implemented as extension ttributes to HTML tags. JavaScript-aware browsers use the event handlers. rowsers that are not JavaScript-aware simply ignore them.

```
<BODY
 onLoad="return setDefaultStatus(self.window,
         'Click on the link to go home.')"
 onUnload="return setDefaultStatus(self.window,'')">
```

ormatting the Text for the Document. The following HTML tags and text ontrol the information that is displayed when the HTML file is loaded. Refer to ıe HTML Brushup box if you need to refresh your memory about HTML ormats.

```
<P>The <CODE>defaultStatus</CODE> message is
displayed when nothing else is in the status bar
at the bottom of the window. The
<CODE>status</CODE> message is displayed in
response to a <CODE>mouseOver</CODE> event.

<P>Move your mouse pointer over "Go Home" and look
at the status bar to see what it is all about.
```

reating Link, URL, and Defining the onMouseOver Event Handler. elow is a line-by-line explanation of the code that creates the hypertext link, dentifies the URL, and defines the `onMouseOver` event handler to call `omeStatus()`.

`<CENTER>`	Center the following anchor.
`<A HREF="http://home.netscape.com" ;`	Start the hypertext link (anchor) and define the hypertext reference to go to Netscape's home page URL.

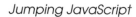

`onMouseOver="return homeStatus(self.window);">Go Home</A>`	Define the `onMouseOver` event handler to return the value returned by a call to `homeStatus()`. The current window, object is passed in as an argument to `homeStatus()`. Specify the text for the anchor to be `Go Home`, and end the anchor.
`</CENTER>`	End centering of text.

UI Guideline – You can provide four kinds of messages in the status bar: progress, completion, instruction, and error messages.

Use progress messages to keep users informed about the status of operations of uncertain duration. Progress messages tell users how the process is coming along. The bar at the bottom of the Navigator browser is a kind of progress message. In addition, the browser tells you the percentage of completion.

Use completion messages to inform users when something is complete. You do not need to display completion messages when the effect of an operation is obvious. It's a good idea to post a completion message after long, complex operations, and as the last step of a progress message.

Use instruction messages to give brief instructions to users and to tell them the consequences of their actions. Make these messages short and easy to read. Start the sentence with a command verb: Do this. Go to there. Load the *filename* file. Access the *URL* location.

Use error messages for the following types of actions:

- When users type invalid information into a text or numeric field
- When an operation cannot be undone
- When users quit a window with unsaved edits
- When the operation will overwrite an existing file

You can also use alert windows, described later in this chapter, to display error messages.

nding the Document. The following two lines of code end the body of the TML document, and the document itself.

```
</BODY>
</HTML>
```

xample of status and defaultStatus Properties with a Timeout

ecause Navigator 2.0 on some platforms overwrites any `defaultStatus` essage you set in a script while it is loading a file, we provide an example of ow to use the timeout methods to work around this bug in the following `indowStatusTimeout.html` script. For more information about timeout ethods, see "Using Timeouts" on page 209.

```
<!--
       windowStatusTimeout.html

    This example uses the window
    object's status and defaultStatus
    properties. Changing either of these
    properties affects what is displayed in the
    status bar at the bottom of a Navigator
    window.

    To show how status and defaultStatus can be
    changed, event handlers are set up to call
    functions. The window object's onLoad event
    handler is used to set defaultStatus, and
    onMouseOver is used for status. onMouseOver
    is an event handler of the link object. When
    the events occur, the functions
    setDefaultStatus() and setStatus() actually
    set the properties.


    Note: A timer is used to delay the call to
    setDefaultStatus() when the onLoad event
    occurs. This timer circumvents a
    Navigator 2.0 browser bug. If you have an
    FCS version of Navigator 2.0, you should be able
    to just set defaultStatus as in the line
    below:

    <BODY onLoad="defaultStatus='My message';
    return true">
```

```
    The bug occurs when the document is loading;
    Navigator indicates progress in the status
    bar, which obscures any defaultStatus message
    you have set. If you set the timer to a
    reasonable amount of time, Navigator should
    be finished and your defaultStatus message
    be set. Timers are not exact in JavaScript
    and page loading times may vary; this workaround
    is merely an example.
-->
<HTML>
<HEAD>
<TITLE>status & defaultStatus w/a Timer</TITLE>
<SCRIPT LANGUAGE="JavaScript">
<!-- HIDE FROM OLD BROWSERS

//
// setDefaultStatus function
//   Change the window object's defaultStatus
//   property.
//
function setDefaultStatus() {
  window.defaultStatus =
    "Click on the link to go home."
  return true
}

//
// setStatus function
//   Change the window object's status property.
//
function setStatus() {
  window.status = "Hey, this isn't our home page!"
  return true
}


// clearDefaultStatus function
//   Clear the defaultStatus message when the page
//   is unloaded.
```

```
function clearDefaultStatus() {
  window.defaultStatus = ""
  return true
}

//
// homeStatus function
//   Change the status messages.
//
function homeStatus() {
  if (!setDefaultStatus())
    return false
  if (!setStatus())
    return false
  return true
}

// STOP HIDING -->
</SCRIPT>
</HEAD>

<!--
    Set up the onLoad event handler. When the
    document is loaded, this event handler is called.
    It, in turn, sets up a timer to work around the
    Navigator bug.

    When the onLoad event handler is executed,
    the function setTimout() is
    called. setTimeout() takes an expression and
    a timeout interval as arguments. On
    completion it returns a timeoutID so you can
    cancel the timer if you want.

    We want to call the function
    setDefaultStatus() when the timer goes off,
    so the expression simply becomes a call to
    setDefaultStatus(). I figured a reasonable
    amount of time for Navigator to finish was 2
    seconds, so I set the timeout interval to
    2000 msec. (1000 msec. = 1 sec.) `id` is
    simply a temporary variable used to catch the
    return value from setTimeout().
```

```
        It's good practice to always catch anything
        returned from a method even if you don't use
        it later, as in our case here.
    -->
    <BODY
    onLoad="id=setTimeout('setDefaultStatus()',2000)";
    onUnload="return clearDefaultStatus()">

    <P>The <CODE>defaultStatus</CODE> message is
    displayed when nothing else is in the status bar
    at the bottom of the window. The
    <CODE>status</CODE> message is displayed in
    response to a <CODE>mouseOver</CODE> event.</P>
    <P>Bug Alert - Navigator 2.0 interferes with
    <CODE>defaultStatus</CODE> being set using an
    <CODE>onLoad</CODE> event. Everything's fine if
    you use a timer and wait for Navigator to get
    done.</P>
    <P>Move your mouse pointer over "Go Home" and
    look at the status bar to see what it is all
    about.</P>

    <!--
         Define the Go Home reference and provide
         URL. When the mouse is moved over the link,
         the onMouseOver event handler gets called and
         in turn calls the homeStatus() function.
    -->
    <P><CENTER>
    <A HREF="http://home.netscape.com"
    onMouseOver="return homeStatus()">Go Home</a>
    </CENTER></P>
    </BODY>
    </HTML>
```

Figure 6–4 shows the result of loading the `windowStatusTimeout.html` script.

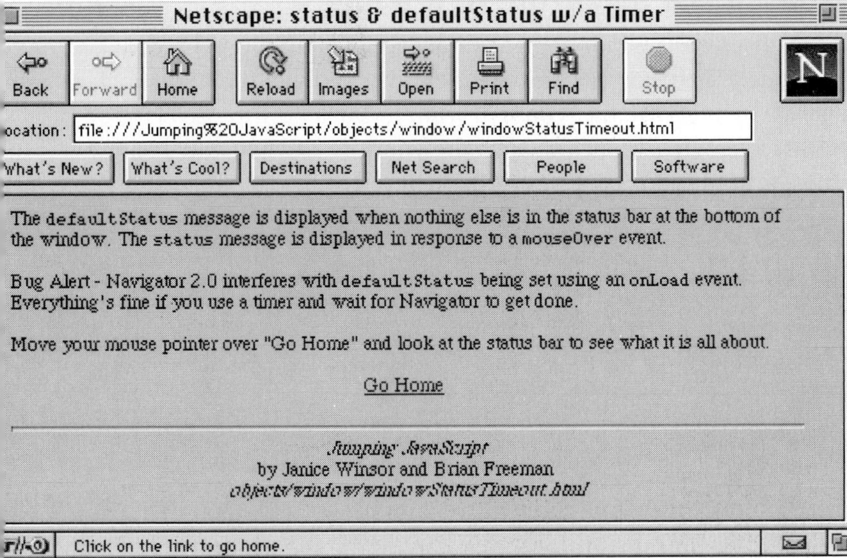

gure 6–4 Result of loading the `windowStatusTimeout`.html

ıe `windowStatusTimeout.html` script is identical to the .`ndowStatus.html` script except for the following line of code:

```
<BODY
onLoad="id=setTimeout('setDefaultStatus()',2000)">
```

ıis line includes within the `<BODY>` tag a temporary variable, `id`, which is used catch the value returned from the `setTimeout()` method. It's good ogramming practice to build in a way to capture the values returned by ethods, even if you don't ever use them in your scripts. The next part of the ıtement is the `setTimeout()` method. Because you want to call the `ɜtDefaultStatus()` function when the timer goes off, you can use it as the gument to the `setTimeout()` method, as we've done here. The `2000` at the .d of the statement represents the time in milliseconds that you want to wait ·fore the method is called. Two thousand milliseconds is two seconds (1000 illiseconds = 1 second).

Controlling the Structure of a Window

You can easily create a window that contains only one document. However, if yo want to create a more complicated window that is divided into distinct sections each with its own HTML file, you will want to learn how to use HTML `<FRAMESET>` tag, in conjunction with the window `frames` and `length` properties, to control the contents of the window.

Property	Value	Gettable	Settable
frames	array of window objects	Yes	No
length	number of defined frames	Yes	No

Using frames, you can create sophisticated windows with their own control ba that are always visible. In addition, you can divide the window into distinct sections. Figure 6–5 shows an example of a window with three frames.

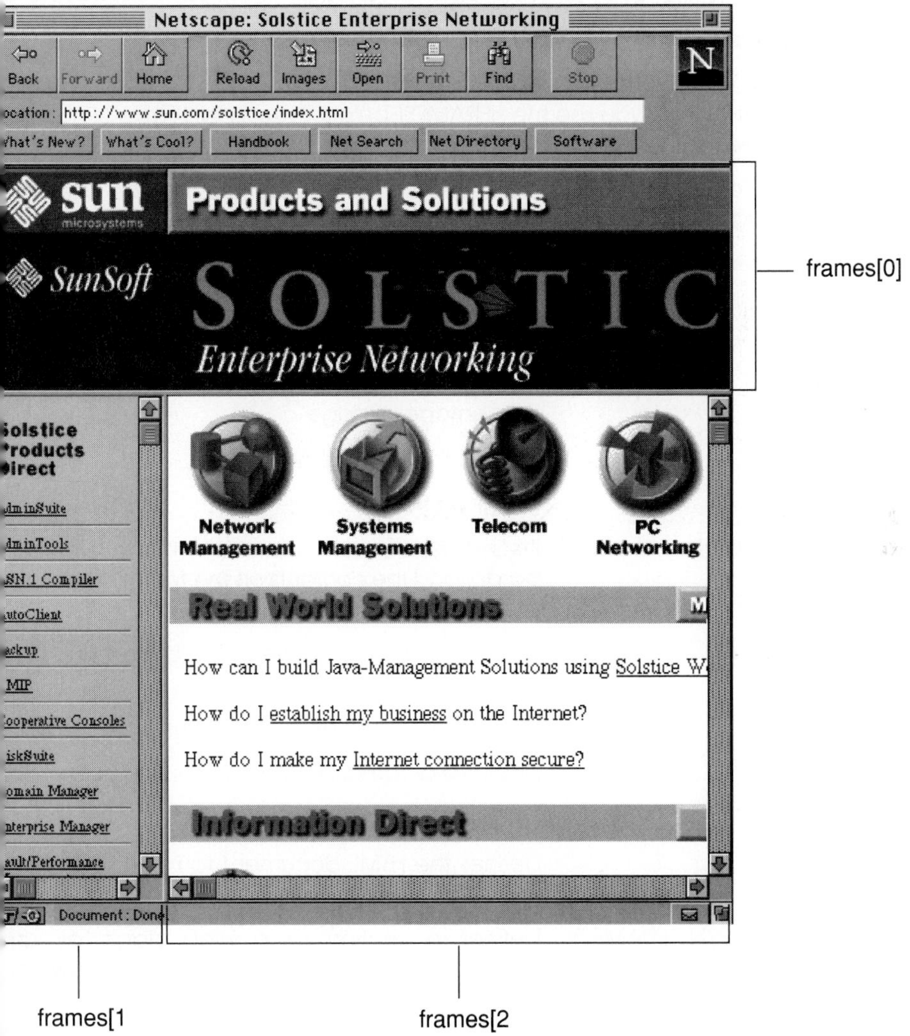

frames[0]

frames[1

frames[2

igure 6–5 Example of a window with multiple frames

ou divide windows into frames by using the `<FRAMESET>` HTML tag. You use e tag in the document that defines the `window` object to specify how to divide e window. Refer to the HTML Brushup box for information on how to create TML frames. For detailed examples of creating frames, see Appendix A, "HTML ames."

HTML Brushup — <FRAME> and <FRAMESET> Tags

Netscape 2.0 and later provide the following HTML extensions you can use to create frames. When you use the <FRAMESET> tag, it replaces the <BODY> tag in an HTML file.

You define a <FRAMESET> to divide up the window into frames. Use the <FRAME> tag to specify which files are displayed in each frame.

<FRAMESET></FRAMESET>	Defines a set of frames in a Web page
COLS	Defines the size of the columns in pixels or percentage of page
ROWS	Defines the size of the rows in pixels or percentage of page
NAME	Defines the variable name
<FRAME>	Defines a frame
MARGINHEIGHT	Defines how much space is left between the border and the contents on the top and bottom of the frame
MARGINWIDTH	Defines the space between the border and the contents on the sides
NAME	Defines the name of the frameset
NORESIZE	Declares a frame to be a fixed size
SCROLLING	Adds a scrollbar as needed
SRC	Defines the HTML document to be loaded into the frame
<NOFRAMES></NOFRAMES>	Defines a section of a Web page as an alternative to be viewed only by browsers without frame capability

You can create and manipulate frames by using the Navigator 2.0 HTML extensions without using JavaScript programs. However, the JavaScript languag provides the `frames` property of the `window` object to enable you to work with different frames from a script.

The frames Property

When you have more than one frame in a window, you need to have a way to identify each specific frame to the JavaScript language. The `frames` property provides that way as an *array* reflecting all the frames in a window. An array is a

ructured way by which you refer to object properties and variable values. In an ray, the properties are named in numerical order, starting with zero (`0`), for ample, `frame[0]`, `frame[1]`, `frame[2]`. For a complete description of rays, see Chapter 29, "Working with Arrays."

---

ote – It is a common programming practice to start numerical sequences with instead of 1.

---

he length Property

ecause you can create a complicated set of frames, the JavaScript language ovides you with a property, named `length`, that you can use to find out how any frames you have created in a parent window.

---

ote – The `length` property returns a count of the number of frames starting e count from 1, not from 0. When a document has three frames, the length is ree, but the frames are numbered 0, 1, and 2.

---

ou will find a `length` property for each array in the JavaScript language. herever you encounter this property, it does the same thing: returns to you the umber of items you have created in a set. This number can be the number of ames in a parent window, the number of radio buttons in a group, the number options in a selection list, or the number of links in a document.

eferring to a Window

ecause you can create complicated window structures with frames and amesets, it's important for you to communicate clearly to the JavaScript nguage the window or portion of a window that you want it to work with.

You can use five window properties, `name`, `parent`, `top`, `window`, and `self` to refer to the `window` object. Although these properties are similar to one another, they each refer to a specific context.

Property	Value	Refers to	Gettable	Settable
name	windowName	Named window	Yes	No
self	windowName	Current window	Yes	No
parent	windowName	Window containing a FRAMESET	Yes	No
top	windowName	Top-most Parent window	Yes	No
window	windowName	Current Window	Yes	No

The `name` property contains a string that represents the window.

The `window` property refers to the current window. The `window` and `self` properties are synonymous.

The `self` property refers to the current window. Because the `window` and `self` properties are synonymous, it's good to get into the habit of using *self* instead of window. If you ever put the code for the page into a frameset, you won't have to revise it.

The `parent` property refers to a window containing a frameset. When you use frames, you have a parent reference so that the interpreter can figure out which portion of the window to act on.

The `top` property refers to the topmost Navigator window in a frameset. This window is at the very top of the hierarchy and contains all subwindows. When you open new windows, you can use this property to refer back to the topmost window.

Examples of frame and Window Naming Properties

The following `simple.html` example creates a window and splits it into two equal frames.

HTML Brushup

The simple.html script contains a few new HTML tags:

<H1></H1>	Head one
<UL></UL>	Unordered (bulleted) list
<LI></LI>	List item. Surrounds individual items in the list Using the </LI> tag to end a list is not mandatory
"	Quotation mark

```
<!--
          simple.html
--!>
<HTML>
<HEAD>
<TITLE>Simple Frame Example</TITLE>
</HEAD>
<BODY>

<H1 ALIGN=CENTER>Frame Example</h1>

<P><A HREF="simple/index.html">simple/index.html
</A> is a basic example of using frames that
splits the window in half horizontally and loads
the same URL into each half. </P>

<P>The files involved are:</P>

<UL>
<LI>index.html contains a FRAMESET that defines
the two frames.  The first frame is given the
name &QUOT;frameA&QUOT; and the second
&QUOT;frameB&QUOT;.
<LI>frame.html contains the contents that are
loaded into each frame.
</UL>

</BODY>
</HTML>
```

Following is the `index.html` file that creates the frames.

```
<!--
    objects/window/frames/simple/index.html

    This example splits the window into
    two equal frames and loads frame.html into
    each half.
-->
<HTML>
<HEAD>
<TITLE>Simple Frame Example</TITLE>
</HEAD>

<FRAMESET ROWS="50%,50%">
  <FRAME NAME="frameA" SRC="frame.html">
  <FRAME NAME="frameB" SRC="frame.html">
</FRAMESET>

</HTML>
```

Following is the `frame.html` file that is loaded by the `index.html` script.

```
<!--
     objects/window/frames/simple/frame.html

    This example shows the window object's frames
    property. It splits the window into two
    frames, loading this document into each. See
    index.html for the complete picture.
-->
<HTML>
<BODY>
<SCRIPT LANGUAGE="JavaScript">
<!-- HIDE FROM OLD BROWSERS

  var mstr = "\n"
  mstr += "This is " + window.name
  document.open()
  document.write(mstr)
  document.close()

// STOP HIDING -->
</SCRIPT>
</BODY>
</HTML>
```

gure 6–6 shows the results of loading the `frames/simple.html` file that ovides a link to the other two scripts that are part of this set.

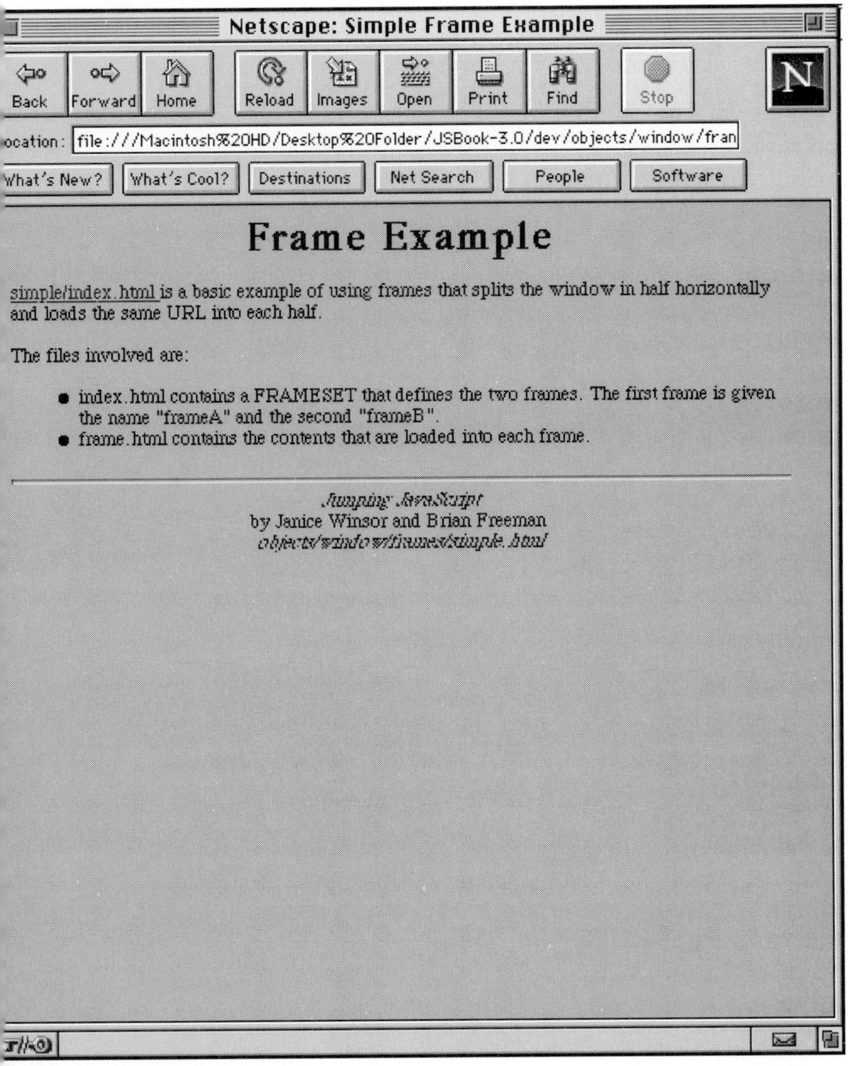

igure 6–6 Results of loading the `frames/simple.html` script

/hen you click on the link, the `index.html` file is loaded, which divides the creen in half and loads the `frame.html` script into each frame, as shown in igure 6–7.

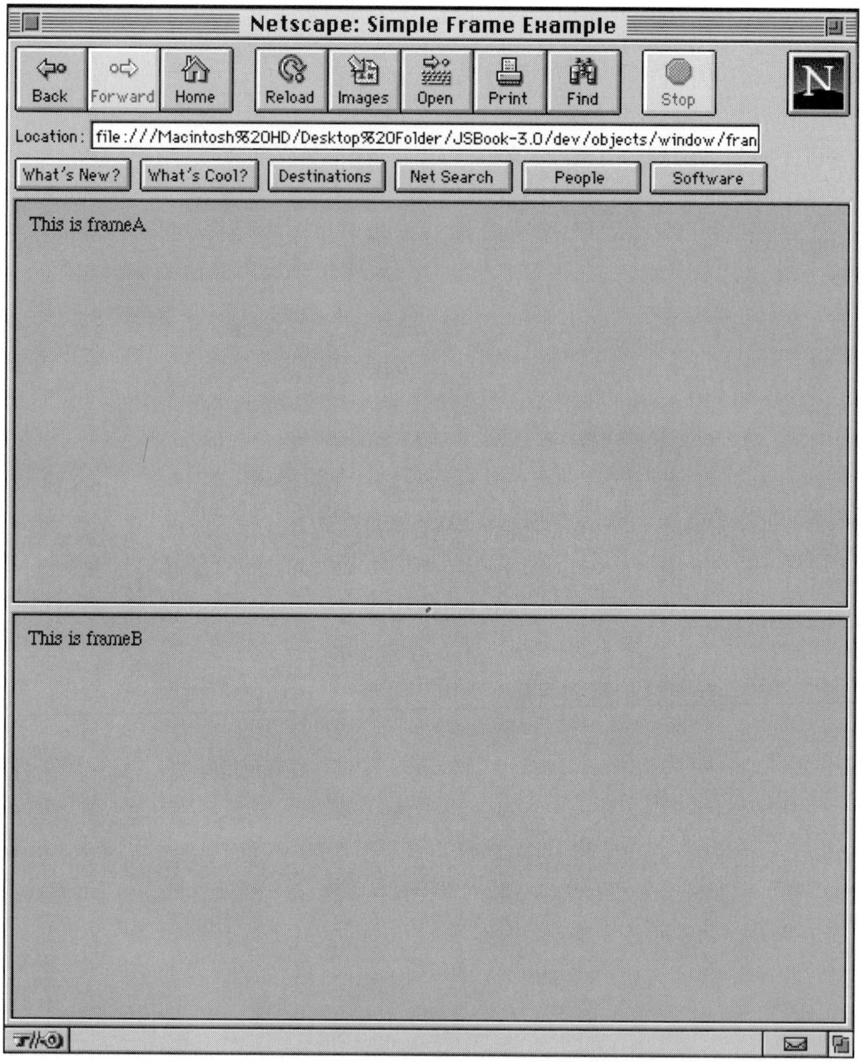

Figure 6–7 Result of clicking on `simple/index.html` link

Another example that is similar to the `simple.html` shows you the difference in the properties for each frame. This example starts with the `properties.html` script. When you load that file and click on the link, the `properties/index.html` script splits the window 50-50 and creates a Display Information button in each frame. When you click on the Display Information button in each frame, an alert window displays the different window-naming properties so that you can see how they differ from one another.

ne following properties.html script starts the sequence.

```
<!--
        properties.html
--!>
<HTML>
<HEAD>
<TITLE>Properties Frame Example</TITLE>
</HEAD>
<BODY>

<H1 ALIGN=CENTER>Frame Example</h1>

<P><A HREF="properties/index.html">properties/index.html
</A> is a basic example of using frames that
splits the window in half horizontally and loads
the same URL into each half. </P>

<P>The files involved are:</P>

<UL>
<LI>index.html contains a FRAMESET that defines
the two frames.  The first frame is given the
name &QUOT;frameA&QUOT; and the second
&QUOT;frameB&QUOT;.
<LI>frame.html contains the contents that are
loaded into each frame.
</UL>

<P>When you have read the information in this
window, click on the properties/index.html link to
create the frames and load the contents.</P>

<P>When you click on the Display Information
button in either frame, information about the
window properties is displayed in an alert
dialog. Notice that parent and top are the
same. Also, the name property has no value
because none was assigned when index.html was
loaded.  I think the only way you can assign a
window name is to create it. The frames
(&QUOT;frameA&QUOT; and &QUOT;frameB&QUOT;) do
have names because they were assigned in the
FRAME definitions.</P>
```

```
<p>This example uses:</p>

<UL>
<LI>FRAME
<LI>FRAMESET
<LI>window
<LI>parent
<LI>self
<LI>top
<LI>frames
<LI>length
</UL>

</BODY>
</HTML>
```

The `properties.html` script loads the following `properties/index.html` script.

```
<!--
   objects/window/frames/properties/index.html

    This example splits the window into
    two equal frames and loads frame.html into
    each half.
-->
<HTML>
<HEAD>
<TITLE>Properties Frame Example</TITLE>
</HEAD>

<FRAMESET ROWS="50%,50%">
  <FRAME NAME="frameA" SRC="frame.html">
  <FRAME NAME="frameB" SRC="frame.html">
</FRAMESET>

</HTML>
```

ne index.html script divides the window into equal frames and loads the llowing frame.html script.

```
<!--
   objects/window/frames/properties/frame.html

    This example shows the window object's frames
    property. It splits the window into two
    frames, loading this document into each. See
    index.html for the complete picture.
-->
<HTML>
<HEAD>
<SCRIPT LANGUAGE="JavaScript">
<!-- HIDE FROM OLD BROWSERS
//
// display window info into an alert dialog
//
function displayWindowInfo()
{
  var mstr = "\n"

  // window
  mstr += "window object:\t" + window + "\n"
  mstr += "window.name:\t" + window.name + "\n"
  mstr += "\n"

  // parent
  mstr += "parent property:\t" + parent + "\n"
  mstr += "parent.name:\t\t" + parent.name + "\n"
  mstr += "parent.length:\t" + parent.length + "\n"
  mstr += "parent.frames[0]:\t" + parent.frames[0] + "\n"
  mstr += "parent.frames[1]:\t" + parent.frames[1] + "\n"
  mstr += "\n"

  // self
  mstr += "self property:\t" + self + "\n"
  mstr += "self.name:\t" + self.name + "\n"
  mstr += "\n"
```

```
  // top
  mstr += "top property:\t" + top + "\n"
  mstr += "top.name:\t\t" + top.name + "\n"
  mstr += "top.length:\t" + top.length + "\n"
  mstr += "top.frames[0]:\t" + top.frames[0] + "\n"
  mstr += "top.frames[1]:\t" + top.frames[1] + "\n"
  mstr += "\n"

  // display it
  alert(mstr)
}
// STOP HIDING -->
</SCRIPT>
</HEAD>
<BODY>

<CENTER><FORM>
<INPUT TYPE="button" VALUE="Display Information"
onClick="displayWindowInfo()">
</FORM></CENTER>

</BODY>
</HTML>
```

Figure 6–8 shows the result of loading the `properties.html` script.

igure 6–8 Result of loading the `properties.html` script

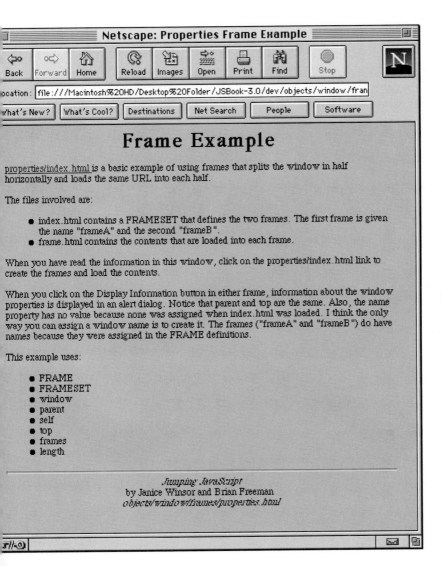

/hen you click on the `properties/index.html` link, the window is divided ıto two frames, each with a Display Information button, as shown in Figure 6–9.

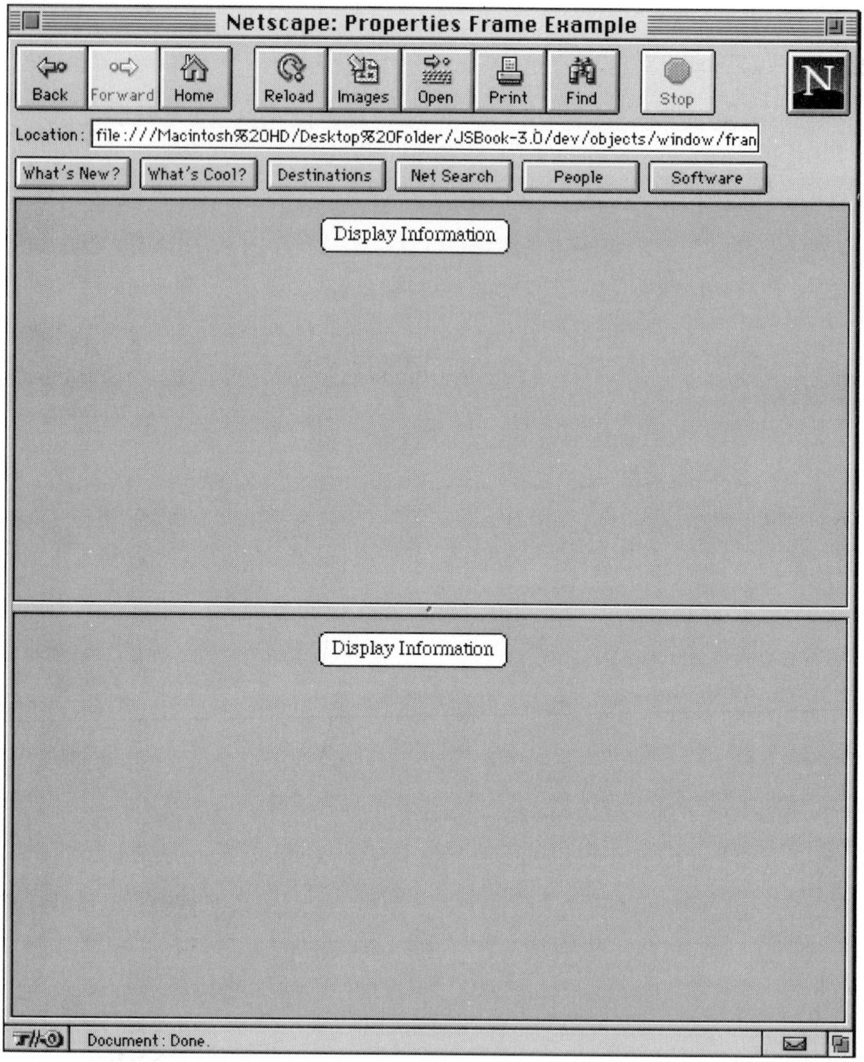

Figure 6–9 Two frames with Display Information buttons

When you click on the button in each frame, an alert window is displayed showing the window naming properties for that frame. Figure 6–10 shows the two alert windows together so you can compare the relationship between the window-naming properties, and how they differ frame by frame.

```
JavaScript Alert:

window object: [object Window]
window.name: frameA

parent property: [object Window]
parent.name:
parent.length: 2
parent.frames[0]: [object Window]
parent.frames[1]: [object Window]

self property: [object Window]
self.name: frameA

top property: [object Window]
top.name:
top.length: 2
top.frames[0]: [object Window]
top.frames[1]: [object Window]

OK
```

```
JavaScript Alert:

window object: [object Window]
window.name: frameB

parent property: [object Window]
parent.name:
parent.length: 2
parent.frames[0]: [object Window]
parent.frames[1]: [object Window]

self property: [object Window]
self.name: frameB

top property: [object Window]
top.name:
top.length: 2
top.frames[0]: [object Window]
top.frames[1]: [object Window]

OK
```

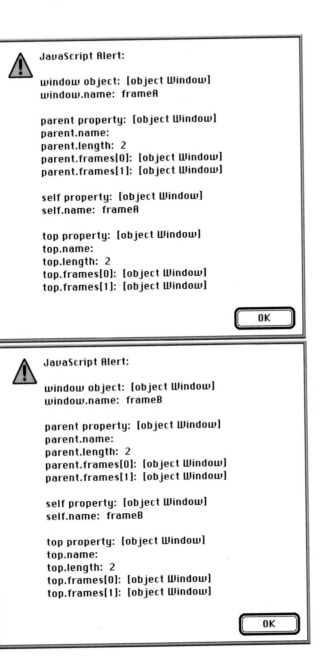

Figure 6–10 Comparing alert windows with window-naming properties

The following list explains the relationship between the window-naming properties shown in Figure 6–10:

- The `window` object is the name of the object, which is Window.
- The `window.name` for the top frame is frameA. The `window.name` for the bottom frame is frameB.
- The `parent.property` is the `window` object that created the frame, and it is the same for both frames.
- The `parent.name` property has no value because none was assigned when the `index.html` file was loaded. A name can be assigned only when the original window is created. The original window name is displayed in the header of the window even when the window is divided into frames and new information is displayed.
- The `parent.length` property is 2, the accurate count of the two frames in the parent window.
- The `parent.frames[0]` property returns the value `[object Window]`, which indicates that the window is the parent object for this frame.
- The `parent.frames[1]` property returns the value `[object Window]`, which indicates that the window is the parent object for this frame.
- The `self` property returns the value `[object Window]`, which indicates that the window is the parent object for this frame.
- The `self.name` property is the name of the frame that is assigned in the `index.html` script, and it reflects the name of the frame in which it is used.
- The `top` property is the same as the `parent` property.
- The `top.name` property has no value because none was assigned when the `index.html` file was loaded.
- The `top.frames[0]` value is the same as `parent.frames[0]`.
- The `top.frames[1]` value is the same as `parent.frames[1]`.

Explanation of Example Scripts

The `index.html` script that creates the frames is very simple:

`<FRAMESET ROWS="50%,50%">`	Create a set of frames with two rows that divide the document area in half.
`<FRAME NAME="frameA" SRC="frame.html">`	Name the first frame `frameA`, and load the file `frame.html` into that frame.
`<FRAME NAME="frameB" SRC="frame.html">`	Name the second frame `frameB`, and load the file `frame.html` into that frame.
`</FRAMESET>`	End the set of frames.

The `frame.html` script formats text in ways that are explained in much more detail in Chapter 28, "Working with Strings and String Objects."

The `frame.html` script does the majority of its work within the `displayWindowInfo()` function. The point of this script is to show you the values returned by the `window`, `parent`, `self`, `top`, `frames`, and `length` properties.

First we define a function named `displayWindowInfo()`.

```
function displayWindowInfo()
{
  var mstr = "\n"
```

The first statement in the function defines a variable, `mstr`, which stands for message string, and initializes it with a value of `\n`.

Note – `\n` is an escaped character that tells Navigator to display a new line at the end of the statement. The JavaScript language has a number of escaped characters that you can use to format JavaScript strings. This script also uses `\t`, which is an escaped character that inserts a tab. For a table of string-formatting escape characters, see Appendix C, "JavaScript Quick Reference."

The next group of statements concatenate text, formatting characters, and properties.

The += assignment operator joins (concatenates) the items in the strings and puts a new line at the end of each item:

```
mstr += "parent property:\t" + parent + "\n"
```

UI Guideline – Be aware that text formatting differs for different platforms. In Windows 95™ Navigator, the tabs in this script display a nicely formatted window. In Macintosh Navigator, the tabs are ignored and are replaced by spaces.

After all of the string formatting, the last element in the function creates an alert window to display the message strings.

```
    alert(mstr)
}
```

The body of the script creates a button labeled Display Information and uses the `onClick` event handler to call the `displayWindowInfo()` function.

```
<CENTER><FORM>
<INPUT TYPE="button" VALUE="Display Information"
onClick="displayWindowInfo()">
</FORM></CENTER>
```

A Three-Frame Window Example

The following, more complicated, example shows you the flexibility of creating frames and further demonstrates how important it is for you to keep track of your frames and window properties This example uses six scripts:

- The first script, `top.html`, provides a link that you click on to create the frames, and an explanation of what the script does.
- The second script, `index.html`, divides the window in half vertically and loads the third script, `frameA.html`, into the left half and the fourth script, `frameB.html`, into the right half.
- The third script, `frameA.html`, further subdivides the left half of the screen into two rows and loads the fifth script, `frameA1.html`, into the top half and the sixth script, `frameA2.html`, into the bottom half.

igure 6–11 shows a diagram of the windows created by this set of scripts, and ıows which window is the `top.document.title` and `arent.document.title`. The `parent.frames[0].document.title`, and `elf.document.title` always refer to the current window.

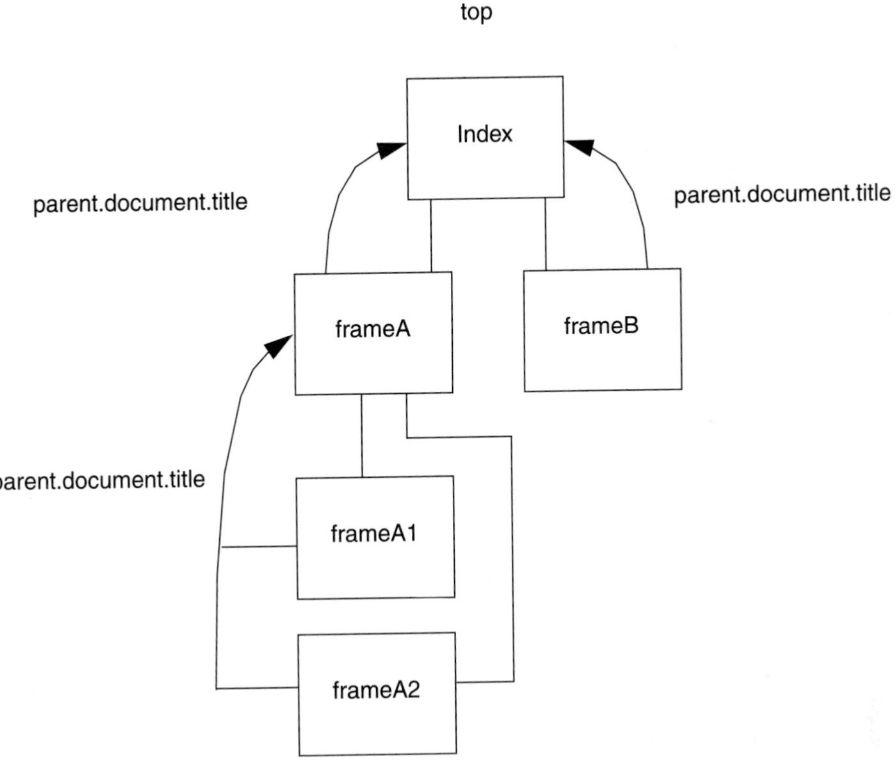

'igure 6–11 Diagram of `parent.document.title` properties

Ɨere is the `top.html` script that creates the link and explains the script example.

```
<!--
    top.html
-->
<HTML>
<HEAD>
   <TITLE>Top Frame Example</TITLE>
</HEAD>
<BODY>

<H1 ALIGN=CENTER>window.top</H1>
```

```
<P><A HREF="top/index.html">top/index.html</A> shows the
window object's top property. </P>

<P>The files involved are:</P>

<UL>
<LI>index.html contains the FRAMESET that defines the two
frames. The first frame is given the name
&QUOT;frameA&QUOT; and the second &QUOT;frameB.&QUOT;</LI

<LI>frameA.html contains a second FRAMESET that defines
two more frames. The first frame is given the name
&QUOT;frameA1&QUOT; and the second
&QUOT;frameA2.&QUOT;</LI>

<LI>frameA1.html contains the contents loaded into
frameA1. frameA is its parent and index.html is top.</LI>

<LI>frameA2.html contains the contents loaded into
frameA2. frameA is its parent and index.html is top.</LI>

<LI>frameB.html contains the contents loaded into frameB
of the FRAMESET.</LI>
</UL>

<P>Multiple ways of getting at the document title are
displayed in each frame. This example is good for showing
dot syntax, frames, and the document window property.
Notice that Navigator's title bar gets the title defined
by index.html.</P>

<P>This example uses the following elements:</P>

<UL>
<LI>FRAME</LI>

<LI>FRAMESET</LI>

<LI>document.title</LI>

<LI>parent.document.title</LI>

<LI>parent.frames[0].document.title</LI>
```

```
<LI>parent.frames[1].document.title</LI>

<LI>parent.frameA.document.title</LI>

<LI>parent.frameB.document.title</LI>

<LI>self.document.title</LI>

<LI>top.document.title</LI>
</UL>

</BODY>
</HTML>
```

ere is the `index.html` script. This script uses multiple frames, splitting the indow into two equal halves and loading `frameA.html` into the left half and `rameB.html` into the right half. It further subdivides frameA into two more ames: frameA1 and frameA2.

```
<!--
      objects/window/frames/top/index.html

     This example shows the window object's top
     property. It uses multiple frames, splitting
     the window into two equal halves and loading
     frameA.html into the left and frameB.html into
     the right. It further subdivides frameA into
     two more frames: frameA1 and frameA2.
-->
<HTML>
<HEAD>
<TITLE>index</TITLE>
</HEAD>

<FRAMESET COLS="50%,50%">
  <FRAME NAME="frameA" SRC="frameA.html">
  <FRAME NAME="frameB" SRC="frameB.html">
</FRAMESET>

</HTML>
```

Iere is the `frameA.html` script that is loaded into the frame on the right side of ne screen by the `index.html` script:

```
<!--
      objects/window/frames/top/frameA.html

    This example shows the window object's top
    property. It uses multiple frames, splitting
    the window into two equal halves and loading
    frameA.html into the left and frameB.html into
    the right. It further subdivides frameA into
    two more frames: frameA1 and frameA2.
-->
<HTML>
<HEAD>
<TITLE>frameA</TITLE>
</HEAD>

<FRAMESET ROWS="50%,50%">
  <FRAME NAME="frameA1" SRC="frameA1.html">
  <FRAME NAME="frameA2" SRC="frameA2.html">
</FRAMESET>

</HTML>
```

Here is the `frameB.html` script that is loaded into the frame on the right side of the screen by the `index.html` script:

```
<!--
      objects/window/frames/top/frameB.html

    This file shows various ways of
    obtaining the document title string. See
    index.html for the complete picture.
-->
<HTML>
<HEAD>
<TITLE>frameB</TITLE>
<SCRIPT LANGUAGE="JavaScript">
<!-- HIDE FROM OLD BROWSERS

var mstr = ""

// document.title
mstr += "document.title = "
mstr += "\"" + document.title + "\"<P>"
```

```
// parent
mstr += "parent.document.title = "
mstr += "\"" + parent.document.title + "\"<P>"

// parent.frames.length
mstr += "parent.frames.length = "
mstr += "\"" + parent.frames.length
mstr += "\"<P>"

// parent.frames[0]
mstr += "parent.frames[0].document.title = "
mstr += "\"" + parent.frames[0].document.title
mstr += "\"<P>"

// parent.frames[1]
mstr += "parent.frames[1].document.title = "
mstr += "\"" + parent.frames[1].document.title
mstr += "\"<P>"

// parent.frameA
mstr += "parent.frameA.document.title = "
mstr += "\"" + parent.frameA.document.title
mstr += "\"<P>"

// parent.frameB
mstr += "parent.frameB.document.title = "
mstr += "\"" + parent.frameB.document.title
mstr += "\"<P>"

// self
mstr += "self.document.title = "
mstr += "\"" + self.document.title + "\"<P>"

// top
mstr += "top.document.title = "
mstr += "\"" + top.document.title + "\"<P>"

document.open()
document.write(mstr)
document.close()
// STOP HIDING -->
</SCRIPT>
</HEAD>
</HTML>
```

Here is the `frameA1.html` script that is loaded into the top half of the left fram created by the `frameA.html` script.

```
<!--
     objects/window/frames/top/frameA1.html

    This file shows various ways of
    obtaining the document title string. See
    index.html for the complete picture.
-->
<HTML>
<HEAD>
<TITLE>frameA1</TITLE>
<SCRIPT LANGUAGE="JavaScript">
<!-- HIDE FROM OLD BROWSERS

var mstr = ""

// document.title
mstr += "document.title = "
mstr += "\"" + document.title + "\"<P>"

// parent
mstr += "parent.document.title = "
mstr += "\"" + parent.document.title + "\"<P>"

// parent.frames.length
mstr += "parent.frames.length = "
mstr += "\"" + parent.frames.length
mstr += "\"<P>"

// parent.frames[0]
mstr += "parent.frames[0].document.title = "
mstr += "\"" + parent.frames[0].document.title
mstr += "\"<P>"

// parent.frames[1]
mstr += "parent.frames[1].document.title = "
mstr += "\"" + parent.frames[1].document.title
mstr += "\"<P>"

// self
mstr += "self.document.title = "
mstr += "\"" + self.document.title + "\"<P>"
```

```
// top
mstr += "top.document.title = "
mstr += "\"" + top.document.title + "\"<P>"

document.open()
document.writeln(mstr)
document.close()

// STOP HIDING -->
</SCRIPT>
</HEAD>
</HTML>
```

Here is the `frameA2.html` script that is loaded into the bottom of Frame A by the `frameA.html` script.

```
<!--
       frames/top/frameA2.html

    This file shows various ways of
    obtaining the document title string. See
    index.html for the complete picture.
-->
<HTML>
<HEAD>
<TITLE>frameA2</TITLE>
<SCRIPT LANGUAGE="JavaScript">
<!-- HIDE FROM OLD BROWSERS

var mstr = ""

// document.title
mstr += "document.title = "
mstr += "\"" + document.title + "\"<P>"

// parent
mstr += "parent.document.title = "
mstr += "\"" + parent.document.title + "\"<P>"

// parent.frames.length
mstr += "parent.frames.length = "
mstr += "\"" + parent.frames.length
mstr += "\"<P>"
```

```
// parent.frames[0]
mstr += "parent.frames[0].document.title = "
mstr += "\"" + parent.frames[0].document.title
mstr += "\"<P>"

// parent.frames[1]
mstr += "parent.frames[1].document.title = "
mstr += "\"" + parent.frames[1].document.title
mstr += "\"<P>"

// self
mstr += "self.document.title = "
mstr += "\"" + self.document.title + "\"<P>"

// top
mstr += "top.document.title = "
mstr += "\"" + top.document.title + "\"<P>"

document.open()
document.write(mstr)
document.close()


// STOP HIDING -->
</SCRIPT>
</HEAD>
</HTML>
```

igure 6–12 shows the result of loading the `top.html` script.

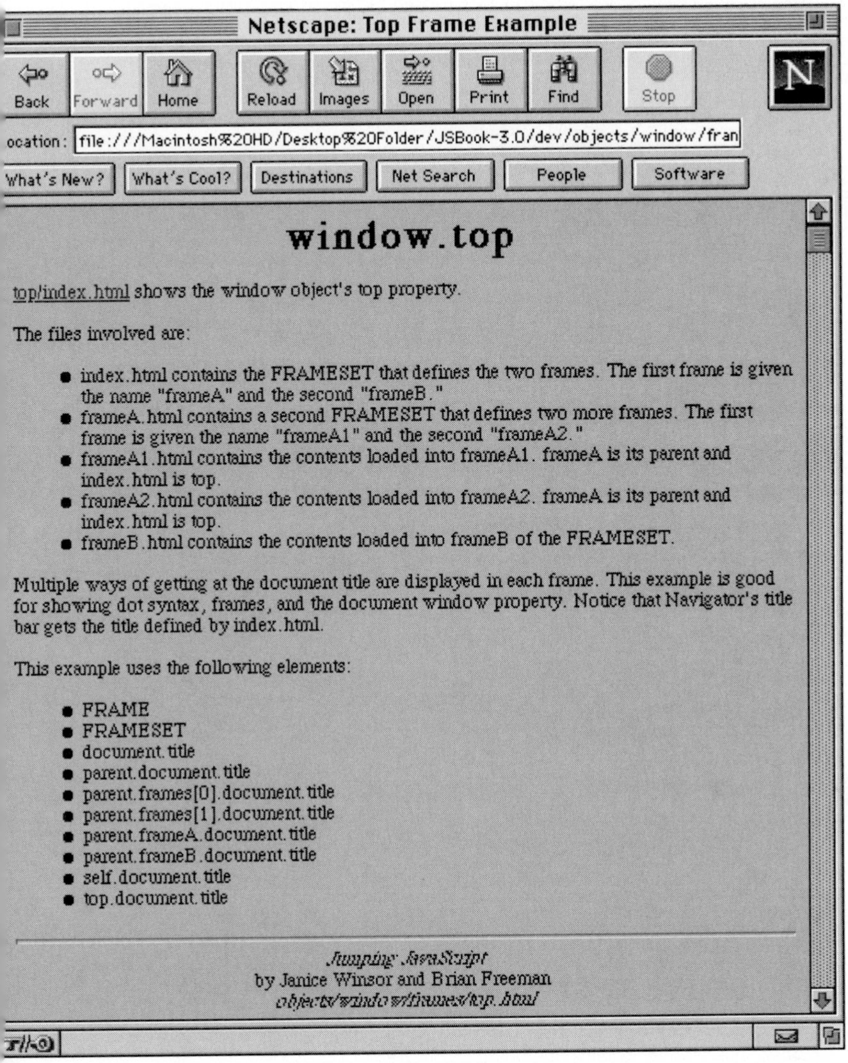

Netscape: Top Frame Example

Back | Forward | Home | Reload | Images | Open | Print | Find | Stop

ocation: file:///Macintosh%20HD/Desktop%20Folder/JSBook-3.0/dev/objects/window/fran

What's New? | What's Cool? | Destinations | Net Search | People | Software

window.top

top/index.html shows the window object's top property.

The files involved are:

- index.html contains the FRAMESET that defines the two frames. The first frame is given the name "frameA" and the second "frameB."
- frameA.html contains a second FRAMESET that defines two more frames. The first frame is given the name "frameA1" and the second "frameA2."
- frameA1.html contains the contents loaded into frameA1. frameA is its parent and index.html is top.
- frameA2.html contains the contents loaded into frameA2. frameA is its parent and index.html is top.
- frameB.html contains the contents loaded into frameB of the FRAMESET.

Multiple ways of getting at the document title are displayed in each frame. This example is good for showing dot syntax, frames, and the document window property. Notice that Navigator's title bar gets the title defined by index.html.

This example uses the following elements:

- FRAME
- FRAMESET
- document.title
- parent.document.title
- parent.frames[0].document.title
- parent.frames[1].document.title
- parent.frameA.document.title
- parent.frameB.document.title
- self.document.title
- top.document.title

Jumping JavaScript
by Janice Winsor and Brian Freeman
objects/window/frames/top.html

igure 6–12 Result of loading the `top.html` script

When you click on the `top/index.html` link, the window is divided into frames, and each frame displays its own properties, as shown in Figure 6–13.

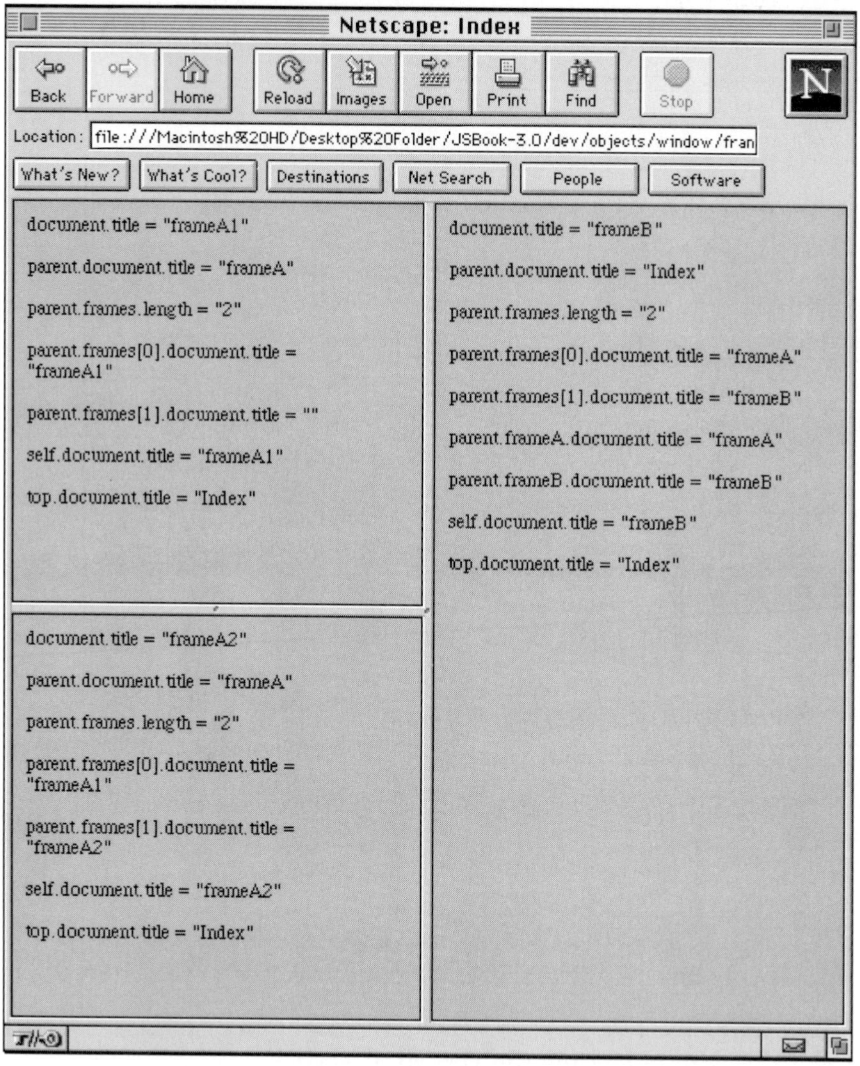

Figure 6–13 Multiple frames with properties

Note – The `length` property in each frame returns a value of 2, not 3. The `length` property counts the number of frames in each frameset, not the total number of frames in the topmost window.

These scripts display the values returned by the properties within each frame. The results are enclosed in quotation marks, which are the result of the \" escaped characters in the script. The output is written to the frame by the `document.write()` property.

Let's look at the values that are returned for the properties, frame by frame. The values in the upper-left frame are as follows:

- The `document.title` property is the name of the HTML document that contains the information loaded into the frame: `frameA1`.
- The `parent.document.title` property is the name of the HTML document that created the original window and split it into two frames: `frameA`.
- The `parent.frames.length` is 2, because the parent document, `frameA`, creates two frames.
- The `parent.frames[0].document.title` property returns the name of the HTML document that created the first frame of this set: `frameA1`.
- The `parent.frames[1].document.title` property returns the name of the HTML document that is loaded into the second frame of this set: `null`. This value is null because the parent for this frame is `frames[0]` and the properties read from top to bottom.

Note – The `parent.frames[1].document.title` property returns a value of null in this case because of the way the page is parsed for layout. The interpreter has not finished laying out the pages when it gets the title values for the different frames. If you create windows with multiple frames from different HTML files, be sure to carefully test your scripts to make sure that you achieve the results you expect. For more information on how the interpreter lays out HTML files, see Chapter 4, "Debugging Scripts."

- The `self.document.title` property is the name of the frame that is assigned in the `frameA.html` script, and it reflects the name of the frame in which it is used: `frameA1`.
- The `top.document.title` property returns the name of the top HMTL document that created the window: `Index`. In this case, top and parent are different because of the multiscript construction of the frames in this window

The values in the lower left frame are as follows:

- The `document.title` property is the name of the HTML document that contains the information loaded into the frame: `frameA2`.
- The `parent.frames.length` is 2, because the parent document, `frameA`, creates two frames.
- The `parent.document.title` property is the name of the HTML document that created the original window and split it into two frames: `frameA`. This value is the same as that for the frame above it.
- The `parent.frames[0].document.title` property returns the name of the HTML document that is loaded into the first frame of this set: `frameA1`.
- The `parent.frames[1].document.title` property returns the name of the HTML document that created the second frame of this set: `frameA2`.
- The `self.document.title` property is the name of the frame that is assigned in the `frameA.html` script, and it reflects the name of the frame in which it is used: `frameA2`.
- The `top.document.title` property returns the name of the top HMTL document that created the window: `index`. In this case, top and parent are different because of the multiscript construction of the frames in this window

ıe values in the right frame are:

The `document.title` property is the name of the HTML document that contains the information loaded into the frame: `frameB`.

The `parent.document.title` property is the name of the HTML document that created the original window and split it into two frames: `index`. This value is different from the value in the left two frames because a different document created this frame.

The `parent.frames.length` is 2, because the parent document, `Index`, creates two frames.

The `parent.frames[0].document.title` property returns the name of the HTML document that is loaded into the first frame of this set: `frameA`.

The `parent.frames[1].document.title` property returns the name of the HTML document that created the second frame of this set: `frameB`.

The `parent.frameA.document.title` property returns the name of the HTML document that is loaded into the first frame of this set: `frameA`.

The `parent.frameA.document.title` property returns the name of the HTML document that created the second frame of this set: `frameB`.

The `self.document.title` property is the name of the frame that is assigned in the `frameA.html` script, and it reflects the name of the frame in which it is used: `frameB`.

The `top.document.title` property returns the name of the top HMTL document that created the window: `index`. In this case, top and parent are different because of the multiscript construction of the frames in this window.

ɔr another example of creating a document with multiple frames that are loaded om different files, see Appendix A, "HTML Frames."

eferencing document, history, and location Objects in a 'indow

ıe `window` object is the top level of the Navigator JavaScript object hierarchy. gure 6–14 shows the top of the object hierarchy. You can see from a glance at ıis figure, that the next three objects in the hierarchy from the window level are ıe `location`, `history`, and `document` objects.

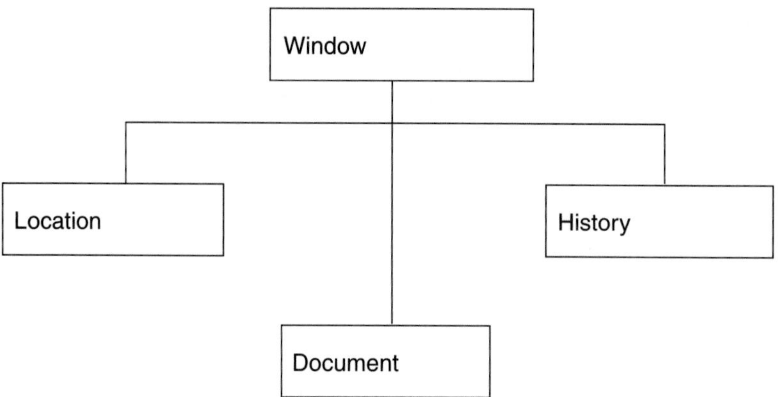

Figure 6–14 Top of the object hierarchy

When you create a `window` object, *instances* of the specific objects: `document`, `history`, and `location` are also created. In other words, when you load a document that creates a window, it also creates `document`, `history`, and `location` objects that are properties of that window.

Property	Value	Gettable	Settable
document	document object	Yes	No
history	history object	Yes	No
location	location object	Yes	Yes

The `document` property refers to an instance of the `document` object, which enables you to work with information about anchors, forms, links, the document title, the current location and URL, and the current colors of a document. For more information about the `document` object, see Chapter 7, "Creating Documents."

The `history` property refers to an instance of the `history` object, which enables you to send the user to somewhere in the history list from within a JavaScript program. For more information about the `history` object, see Chapter 8, "Controlling History."

The `location` property refers to an instance of the `location` object, which enables you to store and display information about the current URL. You can set new location as well as extracting existing information about the location object. For more information about the `location` object, see Chapter 12, "Controlling Location."

xample of Referencing document, history, and location Objects

he following `windowProps.html` script provides an alert that you can use to isplay the properties of a window, including `document`, `history`, and `ocation`. This script uses the generic function defined in the `getProps.js` file escribed in Chapter 4, "Debugging Scripts."

```
<!--
    windowProps.html

    This example displays all the window object's
    properties in an alert dialog.
-->

<HTML>
<HEAD>
<TITLE>Window Properties</TITLE>
<SCRIPT SRC="../../debug/getProps.js"></SCRIPT>
</HEAD>

<BODY>

<CENTER><FORM>
<INPUT TYPE="button"
 VALUE="Display Window Properties"
 onClick="alert(getProps(window,'window',false))">
</FORM></CENTER>

</BODY>
</HTML>
```

igure 6–15 shows the alert that is displayed when you load the `indowProps.html` script and click on the Display Window Properties button.

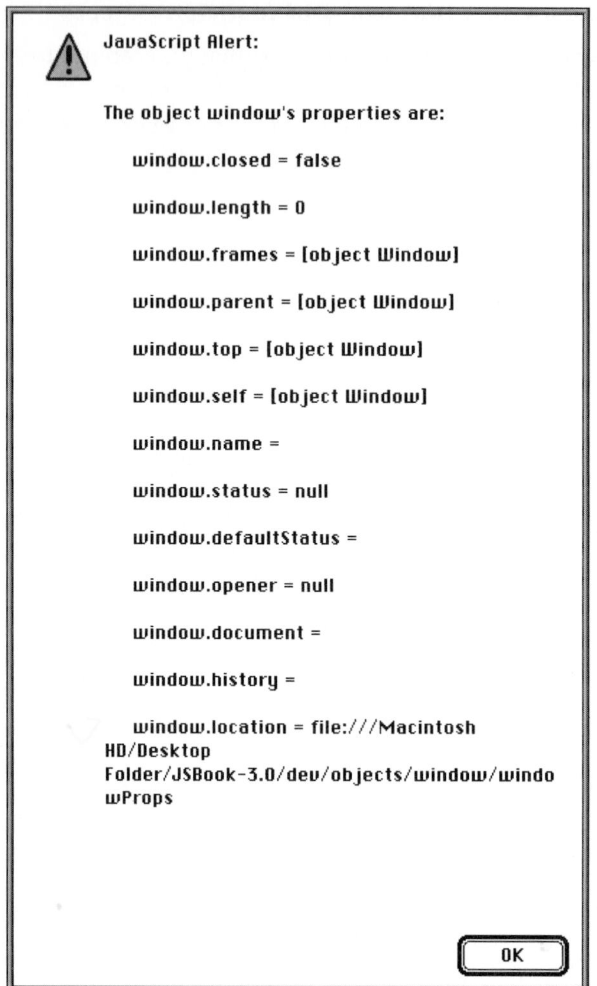

Figure 6–15 Window properties alert

Opening a New Window

When you open a new window, you can specify everything about the window if you want. You use the `window.open()` method to create a new window. Once a window is opened, you cannot change any of its window features.

The following list gives you an idea of the flexibility you have in creating a new window: You can:

Open a new blank window with no HTML document

Open a new window that displays an existing HTML document

Specify the height and width of the window

Specify the user interface elements to be used in the window (toolbar, menubar, scrollbars, resizable)

Duplicate the Go menu history for the new window

Duplicate the "What's New" and other buttons in the row

ou specify the parameters for the `open()` method in the following order. Square ackets (`[ ]`) indicate items that are optional:

Method

(*winVar*) = window.open("*URL*", "*windowName*", ("*windowFeatures*"))

Returns

An instance of the window object; null if the method fails

`winVar` is a reference to the new `window` object or `null` if `open()` failed.

ne `open` method takes the following parameters:

`URL` — Use to specify the location of the HTML document to be loaded. If you do not want to load a document, use an empty string (" ").

`windowName` is an identifier name. You can use this name with the `TARGET` attribute of a `<FORM>` or `<A>` tag. *`windowName`* can contain only alphanumeric or underscore (_) characters.

- *windowFeatures* — An optional, comma-separated list of options and values. If you do not specify any features, the `window` object uses all of the values of the current window. Table 6-2 describes the attributes and values you can use to specify window features.

Table 6-2 Values for windowFeatures Attributes

Option	Value	Description
`toolbar`	[=yes|no]|[=1|0]	Back, Forward, and other buttons in the row
`location`	[=yes|no]|[=1|0]	Field displaying the current URL
`directories`	[=yes|no]|[=1|0]	"What's New" and other buttons in the row
`status`	[=yes|no]|[=1|0]	Status bar at the bottom of window
`menubar`	[=yes|no]|[=1|0]	Menu bar at top of window (except on Macintosh systems, because the menu bar is not in the browser window)
`scrollbars`	[=yes|no]|[=1|0]	Scrollbars are displayed if document is larger than the window
`resizable`	[=yes|no]|[=1|0]	Elements that enable users to resize the window
`width`	=pixels	Width of the window, in pixels
`height`	=pixels	Height of the window, in pixels

You can use any or all of the attributes listed in Table 6-2, and you can put them in any order within the parentheses. Separate the items in the list by commas. Do not put spaces between the options.

Specify window height and width as a positive integer. For example, the method to create a window that is 300 pixels wide and 500 pixels high looks like this:

```
win = self.open("","myWindow","width=300,height=500")
```

or

```
win = window.open("","myWindow","width=300,height=500")
```

oolean values are set to `true` if no value is specified. If `windowName` does not ›ecify an existing window and you do not specify any *`windowFeatures`*, all oolean *`windowFeatures`* are set to `true`. If you specify any Boolean *`indowFeatures`*, all others are set to `false` unless you explicitly set them.

you do not specify width and height of the window, the `window` object may use ıe default size of the window that the browser creates when you choose New /eb Browser from the File menu.

or any of the other attributes, you can specify the attribute by just using the :tribute name or by using the attribute name with a specific value. For example,

```
scrollbars
scrollbars=yes
scrollbars=1
```

l mean the same thing to the `window` object: add scrollbars to the window if the ocument that is displayed is larger than the window.

xamples of open() Method

he following `windowOpen.html` script uses the open method of the `window` oject to open a window when the file is loaded.

```
<!--
    windowOpen.html

    This example shows how to create a window
    object by using the open() method.

    To see how it works, simply load this file
    into your browser and a new window is
    created.
-->
<HTML>
<HEAD>
<TITLE>Window Creation</TITLE>
<SCRIPT LANGUAGE="JavaScript">
<!-- HIDE FROM OLD BROWSERS

  // open the URL "win.html" in a new window and
  // name the new window "win"
  win=open("win.html","win",
           "width=300,height=150")
```

```
  // write a message
  document.open()
  document.writeln("<BR><B>")
  document.writeln("The created window is named:")
  document.writeln(" " + win.name + "</B>")
  document.close()

// STOP HIDING -->
</SCRIPT>
</HEAD>

<BODY>

<P>When you load <KBD>windowOpen.html</KBD>,
<KBD>win.html</KBD> is loaded and displayed
automatically. Above, you should also see a
message denoting the name of the created
window. It corresponds to the second argument in
the <CODE>open()</CODE> call.</P>

</BODY>
</HTML>
```

Following is the `win.html` file that is loaded by the call to `window.open()` in the the `windowOpen.html` file.

```
<!--
    win.html

    This file is used in conjunction with
    windowOpen.html to illustrate the window
    object's open method.
-->
<HTML>
<HEAD>
<TITLE>Opened File</TITLE>
</HEAD>

<BODY>
<CENTER>
<P>This file is win.html</P>
</CENTER>

</BODY>
</HTML>
```

'hen you load the `windowOpen.html` script, a Navigator window and a new 'indow are both opened, as shown in Figure 6–16.

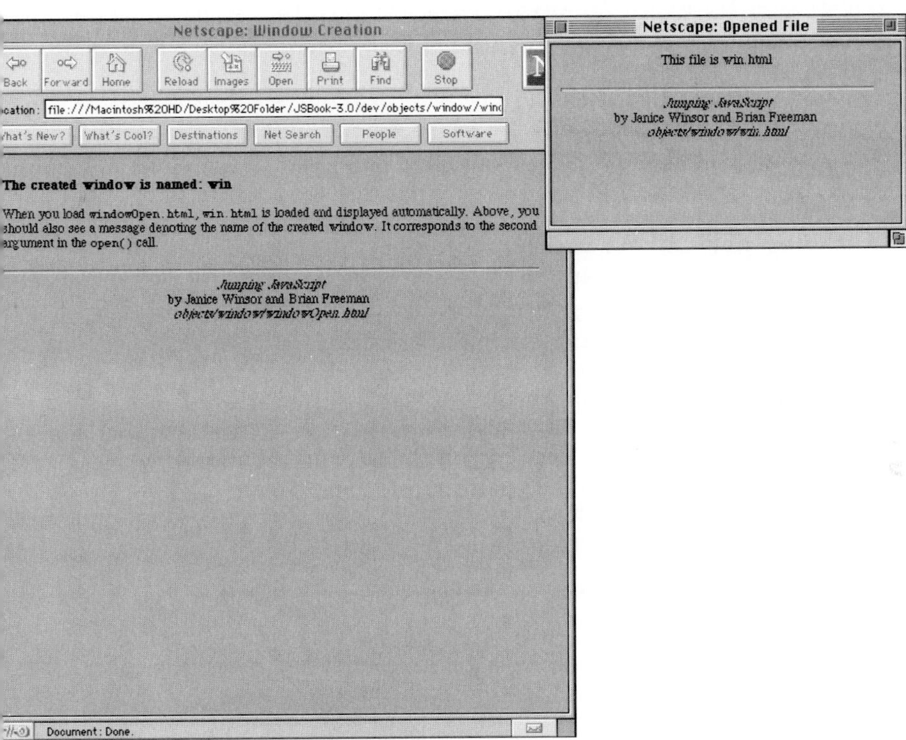

'**igure 6–16** Result of loading the `windowOpen.html` script

'he following `windowOpenDeferred.html` script opens a window containing message when the user clicks on the button.

Bug for open() Method: Netscape Navigator 2.0 Mac and X Versions

In Netscape Navigator 2.0 Mac® and X Versions, the URL that is passed to window.open() fails to load. This bug is currently documented in the FAQ, at:

`http://www.freqgrafx.com/411/jsfaq.html#winopen:`

When you call window.open(), the window is not opened. You need to call window.open() a second time to force the load:

```
function windowOpen(url, name) {
      var newWin = window.open(url, name)
      if (navigator.appVersion.indexOf("2.0")  != -1
        || navigator.appVersion.indexOf("(X11") != -1
        || navigator.appVersion.indexOf("(Mac") != -1)
      {
        newWin = window.open(url, name)
      }
   }
```

The trick here is to call window.open() a second time to force the load. This bug is fixed in the Navigator 3.0 releases.

```
<!--
    windowOpenDeferred.html

    This example uses the window
    object's open() method to open a new window
    when the user clicks on a button. open()
    enables you to display a message to the user
    that does not require any feedback.
-->
<HTML>
<HEAD>
<TITLE>Deferred open()</TITLE>
<SCRIPT LANGUAGE="JavaScript">
<!-- HIDE FROM OLD BROWSERS

//
// Create a window, set its title, and insert a
// message.
//
function openWindow() {
  myWin = window.open("",
```

```
                "myWindow",
                "width=400,height=50")

    myWin.document.write(
        "<HEAD><TITLE>My Window</TITLE></HEAD>")
    myWin.document.write(
        "<CENTER>I did this!</CENTER>")
  }

  // STOP HIDING -->
  </SCRIPT>
  </HEAD>

  <BODY>
  <!--
      When you click on the Create a Window
      button, openWindow() is called.
  -->
  <CENTER>
  <FORM NAME="myform">
  <INPUT TYPE="button" NAME="Button1"
    VALUE="Create a Window!"
    onClick="openWindow()">
  </FORM>
  </CENTER>

  </BODY>
  </HTML>
```

igure 6–17 shows the result of loading the `windowOpenDeferred.html` cript.

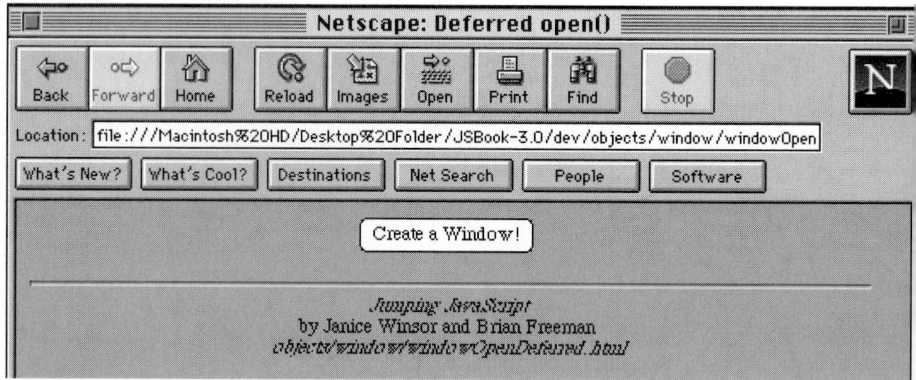

Figure 6–17 Result of loading the `windowOpenDeferred.html` script

When you click on the Create a Window button, a new window is opened, as shown in Figure 6–18.

Figure 6–18 New window

Finding Which Window Is the Opener

The Navigator 3.0 release provides an `opener` property that you can use when you create new windows with the `open()` method. The originating window is considered the "opener" of the new window. You can use the `opener` property to extract information about the originating window. If you use the `opener` property for a file that is loaded directly into the browser, the value is `"null"` because the window was not opened by the `open()` method.

Property	Value	Gettable	Settable
opener	window object or null	Yes	No

xample of window.opener Property

he following `windowWhoOpened.html` script uses the `open()` method to open new window that loads the `windowOpener.html` script. When the `indowOpener.html` script is loaded in this way, it displays the value `[object indow]`, which is the object reference for the originating window.

```
<!--
         windowWhoOpened.html

    This example creates a new window and
    loads windowOpened.html into it.
-->
<HTML>
<HEAD>
<TITLE>Who Opened</TITLE>
<SCRIPT LANGUAGE="JavaScript">
<!-- HIDE FROM OLD BROWSERS

//
// open the given window
//
function windowOpen(win) {
  var newWin = window.open(win, 'myWin')

  if (navigator.appVersion.indexOf("(X11") != -1
   || navigator.appVersion.indexOf("(Mac") != -1)
  {
    newWin = window.open(win, 'myWin')
  }
}

// STOP HIDING -->
</SCRIPT>
</HEAD>

<BODY>
<P>Click on the Open Window button to open
a new window and load windowOpener.html.

<P>The window.opener property for the window
containing the windowOpener.html file shows which
window was used to open the new window.
```

```
<!--
    When you click on the Open Window button,
    windowOpen() opens a new window.
-->
<CENTER>
<FORM NAME="myform">
<INPUT TYPE="button" NAME="Button1"
  VALUE="Open Window!"
  onClick="windowOpen('windowOpener.html')">
</FORM>
</CENTER>

</BODY>
</HTML>
```

Figure 6–19 shows the result of loading the `windowWhoOpened.html` script.

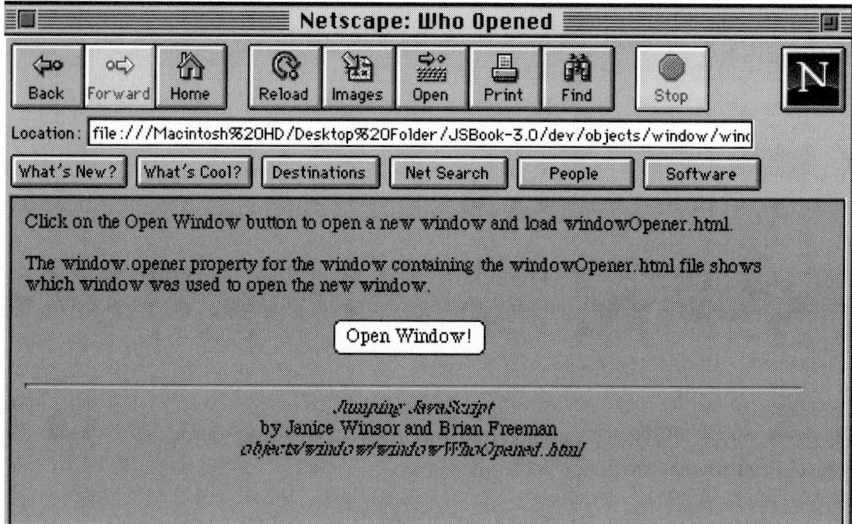

Figure 6–19 Result of loading the `windowWhoOpened.html` script

When you click on the Open Window! button, information about the originating window, or opener, is displayed in the new window, as shown in Figure 6–20.

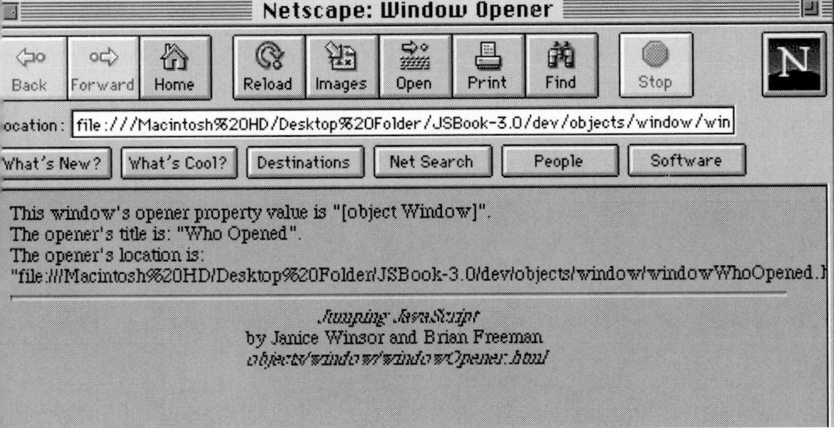

igure 6–20 Window opener information

ou have full access to the properties of the opening window through the `opener` roperty. For example, you can use document properties such as `ocument.title` and `location` as part of `window.opener` statements to eturn the appropriate values. For more information about document properties, e Chapter 7, "Creating Documents."

he following `windowOpener.html` script displays a `null` value when you ad it separately.

```
<!--
       windowOpener.html

    This example displays the window's opener
    property in the body of the document.
-->
<HTML>
<HEAD>
<TITLE>Window Opener</TITLE>
</HEAD>
<BODY>

<P>This window's opener property value is
<SCRIPT LANGUAGE="JavaScript">
<!-- HIDE FROM OLD BROWSERS
  msg_str = ""    // message string

  msg_str += "\"" + window.opener + "\"."
```

```
    // if opener has a value, display more
    // information
    if (window.opener) {
      // display the opener's title
      msg_str += "<BR>The opener's title is: \""
      msg_str += window.opener.document.title + "\"."

      // display the opener's location
      msg_str += "<BR>The opener's location is: \""
      msg_str += window.opener.location + "\"."
    }

    // write into the document
    window.document.open()
    window.document.write(msg_str)
    window.document.close()
  // STOP HIDING -->
  </SCRIPT>

  </BODY>
  </HTML>
```

Figure 6–21 shows the result of loading the `windowOpener.html` script into the browser.

Figure 6–21 Result of `windowOpener.html` script

Using the unescape() Function to Reformat Location Values

You have probably already noticed in illustrations in this book that the location displayed in the Location text field at the top of the browser window contains `%20`. The `%20` is the ASCII representation for the space character, which is part of

he location of the document on a Macintosh system. If you look at the nformation about the opener's location shown in Figure 6–20, you also see everal `%20`s.

'he JavaScript language provides an `unescape()` function that you can use to ormat this information so that the `%20`, and any other ASCII representations of pecial characters are displayed in human-readable form in screen output. To use he `unescape()` function, you simply wrap it around the material you want to eformat.

'o fix the following line from the `windowOpener.html` script that returns the ocation value:

```
msg_str += window.opener.location + "\".";
```

'ou add the `unescape()` function, as shown below:

```
msg_str += unescape(window.opener.location) + "\".";
```

'ou'll find the `unescape()` function in many other examples in this book. 3ecause the information in the Location field of the browser is not controlled by ny scripts that are loaded, you cannot reformat that information. For more nformation on the location object and on using the `unescape()` function, see Chapter 12, "Controlling Location."

Note – The `windowOpener.html` script on the CD-ROM includes the `unescape()` function.

Determining the State of a Newly Opened Window

The Navigator 3.0 release provides a `closed` property that you can use when you create new windows with the `open()` method. The `closed` property is a read-only Boolean property that returns a `true` or `false` value that specifies whether the window has been closed. Once the new window is opened, you can use the `closed` property to determine whether the window is still open or whether it has been closed.

Property	Value	Gettable	Settable
closed	Boolean	Yes	No

Example of Using the closed Property

The following `windowClosed.html` script has buttons that enable you to open and close a second window. When you have opened the window by clicking on the Open Window button, you can click on the Get window.closed button to see the value returned by the `window.closed` property displayed in the text field. Notice that if you click on the Get window.closed button before you have opened the second window, a JavaScript error message is displayed because the window named `win` has not yet been created.

```
<!--
       windowClosed.html
    This example shows you the value of the
    window object's closed property by allowing
    you to open and close a window and then get
    closed's state.

    To see how this script works, click on Open
    Window and then Get window.closed.
    window.closed should equal false. Then click
    on Close Window, followed by Get
    window.closed. The value changes to true.
-->

<HTML>
<HEAD>
<TITLE>Window Closed Property</TITLE>
<SCRIPT LANGUAGE="JavaScript">
<!-- HIDE FROM OLD BROWSERS

var win = null    // the window

//
// open a window, then display the value of the
// closed property.
//
function openIt() {

  // open the URL "win.html" in a new window and
  // name the new window "win"
  win=open("win.html", "win",
           "width=300,height=150")

}
```

```
//
// close the window then display the value of the
// closed property.
//
function closeIt() {
  win.close()
}

//
// update valueForm.textfield with the value of
// the window.closed property
//
function getOpened() {
  if (win.closed) {
    document.valueForm.textField.value = "true"
  } else {
    document.valueForm.textField.value = "false"
  }
}
// STOP HIDING -->
</SCRIPT>
</HEAD>
<BODY>

<P>This example shows you the value of the window
object's closed property by allowing you to open
and close a window and then get closed's
state.</P>
<P>To see how this script works, click on Open
Window and then Get window.closed. window.closed
equals false because the window is open. If
you click on Close Window, then on Get
window.closed, the value changes to true.</P>
<P>If you click on the Get window.closed button
before you click on the Open Window button, you'll
get a JavaScript error message because the window
named win has not yet been created.</P>

<CENTER>
<FORM NAME="myForm">
<INPUT TYPE="button" NAME="Button1"
  VALUE="Open Window"
  onClick="openIt()">
```

```
<INPUT TYPE="button" NAME="Button2"
  VALUE="Close Window"
  onClick="closeIt()">
</FORM>

<FORM NAME="valueForm">
<INPUT TYPE="button" NAME="Button3"
  VALUE="Get window.closed"
  onClick="getOpened()">
<P><B>The value of window.closed = </B>
<INPUT TYPE="text" NAME="textField"
 VALUE=""
 SIZE=5>
</FORM>
</CENTER>
</BODY>
</HTML>
```

Figure 6–22 shows the result of loading the `windowClosed.html` script.

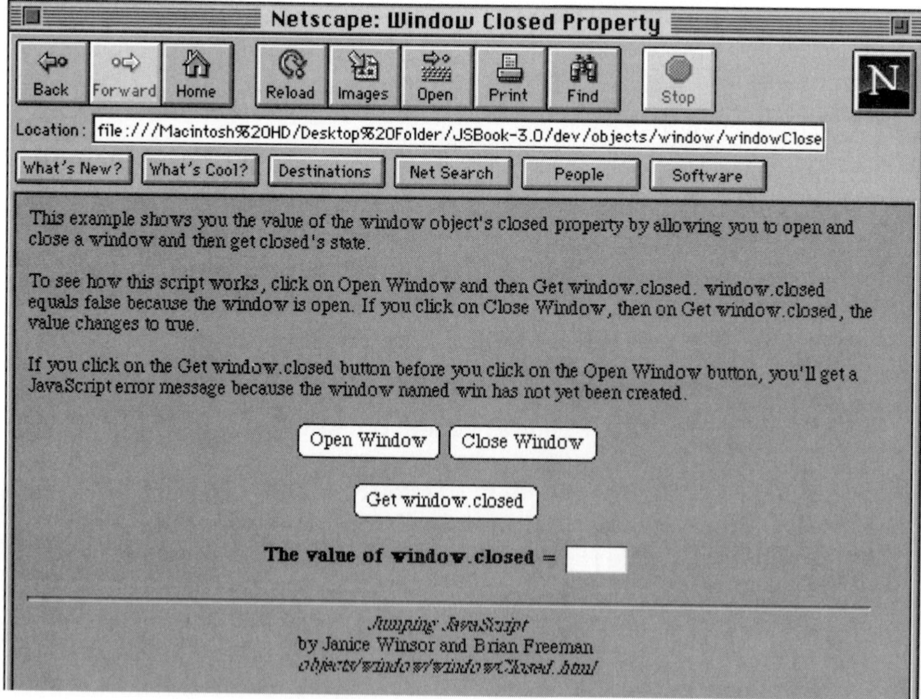

Figure 6–22 Result of loading the `windowClosed.html` script

Displaying Informational Messages in an Alert Window

You can use the `alert()` method to create a *modal window* that displays an informational message, called an *alert*, to the user. While a modal window is displayed, users cannot do anything else in the application until they click on the OK button to dismiss the modal window.

UI Guideline – Use modal windows only when absolutely necessary. Users can quickly get annoyed if they encounter too many modal windows.

Figure 6–23 shows an example of an alert window.

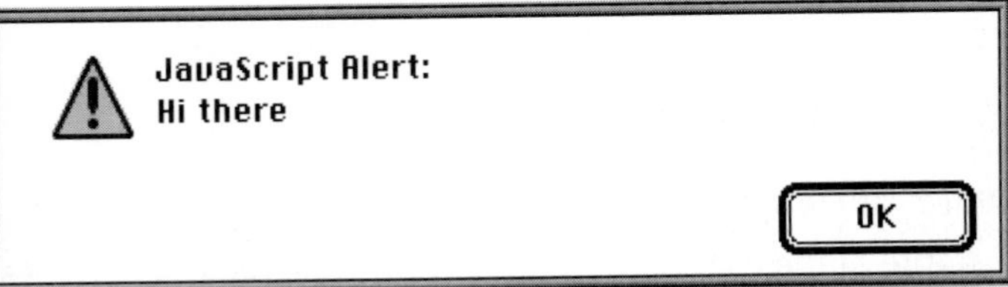

Figure 6–23 Example of an alert window

The JavaScript language provides the window border, size, graphic, JavaScript Alert: text, and OK button. You provide the message text that is displayed in the alert window. The width of the window is fixed, and the JavaScript language automatically adjusts the height of the window to fit the amount of text you provide.

You should use alerts to display only short messages. If you need to display more lengthy messages, create a separate window with scrollbars.

The number of characters displayed on a line can vary depending on font settings and monitor size and resolution. The maximum height of the window depends on the size and resolution of the monitor of each user and the font size. Because you cannot determine what monitor or font settings a user has, we strongly recommend that you restrict any text displayed in an alert window.

Note – If you create very long alerts, be sure to test them. If you create an alert window that is too big to display the OK button, try pressing Return to close the alert window. If the window does not close when you press Return, you may have to reset or reboot your system.

The `alert()` method takes a single parameter that can be a value of any data type. Because the action of this method is to display a modal window, the `alert()` method does not return a value.

Method	Returns
alert(*message*)	Nothing

Example of the alert( ) Method

The following basic example of the `alert()` method for the `window` object uses the `onLoad` event handler in the `BODY` tag. When you load the page into the browser, an alert window is displayed.

```
<!--
    windowAlert.html

    This example of using the window
    object's alert method enables you to
    display a message to the user that does not
    require any feedback.
-->
<HTML>
<HEAD>
<TITLE>Alert Window</TITLE>
<SCRIPT LANGUAGE="JavaScript">
<!-- HIDE FROM OLD BROWSERS

// This function displays an Alert Dialog to the
// user with the message "Hi there" in it. Users
// are required to click on OK to close
// the window before they can continue.
function sayHi() {
  alert("Hi there")
```

```
    return true
  }

  // STOP HIDING -->
  </SCRIPT>
  </HEAD>

  <!--
      When this document is loaded, the function
      sayHi is executed.
  -->
  <BODY onLoad="sayHi()">

  <P>An Alert Dialog should be displayed when you
  load this page.  Click on the OK button to dismiss
  the dialog.<P>

  </BODY>
  </HTML>
```

Figure 6–24 shows the result of loading the `windowAlert.html` script.

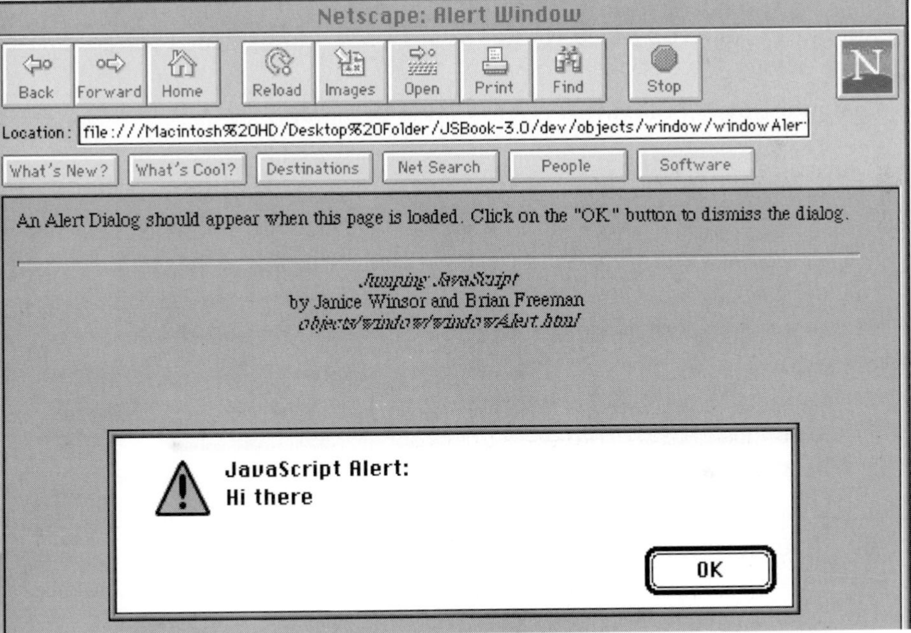

Figure 6–24 Result of loading the `windowAlert.html` script

The window size, border, triangle with the exclamation mark, JavaScript Alert: string, and OK button are automatically created for you by the JavaScript language.

Explanation of the windowAlert.html Script

In this script, the function named `sayHi()` is defined as an `alert()` method that displays a modal window that says `"Hi there."` The following lines of code define the function `sayHi()`.

```
function sayHi() {
  alert("Hi there")
}
```

The quoted string `"Hi there"` between the `alert()` parentheses defines the information that is displayed in the modal window.

The function is called as part of the HTML `BODY` tag:

```
<BODY onLoad="sayHi()">
```

This statement tells the interpreter "After you load the window, call the `sayHi()` function." The `sayHi()` function has already been defined in the `HEAD`.

The body of the HTML document displays a message telling you what should have happened if the script runs successfully:

```
An Alert dialog should be displayed when you loaded this
page.<P>
```

As a reminder, the `<P>` HTML tag starts a new paragraph.

Closing a Window

If you open windows, it's a good idea to provide users with a way to close them as well. You close windows with the `close()` method. You are most likely to use this method to close additional windows that you have opened. If you call the `close()` method directly from the window that you want to close, you do not need to give it a specific object reference. However, because the `document` object also has a `close()` method, scoping rules require you to always reference the window as `self.close()`, `window.close()`, `top.close()`, or `parent.close()`.

When you create a complicated set of windows, it is essential to maintain a record of the additional windows you have opened. Keep track of windows by storing the value returned from the `window.open()` method in a global variable that you can reference later.

Because the action of this method is to close a window, the `close()` method does not take any parameters or return a value.

Method

close()

Returns

Nothing

In the Navigator 3.0 release, the interpreter automatically creates and displays a confirmation window enabling users to confirm whether they want to close the window.

Example of the close() Method

When you click on the Close Window button, the current Navigator window is closed. Because the method closes the current Navigator window, we suggest that you first create a new window by choosing New Navigator Window from the File menu and then load the `windowClose.html` file to test this script.

```
<!--
    windowClose.html

    This example of using the window
    object's close method removes
    the window object from the screen.

    To see how this script works, load this
    example, then click on the Close Window
    button.

    With Navigator 2.0, the window this example
    is loaded into would just go away. Somewhere
    before 3.0 FCS, a confirmation dialog was added by
    Netscape, asking the user to confirm the
    destruction of the window.

    We suggest you load this file into a new
    browser window.
-->
```

```
<HTML>
<HEAD>
<TITLE>Close Window</TITLE>
<SCRIPT LANGUAGE="JavaScript">
<!-- HIDE FROM OLD BROWSERS

// close this window.
function closeWindow() {
  self.close()
}

// STOP HIDING -->
</SCRIPT>
</HEAD>

<BODY>

<P>When you click on the Close Window button,
this window goes away.</P>

<P>We suggest you load this example into a new
browser window before you click on the
button.</P>

<CENTER><FORM>
<INPUT TYPE="button" VALUE="Close Window"
onClick="closeWindow()">
</FORM></CENTER>

</BODY>
</HTML>
```

Figure 6–25 shows the window after you have loaded the `windowClose.html` script but before you close the window.

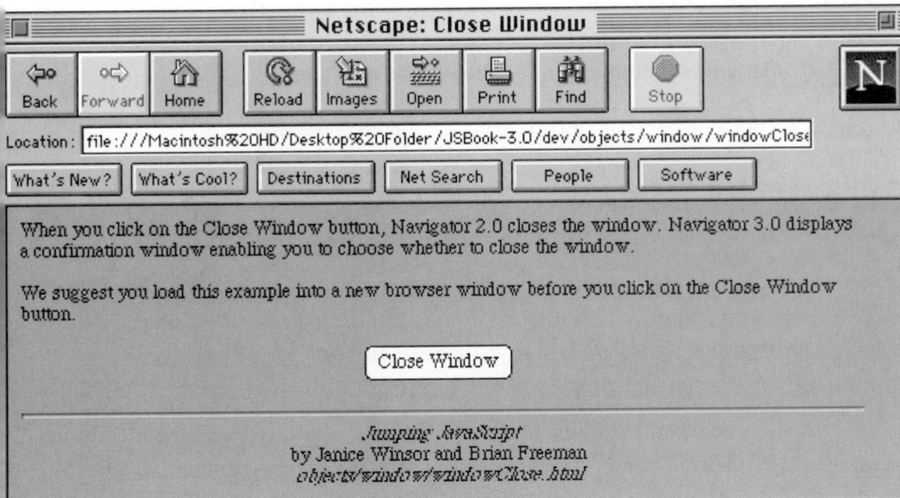

Figure 6–25 Result of loading the `windowClose.html` script

When you click on the Close Window button, in Navigator 3.0 a confirmation window is displayed, as shown in Figure 6–26. In Navigator 2.0, the window just closes.

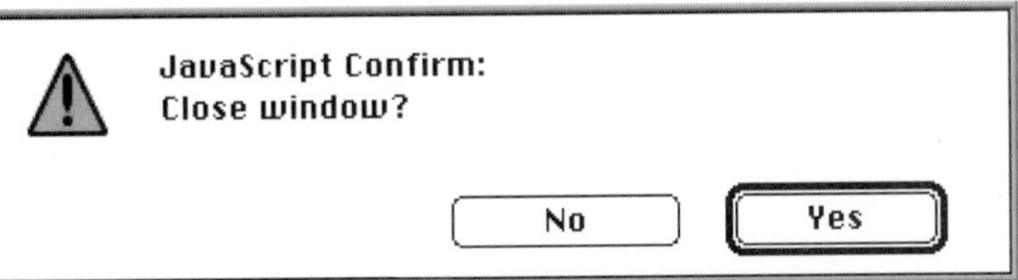

Figure 6–26 Close window confirmation

Displaying a Confirmation Message

Whenever you close a window, it's a good idea to give users a chance to change their minds. You do this by posting a *confirmation message,* using the window `confirm()` method.

You may find other times in your scripts when it would be a good idea to give users a choice about whether to take a certain action. In such cases, you can also use a confirmation window. Figure 6–27 shows an example of a JavaScript confirmation window.

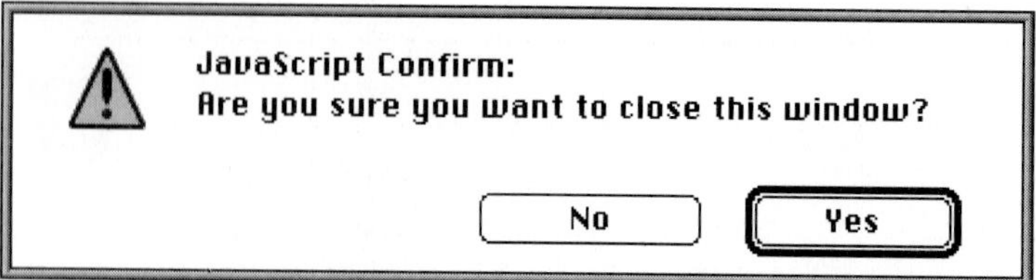

Figure 6–27 JavaScript confirmation window

The JavaScript language provides the window border, size, graphic, JavaScript Confirm: text, and No and Yes buttons. Yes is the default button. You provide the message text that is displayed in the window. The JavaScript language automatically sizes the window to fit the length of your text string.

You should use confirmation windows to display only short messages. If you need to display more lengthy messages, you should create a separate window with scrollbars. The width of confirmation windows is fixed and has the same restrictions as alert windows..

Because the action of this method is to display a message, the parameter for the `confirm()` method is a quoted string containing the message you want to display to your users. Because users can choose one of two actions, the `confirm()` method returns a value of either `true` or `false`.

Method

confirm(*message*)

Returns

true or false

Use the `confirm()` method when you provide your users with a choice that they might want to back out of or before they initiate an action that might be time consuming. For example, it might be useful to display a confirmation window enabling users to decide that they did not really want to close a window.

I Guideline – Be judicial in your use of confirmation windows. Usability tudies show that users quickly learn to automatically click to get rid of those nnoying confirmation windows that are supposed to make them stop and ink. If you display too many confirmation windows, they lose their impact.

---

xample of confirm() Method

ecause the Navigator 3.0 release automatically displays a confirmation window hen you use the `close()` method, we've provided the following `indowConfirm.html` script. It tests for the version of Navigator you are unning and displays a confirmation window if the version of Navigator does not o it for you. This script works in the same way on both Navigator 2.0 and 3.0 eleases.

```
<!--
    windowConfirm.html

    Between Navigator 2.0 FCS and 3.0 FCS, a
    confirmation dialog was added by Netscape
    when the close() method is called.

    This example shows the use of the window
    object's confirm and close methods to create
    our own close confirmation dialog that
    works for either, and hopefully future,
    releases of Navigator.

    To see how this script works, load this
    example, then click on the Close Window
    button.

    The window that this example is loaded into
    is closed if you click on the Yes button in the
    confirmation dialog.

    We suggest you load this file into a new
    browser window.
-->
<HTML>
```

```
<HEAD>
<TITLE>Confirm Window</TITLE>
<SCRIPT LANGUAGE="JavaScript">
<!-- HIDE FROM OLD BROWSERS

// This function should always provide a
// confirmation dialog for the destruction of a
// window.
//
// Navigator 3.0FCS provides its own
// confirmation dialog on close; 2.0 FCS does
// not.
//
function confirmClose() {

  // If the release is 2.0, use confirm() to
  // simulate the dialog. For higher releases,
  // 3.0 and the future, close() should always
  // provide the confirmation dialog.
  //
  if (navigator.appVersion.indexOf("2.") != -1) {
    // 2.0
    if (confirm("Close window?")) {
      close()
    }
  } else {
    // greater than 2.0
    close()
  }
}

// STOP HIDING -->
</SCRIPT>
</HEAD>

<BODY>

<P>When you click on the Nuke the Window button,
you are asked if you want to close this
window. If you click on the Yes button, this window
closes.</P>

<P>We suggest you load this example into a new
browser window before you click on the
```

```
button.</P>

<CENTER><FORM>
<INPUT TYPE="button" VALUE="Nuke the Window"
onClick="confirmClose()">
</FORM></CENTER>

</BODY>
</HTML>
```

Figure 6–28 shows the result of loading the `windowConfirm.html` script.

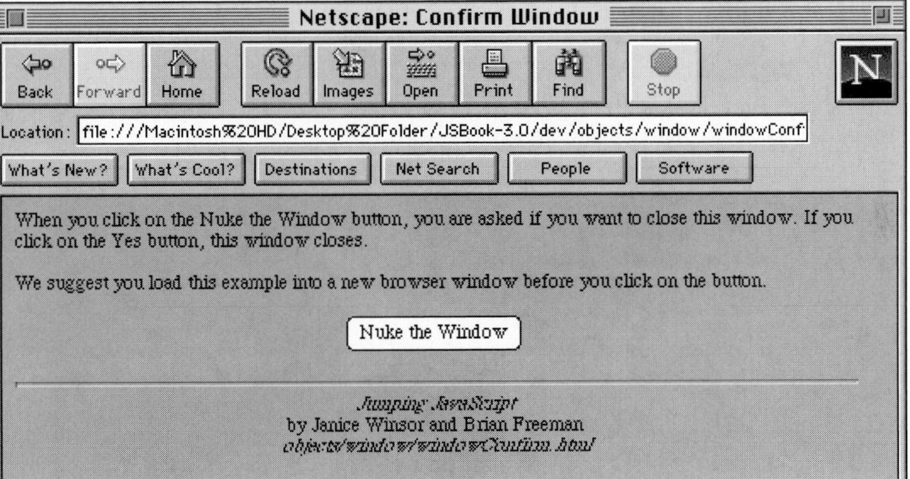

Figure 6–28 Result of loading the `windowConfirm.html` script

Prompting Users for Input

If you want users to provide typed input and to answer questions that require more than a simple yes or no answer, you can use the `prompt()` method. Figure 6–29 shows an example of a JavaScript *prompt window.*

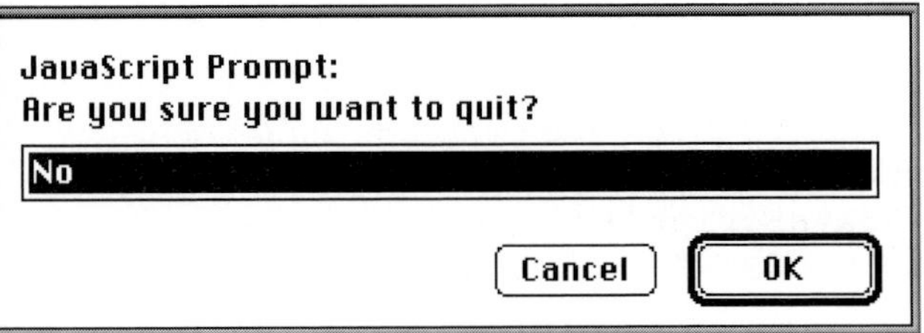

Figure 6–29 JavaScript confirmation window

The JavaScript language provides the window border, size, JavaScript Prompt: text, and Cancel and OK buttons. OK is the default button. You provide the message text that is displayed in the window, and you can write code to control the input that is acceptable. You'll learn how to do this kind of error-checking later in this book. If possible, you should always specify a default reply, so that users can click OK (or press Return) to accept that answer without further typing.

Because the action of this method is to ask a question, the parameters for the `prompt()` method are a quoted string containing the question you want to ask your users, and a `defaultReply`. If you don't have a default reply, enter an empty string (`""`) as the second parameter. If you omit the second parameter, the JavaScript program inserts the string `<undefined>` into the text field.

Method

prompt(*question, defaultReply*)

Returns

String of text entered by user, or null

Example of prompt() Method

In this script example, the question has a yes/no answer. You can use the `prompt()` method in this way, although a confirmation window is probably a better way to present this question. We use this example because it is a simple one to program without introducing additional new JavaScript concepts.

```
<!--
    windowPrompt.html

    This example for the window object's
    prompt method property enables user
    input. Based on the response, action can be
    taken.
-->
<HTML>
<HEAD>
<TITLE>Prompt Window</TITLE>
<SCRIPT LANGUAGE="JavaScript">
<!-- HIDE FROM OLD BROWSERS

//
// This function asks users if they want to
```

```
// exit, that is, destroy, the current window. If the
// user answers Yes, the window is closed.
//
function promptExit() {
  var msg_str = "Are you sure you want to quit?"
  var t_str   = "Yes"
  var f_str   = "No"

  if (prompt(msg_str, f_str) == t_str)
    close()
}

// STOP HIDING -->
</SCRIPT>
</HEAD>

<BODY>

<P>When you Click on the Quit button, you are
asked if you want to close this window.</P>

<P>You can type either Yes or No in response to
the prompt.</P>

<CENTER><FORM>
<INPUT TYPE="button" VALUE="Quit"
 onClick="promptExit()">
</FORM></CENTER>

</BODY>
</HTML>
```

Figure 6–30 shows the window after you have loaded the `windowPrompt.html` script.

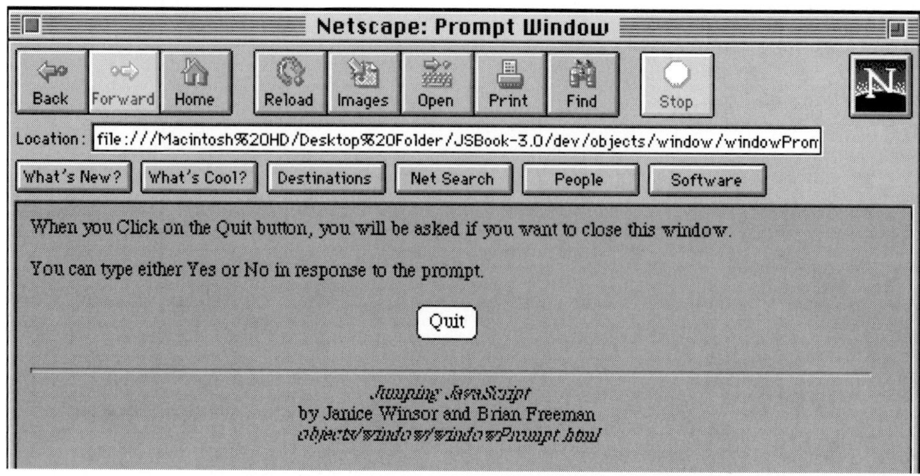

Figure 6–30 Result of loading the `windowPrompt.html` script

Figure 6–31 shows the prompt window. Users can either click on the OK button or press Return to accept the No response, or type Yes. Because of the way the script is written, Yes, with a capital Y is the only new input this window can accept.

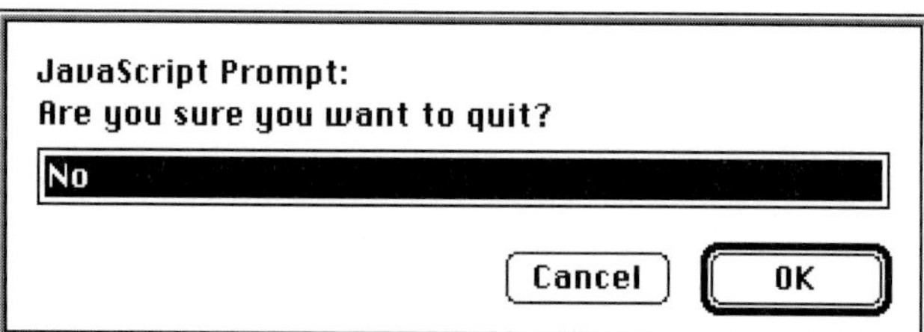

Figure 6–31 Prompt window

Controlling the Input Focus in Windows

Blur and focus are events, which are usually triggered by some user action. On some platforms (Macintosh, Windows 95) you *click to type* in a window. Other platforms (X11, Windows 95 utilities) you can *move the pointer* into and out of the window to control the input focus.

When the user clicks or moves the pointer into a window, the window has *focus*. Only one window object can have focus at a time.

Vhen the user clicks or moves the pointer away from the window object that has ocus, the resulting action is called a *blur*. That is, the window object that had ocus is no longer the focus of the action. You can think of blur as "out of focus" for specific window object.

'he Navigator 3.0 release has added `blur()` and `focus()` methods that enable ou to control how the input focus behaves within a window. When a window as input focus, the window receives a focus event; when input focus is removed rom a window, it receives a blur event.

'ou can use the `blur()` and `focus()` methods with windows, framesets, and ll form elements to control the input focus.

Method

blur()

focus()

Returns

Nothing

Bug for blur() and focus() Method: Netscape Navigator 3.0 Mac and X Versions

In Netscape Navigator 3.0 Mac, the blur() and focus() methods and onBlur and onFocus event handlers do not work at all.

In Netscape Navigator 3.0 X11, the blur() and focus() methods and onBlur and onFocus event handlers work for individual windows, but not for windows in a frameset.

These methods and event handlers work properly only in Netscape Navigator 3.0 for Win95.

This bug is currently documented in the FAQ, at:

http://home/netscape.com/eng/mozilla/3.0/relnotes

Do not design scripts that are dependent on these methods and event handlers until these bugs are fixed.

Example of blur() and focus() Methods

The following `windowBlurFocus.html` script shows how to use the `blur()` and `focus()` methods. It also uses the `onFocus` event handler.

```
<!--
         windowBlurFocus.html

    This example shows a use of the window blur
    and focus methods method.
-->

<HTML>
<HEAD>
<TITLE>Window Blur and Focus</TITLE>
<SCRIPT LANGUAGE="JavaScript">
<!-- HIDE FROM OLD BROWSERS

function setFocus(win) {
  // remove focus from this window
  win.blur()

  // if there are multiple frames, set focus to
  // the first frame.
  if (win.top.length > 0 ) {
   win.top.frames[0].focus()
  }

  message("onFocus")
}

function message(eventstr) {
  var msg_str = ""
  msg_str += "The window received "
  msg_str += "an " + eventstr + " event"
  msg_str += ".\n\r"
  document.aForm.msgField.value += msg_str
}

// STOP HIDING -->
</SCRIPT>
</HEAD>

<BODY onFocus="setFocus(window)">
```

```
<P>When this window receives focus, it calls
blur().

<SCRIPT LANGUAGE="JavaScript">
<!-- HIDE FROM OLD BROWSERS

// add extra text to the message if there are
// multiple frames.
//
if (window.top.length > 0) {
  msg_str = ", then sets focus to the first frame."

  window.document.open()
  window.document.writeln(msg_str)
  window.document.open()
}
// STOP HIDING -->
</SCRIPT>

<FORM NAME="aForm">
<P><B>Messages:</B><BR>
<TEXTAREA
 NAME="msgField"
 ROWS="5"
 COLS="40"
 WRAP="physical"
>
</TEXTAREA>
</FORM>

</BODY>
</HTML>
```

Figure 6–32 shows the result of loading the `windowBlurFocus.html` script.

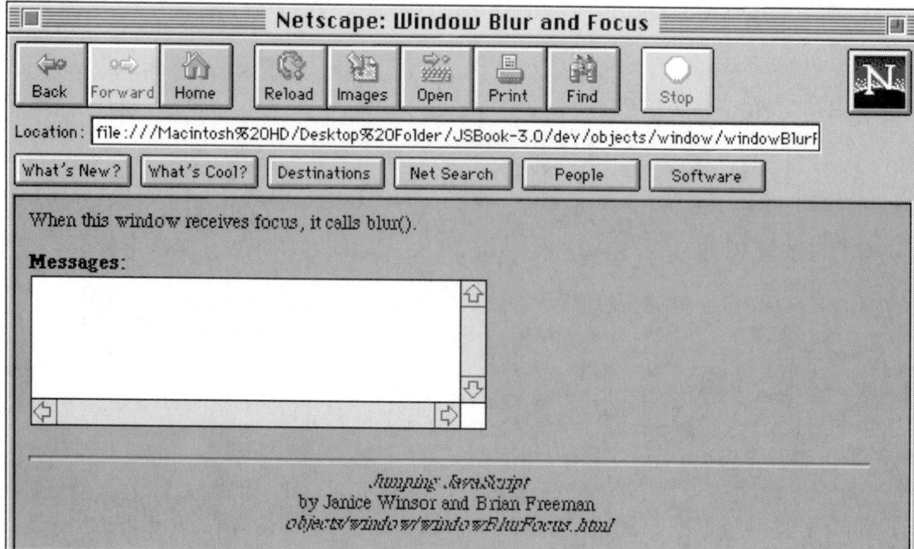

Figure 6–32 Result of loading the `windowBlurFocus.html` script

The following `windowBlurFocusFrame.html` script shows the use of the `blur()` and `focus()` methods in a window with frames. It creates a window with four frames and loads the `windowOnBlurOnFocus.html` file into the top two frames and the `windowBlurFocus.html` file into the bottom two frames. For the complete code of the `windowOnBlurOnFocus.html` file, see "Example of onBlur and onFocus Event Handlers" on page 193.

```
<!--
      windowBlurFocusFrames.html

    This example uses multiple frames to show how
    blur and focus events occur.
-->
<HTML>
<HEAD>
<TITLE>window Blur and Focus with frames</TITLE>
</HEAD>
<FRAMESET ROWS="50%,50%" COLS="50%,50%">
<FRAME SRC="windowOnBlurOnFocus.html" NAME="frame1">
<FRAME SRC="windowOnBlurOnFocus.html" NAME="frame2">
<FRAME SRC="windowBlurFocus.html" NAME="frame3">
<FRAME SRC="windowBlurFocus.html" NAME="frame4">
</FRAMESET>
</HTML>
```

igure 6–33 shows the result of loading the `windowBlurFocusFrame.html` ript.

Netscape: window Blur and Focus with frames

Back Forward Home Reload Images Open Print Find Stop

.ocation: file:///Macintosh%20HD/Desktop%20Folder/JSBook-3.0/dev/objects/window/win

What's New? What's Cool? Destinations Net Search People Software

This window uses an onBlur event handler to set the background color to blue and an onFocus event handler to set the background to white.

When the mouse leaves the window, a blur event is generated and the onBlur event handler changes the background color to blue.

When the mouse enters the window, a focus event is generated and the onFocus event handler changes the background color to white.

Note: You might have to click outside the window to trigger the blur event. Mac users

This window uses an onBlur event handler to set the background color to blue and an onFocus event handler to set the background to white.

When the mouse leaves the window, a blur event is generated and the onBlur event handler changes the background color to blue.

When the mouse enters the window, a focus event is generated and the onFocus event handler changes the background color to white.

Note: You might have to click outside the window to trigger the blur event. Mac users

When this window receives focus, it calls blur() , then sets focus to the first frame.

Messages:

Jumping JavaScript
by Janice Winsor and Brian Freeman
objects/window/windowBlurFocus.html

When this window receives focus, it calls blur() , then sets focus to the first frame.

Messages:

Jumping JavaScript
by Janice Winsor and Brian Freeman
objects/window/windowBlurFocus.html

Document: Done.

igure 6–33 Result of loading the `windowBlurFocusFrame.html` script

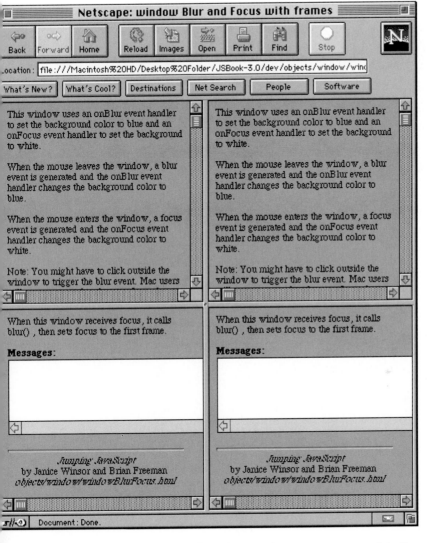

Using Event Handlers to Control Window Focus

The Navigator 3.0 release provides `onBlur` and `onFocus` event handlers to complement the new `blur()` and `focus()` methods.

Event Handler

onBlur

Syntax

<BODY (*other attributes*) onBlur = "*JavaScript code*">

<FRAMESET (*other attributes*) onBlur="*JavaScript code*">

Use the `onBlur` event handler to perform an action when the user clicks away from the window. You include the `onBlur` event handler as an attribute of a `<BODY>` tag for a single-frame document or as an attribute of a `<FRAMESET>` tag for the top window of a multiple-frame document.

Event Handler

onFocus

Syntax

<BODY (*other attributes*) onFocus = "*JavaScript code*">

<FRAMESET (*other attributes*) onFocus="*JavaScript code*">

Use the `onFocus` event handler to perform an action when the user clicks in the window to set the input focus. You include the `onFocus` event handler as an attribute of a `<BODY>` tag for a single-frame document or as an attribute of a `<FRAMESET>` tag for the top window of a multiple-frame document.

Note – Window managers on each platform have different abilities to handle `onBlur` and `onFocus` events. Because of inconsistent behavior across all platforms, we suggest that you do not rely on the use of `onBlur` and `onFocus` event handlers in your scripts.

he Macintosh platform is the most limited, because it is a single-user, click-to-ype platform. You can have only one active window at a time, and regardless f where you move the pointer, the active window gets all of the events. The lacintosh platform cannot respond to `onBlur` and `onFocus` events at the indow level.

he X11 and Win95 platforms do respond to `onBlur` and `onFocus` event andlers, but these handlers behave differently on each of these platforms.

---

xample of onBlur and onFocus Event Handlers

ou've already seen examples of how to use these event handlers in the iscussion of the `blur()` and `focus()` methods. The following code extract hows the use of the `onBlur` and `onFocus` event handlers to change the ackground color of the window when the input focus changes.

```
<BODY
 onBlur="document.bgColor='blue'"
 onFocus="document.bgColor='white'"
>
```

or the complete example, see "Controlling the Input Focus in Windows" on age 186.

he following `windowFocus.html` script shows another example of using the `nBlur` and `onFocus` event handlers. This script provides buttons that you can se to open two small windows, and changes the focus for the windows hemselves, so that they move to the front or the back of the screen as the focus hanges.

---

ote – The `windowFocus.html` script will not work on Macintosh systems ecause it is a single-user, click-to-type platform.

```
<!--
       windowFocus.html

    This example of the window focus method
    allows you to register either an onFocus or
    onBlur event handler on a window and then see
```

```
    the result.
-->

<HTML>
<HEAD>
<TITLE>Window Focus</TITLE>

<!-- include windowOpen() -->
<SCRIPT SRC="../../debug/windowOpen.js"></SCRIPT>

<SCRIPT LANGUAGE="JavaScript">
<!-- HIDE FROM OLD BROWSERS

//
// Create a window that registers an onBlur event
// handler to call focus().
//
function onBlurWindow() {
  var bwin  = null  // blur window
  var wopts = ""    // window options
  var mstr  = ""    // message string

  mstr  += "<HTML>"
  mstr  += "<HEAD>"
  mstr  += "<TITLE>onBlur</TITLE>"
  mstr  += "</HEAD>"
  mstr  += "<BODY onBlur='focus()'>"
  mstr  += "<P>When an onBlur event is received, "
  mstr  += "this window calls focus().</P>"
  mstr  += "<P>In other words, this window  "
  mstr  += "stays at the front of the screen.</P>"
  mstr  += "</BODY>"
  mstr  += "</HTML>"

  wopts += "width=300,height=150"
  bwin   = windowOpen("", "blurWindow", wopts)

  bwin.document.open()
  bwin.document.write(mstr)
  bwin.document.close()
}

//
// Create a window that registers an onFocus event
```

```
// handler to call focus().
//
// Bug Alert: Simply <BODY onFocus="focus()">
// should work, but there is an onFocus bug. The
// following code works around the problem.
//
function onFocusWindow() {
  var fwin  = null  // focus window
  var wopts = ""    // window options
  var mstr  = ""    // message string

  mstr  += "<HTML>"
  mstr  += "<HEAD>"
  mstr  += "<TITLE>onFocus</TITLE>"
  mstr  += "<SCRIPT>"
  mstr  += "var hackObj;"
  mstr  += "function hackIt(obj) {"
  mstr  += "  hackObj = obj;"
  mstr  += "  setTimeout('hackObj.focus()', 0);"
  mstr  += "}"
  mstr  += "</SCRIPT>"
  mstr  += "</HEAD>"
  mstr  += "<BODY onFocus='hackIt(self)'>"
  mstr  += "<P>When an onFocus event is received, "
  mstr  += "this window calls focus().</P>"
  mstr  += "<P>In other words, when you move "
  mstr  += "your pointer over this window, it "
  mstr  += "comes to the front of the screen.</P>"
  mstr  += "</BODY>"
  mstr  += "</HTML>"

  wopts += "width=300,height=150"
  fwin   = windowOpen("", "focusWindow", wopts)

  fwin.document.open()
  fwin.document.write(mstr)
  fwin.document.close()
}

// STOP HIDING -->
</SCRIPT>
</HEAD>
<BODY>
```

```
<P>This example of the window focus method allows
you to register either an onFocus or onBlur
event handler on a window and then see the
result.</P>
<P>Remember, the onFocus event is called when
your pointer enters the window; and the onBlur
event, when your pointer leaves. Calling focus()
when one of these events occurs brings the window
forward, above any other window.</P>

<CENTER>
<FORM NAME="aForm">
<INPUT TYPE="button" NAME="blurBtn"
 VALUE="Create onBlur Window"
 onClick="onBlurWindow()">
<INPUT TYPE="button" NAME="focusBtn"
 VALUE="Create onFocus Window"
 onClick="onFocusWindow()">
</FORM>
</CENTER>

<P>When you click on Create onBlur Window,
click in the primary window to make it active. Notice
that the onBlur window comes to the front of this
window.<P>
<P>When you click on Create onFocus Window,
reposition the window that opens so half of it
is outside this window. Click on this window to
make it active. Now move your mouse over the
onFocus window. Notice that the onFocus window
comes forward, in front of this window.</P>

<P>Neat, isn't it!</P>

</BODY>
</HTML>
```

Figure 6–34 shows the result of loading the `windowFocus.html` script.

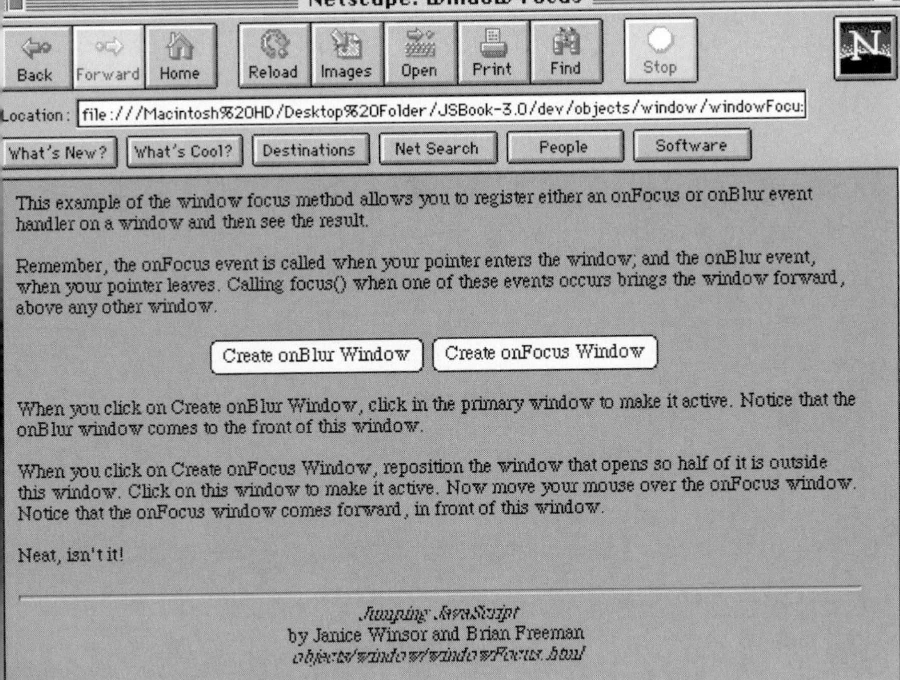

Figure 6–34 Result of loading the `windowFocus.html` script

Click on the Create onBlur Window and Create onFocus Window buttons to open two smaller windows. Move them so they overlap one another, as shown in Figure 6–35.

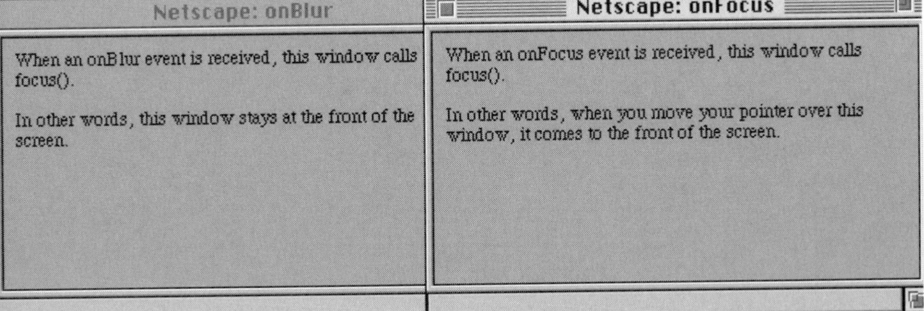

Figure 6–35 Overlapping onBlur and onFocus windows

Experiment with moving the pointer around on the screen and see what happens to the layering of the windows.

The following `windowBlur.html` script is similar to the `windowFocus.html` script, except that the event handlers move the windows to the back of the screen when they receive the events.

```
<!--
        windowBlur.html

    This example of the window blur method allows
    you to register either an onFocus or onBlur
    event handler on a window and then see the
    result.
-->

<HTML>
<HEAD>
<TITLE>Window Blur</TITLE>

<!-- include windowOpen() -->
<SCRIPT SRC="../../debug/windowOpen.js"></SCRIPT>

<SCRIPT LANGUAGE="JavaScript">
<!-- HIDE FROM OLD BROWSERS

//
// Create a window that registers an onBlur event
// handler to call blur().
//
function onBlurWindow() {
  var bwin  = null  // blur window
  var wopts = ""    // window options
  var mstr  = ""    // message string

  mstr  += "<HTML>"
  mstr  += "<HEAD>"
  mstr  += "<TITLE>onBlur</TITLE>"
  mstr  += "</HEAD>"
  mstr  += "<BODY onBlur='blur()'>"
  mstr  += "<P>When an onBlur event is received, "
  mstr  += "this window calls blur().</P>"
  mstr  += "<P>In other words, this window is "
  mstr  += "behind any other windows.</P>"
  mstr  += "</BODY>"
  mstr  += "</HTML>"
  wopts += "width=300,height=150"
```

```
  bwin   = windowOpen("", "blurWindow", wopts)

  bwin.document.open()
  bwin.document.write(mstr)
  bwin.document.close()
}

//
// Create a window that registers an onFocus event
// handler to call blur().
//
// Bug Alert: Simply <BODY onFocus="blur()">
// should work, but there is an onFocus bug. The
// following code works around the problem.
//
function onFocusWindow() {
  var fwin  = null  // focus window
  var wopts = ""    // window options
  var mstr  = ""    // message string

  mstr  += "<HTML>"
  mstr  += "<HEAD>"
  mstr  += "<TITLE>onFocus</TITLE>"
  mstr  += "<SCRIPT>"
  mstr  += "var hackObj;"
  mstr  += "function hackIt(obj) {"
  mstr  += "  hackObj = obj;"
  mstr  += "  setTimeout('hackObj.blur()', 0);"
  mstr  += "}"
  mstr  += "</SCRIPT>"
  mstr  += "</HEAD>"
  mstr  += "<BODY onFocus='hackIt(self)'>"
  mstr  += "<P>When an onFocus event is received, "
  mstr  += "this window calls blur().</P>"
  mstr  += "<P>In other words, when you move "
  mstr  += "your pointer over this window, it "
  mstr  += "moves behind any other windows.</P>"
  mstr  += "</BODY>"
  mstr  += "</HTML>"
  wopts += "width=300,height=150"
  fwin   = windowOpen("", "focusWindow", wopts)

  fwin.document.open()
  fwin.document.write(mstr)
```

```
  fwin.document.close()
}

// STOP HIDING -->
</SCRIPT>
</HEAD>
<BODY>

<P>This example of the window blur method allows
you to register either an onFocus or onBlur event
handler on a window and then see the result.</P>

<P>Remember, the onFocus event gets called when
your pointer enters the window; and the onBlur
event, when your pointer leaves. Calling blur()
when one of these events occurs brings the window
forward, above any other window.</P>

<CENTER>
<FORM NAME="aForm">
<INPUT TYPE="button" NAME="blurBtn"
 VALUE="Create onBlur Window"
 onClick="onBlurWindow()">
<INPUT TYPE="button" NAME="focusBtn"
 VALUE="Create onFocus Window"
 onClick="onFocusWindow()">
</FORM>
</CENTER>

<P>When you click on Create onBlur Window, make
another window active and notice that the onBlur
window moves behind all your other windows.<P>

<P>When you click on Create onFocus Window, move
your pointer into the window and notice that it
moves below your other windows. You might have to
reposition the window to see the effect.</P>

<P>Neat, isn't it!</P>

</BODY>
</HTML>
```

Figure 6–36 shows the result of loading the `windowBlur.html` script.

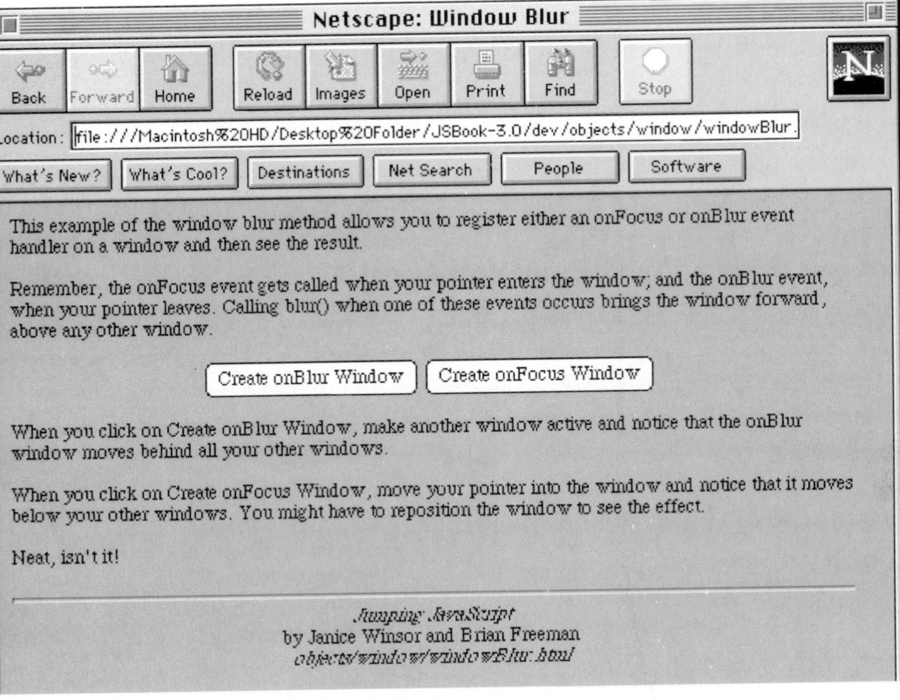

Figure 6–36 Result of loading the `windowBlur.html` script

When you click in the Create onBlurWindow and Create onFocusWindow buttons, small windows are opened. Figure 6–37 shows the onBlur window.

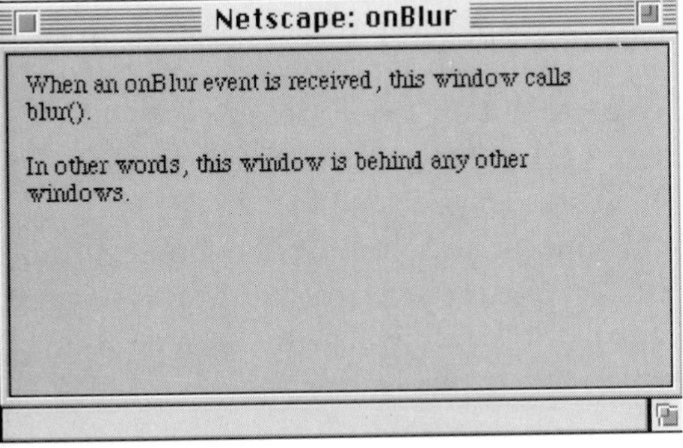

Figure 6–37 onBlur window

It was a challenge taking the screen shot for the onBlur window, because every time I moved the pointer, the window moved to the back of the screen behind other windows. I finally had to move it to a clear space on the screen to be able to take the snapshot. However, the challenge did show me that the `onBlur` event handler definitely was working.

Open both windows and experiment with the behavior on your system by moving the pointer around the screen and over the windows to see what happens.

Moving Around within a Window

The Navigator 3.0 release provides a `scroll()` window method that you can use to scroll to a particular coordinate on the screen. The `scroll()` method does not add scrollbars to a window. Instead, it enables you to move to a specific point within the window. The `(x,y)` arguments are positive, whole numbers that represents the position of a particular *pixel* in the window that you want to move to. `0,0` is the upper-left corner of the window. A pixel is a single dot on a display screen and is a contraction for picture element.

Method

scroll(x,y)

Returns

Nothing

Because the size of a pixel depends on screen resolution, we can't provide guidelines to specify how many pixels are in an inch. On a low-resolution screen, a pixel is much bigger than it is on a high-resolution screen. Because the JavaScript language "scrolls" to the place you specify without giving you any visual feedback, it may be tough to see the results of the `scroll()` method. If you scroll to a position with the current window, the scrollbar does not give you any feedback that the action took place. You can, however, be confident that if you find the proper pixel coordinates, the resultant "scroll" will go to the same point in your document on every screen resolution that displays your page.

Example of scroll() Method

The following examples show how you can incorporate the `scroll()` method in an `HREF`, how you can use the method to create your own scrolling buttons, and how to use those buttons in a frameset.

The following windowScroll.html script provides an HREF at the bottom of the window by adding scroll(0,0) to the HREF statement, as shown below:

```
<A HREF="javascript:scroll(0,0)">here</A>.
```

Clicking on the link takes you back to the upper-left corner of the window.

```
<!--
        windowScroll.html

     Shows a use of the window scroll method. 0,0
     is the top-left corner of the document.
-->

<HTML>
<HEAD>
<TITLE>Window Scroll</TITLE>
</HEAD>
<BODY>

<P>Say you have a bunch of text...
<P>AAAA BBBB CCCC DDDD EEEE FFFF GGGG HHHH ....
...
<P>AAAA BBBB CCCC DDDD EEEE FFFF GGGG HHHH ....
<P>
<P>and you want to go to the top from down
<A HREF="javascript:scroll(0,0)">here</A>.
Just add a scroll(0,0)!

</BODY>
</HTML>
```

Figure 6–38 shows the page after the windowScroll.html file is loaded and you have scrolled to the bottom of the page with the vertical scrollbar.

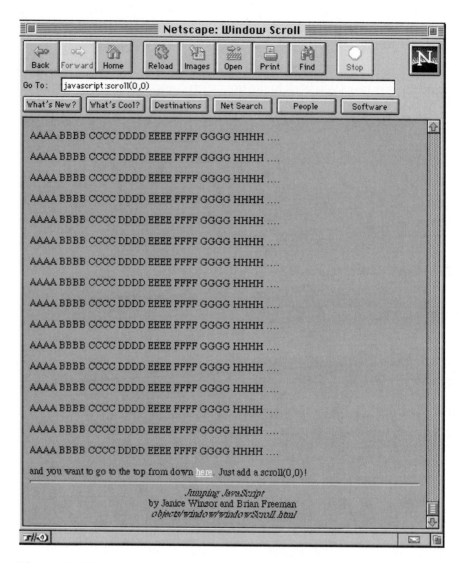

Figure 6–38 `HREF` with `scroll(0,0)`

You can also use the `scroll()` method to create your own scrolling buttons. The following `windowScrollImage.html` file creates a window with two frames and loads an image file into the top frame and the `windowScrollBtn.html` script into the bottom file.

```
<!--
        windowScrollImage.html
-->

<HTML>
<HEAD>
<TITLE>Scroll Image</TITLE>
</HEAD>
<FRAMESET ROWS="80%,20%">
  <FRAMESET ROWS="33%,33%,33%">
    <FRAME NAME="blank" BORDER=0>
    <FRAMESET COLS="33%,33%,33%">
      <FRAME NAME="blank" BORDER=0>
      <FRAME SRC="largeImage.html"   NAME="imgframe"
        BORDER=0>
      <FRAME NAME="blank" BORDER=0>
    </FRAMESET>
    <FRAME NAME="blank" BORDER=0>
  </FRAMESET>
  <FRAME SRC="windowScrollBtns.html" NAME="btnframe">
</FRAMESET>
</HTML>
```

The `windowScrollBtn.html` below shows one way you can create scrolling buttons. This script scrolls in one-pixel increments. To scroll in larger increments, simply adjust the x and y values to increment by a different number of pixels.

```
<!--
        windowScrollBtns.html

    Scrolls the frame around when you click on
    the buttons.
-->

<HTML>
<HEAD>
<TITLE>Scroll Buttons</TITLE>
<SCRIPT LANGUAGE="JavaScript">
<!-- HIDE FROM OLD BROWSERS

var x = 0
var y = 0
```

```
function up(frame) {
  y = y - 1

  // keep in the positive range.
  if ( y < 0 ) {
    y = 0
  }
  frame.scroll(x, y)
}

function down(frame) {
  y = y + 1
  frame.scroll(x, y)
}

function left(frame) {
  x = x - 1

  // keep in the positive range.
  if ( x < 0 ) {
    x = 0
  }
  frame.scroll(x, y)
}

function right(frame) {
  x = x + 1
  frame.scroll(x, y)
}

// STOP HIDING -->
</SCRIPT>
</HEAD>
<BODY>

<CENTER>
<TABLE COLS=3
 CELLSPACING=0 CELLPADDING=0>
<TR>
  <TD></TD>
  <TD>
    <A HREF="javascript:up(parent.frame1)">
      <IMG SRC="../../icons/2ARROW2.GIF">
    </A>
```

```
    </TD>
    <TD></TD>
  </TR>
  <TR>
    <TD>
      <A HREF="javascript:left(parent.frame1)">
        <IMG SRC="../../icons/2ARROW3.GIF">
      </A>
    </TD>
    <TD></TD>
    <TD>
      <A HREF="javascript:right(parent.frame1)">
        <IMG SRC="../../icons/2ARROW4.GIF">
      </A>
    </TD>
  </TR>
  <TR>
    <TD></TD>
    <TD>
      <A HREF="javascript:down(parent.frame1)">
        <IMG SRC="../../icons/2ARROW1.GIF">
      </A>
    </TD>
    <TD></TD>
  </TR>
  </TABLE>
  </CENTER>
  </BODY>
  </HTML>
```

Figure 6–39 shows the result of loading the `windowScrollImage.html` script.

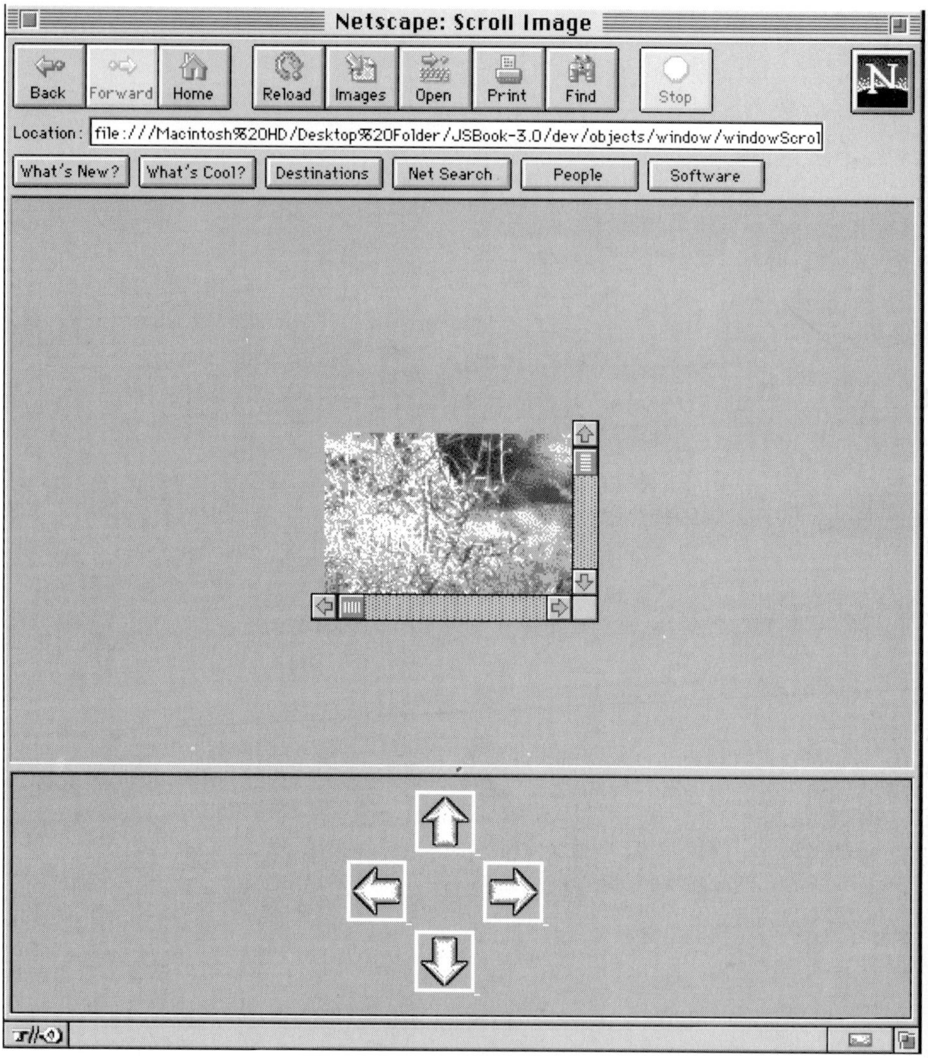

Figure 6–39 Result of `windowScrollImage.html` script

The image is larger than the frame. Although you can use the scrollbars around the image to scroll the image into the frame, you can also click on any of the four arrows in the bottom frame to scroll the lion image in the top frame one pixel at a time in the direction that the arrow points.

As you scroll using the buttons in the bottom frame, notice that the scrollbars around the image change to reflect the current scrolling positions, as shown in Figure 6–40.

Figure 6–40 Scrolling the image, using the scrolling buttons

Using Timeouts

At times you may want to delay the evaluation of an expression for a specific period of time. For example, you might want to set a timeout to display an alert if the user has not performed an action within a specified time period. The JavaScript language provides you with two *timeout* methods for the `window` object to enable you to set specific timeouts: `setTimeout()` and `clearTimeout()`.

Using the `setTimeout()` method is like setting an alarm clock. Because this method evaluates an expression after a specified time period, the parameters for the `setTimeout()` method are a quoted expression and the time, in milliseconds, that you want to delay the execution of the expression. One minute contains 60,000 milliseconds. So, if you want a 15-second delay, you would use a 7500 millisecond delay.

Method

setTimeout("*expression*", *millisecondsDelay*)

Returns

A reference to an object used only with the window.clearTimeouT() method to cancel the evaluation of the expression.

Users can perform other tasks while the timeout clock is running. Once the timer starts, you cannot adjust its time. If you want to adjust the time, you can clear the timeout, using the `clearTimeout()` method, and start another one.

Method

clearTimeout(timeoutIDnumber)

Returns

Nothing

When you use timeouts, provide a way to clear the timeout if the user performs any actions that negate the need for the evaluation of the expression.

Example of Timeouts in a Script

The following `windowTimeout.html` script uses the `setTimeout()` and `clearTimeout()` methods to display a message in the status bar when the clock is running, and to display an alert when the time is up.

```
<!--
    windowTimeout.html

    This example uses the window
    object's clearTimeout and setTimeout
    methods. It also makes use of the window
    object's defaultStatus property.
-->
<HTML>
<HEAD>
<TITLE>clearTimeout & setTimeout</TITLE>
<SCRIPT LANGUAGE="JavaScript">
<!-- HIDE FROM OLD BROWSERS

//
// Description:
//
// When you click on the "Set Timeout" button,
// two timers start up.  The 'alert' timer waits
// for 5 seconds, then displays an alert
// dialog. Meanwhile, the 'message' timer goes
// off roughly every 1/2 second, displaying a
// message in the window's status line.
```

```
//
//
var alertID = null  // holds the alert timer ID
var mesgID  = null  // holds the message timer ID
var ticktock  = true

// switch the message and restart the 'message'
// timer.
function togglemsg() {
  if (ticktock) {
    this.window.defaultStatus = "tick..."
    ticktock = false
  } else {
    this.window.defaultStatus = "tock..."
    ticktock = true
  }
  mesgID=setTimeout("togglemsg()", 500)
}

// activate the 'alert' by displaying an alert
// then restarting the timer.
function timeout() {
  alert("Timeout!")
  alertID=setTimeout("timeout()", 5000)
}

// start them off
function startTiming() {
  alertID=setTimeout("timeout()", 5000)
  mesgID=setTimeout("togglemsg()", 500)
}

// stop the timeouts and clean up
function stopTiming() {
  if (alertID) {
    clearTimeout(alertID)
  }
  if (mesgID) {
    clearTimeout(mesgID)
    this.window.defaultStatus =
      "Timeouts Cleared!"
  }
}
```

```
// STOP HIDING -->
</SCRIPT>
</HEAD>

<P>Control the timers using the buttons below:</P>
<DD>Click on Set Timeout to start the timers.
<DD>Click on Clear Timeout to stop them.

<CENTER><FORM>
<INPUT TYPE="button" VALUE="Set Timeout"
 onClick="startTiming()">
<INPUT TYPE="button" VALUE="Clear Timeout"
 onClick="stopTiming()">
</FORM></CENTER>

</BODY>
</HTML>
```

Figure 6–41 shows the window after you have loaded the `windowTimeout.html` file.

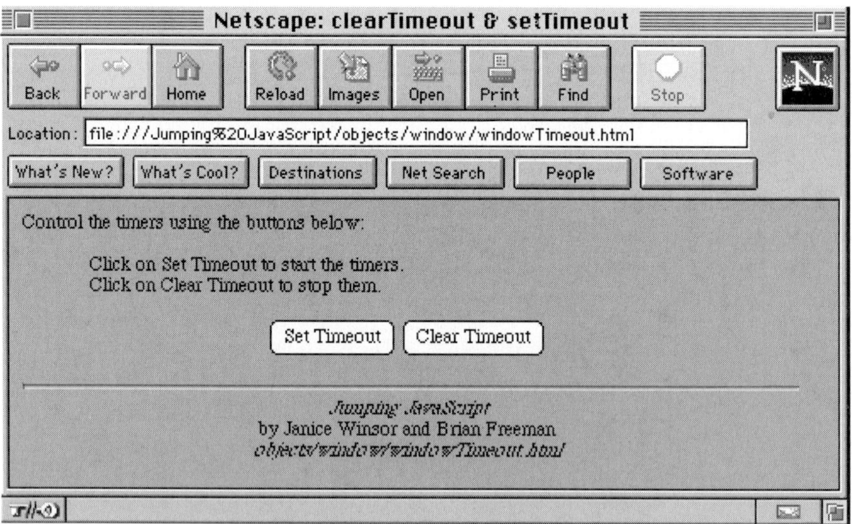

Figure 6–41 Result of loading the `windowTimeout.html` script

When you click on the Set Timeout button, the words tick... and tock... are displayed in the status bar at the bottom of the window, as shown in Figure 6–42.

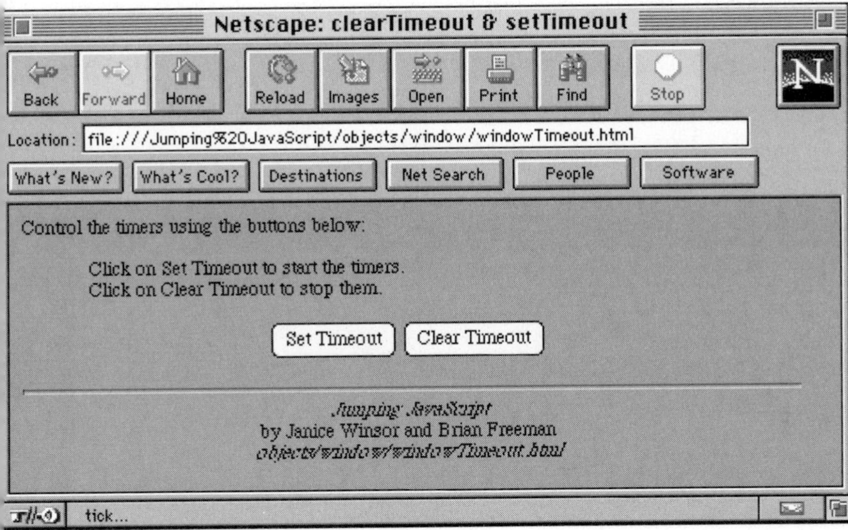

Figure 6–42 Timeout in progress

When the timeout expires, an alert is displayed, as shown in Figure 6–43.

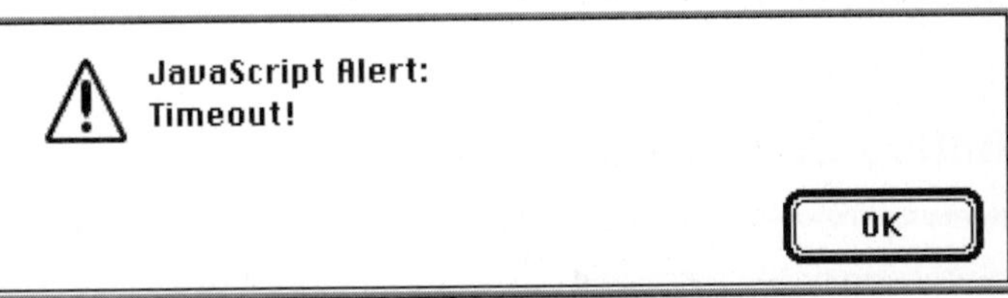

Figure 6–43 Timeout has expired and alert is displayed

When you click on the OK button, the timer starts running again. Click on the Clear Timeout button to stop the timer. A status message is displayed in the status bar, as shown in Figure 6–44.

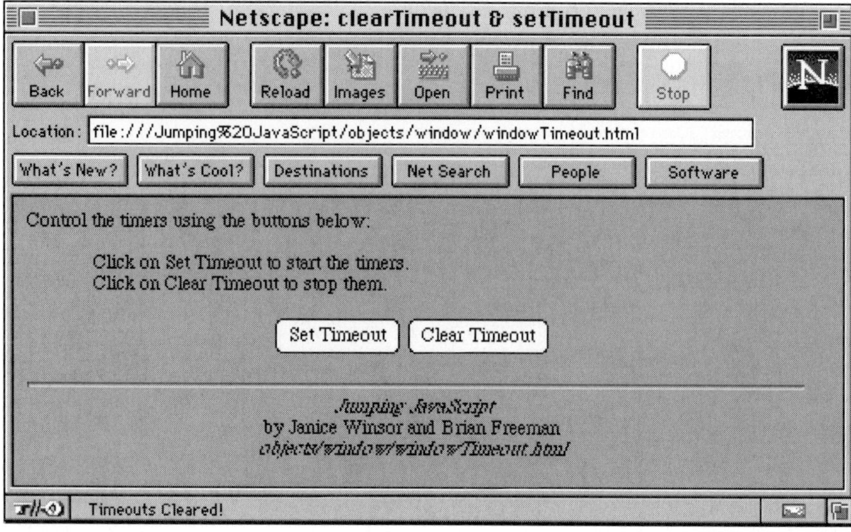

Figure 6–44 Timeouts cleared

Remember, when you use `defaultStatus` messages in your script, you should clear them with the `onUnload` event handler so that your messages do not persist when other files are loaded.

Using Event Handlers on Load and Unload

The `onLoad` and `onUnload` event handlers enable you to perform scripting actions when file load and unload events occur. The load event occurs when the browser finishes loading the window or all of the frames in a frameset. The `onLoad` event handler enables you to execute JavaScript code when the event occurs.

ou include the onLoad event handler as an attribute of a <BODY> tag for a ingle-frame document or as an attribute of a <FRAMESET> tag for the top vindow of a multiple-frame document. When you use onLoad as an attribute of FRAMESET>, the event triggers only after all frames defined by that frameset ave loaded completely.

Event Handler

onLoad

Syntax

<BODY (*other attributes*) onload = "*JavaScript code*">

<FRAMESET (*other attributes*) onLoad="*JavaScript code*">

he unload event occurs when the browser finishes unloading the window or all f the frames in a frameset. The onUnload event handler enables you to execute avaScript code when the event occurs. Use the onUnload event handler only for uick operations that don't interfere with an easy transition from one document o another. The event triggers only after all frames defined by that frameset have nloaded completely.

Event Handler

onUnload

Syntax

<BODY (*other attributes*) onUnload = "*JavaScript code*">

<FRAMESET (*other attributes*) onUnload="*JavaScript code*">

xample of onLoad and onUnload Event Handlers

ou've already seen how to use the onLoad and onUnload event handlers in the vindowStatus.html script shown in "Example of status and defaultStatus roperties" on page 107. The following code extract from that script shows how hese event handlers are used to call functions.

```
<BODY onLoad="return setDefaultStatus()"
onUnload="return clearDefaultStatus()">
```

Using an Event Handler to Capture Interpreter Error Messages

The Navigator 3.0 release provides an `onError` event handler. This new event handler is listed as a property of the `window` object; however, because it works as an event handler, we have included it here. You cannot define an `onError` event handler as an attribute in the `<BODY>` or `<FRAMESET>` tags as you can with other event handlers such as onLoad. Instead, you use the `window.onerror` syntax in your JavaScript code.

You can use this event handler to capture error messages that are generated when the interpreter loads your script. You can either display these messages in a different way or suppress the error messages.

Event Handler

onError

Syntax

window.onerror = *statement*

Note – Be sure you do not capitalize the `E` in this event handler. Because the JavaScript language lists `onerror` as a property, it does not follow the same naming capitalization scheme as the other event handlers. The JavaScript language is case sensitive. If you use `window.onError` in your scripts for the window object, it does not work. To make matters even more confusing, the other `onError` event handlers provided by the JavaScript language do have a capital E.

Example of Capturing and Displaying Error Messages

The following `windowOnerrorHandler.html` script uses the `onerror` event handler to capture error messages and display them in a separate window.

```
<!--
       windowOnerrorHandler.html

    This example shows how to create an onerror
    event handler for a window.

-->

<HTML>
<HEAD>
<TITLE>Window onerror Handler</TITLE>
<SCRIPT LANGUAGE="JavaScript">
<!-- HIDE FROM OLD BROWSERS

// point JavaScript errors to my error handler
window.onerror = errorHandler

// arrays to store the errors in
messageArray    = new Array()
urlArray        = new Array()
lineNumberArray = new Array()

// collect the errors with the error handler
function errorHandler(message, url, lineNumber) {
  messageArray[messageArray.length]
    = message
  urlArray[urlArray.length]
    = url
  lineNumberArray[lineNumberArray.length]
    = lineNumber
  return true
}

// when asked, display the errors received
function displayErrors() {
  //
  // open a new window to display the errors
  win2=window.open('','window2','scrollbars=yes')

  // work around the open bug
  if (navigator.appVersion.indexOf("(X11") != -1
   || navigator.appVersion.indexOf("(Mac") != -1)
  {
    win2=window.open('','window2','scrollbars=yes')
```

```
  }

  // write out the errors
  win2.document.writeln('<B>Error Report</B><P>')

  // loop through the errors received and format them
  for (var i=0; i < messageArray.length; i++) {
    with (win2.document) {
      writeln('<B>Error in file:</B> ' +
               urlArray[i] + '<BR>')
      writeln('<B>Line number:</B> ' +
               lineNumberArray[i] + '<BR>')
      writeln('<B>Message:</B> ' +
               messageArray[i] + '<P>')
    }
  }
  win2.document.close()
}

// STOP HIDING -->
</SCRIPT>
</HEAD>

<BODY onLoad="nonExistentFunction()">

<P>This example shows how to use an onerror event
handler. When this document is loaded, an onLoad
event handler refers to a nonexistent function,
but you don't see the error dialogs. The errors
are captured by the onerror event handler. If
you click on the button below, the error(s) are
displayed in a separate window.

<CENTER><FORM>
<INPUT TYPE="button" VALUE="Display Errors"
 onClick="displayErrors()">
</FORM></CENTER>

</BODY>
</HTML>
```

Figure 6–45 shows the result of loading the `windowOnerrorHandler.html` script.

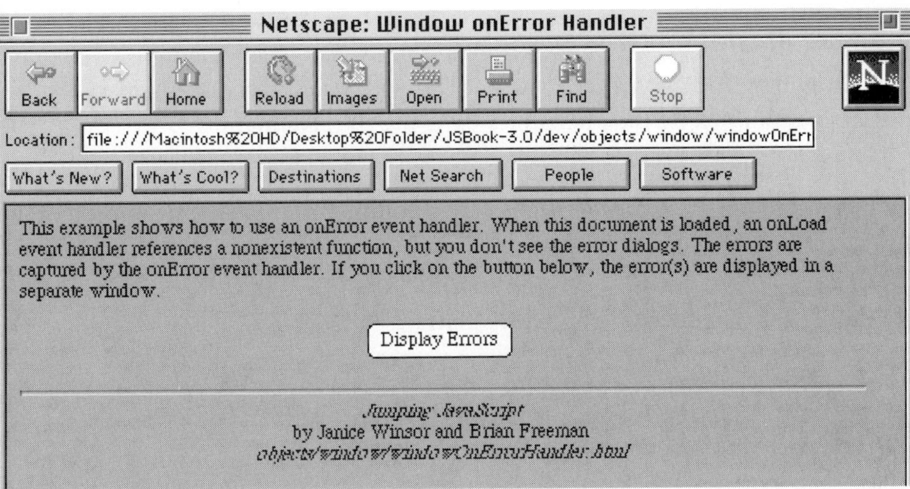

Figure 6–45 Result of loading the `windowOnerrorHandler.html` script

When you click on the Display Errors button, a window opens, showing the error messages generated by the interpreter when the file was loaded, as shown in Figure 6–46.

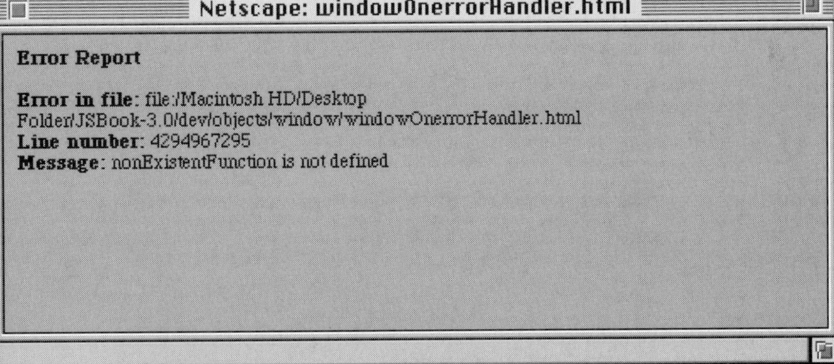

Figure 6–46 Error message window

Explanation of windowOnerrorHandler.html Script

The `windowOnerrorHandler.html` script introduces some new elements. It creates an array to capture the error messages generated by the interpreter. It also uses a `for...with` loop to loop through the array and format the messages. Note that this script uses the `unescape()` function to format the result of `urlArray`. For more information about arrays, see Chapter 29, "Working with Arrays." For more information about creating loops, see Chapter 27, "Creating Loops."

Example of Hiding Error Messages

The following `windowOnerrorNull.html` script suppresses any error messages generated by the interpreter by using the statement:

```
window.onerror = null
```

If you want to see the error messages, add a comment (//) to the beginning of the statement.

```
<!--
         windowOnerrorNull.html

    This script sets the window's onerror event
    handler to null. No JavaScript-generated errors
    are shown to the user.
-->
<HTML>
<HEAD>
<TITLE>Window onerror null</TITLE>
<SCRIPT LANGUAGE="JavaScript">
<!-- HIDE FROM OLD BROWSERS
// turn off JavaScript errors
window.onerror = null

// STOP HIDING -->
</SCRIPT>
</HEAD>

<BODY onLoad="nonExistentFunction()">

<P>This example shows how to turn off JavaScript
errors. When this document was loaded, an onLoad
event handler referenced a nonexistent
function. You should not see any error dialogs.

<P>If you want to see the error message,
add a comment (//) at the beginning of the
 <CODE>window.onerror = null </CODE> statement.

</BODY>
</HTML>
```

Figure 6–47 shows the result of loading the `windowOnerrorNull.html` script.

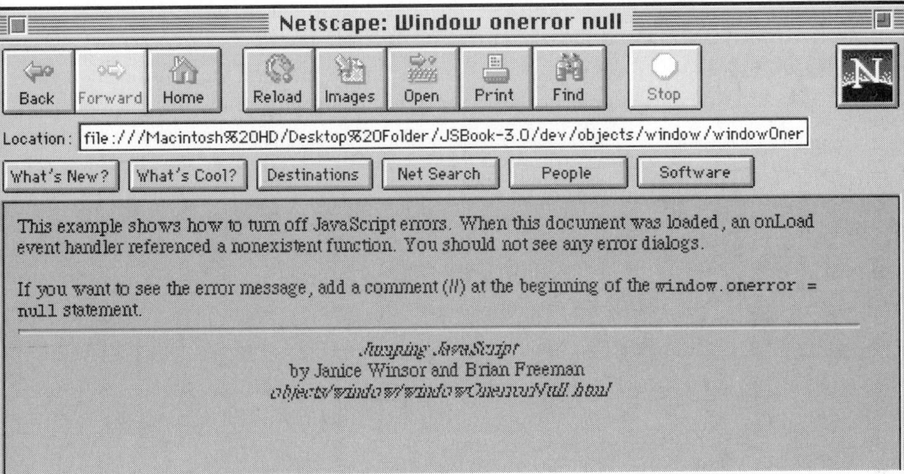

Figure 6–47 Result of loading the `windowOnerrorNull.html` script

Summary of New Terms and Concepts

The new terms and concepts introduced in this chapter are listed in alphabetical order in Table 6-3. The terms and concepts are also included in the glossary at the end of the book.

Table 6-3 Summary of New Terms and Concepts

Term/Concept	Description
alert	A modal window that displays an information or warning message to users. You create an alert by using the `window.alert()` method.
array	A list of properties for an object. The properties are listed in numerical order, starting with zero (0). For example, `frame[0]`, `frame[1]`, `frame[2]`.
blur	The action that occurs when a user clicks or moves the pointer outside of a window so that the focus is removed from it.
click-to-type	To set the insert point by a mouse click in an area of the screen that accepts keyboard input.

Table 6-3 **Summary of New Terms and Concepts (Continued)**

Term/Concept	Description
confirmation window	A message to users displayed in a transitory window that blocks any user input to the application. Users must click on a button in the confirmation window to dismiss it. You create a confirmation message with the `window.confirm()` method.
focus	The action that occurs when a user clicks in a window or frame within a window to indicate which window receives input.
frame	A subwindow within a browser window.
instance	A specific object that is created from HTML code by the browser at runtime.
modal window	A transitory window that displays a message to users and blocks any other input to the application. Users cannot perform any other activities in the application until they click on the OK button to close the modal window.
move pointer	To set the insert point by moving the pointer into an area of the screen that accepts keyboard input.
pixel	A single dot on a display screen. Pixel is a contraction for picture element.
prompt window	A modal window that you use to enable users to provide typed input in response to a question.
status bar	The region at the bottom of the browser window where you can display `status` and `defaultStatus` messages.
timeout	JavaScript `window` object methods that enable you to delay the evaluation of an expression for a specific period of time.

223

CHAPTER 7

- Controlling Document Colors
- Extracting Title, Location, Modification, and Document Referrer Information for a Document
- Working with the anchors Property
- Working with the links Property
- Referencing Forms in a Document
- Referencing Images in a Document
- Referencing Java Applets in a Document
- Finding Plug-ins Embedded in a Document
- Finding the Document Domain
- Storing User-Generated Information: the cookie Property
- Writing into a Document
- Opening, Closing, and Clearing a Document
- Summary of New Terms and Concepts

Creating Documents

The document is the area of the window where an HTML file is loaded and where users interact with the page. The `document` object provides the properties and methods to work with information about anchors, forms, links, the document title, the current location and URL, and the current colors. The rest of the objects that we discuss in this book are below the `document` object in the hierarchy. Figure 7–1 shows this portion of the object hierarchy.

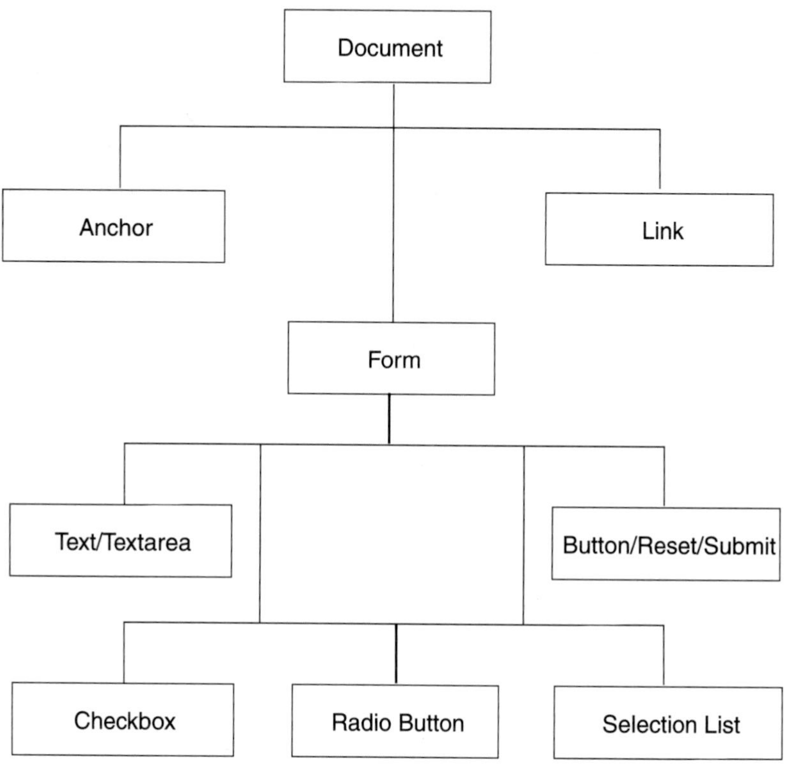

Figure 7–1 The `document` object hierarchy

The Navigator 3.0 release adds `applet`, `area`, and `image` objects to the document hierarchy, as illustrated in Figure 7–2.

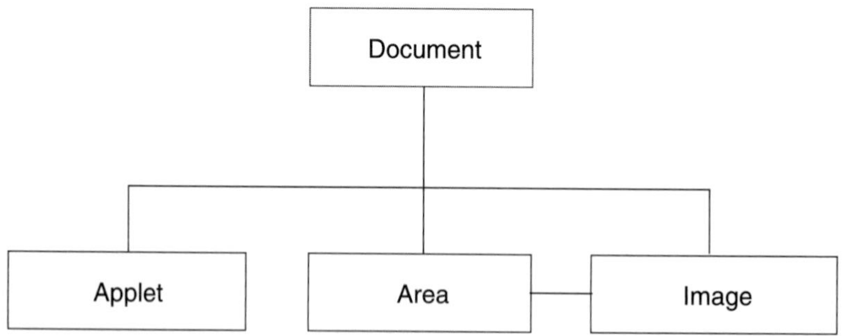

Figure 7–2 New objects in Navigator 3.0

This chapter discusses the properties and methods for the `document` object itself. The other objects are discussed in the chapters that follow.

The properties and methods for the document object are listed in alphabetical order in Table 7-1. The document object has no event handlers.

Table 7-1 Properties and Methods for the document Object

Properties	Methods	Event Handlers
alinkColor	clear()	None
anchors[]	close()	
applets[]*	eval()*	
bgColor	open()	
cookie	toString()*	
domain*	valueOf()*	
embeds[]*	write()	
fgColor	writeln()	
forms		
images[]*		
lastModified		
linkColor		
links		
location		
plugins[]*		
referrer		
title		
URL*		
vlinkColor		

* New in the Navigator 3.0 release.

Controlling Document Colors

The color elements of a document are set by the attributes of the HTML `<BODY>` tag. See the HTML Brushup box for a list of the attributes. You can read these attributes in a script, but you cannot dynamically change the colors of an existing document in a script.

HTML Brushup — Defining Document Colors

You define the color elements of a document by setting the following attributes of the <BODY> HTML tag:

<BODY

(BACKGROUND = "*backgroundImage*")

(BGCOLOR = "*backgroundColor*")

(FGCOLOR = "*foregroundColor*")

(LINK = "*linkColor*")

(ALINK = "*activatedLinkColor*")

(VLINK = "*visitedLinkColor*")>

</BODY>

The attributes are included in square brackets (( )) because they are optional. You can use none, some, or all of these attributes for any document.

The properties that return color values are:

- `bgColor` returns the background color.
- `fgColor` returns the foreground color.
- `linkColor` returns the color of links that have not been visited.
- `alinkColor` returns the color of links that have been activated.
- `vlinkColor` returns the color of links that have been visited.

To set these colors, you need to create a new window and define the color properties for the document as part of the `<BODY>` tag.

Property	Value	Gettable	Settable
alinkColor	hexadecimal triplet string or predefined JavaScript Color	Yes	No
bgColor	hexadecimal triplet string or predefined JavaScript Color	Yes	No
fgColor	hexadecimal triplet string or predefined JavaScript Color	Yes	No
linkColor	hexadecimal triplet string or predefined JavaScript Color	Yes	No
vlinkColor	hexadecimal triplet string or predefined JavaScript Color	Yes	No

Let's take a closer look at how colors are defined. Each specification contains three colors: red, blue, and green. You define colors by specifying the mix of red, blue, and green that makes up the final color. Each color has a decimal value from 0 to 255, with 0 being a complete lack of color and 255 being 100 percent of the color. A color value of 000 is black, and a color of 255255255 is pure white.

However, the JavaScript language uses hexadecimal values to define its colors. Hexadecimal numbers are base 16, with two-digit numbers that are based on the values 0, 1, 2, 3, 4, 5, 6, 7, 8, 9, A, B, C, D, E, and F. The hexadecimal equivalent of the decimal number 255 is the hexadecimal number FF. The following table shows the decimal and hexadecimal values for white and black.

Color	Decimal Value	Hexadecimal Value
white	255255255	FFFFFF
black	000	000000

Hexadecimal numbers are always preceded by a pound sign (#). Although you can omit the pound sign, any time the JavaScript language returns a value, it displays it with a pound sign.

To define a document background color of white, you would assign the value in the following way:

```
document.bgColor = #FFFFFF
```

The JavaScript language does, however, provide a shortcut to defining colors. You can assign a string literal specifying one of the predefined color names, such as `aqua`, `coral`, `ghostwhite`, or `seashell`. For the complete list of predefined colors and their hexadecimal values, see Appendix B, "JavaScript Predefined Colors." Using the string literal color value, you would assign a document background color of white in the following way:

```
document.bgColor = "white"
```

Because the string literal names may not always accurately describe the color, you may have to experiment with some of the colors to find the ones you want.

Example of Setting Document Colors

The `documentColor.html` script below provides a button to open a new window that contains a document with colors specified from the JavaScript list of predefined colors.

```
<!--
          documentColor.html

    An example of creating a document with
    alinkColor, bgColor, fgColor, linkColor, and
    vlinkColor properties set.
-->

<HTML>
<HEAD>
<TITLE>Document Color</TITLE>
<SCRIPT LANGUAGE="JavaScript">
<!-- HIDE FROM OLD BROWSERS

//
// Create a window ...
//
function openWindow() {
  var docStr = ""  // string to write in document
  var wopts = ""   // window options

  // Build the window options
  wopts += "toolbar=yes,"
  wopts += "location=yes,"
```

```
wopts += "directories=yes,"
wopts += "status=yes,"
wopts += "menubar=yes,"
wopts += "scrollbars=yes,"
wopts += "resizable=yes,"
wopts += "copyhistory=yes"

//
// Create the document
//
docStr += "<HEAD>"
docStr += "<TITLE>Document Color</TITLE>"
docStr += "</HEAD>"

docStr += "<BODY "  // tag continues...

// set document.bgColor
docStr += " BGCOLOR=\"#FAEBD7\""  // antiquewhite

// set document.fgColor
docStr += " TEXT=\"brown\""

// use the current document's linkColor
docStr += " LINK=\"" + window.document.linkColor
docStr += "\""

// set document.alinkColor
docStr += " ALINK=\"#000000\""    // black

// set document.vlinkColor
docStr += " VLINK=\"green\""
docStr += ">"        // BODY tag ends here


// BODY content starts here
docStr += "<P>This is some text.</P>"
docStr += "<P>...and some more...</P>"
docStr += "<P>...and more...</P>"
docStr += "<P>...and more.</P>"
docStr += "<A HREF=\"http://home.mcom.com\">"
docStr += "A link to Netscape</A>"

// the document ends here
docStr += "</BODY>"
```

```
  //
  // Create the window and write the document
  // into it.
  win = window.open("", "myWindow", wopts)
  win.document.open()
  win.document.write(docStr)
  win.document.close()
}

// STOP HIDING -->
</SCRIPT>
</HEAD>

<BODY>

<P>Click on Create Window to see a window
with color.</P>

<!--
    When the button is clicked, openWindow()
    is called.
-->
<CENTER>
<FORM NAME="aForm">
<INPUT TYPE="button" NAME="createButton"
  VALUE="Create Window!"
  onClick="openWindow()">
</FORM>
</CENTER>

</BODY>
</HTML>
```

Figure 7–3 shows the result of loading the `documentColor.html` script.

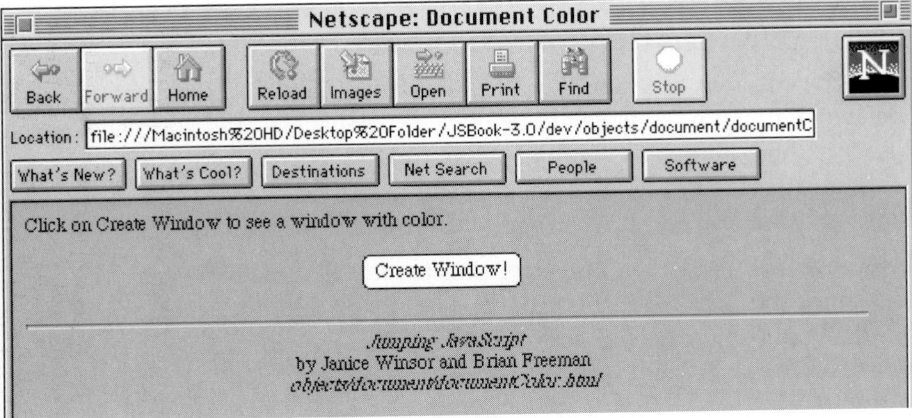

Figure 7–3 Result of loading the `documentColor.html` script

When you click on the Create Window! button, a new window is opened, using the colors defined in the script, as shown in Figure 7–4.

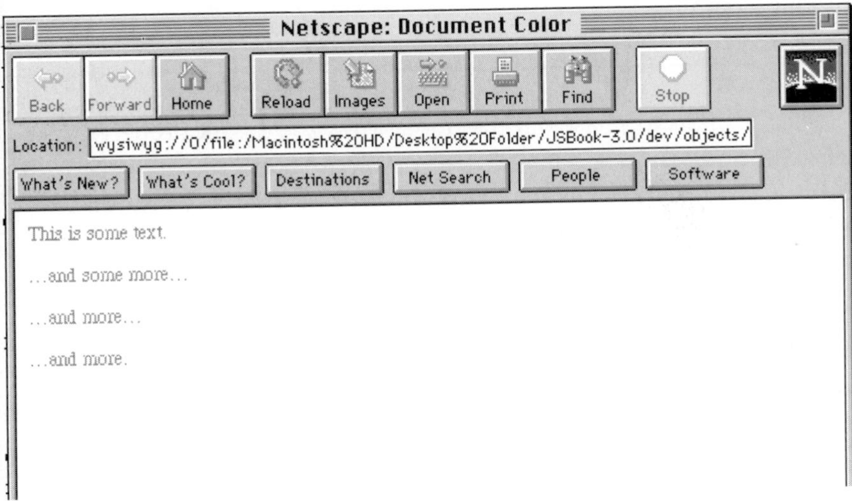

Figure 7–4 Window with new document colors

Extracting Title, Location, Modification, and Document Referrer Information for a Document

The `document.title` property holds the value of the title of the document that is defined within the `<TITLE></TITLE>` HTML tags. The title is displayed in the title bar of the browser window and in the bookmark list if a user marks the page with a bookmark. The title does not appear within the contents of the page. You can use the `document.title` property to retrieve the title of the document.

The `document.location` property holds the full URL of the file that contains the document source code. This property is different from the `location` object because it only holds the URL for the file itself. It is the same as the `location.href` property.

The Navigator 3.0 release provides a `document.URL` property that returns the same value as the `document.location` property. In the Navigator 2.0 release, `document.URL` property was an undocumented feature. It is now included in the Navigator 3.0 documentation. The `document.URL` property works correctly in Navigator 2.0 releases. The `URL` property name (not its value) must be all upper case to work properly.

Note – Netscape plans to phase out the `document.location` property in an (unspecified) future release. To make sure your scripts continue to work with subsequent releases, always use the `document.URL` property instead of the `document.location` property.

The `document.lastModified` property holds the date the file was last modified. You can use this property to inform users of modifications that have been made since they last visited the site.

Note – On Macintosh systems, Navigator 2.0 and 3.0 may not return the correct last modified date for the `document.lastModified` property. The `document.lastModified` property is looking for a particular date format, usually sent by the server. This date format does not match the way that MacOS™ formats the last modified information. If the `document.lastModified` property returns a date with a year of 1926, (as my Mac does), you've stumbled onto this problem. If your Macintosh is set up as a Web server, you may (or may not) find that the `document.lastModified`

property works correctly. Because you do not know which platform your users will be running, we'd suggest that you minimize your use of this property in your scripts.

The `document.referrer` property holds the URL of the page that led to the current page. In other words, if the user got to the current page by clicking on a link from another page, this property contains the URL of the page that contained the originating link. You can use this property to track statistics about which sites refer users to your site.

Property	Value	Gettable	Settable
title	string	Yes	No
lastModified	date string	Yes	No
location	string	Yes	No
referrer	string	Yes	No

Example of Displaying All of the Properties of a Document

The `documentProps.html` script shown below displays all of the properties for the document object in an alert when you click on the Document Properties button. Note that the `documentProps.html` script includes the `getProps.js` script described in Chapter 4, "Debugging Scripts."

```
<!--
        documentProps.html

    Display all the document properties in an
    alert dialog when the button is pressed.
-->

<HTML>
<HEAD>
<TITLE>Document Properties</TITLE>

<!-- Include for displayPropsWin() -->
<SCRIPT SRC="../../debug/getProps.js"></SCRIPT>
<!--
    Include displayPropsWin(), which displays
    the properties of a given object in a new
```

```
    window.
-->
<SCRIPT SRC="../../debug/displayPropsWin.js">
</SCRIPT>
</HEAD>

<BODY>

<P>Click on the button below to display the
document properties of this page.
</P>

<CENTER><FORM>
<INPUT TYPE="button" NAME="docProps"
  VALUE="Document Properties"
  onClick="displayPropsWin(document,'document')">
</FORM></CENTER>

</BODY>
</HTML>
```

Figure 7–5 shows the result of loading the `documentProps.html` script.

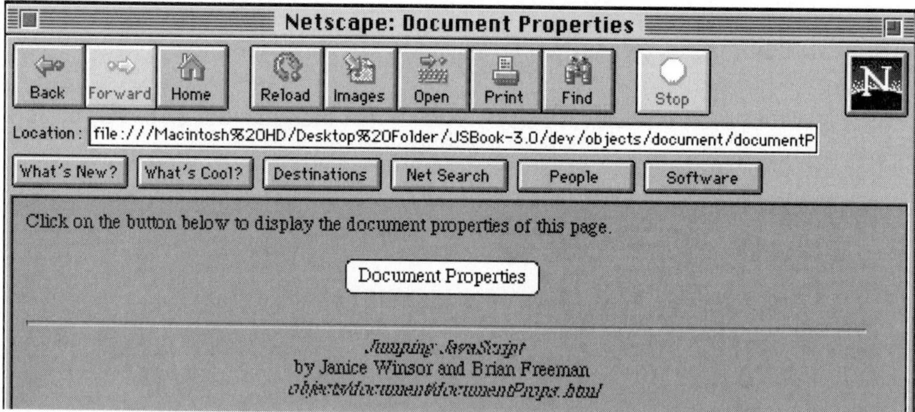

Figure 7–5 Result of loading the `documentProps.html` script

When you click on the Document Properties button, a new window opens, listing all of the `document` object properties, as shown in Figure 7–6.

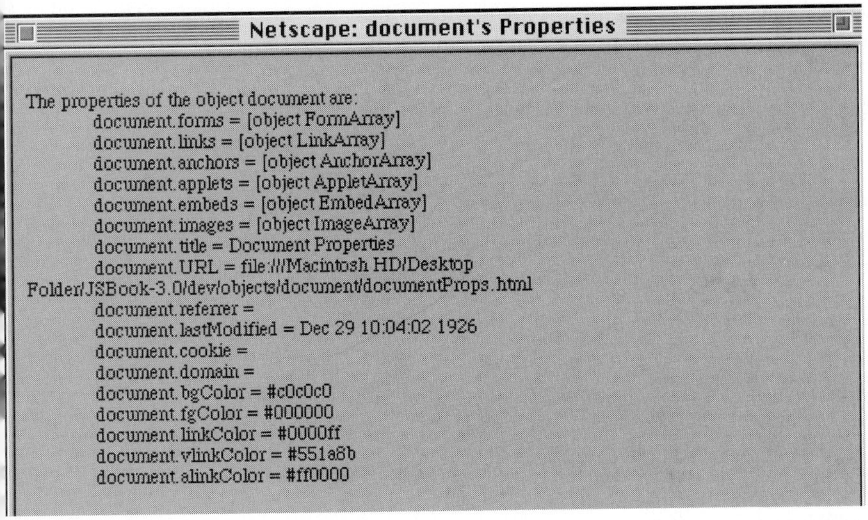

```
Netscape: document's Properties

The properties of the object document are:
        document.forms = [object FormArray]
        document.links = [object LinkArray]
        document.anchors = [object AnchorArray]
        document.applets = [object AppletArray]
        document.embeds = [object EmbedArray]
        document.images = [object ImageArray]
        document.title = Document Properties
        document.URL = file:///Macintosh HD/Desktop
Folder/JSBook-3.0/dev/objects/document/documentProps.html
        document.referrer =
        document.lastModified = Dec 29 10:04:02 1926
        document.cookie =
        document.domain =
        document.bgColor = #c0c0c0
        document.fgColor = #000000
        document.linkColor = #0000ff
        document.vlinkColor = #551a8b
        document.alinkColor = #ff0000
```

Figure 7–6 Document properties window

The property returns the string that is returned from the object for forms, links, anchors, applets, embeds, and images. Note that on Macintosh systems, the `document.lastModified` property returns an incorrect date and year. On my Macintosh, the `document.lastModified` property thinks it's always 1926!

Example of Comparison of location and URL Document Properties

The following `documentURL.html` script shows that the `location` and `URL` properties both return exactly the same value. Note that this script formats the value returned by the `URL` property by passing the message string through the `unescape()` method.

```
<!--
        documentURL.html

     Shows that the document location and URL
     properties are the same.
-->

<HTML>
<HEAD>
<TITLE>Document URL vs. Location</TITLE>
<SCRIPT LANGUAGE="JavaScript">
<!-- HIDE FROM OLD BROWSERS
var mstr = "<BR>"  // message string
```

```
mstr += "<P>document.location = "
mstr += "\"" + document.location + "\"</P>"

mstr += "<P>document.URL = "
mstr += "\"" + document.URL + "\"</P>"

document.open()
document.write(unescape(mstr))
document.close()

// STOP HIDING -->
</SCRIPT>
</HEAD>

<BODY>
</BODY>
</HTML>
```

Figure 7–7 shows the result of loading the `documentURL.html` script.

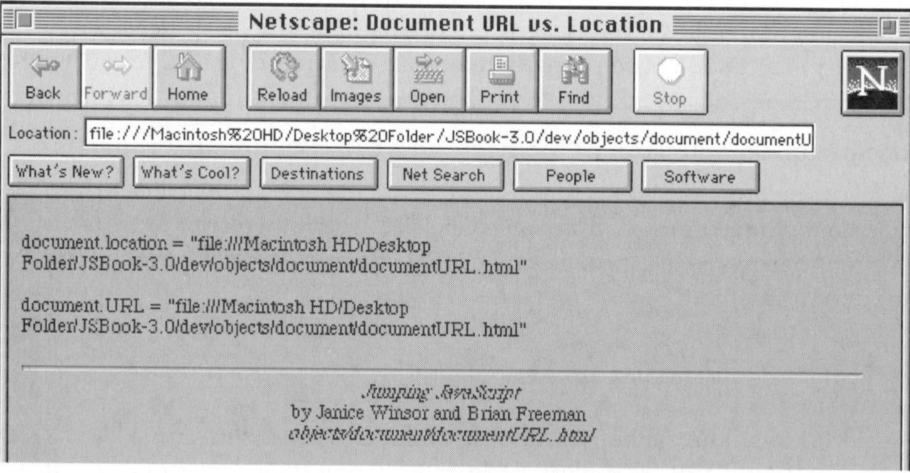

Figure 7–7 Result of loading the `documentURL.html` script

As you can see, the value returned by `document.location` and `document.URL` are identical.

Example of Finding Where a Document Came From

The following `documentWhere.html` script shows how to obtain the `title`, `location`, and `referrer` properties for the `document` object.

```
<!--
          documentWhere.html

    Shows how to obtain the title, location, and
    referrer document object properties.
-->

<HTML>
<HEAD>
<TITLE>Document Where</TITLE>
<SCRIPT LANGUAGE="JavaScript">
<!-- HIDE FROM OLD BROWSERS
var mstr = "<BR>"  // message string

mstr += "<P>The location of this document"
mstr += ", \"" + document.title + "\", is "
mstr += "\"" + document.URL + "\"</P>"
mstr += "<P>The referring document is "
mstr += "\"" + document.referrer + "\"</P>"

document.open()
document.write(unescape(mstr))
document.close()

// STOP HIDING -->
</SCRIPT>
</HEAD>

<BODY>


</BODY>
</HTML>
```

Notice that we've used the `unescape()` method to format the message string to convert any ASCII equivalents for easier human readability. Figure 7–8 shows the result of loading the `documentWhere.html` script.

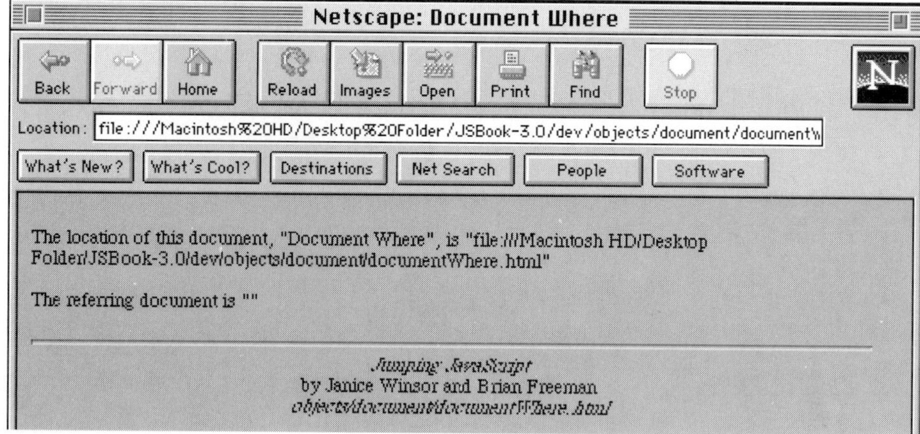

Figure 7–8 Result of loading the `documentWhere.html` script

Working with the anchors Property

Anchors and links are the heart and soul of the World Wide Web. HTML provides you with the basic tools that you need to create anchors and links. The JavaScript `document.anchors[]` array enables you to keep track of the anchors in a document. The `document.anchors.length` property enables you to find out how many anchors you have in a document.

The `anchors` property is useful only if you have anchors in a document. It is an array that contains the value of each anchor and link on the page in the order that they were defined in the HTML code.

Property	Value	Gettable	Settable
anchors	array of anchor objects	Yes	No

Refer to the HTML Brushup box for information on how to create anchors.

HTML Brushup — Creating Anchors

The most commonly used attributes of the <A></A> tags are listed below. At a minimum, you must specify either the URL for the anchor or the name of the destination section in the same page. If you use the NAME attribute, the text of the anchor must match the text of the destination. If you want the anchor to a URL to go to a specific destination on a page, you can specify the URL with a *#name* suffix to load the document and display the page starting at the named location. You can use the TARGET attribute to specify the name of another window or frame used to display the hyperlink.

<A

HREF = "*URL*" | NAME = "*destination*"

(TARGET = "*WindowName*")

>

Text of anchor

</A>

The anchors tag has several other attributes that are rarely used or supported. Understandably, the entire topic of link relationships is under active discussion and subject to change.

Example of Using a Named Anchor

The following `documentAnchorName.html` script shows how to create a named anchor and how to reference it within the same document. This example does not use any JavaScript objects or properties.

```
<!--
        documentAnchorName.html

    This example shows the simplest form of an
    anchor.
-->

<HTML>
<HEAD>
<TITLE>Anchor</TITLE>
</HEAD>
<BODY>

<P>The simplest form of an Anchor object is a
standard HTML &lt;A&gt; tag that contains a NAME
```

```
attribute.</P>

<P>URLs to a page containing an anchor may refer
to the anchor by adding a hash symbol, #,
followed by the anchor name. For example, the
following link is to the anchor named anAnchor at
the bottom of the page:
<PRE>
&lt;A HREF="anchorName.html#anAnchor"&gt;some HTML anchor
text&lt;/A&gt;
</PRE>

Here's a <A HREF="anchorName.html#anAnchor">
live</A> version of the link above.

<P>abcd efg hijk lmnop qrst uv wxy and z</P>
...
<P>abcd efg hijk lmnop qrst uv wxy and z</P>

<A NAME="anAnchor"></A>
<P>Notice that the location field in your browser
changed and that clicking on the browser's Back
button takes you back to where you were.</P>

</BODY>
</HTML>
```

Figure 7–9 shows the result of loading the `documentAnchorName.html` script.

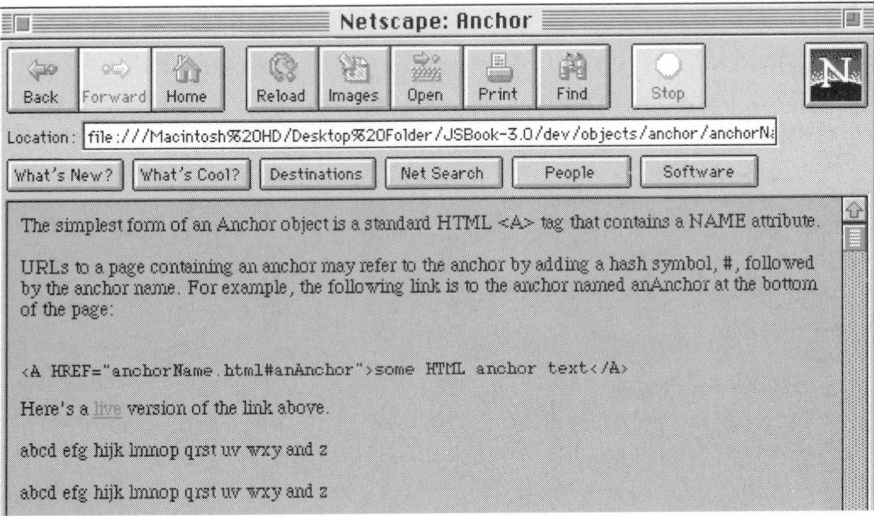

Figure 7–9 Result of loading the `documentAnchorName.html` script

When you click on the live link, the anchor is displayed at the the top of the page, and the Location field changes to show the new location, as shown in Figure 7–10.

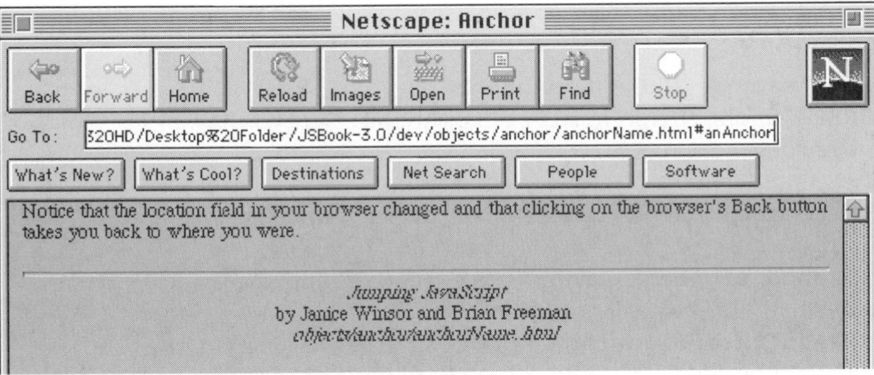

Figure 7–10 Going to a named anchor

Example of an Anchor That Is Also a Link

The following `anchorLink.html` script shows how to create a named anchor and how to reference it within the same document. This example does not use any JavaScript objects or properties.

```
<!--
        anchorLink.html

    This example shows that an anchor can also be
    a link.
-->

<HTML>
<HEAD>
<TITLE>A Link Anchor</TITLE>
</HEAD>
<BODY>

<P>You can make an anchor into a link by adding the
HREF attribute to the standard HTML &lt;A&gt;
tag.</P>

<P>For example, the following link is to the anchor
at the bottom of the page:
<PRE>
&lt;A NAME="topAnchor"
HREF="anchorLink.html#bottomAnchor"&gt;some HTML anchor
text&lt;/A&gt;
</PRE>

Here's a <A NAME="topAnchor"
HREF="anchorLink.html#bottomAnchor">live</A>
version.

<P>abcd efg hijk lmnop qrst uv wxy and z</P>
...
<P>abcd efg hijk lmnop qrst uv wxy and z</P>

<P>And the following anchor is also a link that
takes you back to the <A NAME="bottomAnchor"
HREF="anchorLink.html#topAnchor">top</A> of the
document.</P>

</BODY>
</HTML>
```

Figure 7–11 shows the result of loading the `anchorLink.html` script.

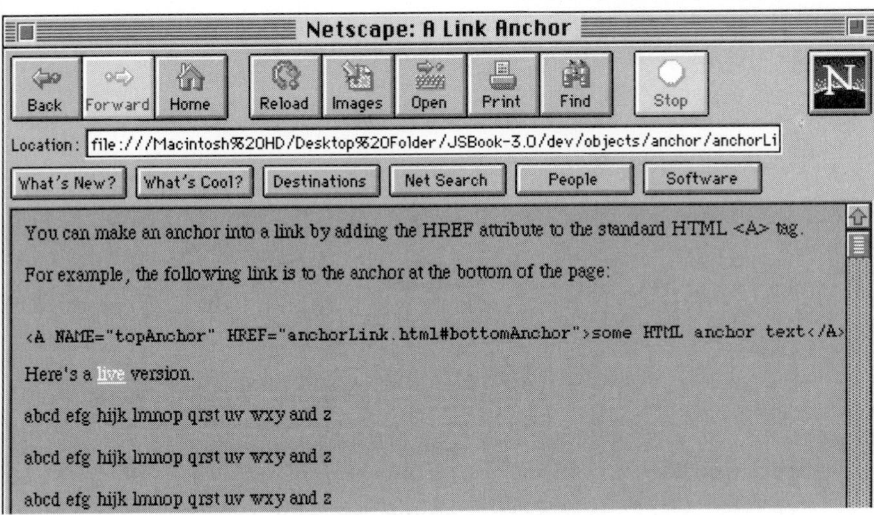

Figure 7–11 Result of loading the `anchorLink.html` script

Clicking on the link takes you to the bottom of the page. At the bottom of the page is another link, shown in Figure 7–12, that takes you back to the top of the page.

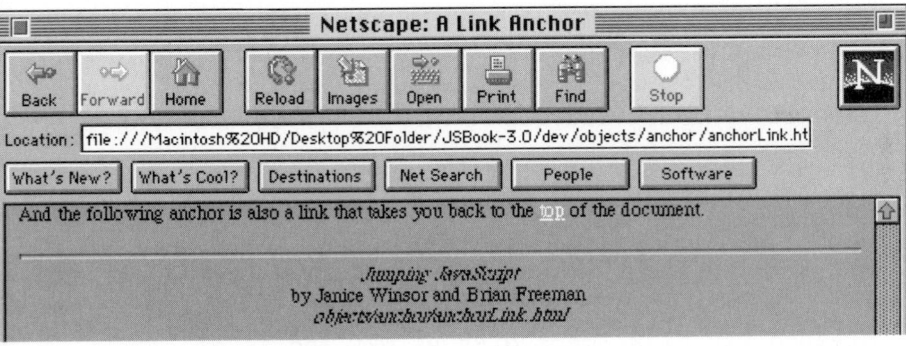

Figure 7–12 Anchor that is a link

Example of a Link to Another Window

The following `anchorTarget.html` script shows how you can create a link to another window. This example does not use any JavaScript objects or properties.

```
<!--
       anchorTarget.html

    This example shows an anchor that is a
    link to another window.
-->
<HTML>
<HEAD>
<TITLE>A Link to Another Window</TITLE>
</HEAD>
<BODY>

<P>An anchor that is a link can load the
document into another window when you include
the TARGET attribute in the Anchor tag. If the
target window does not exist, it is
created. Notice that once the window
is created, any subsequent links to the window
do not create another window but instead
go to the new location.</P>

<P>The following anchor links to a window named
"myWindow".
<PRE>
&lt;A NAME="topAnchor"
HREF="anchorTarget.html#bottomAnchor"
TARGET="myWindow"&gt;some HTML anchor text&lt;/A&gt;
</PRE>

Here's a <A NAME="topAnchor"
HREF="anchorTarget.html#bottomAnchor"
TARGET="myWindow">live</A> version.

<P>abcd efg hijk lmnop qrst uv wxy and z</P>
...
<P>abcd efg hijk lmnop qrst uv wxy and z</P>

<P>And the following anchor is also a link that
takes you back to the <A NAME="bottomAnchor"
HREF="anchorTarget.html#topAnchor">top</A> of the
document.</P>

</BODY>
</HTML>
```

Figure 7–13 shows the result of loading the `anchorTarget.html` script.

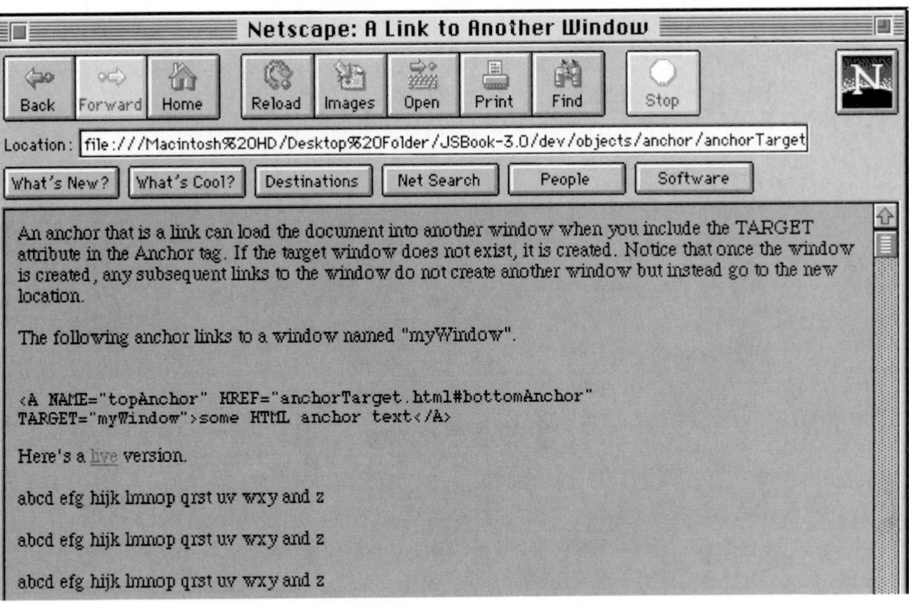

Figure 7–13 Result of loading the `anchorTarget.html` script

Notice that when you click on the live anchor, the browser opens a new window with a copy of the same document. When you click on any of the anchors in the second live window, you always remain within that window.

Another thing to notice is that when you click on the top anchor, in spite of what the text in the window says, it does not actually take you back to the top of the document. Instead, it takes you to the anchor at the top of the window, as shown in Figure 7–14. If you wanted the link to take you to the first line in the document, you would need to add a link at that location in the HTML file. Be sure to test your anchors and make sure that they are doing what you expect.

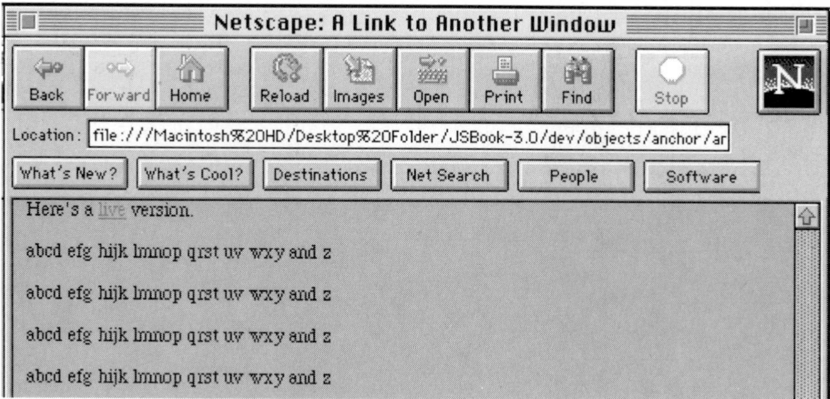

Figure 7–14 Going to the top anchor

Example of Using Anchors to Move Around in a Document

The previous anchor examples provided a review of the basic HTML tags you can use to create anchors. The following `anchors.html` script uses the JavaScript `document.anchors.length` property to enable users to click on buttons to navigate between headings in a page. It also uses the `location` object, which is explained fully in Chapter 12, "Controlling Location."

```
<!--
         anchors.html

     This example shows the use of anchors in a
     document. The anchors are named to correspond
     to their value in the anchors array. 0 and
     (anchors.length - 1) are used to bound the
     Previous and Next buttons for each section.

-->

<HTML>
<HEAD>
<TITLE>Document Anchors </TITLE>
<SCRIPT LANGUAGE="JavaScript">
<!-- HIDE FROM OLD BROWSERS

// change location to the previous anchor until
// the top of the document is reached.
function prevAnchor(currentAnchor) {
  if (currentAnchor <= 0) {
    return
```

```
  } else {
    window.location.hash = currentAnchor - 1
  }
}

// change location to the next anchor until
// the end of the document is reached.
function nextAnchor(currentAnchor) {
  if (currentAnchor >= (document.anchors.length - 1)) {
    return
  } else {
    window.location.hash = currentAnchor + 1
  }
}

// STOP HIDING -->
</SCRIPT>
</HEAD>

<BODY>

<A NAME="0"><H1>Heading Zero</H1>
<FORM>
<INPUT TYPE="button" NAME="prev" VALUE="Previous"
onClick="prevAnchor(0)">
<INPUT TYPE="button" NAME="next" VALUE="Next"
onClick="nextAnchor(0)">
</FORM>
<H2>Filler</H2>
<P>More filler...</P>
<H3>Filler</H3>
<P>More filler...</P>

<H2>Filler</H2>
<P>More filler...</P>
<H3>Filler</H3>
<P>More filler...</P>

<A NAME="1"><H1>Heading One</H1>
<FORM>
<INPUT TYPE="button" NAME="prev" VALUE="Previous"
onClick="prevAnchor(1)">
<INPUT TYPE="button" NAME="next" VALUE="Next"
onClick="nextAnchor(1)">
```

```
</FORM>
<H2>Filler</H2>
<P>More filler...</P>
<H3>Filler</H3>
<P>More filler...</P>

<H2>Filler</H2>
<P>More filler...</P>
<H3>Filler</H3>
<P>More filler...</P>

<A NAME="2"><H1>Heading Two</H1>
<FORM>
<INPUT TYPE="button" NAME="prev" VALUE="Previous"
onClick="prevAnchor(2)">
<INPUT TYPE="button" NAME="next" VALUE="Next"
onClick="nextAnchor(2)">
</FORM>
...
<P>More filler...</P>

</BODY>
</HTML>
```

Figure 7–15 shows the result of loading the `anchors.html` script.

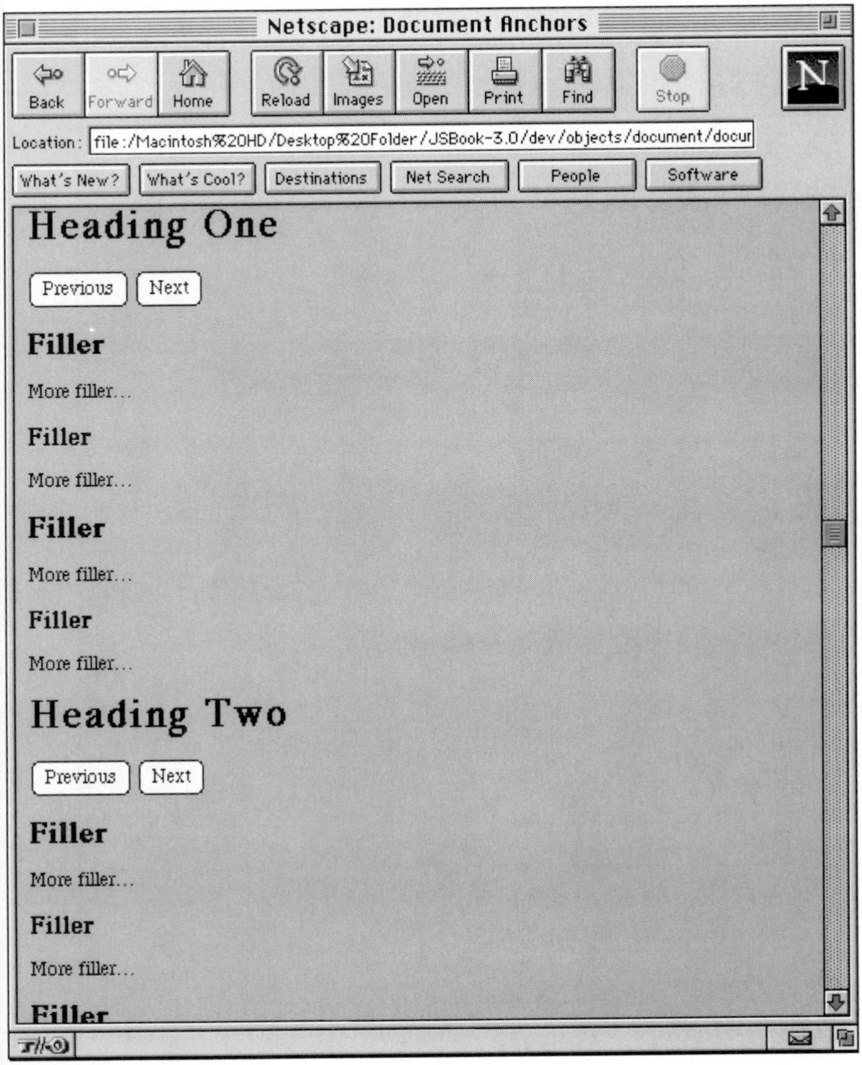

Figure 7–15 Result of loading the `anchors.html` script

Clicking on the Next button moves the next heading to the top of the window, as shown in Figure 7–16. Clicking on the Previous button, takes you back to the previous heading. When you are at the first heading, the Previous button checks to see if you're at the top of the document and does nothing. When you are at the last heading, the Next button checks to see if you're at the bottom of the document and does nothing.

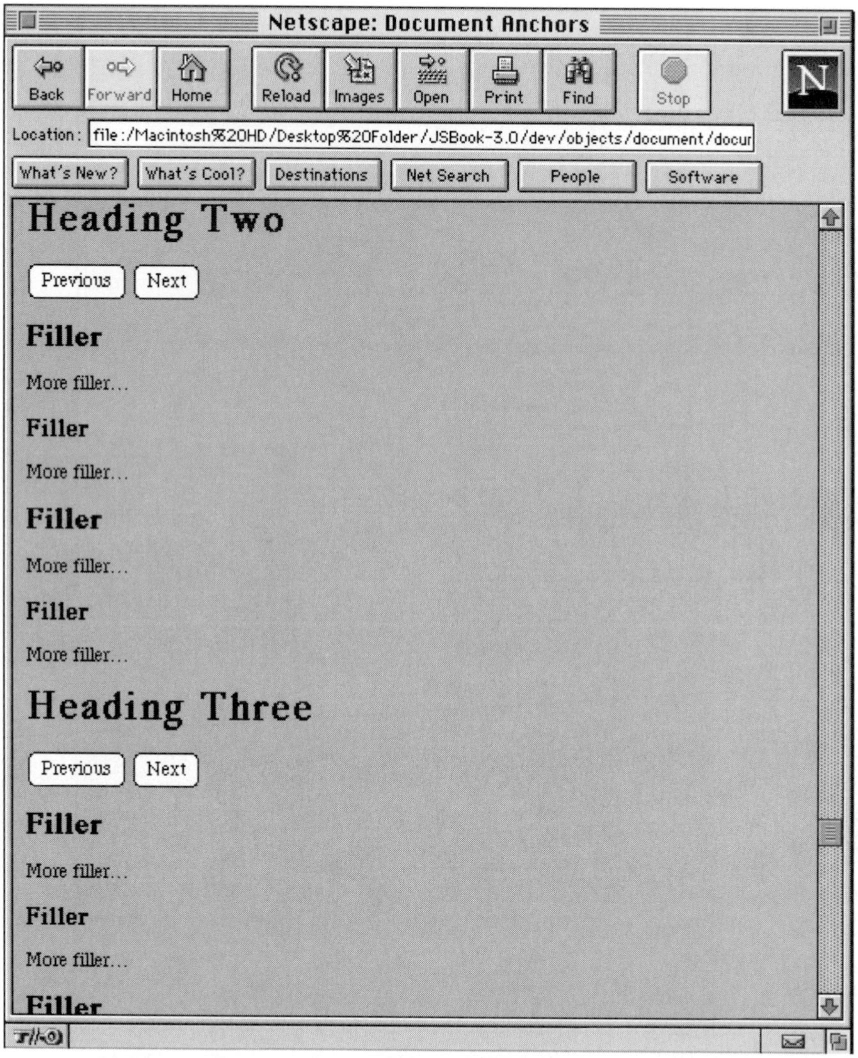

Figure 7–16 Using anchors to move around in a document

Example of Using the Anchors Array

The scripts in the following example use the `document.anchors[]` array to display the values returned for each anchor in the document.

The following `index.html` script creates the frames for the example and loads the `data.html` and `anchors.html` scripts.

```
<!--
   objects/anchor/anchors/index.html

    This frameset defines the page for the
    anchors example.
-->
<HTML>
<HEAD>
<TITLE>Document Anchors</TITLE>
</HEAD>

<FRAMESET COLS="30%,70%">
  <FRAME NAME="anchorsFrame" SRC="anchors.html">
  <FRAME NAME="targetFrame" SRC="data.html">
</FRAMESET>

</HTML>
```

Here is the anchors.html script.

```
<!--
       objects/anchor/anchors/anchors.html

    This example contains anchors. Clicking on
    Display Anchors displays an alert dialog that
    lists the contents of the anchors array for
    this document.
-->

<HTML>
<HEAD>
<!-- Include getProps() -->
<SCRIPT SRC="../../../debug/getProps.js"></SCRIPT>

<SCRIPT LANGUAGE="JavaScript">
<!-- HIDE FROM OLD BROWSERS

// display_anchors
//   Display the contents of the anchors array in
//   an alert dialog.
//
function display_anchors(doc) {
  var msg_str = ""
  var numAnchors = doc.anchors.length
```

```
  msg_str += "\n"
  msg_str += "The anchors array contains:\n"
  for (var i=0; i < numAnchors; i++) {
    msg_str += "     "
    msg_str += "anchors[" + i + "] = "
    msg_str += doc.anchors[i]
    msg_str += "\n"
  }
  alert(unescape(msg_str))
}
// STOP HIDING -->
</SCRIPT>
</HEAD>

<BODY>
<H1>TOC</H1>

<DL>
<DT>
<A HREF="data.html#1"
 TARGET="targetFrame"
>Section One</a>
</DT>

<DT>
<A HREF="data.html#2"
 TARGET="targetFrame"
>Section Two</a>
</DT>

<DT>
<A HREF="data.html#3"
 TARGET="targetFrame"
>Section Three</a>
</DT>

<DT>
<A HREF="data.html#4"
 TARGET="targetFrame"
>Section Four</a>
</DT>

<FORM>
<INPUT TYPE="button" VALUE="Display Anchors"
```

```
onClick="display_anchors(top.frames[1].document)">
</FORM>
</BODY>
</HTML>
```

And here is the data.html script.

```
<!--
       data.html

    Document for the anchor array
    example.
-->

<HTML>
<HEAD>
<TITLE>Location Hash</TITLE>
<BODY>
<CENTER>
<H1>A Gothic Tale</H1>
</CENTER>

<A NAME="S1"><H2>Section One</H2></a>
<P>It was a dark and stormy night. All of the
beagles were safely in their kennels. The bats
flew around the tower, squeaking frantically.</P>

<P>Dosolina stood at the open window wistfully
gazing out over the moors, her long dark tresses
blowing wildly as the wind gusted. Piotor was
long overdue. There were evil things afoot in the
night, and she feared greatly for his safety.</P>

<A NAME="S2"><H2>Section Two</H2></a>
<P>There was something unnatural about the light
flickering through the clouds. The beagles bugled
their howls, protesting their captivity. The dogs
wanted to be out and about, investigating the
strange smells and sensations that were drifting
tantalizingly towards them on the gusting
wind.</P>

<A NAME="S3"><H2>Section Three</H2></a>
<P>Piotor felt the hot breath of the
ravening monsters as they followed closely
```

```
on his heels. He feared for his very life.
He hoped that he could reach the safety
of the tower in the distance before his
strength gave out and the monsters were
upon him. </P>

<A NAME="S4"><H2>Section Four</H2></a>
<P>The skies were clear and the weather balmy,
giving the illusion of innocence.  Dosolina and
Piotor walked with determined steps across the
moors, searching for traces of the monsters that
continuously dogged their very existence.</P>

<P>"Oh, here's a footprint," Piotor cried. "I knew
that there was something tangible in that horrid
blackness that was following me.</P>

<P>"And here's a piece of something ...  Ugh, it
is so disgusting," said Dosolina.  "What is this
awful curse that prevents us from being like
normal folks?"</P>

<P>"We must be brave, and not let them know how
frightened we really are."</P>

</BODY>
</HTML>
```

Figure 7–17 shows the result of loading the anchors example `index.html` script.

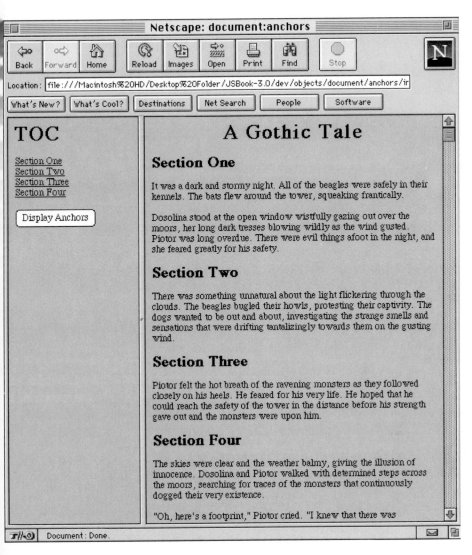

Figure 7–17 Result of loading the `anchors/index.html` script

You can click on the links in the TOC to move each of the four sections to the top of the right frame. When you click on the Display Anchors button, an alert is displayed, showing the values for each of the anchors in the array, as shown in Figure 7–18.

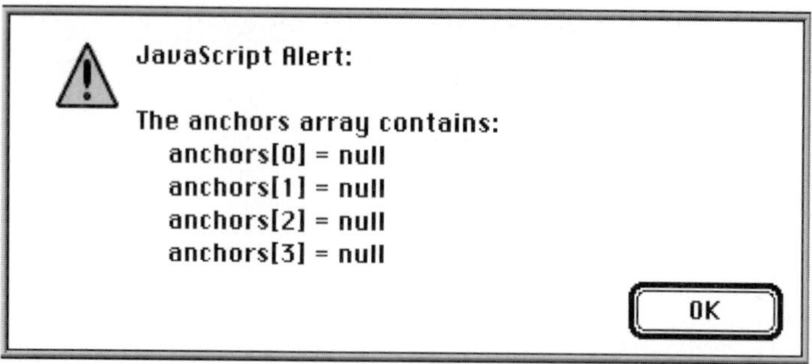

Figure 7–18 Anchors array alert

Working with the links Property

Like the `anchors` property, the `links` property is an array that contains the value of each link on the page in the order in which it was defined in the HTML code. The `links` property is useful if you have links in a document.

Property	Value	Gettable	Settable
links()	array of link objects	Yes	No

You can use the `document.links.length` property to count the number of anchors and links in a document.

Example of Using the links Property

The following `documentLinks.html` script contains two links. When you click on the Display document.links button, another window opens, displaying the values for the links in the document. The `document.links.length` property provides a count of these links.

```
<!--
        documentLinks.html

    This example dumps the contents of the
    document.links array.
-->

<HTML>
<HEAD>
<TITLE>Document Links</TITLE>
<!-- Include for displayPropsWin() -->
```

```
<SCRIPT SRC="../../debug/getProps.js"></SCRIPT>
<!--
    Include displayPropsWin(), which displays
    the properties of a given object in a new
    window.
-->
<SCRIPT SRC="../../debug/displayPropsWin.js">
</SCRIPT>
</HEAD>
<BODY>

<P>Here are some sample links:</P>
<UL>
<LI><A HREF="http://home.mcom.com">Netscape</A>
<LI><A HREF="http://www.sun.com">Sun</A>
</UL>

<CENTER><FORM>
<INPUT TYPE="button" NAME="docProps"
VALUE="Display document.links"
onClick="displayPropsWin(document.links,
   'document.links')">
</FORM></CENTER>

</BODY>
</HTML>
```

Figure 7–19 shows the result of loading the `documentLinks.html` script.

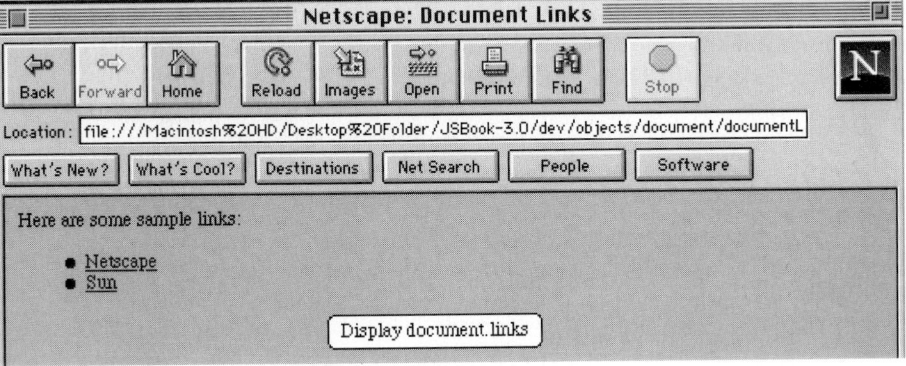

Figure 7–19 Result of loading the `documentLinks.html` script

When you click on the Display document.links button, a window opens, displaying the values for the `document.links` and `document.links.length` properties, as shown in Figure 7–20.

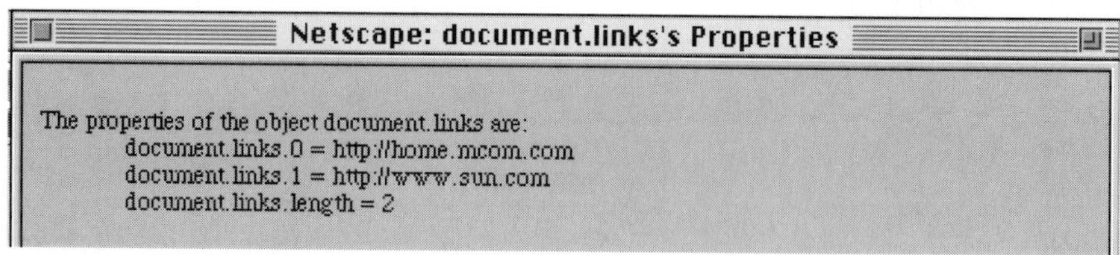

Figure 7–20 Document `links` properties

Referencing Forms in a Document

The `document.forms` property is an array of objects that corresponds to all the forms in a document. These forms are specified by using the `<FORM></FORM>` HTML tag.

Property	Value	Gettable	Settable
forms	array of forms in the document	Yes	No

Example of Referencing Forms in a Document

The following `documentForms.html` script includes the `getProps.js` script to display the properties of the forms in this simple document. The `getProps.js` script is described in Chapter 4, "Debugging Scripts."

```
<!--
         documentForms.html

    This example dumps the contents of the
    document.forms array.
-->

<HTML>
<HEAD>
<TITLE>Document Forms</TITLE>
<!-- Include for displayPropsWin() -->
<SCRIPT SRC="../../debug/getProps.js"></SCRIPT>
```

```
<!--
    Include displayPropsWin(), which displays
    the properties of a given object in a new
    window.
-->
<SCRIPT SRC="../../debug/displayPropsWin.js">
</SCRIPT>
</HEAD>
<BODY>

<CENTER><FORM>
<INPUT TYPE="button" NAME="docProps"
VALUE="Display document.forms"
onClick="displayPropsWin(document.forms,'document.forms')
">
</FORM></CENTER>

</BODY>
</HTML>
```

Figure 7–21 shows the result of loading the `documentForms.html` script.

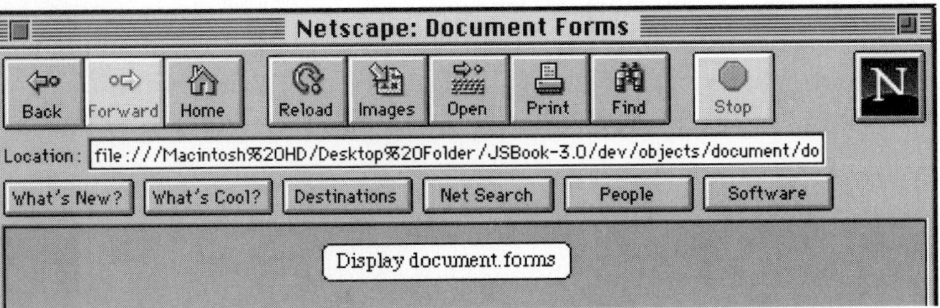

Figure 7–21 Result of loading the `documentForms.html` script

When you click on the Display document.forms button, a new window opens and displays the `document.forms` property information, as shown in Figure 7–22.

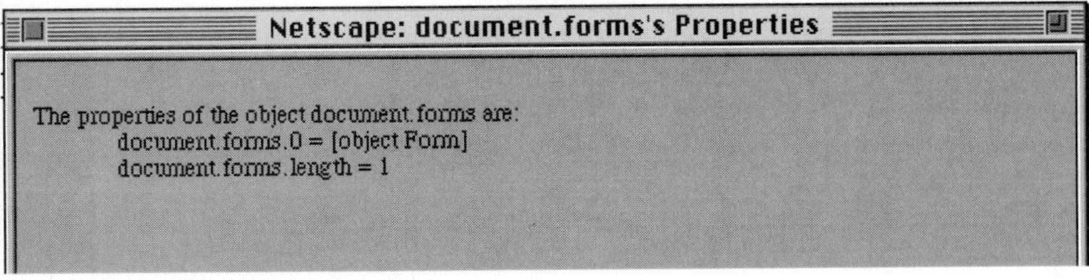

Figure 7–22 Forms property information

This document contains one form. Because forms are an object on their own, we'll take a more detailed look at forms in Chapter 24, "Using Forms to Send Data to a Server."

Referencing Images in a Document

The Navigator 3.0 release provides an `image` object that is created automatically when you include images in an HTML document, using the `<IMG>` HTML tag. For a complete description of the `image` object, see Chapter 9, "Working with Images." As part of this new functionality, the document object now has an `images` property. The `images` property is an array that contains the value of each image on the page in the order in which it was defined in the HTML code.

Property	Value	Gettable	Settable
images	array of images in the document	Yes	No

Refer to the HTML Brushup box for the specific syntax of the `<IMG>` HTML tag.

Example of Using the Images Array

The following `documentImages.html` script loads all of the JPEG files from the images directory. When you click on the Display document.images button, a new window displays the images array information.

```
<!--
          documentImages.html

    This example dumps the contents of the
    document.images array.
-->

<HTML>
<HEAD>
<TITLE>Document Images</TITLE>
<!-- Include for displayPropsWin() -->
<SCRIPT SRC="../../debug/getProps.js"></SCRIPT>
<!--
    Include displayPropsWin(), which displays
    the properties of a given object in a new
    window.
-->
<SCRIPT SRC="../../debug/displayPropsWin.js">
```

HTML Brushup — Incorporating Images

You define which images to incorporate by setting the attributes of the <IMG> HTML tag. The <IMG> tag has the following attributes:

<IMG>

SRC = "*ImageURL*"

(LOWSRC = "*LowResImageURL*")

NAME = "*ImageName*"

WIDTH = "*Pixels*" | "*PercentValue*"

HEIGHT = "*Pixels*" | "*PercentValue*"

(HSPACE = "*Pixels*")

(VSPACE = "*Pixels*")

(BORDER = "*Pixels*")

(ALIGN = "left" | "right" | "top" | "absmiddle" | "absbottom" | "texttop" | "middle" | "baseline" | "bottom")

(ALT = "*DescriptionOfImage*")

(ISMAP)

(USEMAP = "*#AreaMapName*")

(onLoad = "*JavaScript code*")

(onAbort = "*JavaScript code*")

(onError = "*JavaScript code*")

>

```
</SCRIPT>
</HEAD>
<BODY>

<CENTER>
<TABLE BORDER=4>
<CAPTION> [408x264] AyersRock.jpg </CAPTION>
<TR><TD><IMG SRC="../../images/AyersRock.jpg"
NAME="AyersRock" WIDTH=408 HEIGHT=264></TD></TR>
</TABLE><BR><BR>
<TABLE BORDER=4>
<CAPTION> [312x216] Badger.jpg </CAPTION>
<TR><TD><IMG SRC="../../images/Badger.jpg"
NAME="Badger" WIDTH=312 HEIGHT=216></TD></TR>
</TABLE><BR><BR>
<TABLE BORDER=4>
...
<CENTER><FORM>
<INPUT TYPE="button" NAME="imagesProps"
VALUE="Display document.images"
onClick="displayPropsWin(document.images,'document.images
')">
</FORM></CENTER>

</BODY>
</HTML>
```

Figure 7–23 shows the result of loading the `documentImages.html` script.

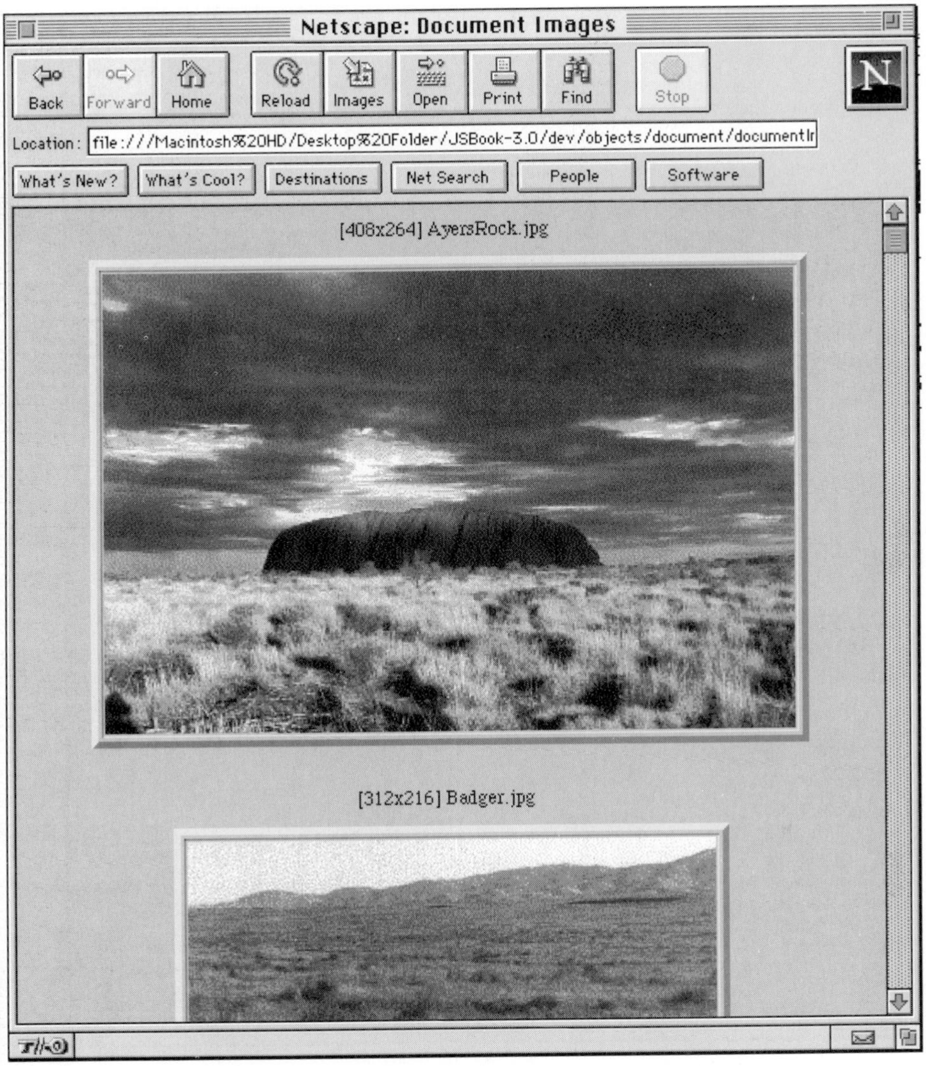

Figure 7–23 Result of loading the `documentImages.html` script

When you click on the Display document.images button, a new window opens and displays the `images` property information, as shown in Figure 7–24.

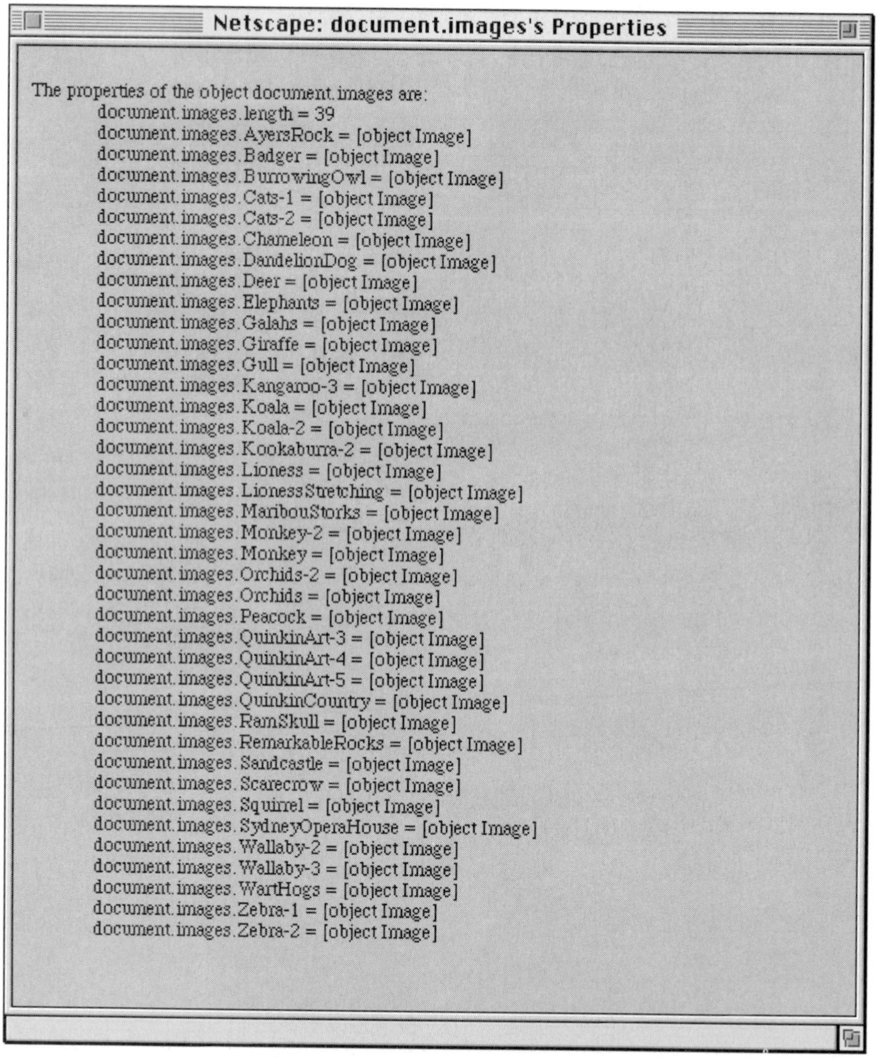

Netscape: document.images's Properties

The properties of the object document.images are:

document.images.length = 39
document.images.AyersRock = [object Image]
document.images.Badger = [object Image]
document.images.BurrowingOwl = [object Image]
document.images.Cats-1 = [object Image]
document.images.Cats-2 = [object Image]
document.images.Chameleon = [object Image]
document.images.DandelionDog = [object Image]
document.images.Deer = [object Image]
document.images.Elephants = [object Image]
document.images.Galahs = [object Image]
document.images.Giraffe = [object Image]
document.images.Gull = [object Image]
document.images.Kangaroo-3 = [object Image]
document.images.Koala = [object Image]
document.images.Koala-2 = [object Image]
document.images.Kookaburra-2 = [object Image]
document.images.Lioness = [object Image]
document.images.LionessStretching = [object Image]
document.images.MaribouStorks = [object Image]
document.images.Monkey-2 = [object Image]
document.images.Monkey = [object Image]
document.images.Orchids-2 = [object Image]
document.images.Orchids = [object Image]
document.images.Peacock = [object Image]
document.images.QuinkinArt-3 = [object Image]
document.images.QuinkinArt-4 = [object Image]
document.images.QuinkinArt-5 = [object Image]
document.images.QuinkinCountry = [object Image]
document.images.RamSkull = [object Image]
document.images.RemarkableRocks = [object Image]
document.images.Sandcastle = [object Image]
document.images.Scarecrow = [object Image]
document.images.Squirrel = [object Image]
document.images.SydneyOperaHouse = [object Image]
document.images.Wallaby-2 = [object Image]
document.images.Wallaby-3 = [object Image]
document.images.WartHogs = [object Image]
document.images.Zebra-1 = [object Image]
document.images.Zebra-2 = [object Image]

Figure 7–24 Document `images` array information

Referencing Java Applets in a Document

A Java *applet* is an application written in the Java language that requires a Java-aware browser such as Netscape Navigator, version 2.0 or later, to run. This property is an array that contains the value of each applet on the page in the order in which it was defined in the HTML code.

Property	Value	Gettable	Settable
applets	array of applets in a document	Yes	No

You can use the `applet` object to read and write all public variables and methods in the applet. You define applets with the `<APPLET></APPLET>` HTML tags. Refer to the HTML Brushup box for the specific syntax.

Example of Including a Java Applet

The following `documentApplets.html` script includes a Java applet in a page and also provides a button that you can click on to display the properties for the applet.

```
<!--
        documentApplets.html

    This example dumps the contents of the
    document.applets array.
-->

<HTML>
<HEAD>
<TITLE>Document Applets</TITLE>
<!-- Include for displayPropsWin() -->
<SCRIPT SRC="../../../debug/getProps.js"></SCRIPT>
<!--
    Include displayPropsWin(), which displays
    the properties of a given object in a new
    window.
-->
<SCRIPT SRC="../../../debug/displayPropsWin.js">
</SCRIPT>
</HEAD>
<BODY>
```

HTML Brushup — Incorporating Java Applets

You define which applets to incorporate by setting the attributes of the <APPLET></APPLET> HTML tags. Note that the <APPLET> tag replaces the <APP> tag as the way to identify and include a Java application.

<APPLET

CODE = "*filename*.class"

WIDTH= *number*

HEIGHT = *number*

(CODEBASE = "*base directory for the applet*")

(ALT = "*alternative character data that is displayed if the browser cannot run the applet*")

(NAME = "*name for the applet instance*")

(ALIGN = LEFT | RIGHT | TOP | TEXTTOP | MIDDLE | ABSMIDDLE | BASELINE | BOTTOM | ABSBOTTOM)

(VSPACE= *number*)

(HSPACE = *number*)>

(ARCHIVE=*JavaClass.zip*)

<PARAM NAME = "*NameOfParameter*" VALUE = "*Value*">

</APPLET>

The minimum set of attributes you can use is CODE, WIDTH, and HEIGHT. CODE provides the name of the file relative to the base URL of the applet that contains the compiled Applet subclass. You cannot reference an applet by using an absolute URL. You can use the optional CODEBASE attribute to define the base directory for the applet.

WIDTH and HEIGHT define, in pixels, the initial width and height of the applet display area.

The attributes included in square brackets (( )) are optional. You can use none, some, or all of these optional attributes for any applet. The VSPACE and HSPACE attributes specify the reserved space around the applet in pixels. You can use the NAME attribute to specify a name for the instance of the applet, to allow applets on the same page to communicate with each other.

You can also include <PARAM> tags and any other elements that would have been allowed at this point in the document within the <APPLET></APPLET> tags. The <PARAM> tag has two attributes: NAME is the name of the parameter, and VALUE is obtained by the applet, using the getParameter() method.

```
<APPLET CODE="Animator.class" width=460 height=160>
<PARAM NAME=imagesource VALUE="images/Beans">
<PARAM NAME=backgroundcolor VALUE="0xc0c0c0">
<PARAM NAME=endimage VALUE=10>
<PARAM NAME=soundsource VALUE="audio">
<PARAM NAME=soundtrack VALUE="spacemusic.au">
<PARAM NAME=sounds
VALUE="1.au|2.au|3.au|4.au|5.au|6.au|7.au|8.au|9.au|0.au"
>
<PARAM NAME=pause VALUE=200>
</APPLET>

<P><A HREF="Animator.java">The source.</A></P>

<CENTER><FORM>
<INPUT TYPE="button" NAME="appletProps"
VALUE="Display document.applets"
onClick="displayPropsWin(document.applets,
  'document.applets')">
</FORM></CENTER>

</BODY>
</HTML>
```

Figure 7–25 shows the result of loading the `documentApplets.html` script.

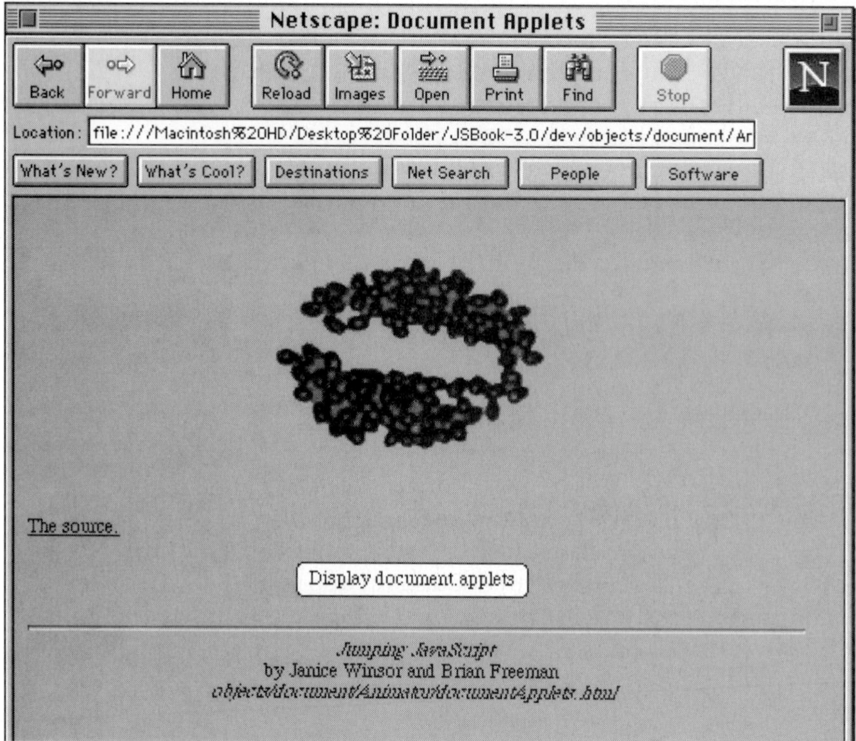

Figure 7–25 Result of loading the `documentApplets.html` script

To start the animation, simply click on the page. To stop the animation, you have to load another page. When you click on the Display document.applets button, a window opens, displaying the applet properties, as shown in Figure 7–26.

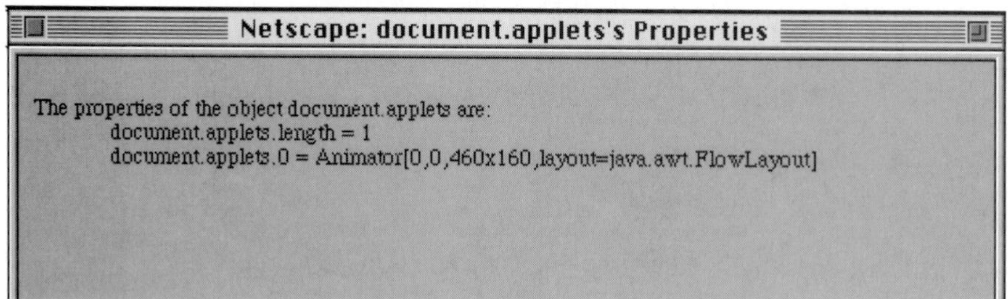

Figure 7–26 Applet properties

Clicking on The source link displays the source for the applet, as shown in Figure 7–27.

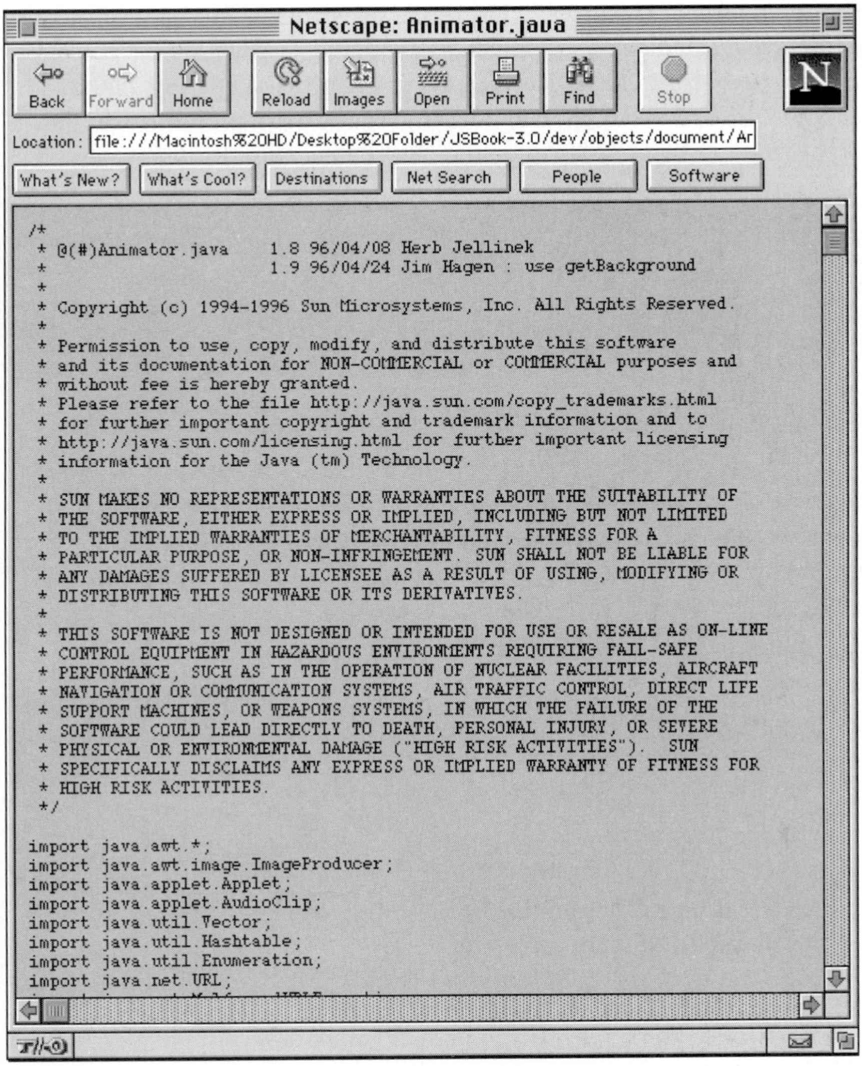

Netscape: Animator.java

Back Forward Home Reload Images Open Print Find Stop

Location: file:///Macintosh%20HD/Desktop%20Folder/JSBook-3.0/dev/objects/document/Ar

What's New? What's Cool? Destinations Net Search People Software

```
/*
 * @(#)Animator.java    1.8 96/04/08 Herb Jellinek
 *                      1.9 96/04/24 Jim Hagen : use getBackground
 *
 * Copyright (c) 1994-1996 Sun Microsystems, Inc. All Rights Reserved.
 *
 * Permission to use, copy, modify, and distribute this software
 * and its documentation for NON-COMMERCIAL or COMMERCIAL purposes and
 * without fee is hereby granted.
 * Please refer to the file http://java.sun.com/copy_trademarks.html
 * for further important copyright and trademark information and to
 * http://java.sun.com/licensing.html for further important licensing
 * information for the Java (tm) Technology.
 *
 * SUN MAKES NO REPRESENTATIONS OR WARRANTIES ABOUT THE SUITABILITY OF
 * THE SOFTWARE, EITHER EXPRESS OR IMPLIED, INCLUDING BUT NOT LIMITED
 * TO THE IMPLIED WARRANTIES OF MERCHANTABILITY, FITNESS FOR A
 * PARTICULAR PURPOSE, OR NON-INFRINGEMENT. SUN SHALL NOT BE LIABLE FOR
 * ANY DAMAGES SUFFERED BY LICENSEE AS A RESULT OF USING, MODIFYING OR
 * DISTRIBUTING THIS SOFTWARE OR ITS DERIVATIVES.
 *
 * THIS SOFTWARE IS NOT DESIGNED OR INTENDED FOR USE OR RESALE AS ON-LINE
 * CONTROL EQUIPMENT IN HAZARDOUS ENVIRONMENTS REQUIRING FAIL-SAFE
 * PERFORMANCE, SUCH AS IN THE OPERATION OF NUCLEAR FACILITIES, AIRCRAFT
 * NAVIGATION OR COMMUNICATION SYSTEMS, AIR TRAFFIC CONTROL, DIRECT LIFE
 * SUPPORT MACHINES, OR WEAPONS SYSTEMS, IN WHICH THE FAILURE OF THE
 * SOFTWARE COULD LEAD DIRECTLY TO DEATH, PERSONAL INJURY, OR SEVERE
 * PHYSICAL OR ENVIRONMENTAL DAMAGE ("HIGH RISK ACTIVITIES").  SUN
 * SPECIFICALLY DISCLAIMS ANY EXPRESS OR IMPLIED WARRANTY OF FITNESS FOR
 * HIGH RISK ACTIVITIES.
 */

import java.awt.*;
import java.awt.image.ImageProducer;
import java.applet.Applet;
import java.applet.AudioClip;
import java.util.Vector;
import java.util.Hashtable;
import java.util.Enumeration;
import java.net.URL;
```

Figure 7–27 Source for `Animator.java`

Finding Plug-ins Embedded in a Document

A plug-in is an application that enhances and expands the capability of another application and is completely integrated within it so that the user is not aware that a plug-in is being used.

The embeds and plugin properties are arrays that contains the value of each plug-in on the page in the order in which it was defined in the HTML code. Both of these properties are identical. The embeds property uses the name of the HTML tag that is used to incorporate plug-ins. The plugin property uses the name of the resource that is defined by the <EMBED></EMBED> HTML tags.

Property	Value	Gettable	Settable
embeds	array	Yes	No
plugins	array	Yes	No

You define plug-ins by using the HTML <EMBED></EMBED> tags. Refer to the HTML Brushup box for the specific syntax.

The document.embeds[ ] and document.plugins[ ] arrays enable you to control the plug-ins and access the data displayed by those plug-ins. The arbitrary attributes that you can define vary from one plug-in to another and must be obtained from the author of each plug-in.

Example of Counting Plug-Ins

The following documentPlugins.html script includes an AVI file in a page and also provides a button that you can click on to display the properties for the plug-in.

```
<!--
         documentPlugins.html

    This example dumps the contents of the
    document.plugins array.
-->

<HTML>
<HEAD>
<TITLE>Document Plugins</TITLE>
<!-- Include for displayPropsWin() -->
<SCRIPT SRC="../../debug/getProps.js"></SCRIPT>

<!--
    Include displayPropsWin(), which displays
    the properties of a given object in a new
    window.
-->
<SCRIPT SRC="../../debug/displayPropsWin.js">
```

HTML Brushup — Embedding Plug-Ins

You define which arbitrary objects you incorporate by setting the attributes of the <EMBED></EMBED> HTML tags. Embedded objects are supported by application-specific plug-ins.

<EMBED

SRC = "*Source URL*"

WIDTH= *number in pixels for the embedded object*

HEIGHT = *number in pixels for the embedded object*

attribute_1="..."

attribute_2="..."

attribute_3="...">

characters

</EMBED>

WIDTH and HEIGHT define, in pixels, the initial width and height of the plug-in display area.

Embedded objects can take arbitrary attributes.

Some examples of plug-in applications are:

- WebFX™ by Paper Software for viewing VRML
- Adobe® Acrobat™ for viewing PDF documents
- Macromedia® Director™ for multimedia
- Apple® QuickTime™ for multimedia

You activate an embedded plug-in application by double-clicking on the image.

```
</SCRIPT>
</HEAD>
<BODY>

<EMBED NAME="bar" SRC="DRAGDROP.AVI"
 WIDTH="346" HEIGHT="251">An AVI file I
found on my system that needs to be replaced
</EMBED>

<CENTER><FORM>
<INPUT TYPE="button" NAME="pluginsProps"
VALUE="Display document.plugins"
onClick="displayPropsWin(document.plugins,'document.plugi
ns')">
</FORM></CENTER>

</BODY>
</HTML>
```

Figure 7–28 shows the result of loading the `documentPlugins.html` script.

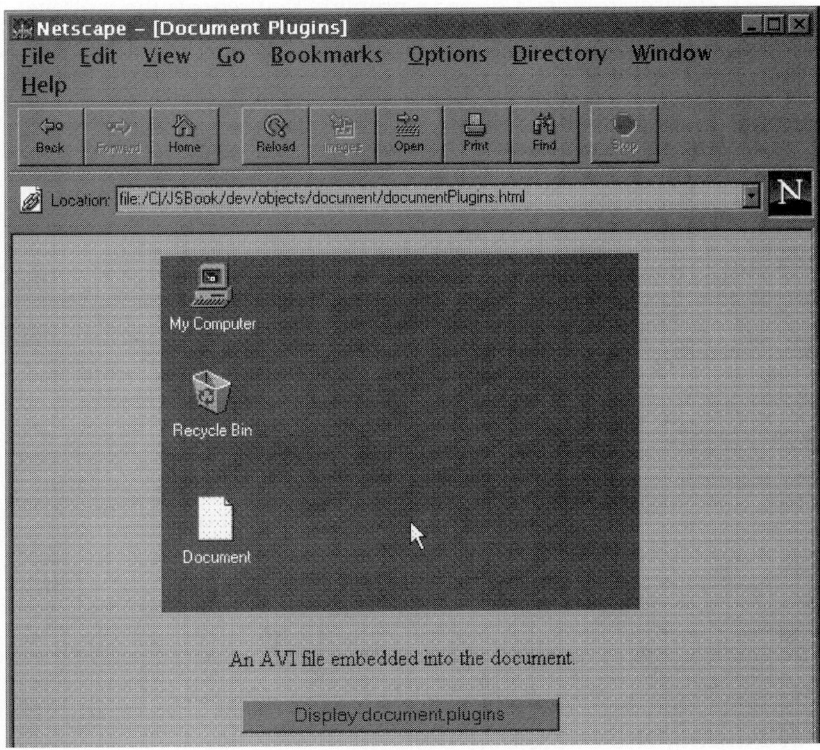

Figure 7–28 Result of loading the `documentPlugins.html` script

Clicking on the Display document.plugins button opens a new window containing a list of the values for the `plugins` array, as shown in Figure 7–29.

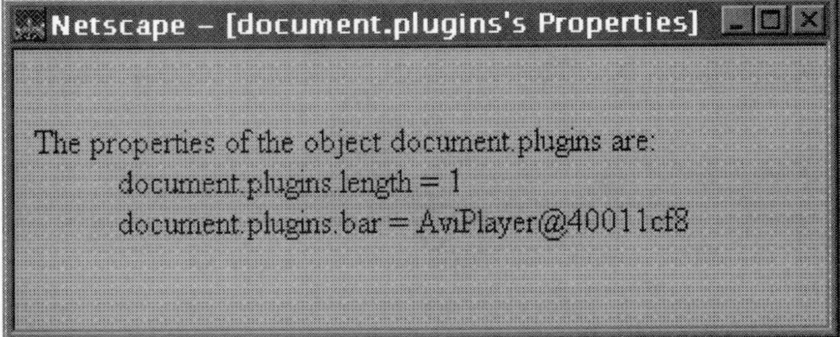

Figure 7–29 Document `plugins` values

Finding the Document Domain

The Navigator 3.0 release provides a `domain` property that returns the top-level Internet domain for a document.

Property	Value	Gettable	Settable
domain	string	Yes	Yes

When data tainting is not enabled, a script running in one window cannot read properties of another window unless that window comes from the same Web server as the host. Large Web sites with multiple servers may have problems with this restriction. The `domain` property initially returns the host name of the Web server that loaded the document. You cannot set the top-level domain with this property, but you can set the value to a domain suffix of itself.

Suppose you have two servers at a Web site, one named `services.frogpond.com` and the other named `www.frogtown.com`. You could not set the domain to `www.frogpond` for a script on `www.frogpond.com`. You can, however, set the `domain` property to `frogpond.com`, and two scripts from `services.frogpond.com` can share properties with a script from `www.frogpond.com`. For more information on data tainting, see Chapter 36, "Controlling Data Tainting."

Example of Finding the Document Domain

The following `documentDomain.html` script prints the value returned by the `document.domain` property.

```
<!--
          documentDomain.html

      Prints out the value of document.domain.
-->

<HTML>
<HEAD>
<TITLE>Document Domain</TITLE>
<SCRIPT LANGUAGE="JavaScript">
<!-- HIDE FROM OLD BROWSERS
var mstr = "<BR>"  // message string

mstr += "<P>document.domain = "
mstr += "\"" + document.domain + "\"</P>"
```

```
document.open()
document.write(unescape(mstr))
document.close()

// STOP HIDING -->
</SCRIPT>
</HEAD>

<BODY>


</BODY>
</HTML>
```

Figure 7–30 shows the result of loading the `documentDomain.html` script. The value returned by the `document.domain` property in this case is nothing because the document was loaded from a file.

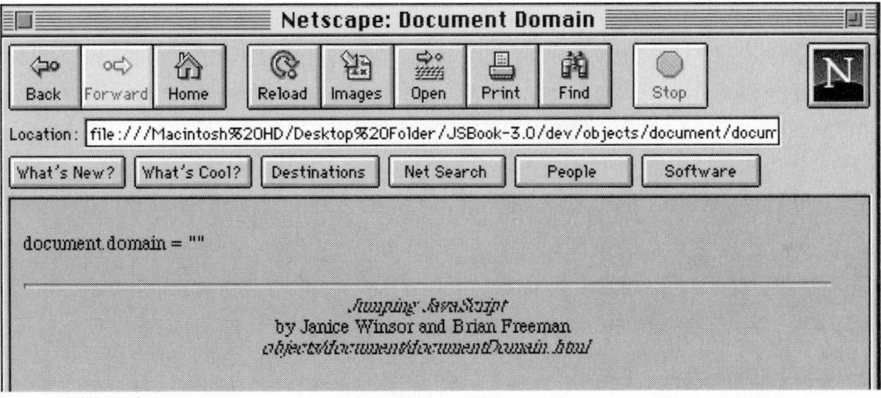

Figure 7–30 Result of loading the `documentDomain.html` script

Figure 7–31 shows the result of loading the `documentDomain.html` script on a system that does not have data tainting enabled.

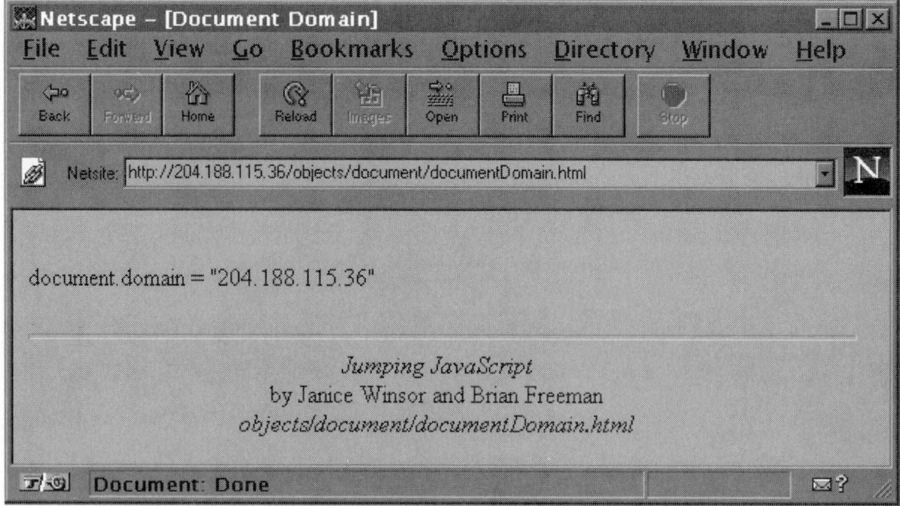

Figure 7–31 Result of loading the `documentDomain.html` script on a domain with an IP address

Notice that the example shown in Figure 7–31 returns an IP address as the document domain. The `document.domain` property returns either an IP address or a name, depending on how your network is set up. Figure 7–32 shows the results of the script when it returns a domain name.

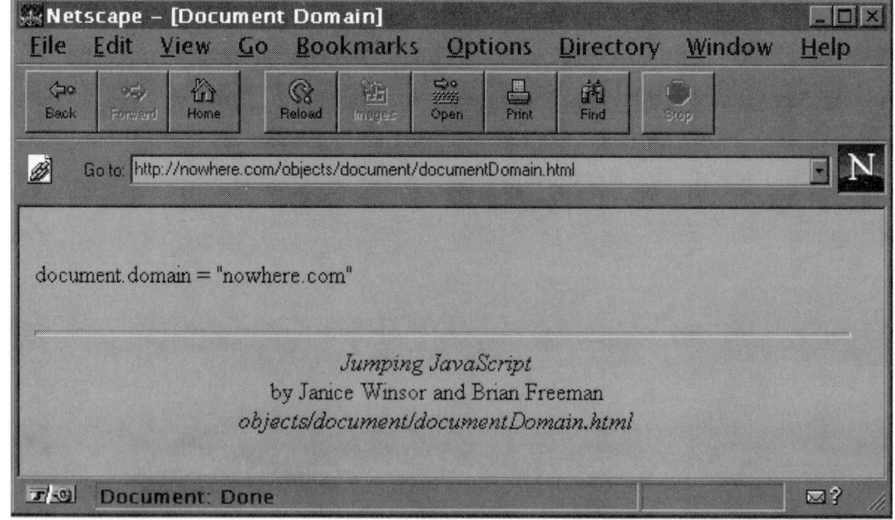

Figure 7–32 Result of loading the `documentDomain.html` script on a domain with a name

Storing User-Generated Information: the cookie Property

When you ask users to fill in information, JavaScript stores that information in a text file on the client system. To enable you to ask for information, the JavaScript language provides the `document.cookie` property. A *cookie* is an entry in a text file called `cookies.txt` (Windows and UNIX platforms) or `MagicCookie` (Macintosh) that is located in the Netscape directory. Typically, this file is used by server-side CGI scripts to store information on the client computer. The JavaScript language can only read to or write from the browser's cookie file.

Property	Value	Gettable	Settable
cookie	string	Yes	Yes

The cookie has the following internal information in addition to its string contents:

- Name of the cookie
- Expiration date
- Path name
- Domain name

Limitations of the cookie Property

The `cookie` property has the following limitations:

- The Netscape environment can create a total of only 300 cookies.
- Each cookie is limited to 4 Kbytes in size, effectively limiting the file to about 1.2 Mbytes.
- A single site can only have 30 cookie entries.
- Sites can only access cookie entries in the same domain.

Because you need to know how to manipulate text in the cookie file before you can effectively use the `cookie` property, we show you how to create a cookie in this chapter and defer any further discussion of the `cookie` property until after you learn how to manipulate text. For the complete cookie story, see Chapter 35, "Controlling Script Input and Output with the cookie Property." You can also refer to `http://home.netscape.com/newsref/std/cookie_spec.html`.

Example of Creating a cookie Property

The following `documentCookie.html` script creates a `cookie` named `ChocolateChip`. This script uses the JavaScript built-in `Date` object to get the date and sets an expiration time for the `cookie`. When the document is loaded, the `checkCookie()` function is called, and an alert displays the information about the `cookie`.

```
<!--
          documentCookie.html

    A document with a cookie. Yum ;-)
-->

<HTML>
<HEAD>
<TITLE>Document Cookie</TITLE>
<SCRIPT LANGUAGE="JavaScript">
<!-- HIDE FROM OLD BROWSERS

//
// sets a cookie for this document.
//
function setCookie() {
  var cstr    = ""      // cookie string
  var now     = null
  var expires = null

  // get the current time and set the expiration
  // time to one minute from now
  now     = new Date()
  expires = new Date(now.getTime() + 60*1000)

  // bake the cookie ;-)
  cstr += "cookieName=ChocolateChip"
  cstr += "; expires=" + expires.toGMTString()

  alert(cstr)
  document.cookie = cstr
}

//
// checkCookies
//
function checkCookies() {
```

```
    if (document.cookie.length > 0) {
      var mstr = ""

      mstr += "This document has the following "
      mstr += "cookies: \"" + document.cookie
      mstr += "\""

      alert(mstr)
    }
    else {
      setCookie()
    }
  }
  // STOP HIDING -->
  </SCRIPT>
  </HEAD>

  <BODY onLoad="checkCookies()">

  <P>More information on cookies can be found in
  the <A HREF=
  "http://home.netscape.com/newsref/std/cookie_spec.html">
  Netscape cookie specification</A>.
  </P>

  </BODY>
  </HTML>
```

Figure 7–33 shows the result of loading the `documentCookie.html` script.

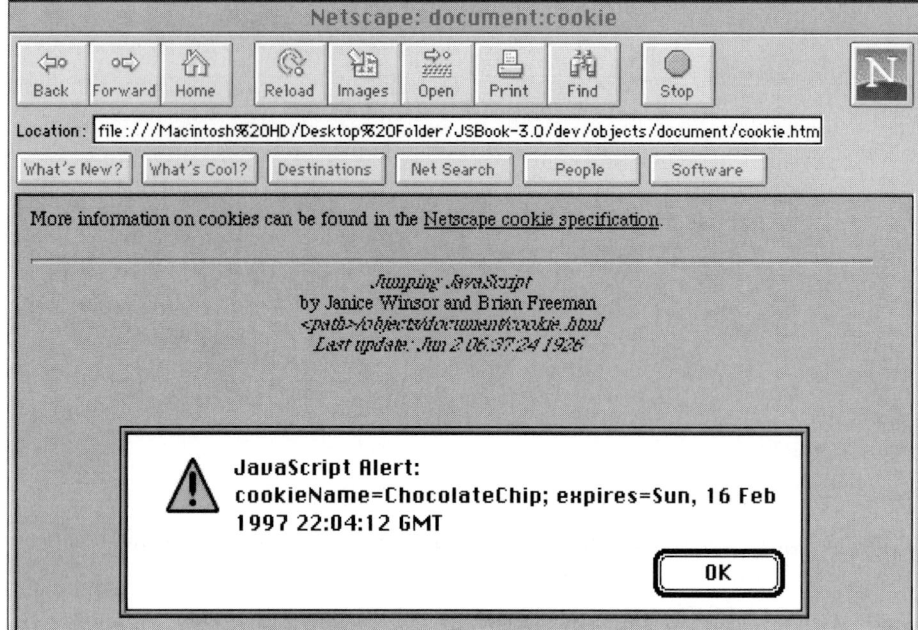

Figure 7–33 Result of loading the `documentCookie.html` script

If you want to see the Netscape specification for the `cookie` property, you can click on the Netscape cookie specification link.

Writing into a Document

As you already know, you write text into a document by using the `write()` and `writeln()` methods. The `write()` method writes the text string defined within the parentheses and quotation marks into the document without doing any formatting. The `writeln()` method writes the defined text string as a separate line in the document.

Method

write("string")

writeln("string")

Returns

Boolean true if successful

For an example of using the `write()` and `writeln()` methods, see "Example of Document Methods" on page 284.

Opening, Closing, and Clearing a Document

You use the `open()`, `close()`, and `clear()` methods to open, close, and clear windows and frames within windows.

Method

open(["mimeType'])

close()

clear()

Returns

Nothing

With the `open()` method, you can specify an optional *MIME* type. MIME is an acronym for Multipurpose Internet Mail Extensions. MIME defines the format of the contents of Internet mail messages and provides a way to include both text and attachments in message bodies. Table 7-2 lists the ***`mimeTypes`*** you can specify as an argument for the `open()` method.

Table 7-2 Mime Types

Mime Type	Description
text/html	A document containing plain ASCII text with HTML formatting. If no mimeType is specified, then text/html is used as the default.
text/plain	A document containing plain ASCII text with end-of-line characters that specify the end of lines in the display.
image/gif	A document with encoded bytes that specify a GIF header and pixel data.
image/jpeg	A document with encoded bites that specify a JPEG header and pixel data.
image/x-bitmap	A document with encoded bytes that specify a bitmap header and pixel data.
plugIn	Loads the specified plug-in and uses it as the destination for the write and writeln methods.

Use the `close()` method to close a window or frame.

Use the `clear()` method to clear the contents of a window or frame.

Example of Document Methods

The three scripts used in this example provide a set of buttons that you can use to experiment with all of the document methods. The following `index.html` script creates the frameset and loads the two additional files.

```
<!--
       objects/document/methods/index.html

    This is the frameset defining page for the
    methods example.
-->
<HTML>
<HEAD>
<TITLE>Document Methods</TITLE>
</HEAD>

<FRAMESET ROWS="20%,80%">
```

```
    <FRAME NAME="outputFrame"
           SRC="blank.html">
    <FRAME NAME="methodFrame"
           SRC="documentMethods.html">
</FRAMESET>

</HTML>
```

The following `blank.html` file is loaded in the top frame when the `index.html` script is loaded.

```
<!--
       objects/document/method/blank.html

    Creates a blank page.
-->
<HTML>
<BODY>
<SCRIPT LANGUAGE="JavaScript">
<!-- HIDE FROM OLD BROWSERS

var dstr = ""     // document string

dstr += "<HTML>"
dstr += "<BODY>"
dstr += "<P>"
dstr += "This page is blank on purpose."
dstr += "</P>"
dstr += "</BODY>"
dstr += "</HTML>"

document.open()
document.write(dstr)
document.close()

// STOP HIDING -->
</SCRIPT>
</BODY>
</HTML>
```

The following `documentMethods.html` file is loaded into the bottom frame when the `index.html` script is loaded.

```
<!--
         documentMethods.html

    This example shows all the document object
    methods.
-->

<HTML>
<HEAD>
<TITLE>Document Methods</TITLE>
</HEAD>

<BODY>

<P>As you read along, click on the buttons to see
what happens in the frame above.</P>

<P>
<FORM>
Normally, you
<INPUT TYPE="button" NAME="openButton"
 VALUE="open()" onClick=
 "top.frames[0].document.open()">
the document; then either
<INPUT TYPE="button" NAME="writeButton"
 VALUE="write()" onClick=
 "top.frames[0].document.write('write...')">
or
<INPUT TYPE="button" NAME="writelnButton"
 VALUE="writeln()" onClick=
 "top.frames[0].document.writeln('writeln...')">
to it; and finally,
<INPUT TYPE="button" NAME="closeButton"
 VALUE="close()" onClick=
 "top.frames[0].document.close()">
it. Notice the messages that appeared after the
close().
</FORM>
</P>

<P>
<FORM>
write() and writeln() look like they
do the about the same thing. writeln() adds a
```

```
newline character after the text it writes, but
HTML ignores the newline in most cases. Only with certain
tags like &lt;PRE&gt; does it make a difference.
You should see the difference here:<BR>
<INPUT TYPE="button" NAME="openButton"
 VALUE="open()" onClick=
 "top.frames[0].document.open()">,
<INPUT TYPE="button" NAME="writeButton"
 VALUE="write(<PRE>)" onClick=
 "top.frames[0].document.write('<PRE>')">,
<INPUT TYPE="button" NAME="writeButton"
 VALUE="write()" onClick=
 "top.frames[0].document.write('write...')">,
<INPUT TYPE="button" NAME="writeButton"
 VALUE="write()" onClick=
 "top.frames[0].document.write('write...')">,
<INPUT TYPE="button" NAME="writelnButton"
 VALUE="writeln()" onClick=
 "top.frames[0].document.writeln('writeln...')">,
<INPUT TYPE="button" NAME="writelnButton"
 VALUE="writeln()" onClick=
 "top.frames[0].document.writeln('writeln...')">,
<INPUT TYPE="button" NAME="writeButton"
 VALUE="write(</PRE>)" onClick=
 "top.frames[0].document.write('</PRE>')">,
<INPUT TYPE="button" NAME="closeButton"
 VALUE="close()" onClick=
 "top.frames[0].document.close()">
</FORM>
</P>

<P>
<FORM>
Sometimes you might want to
<INPUT TYPE="button" NAME="clearButton"
 VALUE="clear()" onClick=
 "top.frames[0].document.clear()">
what's in the document. To make sure it always
clears, the correct sequence is:
<INPUT TYPE="button" NAME="openButton"
 VALUE="open()" onClick=
 "top.frames[0].document.open()">,
<INPUT TYPE="button" NAME="clearButton"
 VALUE="clear()" onClick=
```

```
 "top.frames[0].document.clear()">,
<INPUT TYPE="button" NAME="closeButton"
 VALUE="close()" onClick=
 "top.frames[0].document.close()">.
</FORM>
</P>

<P>Now, it's your turn to play. Try the methods
in different sequences to see what happens.</P>

<CENTER><FORM>
<INPUT TYPE="button" NAME="openButton"
 VALUE="open()" onClick=
 "top.frames[0].document.open()">
</FORM></CENTER>
<CENTER><FORM>
<INPUT TYPE="button" NAME="writeButton"
 VALUE="write()" onClick=
 "top.frames[0].document.write('write...')">
<INPUT TYPE="button" NAME="writeButton"
 VALUE="write(<PRE>)" onClick=
 "top.frames[0].document.write('<PRE>')">
<INPUT TYPE="button" NAME="writeButton"
 VALUE="write(</PRE>)" onClick=
 "top.frames[0].document.write('</PRE>')">
<INPUT TYPE="button" NAME="writelnButton"
 VALUE="writeln()" onClick=
 "top.frames[0].document.writeln('writeln...')">
</FORM></CENTER>
<CENTER><FORM>
<INPUT TYPE="button" NAME="clearButton"
 VALUE="clear()" onClick=
 "top.frames[0].document.clear()">
</FORM></CENTER>
<CENTER><FORM>
<INPUT TYPE="button" NAME="closeButton"
 VALUE="close()" onClick=
 "top.frames[0].document.close()">
</FORM></CENTER>
</BODY>
</HTML>
```

Figure 7–34 shows the result of loading the `index.html` script.

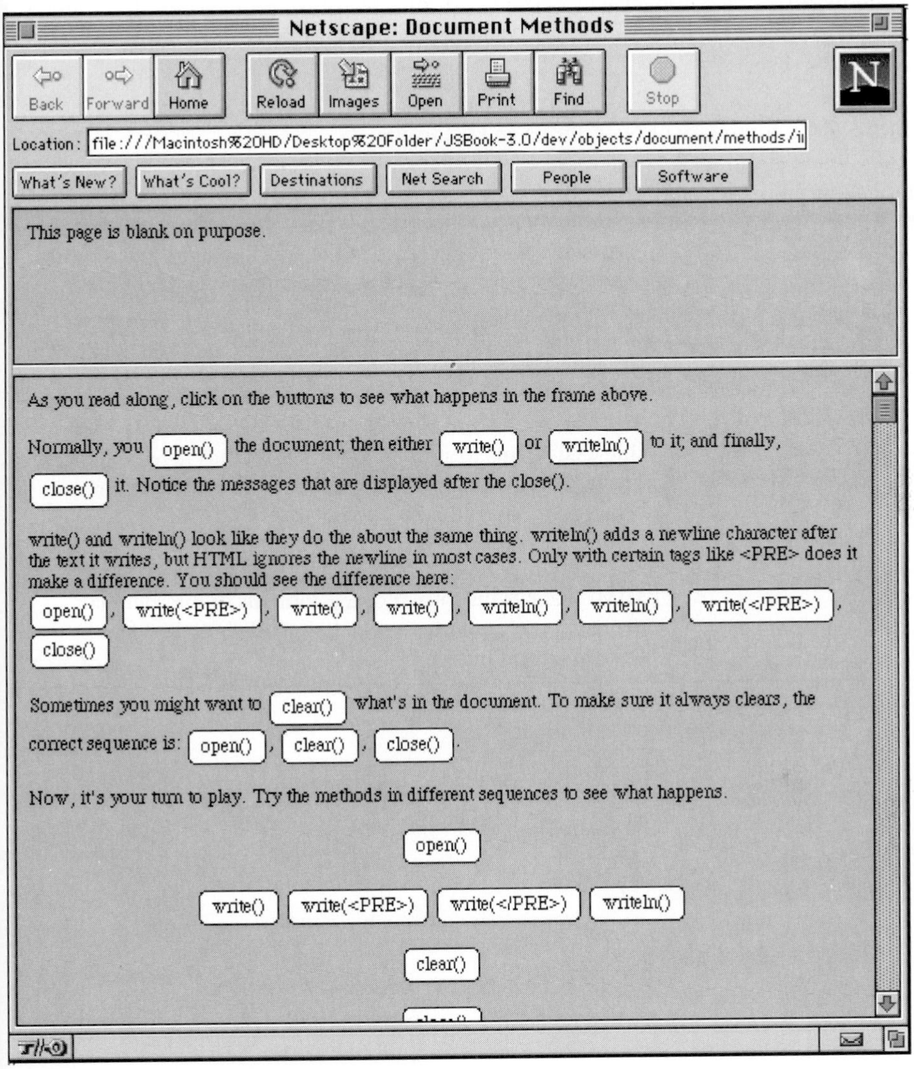

Figure 7–34 Result of loading the `index.html` script

Click on the different buttons and watch what's displayed in the top frame. Notice that after you click on the first `open()` button, the messages from the `write()` and `writeln()` buttons are not displayed until you click on the `close()` button.

Summary of New Terms and Concepts

The new terms and concepts introduced in this chapter are listed in alphabetical order in Table 7-3. The terms and concepts are also included in the glossary at the end of the book

Table 7-3 **Summary of New Terms and Concepts**

Term/Concept	Definition
applet	A small application written in the Java language that requires a Java-aware browser such as Netscape Navigator version 2.0 or later to run.
cookie	An entry in a text file called `cookies.txt` (Windows and UNIX platforms) or `MagicCookie` (Macintosh) that is located in the Netscape directory. Typically, this file is used by server-side CGI scripts to store information on the client computer. The JavaScript language can only read to or write from the browser's cookie file.
MIME	An acronym for Multipurpose Internet Mail Extensions. MIME defines the format of the contents of Internet mail messages and provides a way to include both text and attachments in message bodies.

291

CHAPTER 8

- Displaying history Properties
- Determining the Number of URL Links
- Navigating the History List
- Data Tainting and History Properties
- Extracting Information from the History List
- Summary of New Terms and Concepts

Controlling History

Traditionally, the *history* feature of a program maintains a list or a log of recently executed commands and, in some cases, enables you to navigate through that list. The Web browser version of history maintains a list of URL links that you accessed during the current browsing session. Users access and navigate the history list from a menu or menus. The Navigator history menus are named Go and Bookmarks. In addition, when you click on the Forward or Back buttons in the control panel of the browser, you are stepping forward or backward through the history list, one item at a time.

The `history` object enables you to send the user to somewhere in the history list from within a JavaScript program.

Because users have access to history from the controls in the browser window, you should use the `history` object carefully. Users could easily get confused if you extract URL links from the history list and suddenly take them to some other site on the Web without warning. You should never take users outside of your own Web site without asking for their permission to do so.

The properties and methods for the history object are listed in alphabetical order in Table 8-1. The history object has no event handlers.

Table 8-1 Properties and Methods for the History Object

Properties	Methods	Event Handlers
current*	back()	None
length	eval()*	
next*	forward()	
previous*	go()	
	toString()*	
	valueOf()*	

* New in 3.0 release. These properties and this method work only when data tainting is enabled.

Displaying history Properties

The following historyProps.html script uses the getProps.js script to display the properties for the history object.

```
<!--
       historyProps.html
    This example displays all the history object's
    properties in an alert dialog.
-->

<HTML>
<HEAD>
<TITLE>History Properties</TITLE>
<SCRIPT SRC="../../debug/getProps.js"></SCRIPT>
</HEAD>

<BODY>

<CENTER><FORM>
<INPUT TYPE="button"
 VALUE="Display History Properties"

onClick="alert(getProps(window.history,'history',false))"
>
```

```
</FORM></CENTER>
</BODY>
</HTML>
```

Figure 8–1 shows the alert that is displayed when you load the `historyProps.html` script and click on the Display History Properties button.

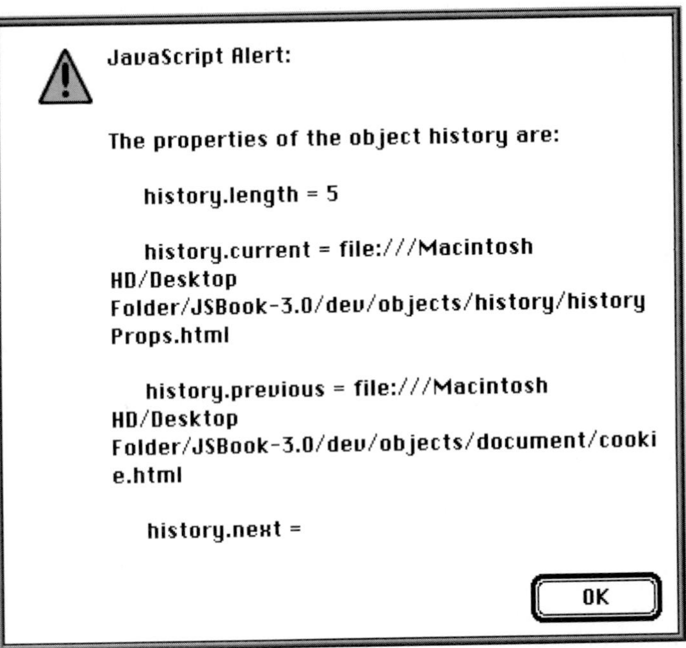

Figure 8–1 history properties

Determining the Number of URL Links

Yo use the `length` property to determine how many URL links are in the history list.

Property	Value	Gettable	Settable
length	number	Yes	No

Use the `length` property to count the items in the history list. This property is useful only as a counter; you cannot determine the location of the current document within the list.

Example of the history.length Property

The following `historyLength.html` script displays the number of items in the history list in an alert window.

```
<!--
          historyLength.html

    Obtain the history.length property and display
    it in an alert dialog.
-->

<HTML>
<HEAD>
<TITLE>History Length</TITLE>
<SCRIPT LANGUAGE="JavaScript">
<!-- HIDE FROM OLD BROWSERS

//
// display history.length in an alert dialog
//
function displayLength() {
  var msg_str = ""

  msg_str += "\n"
  msg_str += "history.length"
  msg_str += " = " + history.length
  msg_str += "\n"

  alert(msg_str)
}

// STOP HIDING -->
</SCRIPT>
</HEAD>

<BODY>
<CENTER>
<P>Click on the Get button to open an
alert dialog that displays the number of
items in the history list.</P>
<FORM>
<INPUT TYPE="button" VALUE="Get"
onClick="displayLength()">
</FORM>
```

```
</CENTER>

</BODY>
</HTML>
```

Figure 8–2 shows the result of loading the `historyLength.html` script.

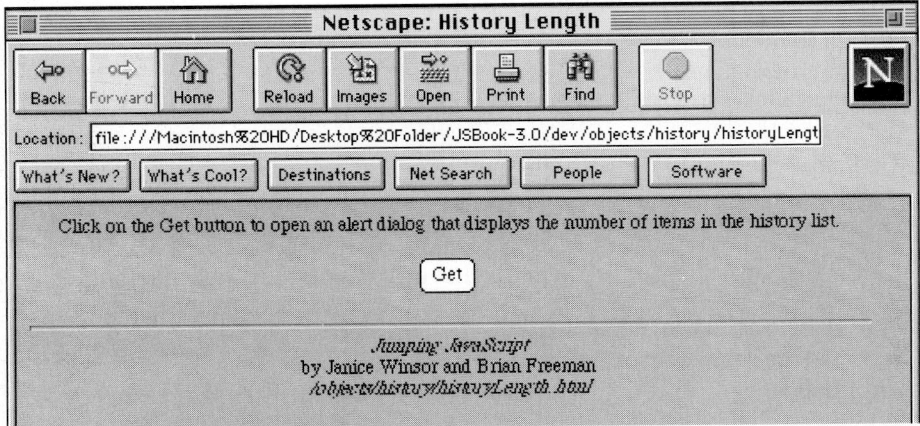

Figure 8–2 Result of loading the `historyLength.html` script

When you click on the Get button, the alert shows the number of items in the history list. In the example shown in Figure 8–3, the history list contains five items.

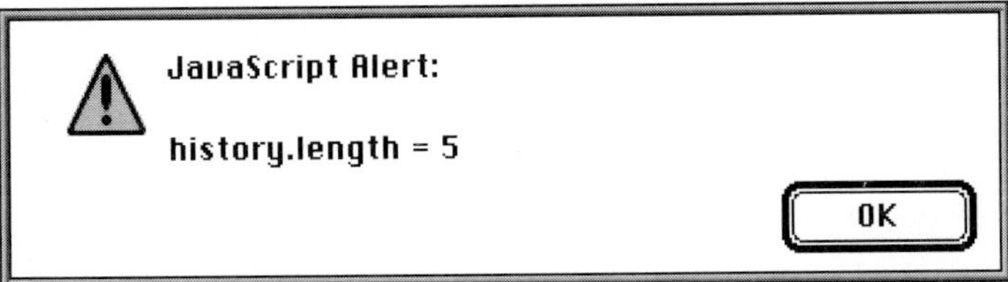

Figure 8–3 Alert showing history length

The `length` property starts counting with the number 1, although the shortcut codes you can use to navigate the history list from the Go menu in Navigator start counting with the number 0. Figure 8–4 shows the Go menu with the five history items that were counted in this example.

Go Bookmarks Options Directory Wir
Back ⌘[
Forward ⌘]
Home
Stop Loading ⌘.
✓History Length ⌘0
Jumping JavaScript Author's Page ⌘1
ref_t-z.html ⌘2
JavaScript Examples ⌘3
Jumping JavaScript Author's Page ⌘4

Figure 8–4 Go menu with history list

Navigating the History List

The `history` object has three methods that enable you to navigate through the history list in a script.

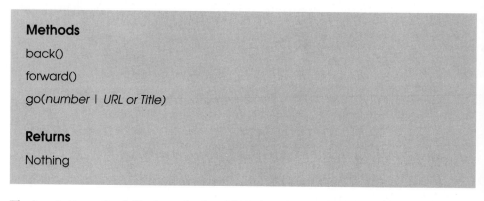

Methods

back()

forward()

go(*number* | *URL or Title*)

Returns

Nothing

The `back()` method displays the last URL that the user visited. The result is the same as if the user clicks on the Back button in the Netscape toolbar.

The `forward()` method displays the next URL in the history list. The result is the same as if the user clicks on the Forward button in the Netscape toolbar. Because your script cannot determine the location in the history list, you may be taking the user to an unexpected location. Use this method with caution, and only after extensive testing. The `forward()` method is most likely to be useful when used in conjunction with the `back()` method in the same script, when you are keeping track of how many steps the script navigates in either direction.

The go() method moves either forward or backward in the list by a specified number. For example, to go back three items in the list, use go(-3). To go forward three items in the list, use go(3). Alternatively, you can specify the URL or a title for the name of a site that is already contained in the history list. The title is the text that is displayed in the Go menu.

Because users have control over navigation through the browser, you need to be very careful about when (or if) you use these methods for the history object.

Example of history.forward() and history.back() Methods

The following historyForward.html script calls the historyBack.html script that follows it. These scripts demonstrate how to use the history.back() and history.forward() methods.

```
<!--
            historyForward.html

      This example adds buttons to the bottom of the
      page implemented with the history object's
      back and forward methods.
-->
<HTML>
<HEAD>
<TITLE>History back() &amp; forward()</TITLE>
</HEAD>
<BODY>
<P>The buttons at the bottom of this page
duplicate Navigator's Back and Forward
buttons. They are implemented with
<CODE>history.back()</CODE> and
<CODE>history.forward().</CODE></P>

<P>Click <A href="historyBack.html">here</A> and
follow the instructions on the next page. Once
you return, click on Forward, down</P>
<CENTER>
<P>||<BR>
||<BR>
...
||<BR>
\/</P>
<CENTER>
HERE
```

```
<FORM>
<INPUT TYPE="button" VALUE="Back"
onClick="history.back()">
<INPUT TYPE="button" VALUE="Forward"
onClick="history.forward()">
</FORM>
</CENTER>
<P>Now have some fun with it.</P>
</BODY>
</HTML>
```

The following `historyBack.html` script is called by the `historyForward.html` script.

```
<!--
       historyBack.html
    This is the second page of the back forward
    example. The buttons at the bottom of the
    page are implemented with the history object's
    back and forward methods.
-->
<HTML>
<HEAD>
<TITLE>History back() &amp; forward()</TITLE>
</HEAD>

<BODY>
<P>Click on Back to return to the previous
 page. It's down</P>

<CENTER>
<P>||<BR>
...
||<BR>
\/</P>
<CENTER>
HERE

<FORM>
<INPUT TYPE="button" VALUE="Back"
onClick="history.back()">
<INPUT TYPE="button" VALUE="Forward"
onClick="history.forward()">
</FORM>
</CENTER>
```

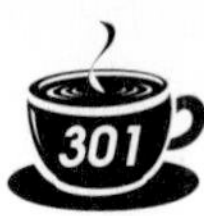


```
<P>Now have some fun with it.</P>
</BODY>
</HTML>
```

Figure 8–5 shows the results of loading the `historyForward.html` script.

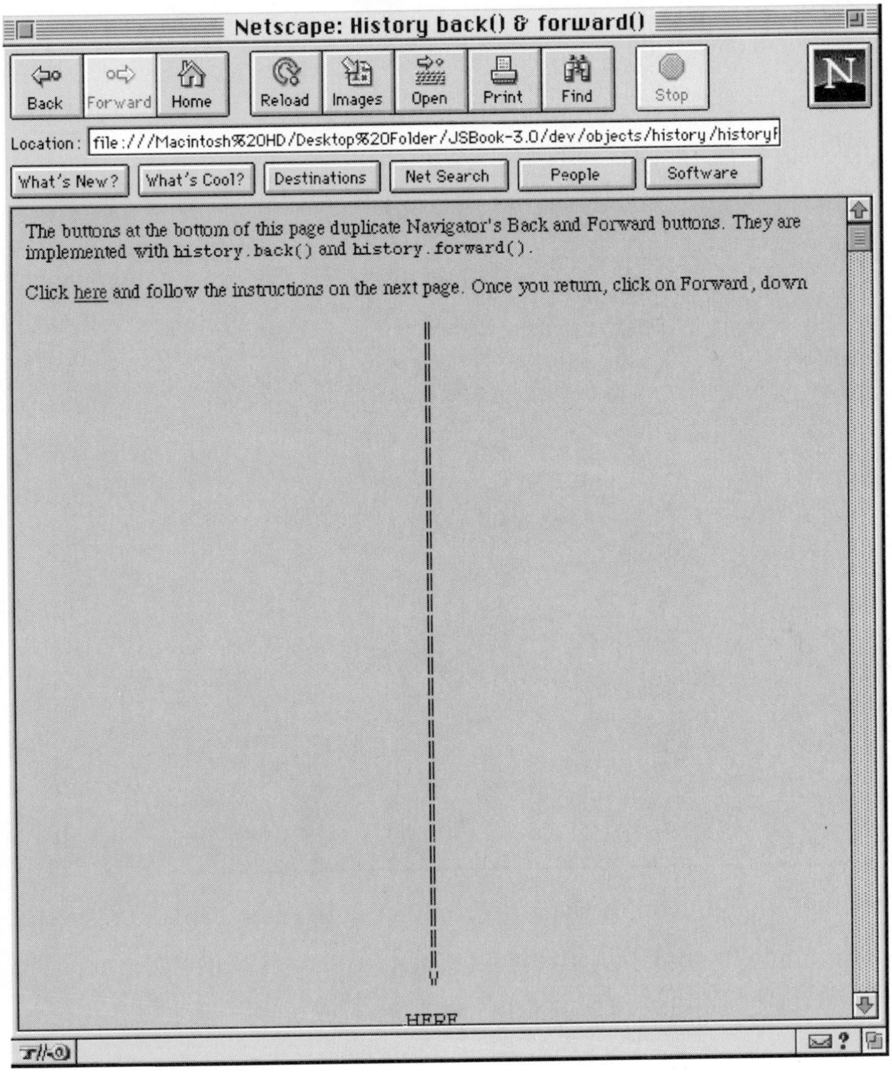

Figure 8–5 Results of `historyForward.html` script

When you click on the here link, the `historyBack.html` script is loaded, as shown in Figure 8–6.

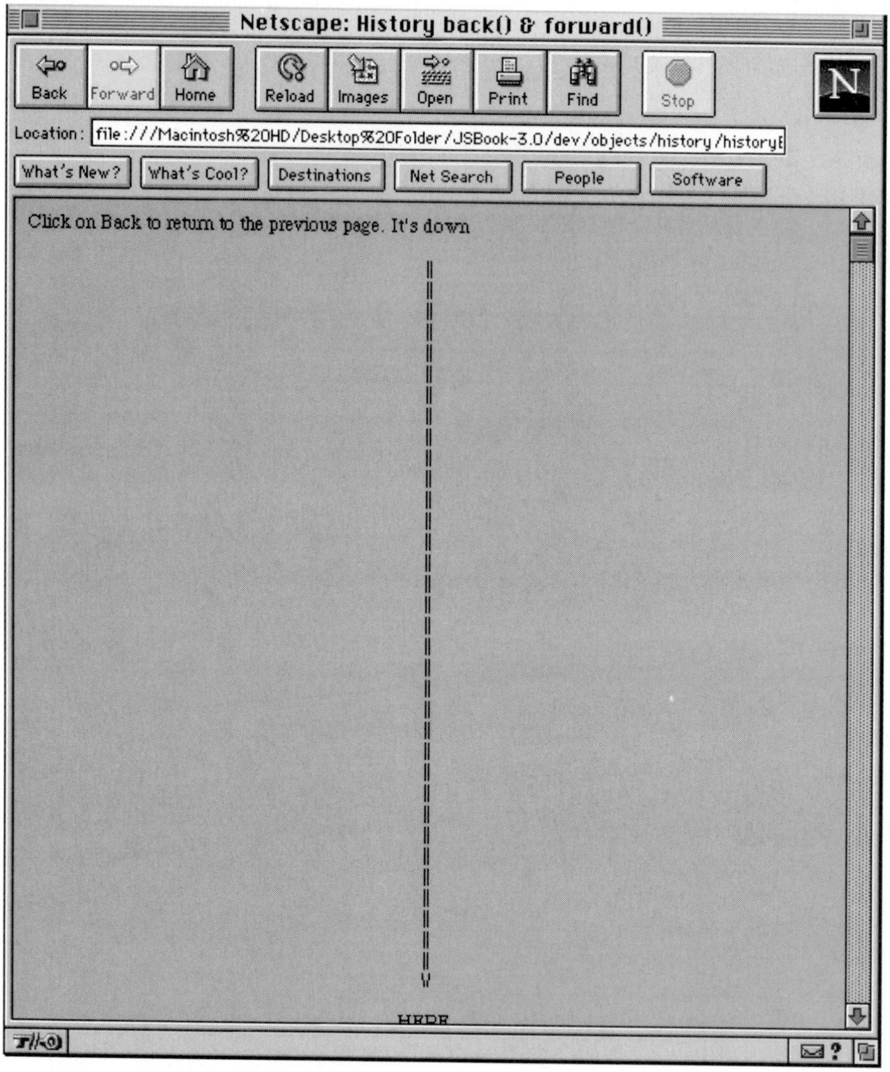

Figure 8–6 Clicking on the here link loads the `historyBack.html` script

Because the buttons are at the bottom of the page, you need to scroll down to get at them, as shown in Figure 8–7.

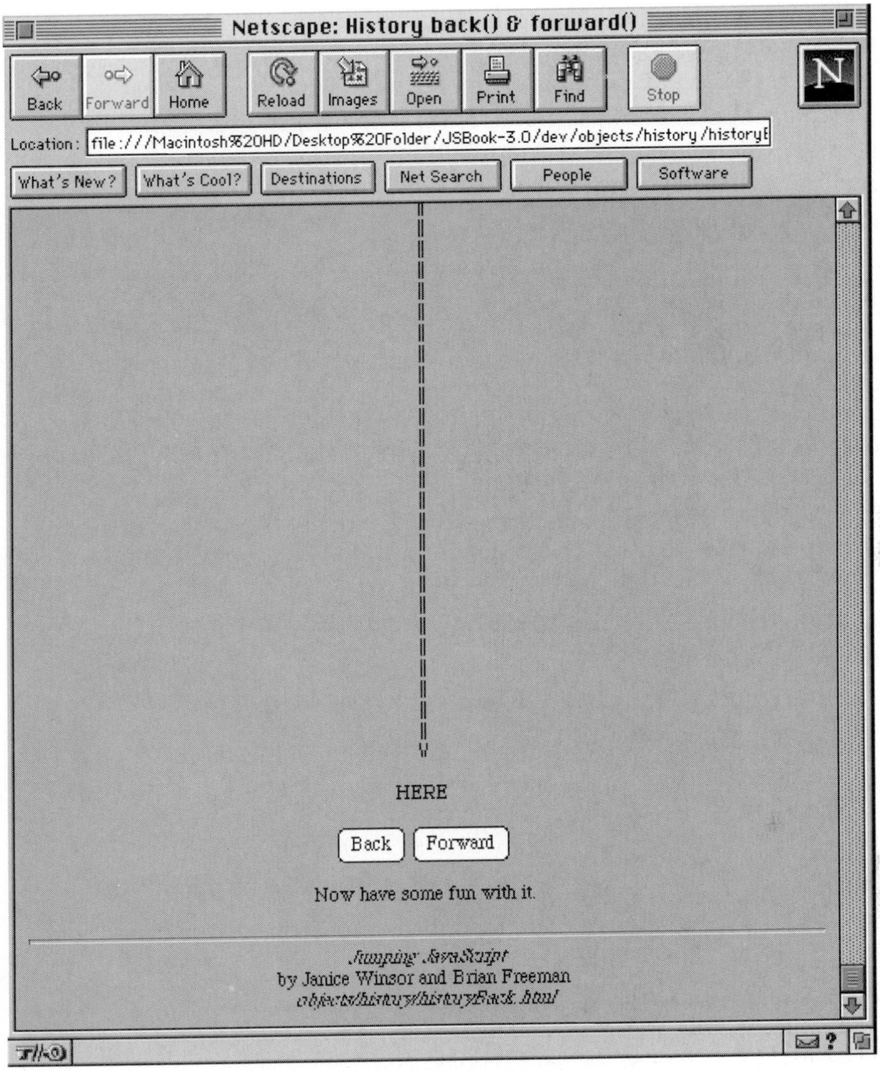

Figure 8–7 Displaying the Back and Forward buttons

Notice that as you move forward and backward by clicking on the Back and Forward buttons, you cannot go any farther forward than the last page of the document because you are at the very end of the history list. However, when you click on the Back button to go back to the first page and then click again on the Back button, you go back to the page that was loaded before you started experimenting with the `historyForward.html` script.

The following example uses three scripts to demonstrate how you can use the `forward()` and `back()` methods to navigate to sections within a document. The first script, `index.html`, creates a document with two frames and loads a different file into each frame. The `toc.html` script creates a set of links for the sections of the document in the other frame and uses the `TARGET` attribute to tell Navigator which frame to operate in. The `doc.html` script contains the section headings and text of the document itself.

HTML Brushup — The TARGET Attribute

When you use frames in a document, you can use the TARGET attribute to help you navigate between frames. The default TARGET is always the current frame, so if you do not specify a target, the document is displayed in the current frame. If you specify a target frame that does not currently exist, a new frame is opened in a new window and given that name.

Begin TARGET names with a number or a letter. TARGET names are case sensitive, so make sure the capitalization of the TARGET name matches the capitalization of the target frame or window.

To set a target for a specific link, you can use the TARGET attribute with the <A> tag, using the following syntax:

<A HREF="*url*.html" TARGET="*window_name*">*Anchor Name*</A>

HTML 3.0 provides a set of predefined target names, described below:

_blank	Load this link into a new unnamed window
_self	Load this link into the current window (default)
_parent	Load the link over the parent (or self if no parent exists)
_top	Load this link at the top level (or self if you are currently at the top)

You load the `index.html` script below to start this example.

```
<!--
   objects/history/navbar/index.html

    This file defines the frameset for the
    navbar example.
-->
<HTML>
<HEAD>
<TITLE>History Navigation Bar</TITLE>
```

```
</HEAD>

<FRAMESET COLS="30%,70%">
  <FRAME NAME="tocFrame" SRC="toc.html">
  <FRAME NAME="docFrame" SRC="doc.html">
</FRAMESET>

</HTML>
```

The `toc.html` script below defines the `HREFs` to the sections in the document and uses the `TARGET` attribute to identify the frame where these sections are loaded.

```
<!--
    objects/history/navbar/toc.html

    History object navbar example table of
    contents frame.
-->

<HTML>
<HEAD>
<TITLE>History TOC</TITLE>
</HEAD>

<BODY>
<H1>TOC</H1>

<DL>
<DT>
<A HREF="doc.html#S1"
 TARGET="docFrame"
>Section One</a>
</DT>

<DT>
<A HREF="doc.html#S2"
 TARGET="docFrame"
>Section Two</a>
</DT>

<DT>
<A HREF="doc.html#S3"
 TARGET="docFrame"
>Section Three</a>
```

```
</DT>

<DT>
<A HREF="doc.html#S4"
 TARGET="docFrame"
>Section Four</a>
</DT>

<FORM>
<INPUT TYPE="button" VALUE="Back"
onClick="top.frames[1].history.back()">
<INPUT TYPE="button" VALUE="Forward"
onClick="top.frames[1].history.forward()">
</FORM>
</BODY>
</HTML>
```

The `doc.html` script below defines the sections and the text for the document that is displayed in the second frame of the window.

```
<!--
    objects/history/navbar/doc.html

    Document for the history object navbar
    example.
-->

<HTML>
<HEAD>
<TITLE>History navbar</TITLE>
</HEAD>

<BODY>
<CENTER>
<H1>A Gothic Tale</H1>
</CENTER>

<A NAME="S1"><H2>Section One</H2></a>
<P>
It was a dark and stormy night. All
of the beagles were safely in their
kennels. The bats flew around the tower,
squeaking frantically.</P>
<P>
```

```
Dosolina stood at the open window
wistfully gazing out over the moors,
her long dark tresses blowing wildly
as the wind gusted. Piotor was long
overdue. There were evil things afoot
in the night, and she feared greatly
for his safety.
</P>

<A NAME="S2"><H2>Section Two</H2></a>
<P>
There was something unnatural
about the light flickering through
the clouds. The beagles bugled their
howls, protesting their captivity. The
dogs wanted to be out and about,
investigating the strange smells and
sensations that were drifting
tantalizingly towards them on the gusting
wind.
</P>

<A NAME="S3"><H2>Section Three</H2></a>
<P>
Piotor felt the hot breath of the
ravening monsters as they followed closely
on his heels. He feared for his very life.
He hoped that he could reach the safety
of the tower in the distance before his
strength gave out and the monsters were
upon him.
</P>

<A NAME="S4"><H2>Section Four</H2></a>
<P>
The skies were clear and the weather
balmy, giving the illusion of innocence.
Dosolina and Piotor walked with
determined steps across the moors,
searching for traces of the monsters
that continuously dogged their very
existence.
</P>
<P>
```

```
"Oh, here's a footprint," Piotor
cried. "I knew that there was something
tangible in that horrid blackness that
was following me."
</P>
<P>
"And here's a piece of something ...
Ugh, it is so disgusting," said Dosolina.
"What is this awful curse that prevents
us from being like normal folks?"
</P>
<P>
"We must be brave, and not let them
know how frightened we really are."
</P>

</BODY>
</HTML>
```

Figure 8–8 shows the results of loading the `index.html` script.

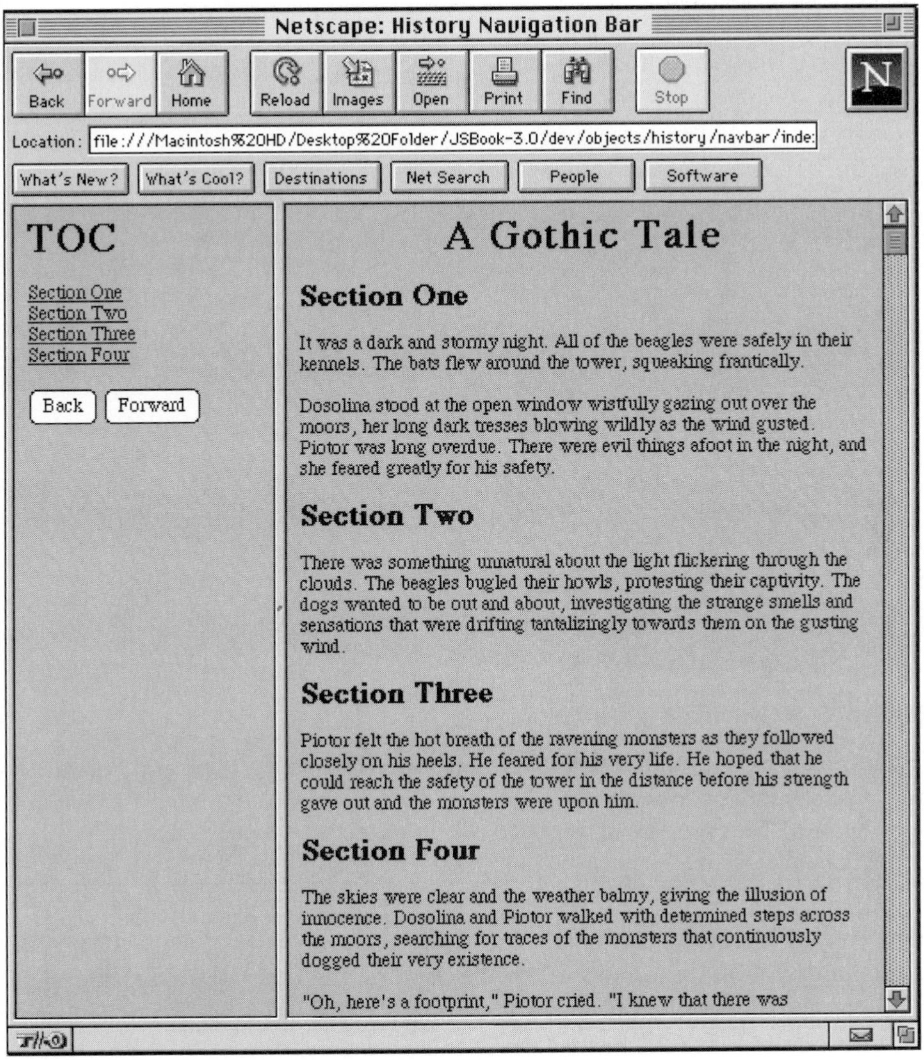

Netscape: History Navigation Bar

Back Forward Home Reload Images Open Print Find Stop

Location: file:///Macintosh%20HD/Desktop%20Folder/JSBook-3.0/dev/objects/history/navbar/inde:

What's New? What's Cool? Destinations Net Search People Software

TOC

Section One
Section Two
Section Three
Section Four

Back Forward

A Gothic Tale

Section One

It was a dark and stormy night. All of the beagles were safely in their kennels. The bats flew around the tower, squeaking frantically.

Dosolina stood at the open window wistfully gazing out over the moors, her long dark tresses blowing wildly as the wind gusted. Piotor was long overdue. There were evil things afoot in the night, and she feared greatly for his safety.

Section Two

There was something unnatural about the light flickering through the clouds. The beagles bugled their howls, protesting their captivity. The dogs wanted to be out and about, investigating the strange smells and sensations that were drifting tantalizingly towards them on the gusting wind.

Section Three

Piotor felt the hot breath of the ravening monsters as they followed closely on his heels. He feared for his very life. He hoped that he could reach the safety of the tower in the distance before his strength gave out and the monsters were upon him.

Section Four

The skies were clear and the weather balmy, giving the illusion of innocence. Dosolina and Piotor walked with determined steps across the moors, searching for traces of the monsters that continuously dogged their very existence.

"Oh, here's a footprint," Piotor cried. "I knew that there was

Figure 8–8 Result of loading the `index.html` script

Figure 8–9 shows the document after you click on the Section Four link.

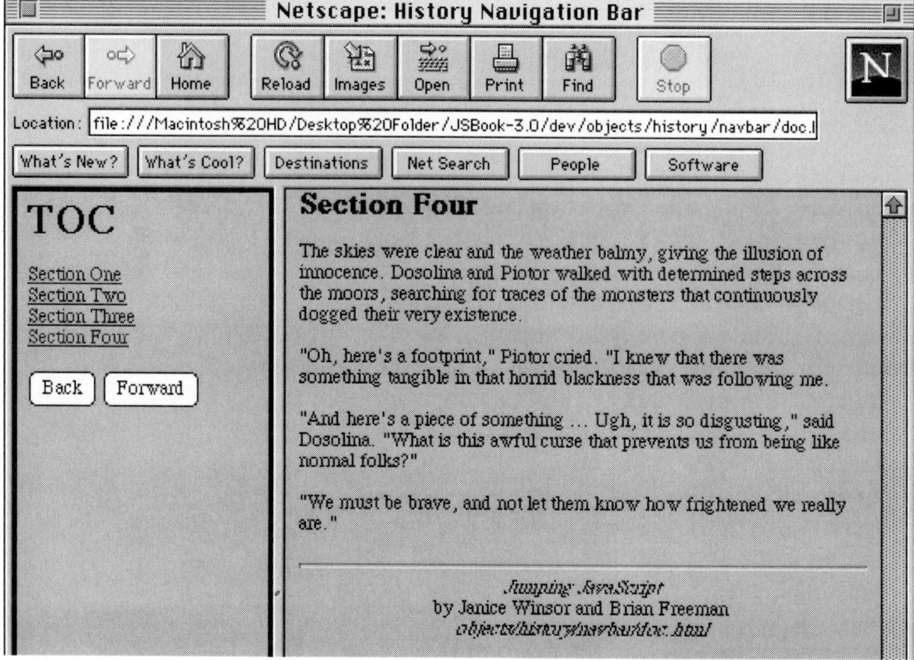

Figure 8–9 Navigating by sections

Experiment by clicking on the different section links and the Back and Forward button to see what happens.

Note – The browser Go menu only records the top-level document, so as you move around with the frames in these examples, the script should work properly; the history feature tracks your movements, but those movements are not incorporated into the history list in the Go menu.

Example of Using Images with forward and back Methods

The following `historyButtons.html` script shows another way you can create your own history navigation buttons. This script opens a second window containing active image areas. The `HREF` for the image contains the properties

that navigate the history list. The script uses the `window.opener` property to control the actions in the main window. For more information on creating active image areas, see Chapter 9, "Working with Images."

```
<!--
          historyButtons.html
     This history object example creates a
     separate control window when the document is
     loaded.
-->
<HTML>
<HEAD>
<TITLE>History Buttons</TITLE>

<!-- include windowOpen() -->
<SCRIPT SRC="../../debug/windowOpen.js"></SCRIPT>

<!-- local functions -->
<SCRIPT LANGUAGE="JavaScript">
<!-- HIDE FROM OLD BROWSERS

// global history control window
var cWin  = null

//
// display the history control window
//
function displayControlWindow() {
  var wopts = ""    // window options
  var dstr  = ""    // document string

  // set up the window options
  wopts += "toolbar=no,"
  wopts += "location=no,"
  wopts += "directories=no,"
  wopts += "status=no,"
  wopts += "menubar=no,"
  wopts += "scrollbars=no,"
  wopts += "resizable=no,"
  wopts += "copyhistory=no,"
  wopts += "width=200,"
  wopts += "height=40"

  // create the window
```

```
  cWin = windowOpen("", "controlWindow", wopts)
  if (cWin == null)
    // couldn't create the window, exit
    return false

  // create the window contents
  dstr += "<HEAD>"
  dstr += "<SCRIPT>"
  dstr += "function goBack() {"
  dstr += "  self.window.opener.history.back()"
  dstr += "}"
  dstr += "function goForward() {"
  dstr += "  self.window.opener.history.forward()"
  dstr += "}"
  dstr += "</SCRIPT>"
  dstr += "</HEAD>"
  dstr += "<BODY>"
  dstr += "<CENTER>"
  dstr += "<H3 ALIGN=center>History Controls</H3>"
  dstr += "<A HREF='javascript:goBack()'>"
  dstr += "<IMG SRC='../../icons/4ARROW3.GIF' "
  dstr += "WIDTH=31 HEIGHT=31></A>"
  dstr += "<A HREF='javascript:goForward()'>"
  dstr += "<IMG SRC='../../icons/4ARROW4.GIF' "
  dstr += "WIDTH=31 HEIGHT=31></A>"
  dstr += "</CENTER>"
  dstr += "</BODY>"

  // write the contents to the window
  cWin.document.open()
  cWin.document.write(dstr)
  cWin.document.close()

  return true
}
// STOP HIDING -->
</SCRIPT>
</HEAD>
<BODY onLoad="displayControlWindow()">
<P>When you load this page, it creates a
History Control window that provides an
alternate set of history navigation buttons.</P>
</BODY>
</HTML>
```

Figure 8–10 shows the result of loading the `historyButtons.html` script.

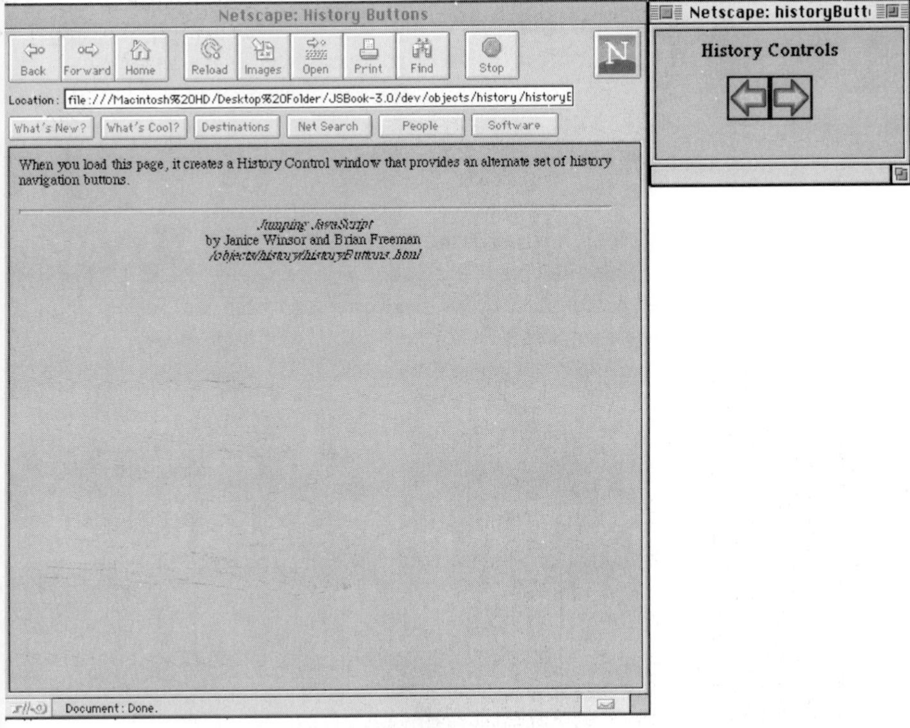

Figure 8–10 Result of `historyButtons.html` script

Click on the buttons in the History Controls window to navigate backward and forward in the history list.

Note – The `historyButtons.html` script does no error checking to determine whether the button is at the beginning and the end of the history list. Without the error checking, if you are at the beginning of the history list and click on the back arrow, the script displays error messages and forces a restart on Macintosh systems. The same thing happens if you are at the end of the history list and click on the forward error. It's good programming practice to include error checking as part of your scripts, especially because you do not know what platform the script will run on.

Example of history.go() Method

The `historyGoForward.html` script below is similar to the `historyForward.html` script example, except that instead of using the `back()` and `forward()` methods, it uses the `go()` method. `go(-1)` moves back one item in the history list, and `go(1)` moves forward one item in the list. If you use the `go()` method to move to specific numbers in the history list, remember that user navigation actions may produce unpredictable results in your scripts.

```
<!--
         historyGoForward.html

     This example adds buttons to the bottom of the
     page implemented with the history object's
     go method.
-->

<HTML>
<HEAD>

<TITLE>History back &amp; forward with go</TITLE>
</HEAD>

<BODY>

<P>The buttons at the bottom of this page
duplicate Navigator's Back and Forward
buttons. They are implemented with
<CODE>history.go()</CODE>.</P>

<P>Click <A href="historyGoBack.html">here</A> and
follow the instructions on the next page. Once you
return, click on Forward, down</P>

<CENTER>
<P>||<BR>
||<BR>
...
||<BR>
\/</P>
<CENTER>
HERE

<FORM>
```

```
<INPUT TYPE="button" VALUE="Back"
onClick="history.go(-1)">
<INPUT TYPE="button" VALUE="Forward"
onClick="history.go(1)">
</FORM>
</CENTER>

</BODY>
</HTML>
```

The `historyGoForward.html` file loads the `historyGoBack.html` file shown below to create the second page.

```
<!--
          historyGoBack.html

    This page is the second part of the back forward
    example. The buttons at the bottom of the
    page are implemented with the history object's
    go method.
-->

<HTML>
<HEAD>
<TITLE>History back &amp; forward with go</TITLE>
</HEAD>

<BODY>

<P>Click on Back to return to the previous
 page. It's down</P>
<CENTER>
<P>||<BR>
||<BR>
...
||<BR>
\/</P>
<CENTER>
HERE

<FORM>
<INPUT TYPE="button" VALUE="Back"
onClick="history.go(-1)">
<INPUT TYPE="button" VALUE="Forward"
```

```
onClick="history.go(1)">
</FORM>
</CENTER>

<P>Remember to have some fun!</P>

</BODY>
</HTML>
```

When you load either the `historyGoForward.html` script or the `historyGoBack.html`, the screens look exactly the same as those shown in Figure 8–5, Figure 8–6, and Figure 8–7. Only the underlying code that controls the behavior of the Back and Forward buttons is different in this example.

Data Tainting and History Properties

The Navigator 3.0 release has three new properties:

- `current`
- `next`
- `previous`

These properties return values only when *data tainting* is enabled. Data tainting is a new security mechanism that is provided in the Navigator 3.0 release. It marks, or taints, any property values or data that should be secure and private. For the complete story on data tainting, and information on how to enable data tainting on your system, see Chapter 36, "Controlling Data Tainting."

Property	Value	Gettable	Settable
current	URL	Yes	No
next	URL	Yes	No
previous	URL	Yes	No

Example of current, previous, and next Properties

Before you load the following `historyTainting.html` script from the CD-ROM, enable data tainting on your system. If you do not enable data tainting, you can run the script, but no values are displayed. This script is an extension of the `historyButtons.html` script. In addition to creating a separate window with back and forward navigation buttons, it also adds three text fields that

display the values of the `current`, `previous`, and `next` properties. Click on the back and forward arrows in the History Controls window to navigate back and forward in the history list and display the hyistory information in the text fields.

```
<!--
          historyTainting.html
      This history object example creates a
      separate control window when the document is
      loaded.  The control window shows the
      previous and next URL in the history list
      and provides forward and back navigation
      buttons.
-->
<HTML>
<HEAD>
<TITLE>Tainted History Properties</TITLE>

<!-- include windowOpen() -->
<SCRIPT SRC="../../debug/windowOpen.js"></SCRIPT>

<!-- local functions -->
<SCRIPT LANGUAGE="JavaScript">
<!-- HIDE FROM OLD BROWSERS

// global history control window
var cWin  = null

//
// display the history control window
//
function displayControlWindow() {
  var wopts = ""     // window options
  var dstr  = ""     // document string

  // set up the window options
  wopts += "toolbar=no,"
  wopts += "location=no,"
  wopts += "directories=no,"
  wopts += "status=no,"
  wopts += "menubar=no,"
  wopts += "scrollbars=no,"
  wopts += "resizable=yes,"
  wopts += "copyhistory=no,"
  wopts += "width=300,"
```

```
  wopts += "height=300"

  // create the window
  cWin = windowOpen("", "controlWindow", wopts)
  if (cWin == null) {
    // couldn't create the window, exit
    return false
  }

  // create the window contents
  dstr += "<HEAD>"
  dstr += "<SCRIPT>"
  dstr += "function goBack() {"
  dstr += "  self.window.opener.history.back();"
  dstr += "}"
  dstr += "function goForward() {"
  dstr += "  self.window.opener.history.forward();"
  dstr += "}"
  dstr += "function displayLocations() {"
  dstr += "  with (self.window.opener.history) {"
  dstr += "    untaint(previous);"
  dstr += "    untaint(current);"
  dstr += "    untaint(next);"
  dstr += "  }"
  dstr += "  with (self.window.document.aForm) {"
  dstr += "    prev.value = "
  dstr += "      self.window.opener.history.previous;"
  dstr += "    cur.value = "
  dstr += "      self.window.opener.history.current;"
  dstr += "    next.value = "
  dstr += "       self.window.opener.history.next;"
  dstr += "  }"
  dstr += "}"
  dstr += "</SCRIPT>"
  dstr += "</HEAD>"
  dstr += "<BODY>"
  dstr += "<H3 ALIGN=center>History Controls</H3>"
  dstr += "<FORM NAME='aForm'>"
  dstr += "<BR>Previous Location:<BR>"
  dstr += "<INPUT TYPE='text' NAME='prev' VALUE=''
SIZE=35>"
  dstr += "<BR>Current Location:<BR>"
 dstr += "<INPUT TYPE='text' NAME='cur' VALUE='' SIZE=35>"
  dstr += "<BR>Next Location:<BR>"
```

```
  dstr += "<INPUT TYPE='text' NAME='next' VALUE=''
SIZE=35>"
  dstr += "</FORM>"
  dstr += "<CENTER>"
  dstr += "<A HREF='' onMouseOver='displayLocations()'"
  dstr += "  onClick='goBack()'>"
  dstr += "<IMG SRC='../../icons/4ARROW3.GIF' "
  dstr += "WIDTH=31 HEIGHT=31></A>"
  dstr += "<A HREF='' onMouseOver='displayLocations()'"
  dstr += "  onClick='goForward()'>"
  dstr += "<IMG SRC='../../icons/4ARROW4.GIF' "
  dstr += "WIDTH=31 HEIGHT=31></A>"
  dstr += "</CENTER>"
  dstr += "</BODY>"

  // write the contents to the window
  cWin.document.open()
  cWin.document.write(dstr)
  cWin.document.close()

  return true
}

// STOP HIDING -->
</SCRIPT>
</HEAD>
<BODY onLoad="displayControlWindow()">

<P>When you load this page, it creates a
History Control window that provides an alternate set
of history navigation buttons.</P>

<P>This version shows the previous, current, and
next items in the history list. You must enable
Data Tainting on your system before you can
see the values.</P>

<P>Because this example uses an onMouseOver
event handler to update the Previous Location,
Current Location, and Next Location fields in the
window, you must move your pointer over one of the
buttons to update the fields.</P>
</BODY>
</HTML>
```

Figure 8–11 shows the result of loading the `historyTainting.html` script.

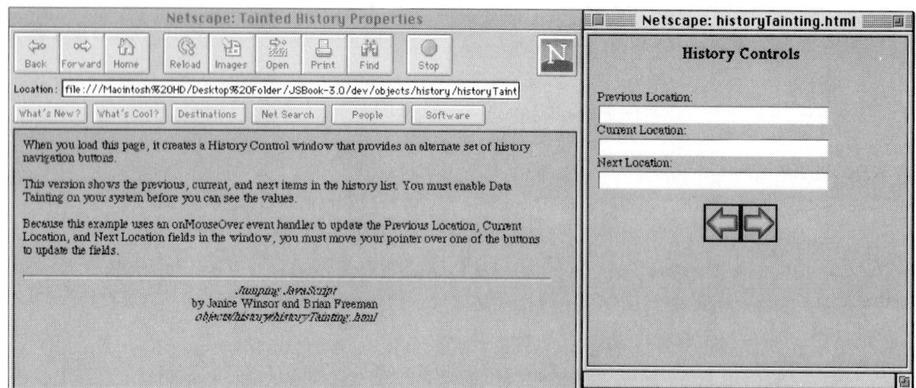

Figure 8–11 Result of loading the `historyTainting.html` script

Extracting Information from the History List

The Navigator 3.0 release provides a new `toString()` method for the `history` object. You can use this method to extract the current history list in a format that you can use to display as a list of links in a document.

The `toString()` method returns values only when *data tainting* is enabled. For the complete story on data tainting and information on how to enable data tainting on your system, see Chapter 36, "Controlling Data Tainting."

Example of toString() Method

The following `historyToString.html` script uses the `toString()` method to display the current history list as part of the page, as shown in Figure 8–12 on 322. It displays the history item and creates a link for it.

```
<!--
         historyToString.html

     This history object example uses the
     toString method to write the current history
     list into the document as it loads.
-->

<HTML>
<HEAD>
<TITLE>History toString</TITLE>
</HEAD>
<BODY>
```

```
<P>This example uses the history toString method
to obtain the current history list. You must enable
data tainting before the script will work properly.</P>

<P>The current history list is:</P>

<SCRIPT LANGUAGE="JavaScript">
<!-- HIDE FROM OLD BROWSERS

// write the contents to the window
self.document.open()
self.document.write(self.history.toString())
self.document.close()

// STOP HIDING -->
</SCRIPT>

</BODY>
</HTML>
```

Figure 8–12 shows the result of loading the `historyToString.html` script. Notice that the history list is automatically displayed as active links.

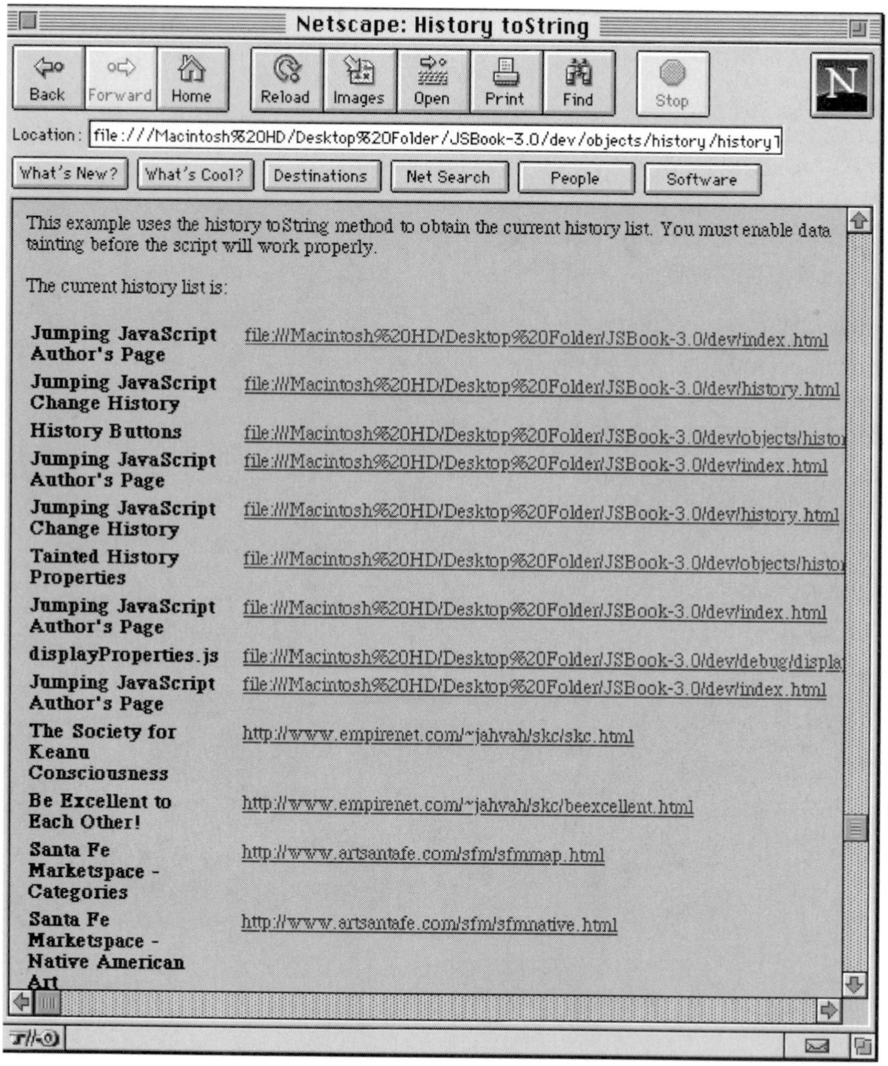

Figure 8–12 Result of loading the `historyToString.html` script

Summary of New Terms and Concepts

The new terms and concepts introduced in this chapter are listed in alphabetical order in Table 8-2. The terms and concepts are also included in the glossary at the end of the book.

Table 8-2 New Terms and Concepts

Term/Concept	Description
data tainting	A security mechanism that marks, or taints, any property values or data that should be secure and private.
history	The list of URL sites a user has visited during the current session.

CHAPTER 9

- Using the src Property
- Prestaging Images with the lowsrc Property
- Checking If an Image Has Completed Loading
- Using Read-Only Image Properties
- Using the Image Constructor
- Using the onLoad Event Handler
- Planning for Error Handling
- Planning for the Stopping of Image Loading

Working with Images

Although HTML has supported incorporating images in Web pages for quite some time, the Navigator 3.0 release is the first one that creates a JavaScript object to enable you to access image properties and use event handlers. Everything in this chapter is new in the Navigator 3.0 release.

The properties and event handlers for the `image` object are listed in alphabetical order in Table 9-1. The `image` object has no methods.

Table 9-1 Properties and Methods for the image Object

Properties	Methods	Event Handlers
`border`	`eval()*`	`onAbort`
`complete`	`toString()*`	`onError`
`height`	`valueOf()*`	`onLoad`
`hspace`		
`lowsrc`		
`name`		

Table 9-1 Properties and Methods for the image Object (Continued)

Properties	Methods	Event Handlers
`src`		
`vspace`		
`width`		

* New in Navigator 3.0.

Use the following syntax for image object properties:

```
imageName.propertyName
imageName.methodName(parameter)
```

You add images by using the HTML `<IMG>` tag. Refer to the HTML Brushup box for the HTML syntax. The HTML attributes set the position and size of the image. You can retrieve these values with the image properties, but you cannot change those values in a script.

You can change the image that is displayed by assigning a new value to the `src` and `lowsrc` properties.

Note – Avoid using the name `image[]` for your image arrays to prevent conflict with the `document.images[]` array.

HTML Brushup — Adding Images

You add an image by using the <IMG> tag and specifying the attributes shown below:

<IMG>

SRC = "*ImageURL*"

(LOWSRC = "*LowResImageURL*")

NAME = "*ImageName*"

WIDTH = "*Pixels*" | "*PercentValue*"

HEIGHT = "*Pixels*" | "*PercentValue*"

(HSPACE = "*Pixels*")

(VSPACE = "*Pixels*")

(BORDER = "*Pixels*")

(ALIGN = "left" | "right" | "top" | "absmiddle" | "absbottom" | "texttop" | "middle" | "baseline" | "bottom")

(ALT = "*DescriptionOfImage*")

(ISMAP)

(USEMAP = "*#AreaMapName*")

(onLoad = "*JavaScript code*")

(onAbort = "*JavaScript code*")

(onError = "*JavaScript code*")

>

Using the src Property

The `src` property enables you to substitute images into the space assigned to an existing image. This property gives you a great deal of flexibility because you can use it to preload images and to substitute them. Using this property, you can substitute images to create animations.

Property	Value	Gettable	Settable
src	URL	Yes	Yes

The height and width of the image space are defined by the initial `HEIGHT` and `WIDTH` attributes defined in the `<IMG>` tag. If you do not define `HEIGHT` and `WIDTH` attributes, any subsequent images are loaded into the dimensions of the first image file that was loaded into the object. If you're loading images of varying sizes, you can circumvent problems by loading the largest image first. Because the Navigator 2.0 release had a bug that required you to specify `WIDTH` and `HEIGHT` attributes for images, we recommend that you always specify them.

Example of Using image.src to Substitute Images

The following `imageSrc.html` script displays a series of images. This script provides a Next Image button that enables users to control the timing of the image display.

```
<!--
         imageSrc.html

     This example shows how assigning a new value
     to the image src property loads a new image.

-->

<HTML>
<HEAD>
<TITLE>Image Src Property</TITLE>
<SCRIPT LANGUAGE="JavaScript">
<!-- HIDE FROM OLD BROWSERS
var currentImage = 0
var    my_images = new Array(16)

my_images[0]  = "../../images/AyersRock.jpg"
my_images[1]  = "../../images/Cats-1.jpg"
my_images[2]  = "../../images/Cats-2.jpg"
my_images[3]  = "../../images/Chameleon.jpg"
my_images[4]  = "../../images/Elephants.jpg"
my_images[5]  = "../../images/Galahs.jpg"
my_images[6]  = "../../images/Kookaburra-2.jpg"
my_images[7]  = "../../images/Lioness.jpg"
my_images[8]  = "../../images/Monkey.jpg"
my_images[9]  = "../../images/Peacock.jpg"
my_images[10] = "../../images/QuinkinArt-3.jpg"
my_images[11] = "../../images/QuinkinArt-4.jpg"
my_images[12] = "../../images/QuinkinArt-5.jpg"
my_images[13] = "../../images/QuinkinCountry.jpg"
my_images[14] = "../../images/Zebra-1.jpg"
```

```
my_images[15] = "../../images/Zebra-2.jpg"

// load an image from the my_images array into
// document.images[0]
//
function loadImage() {
  // adjust currentImage so it cycles through the
  // available images.
  if (currentImage < my_images.length - 1) {
    currentImage++
  } else {
    currentImage = 0
  }

  // load the image
  document.images[0].src = my_images[currentImage]
}

// STOP HIDING -->
</SCRIPT>
</HEAD>
<BODY>

<CENTER>
<IMG SRC="../../images/AyersRock.jpg"
   WIDTH=408
  HEIGHT=264
  HSPACE=0
  VSPACE=0
  BORDER=4>
</CENTER>

<CENTER><FORM>
<INPUT TYPE="button" NAME="nextImage"
  VALUE="Next Image" onClick="loadImage()">
</FORM></CENTER>

</BODY>
</HTML>
```

Figure 9–1 shows the result of loading the `imageSrc.html` script.

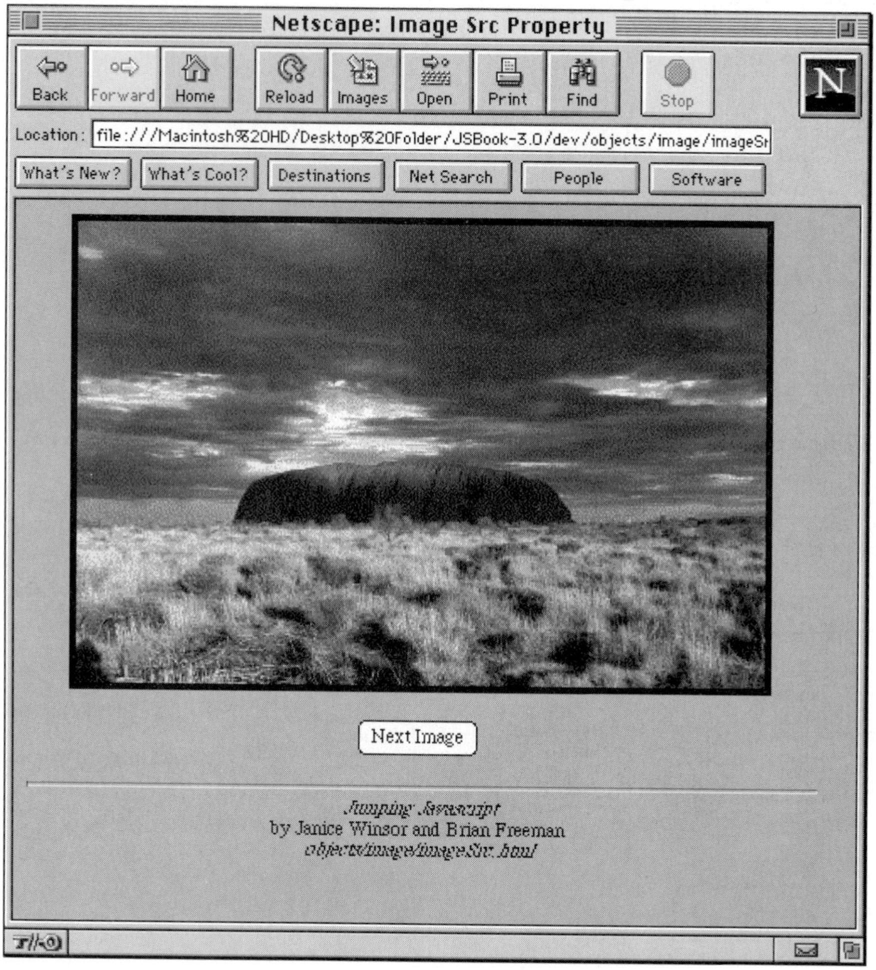

Figure 9–1 Result of loading the `imageSrc.html` script

To display the next image, click on the Next Image button. The next image is displayed, as shown in Figure 9–2.

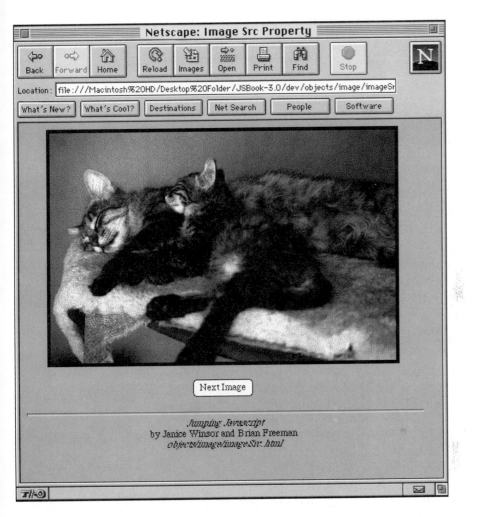

Figure 9–2 Displaying the next image

Notice that as you click on the Next Image button, when you reach the end of the array, the script starts again with the first image in the array.

Prestaging Images with the lowsrc Property

When you have large image files that may take some time to load, you can specify a lower-resolution image to act as a placeholder while the larger image file is being downloaded. You specify the low-resolution image with the `LOWSRC` attribute of the `<IMG>` tag. When the low-resolution image has finished loading,

the HTML automatically loads the image specified by the `SRC` attribute. The JavaScript language (in the 3.0 release) has a `lowsrc` property that you can use in scripts to control behavior of these low-resolution images.

Property	Value	Gettable	Settable
lowsrc	URL	Yes	No

Example of Prestaging Big Images with Low-Resolution Files

The following `imageQuality.html` script provides radio buttons that enable users to choose whether they want to view low- or high-resolution images. When users click on the Low radio button, they can cycle through the array of images and choose which image they want to see at a higher resolution.

This script uses properties of the JavaScript `string` object and the `parseInt()` function to convert a string to an integer. For more information about the `string` object methods and `parseInt()` function, see Chapter 28, "Working with Strings and String Objects."

```
<!--
       imageQuality.html
   This example lets users specify whether
   to view a low- or high-resolution image. When
   users click on the Low radio button, they can
   cycle through the array of images and choose
   which image they want to see at a higher
   resolution.
-->

<HTML>
<HEAD>
<TITLE>Image Quality</TITLE>
<SCRIPT LANGUAGE="JavaScript">
<!-- HIDE FROM OLD BROWSERS

// The names of the images to load.
//
var image_info = new Array()

image_info[0] = "Giraffe 264x408"
image_info[1] = "GuineaFowl 264x408"
image_info[2] = "Koala-2 264x408"
image_info[3] = "Koala 264x408"
```

```
image_info[4] = "Wallaby-3 264x408"
image_info[5] = "WartHogs 264x408"

// The number of images in the image_info
// array.
var amt_images = 6

// The path to the images in the
// image_info array.
//
// Requires a trailing '/'
//
var image_path = "../../images/"


// Obtain the src value for the indicated
// image.
//
function getImageSrc(num) {
  var rstr = ""
  var name = ""

  name = image_info[num].substring(
             0,
             image_info[num].indexOf(' '))

  rstr = image_path + name + ".jpg"

  return rstr
}

// Obtain the lowsrc value for the
// indicated image.
//
function getImageLowsrc(num) {
  var rstr = ""
  var name = ""

  name = image_info[num].substring(
             0,
             image_info[num].indexOf(' '))

  rstr = image_path + name + ".gif"
```

```
  return rstr
}

// Obtain the dimension of the indicated image.
//
function getImageDimension(num) {
  var rstr = ""

  rstr = image_info[num].substring(
              image_info[num].indexOf(' ') + 1,
              image_info[num].length)

  return rstr
}

// Obtain the width of the indicated image.
//
function getImageWidth(num) {
  var   dim = ""
  var width = ""

  dim   = getImageDimension(num)
  width = dim.substring(0, dim.indexOf('x'))

  return parseInt(width, 0)
}

// Obtain the height of the indicated image.
//
function getImageHeight(num) {
  var    dim = ""
  var height = ""

  dim    = getImageDimension(num)
  height = dim.substring(
              dim.indexOf('x') + 1,
              dim.length)
  return parseInt(height, 0)
}


// Image objects constructed from
// image_info
imgs = new Array(6)
```

```
// Create the imgs array from the data in the
// image_info array.
//
function createImgs() {

  // loop through the image_info array
  for (var i=0; i < amt_images; i++) {
    // create the image object and load it.
    imgs[i]         = new Image(
                            getImageWidth(i),
                            getImageHeight(i))
    imgs[i].lowsrc = getImageLowsrc(i)
    imgs[i].src    = getImageSrc(i)
  }
}


// The currently loaded image
//
var current = 0

// Go to an image relative to the current location
//
function goImage(num) {
  if (num < 0) {
    // going backward
    if ((current + num) < 0) {
      // past the start of the array
      // bring back into range
      current =
        (amt_images) + (current + num)
    } else {
      // add a negative number
      current += num
    }
  } else {
    // going forward
    if ((current + num) >= amt_images) {
      // past the end of the array
      // bring back into range
      current =
        (current + num) - (amt_images)
    } else {
```

```
      current += num
    }
  }

  if (high_resolution == true) {
    document.images[0].lowsrc = imgs[current].lowsrc
    document.images[0].src    = imgs[current].src
  } else {
    document.images[0].lowsrc = imgs[current].lowsrc
    document.images[0].src    = imgs[current].lowsrc
  }
}

// go forward in the imgs array
//
function forwardImage(num_str) {
  goImage(parseInt(num_str, 0))
}

// go backward in the imgs array
//
function backImage(num_str) {
  goImage(0 - parseInt(num_str, 0))
}

// image quality
high_resolution = true

// change to low-resolution images
//
function loadLowRes() {
  high_resolution = false
  goImage(0)
}

// change to high-resolution images
//
function loadHighRes() {
  high_resolution = true
  goImage(0)
}

// STOP HIDING -->
</SCRIPT>
```

```
</HEAD>
<BODY onLoad="createImgs()">

<CENTER>
<IMG SRC="../../images/Giraffe.jpg"
  LOWSRC="../../images/Giraffe.gif"
   WIDTH=264 HEIGHT=408 HSPACE=0 VSPACE=0
  BORDER=4>
</CENTER>

<CENTER><FORM>
Image Quality:<BR>
<INPUT TYPE="radio" NAME="resolution"
 VALUE="low" onClick="loadLowRes()">
Low<BR>
<INPUT TYPE="radio" NAME="resolution" CHECKED
 VALUE="high" onClick="loadHighRes()">
High<BR><BR>
<INPUT TYPE="button" NAME="prevBtn"
 VALUE="Previous Image" onClick="backImage(1)">
<INPUT TYPE="button" NAME="nextBtn"
 VALUE="Next Image" onClick="forwardImage(1)">
</FORM></CENTER>

</BODY>
</HTML>
```

Figure 9–3 shows the result of loading the `imageQuality.html` script. The default is to display a high-resolution image, so the low-resolution image loads first, and then the high-resolution image is displayed. This behavior is the default behavior for the Giraffe image, which has a `LOWSRC` and `SRC` image specified in the `<IMG>` tag.

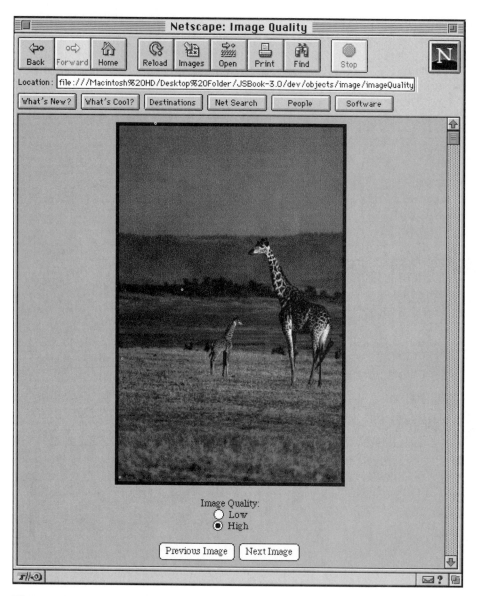

Figure 9–3 Result of loading the `imageQuality.html` script

When you click on the Low radio button, the low-resolution image is displayed, as shown in Figure 9–4.

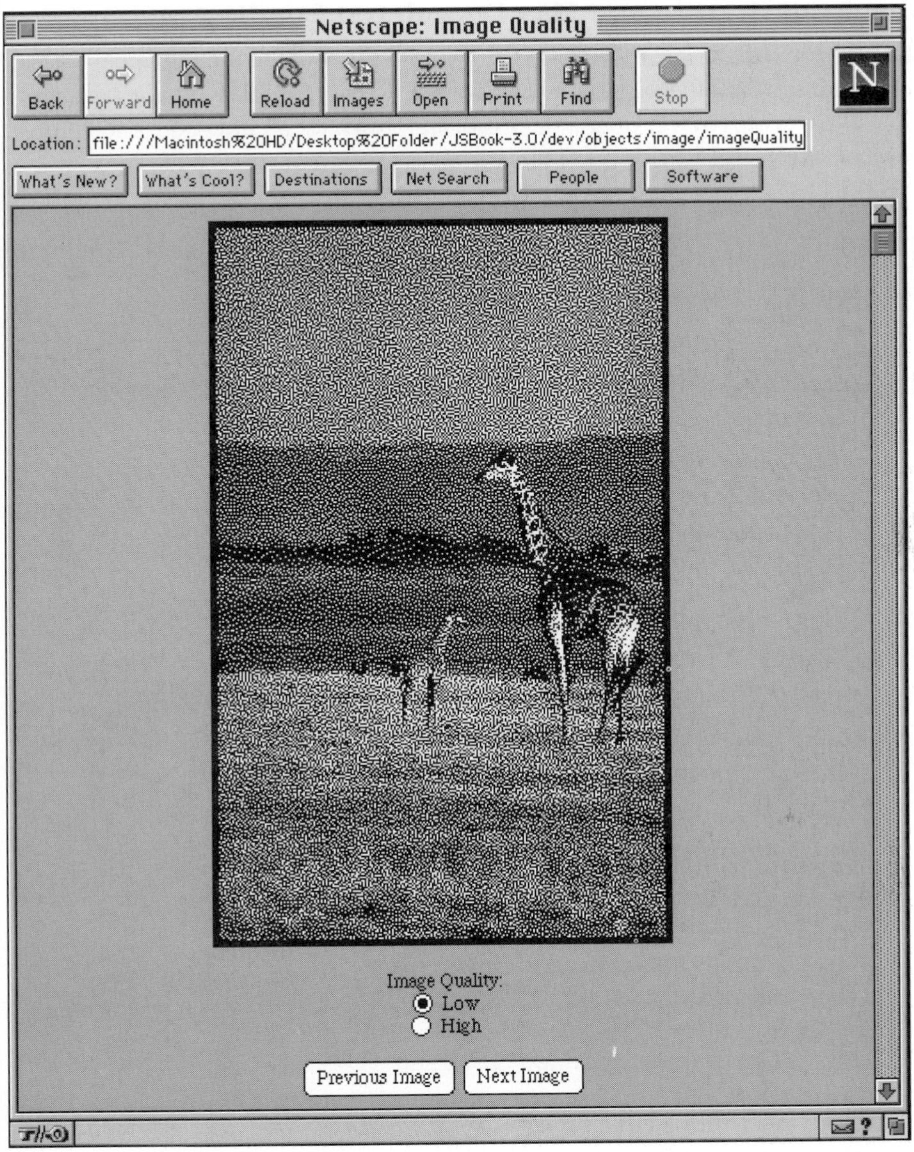

Figure 9–4 Clicking on the Low radio button displays a low-resolution image

You can click on the Next Image or Previous Image button to cycle through an array of low-resolution images.

Checking If an Image Has Completed Loading

At times you may want to check to make sure that an image is completely loaded before you start another action in your scripts. To check on the completion state, you use the `complete` property. If you want to wait for an image to load before you start another action, you use the `image` object `onLoad` event handler.

Property	Value	Gettable	Settable
complete	Boolean	Yes	No

The `complete` property returns a value of `true` if the image has completed loading. It returns a value of `false` if the image is still loading.

You might want to consider using the `complete` property together with the `onError` or `onAbort` event handlers, described later in this chapter, to determine whether an image has completed loading before the error or the abort event takes place.

Example of Checking If an Image Has Completed Loading

The following `imageComplete.html` script displays an alert when the image has completed loading or when you click on the Stop key.

```
<!--
          imageComplete.html
-->

<HTML>
<HEAD>
<TITLE>Image Complete</TITLE>
<SCRIPT LANGUAGE="JavaScript">
<!-- HIDE FROM OLD BROWSERS

// Is the image finished loading
//
function isComplete() {
  var completeTimeout = null

  if (document.images[0].complete == true) {
    var mstr = "\n"

    mstr += "The image " + document.images[0].src
    mstr += "\nis either completely loaded,"
    mstr += " or the loading was interrupted.\n"
```

```
        alert(unescape(mstr))
      } else {
        completeTimeout =
          window.setTimeout(isComplete(), 10)
      }
    }

    // STOP HIDING -->
    </SCRIPT>
    </HEAD>
    <BODY onLoad="isComplete()">

    <P>This example watches the image complete
    property. The complete property is used to
    determine when loading is finished. Either a
    successful load or an abort by the user sets
    complete to true.</P>

    <P>A timeout is used to continually call the
    function isComplete. When complete is true, an alert
    dialog is displayed.</P>

    <CENTER>
    <IMG SRC="../../images/Monkey.jpg"
      NAME="Monkey" WIDTH=408 HEIGHT=264
      HSPACE=0 VSPACE=0 BORDER=4>
    </CENTER>

    </BODY>
    </HTML>
```

Figure 9–5 shows the result of the completed loading of the `imageComplete.html` script.

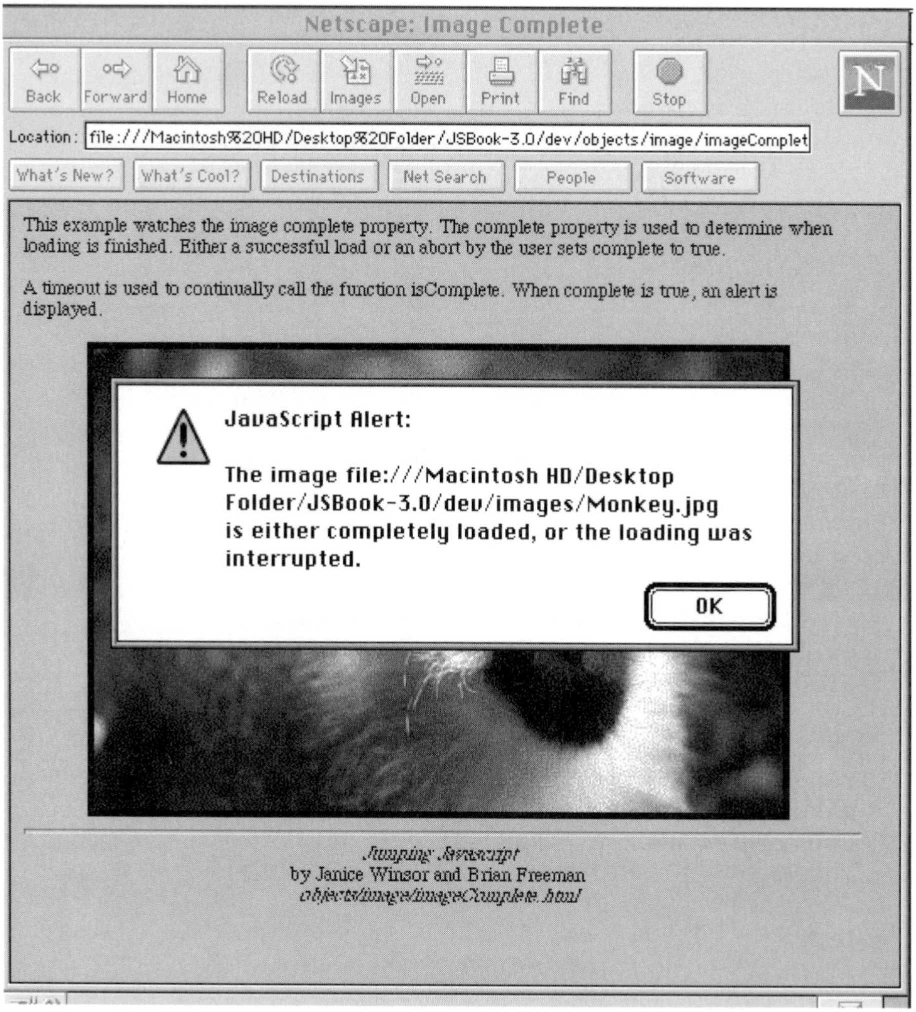

Figure 9–5 Result of loading the `imageComplete.html` script

Using Read-Only Image Properties

The rest of the properties for the `image` object return the value that was set for the attribute in the HTML `<IMG>` tag. Although you can retrieve their values, you cannot change them.

Property	Value	Gettable	Settable
border	pixels	Yes	No
height	pixels	Yes	No
hspace	pixels	Yes	No
name	string	Yes	No
vspace	pixels	Yes	No
width	pixels	Yes	No

Example of Displaying Image Properties

The following `imageProps.html` script displays the properties for two images.

```
<!--
        imageProps.html

    This example displays all the image
    properties in a window when the button
    is clicked.
-->

<HTML>
<HEAD>
<TITLE>Image Properties</TITLE>

<!-- Includes -->
<SCRIPT SRC="../../debug/documentUtils.js"></SCRIPT>
<SCRIPT SRC="../../debug/windowOpen.js"></SCRIPT>
<SCRIPT SRC="../../debug/generateWindow.js"></SCRIPT>
<SCRIPT SRC="../../debug/displayProperties.js"></SCRIPT>

<!-- local functions -->
<SCRIPT LANGUAGE="JavaScript">
<!-- HIDE FROM OLD BROWSERS

// display all the properties of the
// document.images array.
//
function imageProps() {
```

```
  // load an array with the arguments for
  // displayProperties().
  // The order of the arguments is:
  //   obj
  //   obj_name
  //   html
  //
  var displayPropsArgs = new Array(3)
  displayPropsArgs[0] = document.images
  displayPropsArgs[1] = "document.images"
  displayPropsArgs[2] = true

  // generateWindow() creates a window and calls
  // the function passed as the fifth argument. The
  // last argument, an array, holds any arguments
  // you want to pass to the function.
  //
  // In this case, displayProperties() is the
  // function; displayPropsArgs[] is the
  // argument array I want to pass to
  // displayProperties().
  //
  generateWindow("imagePropsWin", "document.images",
                 500, 500, displayProperties,
                 displayPropsArgs)
}
// STOP HIDING -->
</SCRIPT></HEAD>

<BODY>
<CENTER>
<TABLE BORDER=4 WIDTH=412 HEIGHT=268>
  <CAPTION>[408x264] AyersRock.jpg</CAPTION>
  <TR>
    <TD>
      <IMG SRC="../../images/AyersRock.jpg"
   LOWSRC="../../images/AyersRock.gif"
     NAME="AyersRock"
    WIDTH=408
        HEIGHT=264
   HSPACE=0
        VSPACE=0
         ALIGN=absmiddle
   BORDER=4>
```

```
      </TD>
    </TR>
  </TABLE>
  <BR><BR>
  <TABLE BORDER=4 WIDTH=436 HEIGHT=268>
    <CAPTION>[432x264] RamSkull.jpg</CAPTION>
    <TR>
      <TD>
        <IMG SRC="../../images/RamSkull.jpg"
          LOWSRC="../../images/RamSkull.gif"
            NAME="RamSkull"
           WIDTH=432
          HEIGHT=264
          HSPACE=0
          VSPACE=0
           ALIGN=absmiddle
          BORDER=4>
      </TD>
    </TR>
  </TABLE>

  <P>Click on the button below to display the
  properties of the images on this page.</P>

  <P>Keep in mind that the images above are defined
  with both SRC and LOWSRC attributes; thus, the four
  elements in the images array.
  </CENTER>

  <CENTER><FORM>
  <INPUT TYPE="button" NAME="imagePropsBtn"
    VALUE="Image Properties" onClick="imageProps()">
  </FORM></CENTER>

  </BODY>
  </HTML>
```

Figure 9–6 shows the result of loading the `imageProps.html` script and scrolling to the bottom of the page.

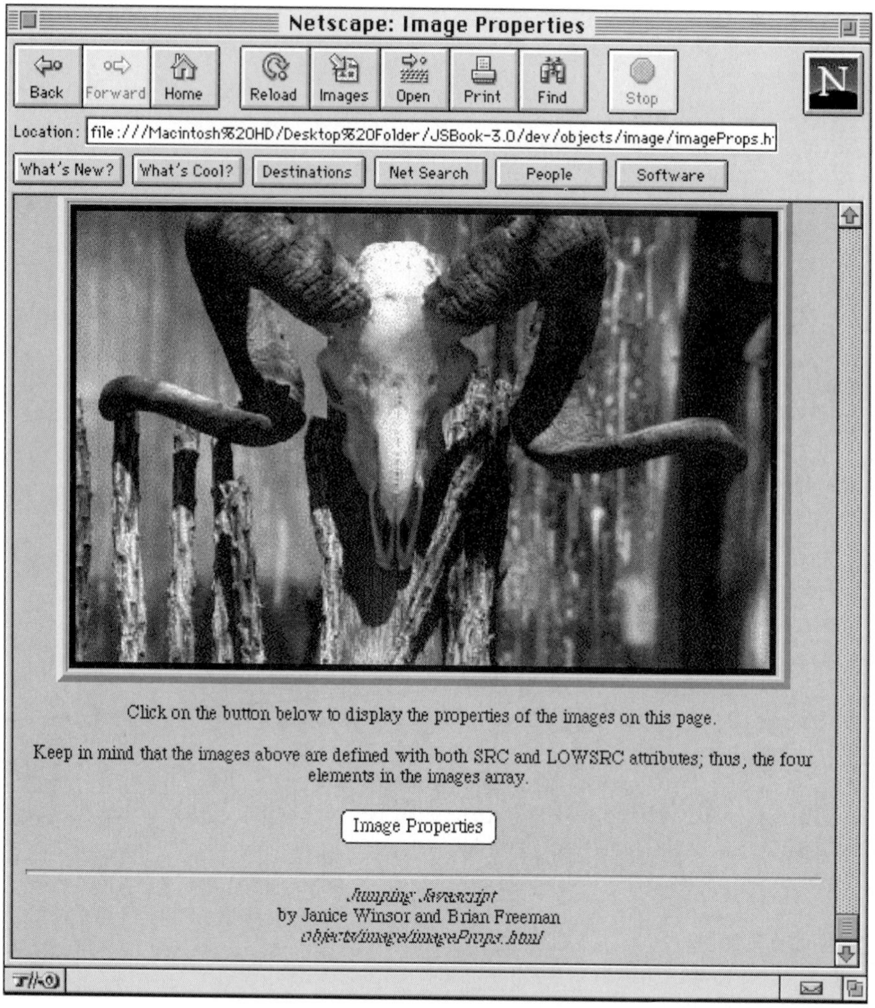

Netscape: Image Properties

Back Forward Home Reload Images Open Print Find Stop

Location: file:///Macintosh%20HD/Desktop%20Folder/JSBook-3.0/dev/objects/image/imageProps.h

What's New? What's Cool? Destinations Net Search People Software

Click on the button below to display the properties of the images on this page.

Keep in mind that the images above are defined with both SRC and LOWSRC attributes; thus, the four elements in the images array.

Image Properties

Jumping Javascript
by Janice Winsor and Brian Freeman
objects/image/imageProps.html

Figure 9–6 Result of loading the `imageProps.html` script

When you click on the Image Properties button, a new window opens, displaying the properties for the images on the page, as shown in Figure 9–7. Because the two images have both `SRC` and `LOWSRC` attributes, the `images` array counts four elements.

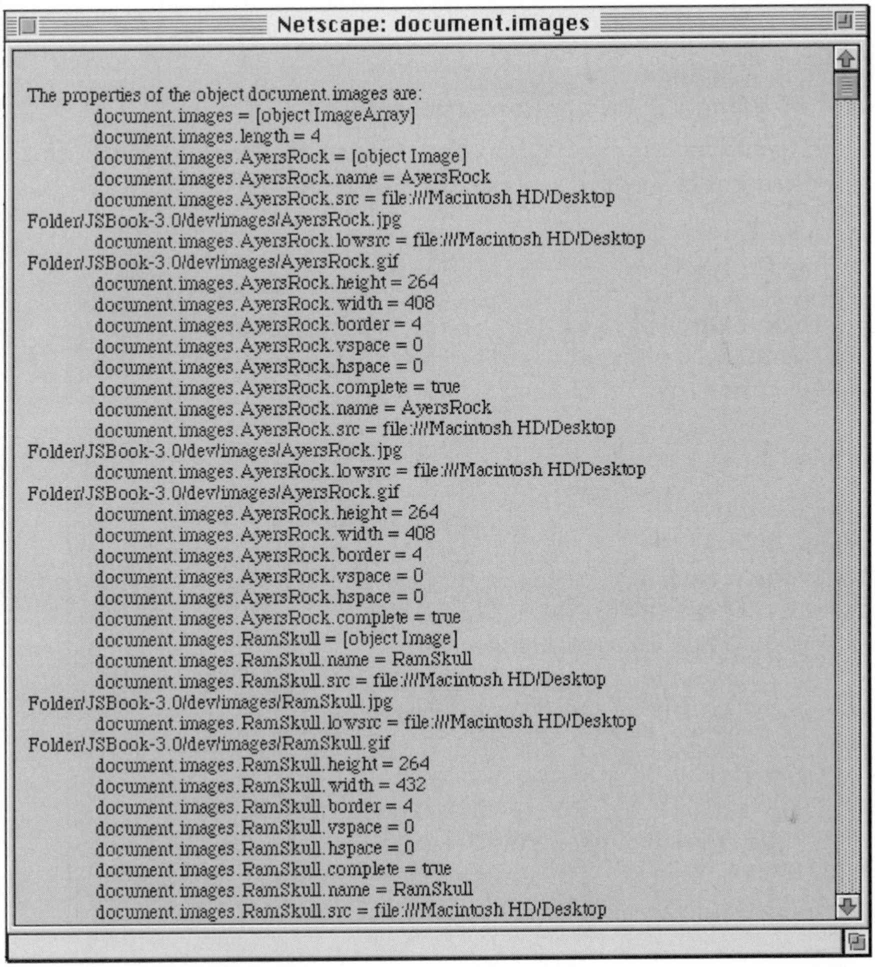

Netscape: document.images

```
The properties of the object document.images are:
        document.images = [object ImageArray]
        document.images.length = 4
        document.images.AyersRock = [object Image]
        document.images.AyersRock.name = AyersRock
        document.images.AyersRock.src = file:///Macintosh HD/Desktop
Folder/JSBook-3.0/dev/images/AyersRock.jpg
        document.images.AyersRock.lowsrc = file:///Macintosh HD/Desktop
Folder/JSBook-3.0/dev/images/AyersRock.gif
        document.images.AyersRock.height = 264
        document.images.AyersRock.width = 408
        document.images.AyersRock.border = 4
        document.images.AyersRock.vspace = 0
        document.images.AyersRock.hspace = 0
        document.images.AyersRock.complete = true
        document.images.AyersRock.name = AyersRock
        document.images.AyersRock.src = file:///Macintosh HD/Desktop
Folder/JSBook-3.0/dev/images/AyersRock.jpg
        document.images.AyersRock.lowsrc = file:///Macintosh HD/Desktop
Folder/JSBook-3.0/dev/images/AyersRock.gif
        document.images.AyersRock.height = 264
        document.images.AyersRock.width = 408
        document.images.AyersRock.border = 4
        document.images.AyersRock.vspace = 0
        document.images.AyersRock.hspace = 0
        document.images.AyersRock.complete = true
        document.images.RamSkull = [object Image]
        document.images.RamSkull.name = RamSkull
        document.images.RamSkull.src = file:///Macintosh HD/Desktop
Folder/JSBook-3.0/dev/images/RamSkull.jpg
        document.images.RamSkull.lowsrc = file:///Macintosh HD/Desktop
Folder/JSBook-3.0/dev/images/RamSkull.gif
        document.images.RamSkull.height = 264
        document.images.RamSkull.width = 432
        document.images.RamSkull.border = 4
        document.images.RamSkull.vspace = 0
        document.images.RamSkull.hspace = 0
        document.images.RamSkull.complete = true
        document.images.RamSkull.name = RamSkull
        document.images.RamSkull.src = file:///Macintosh HD/Desktop
```

Figure 9–7 Image properties

Using the Image Constructor

The JavaScript language provides an image constructor, `Image()`, that you can use to create instances of the `image` object. The main use for this constructor is to enable you to force an image to be downloaded and decoded before you need to display it. For example, you can use the image constructor to download and prestage a set of images for smooth animations. Alternatively, you can download a set of images and display only one of them, saving the other images in memory for immediate display when called in the script.

The syntax for using the image constructor is:

```
myImage=new Image()
```

Example of Using the Image Constructor

The following `imageConstructor.html` script uses the `Image()` constructor to create an array of images that the user can cycle through.

```
<!--
        imageConstructor.html

    This example uses the image constructor,
    Image(), to create an array of images the
    user can cycle through.

-->


<HTML>
<HEAD>
<TITLE>Image Constructor</TITLE>
<SCRIPT LANGUAGE="JavaScript">
<!-- HIDE FROM OLD BROWSERS
var currentImage = 0
var    my_images = new Array(20)

// preload the my_images array
for (var i = 0; i < my_images.length; i++) {
  my_images[i] = new Image(175, 150)
 my_images[i].src = "../../images/Frogs/Frog" + (i + 1) +
".gif"
}

// load an image from the my_images array into
// document.images[0]
//
function loadImage() {
  // adjust currentImage so it cycles through the
  // available images.
  if (currentImage < my_images.length - 1) {
    currentImage++
  } else {
    currentImage = 0
  }
```

```
    // load the image
    document.images[0].src = my_images[currentImage].src
  }

  // STOP HIDING -->
  </SCRIPT>
  </HEAD>
  <BODY>

  <CENTER>
  <IMG SRC="../../images/Frogs/Frog1.gif"
     WIDTH=175
    HEIGHT=150
    HSPACE=0
    VSPACE=0
    BORDER=4>
  </CENTER>

  <CENTER><FORM>
  <INPUT TYPE="button" NAME="nextImage"
    VALUE="Next Image" onClick="loadImage()">
  </FORM></CENTER>

  </BODY>
  </HTML>
```

Figure 9–8 shows the result of loading the `imageConstructor.html` script.

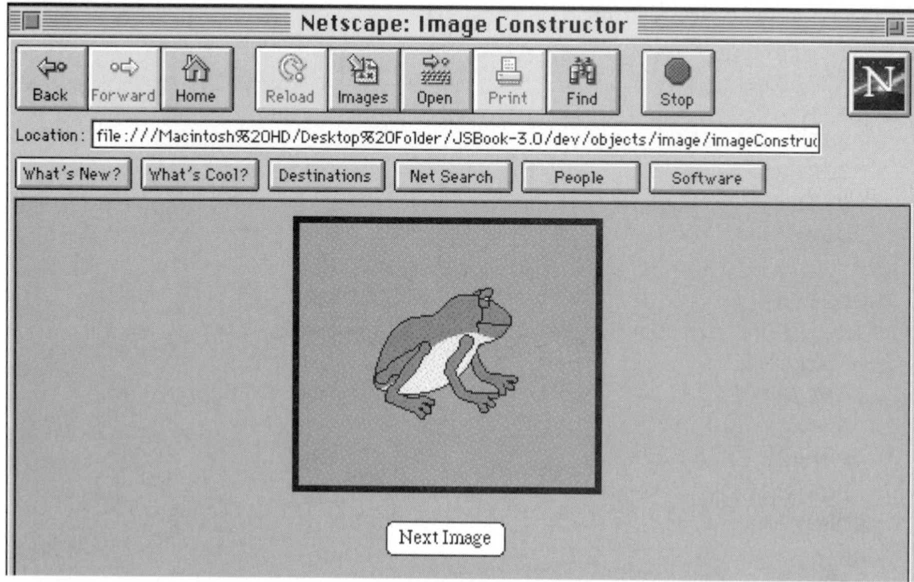

Figure 9–8 Result of loading the `imageConstructor.html` script

When you click on the Next Image button, the next image is loaded, as shown in Figure 9–9. Note that these two images differ slightly.

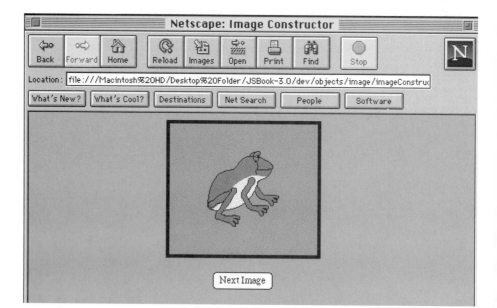

Figure 9–9 Next loaded image

Example of Animation Script

The following `jumpingJavaScript.html` script is a variation on the `imageConstructor.html` script. The `jumpingJavaScript.html` script uses the `Image()` constructor. It automatically displays the next image without any user action and provides some buttons you can use to control the speed and to stop and start the animation.

```
<!--
       jumpingJavaScript.html

    This example performs a simple animation
    sequence, using the onLoad event handler to
    determine when to cycle to the next image.

-->

<HTML>
<HEAD>
<TITLE>Jumping JavaScript Animation</TITLE>
<SCRIPT LANGUAGE="JavaScript">
<!-- HIDE FROM OLD BROWSERS
var currentImage = 0
var      timeout = null
var         frog = new Array(20)
var        delay = 200

for (var i = 0; i < frog.length; i++) {
  frog[i]     = new Image(175, 150)
  frog[i].src = "../../images/Frogs/Frog" + (i + 1) +
".gif"
}

// decrease the delay between image changes
//
function faster() {
  delay -= 50

  if (delay < 0) {
    delay = 0
  }
}

// increase the delay between image changes
//
```

```
function slower() {
  delay += 50

  if (delay > 5000) {
    delay = 5000
  }
}

// load the image with the designated image from
// the frog array.
//
function loadImage(imgNum) {
  // load the image
  document.images[0].src = frog[imgNum].src
}

// load the next image from the frog array into
// document.images[0]. Starts over with 0 when it
// hits the end of the frog array.
//
function nextImage() {
  // adjust currentImage so it cycles through the
  // available frog.
  if (currentImage < frog.length - 1) {
    currentImage++
  } else {
    currentImage = 0
  }

  // set a timeout to load the image
  timeout = setTimeout("loadImage(currentImage)", delay)
}

// stop the animation
//
function stop() {
  clearTimeout(timeout)
}

// STOP HIDING -->
</SCRIPT>
</HEAD>
<BODY>
```

```
<CENTER>
<IMG SRC="../../images/Frogs/Frog1.gif"
   WIDTH=175 HEIGHT=150
  HSPACE=0 VSPACE=0 BORDER=4
  onLoad="nextImage()">
</CENTER>

<CENTER><FORM>
<INPUT TYPE="button" NAME="StopBtn"
  VALUE="Stop" onClick="stop()">
<INPUT TYPE="button" NAME="restartBtn"
  VALUE="Restart" onClick="nextImage()"><BR>
<INPUT TYPE="button" NAME="fasterBtn"
  VALUE="Faster" onClick="faster()">
<INPUT TYPE="button" NAME="slowerBtn"
  VALUE="Slower" onClick="slower()">
</FORM></CENTER>

</BODY>
</HTML>
```

Figure 9–10 shows the result of loading the `jumpingJavaScript.html` script.

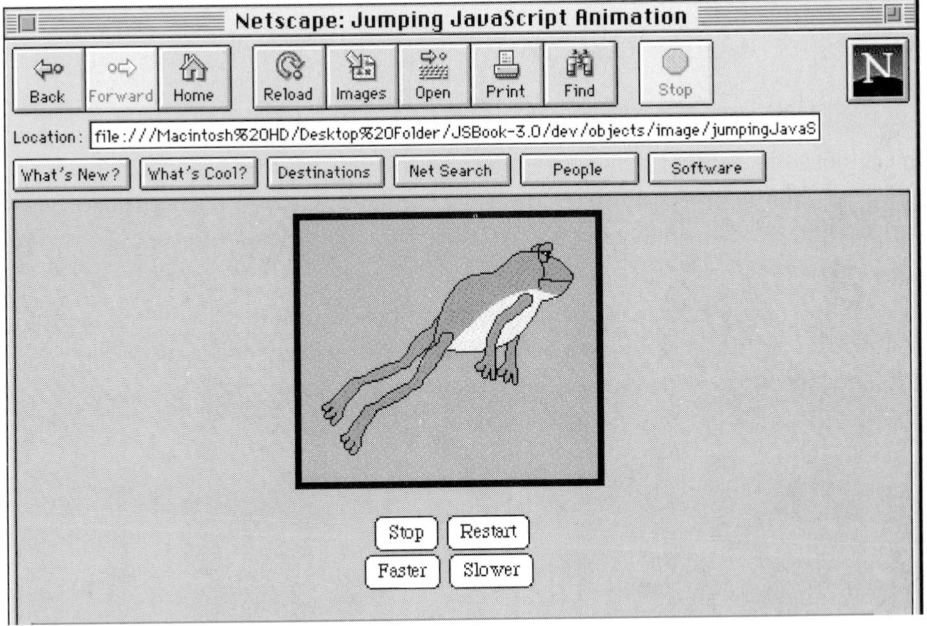

Figure 9–10 Result of loading the `jumpingJavaScript.html` script

The script keeps cycling through the images until you click on the Stop button. Figure 9–11 shows the winking frog image from the animation.

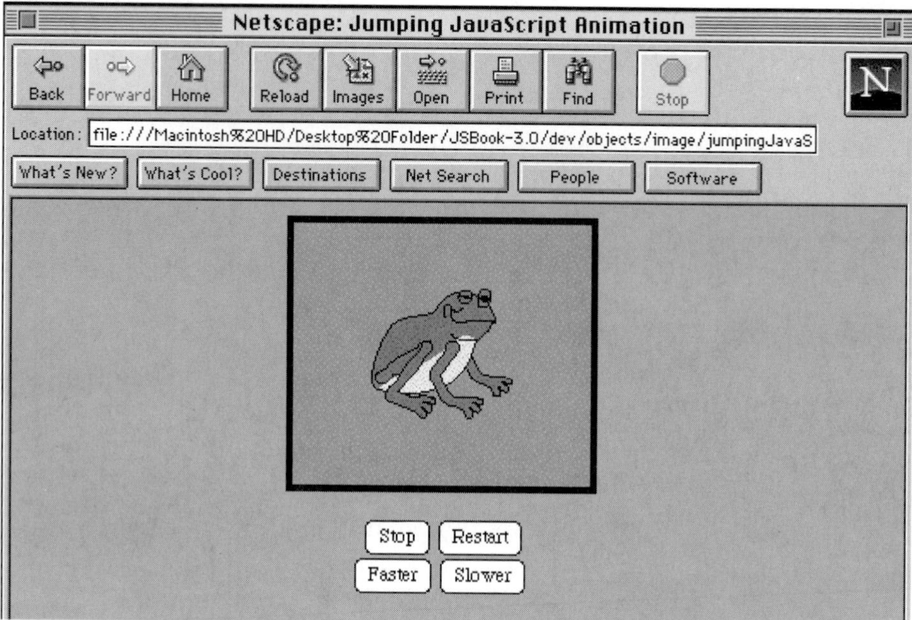

Figure 9–11 Another image in the `jumpingJavaScript.html` animation

Using the onLoad Event Handler

You can use the `onLoad` event handler to perform a scripting action when an image has completed loading. Loading is completed when a `LOWSRC` image is loaded; if no `LOWSRC` image is specified, loading is completed after an `SRC` image is loaded.

The `LOWSRC` and `SRC` images are not connected to one another in the JavaScript image object. When you define a `LOWSRC` image, the image object does not automatically know when the `SRC` image loading is completed.

Event Handler

onLoad

Syntax

<IMG>

SRC = "*ImageURL*"

(onLoad = "*JavaScript code*")

>

Because the onLoad handler responds automatically by events in the HTML <IMG> tags, you should not use the onLoad event handler to load another image unless you include a timeout. For an example of how you can get into trouble with the onLoad event handler, see "Getting into Trouble with the onLoad Event Handler" on page 363.

Using the onLoad Event Handler to Display an Alert

The following imageOnLoad.html script displays an alert when the image is loaded.

```
<!--
       imageOnLoad.html

    This example shows an image onLoad event
    handler that displays an alert.
-->

<HTML>
<HEAD>
<TITLE>Image OnLoad</TITLE>
<SCRIPT LANGUAGE="JavaScript">
<!-- HIDE FROM OLD BROWSERS

// An onLoad event handler
//
function imageLoaded(theImage) {
  if (theImage) {
    alert(unescape(theImage.src) + " was loaded.")
  } else {
```

```
      alert("An image loaded.")
    }
  }

  // STOP HIDING -->
  </SCRIPT></HEAD>
  <BODY>

  <CENTER>
  <IMG SRC="../../images/AyersRock.jpg"
     WIDTH=408 HEIGHT=264
    HSPACE=0 VSPACE=0 BORDER=4
    onLoad="imageLoaded(this)">
  </CENTER>

  </BODY>
  </HTML>
```

Figure 9–12 shows the result of loading the `imageOnLoad.html` script.

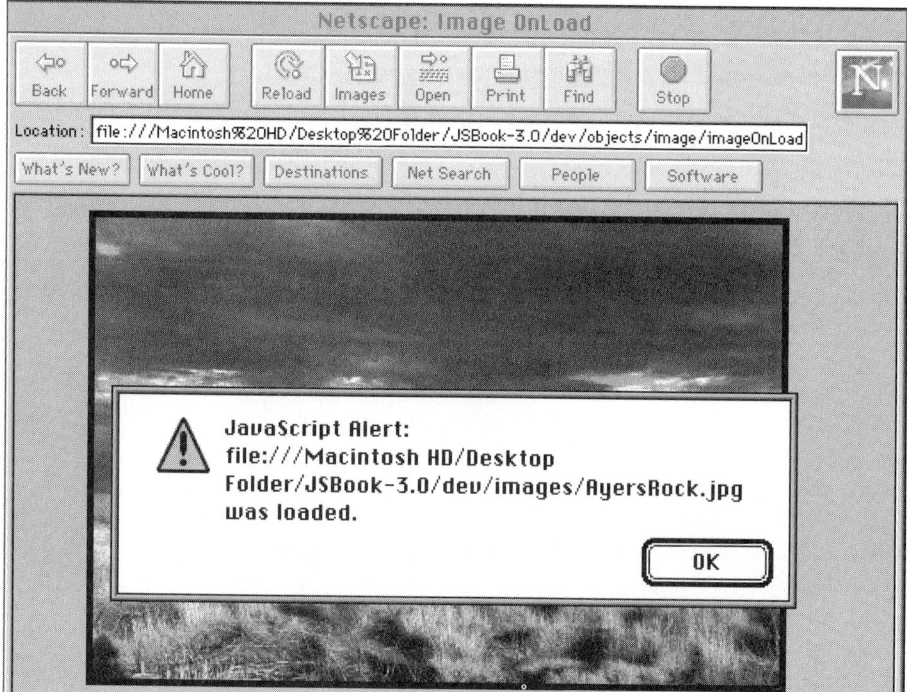

Figure 9–12 Result of loading the `imageOnLoad.html` script

Using the onLoad Event Handler to Create a Slide Show

The following `imageAnimate.html` script creates an array of 16 images. The first image in the array is loaded, and the script then uses the `onLoad` event handler and a timer to determine when to load the next image. It includes a timeout of 1000 microseconds to control the time each image is displayed. You can experiment with this value to create a display time that works for you.

```
<!--
      imageAnimate.html

    This example performs a simple animation
    sequence, using the onLoad event handler to
    determine when to cycle to the next image.

-->

<HTML>
<HEAD>
<TITLE>Image Animation</TITLE>
<SCRIPT LANGUAGE="JavaScript">
<!-- HIDE FROM OLD BROWSERS
var currentImage = 0
var    my_images = new Array(16)

my_images[0]  = "../../images/AyersRock.jpg"
my_images[1]  = "../../images/Cats-1.jpg"
my_images[2]  = "../../images/Cats-2.jpg"
my_images[3]  = "../../images/Chamelion.jpg"
my_images[4]  = "../../images/Elephants.jpg"
my_images[5]  = "../../images/Galahs.jpg"
my_images[6]  = "../../images/Kookaburra-2.jpg"
my_images[7]  = "../../images/Lioness.jpg"
my_images[8]  = "../../images/Monkey.jpg"
my_images[9]  = "../../images/Peacock.jpg"
my_images[10] = "../../images/QuinkinArt-3.jpg"
my_images[11] = "../../images/QuinkinArt-4.jpg"
my_images[12] = "../../images/QuinkinArt-5.jpg"
my_images[13] = "../../images/QuinkinCountry.jpg"
my_images[14] = "../../images/Zebra-1.jpg"
my_images[15] = "../../images/Zebra-2.jpg"

// load the image with the designated image from
// the images array.
//
```

```
function loadImage(imgNum) {
  // load the image
  document.images[0].src = my_images[imgNum]
}

// load the next image from the images array into
// document.images[0]. Starts over with 0 when it
// hits the end of the images array.
//
function nextImage() {
  // adjust currentImage so it cycles through the
  // available images.
  if (currentImage < my_images.length - 1) {
    currentImage++
  } else {
    currentImage = 0
  }

  // set a timeout to load the image
  setTimeout("loadImage(currentImage)", 1000)
}

// STOP HIDING -->
</SCRIPT>
</HEAD>
<BODY>

<CENTER>
<IMG SRC="../../images/AyersRock.jpg"
   WIDTH=408 HEIGHT=264
  HSPACE=0 VSPACE=0 BORDER=4
  onLoad="nextImage()">
</CENTER>

<CENTER><FORM>
<INPUT TYPE="button" NAME="restart"
  VALUE="Restart" onClick="nextImage()">
</FORM></CENTER>

</BODY>
</HTML>
```

Figure 9–13 shows the result of loading the `imageAnimate.html` script with one of the images in the middle of the sequence displayed.

Figure 9–13 Result of loading the `imageAnimate.html` script

Using the onLoad Event Handler to Change the Image Source

The following `imageOnLoadLowHigh.html` script uses the `onLoad` event handler and a timer with a timeout to load a higher-resolution image when the low-resolution image has finished loading. If you click quickly enough on the Next Image button, you can cycle through the low-resolution images before the high-resolution image is loaded. When you stop, the high-resolution image is loaded.

```
<!--
            imageOnLoadLowHigh.html
      This example shows an image onLoad event
      handler that changes the image src property
      to a higher-quality image.
-->
<HTML>
<HEAD>
<TITLE>Image onLoad Low to High</TITLE>
```

```
<SCRIPT LANGUAGE="JavaScript">
<!-- HIDE FROM OLD BROWSERS
var currentImage = 0
var    my_images = new Array(16)

my_images[0]  = "../../images/AyersRock.gif"
my_images[1]  = "../../images/Cats-1.gif"
my_images[2]  = "../../images/Cats-2.gif"
my_images[3]  = "../../images/Chamelion.gif"
my_images[4]  = "../../images/Elephants.gif"
my_images[5]  = "../../images/Galahs.gif"
my_images[6]  = "../../images/Kookaburra-2.gif"
my_images[7]  = "../../images/Lioness.gif"
my_images[8]  = "../../images/Monkey.gif"
my_images[9]  = "../../images/Peacock.gif"
my_images[10] = "../../images/QuinkinArt-3.gif"
my_images[11] = "../../images/QuinkinArt-4.gif"
my_images[12] = "../../images/QuinkinArt-5.gif"
my_images[13] = "../../images/QuinkinCountry.gif"
my_images[14] = "../../images/Zebra-1.gif"
my_images[15] = "../../images/Zebra-2.gif"

// Set the image src property to the JPEG image.
//
// This function is called from a timeout to set
// the image src property.  It strips off the
// gif extension, replaces it with jpg, and
// assigns the resulting value to the src
// property.
//
function setJPEGImage() {
  var curSrc = document.images[0].src
  var newSrc = ""

  newSrc =
    curSrc.substring(0, curSrc.lastIndexOf(".gif"))
  newSrc += ".jpg"
  document.images[0].src = newSrc
}

// Load the JPEG version of the image.
//
// Registered as an onLoad event handler, this
// function loads the JPEG version of the current
```

```
// image.
//
function loadJPEGVersion() {
  var curSrc = document.images[0].src

  // If the curSrc string contains '.gif', change
  // the image to the JPEG version.
  //
  if (curSrc.indexOf(".gif") != -1) {
    //
    // A timeout is used to load the image
    // because we're in an onLoad event handler.
    //
    // When you assign a value to the src
    // property, the image is loaded.  On a
    // successful load, the onLoad event handler
    // is called. But, that's the way it's
    // supposed to work, right?
    //
    // Yes, but there's a problem.  the program is in
    // the onLoad event handler, and this invocation
    // hasn't returned yet. Indirectly, the program
    // winds up recursively calling itself and never
    // returning. Eventually, a stack overflow
    // stops the recursion.
    //
    setTimeout("setJPEGImage()", 1)
  }
}

// Load the next image.
//
// Registered as an onClick event handler, this
// function determines the next image to load. It
// sets a timeout to actually load the image into
// the document.
//
// The available images range from 0 to
// my_images.length - 1. If the next image can be
// loaded without going past the end of the array,
// do so. Otherwise, start over at 0.
//
function loadImage() {
  // adjust currentImage so it cycles through the
```

```
    // available images.
    if (currentImage < my_images.length -1) {
      currentImage++
    } else {
      currentImage = 0
    }

    // load the image.
    //
    // No need to worry about a stack overflow
    // here. The onLoad event handler uses a
    // timeout, and it will return before the user
    // can click on the button again.
    //
    document.images[0].src = my_images[currentImage]
}

// STOP HIDING -->
</SCRIPT>
</HEAD>
<BODY>

<P>This example shows an image onLoad event
handler that changes the image src property to a
higher-quality image. Click on the Next Image
button to cycle through the low-quality images until
you reach one you're interested in. When you stop,
the onLoad event handler loads a higher-
quality image for you.</P>

<CENTER>
<IMG SRC="../../images/AyersRock.gif"
   WIDTH=408 HEIGHT=264
  HSPACE=0 VSPACE=0 BORDER=4
  onLoad="loadJPEGVersion()">
</CENTER>

<CENTER><FORM>
<INPUT TYPE="button" NAME="nextImage"
  VALUE="Next Image" onClick="loadImage()">
</FORM></CENTER>

</BODY>
</HTML>
```

Figure 9–14 shows the result of loading the `imageOnLoadLowHigh.html` script after cycling through several images and waiting for the high-resolution image to load.

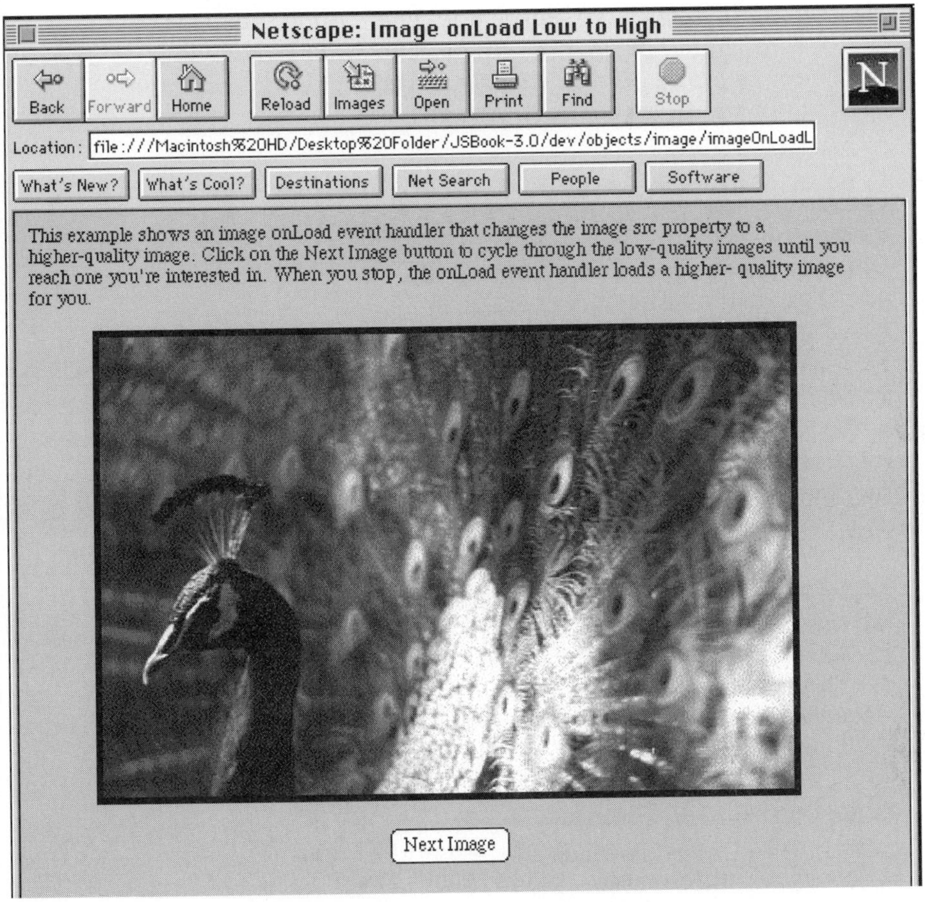

Netscape: Image onLoad Low to High

Back Forward Home Reload Images Open Print Find Stop

Location: file:///Macintosh%20HD/Desktop%20Folder/JSBook-3.0/dev/objects/image/imageOnLoadL

What's New? What's Cool? Destinations Net Search People Software

This example shows an image onLoad event handler that changes the image src property to a higher-quality image. Click on the Next Image button to cycle through the low-quality images until you reach one you're interested in. When you stop, the onLoad event handler loads a higher- quality image for you.

Next Image

Figure 9–14 Result of loading the `imageOnLoadLowHigh.html` script

Getting into Trouble with the onLoad Event Handler

The following `imageOnErrorChange.html` script demonstrates how you can get into trouble when using the `onLoad` event handler to load another image. The script is well commented, so you can follow along in the script and see where the problem occurs.

```
<!--
             imageOnErrorChange.html

    This example intentionally loads an image that
    doesn't exist to show how the image onError
    event handler works. When the onError event
    occurs, the event handler attempts to replace
    it with an alternate image.
-->

<HTML>
<HEAD>
<TITLE>Image OnError</TITLE>
<SCRIPT LANGUAGE="JavaScript">
<!-- HIDE FROM OLD BROWSERS
var currentImage = 0
var    my_images = new Array(3)

my_images[0]  = "../../images/AyersRock.gif"
my_images[1]  = "../../images/Lioness.gif"
my_images[2]  = "../../images/jpgVersionErrors.gif"

// Set the image src property to the JPEG image.
//
// This function is called from a timeout to set
// the image src property.  It strips off the gif
// extension, replaces it with jpg, and assigns
// the resulting value to the src property.
//
function setJPEGImage() {
  var curSrc   = document.images[0].src
  var theImage = new Image(408, 264)
  var newSrc   = ""

  // build the src property
  newSrc =
    curSrc.substring(0, curSrc.lastIndexOf(".gif"))
  newSrc += ".jpg"

  theImage.onerror = loadGIFVersion
  theImage.onload  = null
  theImage.src     = newSrc

  // make the assignment
```

```
    document.images[0].onerror = loadGIFVersion
    document.images[0].onload  = null
    document.images[0].src     = theImage.src
  }

  // Set the image src property to the GIF image.
  //
  // This function is called from a timeout to set
  // the image src property.  It strips off the jpg
  // extension, replaces it with gif, and assigns
  // the resulting value to the src property.
  //
  function setGIFImage() {
    var curSrc   = document.images[0].src
    var theImage = new Image(408, 264)
    var newSrc   = ""

    // build the src property
    newSrc =
      curSrc.substring(0, curSrc.lastIndexOf(".jpg"))
    newSrc += ".gif"

    theImage.onerror = loadJPEGVersion
    theImage.onload  = null
    theImage.src     = newSrc

    // make the assignment
    document.images[0].onerror = loadJPEGVersion
    document.images[0].onload  = null
    document.images[0].src     = theImage.src
  }

  // Load the JPEG version of the image.
  //
  // Registered as an onLoad and onError event
  // handler, this function loads the JPEG version
  // of the current image.
  //
  function loadJPEGVersion() {
    var curSrc = document.images[0].src

    // If the curSrc string contains '.gif', change
    // the image to the JPEG version.
    //
```

```
    if (curSrc.indexOf(".gif") != -1) {
      //
      // A timeout is used to load the image
      // because we're in an onLoad event handler.
      //
      // When you assign a value to the src
      // property, the image is loaded.  Upon a
      // successful load, the onLoad event handler
      // is called. But, that's the way it's
      // supposed to work, right?
      //
      // Yes, but there's a problem.  the program is in
      // the onLoad event handler, and this invocation
      // hasn't returned yet. Indirectly, the program
      // winds up recursively calling itself and never
      // returning. Eventually, a stack overflow
      // stops the recursion.
      //
      setTimeout("setJPEGImage()", 1)
    }
  }

  // Load the GIF version of the image.
  //
  // Registered as an onLoad and onError event
  // handler, this function loads the GIF version
  // of the current image.
  //
  function loadGIFVersion() {
    var curSrc = document.images[0].src

    // If the curSrc string contains '.jpg', change
    // the image to the GIF version.
    //
    if (curSrc.indexOf(".jpg") != -1) {
      // A timeout is used here for the same reason
      // as in loadJPEGVersion.
      setTimeout("setGIFImage()", 1)
    }
  }

  // load an image from the my_images array into
  // document.images[0]
  //
```

```
function loadImage() {
  var theImage = new Image(408, 264)

  // adjust currentImage so it cycles through the
  // available images.
  currentImage++
  if (currentImage >= my_images.length) {
    currentImage = 0
  }

  theImage.onerror = loadGIFVersion
  theImage.onload  = loadJPEGVersion
  theImage.src     = my_images[currentImage]

  // load the image
  document.images[0].onerror = loadGIFVersion
  document.images[0].onload  = loadJPEGVersion
  document.images[0].src     = theImage.src
}

// STOP HIDING -->
</SCRIPT>
</HEAD>
<BODY>

<P>Well, this script doesn't work as intended. What's
supposed to happen is this: a low-resolution image is
loaded, then a high-resolution, using an onLoad
event handler. The third high-resolution image
doesn't exist, so an error is generated. The
onError event handler catches it and tries to
compensate by loading the low-resolution image
again. But, when the error occurs, the image is
given a new width and height. All images
displayed from then on have incorrect
dimensions. Bummer.</P>

<CENTER>
<IMG SRC="../../images/AyersRock.gif"
   WIDTH=408 HEIGHT=264
  HSPACE=0 VSPACE=0 BORDER=4
  onLoad="loadJPEGVersion()"
 onError="loadGIFVersion()">
</CENTER>
```

```
<CENTER><FORM>
<INPUT TYPE="button" NAME="nextImage"
  VALUE="Next Image" onClick="loadImage()">
</FORM></CENTER>

</BODY>
</HTML>
```

Planning for Error Handling

The JavaScript language provides an `onError` event handler for the image object. You can use the `onError` event handler to provide a function that handles cleanup if something goes wrong while an image is downloading.

Event Handler

onError

Syntax

<IMG

SRC = "*ImageURL*"

(onError = "*JavaScript code*")

>

Using the onError Event Handler to Catch Errors

The following `imageOnError.html` script intentionally loads a nonexistent image to force an alert to display when the image is not found.

```
<!--
                imageOnError.html

    This example intentionally loads an image that
    doesn't exist to show how the image onError
    event handler works.
-->

<HTML>
<HEAD>
<TITLE>Image OnError</TITLE>
<SCRIPT LANGUAGE="JavaScript">
```

```
<!-- HIDE FROM OLD BROWSERS

// image onError event handler
//
// Tell the user about the problem
//
function handleError() {

  var mstr = "\n"

  mstr += "The image " + document.images[0].src
  mstr += " did not load properly.\n"
  mstr += "If this problem persists, please "
  mstr += "let the webmaster know.\n"

  alert(unescape(mstr))
  return true
}

// STOP HIDING -->
</SCRIPT>
</HEAD>
<BODY>

<CENTER>
<IMG SRC="../../images/doesntExist.jpg"
   WIDTH=408 HEIGHT=264
  HSPACE=0 VSPACE=0 BORDER=4
 onError="return handleError()">
</CENTER>

</BODY>
</HTML>
```

Figure 9–15 shows the alert that is displayed when you load the `imageOnError.html` script.

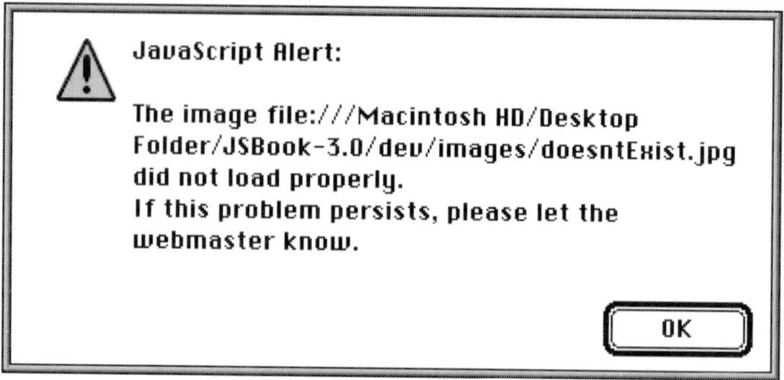

Figure 9–15 Alert that is displayed when you load the `imageOnError.html` script

Planning for the Stopping of Image Loading

The JavaScript language provides an `onAbort` event handler for the `image` object. You can use the `onAbort` event handler to provide a function that handles cleanup when the user clicks on the Stop button in the browser (or uses a keyboard equivalent) to stop loading an image.

Event Handler

onAbort

Syntax

<IMG

SRC = "*ImageURL*"

(onAbort = "*JavaScript code*")

>

Using the onAbort Event Handler When Users Click on the Stop Button

The following `imageOnAbort.html` script displays an alert when the user clicks on the Stop button before the image has completed loading. If you do not have enough time to click on the Stop button before the image has completed loading, use the keyboard equivalent for the Stop button on your platform:

- On Windows or UNIX systems, press the Escape key.
- On Macintosh systems, press the Command key and type a period (`.`).

```
<!--
        imageOnAbort.html

-->

<HTML>
<HEAD>
<TITLE>Image On Abort</TITLE>
<SCRIPT LANGUAGE="JavaScript">
<!-- HIDE FROM OLD BROWSERS

// image onAbort event handler
//
// Display an alert when the event occurs
//
function handleAbort() {

  var mstr = "\n"

  mstr += "Loading of the image "
  mstr += document.images[0].src
  mstr += " was interrupted.\n"

  alert(unescape(mstr))
}

// STOP HIDING -->
</SCRIPT>
</HEAD>
<BODY>

<P>This example displays an alert dialog when the
onAbort event occurs while loading the images
below. To make the event occur, hold down the
Shift key, click on Reload, and immediately click
on the Stop button to interrupt the transfer. If
you don't have enough time, use the keyboard
equivalent for stop:</P>
<UL>
  <LI>On Windows and UNIX systems, press the
  Escape key.
  <LI>On Macintosh systems, press Command and
  type a period (.).
</UL>
```

```
<CENTER>
<IMG SRC="../../images/AyersRock-2.jpg"
  NAME="AyersRock-2" WIDTH=408 HEIGHT=264
  HSPACE=0 VSPACE=0 BORDER=4
  onAbort="handleAbort()">
</CENTER>

</BODY>
</HTML>
```

Figure 9–16 shows the result of loading the `imageOnAbort.html` script.

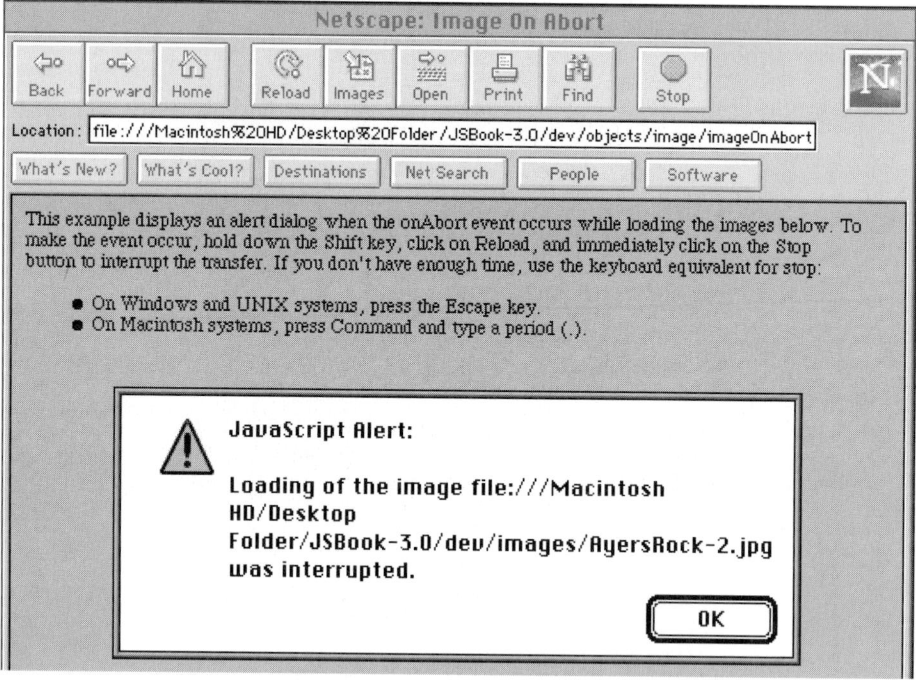

Netscape: Image On Abort
Back
Forward
Home
Reload
Images
Open
Print
Find
Stop
Location: file:///Macintosh%20HD/Desktop%20Folder/JSBook-3.0/dev/objects/image/imageOnAbort
What's New?
What's Cool?
Destinations
Net Search
People
Software
This example displays an alert dialog when the onAbort event occurs while loading the images below. To make the event occur, hold down the Shift key, click on Reload, and immediately click on the Stop button to interrupt the transfer. If you don't have enough time, use the keyboard equivalent for stop:
On Windows and UNIX systems, press the Escape key.
On Macintosh systems, press Command and type a period (.).
JavaScript Alert:
Loading of the image file:///Macintosh HD/Desktop Folder/JSBook-3.0/dev/images/AyersRock-2.jpg was interrupted.
OK

Figure 9–16 Result of loading the `imageOnAbort.html` script

CHAPTER 10

- Applet Files
- Downloading the JDK
- Applet HTML Review
- Using the Java Console
- Adding an Applet to a Script by Using a Class File
- Adding an Applet to a Script by Using an Archive File
- Controlling Applet Parameters from a Script
- Referencing an Applet by Using the document.applet Property
- Applets and LiveConnect
- Summary of New Terms and Concepts

Embedding Java Applets in Your Web Page

An applet is a small application written in the Java language that requires a browser to execute. The Java language is an object-oriented, *device-independent* programming language developed by Sun Microsystems. Any applet can be run in any browser, provided the company that developed the browser has licensed the Java technology from Sun Microsystems and incorporated it as a built-in part of their browser.

Non-Java programs must be compiled to run on a specific platform, such as a specific release of the UNIX operating system, Windows 95, or the Macintosh operating system. To make the Java language device-independent, Java creates a virtual machine. Before Sun engineers started designing the Java language, they wrote down all of the specifications for the language for a hardware chip that, at that time, did not exist. (However, now that the specifications exist for this Java virtual machine, Sun and other companies are designing a Java virtual machine chip. We will soon enter the strange world where virtual and real may be identical.)

Any software written in the Java language and compiled with the Java compiler uses the language of the virtual machine. This process hides the underlying operating system from Java applets and applications.

When a browser licenses the Java technology for inclusion in its browser, the company designing the browser includes the *runtime system* that enables the Java applet or application to be run on a specific hardware platform. Runtime

environments exist for Solaris®, SPARC®, Solaris x86, Windows 95, Windows NT™, and Macintosh systems. You don't really need to understand these technical underpinnings to incorporate Java applets in your Web page.

If you are interested in learning more about the Java language, you can visit the following Web sites:

- The JavaSoft Web site: `http://java.sun.com`
- Netscape's home page: `http://home.netscape.com`
- The Java newsgroup: `comp.lang.java.`*`group_name`*
- The Java-interest mailing list: send e-mail to `java-interest-request@java.MageLang.com`. Include the word `subscribe` in the body of the message.
- Digital Espresso: `http://www.io.org/~mentor/DigitalEspresso.html`
- The Java developer: `http://www.digitalfocus.com/faq`
- Gamelan: `http://www.gamelan.com`
- Mangalam's multiple, wide-area Internet service (WAIS) sources: `http://hornet.mmg.uci.edu/cgi-bin/nph-fwais.pl`

In this chapter we use applets from the Java Developer's Kit sample applets and a Hello applet written by Brian. We recommend John Pew's book, *Instant Java*, published by Sun Microsystems Press/Prentice Hall, 1996, as a source for more applets. The book comes with a companion CD-ROM that contains all of the applets described in the book.

- To download applets from John Pew's home page, visit: `http://www.vivids.com/ij2`

Applet Files

Before we start discussing the `applet` object, newly included in the Navigator 3.0 release, let's take a detailed look at the parts of an applet and review some basics of how you add an applet to your Web page.

To run an applet, you need to have all of the `.class` files associated with the applet. `.class` files are the compiled binary files for the applet. Some applets may have only one `.class` file. Others may have several class files. When an applet has more than one `.class` file, you specify the primary class file, which usually has the same name as the applet.

Some applets may provide you with the compiled `.class` files. Other applets may provide you only with the `.java` file. If all you have access to is the `.java` file, you must obtain the *Java Developer's Kit* (JDK) to get the Java compiler.

The pieces of the JDK that are useful to you are:

- Java Compiler. Use it to compile any Java applets that are not already compiled.
- Applet Viewer. Use it to test your applets before you load them into a browser and for checking for bugs in the browser for a specific platform.
- Sample applets. Experiment with them to see if any of them are useful for your Web site.

The Java Developer's Kit also contains libraries and documentation and a user's guide for the application program interface (API). An API is a series of designed interface standards that define how programmers communicate with functionality in a Java application.

Note – Be warned that the Macintosh version of Netscape Navigator 3.01 may not display applets properly. If you are incorporating applets on a Macintosh, be sure to use the applet viewer to make sure that your applet is displaying and working properly. If you start with the browser, you won't get very far. It also seems that applets work properly from a URL, but not from the file protocol.

Downloading the JDK

You can download the JDK without charge from the JavaSoft Web site or from the Sun ftp site.

- The Web site: `http://www.javasoft.com/products/JDK/1.0.2/installation.html`
- The FTP site: `ftp://ftp.javasoft.com/pub`
  - `ftp://ftp.javasoft.com/pub/JDK-1_0_2-solaris2-sparc.tar.Z`
  - `ftp://ftp.javasoft.com/pub/JDK-1_0_2-solaris2-x86.tar.Z`

- ftp://ftp.javasoft.com/pub/JDK-1_0_2-win32-x86.exe
- ftp://ftp.javasoft.com/pub/JDK-1_0_2-MacOS.sea.bin

For complete instructions on how to install, set up, and run the JDK, we recommend that you refer to *Core Java* by Gary Cornell and Cay S. Horstman, Sun Microsystems Press/Prentice Hall, 1997.

Running the Java Compiler

Once you have the Java compiler installed, running it is easy. You don't need to have any programming skills to run the compiler. You simply give the compiler the command to compile and the name of the `.java` file that you want to compile.

On UNIX and Windows 95 systems, from a command line, you type:

```
javac filename.java
```

When the command is complete, the `.class` files are located in the same directory with the original `.java` file.

On Windows 95 systems, from WinEdit:

1. From the File menu, choose Open and use the dialog box to locate the *`filename`*`.java` source code that you want to compile.
2. From the Project menu, choose Compile. This command opens a temporary DOS shell and runs the Java compiler. When the compiler has finished, a dialog box gives you the option to analyze your results, load the output file, or cancel.
3. Click on the Analyze Results button.
4. From the Project menu, choose Execute to run the compiled code.

On Macintosh systems, double-click on the Java Compiler icon. The "javac" window opens, as shown in Figure 10–1, and the menu bar contains the items File and Edit.

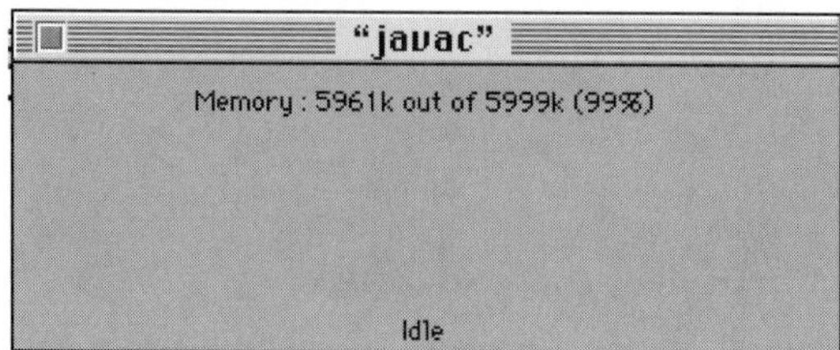

Figure 10–1 Java compiler window

From the File menu, choose Compile file and locate the `.java` file in your file system. Then click on the Open button. While the file is compiling, messages are displayed in the Java compiler window, as shown in Figure 10–2.

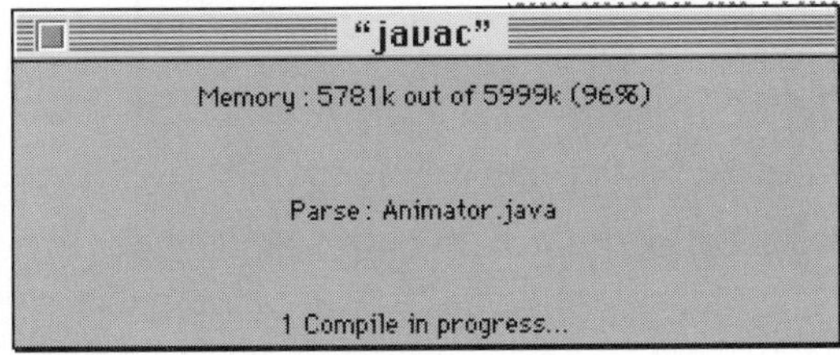

Figure 10–2 Java compiler window during a compile

Running the Applet Viewer

You can run the applet viewer to preview, debug, and test applets in an HTML page before you try them out in a browser.

To run the applet viewer,

On UNIX and Windows 95 systems, from a command line, type:

```
appletviewer filename.html
```

When the command is complete, a window opens, displaying the html file.

On Macintosh systems, double-click on the Applet Viewer icon. The AppletViewer window opens, as shown in Figure 10–3, and the menu bar contains the items File and Edit.

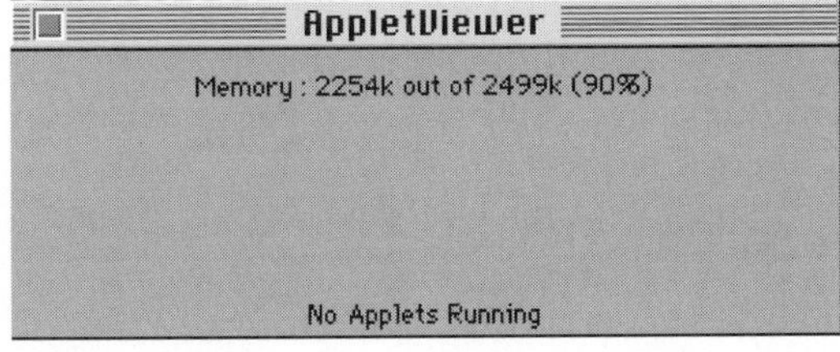

Figure 10–3 Java Applet Viewer window

From the File menu, choose either Open URL or Open Local and locate the `.html` file in your file system. Then click on the Open button. A separate window opens running the applet, as shown in Figure 10–4.

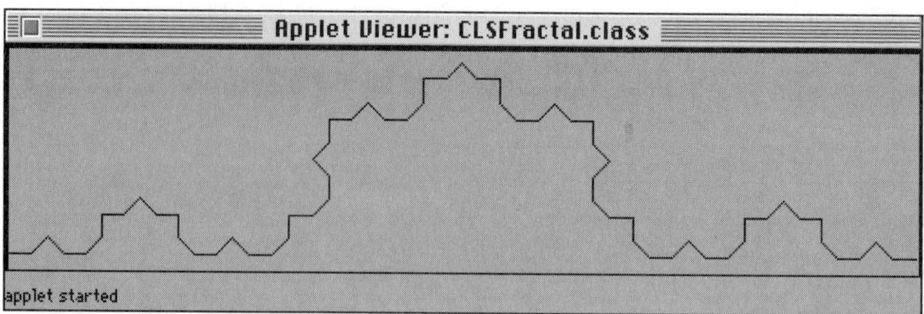

Figure 10–4 Java Applet Viewer window with running applet

The title bar of the window displays the name of the `.class` file that is running.

Applet HTML Review

You can think of the HTML for applets as being divided into two categories:

- The HTML tags and attributes that specify information about the applet to the browser
- The parameters that you can specify to customize an applet

Applet HTML Attributes

This section describes the HTML tags and attributes that you use to include applets in your Web pages.

Note – Although HTML is case insensitive (you can type the tags and attributes in either upper case, lower case, or a mix of cases), the values for the Java applet `PARAM` tags are case sensitive and must match the capitalization used by the Java applet developer.

Table 10-1 describes the applet attributes. Refer to the HTML Brushup box for a review of the HTML applet syntax.

Table 10-1 Applet Attributes

Attribute	Description
`CODE="`*`filename`*`.class"`	Required. The name of the file (or the primary file) that contains the compiled Java program. The class file must be in the same place in the same directory as the `.html` file unless you specify a codebase.
`WIDTH=`*`number`*	Required. The horizontal space, in pixels, that the applet occupies.
`HEIGHT=`*`number`*	Required. The vertical space, in pixels, that the applet occupies.
`MAYSCRIPT`	Enables the applet to access JavaScript. Use this attribute to prevent an applet from accessing JavaScript on a page without your knowledge. If omitted, the applet will not work with JavaScript.
`CODEBASE="`*`directory`*`"`	Optional. The name of the relative directory containing the class files. The codebase directory must be in the same directory as the `.html` file.
`ARCHIVE="`*`filename`*`.zip"`	Optional. To speed loading of applets, Navigator 3.0 permits developers to provide a zip file that contains one or more `.class` files. When the applet has a `.zip` file, you must specify the archive attribute with its name.
`ALIGN`	Optional. The alignment of the applet with the space defined to contain it.
`NAME`	Optional. The name of the applet. Use when you have more than one applet in one page that needs to communicate with the others.
`VSPACE`	The vertical margin around the applet, in pixels.
`HSPACE`	The horizontal margin around the applet, in pixels.

HTML Brushup — Incorporating Java Applets

You define which applets to incorporate by setting the attributes of the <APPLET></APPLET> HTML tags. Note that the <APPLET> tag replaces the <APP> tag as the way to identify and include a Java application.

Note that, unlike the rest of HTML, which does not care about capitalization, the values for the PARAM tags are case sensitive and must match the capitalization of the parameter as defined by the applet.

<APPLET

CODE = "*filename*.class"

WIDTH= *number*

HEIGHT = *number*

MAYSCRIPT

(CODEBASE = "*base directory for the applet*")

(ALT = "*alternative character data that is displayed if the browser cannot run the applet*")

(NAME = "*name for the applet instance*")

(ALIGN = left | right | top | texttop | middle | absmiddle | baseline | bottom | absbottom)

(VSPACE= *number*)

(HSPACE = *number*)

ARCHIVE="*filename.zip*">

</APPLET>

The minimum set of attributes you can use is CODE, WIDTH, and HEIGHT. CODE provides the name of the file relative to the base URL of the applet that contains the compiled applet subclass. You cannot reference an applet by an absolute URL. You can use the optional CODEBASE attribute to define the base directory for the applet. WIDTH and HEIGHT define, in pixels, the initial width and height of the applet display area.

The attributes included in square brackets (( )) are optional. You can use none, some, or all of these optional attributes for any applet. The VSPACE and HSPACE attributes specify the reserved space around the applet in pixels. You can use the NAME attribute to specify a name for the instance of the applet, to allow applets on the same page to communicate with each other.

You can also include <PARAM> tags and any other elements that would have been allowed at this point in the document within the <APPLET></APPLET> tags. The <PARAM> tag has two attributes: NAME is the name of the parameter, and VALUE is obtained by the applet, using the getParameter() method.

Applet Parameters

This section describes applet parameters. When a programmer writes a Java applet, the applet is designed with a set of specific parameters that are made public along with the source code for the applet. These parameters are the elements of the applet that you can customize. You can find out the parameters for a particular applet in one of the following ways:

- Consult the documentation for the applet.
- Contact the programmer (if you know how).
- Review the source code (if you know how).
- Look at the `.html` file that displays the applet (if one is provided).

The best (and sometimes the only) way for you to get information for the parameters is from whatever documentation the programmer provides. Programming styles vary, and you may find some applet design and parameters easier to understand and use than others.

To help you understand how parameters are used, let's start with a simple example. The JDK has a sample applet named NervousText. When you run NervousText in the Applet Viewer, the text jumps around on the screen. Figure 10–5 shows a moment of stillness for the nervous text.

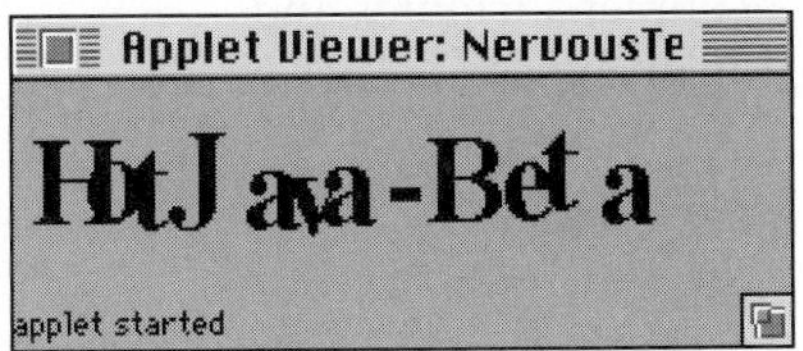

Figure 10–5 NervousText applet

How did the applet decide what text to display? The information is specified in the HTML file included with the applet. Here's the text of the `example1.html` file that was used to start the applet.

```
<TITLE>Nervous Text</TITLE>
<HR>
<APPLET CODE="NervousText.class" WIDTH=200 HEIGHT=50>
<PARAM NAME=text VALUE="HotJava-Beta">
</APPLET>
<HR>
<A HREF="NervousText.java">The source.</A>
```

```
<P>
This applet was originally written by Daniel Wyszynski.
```

As you can see, this applet has one parameter, specified by the following line of code:

```
<PARAM NAME=text VALUE="HotJava-Beta">
```

This parameter has a name of `text` and the value `HotJava-Beta`. If we want to make the text say Jumping JavaScript, we can edit the HTML file and change the line to:

```
<PARAM NAME=text VALUE="Jumping JavaScript">
```

Let's run the applet again. Figure 10–6 shows the result with the new text.

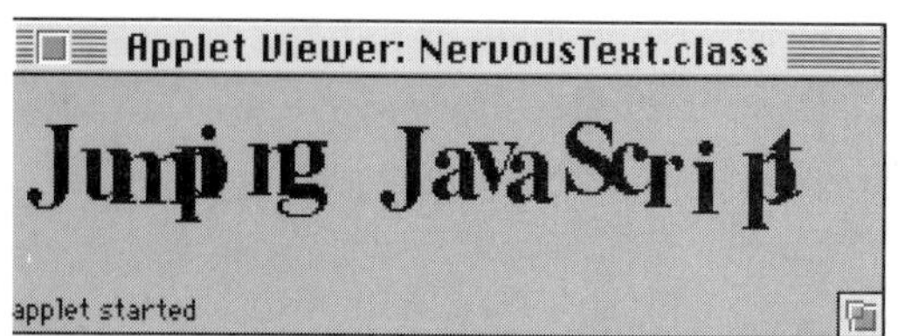

Figure 10–6 NervousText with new text

It may seem a long way to go before you get to JavaScript examples; however, it is important for you to understand how you specify applet attributes and parameters, so that you understand exactly what the JavaScript `applet` object can do for you.

Using the Java Console

Netscape Navigator provides a Java Console window that you can use to view messages from the applet any time you are working with them. The Java Console can be particularly useful if you are having problems incorporating a particular applet in a script.

To open the Java Console, from the Navigator Options menu, choose Show Java Console. The Java Console window is displayed, as shown in Figure 10–7.

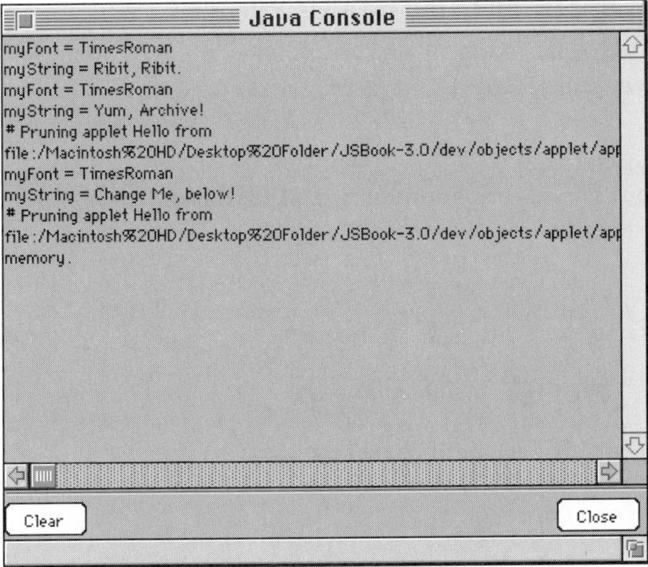

Java Console
myFont = TimesRoman
myString = Ribit, Ribit.
myFont = TimesRoman
myString = Yum, Archive!
# Pruning applet Hello from
file:/Macintosh%20HD/Desktop%20Folder/JSBook-3.0/dev/objects/applet/ap
myFont = TimesRoman
myString = Change Me, below!
# Pruning applet Hello from
file:/Macintosh%20HD/Desktop%20Folder/JSBook-3.0/dev/objects/applet/ap
memory.
Clear
Close

Figure 10–7 Java Console

Adding an Applet to a Script by Using a Class File

To add an applet to a script, you use the HTML `<APPLET></APPLET>` tags. Within those tags, you specify any parameters for the applet that are available to you.

The minimum set of attributes you can use is `CODE`, `WIDTH`, and `HEIGHT`.

The following code extract adds the `Hello.class` applet to the script, specifies the code, width, height, and two parameters.

```
<APPLET CODE="Hello.class" NAME="Hello"
 WIDTH=300 HEIGHT=100>
<PARAM NAME=font VALUE="TimesRoman">
<PARAM NAME=text VALUE="Ribit, Ribit.">
</APPLET>
```

Example of Adding an Applet by Using a Class File

The following `applet.html` script adds the `Hello` applet to a page. This applet has two parameters that you can set: `font` and `text`.

```
<!--
         applet.html
    The Hello applet is embedded in the document.
-->
<HTML>
<HEAD>
<TITLE>Hello Applet</TITLE>
</HEAD>
<BODY>

<P>The Hello applet is embedded below by
specifying the name of the applet's class file in
the CODE attribute. In this case, it's
"Hello.class":</P>
<PRE>
&lt;APPLET CODE="Hello.class" NAME="Hello"
 WIDTH=300 HEIGHT=100&gt;
</PRE>

<P>The two parameters this applet supports are
specified using the PARAM tag:</P>

<PRE>
&lt;PARAM NAME=font VALUE="TimesRoman"&gt;
&lt;PARAM NAME=text VALUE="Ribit, Ribit."&gt;
</PRE>

<P>Here it is in action:</P>

<CENTER>
<APPLET CODE="Hello.class" NAME="Hello"
 WIDTH=300 HEIGHT=100>
<PARAM NAME=font VALUE="TimesRoman">
<PARAM NAME=text VALUE="Ribit, Ribit.">
</APPLET>
</CENTER>

</BODY>
</HTML>
```

Figure 10–8 shows the result of loading the `applet.html` script.

Netscape: Hello Applet

Back Forward Home Reload Images Open Print Find Stop

Location: file:///Macintosh%20HD/Desktop%20Folder/JSBook-3.0/dev/objects/applet/applet.html

What's New? What's Cool? Destinations Net Search People Software

The Hello applet is embedded below by specifying the name of the applet's class file in the CODE attribute. In this case, it's "Hello.class":

```
<APPLET CODE="Hello.class" NAME="Hello"
 WIDTH=300 HEIGHT=100>
```

The two parameters this applet supports are specified using the PARAM tag:

```
<PARAM NAME=font VALUE="TimesRoman">
<PARAM NAME=text VALUE="Ribit, Ribit.">
```

Here it is in action:

Ribit, Ribit.

Jumping JavaScript
by Janice Winsor and Brian Freeman
objects/applet/applet.html

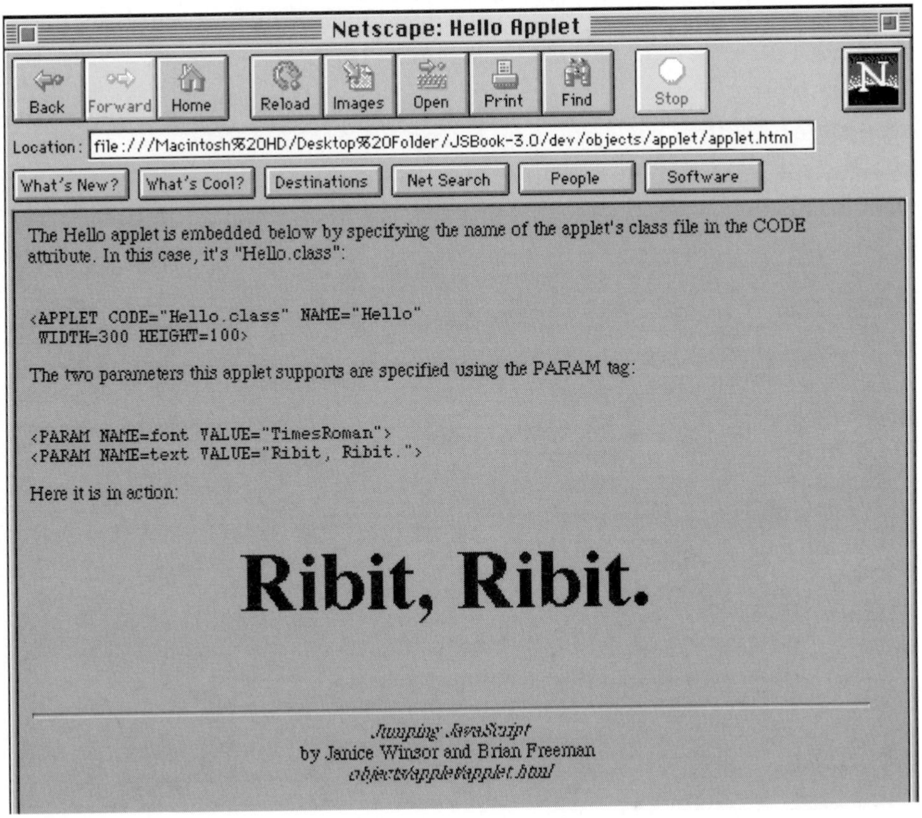

Figure 10–8 Result of loading the `applet.html` script

Adding an Applet to a Script by Using an Archive File

The Navigator 3.0 release provides the `ARCHIVE` attribute. You can improve performance by reducing the time it takes to download an attribute by providing a zip file that contains all of the class files needed to run the applet. You specify the zip file with the `ARCHIVE` attribute. You still must specify the `CODE` attribute. When the zip file contains more than one class file, you specify the primary class file as the value for the `CODE` attribute. The primary class file usually has the same name as the applet.

The following code extract adds the `Hello.class` applet to the script. It specifies the code, archive, width, height, and two parameters.

```
<APPLET ARCHIVE="Hello.zip" CODE="Hello.class"
 NAME="Hello" WIDTH=300 HEIGHT=100>
<PARAM NAME=font VALUE="TimesRoman">
<PARAM NAME=text VALUE="Yum, Archive!">
</APPLET>
```

Example of Adding an Applet by Using an Archive File

The following `appletArchive.html` script adds the `Hello` applet by specifying an archive file. Notice that this script changes the text value that is displayed to read `Yum, Archive!`.

```
<!--
               appletArchive.html
    The Hello applet is embedded by using the
    ARCHIVE attribute.
-->
<HTML>
<HEAD>
<TITLE>Applet Archive Attribute</TITLE>
</HEAD>
<BODY>

<P>Specifying the APPLET tag's ARCHIVE attribute
can reduce an applet's download time. It was
introduced in Navigator 3.0 and uses zip files as
the archive format. Simply archive all the class
files the applet needs in a zip file and add the
ARCHIVE attribute, like so:</P>

<PRE>
&lt;APPLET ARCHIVE="Hello.zip" CODE="Hello.class"
 NAME="Hello" WIDTH=300 HEIGHT=100&gt;
</P>

<CENTER>
<APPLET ARCHIVE="Hello.zip" CODE="Hello.class"
 NAME="Hello" WIDTH=300 HEIGHT=100>
<PARAM NAME=font VALUE="TimesRoman">
<PARAM NAME=text VALUE="Yum, Archive!">
</APPLET>
</CENTER>

</BODY>
</HTML>
```

Figure 10–9 shows the result of loading the `appletArchive.html` script.

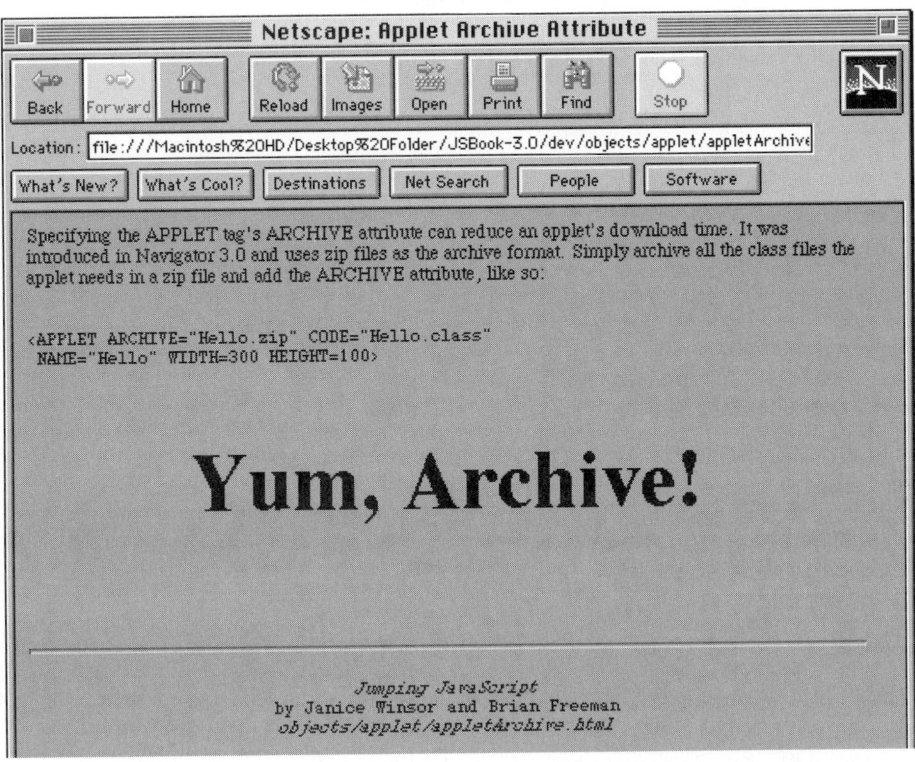

Figure 10–9 Result of loading the `appletArchive.html` script

Controlling Applet Parameters from a Script

You can create scripts that dynamically enable your users to change the parameters for an applet. To control applet parameters, you use the programmer's documentation for each applet to find out what parameters are public and whether the applet has public methods that you can use in your scripts.

Example of Controlling Applet Parameters from a Script

The following `appletParameters.html` script enables users to dynamically change the text of the message and to choose one of four fonts to display the message.

```
<!--
              appletParameters.html

    Parameters are passed to the Hello applet
    from JavaScript.
-->

<HTML>
<HEAD>
<TITLE>Applet Archive Attribute</TITLE>
<SCRIPT LANGUAGE="JavaScript">
<!-- HIDE FROM OLD BROWSERS

// Tell the applet to stop running
function stopApplet() {
  document.applets[0].stop()
}

// Run the applet again
function startApplet() {
  document.applets[0].start()
}

// call the applet's setString public method with
// new string.
function setString(str) {
  document.applets[0].setString(str)
}

// call the applet's setFont public method with
// the new font
function setFont(font) {
  document.applets[0].setFont(font)
}

// STOP HIDING -->
</SCRIPT></HEAD>
<BODY>

<P>You can use the controls below to control the
applet from JavaScript. To see messages from
the applet, Choose Java Console from the
Navigator Options menu.</P>
```

```
<CENTER>
<APPLET ARCHIVE="Hello.zip" CODE="Hello.class"
 NAME="Hello" WIDTH=500 HEIGHT=100>
<PARAM NAME=font VALUE="TimesRoman">
<PARAM NAME=text VALUE="Change Me, below!">
</APPLET>

<FORM NAME="controlForm">
<B>Applet Text:</B><BR>
<INPUT TYPE="text" NAME="textStr" VALUE=""
 SIZE=14 onChange="setString(this.value)"><BR>

<B>Font:</B><BR>
<SELECT NAME="fontSel" SIZE=4

onChange="setFont(this.options[this.selectedIndex].value)
">
 <OPTION VALUE="Courier"> Courier
 <OPTION VALUE="Dialog"> Dialog
 <OPTION VALUE="Helvetica"> Helvetica
 <OPTION VALUE="TimesRoman" SELECTED> Times Roman
</SELECT><BR>
<BR>
<INPUT TYPE="button" NAME="stopBtn"
 VALUE="Stop" onClick="stopApplet()">
<INPUT TYPE="button" NAME="restartBtn"
 VALUE="Restart" onClick="startApplet()">
</FORM>
</CENTER>

</BODY>
</HTML>
```

Figure 10–10 shows the result of loading the `appletParameters.html` script.

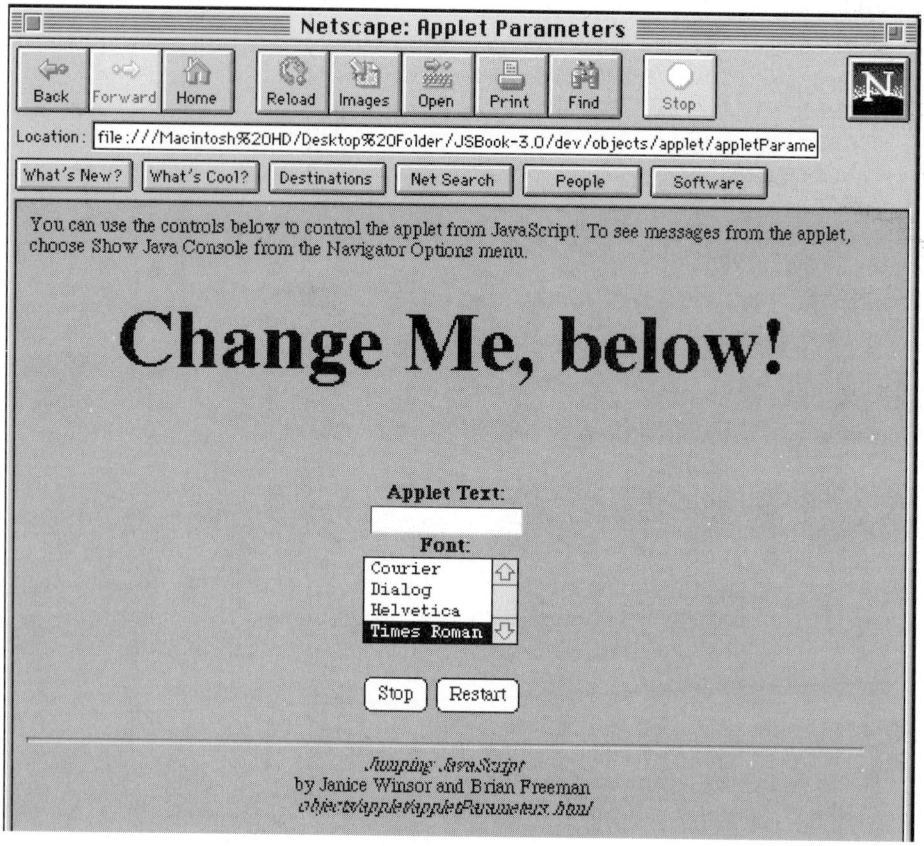

Figure 10–10 Result of loading the `appletParameters.html` script

Figure 10–11 shows the `appletParameters.html` script with new text and a new font.

Netscape: Applet Parameters

Back Forward Home Reload Images Open Print Find Stop

Location: file:///Macintosh%20HD/Desktop%20Folder/JSBook-3.0/dev/objects/applet/appletParame

What's New? What's Cool? Destinations Net Search People Software

You can use the controls below to control the applet from JavaScript. To see messages from the applet, choose Show Java Console from the Navigator Options menu.

An Original Thought

Applet Text:

iginal Thought

Font:

Courier
Dialog
Helvetica
Times Roman

Stop Restart

Jumping JavaScript
by Janice Winsor and Brian Freeman
objects/applet/appletParameters.html

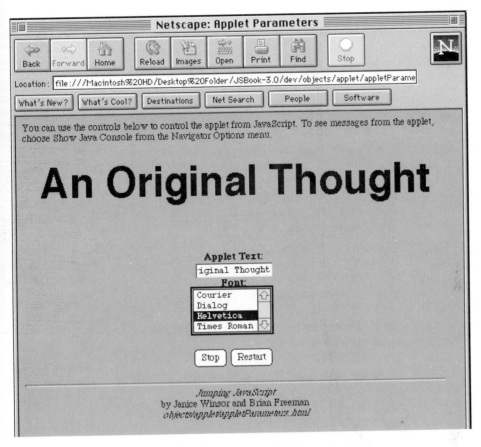

Figure 10–11 Dynamically changing applet parameters

Referencing an Applet by Using the document.applet Property

You can reference an applet by using the `document.applet[]` property or by specifying the name of the applet as a property of the document object, using the following syntax:

```
document.AppletName
```

Example of Referencing an Applet by Using Document Properties

The following `index.html` script uses both the `document.applet[]` array and the `document.AppletName` properties to display information about the applet. This script runs into a known bug because the script cannot reflect the values for these document properties until the applet is loaded. To work around the problem, you need to be sure that the applet is loaded before you try to access it. One way to work around the problem is to create an `onLoad` event handler for the window.

```
<!--
       objects/applet/BarChart/index.html
-->
<HTML>
<HEAD>
<TITLE>Bar Chart Applet</TITLE>
</HEAD>
<BODY>

<P>Embedded below is the Chart applet.</P>

<HR>
<APPLET CODE="Chart.class" NAME="Chart"
 WIDTH=251 HEIGHT=125>
<PARAM NAME=title VALUE="Performance">
<PARAM NAME=columns VALUE="4">
<PARAM NAME=orientation VALUE="horizontal">
<PARAM NAME=scale VALUE="5">
<PARAM NAME=c1 VALUE="10">
<PARAM NAME=c1_color VALUE="blue">
<PARAM NAME=c1_label VALUE="Q1">
<PARAM NAME=c1_style VALUE="striped">
<PARAM NAME=c2 VALUE="20">
<PARAM NAME=c2_color VALUE="green">
<PARAM NAME=c2_label VALUE="Q2">
<PARAM NAME=c2_style VALUE="solid">
<PARAM NAME=c3 VALUE="5">
<PARAM NAME=c3_color VALUE="magenta">
<PARAM NAME=c3_label VALUE="Q3">
<PARAM NAME=c3_style VALUE="striped">
<PARAM NAME=c4 VALUE="30">
<PARAM NAME=c4_color VALUE="yellow">
<PARAM NAME=c4_label VALUE="Q4">
<PARAM NAME=c4_style VALUE="solid">
</APPLET>
<HR>

<P>The applet is accessible in JavaScript through
the document.applets array:</P>
```

```
<SCRIPT LANGUAGE="JavaScript">
<!-- HIDE FROM OLD BROWSERS

var msg = ""

msg += "document.applets[0] = "
msg += document.applets[0]

document.write(unescape(msg))

// STOP HIDING -->
</SCRIPT>

<P>Or through the name given to the applet. In
this case, it's "Chart", and it has a value
of:</P>

<SCRIPT LANGUAGE="JavaScript">
<!-- HIDE FROM OLD BROWSERS

var msg = ""

msg += "document.Chart = "
msg += document.Chart

document.write(unescape(msg))

// STOP HIDING -->
</SCRIPT>

<P>Note: you might receive an error message
stating that JavaScript can't reflect the applet
"Chart". It's not loaded yet. It's a known bug;
just click on Reload and the correct information
is displayed. To work around the problem,
make sure the applet is loaded before you try
to access it. Creating an onLoad event handler on
the window will do the trick.</P>

<P>The source code for this applet is located in
the file <A HREF="Chart.java">Chart.java</A>.</P>

</BODY>
</HTML>
```

Because the document properties cannot access the information for the applet, you'll receive an alert, as shown in Figure 10–12, when you first load the `index.html` script.

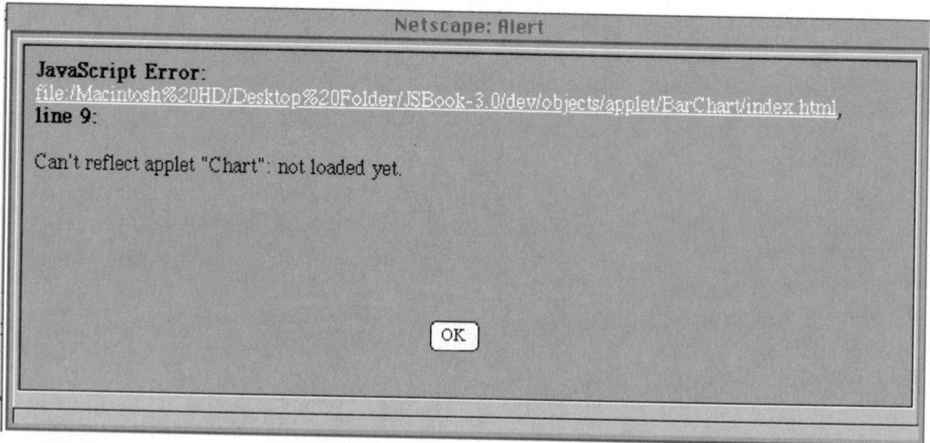

Figure 10–12 Error message alert

Click on the OK button to close the Alert window, then click on the Reload button. The values for the document properties are displayed in the window, as shown in Figure 10–13.

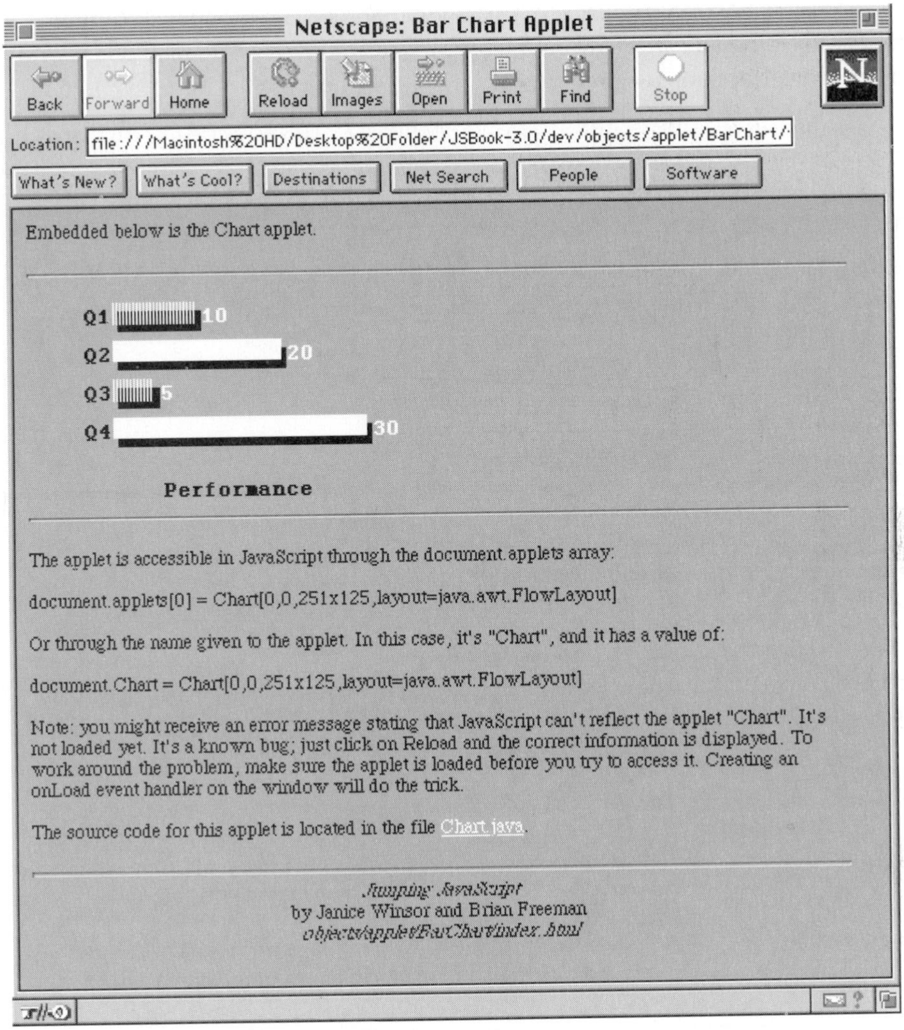

Netscape: Bar Chart Applet

Back Forward Home Reload Images Open Print Find Stop

Location: file:///Macintosh%20HD/Desktop%20Folder/JSBook-3.0/dev/objects/applet/BarChart/

What's New? What's Cool? Destinations Net Search People Software

Embedded below is the Chart applet.

Q1 10
Q2 20
Q3 5
Q4 30

Performance

The applet is accessible in JavaScript through the document.applets array:

document.applets[0] = Chart[0,0,251x125,layout=java.awt.FlowLayout]

Or through the name given to the applet. In this case, it's "Chart", and it has a value of:

document.Chart = Chart[0,0,251x125,layout=java.awt.FlowLayout]

Note: you might receive an error message stating that JavaScript can't reflect the applet "Chart". It's not loaded yet. It's a known bug; just click on Reload and the correct information is displayed. To work around the problem, make sure the applet is loaded before you try to access it. Creating an onLoad event handler on the window will do the trick.

The source code for this applet is located in the file Chart.java.

Jumping JavaScript
by Janice Winsor and Brian Freeman
objects/applet/BarChart/index.html

Figure 10–13 Result of `index.html` script

Applets and LiveConnect

This chapter shows you how to use JavaScript to work with applet parameters and methods. If you want a more sophisticated and robust way to connect to Java applets, you will want to learn more about *LiveConnect*, which became available with the beta Navigator 3.0 release. LiveConnect provides two-way communication between scripts and Java applets or plug-ins. LiveConnect also provides a way for Java applets to write directly to JavaScript. Documenting

LiveConnect is beyond the scope of this book. For a brief introduction to the Java/JavaScript connection through LiveConnect, check out Danny Goodman's excellent introduction, available at:

```
http://developer.netscape.com/news/viewsource/archive/
goodman_liveconnect.html
```

Summary of New Terms and Concepts

The new terms and concepts introduced in this chapter are listed in alphabetical order in Table 10-2. The terms and concepts are also included in the glossary at the end of the book.

Table 10-2 Summary of New Terms and Concepts

Term/Concept	Description
`.class` files	The standard suffix for compiled binary files for an applet.
device-independent language	A language that does not need to be compiled to run on a specific hardware platform. Java is a device-independent language.
Java Developer's Kit (JDK)	The collection of utilities and libraries available free from Sun Microsystems, Inc., that enable you to compile Java source code, view applets, and understand the Java API.
`.java` files	The standard suffix for source code files for Java applets
LiveConnect	A scripting language that provides two-way communications between JavaScript scripts and Java applets or plug-ins.
runtime system	A system that provides basic language services to a device-independent language that enables the language to run on specific hardware platforms.

399

CHAPTER 11

- Embedding a Plug-in in a Document
- Accessing the plugin/embeds Array
- Using the plugin Object Properties
- Updating the List of Plug-ins Available to the Browser
- Checking to Determine if a Plug-in Is Available
- Controlling a Plug-in
- Plug-ins and LiveConnect
- Summary of New Terms and Concepts

Using the plugin Object

Plug-ins expand the capability of basic browsers to handle embedded information such as audio and video. You still need to have the plug-in available on your hard disk. Unlike a helper application, however, the plug-in interacts with the browser in a way that technical people call *transparent* to the user. What this term means is that you don't know that the browser is starting up another application to handle display of the information.

When you start Netscape Navigator 3.0 (and later) releases, you may have noticed that `Registering plug-ins` is one of the status messages that is displayed as Navigator is loading. The Navigator software looks in the Plug-ins directory or folder in the Navigator hierarchy to determine which plug-ins to load at startup. After Navigator is running, you can add new plug-ins to the Plug-ins directory, but Navigator does not recognize them until you quit the current session and start Navigator again.

This chapter uses Apple's QuickTime plug-in for some of its examples. Netscape includes QuickTime as part of the Navigator 3.01 release, so if you are running Navigator 3.01 (or later), you should already have a QuickTime plug-in ready to use.

If you do not have a QuickTime plug-in in your Plug-ins directory, you can either download Navigator 3.01 from Netscape at:

```
http://home.netscape.com
```

or download the QuickTime plug-in from:

```
http://quicktime.apple.com/qt/sw/sw.html
```

Because the file system structure you have depends on what hardware platform you're running, you'll need to figure out for yourself exactly where your Netscape Plug-ins folder is.

You've already seen how to add a plug-in to your document by using the HTML <EMBED> tags, and how to use the `document.embeds` and `document.plugins` properties that are new in the Navigator 3.0 release to access the array of plug-ins in a document. For a review of this information, see Chapter 7, "Creating Documents."

In addition to the `document.embeds` and `document.plugins` properties, the Navigator 3.0 release provides a `plugin` object with its own properties and methods, which are listed in Table 11-1.

Table 11-1 Properties and Methods for the plugin Object

Properties	Methods	Event Handlers
`description`	`eval()*`	None
`filename`	`refresh()`	
`length`	`toString()*`	
`name`	`valueOf()*`	

* New in Navigator 3.0.

The properties and methods for the `plugin` object enable you to deal with plug-ins as the browser sees them rather than as the user sees them. You can use these properties and methods to determine if a plug-in you want users to have available for your script is currently registered with the browser. You can even use these properties and methods to help with installing a plug-in.

The `plugin` object and the `mimeType` object are closely related because a `plugin` object evaluates to an array of MIME types that the plug-in can interpret and use to display its data. For more information on the `mimeType` object, see Chapter 33, "Specifying MIME Types."

Embedding a Plug-in in a Document

The following `plugin.html` script embeds a QuickTime MIDI file in a document. We provide this example as a refresher on how to embed a plug-in in a document. Note that this file uses a URL to load the file, so you should be connected to the Web before you load this script.

```
<!--
         plugin.html

    This example embeds a MIDI file into the
    document.
-->

<HTML>
<HEAD>
<TITLE>Plugin</TITLE>
</HEAD>
<BODY>

<P>This document embeds a QuickTime MIDI file
from the <A HREF="http://www.MediaCity.com/~erweb/">
QuickTime Plug-in Sample Web Site</A>. Give it a
visit when you have a chance.</P>

<P>If you have the QuickTime plug-in installed,
you'll see controls displayed below the plug-in
area as soon as the file starts to load.</P>

<P>You can pick up the QuickTime plug-in from
<A HREF="http://quicktime.apple.com/sw">
quicktime.apple.com</A></P>

<CENTER>
<EMBED ALT="Embedded QuickTime MIDI file."
SRC="http://www.MediaCity.com/~erweb/frame/QuickTimeDemo/
midi/history.mov"
AUTOPLAY=TRUE CONTROLLER=TRUE
PLUGINSPACE="http://quicktime.apple.com"></EMBED>
</CENTER>

</BODY>
</HTML>
```

Figure 11–1 shows the result of loading the `plugin.html` script.

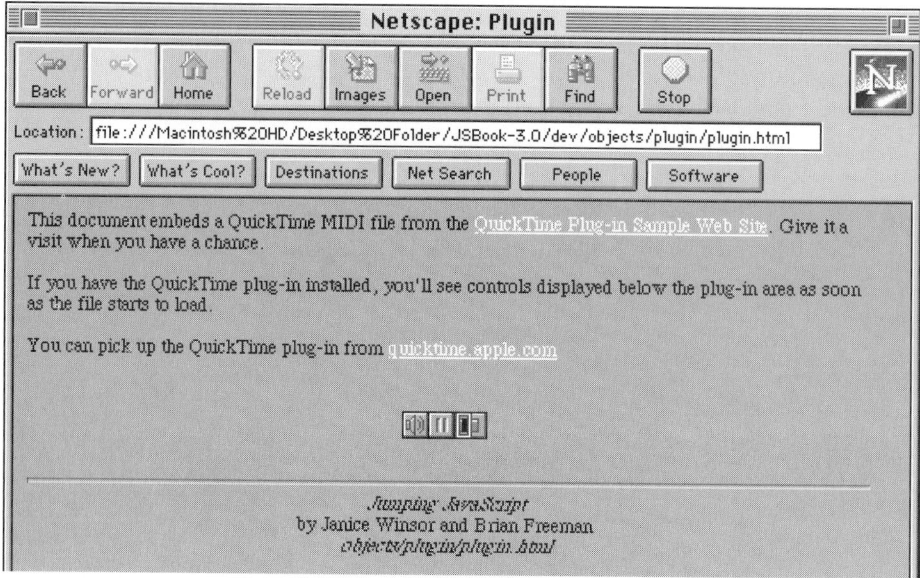

Figure 11–1 Result of loading the `plugin.html` script

Accessing the plugin/embeds Array

You can determine the number of plug-ins in a document by using the `document.plugin` or `document.embeds` properties described in Chapter 7, "Creating Documents." Both of these document properties access the plug-ins embedded in a document in the same way.

As a refresher, we provide another example here. The following `documentEmbeds.html` script includes a plug-in in a document and provides a button that you can click on to display information about the `document.embeds` array. Note that this file uses a URL to load the file, so you should be connected to the Web before you load this script.

```
<!--
          documentEmbeds.html

    This example dumps the contents of the
    document.embeds array.
-->

<HTML>
<HEAD>
```

```
<TITLE>Document Embeds</TITLE>
<!-- Include for displayPropsWin() -->
<SCRIPT SRC="../../debug/getProps.js"></SCRIPT>
<!--
    Include displayPropsWin() which will display
    the properties of a given object in a new
    window.
-->
<SCRIPT SRC="../../debug/displayPropsWin.js">
</SCRIPT>
</HEAD>
<BODY>

<CENTER>
<EMBED NAME="SetThePace" WIDTH=400 Height=175
SRC="http://www.MediaCity.com/~erweb/frame/QuickTimeDemo/
animation/SetThePace.mov"
CONTROLLER=TRUE LOOP=TRUE AUTOPLAY=TRUE
PLUGINSPACE="http://quicktime.apple.com"></EMBED>

<FORM>
<INPUT TYPE="button" NAME="embedsProps"
 VALUE="Display document.embeds"

onClick="displayPropsWin(document.embeds,'document.embeds
')">
</FORM>
</CENTER>

</BODY>
</HTML>
```

Figure 11–2 shows the result of loading the `documentEmbeds.html` script.

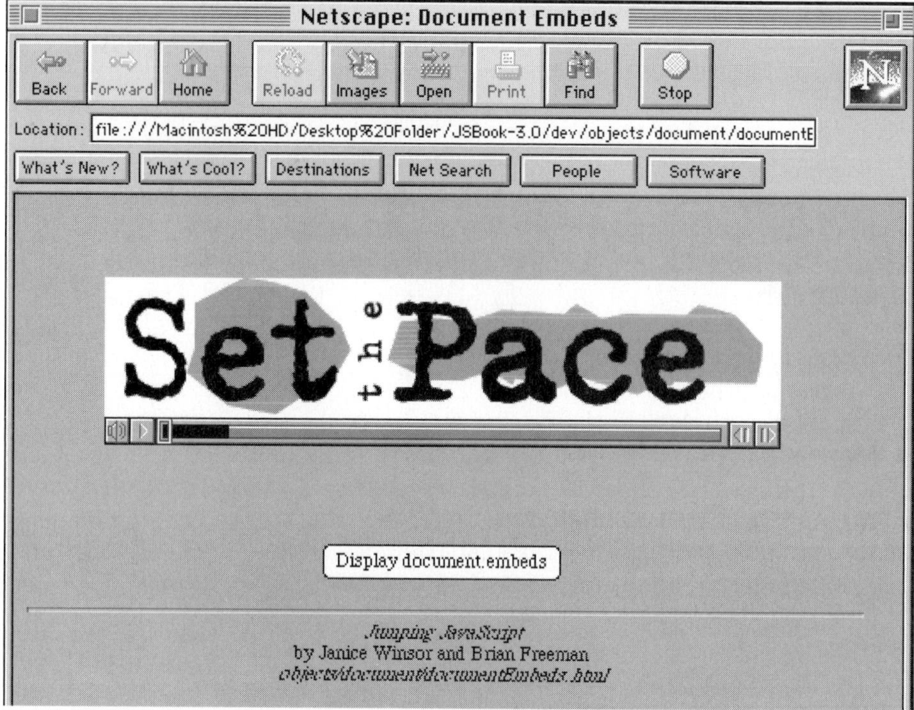

Figure 11–2 Result of loading the `documentEmbeds.html` script

Clicking on the Display document.embeds button displays the properties for the plug-ins embedded in the page, as shown in Figure 11–3. Note that you can click on the plug-in to stop it.

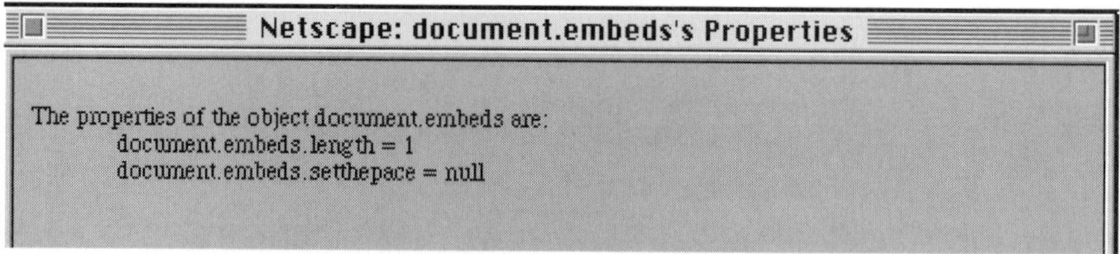

Figure 11–3 Embeds properties

Using the plugin Object Properties

The `description`, `filename`, and `name` properties return descriptive information about the plug-in file. The plug-in supplier provides the name and description. You should be aware that standards do not currently exist that

require plug-in programmers to assign the same name to the plug-in for each platform. What this means is that, once again, you cannot depend on your script working consistently across all platforms.

The `length` property does not count the number of plug-ins. Instead, it returns the number of MIME types that the plug-in recognizes.

Property	Value	Gettable	Settable
description	string	Yes	No
filename	string	Yes	No
length	integer	Yes	No
name	string	Yes	No

Example of Using the plugin Object Properties

The following `pluginProps.html` script contains a button that you can click on to display the list of the plug-ins on your computer that are available to the Navigator browser.

```
<!--
            pluginProps.html

    Display all the plug-in properties in a
    window when the button is pressed.
-->

<HTML>
<HEAD>
<TITLE>Plug-in Properties</TITLE>

<!-- Includes -->
<SCRIPT SRC="../../debug/documentUtils.js"></SCRIPT>
<SCRIPT SRC="../../debug/windowOpen.js"></SCRIPT>
<SCRIPT SRC="../../debug/generateWindow.js"></SCRIPT>

<!-- local functions -->
<SCRIPT LANGUAGE="JavaScript">
<!-- HIDE FROM OLD BROWSERS

// Display plug-in properties of an object
//
// Description:
```

```
//    A function suitable for use as the 'fcn'
//    argument of generateWindow(). See the file
//    generateWindow.js for more information on
//    generateWindow().
//
// Arguments:
//    args - an array with three elements in the
//           following order:
//       obj      - the object to obtain properties from
//       obj_name - a string representing the object
//       html     - generate html output?
//
// Return Value
//     string of the form:
//       object_name.property = "value"
//       object_name.property = "value"
//       ...
//
function displayPluginProperties(args) {
  var rvalue = ""

  // convert args array elements to more usable
  // variable names
  var      obj = args[0]
  var obj_name = args[1]
  var     html = args[2]

  // make sure we have the correct number of arguments
  if (args.length != 3) {
    return null
  }

  rvalue += newline(html)
  rvalue += "The properties of the object "
  rvalue += obj_name + " are:"
  rvalue += newline(html)

  rvalue += obj_name + " = " + obj
  rvalue += newline(html)
  rvalue += obj_name + ".length = " + obj.length
  rvalue += newline(html)

  // loop through all the object's properties
  for (var i = 0; i < obj.length; i++) {
```

```
    var plugin = obj[i]
    rvalue += obj_name + "[" + i + "] = " + plugin
    rvalue += newline(html)

    // loop through all the plug-in's properties
    for (var j in plugin) {
      rvalue += obj_name + "[" + i + "]." + j
      rvalue += " = " + plugin[j]
      rvalue += newline(html)
    }

    // there's a mimeType array here, too
    for (var k = 0; k < plugin.length; k++) {
      var mimetype = plugin[k]

      // mimeType object
      rvalue += obj_name + "[" + i + "][" + k
      rvalue += "] = " + mimetype
      rvalue += newline(html)

      // mimeType.type property
      rvalue += obj_name + "[" + i + "][" + k
      rvalue += "].type = " + mimetype.type
      rvalue += newline(html)

// Just display the mimeType's type property to
// reduce the amount of information.
//
// Delete or comment out the mimeType.type block
// above and uncomment the lines below to see all
// the mimeType properties.
//
//      for (var l in mimetype) {
//        rvalue += obj_name + "[" + i + "][" + k
//        rvalue += "]." + l + " = " + mimetype[l]
//        rvalue += newline(html)
//      }
    }
  }
  return unescape(rvalue)
}

// display all the properties of the
// navigator.plugins array.
```

```
//
function pluginProps() {

  // load an array with the arguments for
  // displayProperties().
  // The order of the arguments is:
  //   obj
  //   obj_name
  //   html
  //
  var displayPropsArgs = new Array(3)
  displayPropsArgs[0] = navigator.plugins
  displayPropsArgs[1] = "navigator.plugins"
  displayPropsArgs[2] = true

  // generateWindow() creates a window and calls
  // the function passed as the 5th argument. The
  // last argument, an array, holds any arguments
  // you want to pass to the function.
  //
  // In this case, displayProperties() is the
  // function and displayPropsArgs[] is the
  // argument array I want to pass to
  // displayProperties().
  //
  generateWindow("pluginPropsWin", "navigator.plugins",
                 500, 500, displayPluginProperties,
                 displayPropsArgs)
}
// STOP HIDING -->
</SCRIPT>
</HEAD>

<BODY>
<P>The plugin object is a property of the
navigator object that enables you to determine all
all the plug-ins currently installed on the
client.</P>

<P>Each element of the navigator object's plugin
array contains a plugin object. The plugin object
has properties for its name and description as
well as an array of mimeTypes objects for the
MIME types supported by that plug-in.</P>
```

```
<P>Click on the Plug-in Properties button to display
the plug-ins installed on this client.</P>

<CENTER><FORM>
<INPUT TYPE="button" NAME="pluginPropsBtn"
  VALUE="Plug-in Properties"
  onClick="pluginProps()">
</FORM></CENTER>

</BODY>
</HTML>
```

Figure 11–4 shows the result of loading the `pluginProps.html` script.

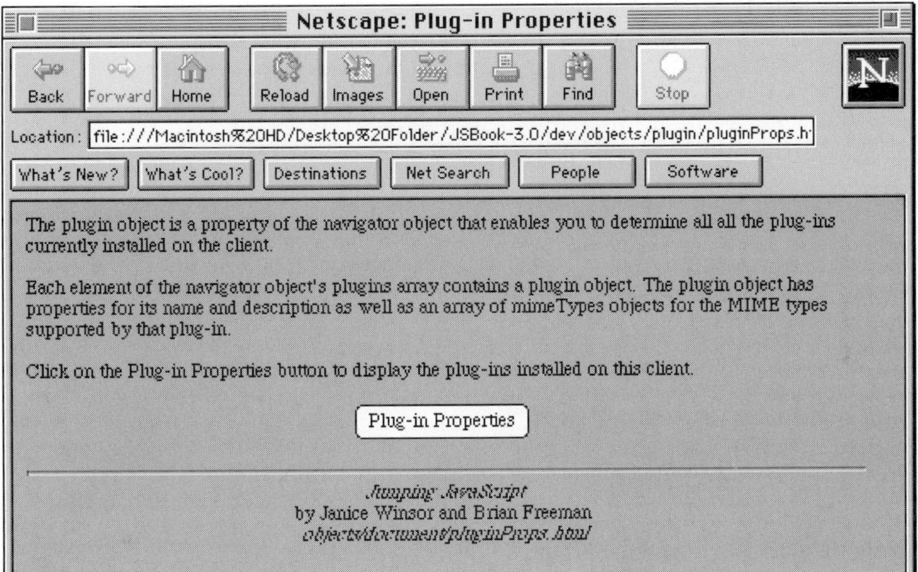

Figure 11–4 Result of loading the `pluginProps.html` script

When you click on the Plug-in Properties button, a new window opens, as shown in Figure 11–5. It contains a list of the properties and MIME types for the plug-ins on your computer that are available to the Navigator browser.

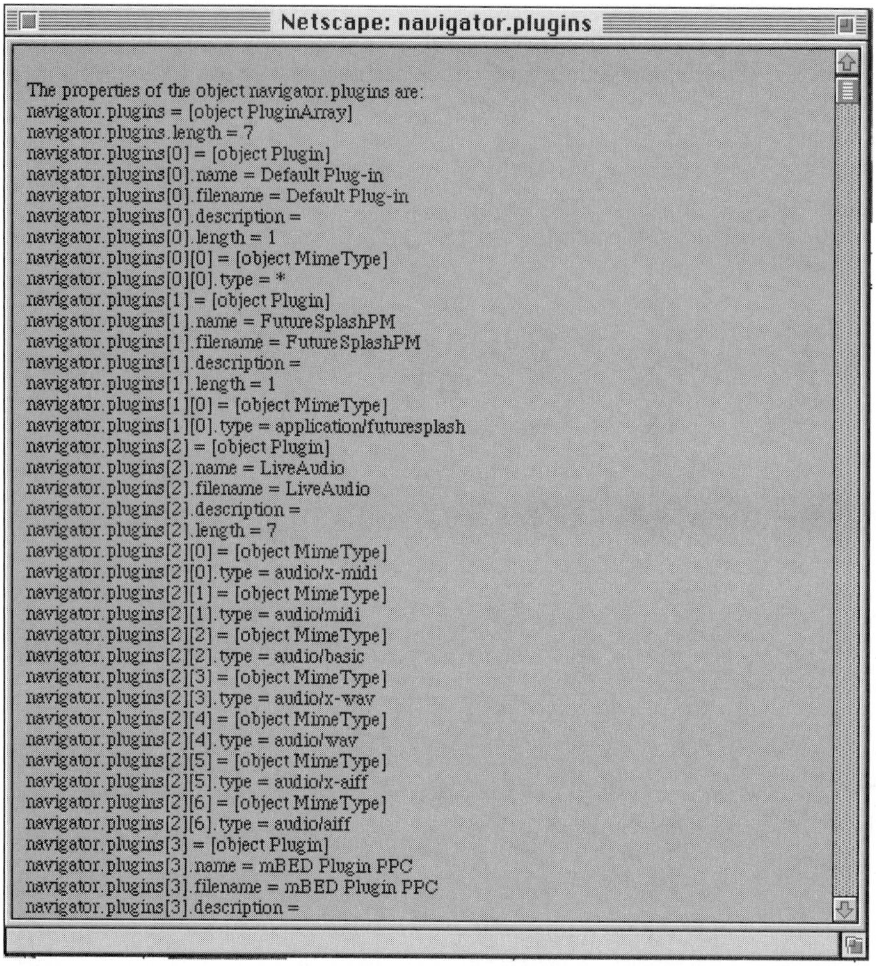

Netscape: navigator.plugins

```
The properties of the object navigator.plugins are:
navigator.plugins = [object PluginArray]
navigator.plugins.length = 7
navigator.plugins[0] = [object Plugin]
navigator.plugins[0].name = Default Plug-in
navigator.plugins[0].filename = Default Plug-in
navigator.plugins[0].description =
navigator.plugins[0].length = 1
navigator.plugins[0][0] = [object MimeType]
navigator.plugins[0][0].type = *
navigator.plugins[1] = [object Plugin]
navigator.plugins[1].name = FutureSplashPM
navigator.plugins[1].filename = FutureSplashPM
navigator.plugins[1].description =
navigator.plugins[1].length = 1
navigator.plugins[1][0] = [object MimeType]
navigator.plugins[1][0].type = application/futuresplash
navigator.plugins[2] = [object Plugin]
navigator.plugins[2].name = LiveAudio
navigator.plugins[2].filename = LiveAudio
navigator.plugins[2].description =
navigator.plugins[2].length = 7
navigator.plugins[2][0] = [object MimeType]
navigator.plugins[2][0].type = audio/x-midi
navigator.plugins[2][1] = [object MimeType]
navigator.plugins[2][1].type = audio/midi
navigator.plugins[2][2] = [object MimeType]
navigator.plugins[2][2].type = audio/basic
navigator.plugins[2][3] = [object MimeType]
navigator.plugins[2][3].type = audio/x-wav
navigator.plugins[2][4] = [object MimeType]
navigator.plugins[2][4].type = audio/wav
navigator.plugins[2][5] = [object MimeType]
navigator.plugins[2][5].type = audio/x-aiff
navigator.plugins[2][6] = [object MimeType]
navigator.plugins[2][6].type = audio/aiff
navigator.plugins[3] = [object Plugin]
navigator.plugins[3].name = mBED Plugin PPC
navigator.plugins[3].filename = mBED Plugin PPC
navigator.plugins[3].description =
```

Figure 11–5 Plug-in properties

Example of Displaying Plug-in File Names

The following `pluginFilename.html` script uses the `filename` property to display a list of the file names of all of the plug-ins that are available to the browser.

```
<!--
                    pluginFilename.html
-->

<HTML>
<HEAD>
```

```
<TITLE>Plugin Filename</TITLE>
<SCRIPT LANGUAGE="JavaScript">
<!-- HIDE FROM OLD BROWSERS

// List the filenames of the installed Plug-ins
//
function pluginFiles() {
  var instPlugins = navigator.plugins
  var     rvalue = ""

  for (var i = 0; i < instPlugins.length; i++) {
    var p = instPlugins[i]

    rvalue += "<DD>" + p.filename
  }
  return unescape(rvalue)
}

// STOP HIDING -->
</SCRIPT>
</HEAD>
<BODY>

<P>By extracting the plugin object's filename
property, this example displays a list of the
files used by the installed Plug-ins.</P>

<P>The files are:</P>

<SCRIPT LANGUAGE="JavaScript">
<!-- HIDE FROM OLD BROWSERS

document.write("<DL>")
document.write(pluginFiles())
document.write("</DL>")

// STOP HIDING -->
</SCRIPT>

</BODY>
</HTML>
```

Figure 11–6 shows the result of loading the `pluginFilename.html` script.

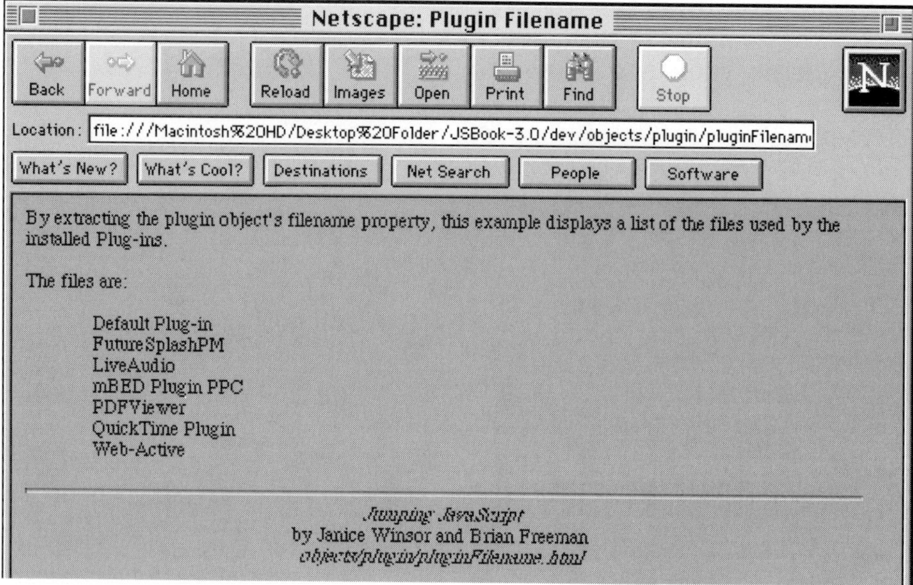

Figure 11–6 Result of loading the `pluginFilename.html` script

Example of Displaying Plug-in Names

The following `pluginName.html` file uses the `name` property of the `plugin` object to display a list of plug-in names. Notice that on this computer, the `filename` and the `name` of the plug-ins are the same. The file name and the name are assigned by the creator of the plug-in and may not always be identical. The `pluginName.html` script formats the display as a numbered list.

```
<!--
                 pluginName.html
-->

<HTML>
<HEAD>
<TITLE>Plugin Name</TITLE>
<SCRIPT LANGUAGE="JavaScript">
<!-- HIDE FROM OLD BROWSERS

// List the installed plug-ins by name
//
function installedPlugins() {
  var instPlugins = navigator.plugins
  var      rvalue = ""
```

```
    for (var i = 0; i < instPlugins.length; i++) {
      var p = instPlugins[i]

      rvalue += "<LI>" + p.name
    }
    return unescape(rvalue)
  }

  // STOP HIDING -->
  </SCRIPT>
  </HEAD>
  <BODY>

  <P>By extracting the plugin object's name
  property, this example displays a list of the
  plug-ins available to this browser.</P>

  <P>The available plug-ins are:</P>

  <SCRIPT LANGUAGE="JavaScript">
  <!-- HIDE FROM OLD BROWSERS

  document.write("<OL>")
  document.write(installedPlugins())
  document.write("</OL>")

  // STOP HIDING -->
  </SCRIPT>

  </BODY>
  </HTML>
```

Figure 11–7 shows the result of loading the `pluginName.html` script.

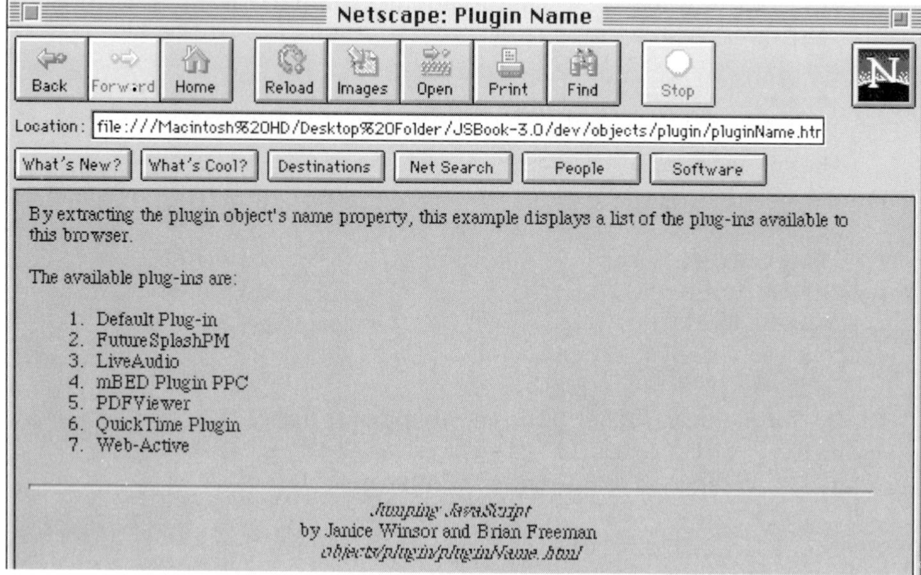

Figure 11–7 Result of loading the `pluginName.html` script

Updating the List of Plug-ins Available to the Browser

Because Navigator builds its list of installed plug-ins when you start it, if you add a new plug-in file, you would have to quit Navigator and restart it before the new plug-in is recognized. The `plugin` object provides a `refresh()` method that enables you to rebuild the plug-in list from a script to add any new plug-ins without needing to quit and restart the browser.

Methods

refresh()

Syntax

navigator.plugins.refresh()

Returns

Nothing

The `refresh()` method is used only to add a new plug-in to the list. If you remove a plug-in, it still remains in the `plugins[]` array for the current session, although the removed plug-in may not be available to the browser.

Example of Updating the List of Plug-ins Available to the Browser

The following `pluginRefresh.html` script uses the `refresh()` method as part of a function that is called by the `onClick` event handler for the Refresh button. Clicking on the button updates the list of plug-ins that are available to the browser. This example does not add any plug-ins to the system, so the `refresh()` method does not actually add a plug-in to the list. You would use this method as part of a helper script that enabled users to add a plug-in to their system and use it without quitting Navigator and restarting it again.

```
<!--
               pluginRefresh.html
-->

<HTML>
<HEAD>
<TITLE>Plugin Refresh</TITLE>
<SCRIPT LANGUAGE="JavaScript">
<!-- HIDE FROM OLD BROWSERS

// refresh the plug-ins
function pluginRefresh() {
  navigator.plugins.refresh(true)
}

// STOP HIDING -->
</SCRIPT>
</HEAD>

<BODY>

<P>If you use an argument of true for the plugin
object's refresh method, Navigator looks for any
newly installed plug-ins and updates itself. Without
the refresh method, you would have to restart
Navigator for your change to take effect.</P>

<P>This method is provided mainly for plug-in
installation.</P>
```

```
<P>Give it a try, what could it hurt ;-)</P>

<CENTER><FORM>
<INPUT TYPE="button" NAME="btn" VALUE="Refresh"
 onClick="pluginRefresh()">
</FORM><CENTER>

</BODY>
</HTML>
```

Figure 11–8 shows the result of loading the `pluginRefresh.html` script.

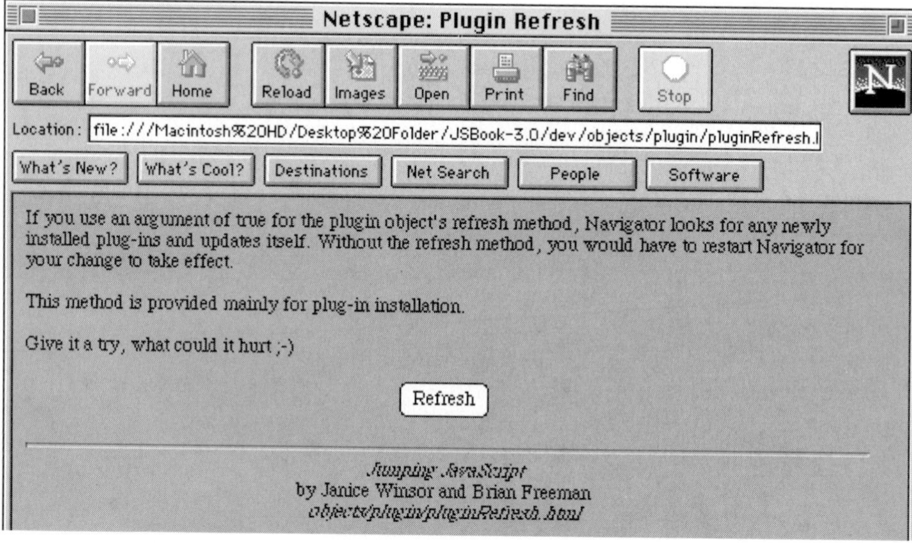

Figure 11–8 Result of loading the `pluginRefresh.html` script

Checking to Determine if a Plug-in Is Available

You can use the `plugin` property of the `navigator` object to determine if a plug-in is available on a client computer. If the plug-in is not available, you can display an alternative message. For more information about the `navigator` object, see Chapter 32, "Using the navigator Object."

Example of Checking to Determine if a Plug-in Is Available

The following `pluginAvailable.html` script uses the `navigator.plugins` property to check to see whether the LiveAudio plug-in is available. If it is not available on the client system, a message is displayed in place of the plug-in.

```
<!--
              pluginAvailable.html

    By checking if the desired plug-in is
    available before embedding it into the
    document, the viewer is always provided with
    an appropriate behavior.
-->

<HTML>
<HEAD>
<TITLE>Plug-in Available</TITLE>
</HEAD>
<BODY>

<P>If the LiveAudio plug-in is available, you'll
see controls below and a MIDI file will play.</P>

<CENTER>
<SCRIPT LANGUAGE="JavaScript">
<!-- HIDE FROM OLD BROWSERS

var plugin = navigator.plugins["LiveAudio"]
var    msg = ""

if (plugin) {
  msg += "<EMBED SRC='../../media/Hero.mid'"
  msg += "  WIDTH=200 HEIGHT=100></EMBED>"
} else {
  msg += "<P>Otherwise, you'll see this message."
}

document.write(msg)

// STOP HIDING -->
</SCRIPT>
</CENTER>

</BODY>
</HTML>
```

Figure 11–9 shows the result of loading the `pluginAvailable.html` script when the plug-in is available.

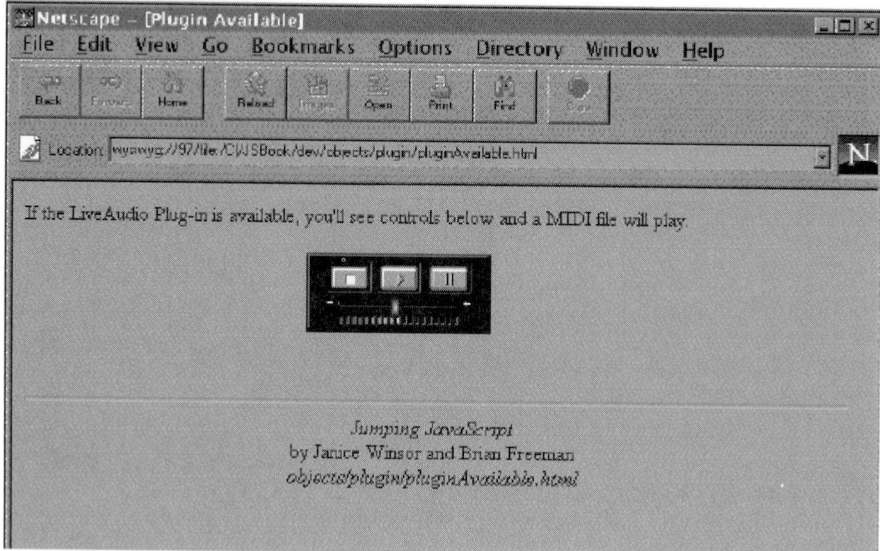

Figure 11–9 Result of loading the `pluginAvailable.html` script when the plug-in is available

If no plug-in is available, the page loads and leaves a blank space for the plug-in as shown in Figure 11–10.

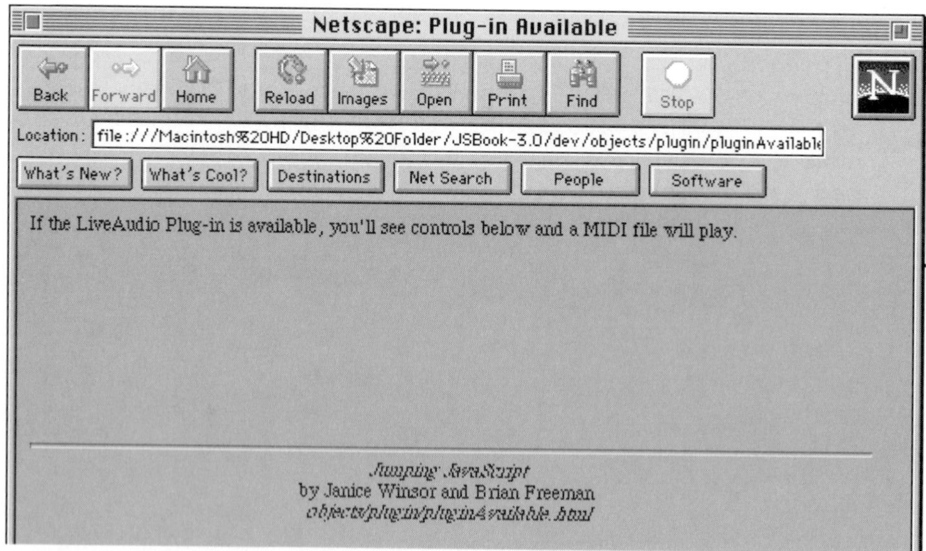

Figure 11–10 Result of loading the `pluginAvailable.html` script when the plug-in is not available

Controlling a Plug-in

When you have access to plug-in source code or documentation, you can control the behavior of the plug-in from within your script. For more information about plug-ins see the *Netscape Developer's Guide to Plug-Ins* by Doug Young, published by Prentice Hall Professional Technical Reference, 1996

Example of Controlling a Plug-in from a Script

We include the following `Music.html` script from the *Netscape Developer's Guide to Plug-Ins* by permission of Doug Young. This script provides a dummy `doNothing()` function that displays an alert if the plug-in is not available. Otherwise, the LiveAudio plug-in is used to stop any plug-in that is currently playing and start the new sound.

The sound files are embedded as shown in the following script extract:

```
<embed src="keyboard.aiff" name="keyboard"
       hidden=true volume= 100% autostart=false>
```

For each sound file, `src` specifies the audio file, `name` specifies the `soundName` for the embedded sound file, `hidden` set to `true` means that the file is not visible, `volume` is set to the maximum of 100 percent, and `autostart` is set to `false` so that the audio file is not automatically played when you load the plug-in.

```
<html>
<head>
<script language="JavaScript">

function doNothing() {} // A dummy function

// Use an audio plugin to play a named sound

function playSound ( soundName )
{
   // Get the plugin used to play this sound

   plugin = document.plugins[soundName];

   // Print the name of the sound in the status area
   window.status = soundName

   if ( plugin != null )
   {
       // If the needed plugin was found, stop any
       // plugin currently playing, and start the
       // new sound. Arrange for the new sound
```

```
        // to stop after 2 seconds.

        plugin.StopAll();
        plugin.play(false);
        setTimeout('plugin.stop()', 2000);
    }
}

</script>
</head>
<title> Sound Sampler </title>

<body bgcolor=#ffffff>

<h2>
Point to an instrument to hear how it sounds
</h2>

<! Embed an audio plugin for each sound to be
   played.>

<embed src="keyboard.aiff" name="keyboard"
       hidden=true volume= 100% autostart=false>
<embed src="guitar.aiff" name="guitar"
       hidden=true volume=100% autostart=false>
<embed src="drums.aiff" name="drums"
       hidden=true volume= 100% autostart=false>
<embed src="violin.aiff  name="violin"
       hidden=true volume=100% autostart=false>

<! Include each image inside an anchor tag. The href
   points to a dummy function. The sole purpose of the
  anchor is to support the onMouseOver event,
  which calls playSound() with the appropriate
  sound as an argument >

<a href="doNothing()"
   onMouseOver="playSound('violin'); return true;">
  <img src="violin.gif"  border=0> </a>

<a href="doNothing()"
   onMouseOver="playSound('guitar'); return true;">
  <img src="guitar.gif"  border=0> </a>
```

```
<a href="doNothing()"
   onMouseOver="playSound('keyboard');
       return true;">
   <img src="keyboard.gif"  border=0> </a>

<a href="javascript:doNothing()"
   onMouseOver="playSound('drums'); return true;">
   <img src="drums.gif"  border=0> </a>

</body>
</html>
```

Figure 11–11 shows the result of loading the `Music.html` script.

Figure 11–11 Result of loading the `Music.html` script

Moving the pointer over the musical instrument displays the name of the instrument in the status area and plays its sound.

Plug-ins and LiveConnect

This chapter shows you how to use JavaScript to work with plug-ins. If you want a more sophisticated and robust way to connect to plug-ins, you will want to learn more about LiveConnect, which became available with the beta Navigator 3.0 release. LiveConnect provides two-way communication between scripts and Java applets or plug-ins. Documenting LiveConnect is beyond the scope of this book. For a brief introduction to the Java/JavaScript connection through LiveConnect, we suggest that you check out the LiveConnect/Plug-in Developer's guide available at:

```
http://home.netscape.com/eng/mozilla/3.0/handbook/
plugins/index.html
```

Summary of New Terms and Concepts

The new terms and concepts introduced in this chapter are listed in alphabetical order in Table 11-2. The terms and concepts are also included in the glossary at the end of the book.

Table 11-2 Summary of New Terms and Concepts

Term/Concept	Description
transparent	Any application or process that is started automatically so that no user action is required. Another use for this term is to describe a system that passes through all data exactly as it is received.

PART THREE

Navigating on the Web

CHAPTER 12

- Using the location Object Without Any Properties
- Properties of the location Object
- Referencing the Complete URL
- Referencing the Protocol
- Referencing the Host, Host Name, and Port
- Referencing the Path Name
- Referencing the Hash
- Referencing Search Queries
- Reloading a Document from a Script
- Replacing a URL in the History List
- Summary of New Terms and Concepts

Controlling Location

An important part of writing JavaScript programs is storing and using information about the current URL and any URL that you use as a link.

To control the URLs in scripting, the JavaScript language provides two built-in objects:

- `location`
- `link`

In addition, you can use the `anchor` property and HTML `HREF` tags to control URLs. This chapter describes the `location` object. For information on links and anchors, see Chapter 14, "Working with Links."

Use the `location` object to store and display information about the current URL. The `location` object is a property of the `window` object. It represents information about the URL of any currently open window.

Using the location Object Without Any Properties

Referencing the `location` object without any properties displays the complete URL. The following `location.html` script uses the `location` object to display the URL for the current window.

```
<!--
         location.html

    This example obtains the current
    location of this file. When the button is
    clicked, the function displayLocation()
    pops up an alert dialog with the value of the
    current location.
-->

<HTML>
<HEAD>
<TITLE>Current Location</TITLE>
<SCRIPT LANGUAGE="JavaScript">
<!-- HIDE FROM OLD BROWSERS

//
// displayLocation - display in an alert dialog
// the location of this file.
//
function displayLocation() {
  var msg_str = "\n"

  msg_str += "The location of this file is "
  msg_str += "\"" + location + "\""
  msg_str += "\n"
  alert(unescape(msg_str))
}
// STOP HIDING -->
</SCRIPT>
</HEAD>

<BODY>

<P>Click on the Get Location button to see the location
of this file.

<CENTER><FORM>
<INPUT TYPE="button" VALUE="Get Location"
 onClick="displayLocation()">
</FORM></CENTER>

</BODY>
</HTML>
```

Figure 12–1 shows the result of loading the `location.html` script.

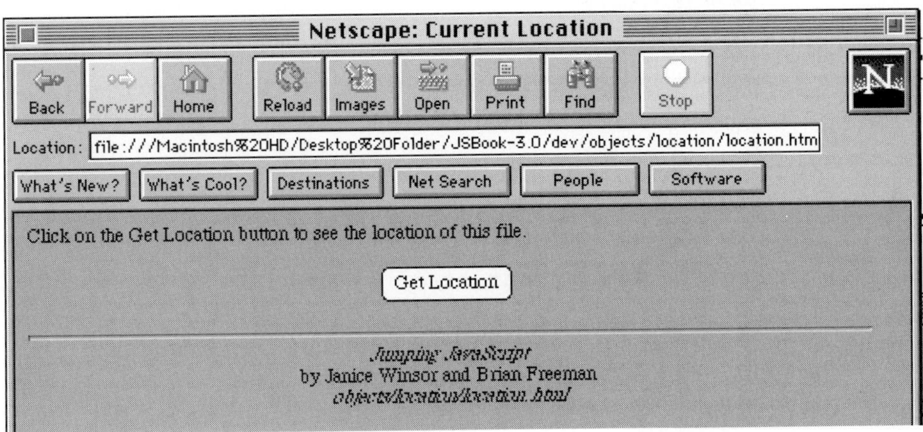

Figure 12–1 Result of loading the `location.html` script

When you click on the Get Location button, an alert window is displayed, showing the location of the HTML document, as shown in Figure 12–2.

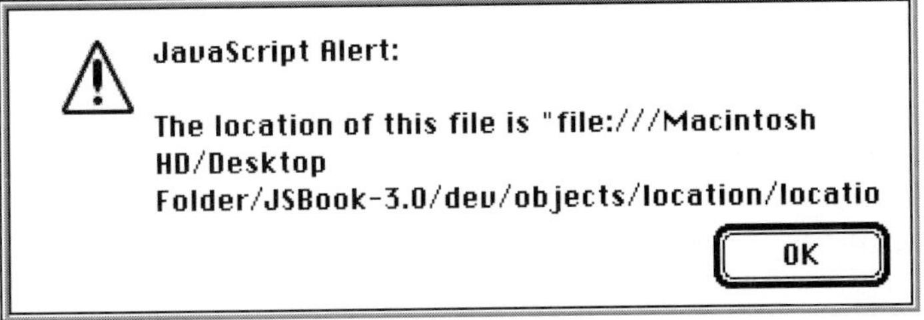

Figure 12–2 Alert window with location of document

The `location.html` script uses the `unescape()` function to format the output to replace `%20` with a space on Macintosh systems. For more information about the `unescape()` function, see Chapter 6, "Creating Windows."

You can also use the `location` object to specify a URL to load in the window, as shown in the following `locationAssignment.html` script. This script works best if you are already connected to the Web before you load the script.

UI Guideline – Be careful about designing scripts that load different URLs. Make sure you do not unexpectedly take your users to different sites without warning.

```
<!--
        locationAssignment.html

    This example assigns a value to the location
    object. You'll see this page load, then it'll
    convert to Netscape's home page.
-->

<HTML>
<HEAD>
<TITLE>Location Assignment</TITLE>
<SCRIPT LANGUAGE="JavaScript">
<!-- HIDE FROM OLD BROWSERS

window.location = "http://home.netscape.com"

// STOP HIDING -->
</SCRIPT>
</HEAD>

<BODY>

<CENTER>
<h2>Now you see it, and now you don't...</h2>
</CENTER>

</BODY>
</HTML>
```

Figure 12–3 shows the result of loading the `locationAssignment.html` script.

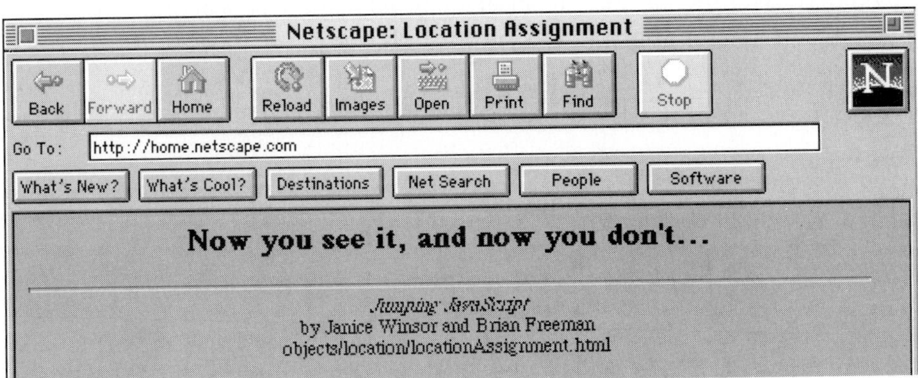

Figure 12–3 Result of loading the `locationAssignment.html` script

After a few moments, the URL specified by the `location` object is loaded, as shown in Figure 12–4.

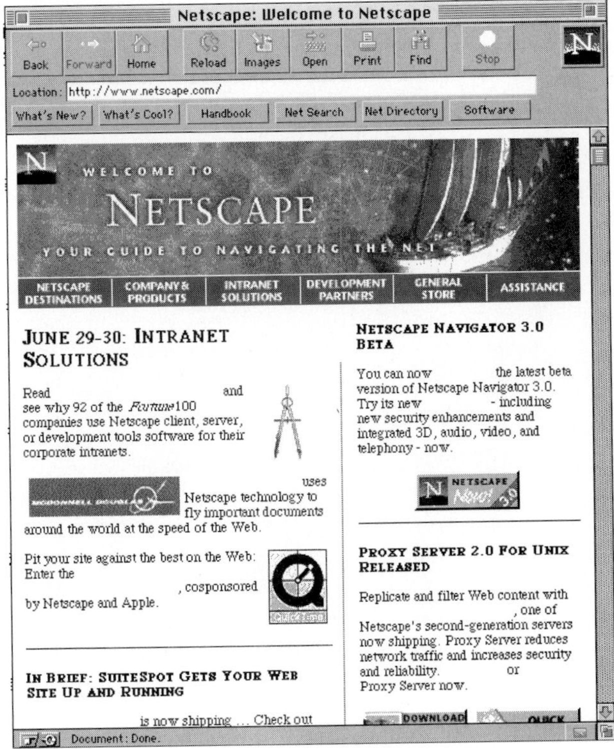

Figure 12–4 Location URL specified in script

Properties of the location Object

The properties for the `location` object are listed in alphabetical order in Table 12-1. The `location` object has no event handlers.

Table 12-1 Properties and Methods for the location Object

Properties	Methods	Event Handlers
`hash`	`eval()*`	None
`host`	`reload()*`	
`hostname`	`replace()*`	
`href`	`toString()*`	
`pathname`	`valueOf()*`	
`port`		
`protocol`		
`search`		

* New in the Navigator 3.0 release.

The `location` object has the eight properties listed below.

Property	Value	Gettable	Settable
hash	string	Yes	Yes
host	string	Yes	Yes
hostname	string	Yes	Yes
href	URL	Yes	Yes
pathname	string	Yes	Yes
port	string	Yes	Yes
protocol	string	Yes	Yes
search	string	Yes	Yes

You use most of the properties for the `location` object to get relevant information that you need from the URL, such as the host, path name, or protocol. The `location` object stores the relevant information from the current URL. Most of the properties for the `location` object are used to control network information, including information about the physical location of the document on the network, the host server, and the protocol being used.

Because the `location` object properties divide the URL into specific components, you need to understand the individual pieces of the URL. Dividing a statement into its constituent parts is called parsing. When you *parse* a statement, you analyze a series of words to determine their collective meaning.

Let's look at a URL that contains all of the possible location object properties:

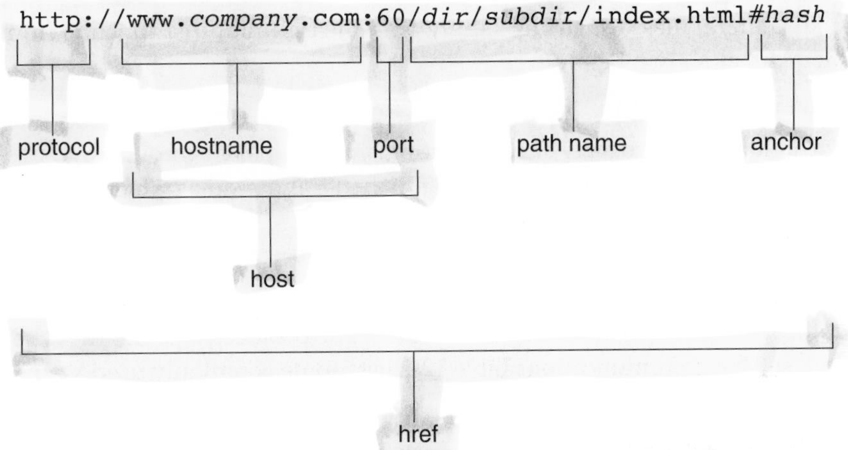

As you can see from this diagram, the `host` property is made up of the `hostname` and the `port`. The `href` property contains the entire URL.

Use the `location` object when you need to extract information about a URL for a script.

Referencing the Complete URL

When you want to reference the complete URL, you use the `location.href` property. We discuss this property first because it is probably the most commonly used property for the `location` object.

When you extract a URL value for the `location.href` property, that value might be encoded with ASCII equivalents of nonalphanumeric characters. These ASCII values include the percent symbol (`%`) and the ASCII numeric value. You've already seen examples of these encoded values in the URLs for the examples in this book. The `%20` represents the ASCII value for a space.

If you want to extract the URL and display the information as a string in your documents, you can manipulate the ASCII equivalents. You can pass a string with ASCII equivalents through the `unescape()` function to remove them so you can display the URL in your documents. The `location.html` script shown in "Using the location Object Without Any Properties" on page 427 uses the `unescape()` function in the following statement.

```
alert(unescape(msg_str))
```

To display a literal message string, simply omit the `unescape()` function from the statement, as shown below:

```
alert(msg_str)
```

If you need to send a properly encoded string, you can pass it through the `escape()` function to restore the ASCII equivalents and send a properly encoded string to CGI programs on servers.

Referencing the Protocol

The protocol is the first component of any URL. The protocol specifies the type of protocol used for communication. Table 12-2 lists some commonly used Web protocols.

Table 12-2 Common World Wide Web Protocols

Protocol	Description
`http:`	Hypertext transfer protocol
`ftp:`	File transfer protocol
`file:`	Protocol for loading a local file
`mailto:`	Mail protocol
`javascript:`	A URL pseudoprotocol that you can use to evaluate expressions and return results

Note – The trailing colon is part of the protocol, but the slashes following the colon are not part of the protocol. The only `location` property that includes the slash delimiters is `location.href`.

Example of Referencing Different Protocols

The following set of scripts creates an analyzer that you can use to explore properties of different protocols. The following `index.html` script defines the frameset for the analyzer example.

```
<!--
       objects/location/analyzer/index.html

    This frameset defines the page for the
    Location Analyzer. The analyzer is loaded into
    the left frame and a target URL into the
    right. Clicking on one of the links provided
    in the analyzer assigns that URL
    to targetFrame.location. Typing your own
    URL into the text field and pressing Return
    assigns your URL to targetFrame.location.
    After the URL is loaded, click on the Analyze
    Location button to display the location object's
    properties for the loaded URL.
-->
<HTML>
<HEAD>
<TITLE>Location Analyzer</TITLE>
</HEAD>

<FRAMESET COLS="50%,50%">
  <FRAME NAME="analyzerFrame" SRC="analyzer.html">
  <FRAME NAME="targetFrame" SRC="image.html">
</FRAMESET>

</HTML>
```

The following `image.html` script contains the definition for the image that is included in one frame of the analyzer.

```
<!--
          image.html
-->

<HTML>
<HEAD>
<TITLE>Image File</TITLE>
</HEAD>
<BODY>

<CENTER>
<IMG SRC="../../../images/Kangaroo-3.jpg">
</CENTER>

</BODY>
</HTML>
```

The following analyzer.html script contains text and the set of buttons that are loaded into the left frame of the analyzer example.

```
<!--
    objects/location/analyzer/analyzer.html

    This script is the heart of the Location
    Analyzer. index.html defines the framesets,
    and this file gets loaded into the left
    frame. A target URL is loaded into the right
    frame. When you click on one of the links provided
    in the analyzer, the code assigns that URL
    to targetFrame.location. Typing your own
    URL into the text field and clicking on the Analyze
    Location button assigns your URL to targetFrame.

    After the URL is loaded, clicking on Analyze
    Location displays the location object's
    properties for the loaded URL.
-->
<HTML>
<HEAD>
<TITLE>Location Analyzer</TITLE>
<SCRIPT LANGUAGE="JavaScript">
<!-- HIDE FROM OLD BROWSERS
```

```
/*
** Script Maintenance variables
*/

// Debugging messages
//   'true' turns them on
//   'false' turns them off
//
debug = true;


/*
** Utility functions
*/

// newline
//
function newline(html) {
  var rvalue = ""

  if (html)
    rvalue += "<BR>"
  else
    rvalue += "\n"

  return rvalue
}

// indent
//
function indent(html) {
  var rvalue = ""

  if (html)
    rvalue += "<DD>"
  else
    rvalue += "     "

  return rvalue
}
```

```
// Array object
//   Creation method
//
function Array(n) {
   this.length = n;
   for (var i = 1; i <= n; i++) {
     this[i] = 0
   }
   return this
}

// setStatus
//   Change the window object's status property to
//   the supplied string.
//
function setStatus(string) {
  var rvalue = false      // the value returned

  if (string == "") {
    if (debug == true) {
      alert("\nNull string passed to setStatus()")
    }
  }
  else {
    window.status = string
    rvalue = true
  }
  return rvalue
}

// getProps
//
// Get the properties for the given object
//
// Arguments:
//    obj      - obtain properties from this
//               object
//    obj_name - a string representing the
//               object name
//    html     - generate html output?
//
// Return Value
//    string of the form:
//      object_name.property = "value"
```

```
//      object_name.property = "value"
//      ...
//
//
function getProps(obj, obj_name, html) {
  var rvalue = ""

  rvalue += newline(html)
  rvalue += "The object " + obj_name + "'s "
  rvalue += "properties are:"
  rvalue += newline(html)

  for (var i in obj) {
    rvalue += indent(html)
    rvalue += obj_name + "." + i
    rvalue += " = " + obj[i]
    rvalue += newline(html)
  }
  rvalue += newline(html)

  return rvalue
}


/*
** Global Program Data
*/

// Message object
//   Creation method
//
// Description:
//   Each instance of this object stores a message
//   string to be displayed to the user.
//
// Properties:
//   id     - the id given to this message
//   string - the message string
//
function Message(id, string) {
  this.id     = id;
  this.string = string;
}
```

```
// onMouseOver Messages Array
//   The messages displayed to the user when an
//   onMouseOver event occurs.
//
overMsgs = new Array(7);

// Load the OverMsgs Array
overMsgs[1]= new Message(1,
  "Sun Microsystems")
overMsgs[2] = new Message(2,
  "JavaScript Authoring Guide\'s hash description")
overMsgs[3] = new Message(3,
  "AltaVista query for JavaScript")
overMsgs[4] = new Message(4,
  "Netscape\'s PowerPack lives here")
overMsgs[5] = new Message(5,
  "A test file")
overMsgs[6] = new Message(6,
  "Enter a URL to analyze.")

/*
** Program Methods
*/

// navigateTo
//
function navigateTo(url) {
  var rvalue = false     // return value

  if (url == "") {
    if (debug == true) {
      alert("navigateTo() passed a null URL.")
    }
    return false
  }
  else {
    parent.targetFrame.location = url
    rvalue = true
  }
  return rvalue
}
```

```
// analyze
//
// This method implements the Analyze Location
// button. If targetField contains a value, we
// navigate there. If targetField is empty, the
// location is analyzed.
//
function analyze() {
  // holds the message string sent to the alert
  // dialog.
  var msg_str = ""

  if (document.forms[0].targetField.value != "") {
    navigateTo(document.forms[0].targetField.value)
    document.forms[0].targetField.value = ""
  }
  else {
    msg_str += getProps(parent.targetFrame.location,
   "targetFrame.location", false)
    alert(unescape(msg_str))
  }
}

// display_hash
//   Display supplied location object's hash
//   property in an alert dialog.
//
// Arguments:
//   win  - The window to get the location of
//
function display_hash(win) {
  var msg_str = ""

  msg_str += "\"" + win.location.hash + "\""
  alert(unescape(msg_str))
}

// display_host
//   Display supplied location object's host
//   property in an alert dialog.
//
// Arguments:
//   win  - The window to get the location of
//
```

```
function display_host(win) {
  var msg_str = ""

  msg_str += "\"" + win.location.host + "\""
  alert(unescape(msg_str))
}

// display_hostname
//   Display supplied location object's hostname
//   property in an alert dialog.
//
// Arguments:
//   win  - The window to get the location of
//
function display_hostname(win) {
  var msg_str = ""

  msg_str += "\"" + win.location.hostname + "\""
  alert(unescape(msg_str))
}

// display_href
//   Display supplied location object's href
//   property in an alert dialog.
//
// Arguments:
//   win  - The window to get the location of
//
function display_href(win) {
  var msg_str = ""

  msg_str += "\"" + win.location.href + "\""
  alert(unescape(msg_str))
}

// display_pathname
//   Display supplied location object's pathname
//   property in an alert dialog.
//
// Arguments:
//   win  - The window to get the location of
//
```

```
function display_pathname(win) {
  var msg_str = ""

  msg_str += "\"" + win.location.pathname + "\""
  alert(unescape(msg_str))
}

// display_port
//   Display supplied location object's port
//   property in an alert dialog.
//
// Arguments:
//   win  - The window to get the location of
//
function display_port(win) {
  var msg_str = ""

  msg_str += "\"" + win.location.port + "\""
  alert(unescape(msg_str))
}

// display_protocol
//   Display supplied location object's protocol
//   property in an alert dialog.
//
// Arguments:
//   win  - The window to get the location of
//
function display_protocol(win) {
  var msg_str = ""

  msg_str += "\"" + win.location.protocol + "\""
  alert(unescape(msg_str))
}

// display_search
//   Display supplied location object's search
//   property in an alert dialog.
//
// Arguments:
//   win  - The window to get the location of
//
```

```
function display_search(win) {
  var msg_str = ""

  msg_str += "\"" + win.location.search + "\""
  alert(unescape(msg_str))
}

// STOP HIDING -->
</SCRIPT>
</HEAD>
<BODY>

<H2>Location Analyzer</H2>

<P><B>Note</B>: On Navigator 2.02 and greater,
this example requires you to enable data
tainting:</P>
<UL>
<LI>On UNIX systems, use the setenv command if
you are running csh.
  <OL>
  <LI>Exit your current Navigator.
  <LI>Type "setenv NS_ENABLE_TAINT true" in a shell.
  <LI>Restart Navigator from the same shell.
  </OL>
<LI>On Windows systems, use the set command.
   <OL>
   <LI>Exit your current Navigator.
   <LI>Add "SET NS_ENABLE_TAINT=TRUE" to your
   autoexec.bat
   <LI>Restart your computer.
   <LI>Restart Navigator.
   </OL>
<LI>On Macintosh systems, you need to download an
application named ResEdit to set the environment
variable. Refer to the Data Tainting chapter for
instructions on how to perform this task.
</UL>

<P>Now, on to the example...</P>

<P>Use one of the samples below or supply your
own in the text field to experiment with the
location object.
```

```
<h3> Samples: </h3>
<LI>
<A HREF="http://www.sun.com:80"
 TARGET="targetFrame"
 onMouseOver="return setStatus(overMsgs[1].string)"
>http</A>
protocol with port
</LI>

<LI>
<A
HREF="http://home.netscape.com/eng/mozilla/Gold/handbook/
javascript/ref_h-l.html#hash_property"
 TARGET="targetFrame"
 onMouseOver="return setStatus(overMsgs[2].string)"
>http</A>
protocol with hash
</LI>

<LI>
<A HREF="http://altavista.digital.com/cgi-
bin/query?pg=aq&what=web&fmt=.&q=%22JavaScript+Books%22&r
=&d0=&d1="
 TARGET="targetFrame"
 onMouseOver="return setStatus(overMsgs[3].string)"
>http</A>
protocol with search
</LI>

<LI>
<A HREF="ftp://ftp20.netscape.com/pub/powerpack"
 TARGET="targetFrame"
 onMouseOver="return setStatus(overMsgs[4].string)"
>ftp</A>
protocol
</LI>

<LI>
<A HREF="test.html"
 NAME="fileLink"
 TARGET="targetFrame"
 onMouseOver="return setStatus(overMsgs[5].string)"
>file</A>
```

```
protocol
</LI>

<P>Type your own URL in the field below, click
Analyze Location, wait for your URL to load, then
click on the Analyze Location button a second time
to get the location information.</P>

<CENTER><FORM>
<INPUT TYPE="text" NAME="targetField" VALUE=""
 onChange="navigateTo(this.value)"
 onFocus="return setStatus(overMsgs[6].string)">

<INPUT TYPE="button" VALUE="Analyze Location"
onClick="analyze()">

<INPUT TYPE="button" VALUE="location.hash"
onClick="display_hash(parent.targetFrame)">

<INPUT TYPE="button" VALUE="location.host"
onClick="display_host(parent.targetFrame)">

<INPUT TYPE="button" VALUE="location.hostname"
onClick="display_hostname(parent.targetFrame)">

<INPUT TYPE="button" VALUE="location.href"
onClick="display_href(parent.targetFrame)">

<INPUT TYPE="button" VALUE="location.pathname"
onClick="display_pathname(parent.targetFrame)">

<INPUT TYPE="button" VALUE="location.port"
onClick="display_port(parent.targetFrame)">

<INPUT TYPE="button" VALUE="location.protocol"
onClick="display_protocol(parent.targetFrame)">

<INPUT TYPE="button" VALUE="location.search"
onClick="display_search(parent.targetFrame)">
</FORM></CENTER>

</BODY>
</HTML>
```

Figure 12–5 shows the result of loading the `analyzer/index.html` script.

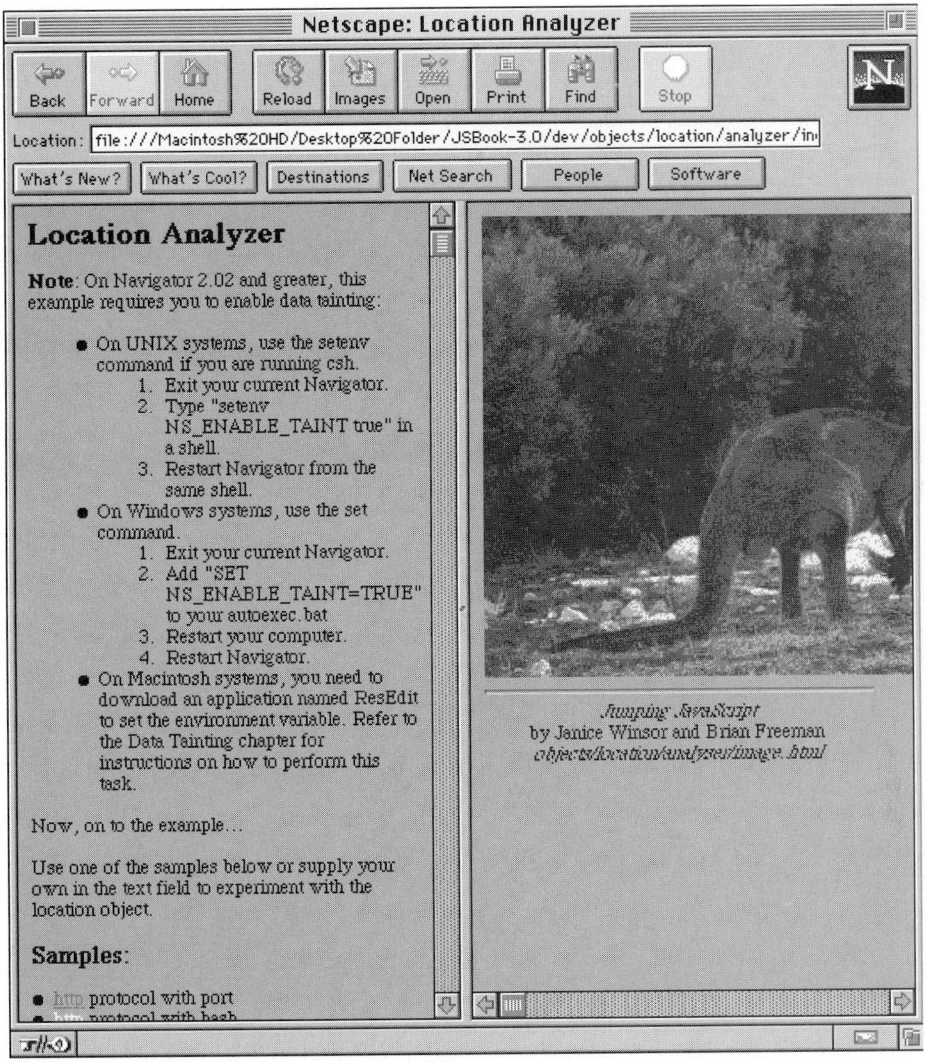

Figure 12–5 Result of loading the `analyzer/index.html` script

Click on one of the sample links to load a file into the right frame. Figure 12–6 shows the link for <u>http</u> protocol with port.

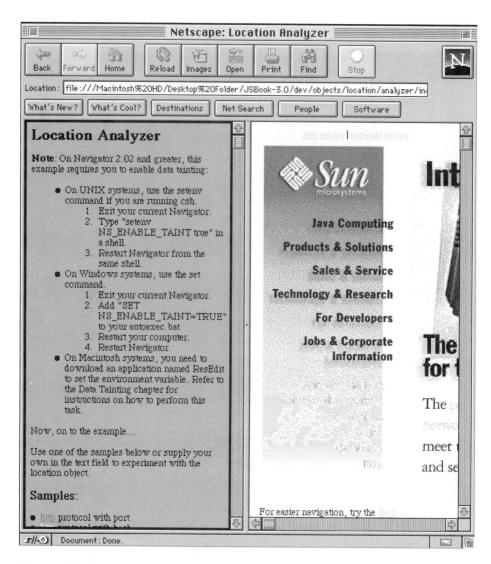

Figure 12–6 Result of clicking on the http protocol with port link

Scroll down to the bottom of the left frame to see the analyzer controls shown in Figure 12–7.

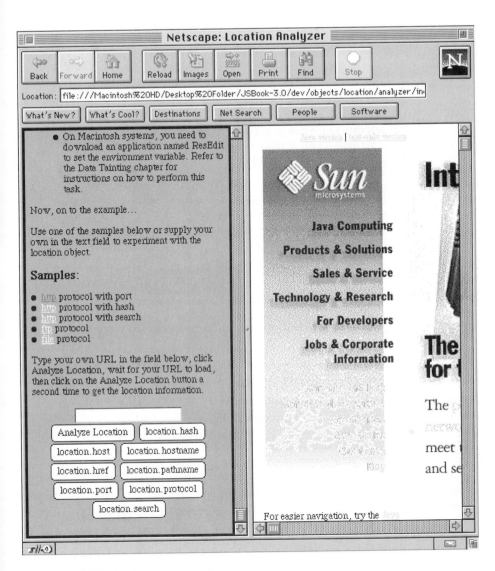

Figure 12–7 Analyzer controls

Clicking on the buttons displays alerts showing the values returned by each property. Figure 12–8 shows the alert that is displayed by clicking on the Analyze Location button.

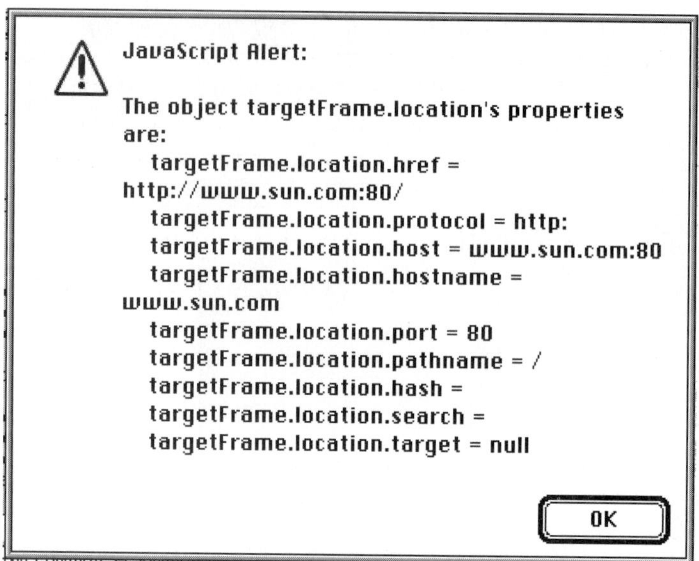

Figure 12–8 Result of clicking on the Analyze Location button

Referencing the Host, Host Name, and Port

The host name of a URL is typically the name of the server that stores the document you are viewing in the browser. Most Web sites include not only the domain name, such as `netscape.com`, but the `www.` prefix as well. The host name does not include the port number, if one is specified.

Most Web sites today do not need to specify a port number as part of their URL. 80 is the most commonly specified port number. You'll see port numbers mostly in URLs to sites that do not have a domain name, or in less popular protocols. You can retrieve the port value by using the `port` property. It's likely that you won't have much use for this property.

The `host` property describes both the host name and the port of a URL. If a port is not specified, then `location.host` and `hostname` both return the same value and can be used interchangeably.

Data Tainting

The Navigator 3.0 release implements a new security model that is based on a concept known as *data tainting*. This concept is used in the Perl programming language. Data tainting marks, or taints, any property values or data that should be secure and private. This tainting enables the JavaScript language to keep close tabs on data that is supposed to be private to the client and to distinguish it from data that is not private. The reason we mention data tainting here is that, because

of the increased security provided by data tainting, you may not be able to retrieve values from the host or hostname properties if the page you are accessing comes from a different server than where the script resides. Tainting is an advanced concept, and it is described in more detail, along with the new methods that are provided to check for tainting and to untaint data, in Chapter 36, "Controlling Data Tainting."

Example of Using the host, host name, and port Properties

The following `locationHost.html` script uses the `host`, `hostname`, and `port` properties.

```
<!--
       locationHost.html

   This example shows how location.host and
   location.hostname can return the same value.
-->

<HTML>
<HEAD>
<TITLE>Comparing Location Host and Hostname</TITLE>
<SCRIPT SRC="../../debug/windowOpen.js"></SCRIPT>
<SCRIPT LANGUAGE="JavaScript">
<!-- HIDE FROM OLD BROWSERS
var myWin = ""

//
// Load Window
//
function loadWindow(dest_url) {
  var wopts = ""    // window options

  // Create the window
  wopts += "toolbar=yes,"
  wopts += "location=yes,"
  wopts += "directories=yes,"
  wopts += "status=yes,"
  wopts += "menubar=yes,"
  wopts += "scrollbars=yes,"
  wopts += "resizable=yes,"
  wopts += "copyhistory=yes,"

  myWin = windowOpen("", "myWindow", wopts)
```

```
  if (myWin == "")
    // couldn't create the window, exit
    return false

  myWin.location.href = dest_url
  return true
}

// display_host
//   Display supplied location object's host
//   property in an alert dialog.
//
// Arguments:
//   win  - The window to get the location of
//
function display_host(win) {
  var msg_str = ""

  msg_str += "\"" + win.location.host + "\""
  alert(unescape(msg_str))
}

// display_hostname
//   Display supplied location object's hostname
//   property in an alert dialog.
//
// Arguments:
//   win  - The window to get the location of
//
function display_hostname(win) {
  var msg_str = ""

  msg_str += "\"" + win.location.hostname + "\""
  alert(unescape(msg_str))
}
```

```
// display_port
//   Display supplied location object's port
//   property in an alert dialog.
//
// Arguments:
//   win  - The window to get the location of
//
function display_port(win) {
  var msg_str = ""

  msg_str += "\"" + win.location.port + "\""
  alert(unescape(msg_str))
}

// STOP HIDING -->
</SCRIPT>
</HEAD>

<BODY>
<P><B>Note</B>: On Navigator 2.02 and greater,
this example requires you to enable data
tainting:</P>
<UL>
<LI>On UNIX systems, use the setenv command if
you are running csh.
  <OL>
  <LI>Exit your current Navigator.
  <LI>Type "setenv NS_ENABLE_TAINT true" in a shell.
  <LI>Restart Navigator from the same shell.
  </OL>
<LI>On Windows systems, use the set command.
   <OL>
   <LI>Exit your current Navigator.
   <LI>Add "SET NS_ENABLE_TAINT=TRUE" to your
   autoexec.bat
   <LI>Restart your computer.
   <LI>Restart Navigator.
   </OL>
<LI>On Macintosh systems, you need to download an
application named ResEdit to set the environment
variable. Refer to the Data Tainting chapter for
instructions on how to perform this task.
</UL>
```

```
<P>Now, on to the example...</P>
<DL>
<DT>Given the URL "http://www.sun.com:80/index.html"
<DD><B>location.hostname</B> becomes "www.sun.com",
<DD><B>location.port</B> becomes "80",
<DD>and <B>location.host</B> becomes the combination
 of the previous two, that is, "www.sun.com:80"
</DL>

<P>Note that "80" is a common port number. So, you
can still get to www.sun.com without specifying the
port. In this case, location.hostname is equal
to location.host. Now, give it a try.
</P>

<FORM>
<INPUT TYPE="button" NAME="openbutton"
  VALUE="http://www.sun.com:80 window"
  onClick="return(loadWindow('http://www.sun.com:80'))">

<INPUT TYPE="button" NAME="openbutton"
  VALUE="http://www.sun.com window"
  onClick="return(loadWindow('http://www.sun.com'))">

<INPUT TYPE="button" NAME="closebutton"
  VALUE="Close window"
  onClick="myWin.close()">
</FORM>

<FORM>
<INPUT TYPE="button" VALUE="location.hostname"
onClick="display_hostname(myWin)">

<INPUT TYPE="button" VALUE="location.port"
onClick="display_port(myWin)">

<INPUT TYPE="button" VALUE="location.host"
onClick="display_host(myWin)">

</FORM>

</BODY>
</HTML>
```

Figure 12–9 shows the result of loading the `locationHost.html` script.

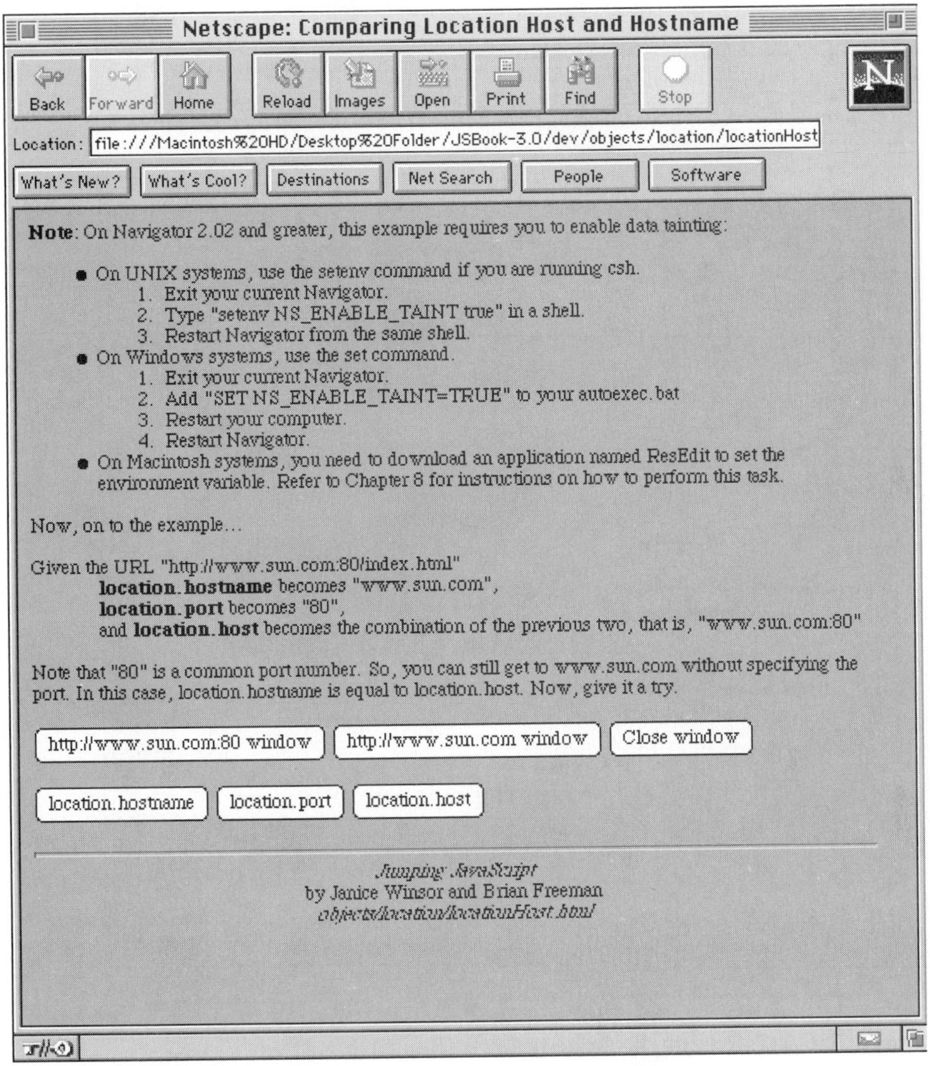

Figure 12–9 Result of loading the `locationHost.html` script

Clicking on either the http://www.sun.com:80 window button or the http://www.sun.com window button opens a new window and displays Sun's home page, as shown in Figure 12–10.

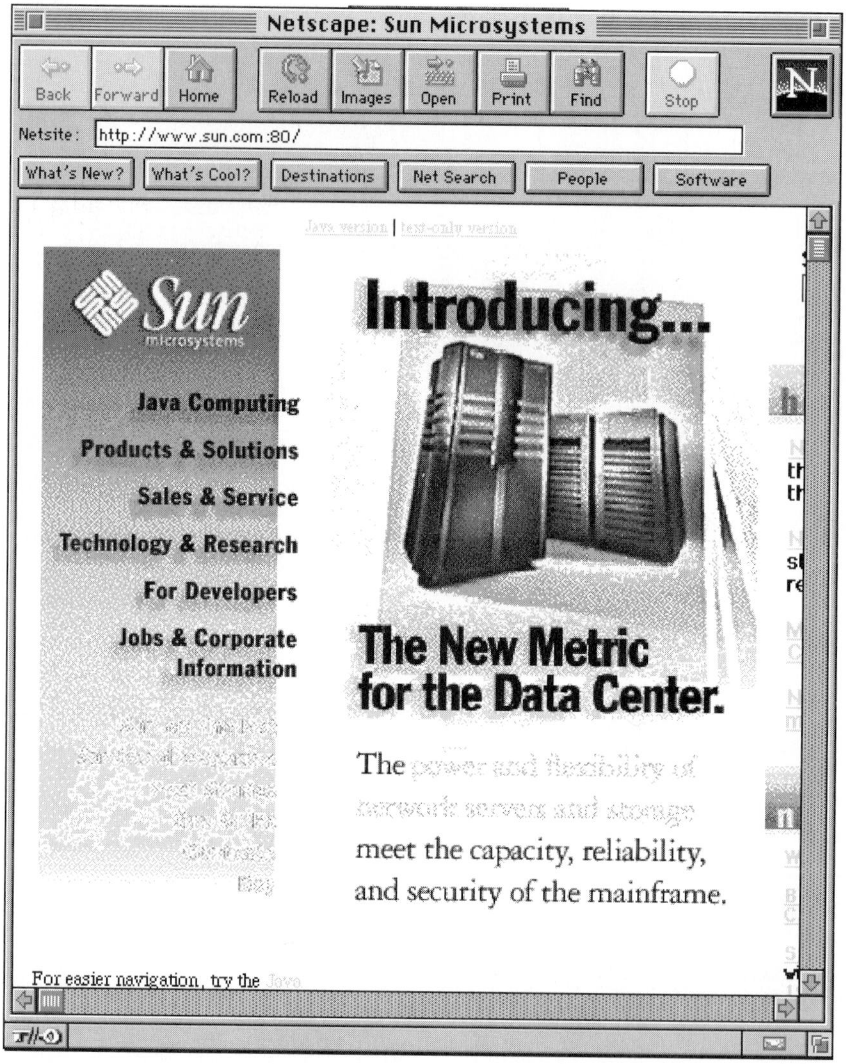

Figure 12–10 Result of clicking on either http button

After you access a location by clicking on either the http://www.sun.com:80 window button or the http://www.sun.com window button, you can click on the location buttons to see what value is returned for each property. Figure 12–11 shows the result of clicking on the location.hostname button.

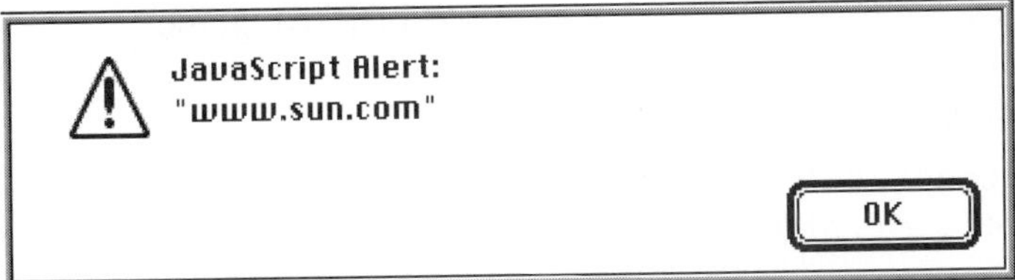

Figure 12–11 Result of clicking on the location.hostname button

Figure 12–12 shows the result of clicking on the location.port button.

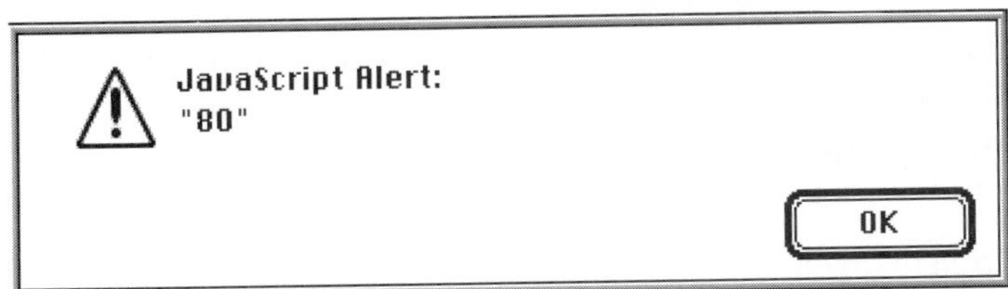

Figure 12–12 Result of clicking on the location.port button

Figure 12–13 shows the result of clicking on the location.host button.

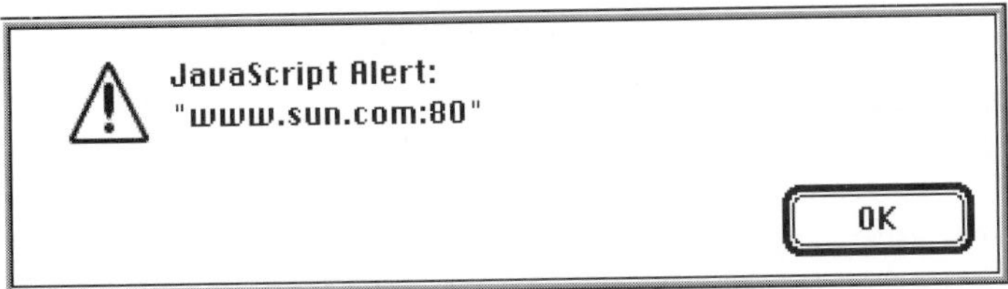

Figure 12–13 Result of clicking on the location.host button

Referencing the Path Name

The path name specifies the location of the directories and files on the server. The server name is not part of the path name. For example, the path name is `/dir/dir/index.html`, not `www.company.com/dir/dir/index.html`.

If the URL references a file in the *root directory*, which is the very top of the file system hierarchy, then the `pathname` property is a slash (/) followed by the name of the document: `/index.html`, for example.

Referencing the Hash

You may see a hash mark (#) near the end of a URL. The hash mark is a URL convention that marks an anchor that the user has clicked on to navigate through a document. When you click on a specific anchor, the information is added to the

URL in the Location text field. In the following example, I clicked on the Operators link in the JavaScript Authoring Guide that is in a file named Examples on my Macintosh desktop.

```
file:///Macintosh%20HD/Desktop%20Folder/Examples/dev/
AuthoringGuide/expr.html#operators
```

In your scripts, you can navigate to another hash in the same document by adjusting the `hash` property in the same way that you can jump to another URL location by using the `window.location` property.

Example of Using the hash Property

The following `index.html` script works with the `data.html` and `hash.html` scripts shown after this script to enable you to navigate between sections and to display the value returned by the `hash` property in an alert window.

```
<!--
    objects/location/hash/index.html

    This frameset defines the page for the
    location.hash example.
-->
<HTML>
<HEAD>
<TITLE>Location Hash</TITLE>
</HEAD>

<FRAMESET COLS="30%,70%">
  <FRAME NAME="hashFrame" SRC="hash.html">
  <FRAME NAME="targetFrame" SRC="data.html">
</FRAMESET>

</HTML>
```

The following `hash.html` file shows the `hash` property for the `location` object, and loads the `data.html` file.

```
<!--
           hash.html

    This example show the location object's hash
    property.
-->

<HTML>
<HEAD>
```

```
<TITLE>Location Hash</TITLE>
<SCRIPT LANGUAGE="JavaScript">
<!-- HIDE FROM OLD BROWSERS

// display_hash
//   Display supplied location object's hash
//   property in an alert dialog.
//
// Arguments:
//   win  - The window to get the location of
//
function display_hash(win) {
  var msg_str = ""

  msg_str += "\"" + win.location.hash + "\""
  alert(unescape(msg_str))
}


// STOP HIDING -->
</SCRIPT>
</HEAD>

<BODY>
<H1>TOC</H1>

<DL>
<DT>
<A HREF="data.html#S1"
 TARGET="targetFrame"
>Section One</A>
</DT>

<DT>
<A HREF="data.html#S2"
 TARGET="targetFrame"
>Section Two</A>
</DT>

<DT>
<A HREF="data.html#S3"
 TARGET="targetFrame"
>Section Three</A>
</DT>
```

```
<DT>
<A HREF="data.html#S4"
 TARGET="targetFrame"
>Section Four</A>
</DT>

<FORM>
<INPUT TYPE="button" VALUE="Get location.hash"
onClick="display_hash(top.frames[1])">
<FORM>
</BODY>
</HTML>
```

The following `data.html` script provides the data for each of the four sections.

```
<!--
           data.html

    Document for the location object's hash
    example.
-->

<HTML>
<HEAD>
<TITLE>Location Hash</TITLE>
</HEAD>

<BODY>
<CENTER>
<H1>A Gothic Tale</H1>
</CENTER>

<A NAME="S1"><H2>Section One</H2></a>
<P>
It was a dark and stormy night. All
of the beagles were safely in their
kennels. The bats flew around the tower,
squeaking frantically.<P>
Dosolina stood at the open window
wistfully gazing out over the moors,
her long dark tresses blowing wildly
as the wind gusted. Piotor was long
overdue. There were evil things afoot
in the night, and she feared greatly
```

```
for his safety.
</P>

<A NAME="S2"><H2>Section Two</H2></a>
<P>
There was something unnatural
about the light flickering through
the clouds. The beagles bugled their
howls, protesting their captivity. The
dogs wanted to be out and about,
investigating the strange smells and
sensations that were drifting
tantalizingly towards them on the gusting
wind.
</P>

<A NAME="S3"><H2>Section Three</H2></a>
<P>
Piotor felt the hot breath of the
ravening monsters as they followed closely
on his heels. He feared for his very life.
He hoped that he could reach the safety
of the tower in the distance before his
strength gave out and the monsters were
upon him.
</P>
<A NAME="S4"><H2>Section Four</H2></a>
<P>
The skies were clear and the weather
balmy, giving the illusion of innocence.
Dosolina and Piotor walked with
determined steps across the moors,
searching for traces of the monsters
that continuously dogged their very
existence.
</P>
<P>
"Oh, here's a footprint," Piotor
cried. "I knew that there was something
tangible in that horrid blackness that
was following me."
</P>
<P>
"And here's a piece of something ...
```

```
Ugh, it is so disgusting," said Dosolina.
"What is this awful curse that prevents
us from being like normal folks?"
</P>
<P>
"We must be brave, and not let them
know how frightened we really are."
</P>

</BODY>
</HTML>
```

Figure 12–14 shows the result of loading the `index.html` file.

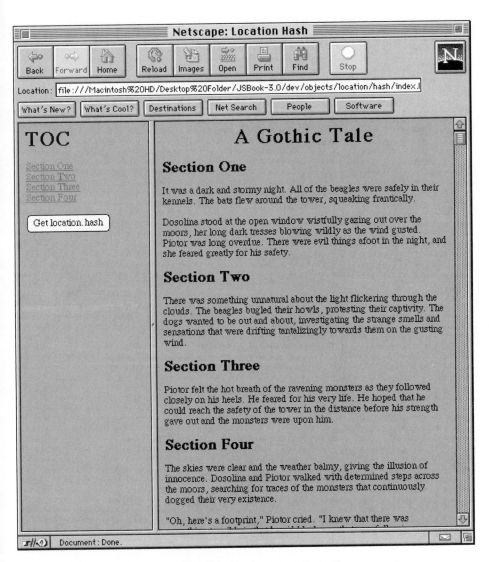

Figure 12–14 Result of loading the `index.html` file

Clicking on any of the links in the TOC column moves the section title to the top of the window. Figure 12–15 shows the page after a user clicks on the Section Three link.

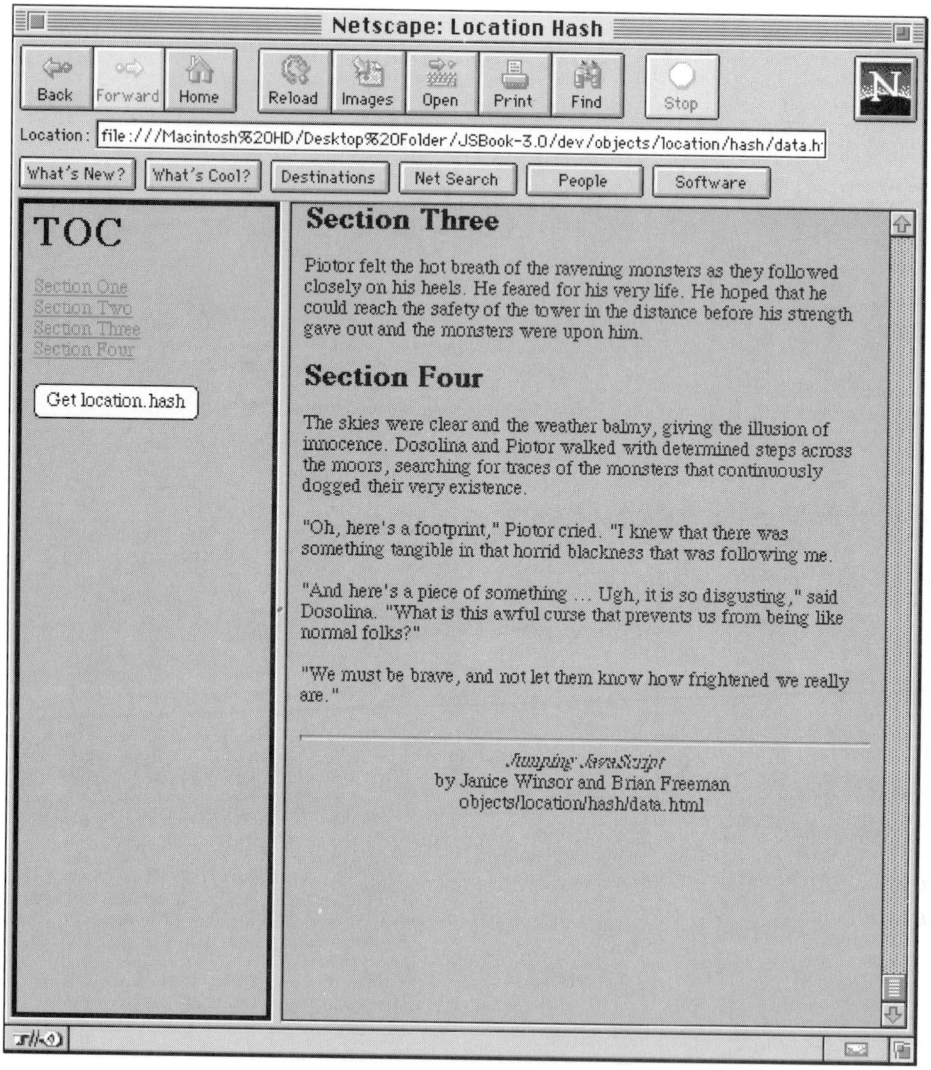

Figure 12–15 Page after clicking on Section Three link

Clicking on the Get location.hash button at any time displays an alert with the value returned by the `hash` property, as shown in Figure 12–16.

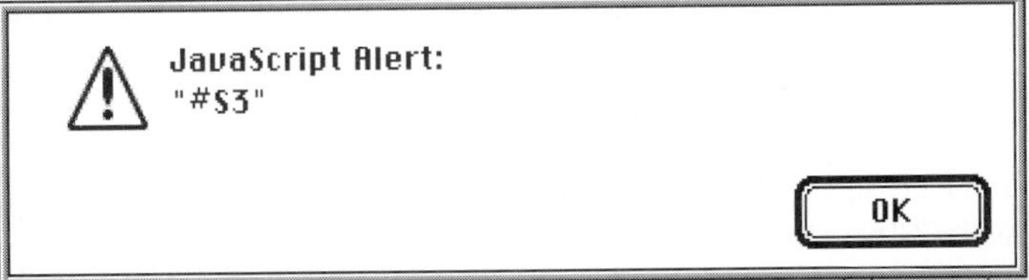

Figure 12–16 `location.hash` alert

Referencing Search Queries

When you use a web search service to look for matches for information, you enter into the keyword field, those search queries are added to the end of the URL. After you type `Kevin Kostner` into the search field and click on the search button from the Lycos home page, the following string is displayed in the Location field:

```
http://www.lycos.com/cgi-
bin/pursuit?cat=lycos&query=Kevin+Kostner&x=35&y=8
```

After you log in to the Columbia House video club, type `Tin Cup` into the search field, and click on the search button, the following string is displayed in the Location field:

```
http://www.columbiahouse.com/vc/cgis/member_search?sid=51
85512097220518678232405 8&searchtype=1&searchfor=Tin+Cup
```

Note that everything at the end of the line, including the question mark is considered the search. Each search engine, which is usually a CGI program running on a server, has its own formula for the queries users submit. These search queries are encoded and are not easy or obvious to interpret. Before you write a script using the `location.search` property, be sure you understand the search engine format completely.

Example of Using location Object Properties

The `locationProps.html` script below shows all of the properties of the `location` object. This script uses the `for (var i in obj)` loop to cycle through all of the properties for the object. For more information about this kind of looping statement, see Chapter 27, "Creating Loops."

```
<!--
        locationProps.html

    This example shows all of the properties of
    the location object. The location of this
    document is used as the location.
```

```
-->

<HTML>
<HEAD>
<TITLE>Location Properties</TITLE>
<SCRIPT LANGUAGE="JavaScript">
<!-- HIDE FROM OLD BROWSERS

/*
** Get the properties for the given object
**
** Arguments:
**    obj      - obtain properties from this
**               object
**    obj_name - a string representing the
**               object name
**
** Return Value
**    string of the form:
**      object_name.property = "value"
**      object_name.property = "value"
**      ...
**
*/
function getProps(obj, obj_name) {
  var retval = ""

  retval += "The object " + obj_name + "'s "
  retval += "properties are:"
  for (var i in obj) {
    retval += "<DD>"
    retval += obj_name + "." + i
    retval += " = " + obj[i] + "</DD>"
  }
  retval += "<P>"

  return retval
}
// STOP HIDING -->
</SCRIPT>
</HEAD>

<BODY>
<HR>
```

```
<P>Most properties below are blank because the
protocol is "file." If this document was on a
server, you would see other properties filled in.

<SCRIPT LANGUAGE="JavaScript">
<!-- HIDE FROM OLD BROWSERS

document.write(getProps(location, "location"))

// STOP HIDING -->
</SCRIPT>

</BODY>
</HTML>
```

Figure 12–17 shows the result of loading the `locationProps.html` script.

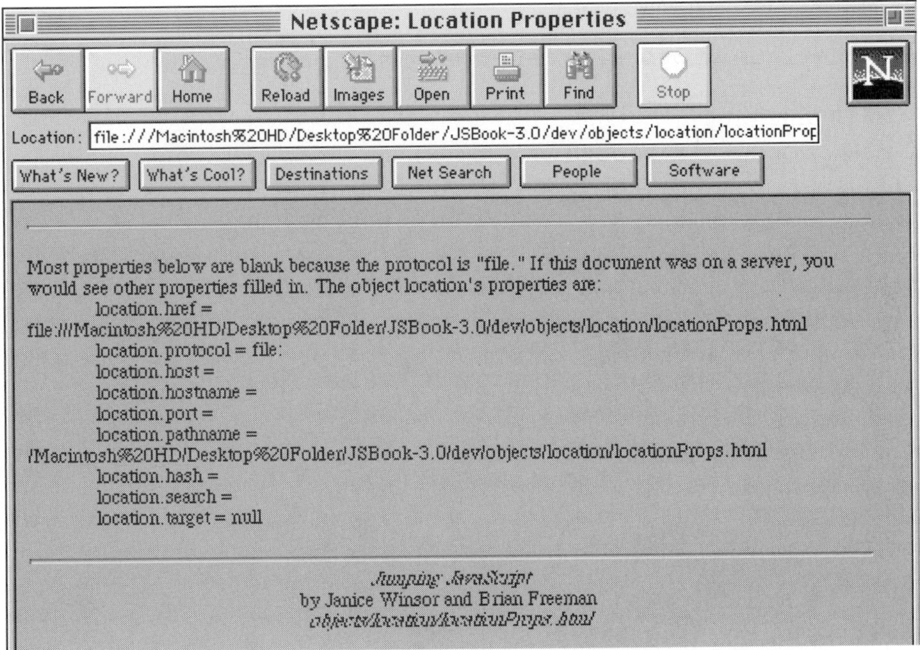

Figure 12–17 Result of `locationProps.html` script

Most of the location properties in the `locationProps.html` window are blank because the file is loaded locally, using the `file` protocol. Notice, once again, the output has the `%20` instead of spaces in the location name.

The `locationPropsUnescape.html` script shown below is exactly the same as the `locationProps.html` script, except that the results are passed through the `unescape()` JavaScript function. The `unescape()` function replaces the `%20` with spaces in the results that are displayed in the document.

```
<!--
      locationPropsUnescape.html

    This example shows all of the properties of
    the location object and uses unescape().
-->

<HTML>
<HEAD>
<TITLE>Unescaped Location Properties</TITLE>
<SCRIPT LANGUAGE="JavaScript">
<!-- HIDE FROM OLD BROWSERS

/*
** Get the properties for the given object
**
** Arguments:
**    obj       - obtain properties from this
**                object
**    obj_name - a string representing the
**                object name
**
** Return Value
**    string of the form:
**      object_name.property = "value"
**      object_name.property = "value"
**      ...
**
*/
function getProps(obj, obj_name) {
  var retval = ""

  retval += "The object " + obj_name + "'s "
  retval += "properties are:"
  for (var i in obj) {
    retval += "<DD>"
    retval += obj_name + "." + i
    retval += " = " + obj[i] + "</DD>"
  }
```

```
    retval += "<P>"

    return retval
  }
  // STOP HIDING -->
  </SCRIPT>
  </HEAD>

  <BODY>
  <HR>

  <P>Most properties below are blank because the
  protocol is "file." If this document was on a
  server, you would see other properties filled in.

  <SCRIPT LANGUAGE="JavaScript">
  <!-- HIDE FROM OLD BROWSERS

  document.write(unescape(getProps(location,
                          "location")))

  // STOP HIDING -->
  </SCRIPT>

  </BODY>
  </HTML>
```

Figure 12–18 shows the results of loading the `locationPropsUnescape.html` script.

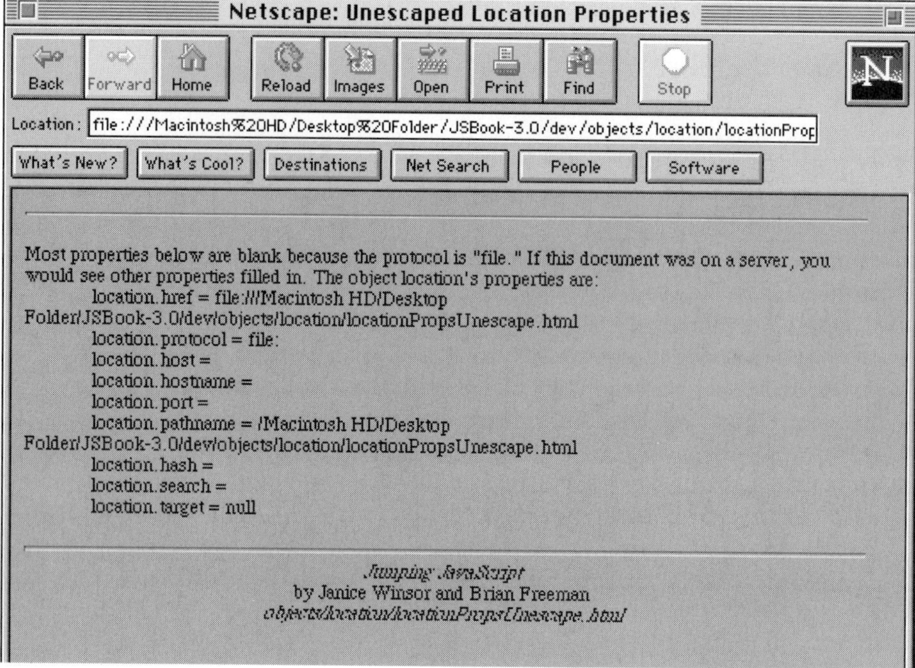

Figure 12–18 Results of `locationPropsUnescape.html` script

Let's take a closer look at the statement that includes the `unescape()` function in the `locationPropsUnescape.html` script.

```
document.write(unescape(getProps(location, "location")))
```

Note – This statement is an excellent example of the importance of keeping track of open and closed parentheses. The three close parentheses at the end of this statement match the open parenthesis for `document.write`, for the `unescape` function, and for the `getProps` function.

As you can see, the way you use the `unescape()` function is to include the things you want to be reformatted within the parentheses of the function.

In this case, the information included within the unescape parentheses is:

```
getProps(location, "location")
```

This statement is the `getProps` function, defined in the head of this script, and the specific object and the name of the object for which to get properties.

Reloading a Document from a Script

The Navigator 3.0 release provides a `reload()` method for the `location` object that you can use to force a reload of a document from a script.

Method

reload()

Returns

Nothing

Example of Reloading a Document from a Script

The following `locationReload.html` script contains an `onClick` event handler for the Reload button. When the user clicks on the Reload button, the document is reloaded.

```
<!--
          locationReload.html

     This example of the location reload method
     enables the user to force a reload of the
     document by clicking on a button.
-->

<HTML>
<HEAD>
<TITLE>Location Reload</TITLE>
</HEAD>
<BODY>

<H1 ALIGN="center">The Cat Cam!</H1>

<P ALIGN="center">To see what the kids are up to,
click on Reload.</P>

<CENTER>
<IMG SRC="../../images/Cats-1.jpg"
     ALT="Is Fluffy home?">
```

```
<FORM>
<INPUT TYPE="button" NAME="reload"
 VALUE="Reload" onClick="window.location.reload()">
</FORM>
</CENTER>

</BODY>
</HTML>
```

Figure 12–19 shows the result of loading the `locationReload.html` script.

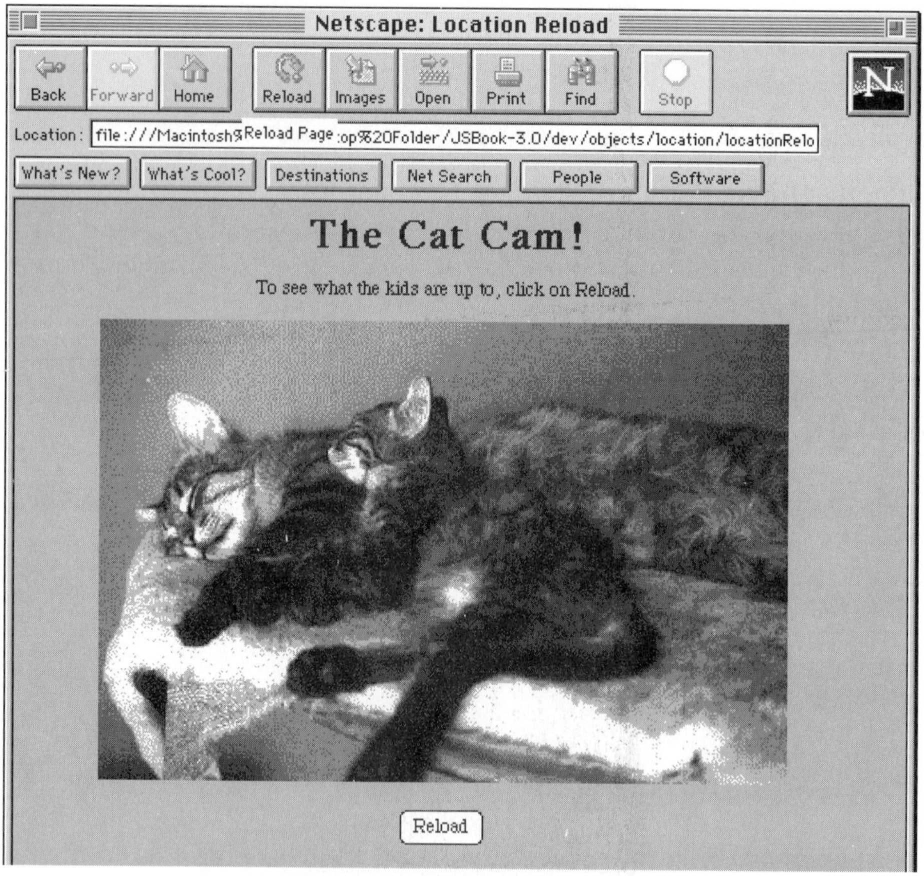

Figure 12–19 Result of loading the `locationReload.html` script

Clicking on the Reload button reloads the page.

Replacing a URL in the History List

The Navigator 3.0 release provides a `replace()` method for the `location` object that you can use to replace a URL in the history list with a new URL that you specify in a script. When you use the `replace()` method, the URL overwrites the current entry in the history list. Because the previous URL is removed from the history list, it is not available to the system when you click on the Back button.

Method

replace()

Returns

Nothing

When a script has multiple frames, users sometimes end up with quite a few entries in the history list. When users click on the Back button, they must navigate through all of the links before they can get out of the page. When you use the `replace()` method, users can click on the Back button to go directly to the previous URL.

Example of Replacing a URL in the History List

The following `locationReplace.html` script uses the `replace()` method to replace the URL in the history list.

```
<!--
         locationReplace.html

     This example uses the location object's
     replace method.
-->

<HTML>
<HEAD>
<TITLE>Location Replace</TITLE>
<SCRIPT LANGUAGE="JavaScript">
<!-- HIDE FROM OLD BROWSERS

//
// Go to the new anchor name without keeping a
// history of it.
```

```
//
function goToAnchor(name) {
  var loc = ""

  loc = "locationReplace.html#" + name
  window.location.replace(loc)
}

//
//   Change the window object's status property
//
function setStatus(win, msg_str) {
  win.status = msg_str
  return true
}

// STOP HIDING -->
</SCRIPT>
</HEAD>
<BODY>

<CENTER>
<H1>A Gothic Tale</H1>
</CENTER>

<A NAME="S1"><H2>Section One</H2></a>

<A HREF="javascript:goToAnchor('S2')"
onMouseOver="return setStatus(self,'Next Section')">
Next</A>

<P>
It was a dark and stormy night. All of the
beagles were safely in their kennels. The bats
flew around the tower squeaking frantically.
<P>
Dosolina stood at the open window wistfully
gazing out over the moors, her long dark tresses
blowing wildly as the wind gusted. Piotor was
long overdue. There were evil things afoot in the
night and she feared greatly for his safety.
</P>
```

```
<A NAME="S2"><H2>Section Two</H2></A>

<A HREF="javascript:goToAnchor('S1')"
onMouseOver="return setStatus(self,'Previous Section')">
Prev</A>
<A HREF="javascript:goToAnchor('S3')"
onMouseOver="return setStatus(self,'Next Section')">
Next</A>

<P>
There was something unnatural about the light
flickering through the clouds. The beagles bugled
their howls, protesting their captivity. The dogs
wanted to be out and about, investigating the
strange smells and sensations that were drifting
tantalizingly towards them on the gusting wind.
</P>

<A NAME="S3"><H2>Section Three</H2></a>

<A HREF="javascript:goToAnchor('S2')"
onMouseOver="return setStatus(self,'Previous Section')">
Prev</A>
<A HREF="javascript:goToAnchor('S4')"
onMouseOver="return setStatus(self,'Next Section')">
Next</A>

<P>
Piotor felt the hot breath of the ravening
monsters as they followed closely on his
heels. He feared for his very life.  He hoped
that he could reach the safety of the tower in
the distance before his strength gave out and the
monsters were upon him.
</P>

<A NAME="S4"><H2>Section Four</H2></a>

<A HREF="javascript:goToAnchor('S3')"
onMouseOver="return setStatus(self,'Previous Section')">
Prev</A>
```

```
<P>
The skies were clear and the weather balmy,
giving the illusion of innocence.  Dosolina and
Piotor walked with determined steps across the
moors searching for traces of the monsters that
continuously dogged their very existence.
</P>
<P>
"Oh, here's a footprint," Piotor cried. "I knew
that there was something tangible in that horrid
blackness that was following me.
</P>
<P>
"And here's a piece of something ...  Ugh, it is
so disgusting," said Dosolina.  "What is this
awful curse that prevents us from being like
normal folks?"
</P>
<P>
"We must be brave and not let them know how
frightened we really are."
</P>


<A HREF="javascript:goToAnchor('S4')"
onMouseOver="return setStatus(self,'Previous Section')">
Prev</A>

</BODY>
</HTML>
```

Figure 12–20 shows the result of loading the `locationReplace.html` script.

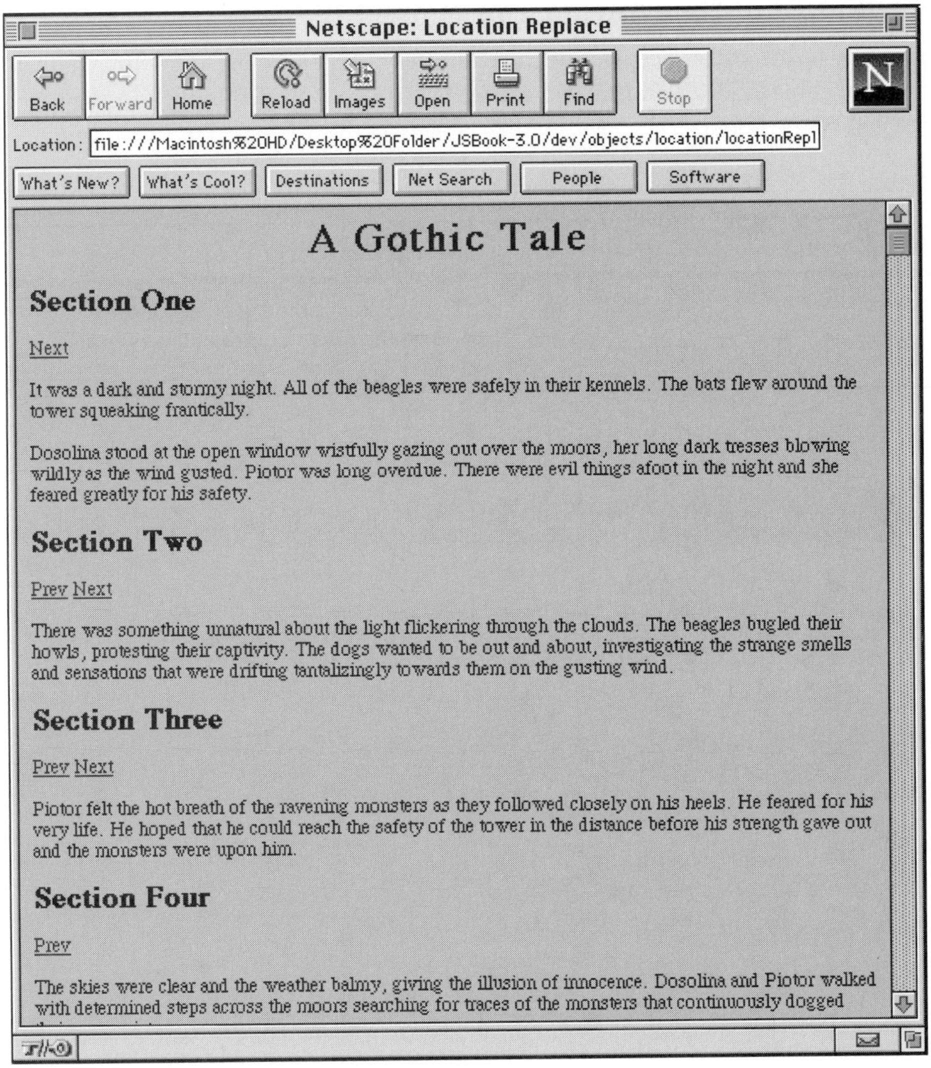

Netscape: Location Replace

Back Forward Home Reload Images Open Print Find Stop

Location: file:///Macintosh%20HD/Desktop%20Folder/JSBook-3.0/dev/objects/location/locationRepl

What's New? What's Cool? Destinations Net Search People Software

A Gothic Tale

Section One

Next

It was a dark and stormy night. All of the beagles were safely in their kennels. The bats flew around the tower squeaking frantically.

Dosolina stood at the open window wistfully gazing out over the moors, her long dark tresses blowing wildly as the wind gusted. Piotor was long overdue. There were evil things afoot in the night and she feared greatly for his safety.

Section Two

Prev Next

There was something unnatural about the light flickering through the clouds. The beagles bugled their howls, protesting their captivity. The dogs wanted to be out and about, investigating the strange smells and sensations that were drifting tantalizingly towards them on the gusting wind.

Section Three

Prev Next

Piotor felt the hot breath of the ravening monsters as they followed closely on his heels. He feared for his very life. He hoped that he could reach the safety of the tower in the distance before his strength gave out and the monsters were upon him.

Section Four

Prev

The skies were clear and the weather balmy, giving the illusion of innocence. Dosolina and Piotor walked with determined steps across the moors searching for traces of the monsters that continuously dogged

Figure 12–20 Result of loading the `locationReplace.html` script

Click on different links in this document to move around, and then click on the Back button. Notice that you go back to the previous URL. To see the difference between a script that uses the `replace()` method and one that doesn't, load the `location/hash/index.html` script, click on several links, and then click on the Back button.

Summary of New Terms and Concepts

The new terms and concepts introduced in this chapter are listed in alphabetical order in Table 12-3. The terms and concepts are also included in the glossary at the end of the book.

Table 12-3 New Terms and Concepts

Term/Concept	Description
root directory	The directory at the very top of the file system hierarchy; represented as a slash (/).

479

CHAPTER 13

- Emulating an onClick Event Handler for the area Object
- Displaying a Status Message with an onMouseOver Event Handler
- Clearing a Status Message with an onMouseOut Event Handler
- Creating an Image Map

Creating Active Image Areas

You can create image map areas that are active links. Although the HTML definitions of image maps are quite different from links, from the user's perspective, they work in much the same way.

The Navigator 3.0 release provides an `area` object which is almost the same as the `link` object. You can control client-side maps that are created using the HTML `<MAP></MAP>` tags with the properties and event handlers listed in alphabetical order in Table 13-1.

Table 13-1 Properties and Methods for the area Object

Properties	Methods	Event Handlers
`links.length`	`eval()*`	`onMouseOver`
`links[index].target`	`toString()*`	`onMouseOut`
`[location` *`object properties`*`]`	`valueOf()*`	

* New in Navigator 3.0.

The `area` object does not have properties of its own; however, you can use the `target` property of the `links` object to specify a window or frame as the target for the URL. For information on how to use `links` object properties, see Chapter 14, "Working with Links."

To the JavaScript language, a link and an image map are the same as a `location` object. If you need to refer to the `area` object, you can access the same properties for that link as you can for any `location` object. In this way, you can conveniently deal with all of the URL data in the same way. For information about the properties of the `location` object, see Chapter 12, "Controlling Location."

Property	Value	Gettable	Settable
links.length	number	Yes	No
links(index).target	string	Yes	Yes
hash	string	Yes	Yes
host	string	Yes	Yes
hostname	string	Yes	Yes
href	string	Yes	Yes
pathname	URL	Yes	Yes
port	string	Yes	Yes
protocol	string	Yes	Yes
search	string	Yes	Yes

When you want an image to have an active area, you must create a link between the `<IMG>` and the `<MAP>` tags by using the `USEMAP` attribute. The `USEMAP` attribute value is the hash mark (#) followed by the map name. For the HTML syntax for the `<IMG>` tag, see Chapter 9, "Working with Images." For the syntax for the HTML `<MAP></MAP>` tags, refer to the HTML Brushup box.

Emulating an onClick Event Handler for the area Object

The `area` object does not have its own `onClick` event handler because when the user clicks on the `area` object, the default action is to go to the URL specified in the `HREF` attribute. You can, however, emulate an event handler to perform a different action by specifying the `javascript:` protocol in the URL for the `HREF` attribute and specifying an action or calling a function that performs the action

---

HTML Brushup — Creating Image Maps

You use the <MAP></MAP> tags to name and describe a client-side image map. The map defines a set of areas on an image that can be clicked on for hyperlinks. The NAME you assign to the map is the same name that you use with the USEMAP attribute of the <IMG> tag to specify that you want to use the image as an image map.

<MAP NAME="*areaMapName*"

<AREA

COORDS="*x1,y1,x2,y2,...*" | "*x-center,y-center,radius*"

HREF = "*URL*"

(NOHREF)

(SHAPE = "*rect*" | "*poly*" | "*circle*" | "*default*")

(TARGET = "*WindowName*")

(onMouseOver = "*JavaScript code*")

(onMouseOut = "*JavaScript code*")

>

</MAP>

To get coordinates for an image map, use an application or applet that displays coordinates such as the ImageMap applet in the *Instant Java* book by John Pew, published by SunSoft Press and Prentice Hall. When you run ImageMap with `TestMode` set to true, coordinates for the pointer location are displayed in the footer.

---

that you want to occur when the user clicks on the area. Note that you cannot use the `javascript:` protocol in the URL alone; you must provide some associated code.

Example of Using the javascript: Protocol to Emulate an OnClick Event Handler

The following `areaOnClick.html` script defines a rectangular area in the middle of the wildebeest image and uses the `javascript:` protocol to call the `onClickHandler()` function that is defined at the top of the script. This function displays an alert.

```
<!--
                areaOnClick.html
-->

<HTML>
<HEAD>
<TITLE>Area onClick</TITLE>
<SCRIPT LANGUAGE="JavaScript">
<!-- HIDE FROM OLD BROWSERS

//
function onClickHandler() {
  alert("An onClick event handler was simulated.")
}

// STOP HIDING -->
</SCRIPT>
</HEAD>
<BODY>

<P>This example simulates the onClick event
handler by using the javascript protocol for the
area's HREF attribute. The area object does not
really have an onClick event handler.</P>

<P>When you click on the image, an alert is
displayed.</P>

<MAP NAME="theMap">
  <AREA    NAME="onClickArea"
         COORDS="100,75,300,230"
           HREF="javascript:onClickHandler()"
          SHAPE="rect"
  >
</MAP>

<CENTER>
<TABLE BORDER=4 WIDTH=412 HEIGHT=268>
  <CAPTION>Wildebeest.jpg [408x264]</CAPTION>
  <TR>
    <TD>
      <IMG SRC="../../images/Wildebeest.jpg"
     NAME="Wildebeest"
        USEMAP="#theMap"
```

```
            WIDTH=408
           HEIGHT=264
      HSPACE=0
           VSPACE=0
            ALIGN=absmiddle
      BORDER=4>
       </TD>
     </TR>
   </TABLE>
   </CENTER>

   </BODY>
   </HTML>
```

If you have a color monitor, any image that has an image map is displayed with a blue border. Images without an image map have a black border. As you move the pointer over the image, notice that it changes when you move within the area defined as the image map. On Macintosh and Windows 95 systems, the arrow changes to the pointing hand. Figure 13–1 shows the result of loading the `areaOnClick.html` script after clicking on the active image area. Notice that the `HREF` is automatically displayed in the status area just as it is any time the user clicks on a text anchor.

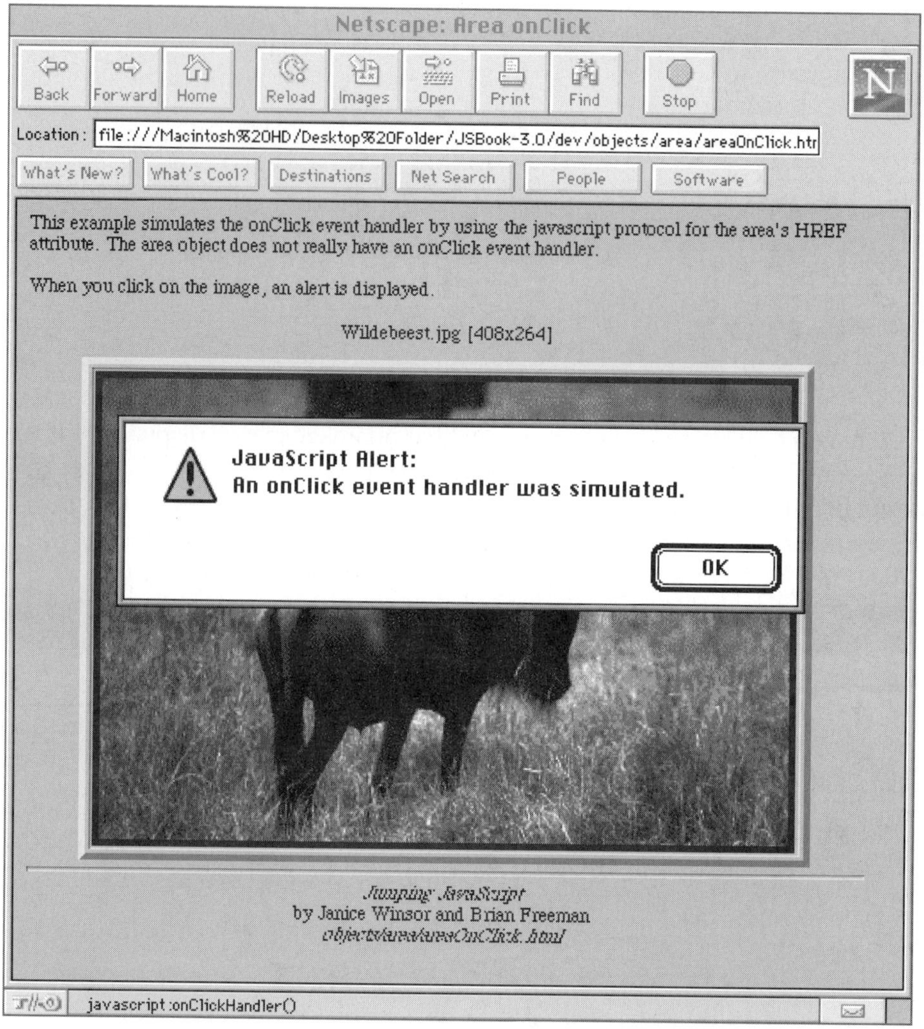

Figure 13–1 Result of loading the `areaOnClick.html` script

Displaying a Status Message with an onMouseOver Event Handler

You can use the `onMouseOver` event handler to display a status message in the status bar at the bottom of the window when the user moves the pointer into the area defined as an image map. In this way, users can move the pointer around in

the window and determine where the active image area is by looking at the message in the status bar as well as by the way the pointer changes as it moves into and out of image map areas.

Event Handler

onMouseOver

onMouseOut

Syntax

```
<MAP NAME="areaMapName"
    <AREA
        COORDS="x1,y1,x2,y2,..." | "x-center,y-center,radius"
        HREF = "URL"
        (NOHREF)
        (SHAPE = "rect" | "poly" | "circle" | "default")
        (TARGET = "WindowName")
        (onMouseOver = "JavaScript code;return true")
        (onMouseOut = "JavaScript code;return true")
    >
</MAP>
```

Notice that the `onMouseOver` event handler requires that you return a value of `true` for the status message to display properly.

Example of Displaying a Status Message with an onMouseOver Event Handler

The following `areaOnMouseOver.html` script displays the message `over area` when you move the pointer into an active image area. When you click in the image area, you make a big geographical leap from the peacock photograph that was taken at the Mt. Kenya Safari Club in Africa to the `GoneTroppo.html` script that describes adventures in Queensland, Australia. You'll see more of the `GoneTroppo.html` script in other examples later in this chapter.

```
<!--
              areaOnMouseOver.html
-->

<HTML>
<HEAD>
<TITLE>Area onMouseOver</TITLE>
</HEAD>
<BODY>

<P>This example creates an onMouseOver event
handler to change the window status area when the
pointer is on the image.</P>

<MAP NAME="theMap">
  <AREA     NAME="aSpot"
         COORDS="204,132,100"
           HREF="GoneTroppo/GoneTroppo.html"
          SHAPE="circle"
    onMouseOver="self.status='over area';return true"
  >
</MAP>
<CENTER>
<TABLE BORDER=4 WIDTH=412 HEIGHT=268>
  <CAPTION>Peacock.jpg [408x264]</CAPTION>
  <TR>
    <TD>
      <IMG SRC="../../images/Peacock.jpg"
     NAME="Peacock"
        USEMAP="#theMap"
         WIDTH=408
        HEIGHT=264
   HSPACE=0
        VSPACE=0
         ALIGN=absmiddle
   BORDER=4>
    </TD>
  </TR>
</TABLE>
</CENTER>

</BODY>
</HTML>
```

Figure 13–2 shows the result of loading the `areaOnMouseOver.html` file and moving the pointer into the active image area.

Netscape: Area onMouseOver

Back Forward Home Reload Images Open Print Find Stop

Location: file:///Macintosh%20HD/Desktop%20Folder/JSBook-3.0/dev/objects/area/areaOnMouseO

What's New? What's Cool? Destinations Net Search People Software

This example creates an onMouseOver event handler to change the window status area when the pointer is on the image.

Peacock.jpg [408x264]

Jumping JavaScript
by Janice Winsor and Brian Freeman
objects/area/areaOnMouseOver.html

over area

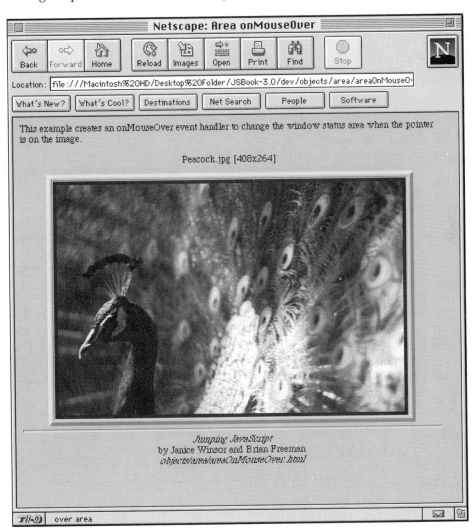

Figure 13–2 Result of loading the `areaOnMouseOver.html` script

Notice that when you move the pointer out of the active image area, the message is cleared from the status bar.

Figure 13–3 shows the beginning of the `GoneTroppo.html` file that is loaded when you click in the active image area.

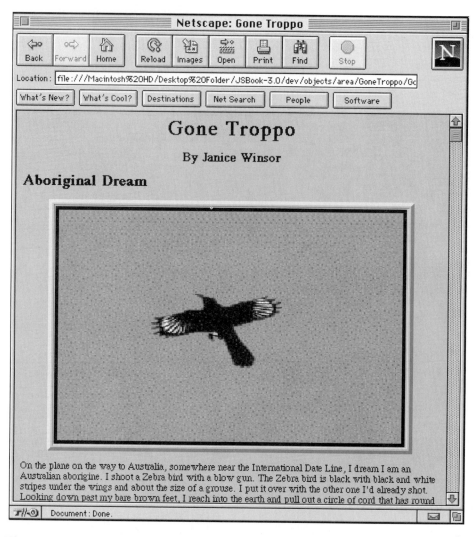

Figure 13–3 Beginning of the `GoneTroppo.html` script

Clearing a Status Message with an onMouseOut Event Handler

Even though using the `onMouseOver` event handler seems both to display and clear messages from the status area, it's good programming practice to specifically clear messages from the status bar. You can use the `onMouseOut` event handler to clear out old messages. If you use the `onMouseOver` event

handler without a matching onMouseOut event handler, there may be times when the status message "sticks" in the status bar and persists even when it is no longer appropriate.

The onMouseOut event handler also requires you to return a value of true for the message to display properly.

Example of Clearing a Message from the Status Bar

The following areaOnMouseOut.html script is similar to the areaOnMouseOver.html script, except that it defines a polygon as the image area. The polygon roughly follows the shape of the body of the lioness (without the ears). When you define a polygon, you specify an x and y coordinate for each point in the polygon. Remember that the polygon must be a closed shape.

The script also includes an onMouseOut statement as part of the map definition:

```
onMouseOut="self.status='';return true"
```

This statement contains an empty string of single quotes with no space between them ('') following the equal sign.

When you click in the image area, the areaOnMouseOut.html script makes a big geographical shift from the lioness in Kenya to the Australian tropics.

```
<!--
               areaOnMouseOut.html
-->

<HTML>
<HEAD>
<TITLE>Area onMouseOut</TITLE>
</HEAD>
<BODY>

<P>This example creates an onMouseOver event
handler to change the window status area to "over
area" and an onMouseOut event handler to blank
the area when you move your mouse away.</P>

<MAP NAME="theMap">
  <AREA    NAME="aSpot"
       COORDS="100,100,100,200,400,200,400,100,100,100"
         HREF="GoneTroppo/GoneTroppo.html"
        SHAPE="poly"
    onMouseOver="self.status='over area';return true"
     onMouseOut="self.status='';return true"
  >
```

```
</MAP>
<CENTER>
<TABLE BORDER=4 WIDTH=412 HEIGHT=268>
  <CAPTION>Lioness.jpg [408x264]</CAPTION>
  <TR>
    <TD>
      <IMG SRC="../../images/Lioness.jpg"
     NAME="Lioness"
        USEMAP="#theMap"
         WIDTH=408
        HEIGHT=264
   HSPACE=0
        VSPACE=0
         ALIGN=absmiddle
   BORDER=4>
    </TD>
  </TR>
</TABLE>
</CENTER>

</BODY>
</HTML>
```

Figure 13–4 shows the result of loading the `areaOnMouseOut.html` script, with the over area message in the status bar.

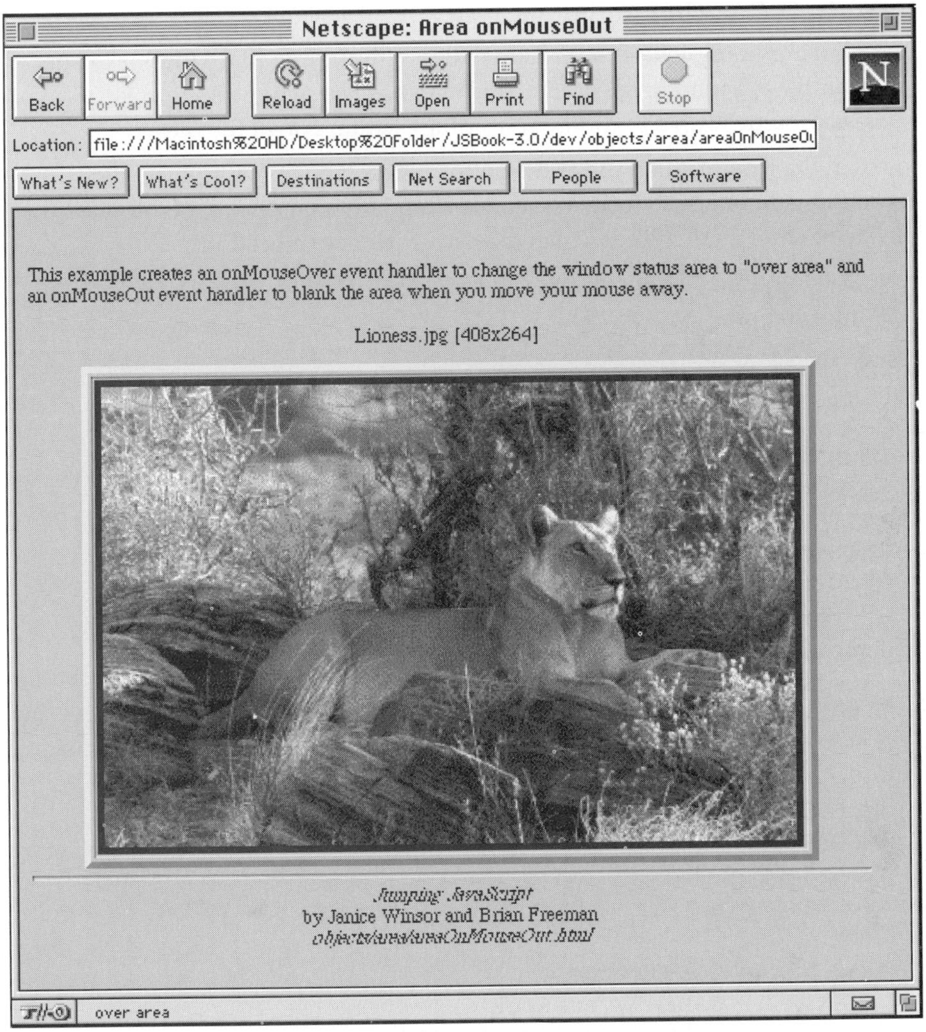

Figure 13–4 Result of loading the `areaOnMouseOut.html` script

Clicking on the image area loads the `GoneTroppo.html` file (Figure 13–3).

Creating an Image Map

You can create an image map that contains more than one active area. The areas can be of different shapes because you define each one individually. When you create such a map, you may want to give your users additional visual cues that tell them where they can click.

Example of Creating an Image Map

The following example uses a set of five files. The starting place for our image map example is a map of Australia. This map has five active image areas. Two of the areas provide HREFs to different headings within one of the files.

Note that the icon of Australia at the bottom of each page is simply a link surrounding an image to form a clickable icon. This icon acts as a button to take you back to the big map so you can do some further exploration.

The following GoneTroppo/index.html file creates the image map with the HREF information.

```
<!--
       objects/area/GoneTroppo/index.html
-->
<HTML>
<HEAD>
<TITLE>Gone Troppo</TITLE>
<SCRIPT LANGUAGE="JavaScript">
<!-- HIDE FROM OLD BROWSERS
// set the status area
function setStatus(str) {
  self.status = str
  return true
}

// STOP HIDING -->
</SCRIPT>
</HEAD>
<BODY>

<MAP NAME="GoneTroppo">
  <AREA     NAME="AyersRock"
        COORDS="230,170,300,190"
          HREF="AyersRock.html"
         SHAPE="rect"
     onMouseOut="return setStatus('')"
    onMouseOver="return setStatus('Ayers Rock')"
  >
  <AREA     NAME="Sydney"
        COORDS="340,240,400,260"
          HREF="Sydney.html"
         SHAPE="rect"
     onMouseOut="return setStatus('')"
    onMouseOver="return setStatus('Sydney')"
```

```
  >
  <AREA    NAME="Jowalbinna"
        COORDS="325,75,25"
          HREF="GoneTroppo.html#Jowalbinna"
         SHAPE="circle"
    onMouseOut="return setStatus('')"
   onMouseOver="return setStatus('Jowalbinna')"
  >
  <AREA    NAME="CoralSea"
        COORDS="340,10,390,50"
          HREF="GoneTroppo.html#CSea"
         SHAPE="rect"
    onMouseOut="return setStatus('')"
   onMouseOver="return setStatus('The Coral Sea')"
  >
  <AREA    NAME="KangarooIsland"
        COORDS="275,275,25"
          HREF="KangarooIsland.html"
         SHAPE="circle"
    onMouseOut="return setStatus('')"
   onMouseOver="return setStatus('Kangaroo Island')"
  >
</MAP>

<CENTER>
<TABLE BORDER=4 WIDTH=412 HEIGHT=268>
  <CAPTION><B>Australia</B></CAPTION>
  <TR>
    <TD>
      <IMG SRC="../../../images/Australia468x396.jpg"
     NAME="Australia"
        USEMAP="#GoneTroppo"
         WIDTH=468
        HEIGHT=396
    HSPACE=0
        VSPACE=0
         ALIGN=absmiddle
    BORDER=4>
     </TD>
  </TR>
</TABLE>
</CENTER>
</BODY>
</HTML>
```

Figure 13–5 shows the result of loading the `GoneTroppo/index.html` file. The map itself does not show the active image areas, so this screen shot is overlaid with graphics and annotated to show (roughly) the location of the active image areas and how they are identified.

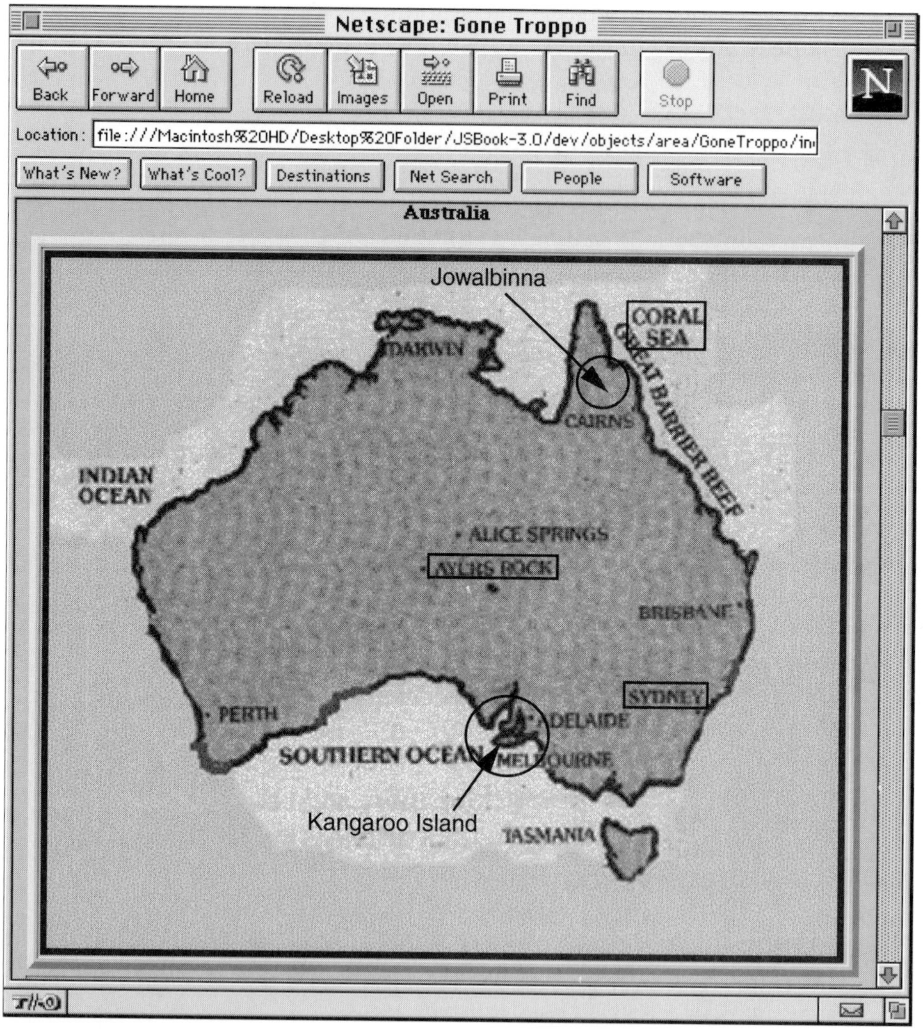

Figure 13–5 Result of loading the `GoneTroppo/index.html` file

Moving the pointer over the map identifies the five locations. When you click on the Kangaroo Island area, the following `KangarooIsland.html` script is loaded. This script contains nine photos that were taken on Kangaroo Island.

```
<!--
               KangarooIsland.html
-->

<HTML>
<HEAD>
<TITLE>Kangaroo Island Images</TITLE>
<SCRIPT LANGUAGE="JavaScript">
<!-- HIDE FROM OLD BROWSERS
var img = new Array(9)

img[00] = "Goanna.jpg 432x264"
img[01] = "Kangaroo-3.jpg 432x264"
img[02] = "KangarooIsland.jpg 432x264"
img[03] = "Koala-2.jpg 264x408"
img[04] = "Koala.jpg 264x408"
img[05] = "RemarkableRocks.jpg 432x264"
img[06] = "SealNursing.jpg 408x264"
img[07] = "Wallaby-2.jpg 432x264"
img[08] = "Wallaby-3.jpg 264x408"

function displayImage(image_num, image_path) {
  var         rstr = ""
  var   image_file = ""
  var   image_name = ""
  var    image_dim = ""
  var  image_width = ""
  var image_height = ""

  image_file   = img[image_num].substring(0,
img[image_num].indexOf(' '))
  image_name   = image_file.substring(0,
image_file.lastIndexOf('.'))
  image_dim    =
img[image_num].substring(img[image_num].indexOf(' ') + 1,
img[image_num].length)
  image_width  = image_dim.substring(0,
image_dim.indexOf('x'))
  image_height =
image_dim.substring(image_dim.indexOf('x') + 1,
image_dim.length)

  rstr += "<TABLE BORDER=4><CAPTION> [ " + image_dim + " ] "
  rstr += image_file + " </CAPTION>\n"
```

```
  rstr += "<TR><TD><IMG SRC='" + image_path + image_file +
"' "
  rstr += "NAME='" + image_name + "' "
  rstr += "WIDTH=" + image_width + " "
  rstr += "HEIGHT=" + image_height
  rstr += "></TD></TR>\n"
  rstr += "</TABLE><BR><BR>\n"

  return rstr
}

// STOP HIDING -->
</SCRIPT>
</HEAD>
<BODY>

<CENTER>
<SCRIPT LANGUAGE="JavaScript">
<!-- HIDE FROM OLD BROWSERS

for (var i=0; i < img.length; i++) {
  document.write( displayImage(i, "../../../images/") )
}

// STOP HIDING -->
</SCRIPT>
</CENTER>

<A HREF="index.html"
onMouseOver="self.status='Go Back';return true"
onMouseOut="self.status='';return true">
<IMG SRC="../../../icons/AustraliaIcon.jpg"
WIDTH=64 HEIGHT=54></A>

</BODY>
</HTML>
```

Figure 13–6 shows the result of loading the `KangarooIsland.html` script.

Figure 13–6 Result of loading the `KangarooIsland.html` script

The Australia icon at the bottom of the page is surrounded by a link. Scroll to the bottom of the page and click on the image map to go back to the Australia map.

From the map, clicking on the Sydney image area loads the following `Sydney.html` script. This script contains one image — the famous Sydney Opera House.

```
<!--
                    Sydney.html
-->

<HTML>
<HEAD>
<TITLE>Sydney Images</TITLE>
<SCRIPT LANGUAGE="JavaScript">
<!-- HIDE FROM OLD BROWSERS
var img = new Array(1)

img[00] = "SydneyOperaHouse.jpg 432x264"

function displayImage(image_num, image_path) {
  var         rstr = ""
  var   image_file = ""
  var   image_name = ""
  var    image_dim = ""
  var  image_width = ""
  var image_height = ""

  image_file   = img[image_num].substring(0,
img[image_num].indexOf(' '))
  image_name   = image_file.substring(0,
image_file.lastIndexOf('.'))
  image_dim    =
img[image_num].substring(img[image_num].indexOf(' ') + 1,
img[image_num].length)
  image_width  = image_dim.substring(0,
image_dim.indexOf('x'))
  image_height =
image_dim.substring(image_dim.indexOf('x') + 1,
image_dim.length)

  rstr += "<TABLE BORDER=4><CAPTION> [ " + image_dim + " ] "
  rstr += image_file + " </CAPTION>\n"
  rstr += "<TR><TD><IMG SRC='" + image_path + image_file +
"' "
  rstr += "NAME='" + image_name + "' "
  rstr += "WIDTH=" + image_width + " "
  rstr += "HEIGHT=" + image_height
  rstr += "></TD></TR>\n"
  rstr += "</TABLE><BR><BR>\n"
```

```
    return rstr
  }

  // STOP HIDING -->
  </SCRIPT>
  </HEAD>
  <BODY>

  <CENTER>
  <SCRIPT LANGUAGE="JavaScript">
  <!-- HIDE FROM OLD BROWSERS

  for (var i=0; i < img.length; i++) {
    document.write( displayImage(i, "../../../images/") )
  }

  // STOP HIDING -->
  </SCRIPT>
  </CENTER>

  <A HREF="index.html"
  onMouseOver="self.status='Go Back';return true"
  onMouseOut="self.status='';return true">
  <IMG SRC="../../../icons/AustraliaIcon.jpg"
  WIDTH=64 HEIGHT=54></A>

  </BODY>
  </HTML>
```

Figure 13–7 shows the result of loading the `Syndey.html` script.

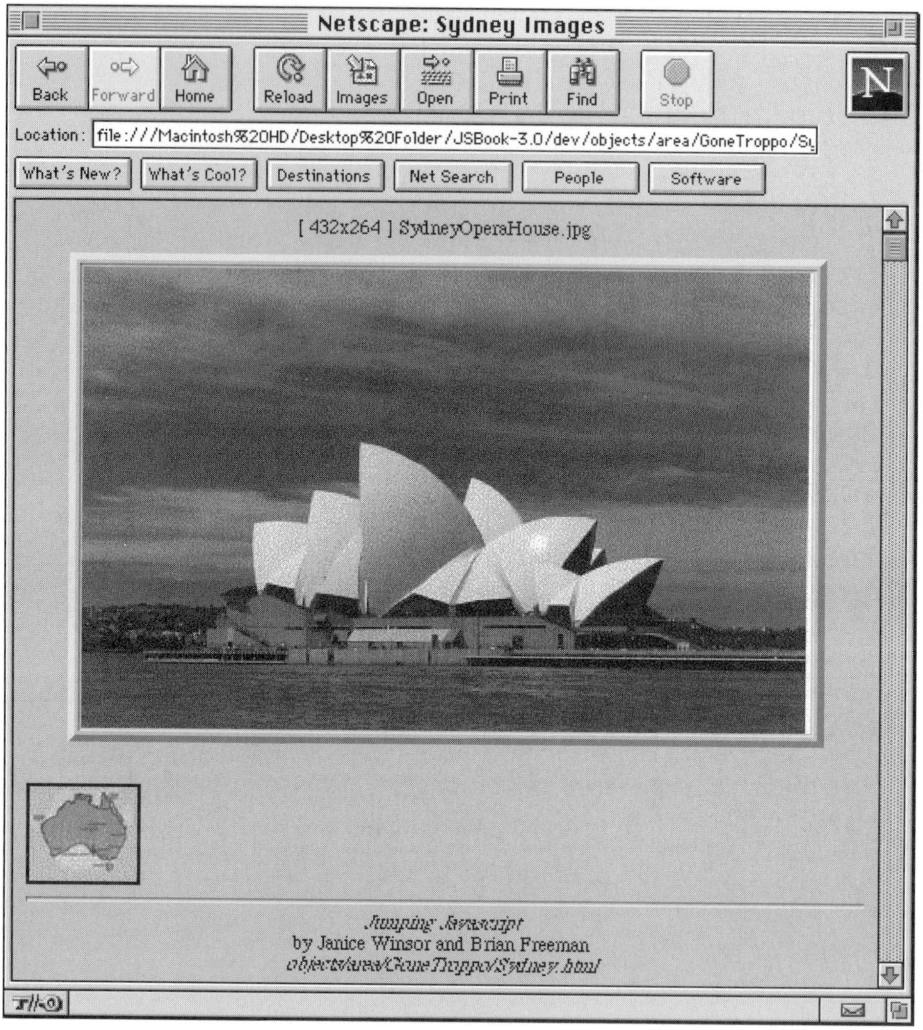

Figure 13–7 Result of loading the `Sydney.html` script

The Australia icon at the bottom of the page is surrounded by a link. Click on it to go back to the Australia map.

Clicking on the Ayers Rock image area loads the following `AyersRock.html` script that contains two photos of Ayers Rock.

```
<!--
          AyersRock.html
-->

<HTML>
<HEAD>
<TITLE>AyersRock Images</TITLE>
<SCRIPT LANGUAGE="JavaScript">
<!-- HIDE FROM OLD BROWSERS
var img = new Array(2)

img[00] = "AyersRock.jpg 408x264"
img[01] = "AyersRock-2.jpg 408x264"

function displayImage(image_num, image_path) {
  var         rstr = ""
  var   image_file = ""
  var   image_name = ""
  var    image_dim = ""
  var  image_width = ""
  var image_height = ""

  image_file   = img[image_num].substring(0,
img[image_num].indexOf(' '))
  image_name   = image_file.substring(0,
image_file.lastIndexOf('.'))
  image_dim    =
img[image_num].substring(img[image_num].indexOf(' ') + 1,
img[image_num].length)
  image_width  = image_dim.substring(0,
image_dim.indexOf('x'))
  image_height =
image_dim.substring(image_dim.indexOf('x') + 1,
image_dim.length)

  rstr += "<TABLE BORDER=4><CAPTION> [ " + image_dim + " ] "
  rstr += image_file + " </CAPTION>\n"
  rstr += "<TR><TD><IMG SRC='" + image_path + image_file +
"' "
  rstr += "NAME='" + image_name + "' "
  rstr += "WIDTH=" + image_width + " "
  rstr += "HEIGHT=" + image_height
  rstr += "></TD></TR>\n"
  rstr += "</TABLE><BR><BR>\n"
```

```
  return rstr
}

// STOP HIDING -->
</SCRIPT>
</HEAD>
<BODY>

<CENTER>
<SCRIPT LANGUAGE="JavaScript">
<!-- HIDE FROM OLD BROWSERS

for (var i=0; i < img.length; i++) {
  document.write( displayImage(i, "../../../images/") )
}

// STOP HIDING -->
</SCRIPT>
</CENTER>

<A HREF="index.html"
onMouseOver="self.status='Go Back';return true"
onMouseOut="self.status='';return true">
<IMG SRC="../../../icons/AustraliaIcon.jpg"
WIDTH=64 HEIGHT=54></A>

</BODY>
</HTML>
```

Figure 13–8 shows the result of loading the `AyersRock.html` script.

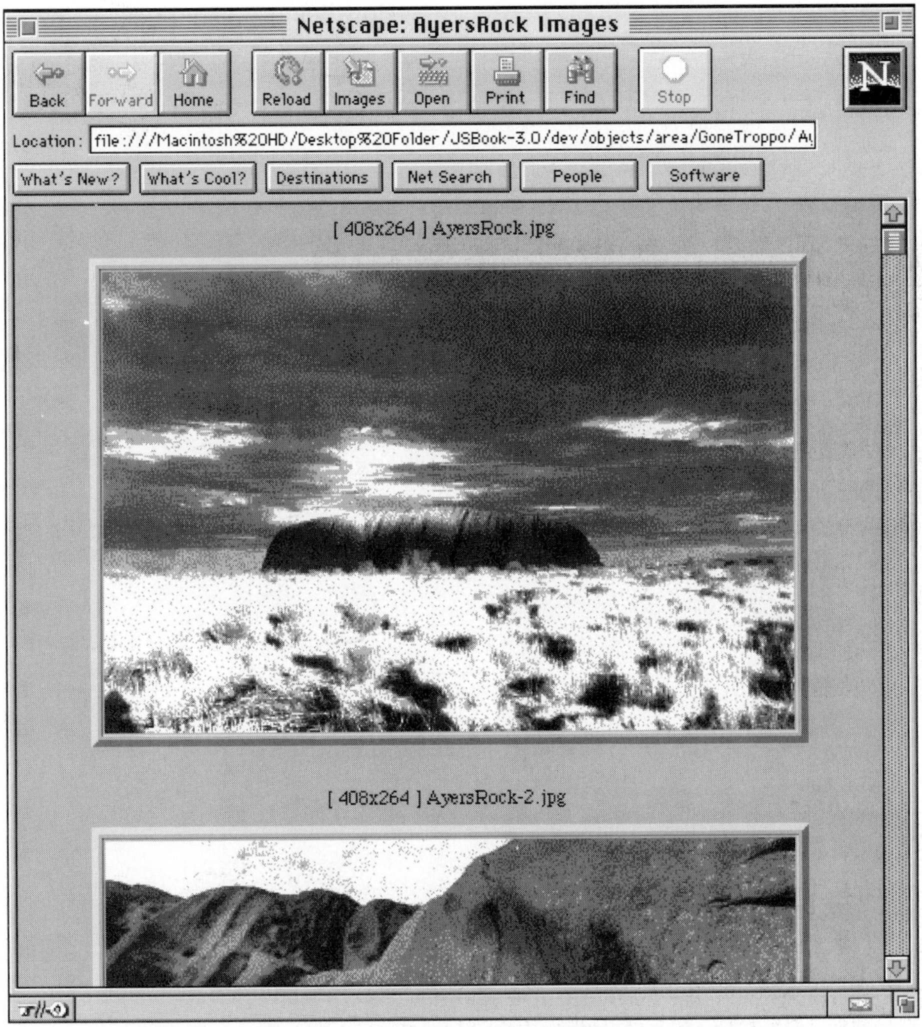

Figure 13–8 Result of loading the `AyersRock.html` script

Now we get to the fun stuff. Clicking on the Jowalbinna area loads the following `GoneTroppo.html` script. This script contains the photographs and accompanying text of the complete Gone Troppo story. The `HREF` goes to the Jowalbinna heading, which is somewhere in the middle of the Gone Troppo story. Refer to the CD-ROM for the complete `GoneTroppo.html` script.

Figure 13–9 shows the result of clicking on the Jowalbinna image area.

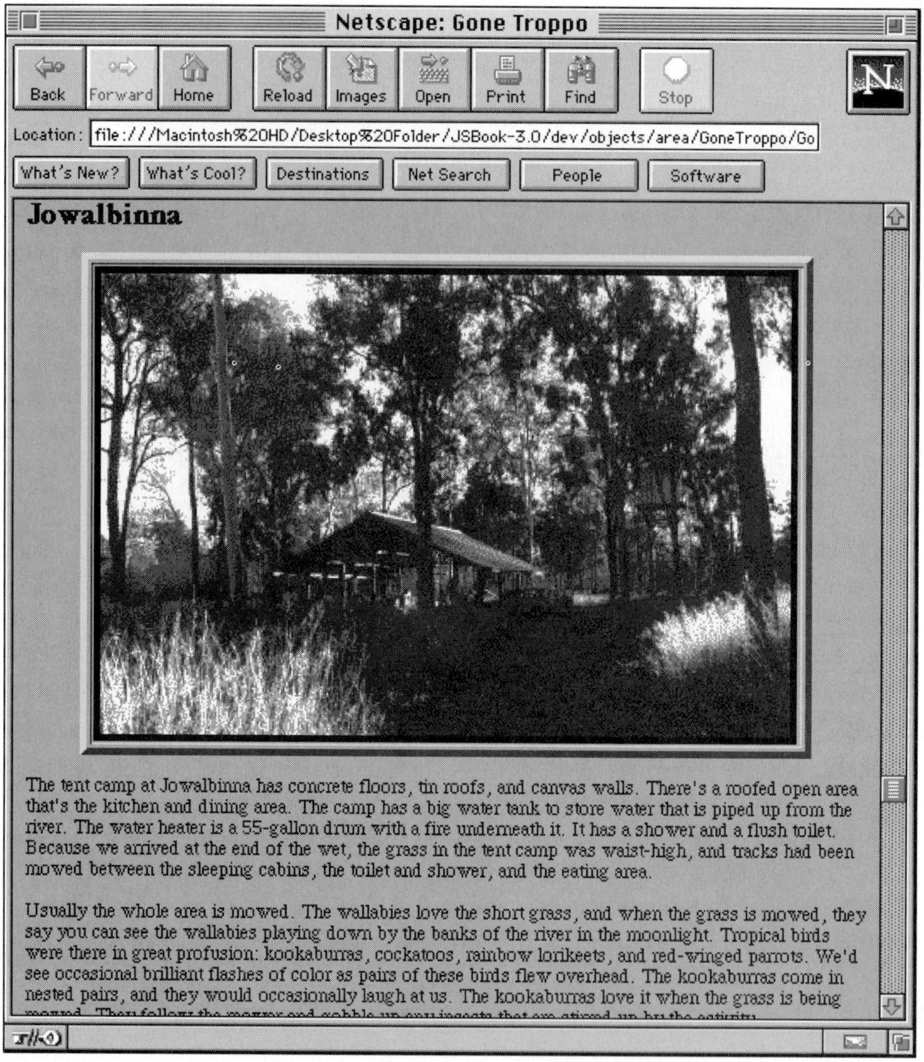

Figure 13–9 Result of clicking on the Jowalbinna image area

The only link you haven't yet traversed is the Coral Sea link. When you click on this link, the `HREF` takes you to the Coral Sea heading in the `GoneTroppo.html` script. Figure 13–10 shows the result of clicking on the Coral Sea image area.

Netscape: Gone Troppo

Back Forward Home Reload Images Open Print Find Stop

Location: file:///Macintosh%20HD/Desktop%20Folder/JSBook-3.0/dev/objects/area/GoneTroppo/Gc

What's New? What's Cool? Destinations Net Search People Software

The Coral Sea

From Cairns in Queensland, we take a four-wheel-drive excursion into the heart of the tropics. We are blessed to be the only people on the excursion, so the two of us and our Kiwi guide Kevin (from New Zealand) take off. Because we do not need to compromise with other tourists, we get to go to places that are off the beaten tourist track. We go through the tropical rain forests filled with beautiful butterflies. The most spectacular are the electric-blue Ulysses butterflies. Instead of going to Cape Tribulation on the Coral Sea, Kevin takes us to a beautiful tropical beach. The three of us are the only people on the beach.

Percy Tresize

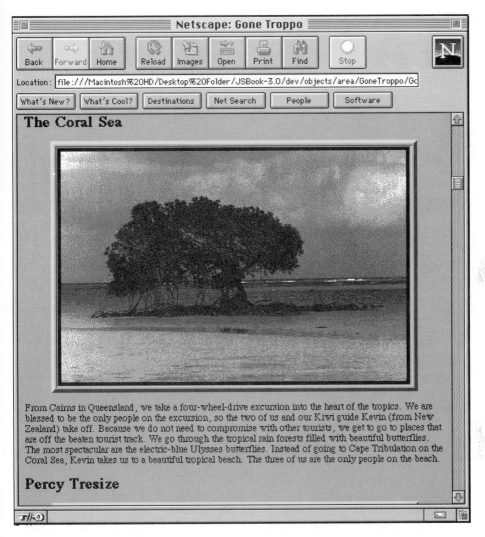

Figure 13–10 Result of clicking on the Coral Sea image area

CHAPTER 14

- Determining the Number of Links in a Document
- Specifying the Link Target Location
- Using an onClick Event Handler Before a Link Is Navigated
- Displaying a Status Message with onMouseOver
- Clearing a Status Message with onMouseOut
- Using Other Protocols with a Link

Working with Links

This chapter describes how to work with links. Hypertext links are the heart and soul of the World Wide Web. Using links, you can hop, skip, and jump from topic to topic. For each hypertext link in an HTML document, the JavaScript language creates a `link` object.

The properties and event handlers for the `link` object are listed in alphabetical order in Table 14-1. The `link` object has no methods.

Table 14-1 **Properties and Methods for the link Object**

Properties	Methods	Event Handlers
`links.length`	`eval()*`	`onClick`
`links[`*`index`*`].target`	`toString()*`	`onMouseOut*`
`[location `*`object properties`*`]`	`valueOf()*`	`onMouseOver`

* New in Navigator 3.0.

To the JavaScript language, a link is similar to the `location` object. If you need to refer to a link, you can access the same properties for that link as you can for any `location` object. In this way, you can conveniently deal with all of the URL data in the same way.

Creating a JavaScript link is the same as creating an HTML link, with the addition of three event handlers: `onClick`, `onMouseOver`, and (new in 3.0) `onMouseOut`. If the script is loaded on a browser that is not JavaScript enabled, the link is created but the events defined in the script are ignored.

When you create a multiframe or multiwindow environment, you must be careful to specify the `TARGET=` attribute with the name of the frame or window in which you want the contents of the URL to be displayed. If you don't target a specific window, the browser replaces the window that contains the link with the new page. Refer to the HTML Brushup box for the HTML syntax for creating anchors, links, and targets.

HTML Brushup — Creating Anchors and Links

You use the <A></A> tags to create anchors and the HREF attribute to specify the link for that anchor. The most commonly used attributes of the <A></A> tags are listed below. At a minimum, you must specify either the URL for the anchor or the name of the destination section in the same page. If you use the NAME attribute, the text of the anchor must match the text of the destination tag. If you want the anchor to a URL to go to a specific destination tag on a page, you can specify the URL with a *#name* suffix to load the document and display the page starting at the named location. You can use the TARGET attribute to specify the name of another window or frame used to display the hyperlink.

<A

HREF = "*URL*" | NAME = "*destinationTag*"

(TARGET = "*WindowName*")

(onClick = " *JavaScript code*")

(onMouseOver = " *JavaScript code*")

(onMouseOut = " *JavaScript code*")>

Text of anchor

</A>

The anchor tag has several other attributes that are rarely used or supported. Understandably, the entire topic of link relationships is under active discussion and subject to change.

UI Guideline – As you design your links, consider building the `onMouseOver` event handlers into your link definitions. In that way, you can use the `window.status` property to display a user-friendly message in the status bar at the bottom of the window when the user moves the mouse pointer over the link. When you use the `onMouseOver` event handler, it's a good idea to also use it in combination with the `onMouseOut` event handler (new in 3.0) to clear the message from the status bar.

Determining the Number of Links in a Document

Just as the `length` property for other objects returns the number of items in the list, so the `link.length` property returns the number of links in the document. If no links are defined, the value is zero (0).

Property	Value	Gettable	Settable
links.length	number	Yes	No

Example of Determining the Number of Links in a Document

The following `linkArea.html` script uses an image map as a link. It also uses the `length` property to create an array of links.

```
<!--
         linkArea.html

  This example shows how to define image areas
  as links and use the length property to create
  an array.
-->

<HTML>
<HEAD>
<TITLE>Link </TITLE>
</HEAD>

<MAP NAME="GoneTroppoMap">
  <AREA NAME="ZebraBird" COORDS="0,0,83,54"
```

```
    HREF="../../images/ZebraBird.jpg">
   <AREA NAME="WallabyGrass" COORDS="0,54,83,108"
    HREF="../../images/WallabyGrass.jpg">
   <AREA NAME="Jowalbinna" COORDS="0,108,83,162"
    HREF="../../images/Jowalbinna.jpg">
   <AREA NAME="CoralSea" COORDS="83,0,166,54"
    HREF="../../images/CoralSea.jpg">
   <AREA NAME="TreeFrog" COORDS="83,54,166,108"
    HREF="../../images/TreeFrog.jpg">
   <AREA NAME="Kookaburra-2" COORDS="83,108,166,162"
    HREF="../../images/Kookaburra-2.jpg">
   <AREA NAME="Maylie" COORDS="166,0,249,54"
    HREF="../../images/Maylie.jpg">
   <AREA NAME="TermiteCastles-1"
    COORDS="166,54,249,108"
    HREF="../../images/TermiteCastles-1.jpg">
   <AREA NAME="QuinkinCountry-2"
    COORDS="166,108,249,162"
    HREF="../../images/QuinkinCountry-2.jpg">
</MAP>
<BODY>

<CENTER>
<IMG SRC="GoneTroppo.jpg" WIDTH=249 HEIGHT=162
USEMAP="#GoneTroppoMap">
</CENTER>

<P>The image areas are accessible through the
document.links array. Clicking on each picture
displays its full-size image. The areas defined
above are:

<SCRIPT LANGUAGE="JavaScript">
<!-- HIDE FROM OLD BROWSERS

var dstr = "<UL>"

for(var i=0; i<document.links.length; i++) {
  dstr += "<LI><A HREF=" + document.links[i].href
  dstr += ">link[" + i + "]</A>\n"
}
dstr += "</UL>"

document.open()
```

```
document.write(dstr)
document.close()

// STOP HIDING -->
</SCRIPT>


</BODY>
</HTML>
```

Figure 14–1 shows the result of loading the `linkArea.html` script.

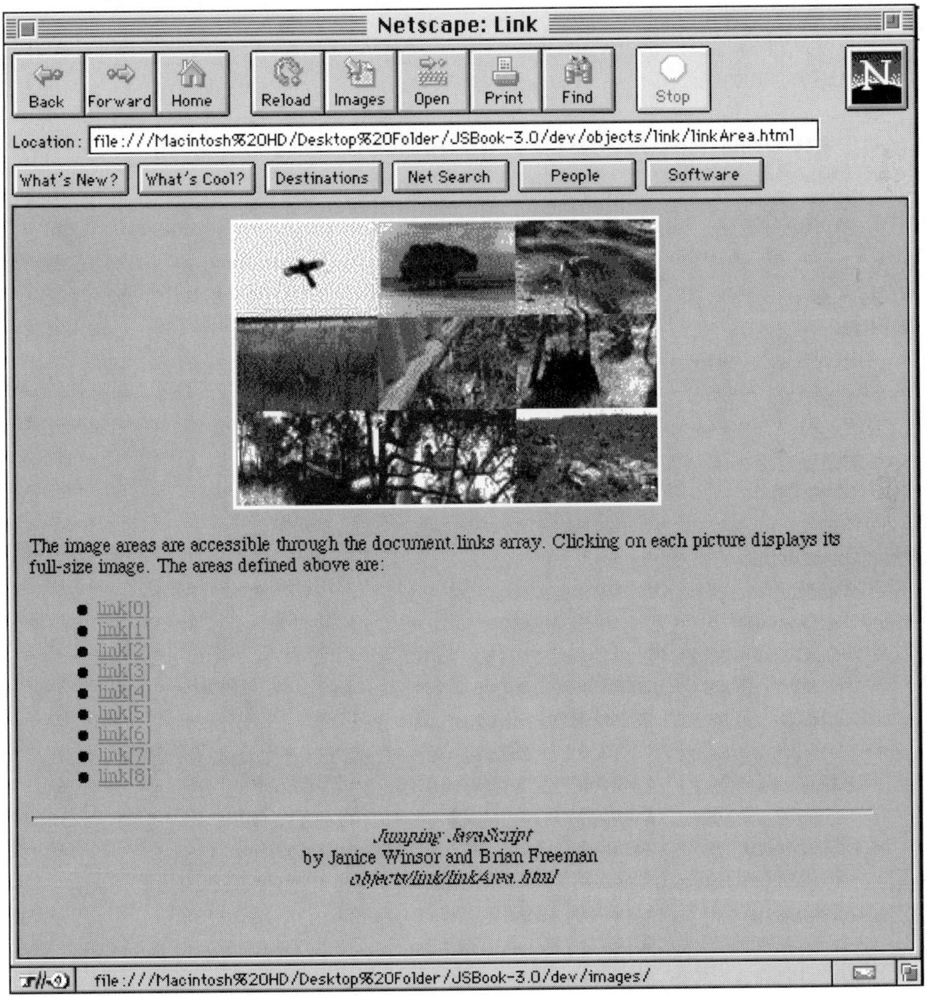

Figure 14–1 Result of loading the `linkArea.html` script

You can click on either the small photograph in the image map or on the link to display the full-size image.

Specifying the Link Target Location

You can specify a target location to be used when the user clicks on a link by using the `links[index].target` property. If you do not specify a particular window or frame as the place where the URL is loaded, the browser replaces the window that contains the link with a new page.

Property	Value	Gettable	Settable
links(index).target	string	Yes	No

Using an onClick Event Handler Before a Link Is Navigated

When users click on a link, the action that results is usually determined by the `HREF=` attribute, which determines which URL to load. You can use the `onClick` event handler to perform some action, such as error checking or validation, before the link is navigated. The `onClick` event handler always executes before the link is navigated, so you can also use it to prevent the link from being activated until some condition is met. `onClick` is also an event handler for the `button` object. You'll see how to script a response to a click on a button in Chapter 19, "Activating Buttons in a Document."

Event Handler

onClick

Syntax

<A HREF="*URL*" onClick="*JavaScript code*" >

Displaying a Status Message with onMouseOver

You can use the `onMouseOver` event handler in conjunction with the `window.status` property to help users understand what will happen when they click on a link.

Event Handler

onMouseOver

Syntax

```
<A HREF="URL" ;
  onMouseOver="functionName();
  return true">;
  anchorName
</A>
```

Note – You must always end the `onMouseOver` event handler by returning a value of `true` or the message in the status bar is not displayed.

Example of Displaying a Status Message with onMouseOver

The following `linkOnMouseOver.html` script uses the `onClick` and `onMouseOver` event handlers. The `onMouseOver` event handler is used in conjunction with the `window.status` property to display the URL of the link in the footer when the user moves the pointer over the link.

Notice that the `HREF` is defined as an empty string in the following statement:

```
<P><A HREF="" onClick="this.href=destURL"
onMouseOver="window.status=destStr; return true">
Go there</A>
```

If you don't define the `HREF` attribute as an empty string, the `Go there` link is not active. In this statement, the `destURL` variable determines the destination for the link.

```
<!--
        linkOnMouseOver.html

    This example of the link object's onMouseOver
    method shows the destination when the user
    moves the pointer over the go there link.

-->

<HTML>
<HEAD>
<TITLE>Link onMouseOver Event Handler</TITLE>
<SCRIPT LANGUAGE="JavaScript">
<!-- HIDE FROM OLD BROWSERS

// default the destination to Netscape
var destURL = "http://home.netscape.com"
var destStr = "Netscape"

// STOP HIDING -->
</SCRIPT>
</HEAD>

<BODY>

<P>Choose your destination:

<FORM>
<INPUT TYPE="radio" NAME="destination"

onClick="destURL='http://home.netscape.com';destStr='Nets
cape'"
 CHECKED>
Netscape Home Page<BR>
<INPUT TYPE="radio" NAME="destination"
 onClick="destURL='http://www.sun.com';destStr='Sun'">
Sun Home Page<BR>
<INPUT TYPE="radio" NAME="destination"

onClick="destURL='http://java.sun.com';destStr='JavaSoft'
">
JavaSoft Home Page<BR>
</FORM>
```

```
<P><A HREF="" onClick="this.href=destURL"
onMouseOver="window.status=destStr; return true">
Go there</A>

</BODY>
</HTML>
```

Figure 14–2 shows the result of loading the `linkOnMouseOver.html` script.

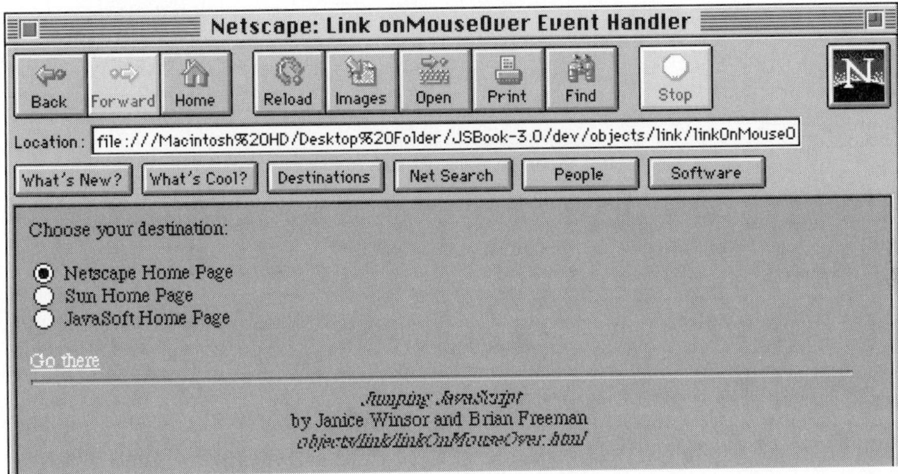

Figure 14–2 Result of loading `linkOnMouseOver.html` script

You can choose the link you want to go to by clicking on one of the radio buttons. Moving the pointer over the Go there link (without clicking the mouse) displays the location for the selected radio button in the status bar at the bottom of the window, as shown in Figure 14–3.

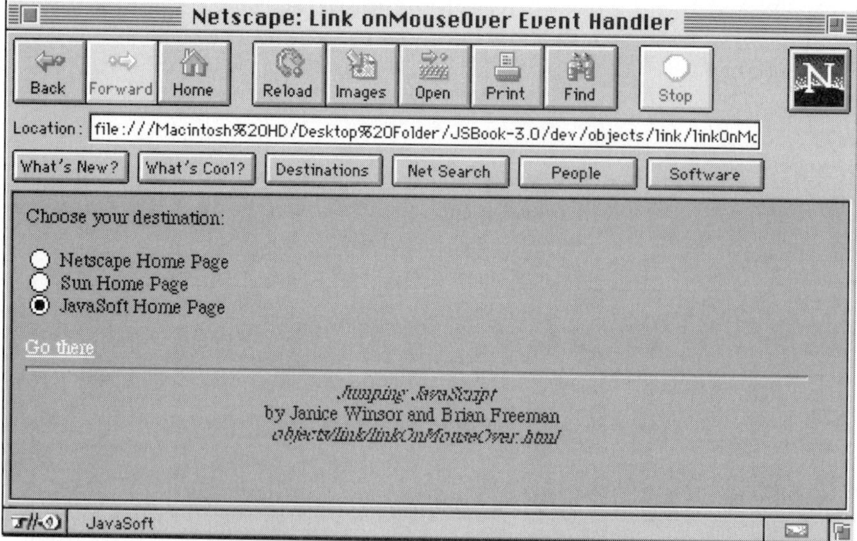

Figure 14–3 URL displayed in status bar

Clearing a Status Message with onMouseOut

In Navigator 2.0, some platforms had problems with clearing status messages from the status bar. Navigator 3.0 provides an `onMouseOut` event handler that you can use to clean up the status bar within each script. Even though you test your script on the platform you are using, you cannot know what platform or what browser release your users have. Therefore, it's always a good idea to make your scripts as fail-safe as possible.

Use the `onMouseOut` event handler in conjunction with the `window.status` property to clear the status message from the status bar when the user moves the pointer off the link.

Event Handler

onMouseOut

Syntax

<A HREF="*URL*" ;
onMouseOut="*functionName*();
return true">;
anchorName
</A>

Note – You must always end the `onMouseOut` event handler by returning a value of `true` or the message in the status bar is not cleared.

Example of Clearing a Status Message with onMouseOut

The following `linkOnMouseOut.html` script is similar to the `linkOnMouseOver.html` script with the addition of the `onMouseOut` event handler.

```
<!--
          linkOnMouseOut.html

      This example of the link object's onMouseOut
      method shows the destination to users in
      the status area when they move their pointer
      over the go there link. When they move their
      pointer off the go there link, the status
      area is cleared.
-->

<HTML>
<HEAD>
<TITLE>Link onMouseOut Event Handler</TITLE>
```

```
<SCRIPT LANGUAGE="JavaScript">
<!-- HIDE FROM OLD BROWSERS

// default the destination to Netscape
var destURL = "http://home.netscape.com"
var destStr = "Netscape"

// STOP HIDING -->
</SCRIPT>
</HEAD>

<BODY>

<P>Choose your destination:

<FORM>
<INPUT TYPE="radio" NAME="destination"

onClick="destURL='http://home.netscape.com';destStr='Nets
cape'"
 CHECKED>
Netscape Home Page<BR>
<INPUT TYPE="radio" NAME="destination"
 onClick="destURL='http://www.sun.com';destStr='Sun'">
Sun Home Page<BR>
<INPUT TYPE="radio" NAME="destination"

onClick="destURL='http://java.sun.com';destStr='JavaSoft'
">
JavaSoft Home Page<BR>
</FORM>

<P>
<A HREF="" onClick="this.href=destURL"
 onMouseOver="window.status=destStr; return true"
 onMouseOut="window.status=''; return true">
Go there</A>

</BODY>
</HTML>
```

Figure 14–4 shows the result of loading the `linkOnMouseOut.html` script.

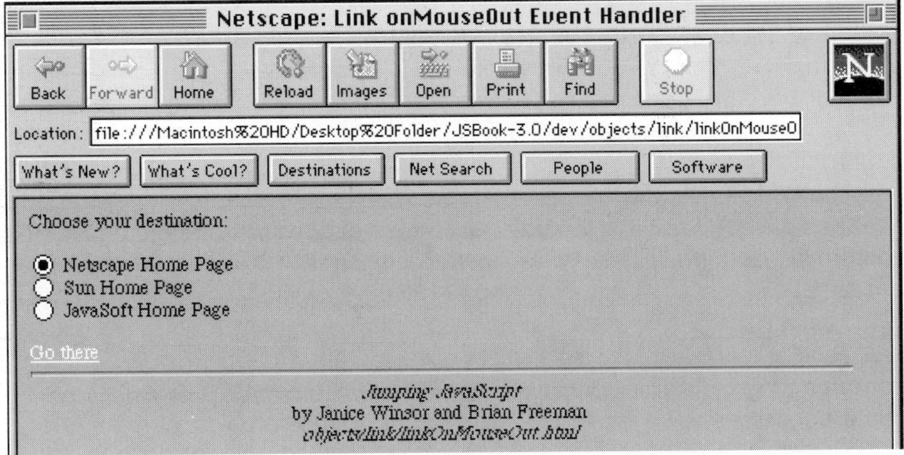

Figure 14–4 Result of loading the `linkOnMouseOut.html` script

From the user's point of view, this script works in exactly the same way as the `linkOnMouseOver.html` script. The difference is behind the scenes in the way the event handlers are programmed.

Using Other Protocols with a Link

You can create links to protocols other than `http`. For example, you can link to the `javascript`, `mailto`, or `ftp` protocols.

Example of Linking to the javascript Protocol

The following `linkJSProtocol.html` script uses links to the `javascript` protocol and `history` object methods to create forward and backward buttons at the bottom of the page.

```
<!--
              linkJSProtocol.html

    This example uses the javascript protocol in
    the link object's URL to add simple back and
    forward buttons to the bottom of the page.
-->

<HTML>
<HEAD>
<TITLE>Link JavaScript Protocol</TITLE>
</HEAD>

<BODY>
```

```
<P>Now is the time for all good men to come to
the aid of their country (or any other text that
might be appropriate).</P>

<CENTER>
<A HREF="javascript:history.go(-1)"
onMouseOver="self.status='Go Back';return true"
onMouseOut="self.status='';return true">
<IMG SRC="../../icons/4ARROW3.GIF"></A>

<A HREF="javascript:history.go(1)"
onMouseOver="self.status='Go Forward';return true"
onMouseOut="self.status='';return true">
<IMG SRC="../../icons/4ARROW4.GIF"></A>
</CENTER>

</BODY>
</HTML>
```

Figure 14–5 shows the result of loading the `linkJSProtocol.html` script.

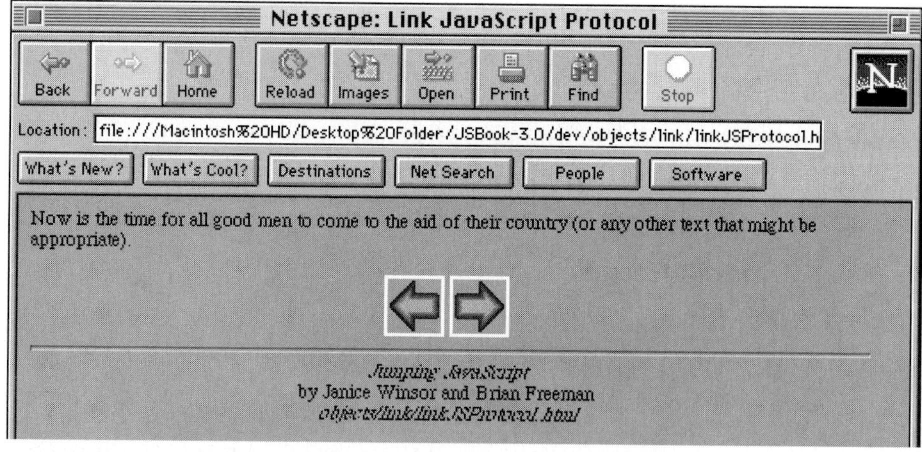

Figure 14–5 Result of loading the `linkJSProtocol.html` script

PART FOUR

Getting User Input

CHAPTER 15

- Retrieving the Form That Contains the Object
- Determining the Type of a form Object
- Evaluating Expressions
- Converting an Object to a String
- Determining the Value of an Object

Introducing form Objects

Forms provide a way to gather user input and send it to a server. When you define forms by using the HTML `<FORM></FORM>`tags, the JavaScript language automatically creates a `form` object as well as objects for each user interface element in the form. The `elements` array of the `form` object stores references to the user interface objects contained in the form. The references are stored in the `elements` array in the order in which they are defined in the HTML page. The input element objects that relate to a form share common properties, methods, and event handlers in addition to the properties, methods, and event handlers that are specific to each input element.

Every time you specify one of the following input types, a corresponding JavaScript object of the same name is stored in the `elements` array of the form that contains it:

- `button`
- `checkbox`
- `fileUpload`
- `hidden`
- `password`
- `radio`
- `reset`
- `select`

- submit
- text
- textarea

When you use the <TEXTAREA></TEXTAREA> tags, the JavaScript language automatically references the corresponding textarea object.

The Navigator 3.0 release provides a new fileUpload object with its own properties, methods, and event handlers that you can use to specify a file that you can attach to a form and upload along with it to a server.

The chapters in this part provide detailed information about how to create each of these user interface elements with the proper HTML tags and how to use the properties, methods, and event handlers of the corresponding JavaScript object.

The last chapter in this part provides information on how to use the properties, methods, and event handlers of the form object itself to submit to a server information gathered in the form.

The common properties and methods for the form input objects are listed in Table 15-1.

Table 15-1 Common Properties and Methods for form Input Objects

Properties	Methods	Event Handlers
form*	eval()*	None
type*	toString()*	
	valueOf()*	

* New in Navigator 3.0 release.

Retrieving the Form That Contains the Object

You can use the form property to retrieve the form that contains the object.

Property	Value	Gettable	Settable
form	string	Yes	No

The following `textForm.html` script contains two buttons that reference the text field in the form by using different object references. The first button calls `select()` on the text field by referencing the `document` object. The second button calls `select()` on the text field by using the `form` property with the following statement:

```
onClick="this.form.textField.select()"
```

The result of clicking on each button looks the same to the user. The only difference is in the underlying object reference in the script.

```
<!--
         textForm.html

    This example shows how the form property of
    the text object can be used to access other
    elements within the containing form.
-->

<HTML>
<HEAD>
<TITLE>Text Form Property</TITLE>
</HEAD>

<BODY>

<P>Below is a form that contains a text object and
two button objects. When clicked, both buttons
call select() on the text object, using different object
references.</P>

<P>The Use document Object button references the
textField by using the document object:</P>

<DT>document.forms[0].elements[0].select()</DT>

<P>The Use form Property button references the
textField by using the text object's form
property:</P>

<DT>this.form.textField.select()</DT>

<P>If you click in the text field and then click
on the Use document Object button, the text in the
text field is selected. Click in the text
```

```
field again to unselect the text, and then click on the
Use form Property button. The text in the text
field is selected again.</P>

<DIV ALIGN = LEFT>
<FORM>
<B>A Text Field: </B><BR>
<INPUT
 TYPE="text"
 NAME="textField"
 VALUE="Some Text"
 SIZE=50
>
<BR>
<INPUT
 TYPE="button"
 NAME="btn1"
 VALUE="Use document Object"
 onClick="document.forms[0].elements[0].select()"
>
<BR>
<INPUT
 TYPE="button"
 NAME="btn2"
 VALUE="Use form Property "
 onClick="this.form.textField.select()"
>
</FORM>
</DIV>

</BODY>
</HTML>
```

Figure 15–1 shows the result of loading the `textForm.html` script.

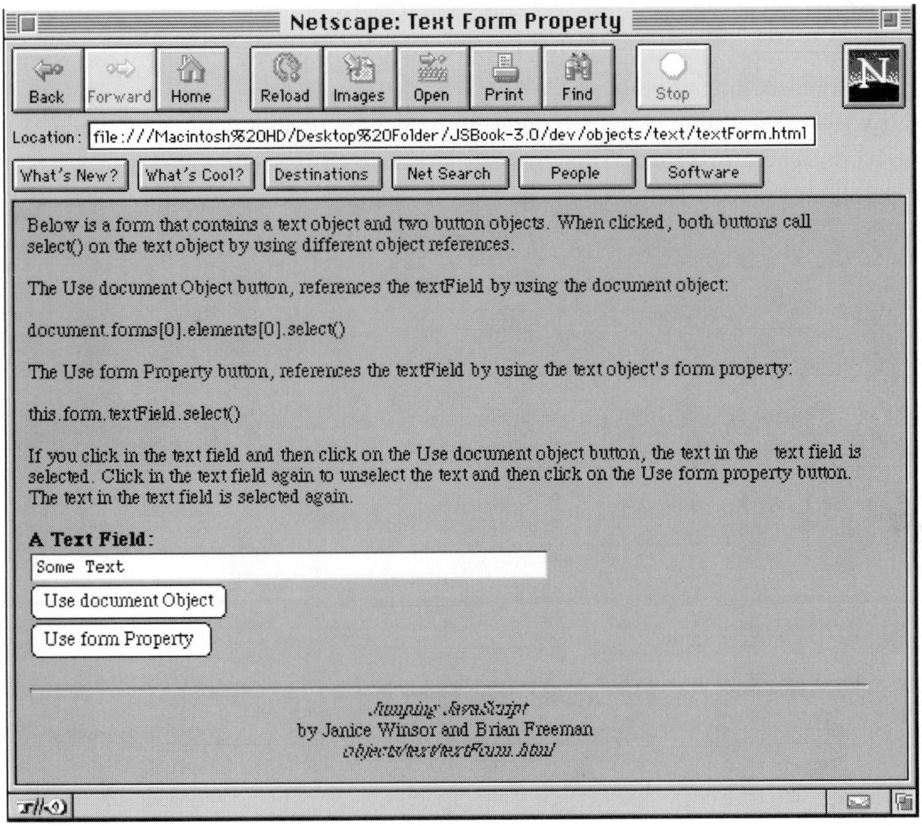

Figure 15–1 Result of loading the `textForm.html` script

Click in the text field and then click on the Use document Object button; the text in the text field is selected. Click in the text field again to unselect the text and then click on the Use form Property button. The text in the text field is selected again by using a different object reference.

Determining the Type of a form Object

The `type` property has been added to the available properties for all of the `form` element objects in the Navigator 3.0 release. This property enables you to test your scripts programmatically to determine the type of any or all of the elements you have created in a form. This property is very useful when you start writing more advanced scripts.

Property	Value	Gettable	Settable
type	string	Yes	No

Table 15-2 shows the value of the `type` property that is assigned to each form element.

Table 15-2 **Value of type Property for Each form Element**

HTML Element	Value of type Property
`INPUT TYPE="button"`	`"button"`
`INPUT TYPE="checkbox"`	`"checkbox"`
`INPUT TYPE="file"`	`"file"`
`INPUT TYPE="hidden"`	`"hidden"`
`INPUT TYPE="password"`	`"password"`
`INPUT TYPE="radio"`	`"radio"`
`INPUT TYPE="reset"`	`"reset"`
`INPUT TYPE="submit"`	`"submit"`
`INPUT TYPE="text"`	`"text"`
`SELECT`	`"select-one"`
`SELECT MULTIPLE`	`"select-multiple"`
`TEXTAREA`	`"textarea"`

Example of Determining the Type of a Form

The following `textType.html` script creates a text field and a button. When you click on the button, an alert displays the type for the text field.

```
<!--
         textType.html
-->

<HTML>
<HEAD>
<TITLE>Text type Property</TITLE>
<SCRIPT LANGUAGE="JavaScript">
<!-- HIDE FROM OLD BROWSERS

function displayType(theform) {
  var msg_str = ""

  for (var e=0; e < theform.length; e++) {
    msg_str += "\n" + theform.elements[e].name
    msg_str += " = " + theform.elements[e].type
  }
  alert(msg_str)
}

// STOP HIDING -->
</SCRIPT>
</HEAD>

<BODY>

<P>Below is a form containing a text field.</P>

<P>The button below it displays the text object's
type property.

<FORM NAME="aForm">
<B>Type Some Text: </B><BR>
<INPUT
 TYPE="text"
 NAME="textField"
 VALUE=""
 SIZE=50
>
</FORM>
```

```
<CENTER>
<FORM NAME="btnForm">
<INPUT TYPE="button" NAME="displayBtn"
 VALUE="Display type Property"
 onClick="displayType(aForm)">
</FORM>
</CENTER>

</BODY>
</HTML>
```

Figure 15–2 shows the result of loading the `textType.html` script.

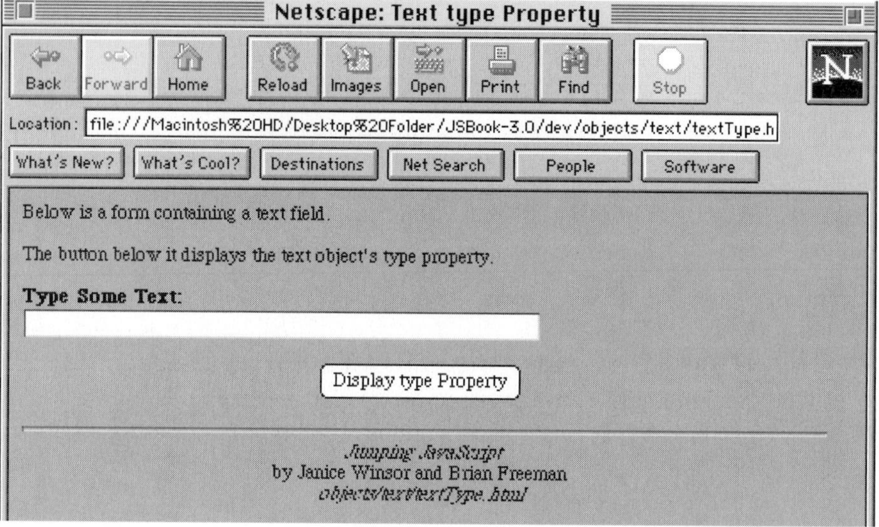

Figure 15–2 Result of loading the `textType.html` script

When you click on the Display type Property button, an alert is displayed, showing the type of the object, as shown in Figure 15–3.

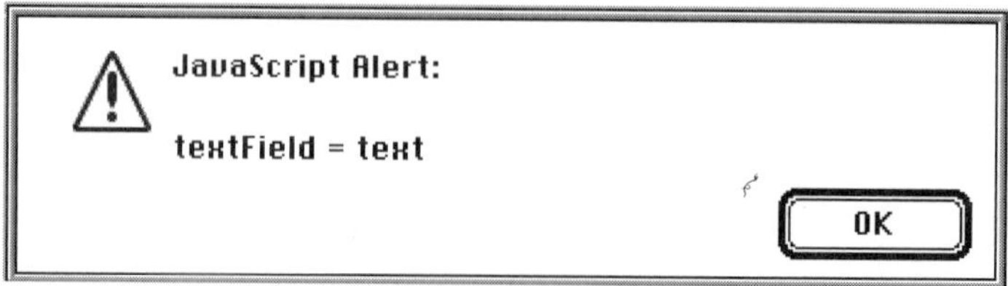

Figure 15–3 Alert showing object type

Evaluating Expressions

You can use the `eval()` method to evaluate a string of JavaScript code. If the string represents an expression, `eval()` evaluates the expression. If the string represents one or more JavaScript statements, `eval()` performs the statements. For more information about the `eval()` method, see "Evaluating Text Expressions" on page 802.

Converting an Object to a String

You can use the `toString()` method to return the string representation of the object. Every object has a built-in `toString()` method. You can create your own function to replace the default `toString()` method. To do so, use the function `prototype` property. For example, if you have an object `Frog`, assign your function to the `prototype` property after you have created an instance of `Frog`, as shown below.

```
MyFrog = new Frog()
MyFrog.prototype.toString = Your function
```

For more information about the `prototype` property, see "Creating Custom String Functions" on page 809.

Determining the Value of an Object

You can use the `valueOf()` method to return the primitive value associated with the object, if there is one. If there is no primitive value, then this method returns the object itself. This method returns the primitive Boolean value for Boolean objects, the string associated with a `String` object, and the function associated with a `Function` object.

CHAPTER 16

- Defining Text Fields
- The text Object
- Naming text Objects
- Getting and Setting text Object Values
- Getting a Default Value for a text Object
- Setting the Input Focus
- Removing Input Focus
- Automatically Selecting Text
- Using the onChange Event Handler to Validate Data
- Catching an Event when the Text Field Has the Focus
- Catching an Event when Text Is Selected
- Catching an Event when a Text Field Loses the Focus
- Catching an Event when the User Changes to Another Text Field
- Summary of New Terms and Concepts

Adding Text Fields to a Document

The text object enables you to capture text that users type into a single line in your Web page. Use the textarea object if you want to enable users to enter multiple lines of text. This chapter describes how to create text fields and how to use the JavaScript text object to evaluate their contents and use them in scripts. For information on how to create text areas, see Chapter 18, "Adding Text Areas to a Document." For information on how to send text data to a server, see Chapter 24, "Using Forms to Send Data to a Server." For information on manipulating text, see Chapter 28, "Working with Strings and String Objects."

Defining Text Fields

You defined text elements with the <FORM></FORM> and <INPUT> HTML tags. The visual design of the text fields and text areas that are created depends on the operating system the particular browser runs on. Figure 16–1 shows an example of a text field for the Macintosh system.

Figure 16–1 Text field style for the Macintosh system

The only part of the text field itself that you can control is the number of characters that it contains and whether the text field contains a default value. The JavaScript language controls the rest of the visual elements. The color, height, and width of the text area are automatically created to accommodate the number of characters you assign to the text field. If you assign a long size to the text field, the text field created is long enough to accommodate the characters, even if it is wider than the page. In addition, each operating system controls the feedback when the user clicks in a text field or highlights text. You cannot control any of these elements in a JavaScript program.

HTML Brushup — Creating Text Fields

You create a text field by using the <FORM></FORM> HTML tags and specifying the parts of the text field using the <INPUT> tag with NAME and VALUE attributes, as shown below:

<FORM>

<INPUT TYPE = "text"

NAME = "*Field Name*"

VALUE = "*Contents*"

SIZE = "*Character Count*"

onBlur = "*JavaScript code*"

onChange = "*JavaScript code*"

onFocus = "*JavaScript code*"

onSelect = "*JavaScript code*">

</FORM>

You use the attributes to specify a name for the field. This name is not the same as the label for the text field but is the name you use in your script to identify the specific text field. You can create an empty text field by specifying VALUE="", or you can enter a default value. The size you specify is the number of characters users can type in the field. Browsers display text in a monospace font, usually Courier.

The <FORM></FORM> HTML tags also have NAME, TARGET, ACTION, METHOD, and ENCTYPE attributes that you must set if you create a form that sends input to a Web server. For more information about creating forms that interact with the server, see Chapter 24, "Using Forms to Send Data to a Server."

Example of Creating a Text Field

The following `text.html` script shows how to create one right-aligned text field with a label and predefined contents.

```
<!--
            text.html

    This example creates a text field in a HTML
    form.
-->

<HTML>
<HEAD>
<TITLE>Text</TITLE>
</HEAD>

<BODY>

<P>Below is a form containing a text field.</P>

<DIV ALIGN = RIGHT>
<FORM>
<B>Type Some Text: </B><BR>
<INPUT
 TYPE="text"
 NAME="textField"
 VALUE=""
 SIZE=50
>
</FORM>
</DIV>

</BODY>
</HTML>
```

Figure 16–2 shows the results of loading the `text.html` script.

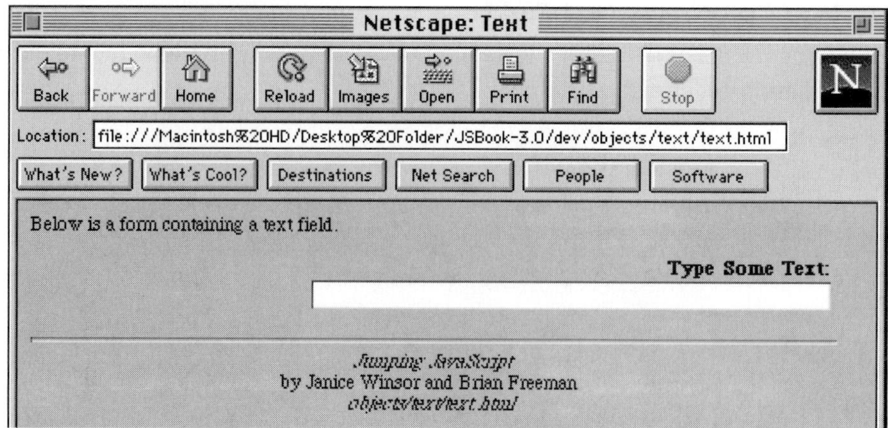

Figure 16–2 Result of loading the `text.html` script

UI Guideline – When creating text fields, always provide a label for each text field. Keep the label short and easy to read. Consider formatting all text field labels in the same way. Use initial capital letters, a bold font, and a colon following the name. Users should be able to tell at a glance what kind of information you expect them to type into the text field. Always position labels in the same way, either above or to the left of the text field. Because you cannot depend on consistent alignment, consider left-aligning your labels above each text field so that the text fields themselves always start at the left margin. Remember when designing your text fields that different operating systems may display text fields in a different way than you expect.

---

text Object Terminology

The terms in this section describe how the system responds to user actions on text.

Focus: When the user clicks in a text field, the field has *focus*: any characters you type go into this field. If text is selected, the text is highlighted. If no text is selected, the insert pointer (usually a horizontal bar or I-beam) flashes. Only one `text` object can have focus at a time.

Blur: When the user clicks away from the `text` object that has focus, the resulting action is called a *blur*. That is, the field that had focus is no longer the focus of the action. You can think of blur as "out of focus" for a specific text field.

Select: When the user highlights text by pressing the mouse button, dragging the pointer, and then releasing the mouse button, this action is a *select*; text is selected.

Change: When the user makes any alteration to the contents of a text field and then either tabs or clicks away from the field to blur the focus, this action is a *change*. Note that the change does not take effect until the user blurs the focus.

Be aware that a user's interaction with a field may trigger more than one event with a single action. For example, when a user highlights text, the field has both a focus and select event. If your script defines actions for the `onFocus` and `onSelect` event handlers that conflict, unexpected results may occur.

Text Field Locations

The default location for text fields on a single line is to align the text field with the left margin. Figure 16–3 shows the location and spacing for a text field with a label left-aligned above the text field on a Macintosh computer. This label is followed by `<BR>`. If you want more space between the label and the text field, you can use `<P>` instead.

Figure 16–3 Default text field alignment (Macintosh)

You can center the label and text field by surrounding the `<FORM></FORM>` definition with `<CENTER></CENTER>` tags, as shown in the following code extract.

```
<CENTER>
<FORM>
<B>Type Some Text: </B><BR>
<INPUT
 TYPE="text"
 NAME="textField"
 VALUE=""
 SIZE=50
>
</FORM>
</CENTER>
```

Figure 16–4 shows the results of this code sample on a Macintosh computer.

Figure 16–4 Centered text field and label (Macintosh)

HTML Brushup — <DIV></DIV> Tags

An alternative HTML tag that you can use to format text fields, as well as any other form element, is the <DIV> tag (explicit divisions). This tag is a Netscape 2.0 extension that is a proposed replacement for the nonstandard <CENTER> tag. The <DIV> tag accepts the ALIGN attribute with the possible values of LEFT | RIGHT | CENTER.

Below is an example of a right-aligned text field and its label:

```
<DIV ALIGN=RIGHT>
<FORM>
<B>Type Some Text: </B><BR>
<INPUT
 TYPE="text"
 NAME="textField"
 VALUE=""
 SIZE=50
>
</FORM>
</DIV>
```

Figure 16–5 shows an example of a right-aligned text field and label. See the HTML Brushup box for an example of the code that generates this alignment.

Figure 16–5 Right-aligned text field and label (Macintosh)

You can put the label in front of the text field as shown in Figure 16–6. However, if you have two or more text fields grouped together with this format, it's likely that the labels will not align properly giving your page a ragged look.

Type Some Text:

Figure 16–6 Label in front of text field

The text Object

Once you have created a text field, you use the properties, methods, and event handlers listed in alphabetical order in Table 16-1 to extract information about the text field and to trigger events based on user actions in the text fields.

Table 16-1 Properties, Methods, and Event Handlers for the text Object

Properties	Methods	Event Handlers
`defaultValue`	`blur()`	`onBlur`
`form*`	`eval()*`	`onChange`
`name`	`focus()`	`onFocus`
`type*`	`select()`	`onSelect`
`value`	`toString()*`	
	`valueOf()*`	

* New in the Navigator 3.0 release.

Another use for text fields is to use them to display the results of a script calculation or other processing. The JavaScript language does not provide read-only text fields, so you cannot prohibit users from changing the contents of a results field. You can, however, use the `onChange` event handler to recalculate the results if a user does change the contents of the field or simply write HTML into another document

---

UI Guideline – Design a different look for text fields that display results of script calculations than for text fields for user input. Position them alone on a page or as part of a table. You can also label the fields in a different way to communicate to users that these text fields are different.

A page with `text` objects is loaded by using its default values when users quit and restart the browser or when they load the page from the Location or Open File items in the File menu.

However, `text` objects save and remember values entered by users in the browser's *disk cache*, which is a memory buffer area that contains a large block of information read from or to be written to the disk. This means that if users navigate to other pages and return to your page by clicking on the Back button or by choosing your page from the Go or Bookmarks menu, any values that were entered into the text fields are retained.

To extract the current data from a `text` object, use the following syntax:

```
document.formName.fieldName.value
```

`text` object values are always returned as strings. When you have obtained the string value, you can use the string object methods to parse the string or otherwise manipulate it for use in your script. String object methods are described in Chapter 28, "Working with Strings and String Objects."

Naming text Objects

`text` object names are important in identifying individual text fields within your JavaScript program as well as in submitting information to CGI scripts on a server.

Property	Value	Gettable	Settable
name	string	Yes	No

Text object names must be a contiguous string of numbers and characters with no spaces. Assign unique and descriptive names to your text objects to help you read and debug your scripts. Using names that are the same or similar to the labels you display on the page for your users can minimize confusion and provide you with an easy way to refer back to the arrangements of text fields in your page design.

Although we strongly recommend that you use unique names for your text objects, you can assign the same name to a series of related fields. Any time you reuse a name for the same object type, the JavaScript program uses an indexed array for that name. For example, if you define three fields with the name `price`, you would get the `value` property for each field with the following statements:

```
data = document.forms[0].price[0],value
data = document.forms[0].price[1],value
data = document.forms[0].price[2],value
```

You may find this construction useful if you want to cycle through all of the fields in a form to find out which are blank. However, you probably would find it difficult elsewhere in the script to determine which price you have gotten from the script.

Getting and Setting text Object Values

You can use the `value` property to extract the contents of a `text` object and to change that value.

Property	Value	Gettable	Settable
value	string	Yes	Yes

All values returned by `text` objects are string values. If you ask your users to enter numbers and you want to use those values in numeric calculations, you must convert the data from a string to a number (for example, from "76" to 76) before you can do any mathematical operations on the value. The Boolean values `true` and `false` are also converted to their string values of `"true"` and `"false"`.

When you want to display a value in a `text` object, you use the `value` property. You can use the `value` property in this way to assign a default value to a text field or to display the results of a computation or to display other information that you have extracted with your script.

Example of Using the text.value Property

The following `textValue.html` script shows how to extract the text value from the State field and convert it to upper case, using the `toUpperCase()` method of the `String` object. It also gives you a preview of using the `focus()` method and the `onFocus` and `onChange` event handlers. This script also uses the `this` keyword as an easy way to provide local references to individual text fields without referring to them by name. For more information on the `this` keyword, see Chapter 5, "Introducing Objects."

```
<!--
        textValue.html
-->

<HTML>
<HEAD>
<TITLE>Text Value</TITLE>
</HEAD>
```

```
<BODY
 onLoad="document.userAddress.nameField.focus()">
<TABLE WIDTH="100%" CELLPADDING=5>
  <TR>
    <TD>
      <P>This script shows event handlers, methods,
       and properties:

      <OL>
        <LI> An onLoad event handler is registered
        to set the focus to nameField.<P>
        <LI> select() is used in onFocus event
        handlers on each text field to highlight the
        contents when the field gets the
        focus.<P>You might have to enter some text
        in the fields, then use TAB to move around
        to see the effect. Or, click in the field,
        then move the pointer out of the browser
        window and then back in.  Also, try
        removing the onFocus lines in the script
        to see the difference.<P>
        <LI> An onChange event handler is
        registered on the stateField. After you
        change it, the contents are converted to
        upper case.
      </OL>
    </TD>
  </TR>
</TABLE>

<TABLE WIDTH="100%" CELLPADDING=5>
  <TR>
    <TH>Description
    <TH>Input FORM
  </TR>
  <TR>
    <TD>
      <P>This example shows the text.value
      property as well as some interesting page
      layout.</P>

      <P>This page is formatted as a table. One row
      contains this text column and the FORM on the right.
```

```
    The FORM contains another TABLE to align the City,
    State, and Zip labels with the text fields
    below them.</P>

    <P>The description at the top of the page is
    another table.</P>
  </TD>
  <TD>
    <FORM NAME="userAddress">
    <P><B>Name:</B><BR>
    <INPUT TYPE="text" NAME="nameField"
     VALUE="" SIZE=50
     onFocus="this.select()"
     ></P>
    <P><B>Address:</B><BR>
    <INPUT TYPE="text" NAME="addressField"
     VALUE="" SIZE=50
     onFocus="this.select()"
     ></P>
    <TABLE CELLSPACING=0 CELLPADDING=0>
<TR>
  <TD><B>City:</B></TD>
  <TD><B>State:</B></TD>
  <TD><B>Zip:</B></TD>
</TR>
<TR>
  <TD>
  <INPUT TYPE="text" NAME="cityField"
   VALUE="" SIZE=32
        onFocus="this.select()"
        >
  </TD>
  <TD>
  <INPUT TYPE="text" NAME="stateField"
   VALUE="CA" SIZE=2
        onFocus="this.select()"
        onChange="this.value=
          this.value.toUpperCase()"
        >
  </TD>
  <TD>
  <INPUT TYPE="text" NAME="zipField"
   VALUE="99999-9999" SIZE=10
        onFocus="this.select()"
```

```
              >
          </TD>
        </TR>
           </TABLE>
           <P><B>Comment:</B><BR>
           <INPUT TYPE="text" NAME="commentField"
            VALUE="" SIZE=50
            onFocus="this.select()"
            ></P>
           </FORM>
        </TD>
      </TR>
    </TABLE>

    </BODY>
    </HTML>
```

Figure 16–7 shows the results of loading the `textValue.html` script.

HTML Brushup — Ordered Lists

In addition to the table formatting tags, this script uses the <OL></OL> HTML tags to create an ordered list. The <OL> tag has the following attributes:

COMPACT	The browser reduces the indentation, space between sequence numbers and list items, or both. Some browsers cannot compact and so do nothing.
START=*n*	Specify the number you want to use to start the list. If you do not specify a START attribute, the default is to start the list with the number 1.
TYPE=A | a | I | i | 1	Specify the numbering style for ordered lists. A uses capital letters. a uses lowercase letters, I uses capital Roman numerals, i uses lowercase Roman numerals, 1 uses Arabic numerals. If you do not specify a TYPE, the default is to use Arabic numerals.
<LI>	Use to start each line within the ordered list.

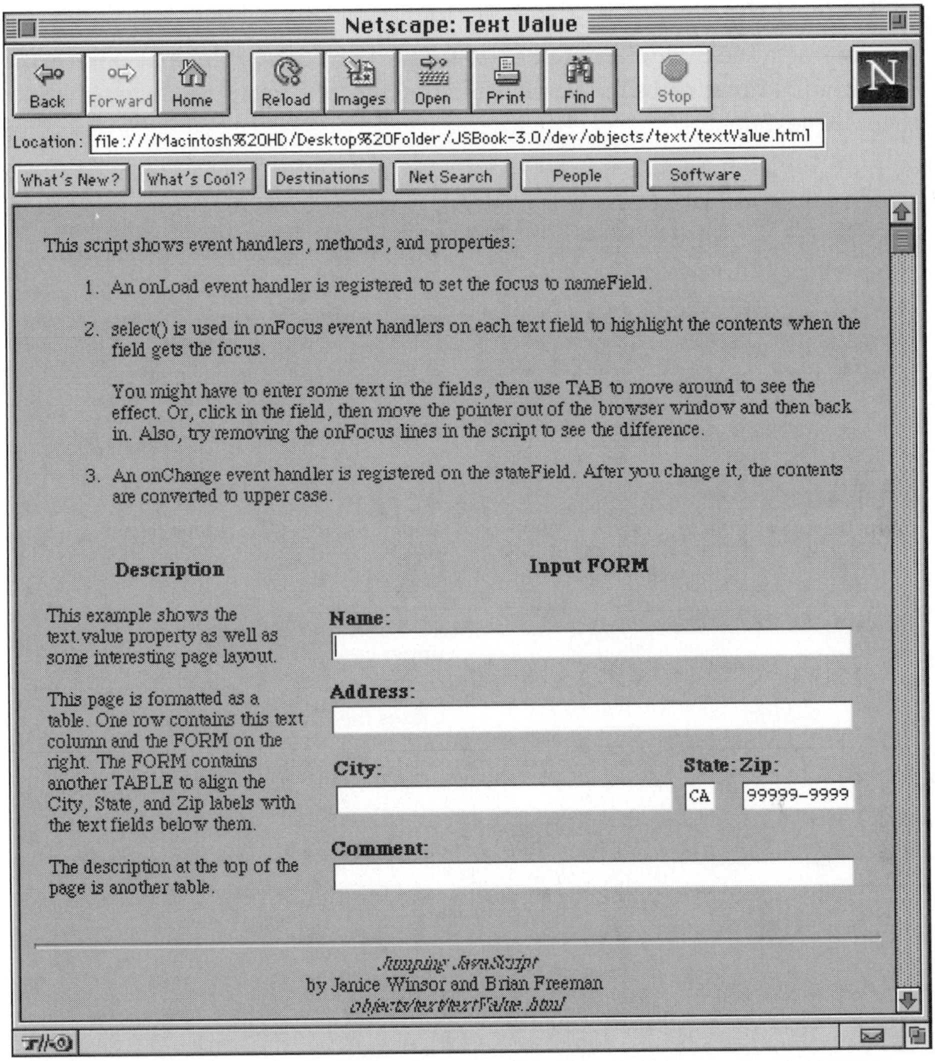

Netscape: Text Value

Back | Forward | Home | Reload | Images | Open | Print | Find | Stop

Location: file:///Macintosh%20HD/Desktop%20Folder/JSBook-3.0/dev/objects/text/textValue.html

What's New? | What's Cool? | Destinations | Net Search | People | Software

This script shows event handlers, methods, and properties:

1. An onLoad event handler is registered to set the focus to nameField.
2. select() is used in onFocus event handlers on each text field to highlight the contents when the field gets the focus.

   You might have to enter some text in the fields, then use TAB to move around to see the effect. Or, click in the field, then move the pointer out of the browser window and then back in. Also, try removing the onFocus lines in the script to see the difference.
3. An onChange event handler is registered on the stateField. After you change it, the contents are converted to upper case.

Description	**Input FORM**
This example shows the text.value property as well as some interesting page layout. This page is formatted as a table. One row contains this text column and the FORM on the right. The FORM contains another TABLE to align the City, State, and Zip labels with the text fields below them. The description at the top of the page is another table.	**Name:** **Address:** **City:** **State: Zip:** CA 99999-9999 **Comment:**

Jumping JavaScript
by Janice Winsor and Brian Freeman
objects/text/textValue.html

Figure 16–7 Result of loading the `textValue.html` script

Type some text in the text fields and move from field to field to see the results. You may have to tab between fields to see the highlighting. You can press Shift/Tab to move to the previous text field. On the Macintosh platform, clicking in the window briefly flashes the highlight, but the text does not remain highlighted. When the text is highlighted, the next character you type replaces the highlighted text. Notice that in the Navigator browser you cannot press Return to move from text field to text field.

Analysis of the textValue.html Script

Let's look at a line-by-line description of the portion of the script that extracts the value from the `stateField` text field and converts it to upper case when the user leaves the text field

`<TD>`	Starts table data HTML tag.
`<INPUT TYPE="text" NAME="stateField"`	Defines the input type as text and name the field `stateField.`
`VALUE="CA" SIZE=2`	Sets the default value to CA and the size of the text field to two characters.
`onFocus="this.select()"`	When this text field receives a focus event, select the contents.
`onChange="this.value=`	When the text field changes focus, extract the contents.
`this.value.toUpperCase()"`	Change the contents of the text field to upper case.
`>`	Closes the `<INPUT>` tag.
`</TD>`	Ends the table data definition.

Getting a Default Value for a text Object

When you want to determine the default value for a `text` object, you use the `defaultValue` property.

Property	Value	Gettable	Settable
defaultValue	string	Yes	No

Because you can extract the default value for a `text` object, you can also restore it by using the `value` property if you need to. The value returned by the `defaultValue` property is the string defined for the `text` object in the `VALUE` attribute of the form. You can use this property to reset individual text fields.

Note – Because not all of the user interface elements you can use in a form have a `defaultValue` property, you might want to use the `reset` button object to return all objects in a form to their default values. The `reset` object is described in Chapter 19, "Activating Buttons in a Document."

Example of Using the defaultValue Property

The following `textDefaultValue.html` script uses the default `value` property to reset the value of each text field to its initial value.

```
<!--
         textDefaultValue.html
-->

<HTML>
<HEAD>
<TITLE>Text defaultValue</TITLE>
<SCRIPT LANGUAGE="JavaScript">
<!-- HIDE FROM OLD BROWSERS

//
// Reset a form to its default values
//
// Limitation: not all objects contained in a
// form have a defaultValue property. Only use
// this method if you know your form contains
// objects with defaultValue.
//
function defaultForm(theForm) {
  for (var e=0; e < theForm.length; e++) {
    theForm.elements[e].value =
      theForm.elements[e].defaultValue
  }
}

// STOP HIDING -->
</SCRIPT>
</HEAD>
```

```
<BODY
 onLoad="document.userAddress.nameField.focus()">

<TABLE WIDTH="100%" CELLPADDING=5>
  <TH>Description
  <TH>Input FORM
  <TR>
    <TD>
      <P>This example shows how you might set all
      the fields in a form to their default
      value.</P>

      <P>Normally, you would use a reset object,
      but this example shows how to script it.</P>

      <P>Type something into the fields, then
      click on the Defaults button.</P>

      <P>Notice after you click on Defaults, the
      label is removed from the button, which
      is why you should use a reset object
      instead. Not all objects contained in a
      form have a defaultValue property.
    </TD>
    <TD>
      <FORM NAME="userAddress">
      <P><B>Name:</B><BR>
      <INPUT TYPE="text" NAME="nameField"
       VALUE="" SIZE=50
       onFocus="this.select()"
       ></P>
      <P><B>Address:</B><BR>
      <INPUT TYPE="text" NAME="addressField"
       VALUE="" SIZE=50
       onFocus="this.select()"
       ></P>
      <TABLE CELLSPACING=0 CELLPADDING=0>
   <TR>
     <TD><B>City:</B></TD>
     <TD><B>State:</B></TD>
     <TD><B>Zip:</B></TD>
   </TR>
```

```
    <TR>
      <TD>
      <INPUT TYPE="text" NAME="cityField"
       VALUE="" SIZE=32
            onFocus="this.select()"
            >
      </TD>
      <TD>
      <INPUT TYPE="text" NAME="stateField"
       VALUE="CA" SIZE=2
            onFocus="this.select()"
            onChange="this.value=
              this.value.toUpperCase()"
            >
      </TD>
      <TD>
      <INPUT TYPE="text" NAME="zipField"
       VALUE="99999-9999" SIZE=10
            onFocus="this.select()"
            >
      </TD>
    </TR>
        </TABLE>
        <P><B>Comment:</B><BR>
        <INPUT TYPE="text" NAME="commentField"
         VALUE="" SIZE=50
         onFocus="this.select()"
         ></P>
        <P>
        <INPUT TYPE="button" NAME="defaultBtn"
         VALUE="Defaults"
         onClick="defaultForm(this.form)"
         ></P>
        </FORM>
      </TD>
    </TR>
  </TABLE>


  </BODY>
  </HTML>
```

Figure 16–8 shows the result of loading the `textDefaultValue.html` script.

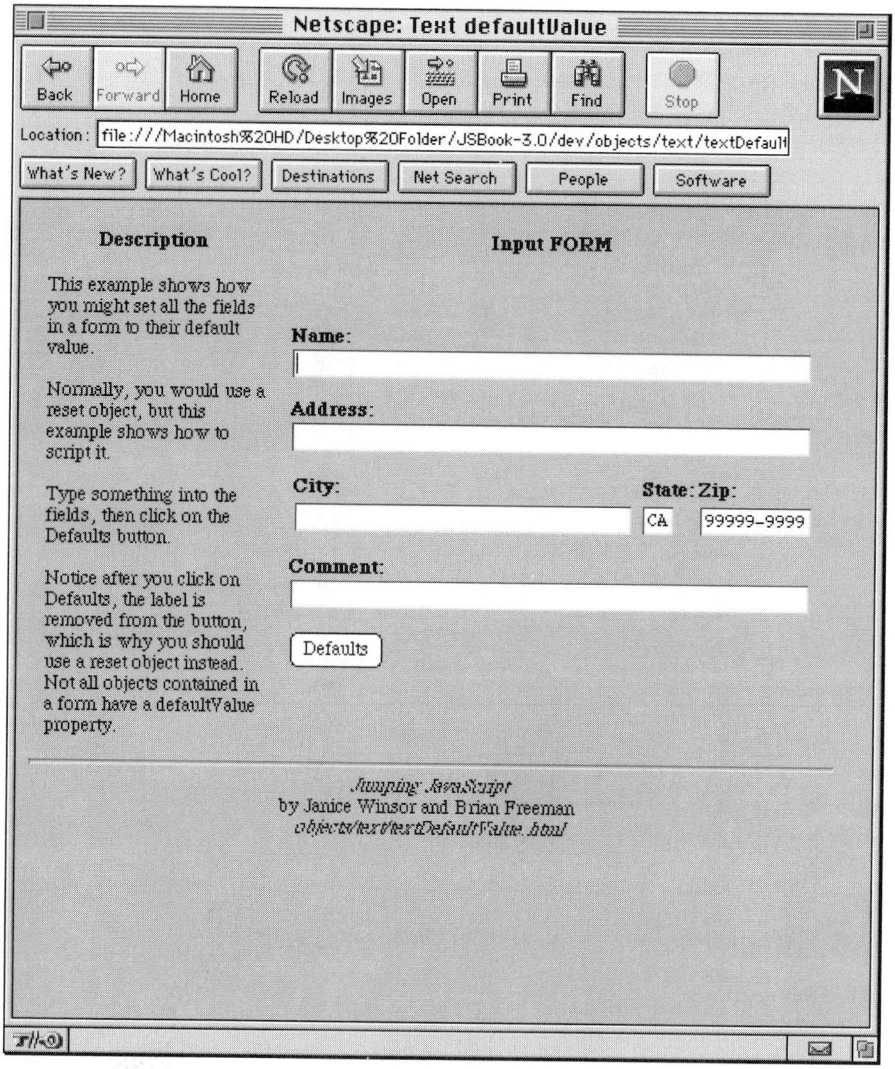

Figure 16–8 Result of loading the `textDefaultValue.html` script

When you type text into the fields and then click on the Defaults button, the values are reset to their default values.

Analysis of textDefaultValue.html Script

The `textDefaultValue.html` script is a modification of the `textValue.html` script. The script is modified by adding the `defaultForm()` function shown below:

```
function defaultForm(theForm) {
  for (var e=0; e < theForm.length; e++) {
    theForm.elements[e].value =
      theForm.elements[e].defaultValue
  }
}
```

This function creates a `for` loop that cycles through all the elements in the form, resetting them to their default values. The variable `e` in the `for` loop is used as an index to the elements in the `form` object array. It is initialized to `0` and ranges to one less than the number of elements in the form. For more information about how to create loops, see Chapter 27, "Creating Loops."

Setting the Input Focus

When you want to programmatically set the input focus to a text object, use the `focus()` method.

Methods

focus()

Returns

Nothing

The `focus()` method sets the flashing insert pointer at the beginning of the text field you specify, which means that the field is ready for users to type something into it. It's a good idea to set the focus to the first text field in a form. You also use the `focus()` method as the first step to performing another action in a specific text field. That way, you can be sure that the script is operating on the correct element. The following extract from the `textValue.html` file sets the input focus to the first text field when the document is loaded.

```
<BODY
 onLoad="document.userAddress.nameField.focus()">
<BODY
```

See "Example of Using the text.value Property" on page 543 for the complete script.

Removing Input Focus

The text objects provide a `blur()` method that you can use to remove input focus from a text field.

Method

blur()

Returns

Nothing

When you use the `blur()` method, the insert point is removed from the text field.

Example of focus( ) and blur( ) Methods

The following `textFocusBlur.html` script has three text fields and a message text area. The message text area displays information about the `focus()` and `blur()` methods as you click in and out of any of the three text fields.

```
<!--
          textFocusBlur.html
-->

<HTML>
<HEAD>
<TITLE>Text focus and blur</TITLE>
<SCRIPT LANGUAGE="JavaScript">
<!-- HIDE FROM OLD BROWSERS

function message(eventstr, fieldstr) {
  var msg_str = ""

  msg_str += "A " + eventstr + " event"
  msg_str += " was received on " + fieldstr
  msg_str += ".\n\r"
  document.blurForm.msgField.value += msg_str
}
// STOP HIDING -->
</SCRIPT>
</HEAD>

<BODY>
<P>This example shows the difference
```

```
between the focus and blur events.
When you click in a field, it receives a focus
event. When you then move out of the field, it
receives a blur event. You can move out of the
field either by pressing the Tab key or by
clicking in another field.

<FORM NAME="blurForm">
<P><B>Field A:</B><BR>
<INPUT TYPE="text" NAME="fieldA"
 VALUE="" SIZE=50
 onFocus="message('focus','fieldA')"
 onBlur="message('blur','fieldA')"
></P>

<P><B>Field B:</B><BR>
<INPUT TYPE="text" NAME="fieldB"
 VALUE="" SIZE=50
 onFocus="message('focus','fieldB')"
 onBlur="message('blur','fieldB')"
></P>

<P><B>Field C:</B><BR>
<INPUT TYPE="text" NAME="fieldC"
 VALUE="" SIZE=50
 onFocus="message('focus','fieldC')"
 onBlur="message('blur','fieldC')"
></P>

<P><B>Messages:</B><BR>
<TEXTAREA
 NAME="msgField"
 ROWS="20"
 COLS="45"
 WRAP="physical"
>
</TEXTAREA>
</P>
</FORM>

</BODY>
</HTML>
```

Figure 16–9 shows the result of loading the `textFocusBlur.html` script and clicking first in Field A, then in Field B.

Netscape: Text focus and blur

Back | Forward | Home | Reload | Images | Open | Print | Find | Stop

Location: file:///Macintosh%20HD/Desktop%20Folder/JSBook-3.0/dev/objects/text/textFocusBlur.h

What's New? | What's Cool? | Destinations | Net Search | People | Software

This example shows the difference between the focus and blur events. When you click in a field, it receives a focus event. When you then move out of the field, it receives a blur event. You can move out of the field either by pressing the Tab key or by clicking in another field.

Field A:

Field B:

Field C:

Messages:

```
A focus event was received on fieldA.
A blur event was received on fieldA.
A focus event was received on fieldB.
A blur event was received on fieldB.
A focus event was received on fieldC.
A blur event was received on fieldC.
A focus event was received on fieldB.
```

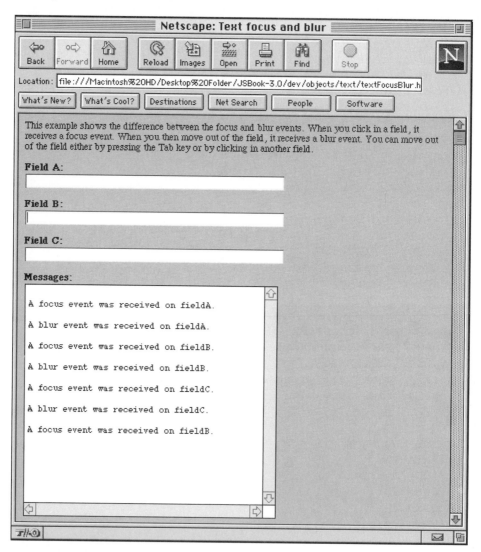

Figure 16–9 Result of loading the `textFocusBlur.html` script

Automatically Selecting Text

The text objects provide a `select()` method that you can use to automatically highlight the contents of a `text` object.

Method

select()

Returns

Nothing

When you use this method in a script, all of the text in a `text` object is highlighted. You might use this method when validating the contents of a text field. If the user enters incorrect information, such as typing alphabetical characters in a numeric text field, after you alert users to the mistake, you can finish by selecting the text. Because any text that is highlighted is deleted when users type the next character, not only do you save users the trouble of selecting the text themselves, but you also draw their attention to the area on the page where the problem occurred.

To make sure that the selection occurs in the right field, you should use both the `focus()` and `select()` methods, in that order. When you use this technique, you guarantee that the focus is on the proper text field before you select the text. You do not need to use the `onSelect` event handler with the `select()` method.

The following extract from the `textValue.html` file selects the contents of the text field when it receives the input focus.

```
<TD>
   <INPUT TYPE="text" NAME="cityField"
    VALUE="" SIZE=32
         onFocus="this.select()"
         >
   </TD>
```

See "Example of Using the text.value Property" on page 543 for the complete script.

Using the onChange Event Handler to Validate Data

Of the four text object event handlers, `onChange` is probably the most useful. You can use it to validate the data users type into a text field as soon as they move out of the text field.

Event Handler

onChange

Syntax

<INPUT

TYPE="text"

NAME="*fieldName*"

VALUE="*value*" SIZE=*n*

onChange="*JavaScript code*"

>

It's good practice to do your data validation field by field instead of waiting until the form is completed (or not doing any validation at all).

Example of Validating Text by Using the onChange Event Handler

The following `textValueVerify.html` script is similar to the `textValue.html` script shown in "Example of Using the text.value Property" on page 543, except that it implements a data validation function for the Zip text field.

```
<!--
          textValueVerify.html
-->

<HTML>
<HEAD>
<TITLE>Text Verify Values</TITLE>
<SCRIPT LANGUAGE="JavaScript">
<!-- HIDE FROM OLD BROWSERS
```

```
//
// is the string a number?
//
function isANum(str) {
  for (var i=0; i < str.length; i++) {
    var ch = str.substring(i, i+1)
    if (ch < "0" || ch > "9") {
      return false
    }
  }
  return true
}

//
// is the string a zip code?
// Accepted formats are:
//   99999
//   999999999
//   99999 9999
//   99999-9999
//
function isAZip(str) {
  if (str.length == 5 ||
      str.length == 9 ||
      str.length == 10) {

    // the first two cases are all numeric
    if (str.length == 5 || str.length == 9) {
      return isANum(str)
    }

    // the last two are somewhat similar, so
    // just loop through and find out if the dash or
    // space is in the right spot.
    for (var i=0; i < str.length; i++) {
      var chr = str.charAt(i)
      if (chr < "0" || chr > "9") {
   if (i != 5 && (chr == "-" || chr == " ")) {
     return false
   }
      }
    }
    return true
   }
```

```
  else {
    return false
  }
}

//
// verify the zip code is valid; if not, tell the
// users and make them reenter.
//
function verifyZip(form) {
  if (!isAZip(form.zipField.value)) {
    alert("Please enter a zip of the form 99999-9999")
    form.zipField.focus()
    form.zipField.select()
  }
}


// STOP HIDING -->
</SCRIPT>
</HEAD>

<BODY
 onLoad="document.userAddress.nameField.focus()">
<TABLE WIDTH="100%" CELLPADDING=20>
  <TR>
    <TD>

      <P>JavaScript does several things in this FORM:

      <OL>
        <LI> Registers an onLoad event handler
        to set the focus to nameField.<P>

        <LI> Uses select() in onFocus event
        handlers on each text field to highlight
        the contents when the field obtains
        focus. You might have to enter some text
        in the fields and then use TAB to move around
        to see the effect. Or click in the field,
        then move your pointer out of the browser
        window and then back in. Also, try removing
        the onFocus lines to see the difference.<P>
```

```
        <LI> Registers an onChange event handler
        on the stateField. After you leave the field,???
        the value is converted to upper case.<P>

        <LI>Registers an onChange event handler
        on the zipField to validate the
        zip code. If an invalid zip is supplied,
        the user is asked to reenter. focus() and then
        select() are called on zipField.<P>
      </OL>
    </TD>
  </TR>
</TABLE><TABLE WIDTH="100%" CELLPADDING=20>
  <TR>
    <TH>Description
    <TH>Input FORM
  </TR>
  <TR>
    <TD>
      <P>This example expands on textValue.html to
      show field validation and using focus and
      select together. </P>

      <P>This page is formatted as a table. One row
     contains this text column and the FORM on the right.
      The FORM contains another TABLE to align the City,
      State, and Zip labels with the text fields
      below them.</P>

      <P>The description at the top of the page is another
      TABLE.</P>
    </TD>
        <TD>
      <FORM NAME="userAddress">
      <P><B>Name:</B><BR>
      <INPUT TYPE="text" NAME="nameField"
       VALUE="" SIZE=50
       onFocus="this.select()"
       ></P>
      <P><B>Address:</B><BR>
      <INPUT TYPE="text" NAME="addressField"
       VALUE="" SIZE=50
       onFocus="this.select()"
       ></P>
```

```
      <TABLE CELLSPACING=0 CELLPADDING=0>
   <TR>
     <TD><B>City:</B></TD>
     <TD><B>State:</B></TD>
     <TD><B>Zip:</B></TD>
   </TR>
   <TR>
     <TD>
     <INPUT TYPE="text" NAME="cityField"
      VALUE="" SIZE=32
           onFocus="this.select()"
           >
     </TD>
     <TD>
     <INPUT TYPE="text" NAME="stateField"
      VALUE="CA" SIZE=2
           onFocus="this.select()"
           onChange="this.value=
             this.value.toUpperCase()"
           >
     </TD>
     <TD>
     <INPUT TYPE="text" NAME="zipField"
      VALUE="99999-9999" SIZE=10
           onFocus="this.select()"
           onChange="verifyZip(this.form)"
           >
     </TD>
   </TR>
      </TABLE>
      <P><B>Comments:</B><BR>
      <INPUT TYPE="text" NAME="commentField"
       VALUE="" SIZE=50
       onFocus="this.select()"
       ></P>
      </FORM>
    </TD>
  </TR>
</TABLE>

</BODY>
</HTML>
```

Figure 16–10 shows the results of loading the `textValueVerify.html` script.

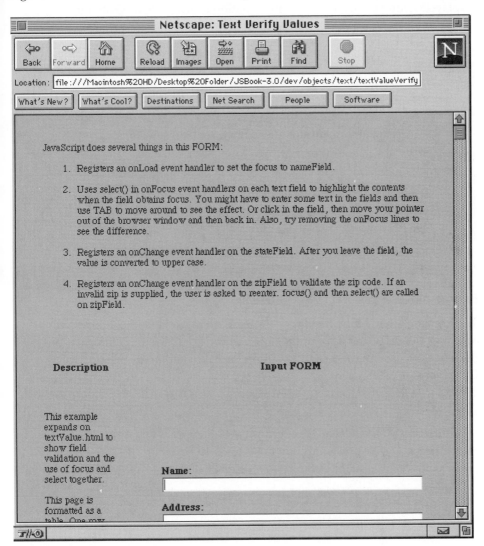

Figure 16–10 Result of loading the `textValueVerify.html` script

Loading the script does not, however, show the interesting features of this script. Load the script into your browser and either type an incorrect zip code into the Zip text field or delete the default zip code. An incorrect zip code is one that is blank or that contains alphabetic or symbol characters instead of numbers. When a user types an incorrect zip code and then leaves the text field, an alert is displayed telling the user that the information is incorrect, as shown in Figure 16–11.

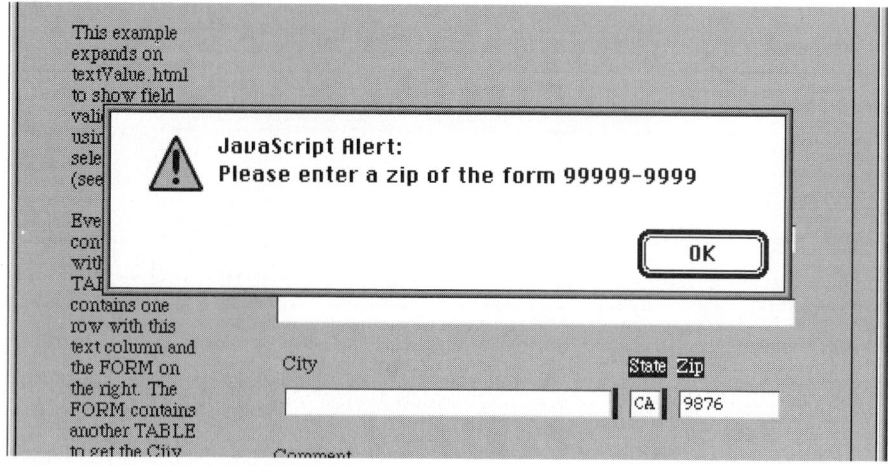

Figure 16–11 Incorrect zip code alert

The functions that define the data validation on this text field contain some scripting elements that have not yet been introduced. For more information on the elements used in the `isAZIP()` function, see Chapter 26, "Testing for Conditions."

UI Guideline – Notice that the alert tells users not only that they have committed an error, but what they need to do to correct it. Be sure to help your users as much as possible to understand what they need to do to get it right.

Catching an Event when the Text Field Has the Focus

You can use the `onFocus` event handler to catch an event when the text field has the focus.

Event Handler

onFocus

Syntax

```
<INPUT
TYPE="text"
NAME="fieldName"
VALUE="value" SIZE=n
onFocus="JavaScript code"
>
```

The following extract from the `textValue.html` file uses both the `onFocus` and `onChange` event handlers and the `select()` method to select the contents of the text field when it receives the input focus and to convert the contents to upper case when the user clicks outside of the text field.

```
<TD>
    <INPUT TYPE="text" NAME="stateField"
     VALUE="CA" SIZE=2
          onFocus="this.select()"
          onChange="this.value=
            this.value.toUpperCase()"
          >
    </TD>
```

See "Example of Using the text.value Property" on page 543 for the complete script.

Catching an Event when Text Is Selected

You can use the `onSelect` event handler to catch an event when text is selected.

Event Handler

onSelect

Syntax

```
<INPUT
TYPE="text"
NAME="fieldName"
VALUE="value" SIZE=n
onSelect="JavaScript code"
>
```

Catching an Event when a Text Field Loses the Focus

You can use the `onBlur` event handler to determine when a text field loses the focus.

Event Handler

onBlur

Syntax

```
<INPUT
TYPE="text"
NAME="fieldName"
VALUE="value" SIZE=n
onBlur="JavaScript code"
>
```

Catching an Event when the User Changes to Another Text Field

You can use the `onChange` event handler to verify data when the user leaves the text field.

Event Handler

onChange

Syntax

<INPUT

TYPE="text"

NAME="*fieldName*"

VALUE="*value*" SIZE=*n*

onChange="*JavaScript code*"

>

Example Using text Object Event Handlers

The following `textAddressForm.html` script uses the `onBlur`, `onChange`, and `onFocus` event handlers to control and verify the contents of each text field.

```
<!--
        textAddressForm.html

     This example creates text fields in an HTML
     form and uses the onBlur, onChange, and onFocus
     event handlers.
-->

<HTML>
<HEAD>
<TITLE>Address Input Form</TITLE>
<SCRIPT LANGUAGE="JavaScript">
<!-- HIDE FROM OLD BROWSERS

function required(val) {
  return
}
```

```
function verify(val) {
  return
}

// STOP HIDING -->
</SCRIPT>
</HEAD>

<BODY>

<P>The following form contains text fields that
have onBlur, onChange, and onFocus event handlers
to control the contents of each text field.</P>

<FORM>
<B>First Name: </B><BR>
<INPUT
 TYPE="text"
 NAME="firstName"
 VALUE=""
 SIZE=25
 onBlur="required(this.value)"
 onChange="verify(this.value)"
 onFocus="this.select()"
>

<BR><B>Last Name: </B><BR>
<INPUT
 TYPE="text"
 NAME="lastName"
 VALUE=""
 SIZE=25
 onBlur="required(this.value)"
 onChange="verify(this.value)"
 onFocus="this.select()"
>

<BR><B>Street Address: </B><BR>
<INPUT
 TYPE="text"
 NAME="address"
 VALUE=""
 SIZE=50
 onBlur="required(this.value)"
```

```
 onChange="verify(this.value)"
 onFocus="this.select()"
>

<BR><B>City: </B><BR>
<INPUT
 TYPE="text"
 NAME="city"
 VALUE=""
 SIZE=30
 onBlur="required(this.value)"
 onChange="verify(this.value)"
 onFocus="this.select()"
>

<B>State: </B>
<INPUT
 TYPE="text"
 NAME="state"
 VALUE="CA"
 SIZE=2
 onBlur="required(this.value)"
 onChange="this.value=this.value.toUpperCase();"
 onFocus="this.select()"
>

<B>Zip: </B>
<INPUT
 TYPE="text"
 NAME="zip"
 VALUE=""
 SIZE=5
 onBlur="required(this.value)"
 onChange="verify(this.value)"
 onFocus="this.select()"
>

<B>-</B>
<INPUT
 TYPE="text"
 NAME="zip4"
 VALUE=""
 SIZE=4
 onBlur="verify(this.value)"
```

```
  onChange="verify(this.value)"
  onFocus="this.select()"
>
</FORM>

</BODY>
</HTML>
```

Figure 16–12 shows the result of loading the `textAddressForm.html` script.

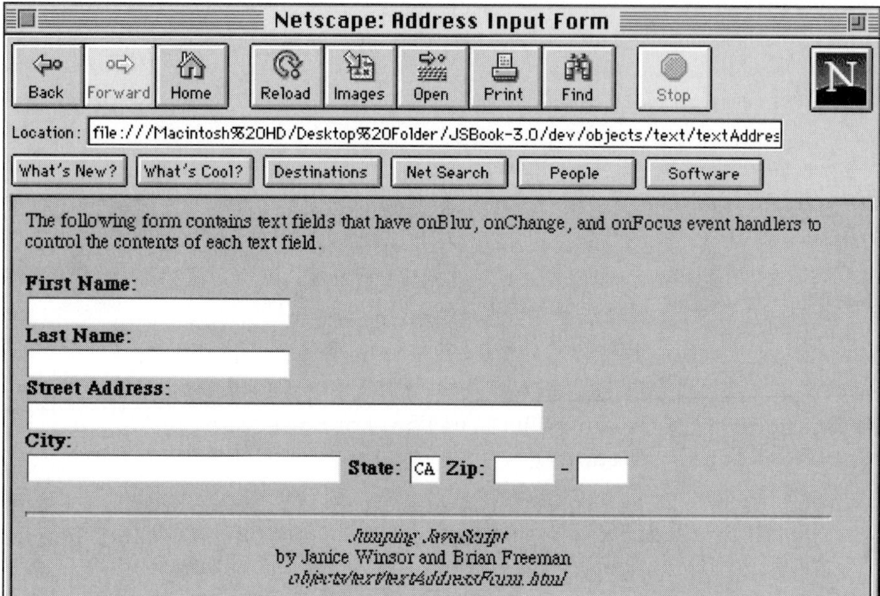

Figure 16–12 Result of loading the `textAddressForm.html` script

Type information into the text field and see what happens. Compare what you expect to happen with the statements in the script. You can expand on this script to do even more validation and error checking than is shown in this example.

Summary of New Terms and Concepts

The new terms and concepts introduced in this chapter are listed in alphabetical order in Table 16-2. The terms and concepts are also included in the glossary at the end of the book.

Table 16-2 Summary of New Terms and Concepts

Term/Concept	Description
change	The event that occurs when a user makes any alteration to the contents of a text field and then either tabs or clicks away from the field to blur the focus.
disk cache	A memory buffer area that contains a large block of information read from or to be written to the disk.
select	The event that occurs when a user highlights text by pressing the mouse button, dragging the pointer, and then releasing the mouse button.

CHAPTER 17

- Defining a Password Field
- The password Object

Adding Password Fields to a Document

The `password` object enables you to retrieve a password that users type into a single line in your Web page. This chapter describes how to create password fields and how to use the JavaScript `password` object to evaluate the password and use it in scripts.

Defining a Password Field

You defined a password field with the `<FORM></FORM>` and `<INPUT>` HTML tags. The visual design of password fields depends on the operating system the particular browser runs on. Figure 17–1 shows an example of a password field for the Macintosh system.

Password:

Figure 17–1 Password field style for the Macintosh system

The only part of the password field itself that you can control is the number of characters that it contains. The JavaScript language controls the rest of the visual elements of password fields. The color, height, and width of the text area are automatically created to accommodate the number of characters you assign to the password field. If you assign a long size to the password field, the password field created is long enough to accommodate the characters, even if it is wider than the

page. In addition, each operating system controls the feedback when the user clicks in a password field or highlights text. You cannot control any of these elements in a JavaScript program.

HTML Brushup — Creating a Password Field

You create a password field by using the <FORM></FORM> HTML tags and specifying the parts of the password field, using the <INPUT> tag with NAME and VALUE attributes, as shown below:

<FORM>

<INPUT TYPE = "password"

NAME = "*Field Name*"

VALUE = "*Contents*"

SIZE = "*Character Count*"

onBlur = "*JavaScript code*"

onChange = "*JavaScript code*"

onFocus = "*JavaScript code*"

onSelect = "*JavaScript code*">

</FORM>

You use the attributes to specify a name for the field. This name is not the same as the label for the password field but is the name you use in your script to identify the specific text field. You can create an empty text field by specifying VALUE="", or you can enter a default value. The size you specify is the number of characters users can type in the field. Browsers display text in a monospace font, usually Courier.

Example of Creating a Password Field

The following `password.html` script shows how to create one password field with a label and no contents.

```
<!--
         password.html
-->
<HTML>
<HEAD>
<TITLE>Password</TITLE>
</HEAD>
```

```
<BODY>

<P>The form below contains a single password
object. When you type into it, your input is
displayed as asterisks to prevent others from
seeing your password.

<FORM>
<BR><B>Password:</B>
<INPUT
 TYPE="password"
 NAME="userPasswd"
 VALUE=""
 SIZE=30
>
</FORM>

</BODY>
</HTML>
```

Figure 17–2 shows the results of loading the `password.html` script.

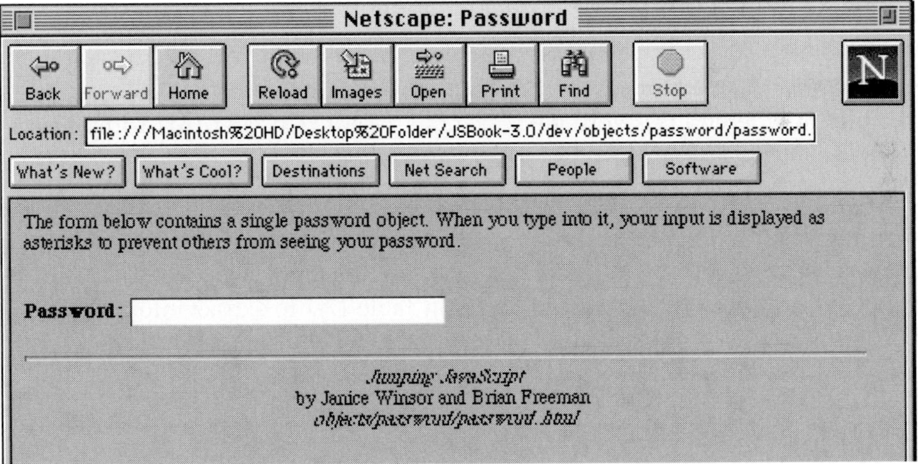

Figure 17–2 Result of loading the `password.html` script

UI Guideline – When creating password fields, always provide a Password label. Format the label for password fields in the same way as for the other text fields in your page. Use initial capital letters, a bold font, and a colon following the name. Users should be able to tell at a glance that the field is a password field. Because you cannot depend on consistent alignment, consider left-aligning your labels above a password field and other text fields so that the text fields themselves always start at the left margin. Remember when designing your password and text fields that different operating systems may display text fields in a different way than you expect.

Password Field Locations

The default location for password fields on a single line is to align the field with the left margin. Figure 17–3 shows the location and spacing for a password field with a label left-aligned above the text field on a Macintosh computer. This label is followed by `<BR>`. If you want more space between the label and the text field, you can use `<P>` instead.

Password:

Figure 17–3 Default password field alignment

As with other text fields, you can change the location of the text field by using `<CENTER></CENTER>` or `<DIV ALIGN=center | right></DIV>` tags. For examples of different password field locations, refer to Chapter 16, "Adding Text Fields to a Document."

The password Object

Once you have created a password field, you use the properties, methods, and event handlers listed in alphabetical order in Table 17-1 to extract information about the `password` object and to initiate actions when users correctly enter a password.

Table 17-1 Properties, Methods, and Event Handlers for the password Object

Properties	Methods	Event Handlers
`defaultValue`	`blur()`	`onBlur`
`form`	`eval()*`	`onChange`
`name`	`focus()`	`onFocus`
`type*`	`select()`	
`value`	`toString()*`	
	`valueOf()*`	

* New in the Navigator 3.0 release.

In Navigator 2.0, a script cannot extract the contents of the field (the `value` property) unless that value has been set as part of the `VALUE` attribute when the script was written.

In Navigator 3.0 and later releases, scripts can treat a `password` object exactly like a `text` object. Because scripts can now access properties of the `password` object that were blocked in previous releases, the `value` property can return the unencrypted value for a `password` object and store it in a cookie file. Storing unencrypted passwords is a potential security loophole. If you store passwords in a local cookie file, use an encryption algorithm on the value of a password object before you store it. Most password-protected sites routinely encrypt passwords before they are sent to a cookie file. If a user modifies a password field, you cannot evaluate it accurately unless data tainting is enabled.

To extract the current value from a `password` object, use the following syntax:

```
document.formName.fieldName.value
```

Password object values are always returned as strings. When you have obtained the string value, you can use the `document.cookie` property to store a user's password for your site.

Most interaction with passwords is handled by a CGI script on a server.

Note – HTML password fields hide the password when users type it into the password field, but the information is exchanged with the server in a way that is not secure. In addition, because you must define the password in the `VALUE` attribute, anyone who views the page as HTML can see the password.

The properties, methods, and event handlers for the password object are the same as those for the `text` and `textarea` objects except that the properties are read-only. For examples, refer to Chapter 16, "Adding Text Fields to a Document."

CHAPTER 18

- Defining Text Areas
- The textarea Object

Adding Text Areas to a Document

The `textarea` object enables you to capture text that users type into a multiple-line text area in your Web page. Users can enter up to 32,700 characters in a text area. Use the `text` object if you want to enable users to enter single lines of text. This chapter describes how to create text areas. For information on how to add text fields to your page, see Chapter 16, "Adding Text Fields to a Document." For information on how to send text data to a server, see Chapter 24, "Using Forms to Send Data to a Server." For information on manipulating text, see Chapter 28, "Working with Strings and String Objects."

Defining Text Areas

You defined text areas with the `<FORM></FORM>` HTML tags. Unlike the text object, which you create by using the `<INPUT>` tag, the text area has its own `<TEXTAREA></TEXTAREA>` HTML tags. The visual design of the text areas that are created depends on the operating system the particular browser runs on. Figure 18–1 shows an example of a text area for the Macintosh system.

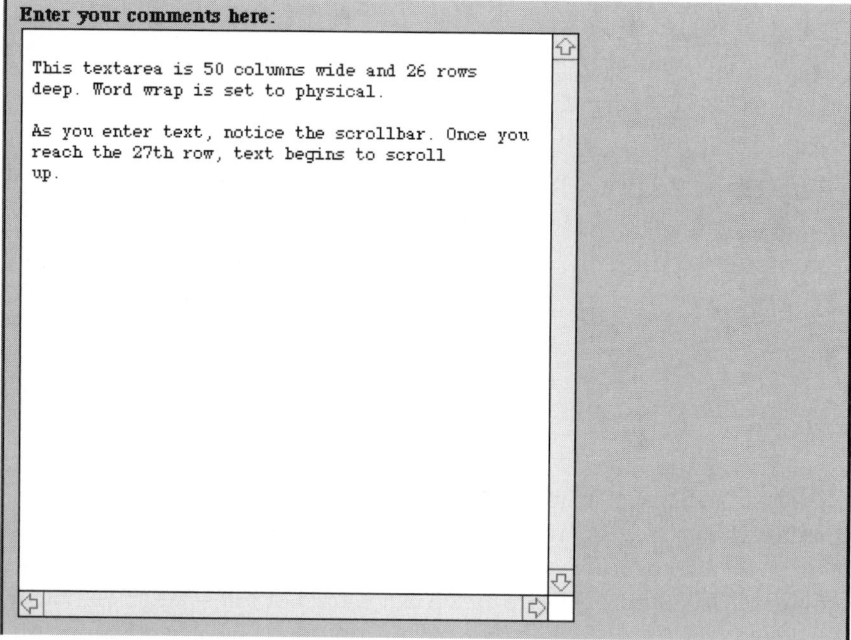

Enter your comments here:
This textarea is 50 columns wide and 26 rows
deep. Word wrap is set to physical.
As you enter text, notice the scrollbar. Once you
reach the 27th row, text begins to scroll
up.

Figure 18–1 Text area style for the Macintosh system

The parts of the text area itself that you can control are:

- The `ROW` attribute, which sets the number of rows (the number of lines in the text area)
- The `COLS` attribute, which sets the number of columns (the number of characters on a line)
- The `WRAP` attribute, which sets how the text wraps: off, virtual, or physical

Scrollbars are automatically created for the text area. The way the scrollbars behave depends on how you set the `WRAP` attribute. When you set `WRAP = "off"`, any text the user inputs does not automatically wrap when it reaches the end of the line. Instead, the horizontal scrollbar at the bottom of the text area is activated, and the text stretches out in one long horizontal line. If you do not specify a value for the `WRAP` attribute, the system uses `off` as the default.

When you set `WRAP = "virtual"`, the text wraps at the end of each row without requiring a new line, but the text is sent exactly as typed.

When you set `WRAP = "physical"`, the text wraps at the end of each row and sends new lines at the wrap points as if the user had typed them.

The JavaScript language controls the rest of the visual elements of text areas, including the color of the area, its text, and the design of the scrollbars. In addition, each operating system controls the feedback when the user clicks in a text field or highlights text. You cannot control any of these elements in a JavaScript program.

HTML Brushup — Creating Text Areas

You create a text area by using the <FORM></FORM> HTML tags and specifying the parts of the text field by using the <TEXTAREA></TEXTAREA> tags with NAME and VALUE attributes, as shown below:

<FORM>

<TEXTAREA

(NAME = "*Field Name*")

(ROWS = "*NumberOfRows*")

(COLS = "*NumberOfColumns*")

(WRAP = "off" | "virtual" | "physical")

(onBlur = "*JavaScript code*")

(onChange = "*JavaScript code*")

(onFocus = "*JavaScript code*")

(onSelect = "*JavaScript code*")>

(defaultText

</TEXTAREA>

</FORM>

You use the attributes to specify a name for the field. This name is the name you use in your script to identify the specific text field. You specify the size by using a number as the value for the ROWS and COLUMNS attributes. You specify the way text wraps by using the WRAP attribute.

You create an empty text area by not including any text between the end of the <TEXTAREA> tag and the beginning of the </TEXTAREA> tag. If you enter text, all text formatting, including white space, is considered to be part of the default text.

Example of Creating a Text Field

The following `textarea.html` script shows how to create a text area with a label and predefined contents. The script does not show how to do anything with the contents of the area.

```
<!--
        textarea.html

    This example creates a single text area in a
    form.
-->

<HTML>
<HEAD>
<TITLE>A Text Area</TITLE>
</HEAD>

<BODY>

<P>Below is a form that contains a text area.</P>

<FORM>
<B>Enter your comments here:</B>
<TEXTAREA
 NAME="comments"
 ROWS="26"
 COLS="80"
 WRAP="physical"
>
This textarea is 80 columns wide and 26 rows
deep. Word wrap is set to physical.

Notice the scrollbars. As you enter text, notice
that the text wraps when you reach the end of
each row. When you reach the 27th row, the
scrollbars are activated and text begins to
scroll up.

</TEXTAREA>
</FORM>

</BODY>
</HTML>
```

Figure 18–2 shows the results of loading the `textarea.html` script.

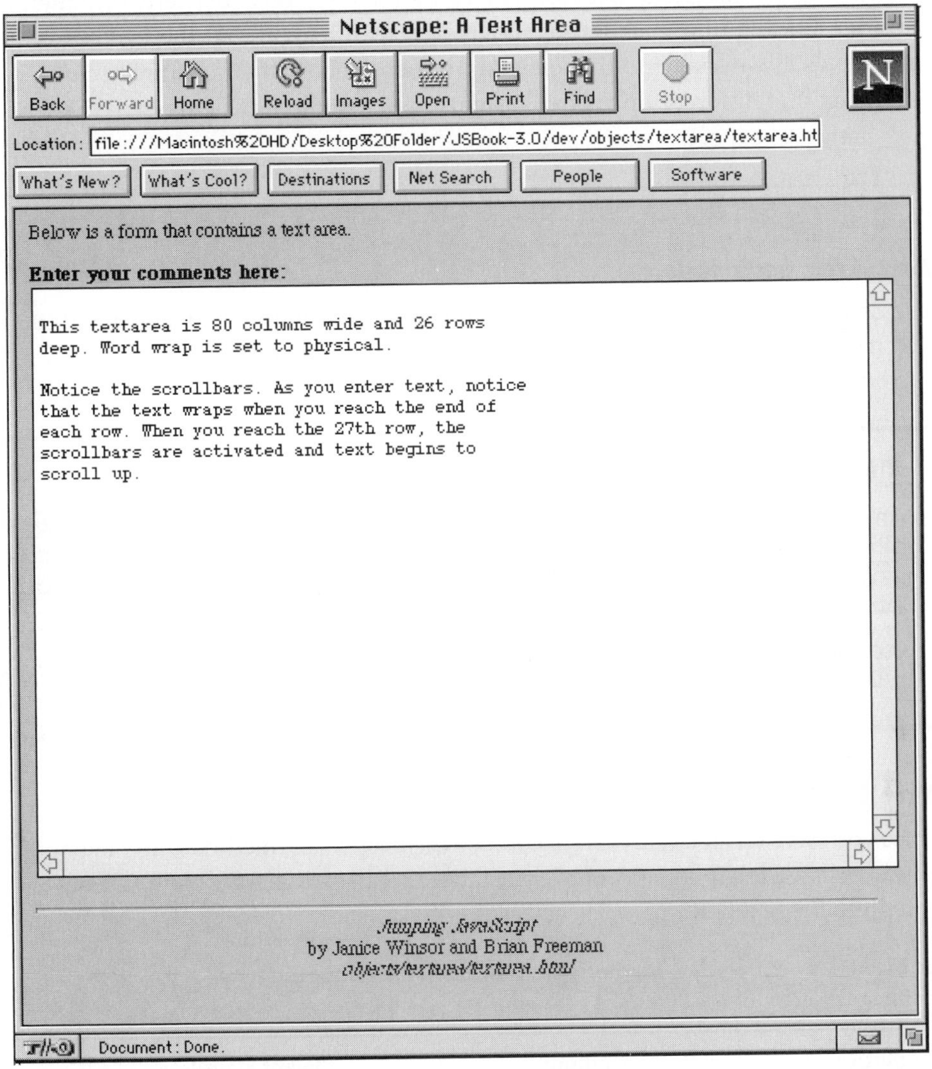

Figure 18–2 Result of `textarea.html` script

UI Guideline – When creating text areas, always provide a label. Keep the label short and easy to read. Consider formatting all text area labels in the same way. Use initial capital letters, a bold font, and a colon following the name. Users should be able to tell at a glance what kind of information you expect them to type into the text area. Always position labels in the same way, either above or to the left of the text field. Because you cannot depend on consistent alignment, consider left-aligning your labels above each text field so that the text fields themselves always start at the left margin. Remember when designing your text fields that different operating systems may display text fields in a different way than you expect.

Text Area Locations

The default location for text areas on a single line is to align the text area with the left margin, as shown in Figure 18–2. You can center the label and text field by surrounding the `<FORM></FORM>` definition with `<CENTER></CENTER>` tags

---

HTML Brushup — <DIV></DIV> Tags

An alternative HTML tag that you can use to format text areas, as well as any other form element, is the <DIV> tag. This tag is a Netscape 2.0 extension that is a proposed replacement for the nonstandard <CENTER> tag. The <DIV> tag accepts the ALIGN attribute with the possible values of LEFT | RIGHT | CENTER.

Use the <DIV ALIGN=right | left | center> before the <FORM> tag and the </DIV> tag after the </FORM> tag.

The textarea Object

Once you have created a text area, you use the properties, methods, and event handlers listed in alphabetical order in Table 18-1 to extract information users enter into the text field.

Table 18-1 **Properties, Methods, and Event Handlers for the textarea Object**

Properties	Methods	Event Handlers
`defaultValue`	`blur()`	`onBlur`
`form*`	`eval()*`	`onChange`
`name`	`focus()`	`onFocus`

Table 18-1 Properties, Methods, and Event Handlers for the textarea Object (Continued)

Properties	Methods	Event Handlers
`type*`	`select()`	`onSelect`
`value`	`toString()*`	
	`valueOf()*`	

* New in the Navigator 3.0 release.

These properties, methods, and event handlers are the same as those for the `text` object except that the properties are read-only. For examples of how to use them, refer to Chapter 16, "Adding Text Fields to a Document."

CHAPTER 19

- Defining the Button Action
- Referencing Button Names and Values
- The click Method
- submit and reset Objects
- Summary of New Terms and Concepts

Activating Buttons in a Document

You can use the `button` object to specify what happens when a user clicks on a button and to extract the name and value of buttons you defined with the `<FORM></FORM>` and `<INPUT>` HTML tags. The visual design of the buttons that are created depends on the operating system the particular browser runs on. Figure 19–1 shows examples of the buttons for Macintosh, Windows 95, and X Window™ systems.

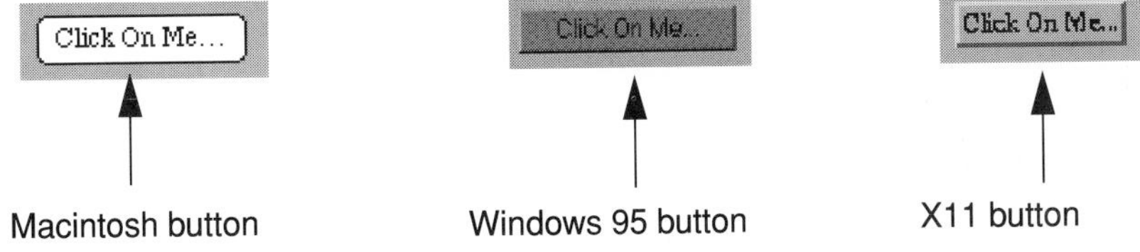

Figure 19–1 Button styles for Macintosh, Windows 95, and X systems

Because each operating system generates buttons in a different way, you may find that your button formatting is not consistent across all platforms.

The only part of the button itself that you can control is the text. The JavaScript language controls the rest of the visual elements of buttons. The color, height, and width of the button are automatically created to accommodate the length of the value you assign to the button. If you assign a lengthy value to the button, the button makes itself wide enough to accommodate the text, even if it is wider than

the page. If you include carriage returns or new line formatting as part of the value, they are displayed as characters. In addition, each operating system controls the feedback when the user clicks on a button. You cannot control any of these elements in a JavaScript program. You cannot assign an image to a button's appearance with Navigator 2.0 and 3.0 releases. You can, however, create a mouse-sensitive image map that acts like a link. For more information on images, see Chapter 9, "Working with Images."

HTML Brushup — Creating Buttons

You create buttons by using the <FORM></FORM> HTML tags and specifying the parts of the button as part of the <INPUT> tag with NAME and VALUE attributes, as shown below:

```
<FORM>
<INPUT TYPE = "button"
(NAME = "Button Name")
VALUE = "Button Text"
onClick = "JavaScript code"
onFocus = "JavaScript code"
onBlur = "JavaScript code">
</FORM>
```

You also include the onClick() event handler as part of the <INPUT> tag. See "Defining the Button Action" on page 592 for a description of the onClick() event handler.

The <FORM></FORM> HTML tags also have NAME, TARGET, ACTION, METHOD, and ENCTYPE attributes that you must set if you create a form that sends input to a Web server. For more information about creating forms that interact with the server, see Chapter 24, "Using Forms to Send Data to a Server."

UI Guideline – When creating button labels, keep button text short (no more than two or three words). Users should be able to tell at a glance what action to expect if they click on a button. Make sure the label of the button describes the action that results when your users click on the button. Use verbs as labels for

buttons that perform an action, such as Back, Forward, Display Information, or Close Window. Use initial capital letters for each word of the label to make sure all of your buttons have the same look.

The default position for buttons on a single line is to align them with the left margin. The following code extract creates two buttons with the default alignment. Navigator automatically creates the space between the two buttons.

```
<FORM>
<INPUT TYPE="button" VALUE="Set Timeout"
 onClick="startTiming()">
<INPUT TYPE="button" VALUE="Clear Timeout"
 onClick="stopTiming()">
</FORM>
```

You can omit the `NAME` attribute because you usually do not need to refer to buttons by name in your scripts.

Figure 19–2 shows the location and spacing between the buttons created by this code.

Figure 19–2 Default button alignment

You can center the buttons by surrounding the `<FORM></FORM>` definition with `<CENTER></CENTER>` tags, as shown in the following code extract.

```
<CENTER>
<FORM>
<INPUT TYPE="button" VALUE="Set Timeout"
 onClick="startTiming()">
<INPUT TYPE="button" VALUE="Clear Timeout"
 onClick="stopTiming()">
</FORM>
</CENTER>
```

Figure 19–3 shows the location and spacing between the buttons created by this code on a Macintosh computer.

Figure 19–3 Centered buttons

You can also position buttons by using the `<DIV ALIGN="where"></DIV>` tags. For an example of how to use these tags, see Chapter 16, "Adding Text Fields to a Document."

The properties, methods, and event handlers for the `button` object are listed in alphabetical order in Table 19-1.

Table 19-1 **Properties, Methods, and Event Handlers for the button Object**

Properties	Methods	Event Handlers
name	click()	onBlur
form*	eval()*	onClick
type*	toString()*	onFocus
value	valueOf()*	

* New in the Navigator 3.0 release.

Defining the Button Action

Because you create and name buttons by using attributes for the HTML `<INPUT>` tag, you may find that for basic scripts, the only JavaScript component of the `button` object that you need to use is the `onClick` event handler. For that reason, we describe the event handler first.

The button object has one event handler, onClick, that you use to specify what you want to happen when users click on the button.

Event Handler

onClick

Syntax

<FORM>

<INPUT TYPE = "button"

NAME = "*Button Name*"

VALUE = "*Button Text*"

onClick = "*JavaScript code*">

</FORM>

All button action takes place in response to the onClick event handler that specifies the JavaScript code or function that you want to take effect when users click on the button. A *click* takes place when users move the mouse pointer onto a button and press and release the mouse button. The event happens only after the mouse button is released, not while the mouse button is held down.

Example of onClick Event Handler

The following button.html script creates a button with an onClick event handler that displays an alert when the user clicks on the button.

```
<!--
          button.html
-->

<HTML>
<HEAD>
<TITLE>A Button</TITLE>
</HEAD>

<BODY>

<P>This script defines a form that contains a single
button. The button has an onClick event handler
registered that displays an alert dialog when
the button is clicked.</P>
```

```
<FORM>
<INPUT
 TYPE="button"
 NAME="myButton"
 VALUE="Click On Me..."
 onClick="alert('Ouch!')"
>
</FORM>

</BODY>
</HTML>
```

Figure 19–4 shows the result of loading the `button.html` script.

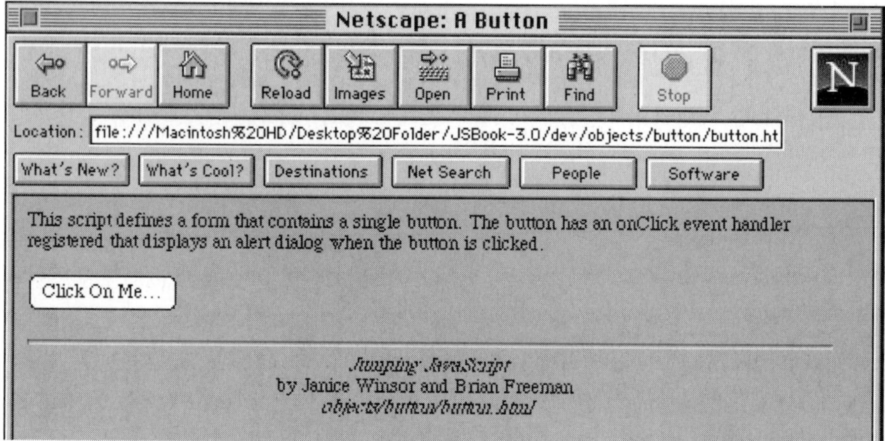

Figure 19–4 Result of loading the `button.html` script

When you click on the button, the `onClick` event handler displays an alert dialog, as shown in Figure 19–5.

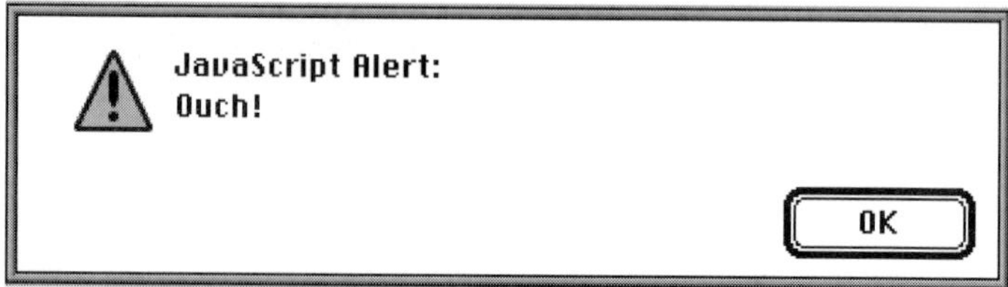

Figure 19–5 The `onClick` event handler displays an alert when you click on the button

Referencing Button Names and Values

The button object has two properties that enables you to get the name and value assigned to the button.

Property	Value	Gettable	Settable
name	string	Yes	No
value	string	Yes	No

If you want to extract the value from a button object, you must give the button a name. You are not likely to use these properties unless you want to extract the name of a button that the user has clicked on. The button object has the name and value properties to be consistent with the other user interface objects. With radio buttons, check boxes, selection lists, and text objects, you need to assign a name to the object so that you can extract the value set by the user. You'll see examples of how to use these properties in Chapter 21, "Using Radio Buttons and Hidden Objects."

The click Method

The button object has one method that enable you to activate a button from a script without having a user click on the button.

Method

click()

Returns

Nothing

Because you include buttons in a script so users can click on them, the click() method is not one you're likely to use much.

Note – The `click()` method does not work properly in any of the Navigator 2.0 releases and may not work properly on some platform implementations of the Navigator 3.0 release.

Example of Using the click() Method

When the `click()` method works properly, the following `buttonClick.html` script should automatically click on the Click On Me button and display an alert.

```
<!--
       buttonClick.html
-->
<HTML>
<HEAD>
<TITLE>Button Click Method</TITLE>
<SCRIPT LANGUAGE="JavaScript">
<!-- HIDE FROM OLD BROWSERS

function startTiming() {
  var alertID

  alertID=setTimeout(
    "document.myForm.myButton.click()", 100)
}

// STOP HIDING -->
</SCRIPT>
</HEAD>

<BODY onLoad="startTiming()">

<P>This script sets a timeout when the
document is loaded that should automatically
click the Click On Me button and display an alert.
</P>
<P>In most releases, when the timer goes off,
the button does not receive the click event.
You can click on the button yourself to see
the alert.
```

```
<FORM NAME="myForm">
<INPUT TYPE="button" NAME="myButton"
 VALUE="Click On Me"
 onClick="alert('Ouch!')"
>
</FORM>

</BODY>
</HTML>
```

If the script works properly, your page should look like Figure 19–6 without any action on your part.

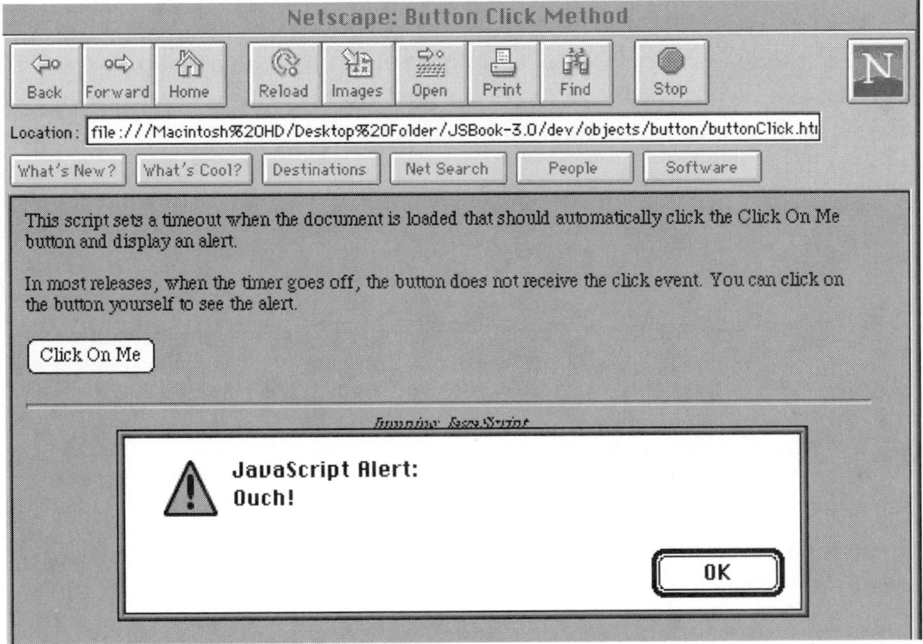

Figure 19–6 Result of loading the `buttonClick.html` script

Security Loophole with click() Method

In the October issue of JavaWorld, Gordon McComb discusses how "wiley [sic] Webmasters can again employ JavaScript to collect e-mail addresses of visitors without their knowledge." Using the `click()` method in combination with the `hidden` object and the `submit` object, creative hackers can extract information from users without their permission. Fortunately, in Netscape's Options, Network Preferences, Protocols tab, the default is to provide a check mark for the option that displays an alert any time you perform an action that submits a form by e-mail. You can disable the Submitting a Form by Email option if you want, so that forms are automatically submitted without notifying you. For the complete text of this article, see `http://www.javaworld.com/javaworld/jw-10-1996/jw-10-jsbug.html`. Although this URL is correct, you may have to start at the top level and work your way down to it.

submit and reset Objects

The JavaScript language provides two special cases of the `button` object: `submit` and `reset`. These two types of button objects perform their own special operations.

The Submit button automatically sends the data from the `<FORM></FORM>` definition to the URL listed in the `ACTION` attribute, in a format specified by the `METHOD` attribute. If your HTML page is communicating with a CGI program on the server, you do not need to write special script to perform these actions. All you need to do to create a submit button is to set `TYPE="submit"`, as shown in the following example:

```
<FORM>
<INPUT TYPE="submit" VALUE="Submit"
</FORM>
```

UI Guideline – Although you can use any value for the `submit` button object, we strongly recommend that you use the word `Submit` as the value.

You can see an example of how to use the `submit` object in Chapter 24, "Using Forms to Send Data to a Server."

The Reset button restores all elements with the form to their default values: text objects, selection lists, checkboxes, and radio button groups. The most common use of this special button is to clear entry fields of the last data entered by the user. All you need to do to create a Reset button is to set `TYPE="reset"`, as shown in the following example:

```
<FORM>
<INPUT TYPE="reset" VALUE="Reset"
 onClick="JavaScript code">
</FORM>
```

UI Guideline – Although you can use any value for the `reset` button object, we strongly recommend that you use the word `Reset` as the value.

Example of the reset Object

The following `reset.html` script contains a Reset button that you can use to return the form elements to their default values.

```
<!--
          reset.html
-->
<HTML>
<HEAD>
<TITLE>Reset Button</TITLE>
</HEAD>
<BODY>
<P>The form below contains a Reset button. When
you click on it, all the other form objects are
returned to their default values.</P>

<FORM NAME="userForm">
<P><B>Gender:</B>
<INPUT TYPE="hidden"
 NAME="answer" VALUE="gender-m">
<INPUT TYPE="radio"
 NAME="genderRadio" VALUE="gender-m"
 CHECKED
 onClick="userForm.answer.value='gender-m'"
> Male
<INPUT TYPE="radio"
 NAME="genderRadio" VALUE="gender-f"
 onClick="userForm.answer.value='gender-f'"
> Female
<P><B>First Name:</B><BR>
<INPUT TYPE="text"
 NAME="firstName" VALUE="" SIZE=20
><BR>
<B>M.I.:</B><BR>
<INPUT TYPE="text"
 NAME="middleInitial" VALUE="" SIZE=1
```

```
><BR>
<B>Last Name:</B><BR>
<INPUT TYPE="text"
 NAME="lastName" VALUE="" SIZE=30
><BR>
<P>
<INPUT TYPE="reset"
 NAME="resetBtn" VALUE="Reset"
>
</FORM>
</BODY>
</HTML>
```

Figure 19–7 shows the result of loading the `reset.html` script.

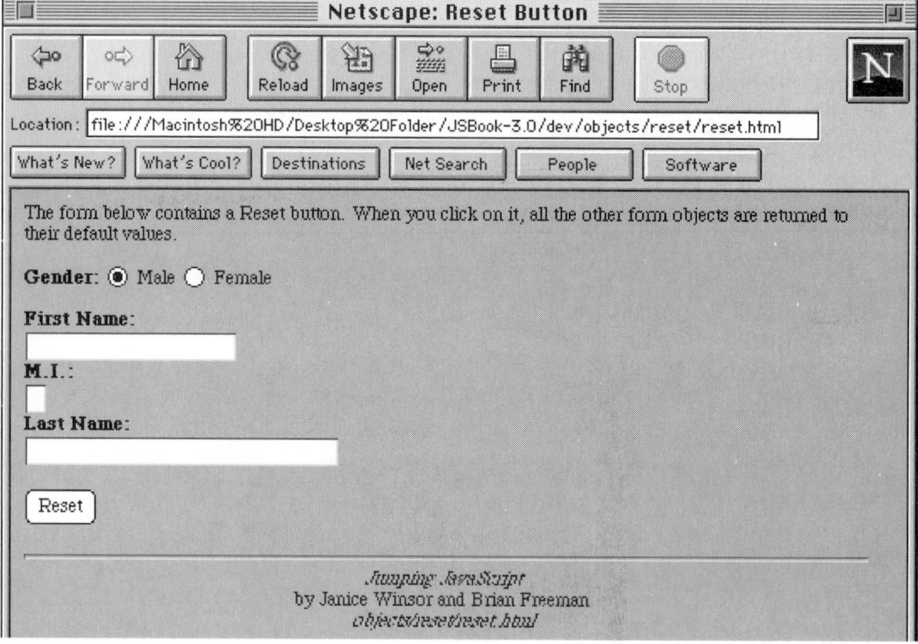

Figure 19–7 Results of loading the `reset.html` script

This script gives you a preview of how to create radio buttons. For more information about how to create radio buttons, see Chapter 21, "Using Radio Buttons and Hidden Objects." Although some might argue whether Male or Female should be the default setting, it's just an example. If you don't like the

default setting, you can edit the script to rewrite it your way. When you click on the Female radio button or type text in the text fields, you can return the form to its original state by clicking on the Reset button.

Summary of New Terms and Concepts

The new terms and concepts introduced in this chapter are listed in alphabetical order in Table 19-2. The terms and concepts are also included in the glossary at the end of the book.

Table 19-2 **Summary of New Terms and Concepts**

Term/Concept	Description
click	The event that occurs when users move the mouse pointer onto a button and press and release the mouse button.

CHAPTER 20

- Defining Check Boxes
- The checkbox Object
- Getting checkbox Object Names
- Getting checkbox Object Values
- Getting and Setting Check Marks
- Getting a Default Value for a checkbox Object
- Determining the Type of a Form Object
- Clicking on a Check Box
- Performing Script Actions onClick

Using Check Boxes

Check boxes enable you to provide a graphical way for users to choose a Yes or No answer to a question or to make an On or Off choice. When the box contains a check, the label text is true. When the box is empty, the label text is false. Each check box is independent of other check boxes. If you want to provide a set of interrelated Yes/No elements, use a group of radio buttons. For information about how to use radio buttons, see Chapter 21, "Using Radio Buttons and Hidden Objects."

Defining Check Boxes

You defined check boxes with the `<FORM></FORM>` and `<INPUT>` HTML tags. The visual design of the check boxes that are created depends on the operating system the particular browser runs on. Figure 20–1 shows an example of check boxes for the Macintosh system.

Figure 20–1 Check box style for the Macintosh system

The only part of the check box itself that you can control is its label and the default state. The JavaScript language controls the rest of the visual elements of check boxes. The color, height, and width of the check box are automatically created. In addition, each operating system controls the feedback (checked or blank) when the user clicks in a check box. You cannot control any of these elements in a JavaScript program.

HTML Brushup — Creating Check Boxes

You create a check box by using the <FORM></FORM> HTML tags and specifying the parts of the check box by using the <INPUT> tag with NAME and VALUE attributes, as shown below. If you want the default state of the box to be checked, you include the CHECKED attribute:

<FORM>

<INPUT TYPE = "checkbox"

NAME = "*Box Name*"

VALUE = "*checkboxValue*"

(CHECKED)

onClick = "*JavaScript code*"

checkboxLabel

</FORM>

The <FORM></FORM> HTML tags also have NAME, TARGET, ACTION, METHOD, and ENCTYPE attributes that you must set if you create a form that sends input to a Web server. For more information about creating forms that interact with the server, see Chapter 24, "Using Forms to Send Data to a Server."

Check box names must be a contiguous string of numbers and characters with no spaces. Assign unique and descriptive names to your check boxes to help you read and debug your scripts.

Example of Creating a Check Box

The following `checkbox.html` script shows how to create check boxes with labels and checked default state. Each check box has an `onClick` event handler that displays an alert showing the value of the check box when it is clicked. This example shows that you can initiate scripting actions when users click on a check box. Because the check box itself gives users feedback, you do not need to also display an alert to show that the box has changed state. You might, however, want to display an alert in certain situations when users click on a particular check box.

```
<!--
         checkbox.html
-->
<HTML>
<HEAD>
<TITLE>Checkbox</TITLE>
</HEAD>

<BODY>

<P>Below is a form that contains a single
check box. The check box has an onClick event
handler registered that displays an alert
dialog containing its value when clicked.</P>

<FORM>
<INPUT
 TYPE="checkbox"
 NAME="myCheckbox"
 CHECKED
 onClick="(this.checked) ?
           this.value='on' :
           this.value='off' ;
         alert(this.value)"
>
Click on the box
</FORM>

<P>Below is a form that contains multiple
check boxes. Notice that checking one does not
affect the settings of the others. If you want a
group of dependent settings, use radio
buttons.</P>

<FORM>
<INPUT
 TYPE="checkbox"
 NAME="cb_one"
 CHECKED
 onClick="(this.checked) ?
           this.value='on' :
           this.value='off' ;
         alert(this.value)"
>
```

```
One
<INPUT
 TYPE="checkbox"
 NAME="cb_two"
 CHECKED
 onClick="(this.checked) ?
            this.value='on' :
            this.value='off' ;
          alert(this.value)"
>
Two
<INPUT
 TYPE="checkbox"
 NAME="cb_three"
 CHECKED
 onClick="(this.checked) ?
            this.value='on' :
            this.value='off' ;
          alert(this.value)"
>
Three
</FORM>

</BODY>
</HTML>
```

Figure 20–2 shows the results of loading the `checkbox.html` script.

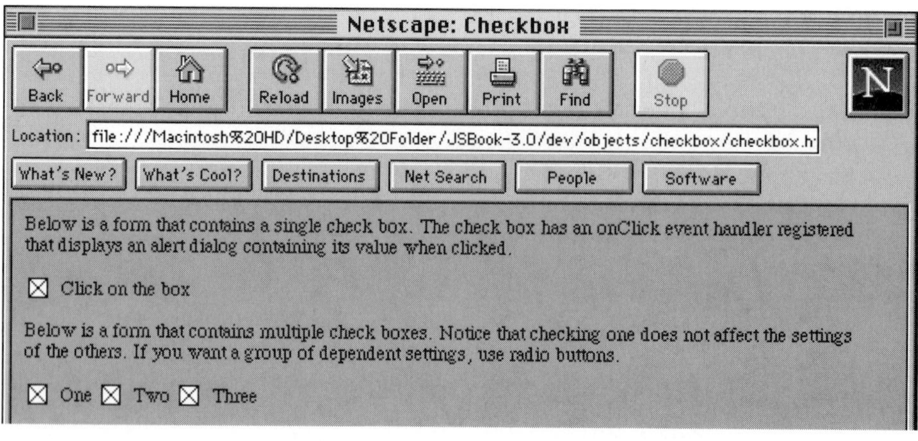

Figure 20–2 Result of loading the `checkbox.html` script

UI Guideline – When creating check boxes, be sure to use them only to toggle between On/Off or Yes/No settings. Do not use check boxes to initiate processes. When choosing labels for check boxes, keep the label short and easy to read. Consider formatting all check box labels in the same way. Use initial capital letters for the label. Users should be able to tell at a glance what kind of setting they are choosing or what kind of information you expect a Yes or No answer to.

Always position labels in the same way, either to the left or to the right of the check box. Because you cannot depend on consistent alignment, consider putting the check box on the left and the label on the right so that the check boxes are always aligned with one another. Remember when designing your check boxes that different operating systems may display check boxes in a different way than you expect. If you put the label on the left, follow it with a colon.

You can use check boxes for a single control, but they are best used in groups. When arranged in a matrix, check boxes provide a compact way to enable users to set groups of related properties. Use a matrix of check boxes when you would otherwise have to repeat labels.

When you use check boxes in a matrix, consider using the `<TABLE></TABLE>` HTML tags to format the matrix. Remember, however, that these tags are an HTML 2 extension and may not be supported on all browsers.

Check Box Locations

The placement of check boxes depends on the HTML code that defines them. Figure 20–3 shows the location and spacing for a check box followed by a label.

☒ Click on the Box

Figure 20–3 Default checkbox alignment

You can put the label in front of the check box by putting the `checkboxLabel` before the `<INPUT>` tag, as shown in the following code extract.

HTML Brushup — <TABLE></TABLE> Tags

The following list describes the basic HTML attributes for the <TABLE></TABLE> tags, in alphabetical order.

BORDER=*n*	This optional attribute creates borders around the table, using the width specified by the number *n*, in pixels.
CAPTION	Use to create a caption for the table.
CELLPADDING=*n*	Specifies the number of pixels between the edge of a cell and its contents. If you do not use this attribute, the default cell padding is one pixel.
CELLSPACING=*n*	Specifies the number of pixels between adjacent cells in a table and along the outer edges of cells along the edges of a table. If you do not use this attribute, the default cell spacing is 2 pixels.
COLS=*n*	Specifies the number of columns in the table.
RULES	Specifies where rules are drawn in the inside of the table. Rules takes the following values: NONE (no rules), GROUPS (put rules between groups), ROWS (horizontal rules between all rows), COLS (vertical rules between all columns), or ALL (lines between everything). Note that setting RULES=ALL is the same as setting the BORDER attribute.
WIDTH=*n* or *n*%	Specifies the width of the table. You can enter the width in pixels or specify it as a percentage of the width of the page.

You start each row in a table with the <TR> table row tag. <TR> takes the following attributes:

ALIGN=left | right	Controls text alignment within table cells, not the alignment of the table within the text flow.
VALIGN	Sets the default vertical alignment for the table cells. VALIGN takes one of four values: TOP, MIDDLE, BOTTOM, and BASELINE. You can override this alignment for individual cells by specifying an alignment attribute with the cell tag.

```
<FORM>
<B>Click on the box:</B>
<INPUT
 TYPE="checkbox"
 NAME="myCheckbox"
 CHECKED
 onClick="(this.checked) ?
            this.value='on' :
            this.value='off' ;
          alert(this.value)"
>
</FORM>
```

Figure 20–4 shows the results of this code sample on a Macintosh computer.

Click on the Box: ☒

Figure 20–4 Label and check box

Figure 20–5 shows an example of a right-aligned check box and label. See the HTML Brushup box for an example of the code that generates this alignment.

Click on the Box: ☒

Figure 20–5 Right-aligned check box and label (Macintosh)

The following `checkboxTable.html` script shows several different check box matrixes created with the `<TABLE></TABLE>` tags:

```
<!--
          checkboxTable.html
-->
<HTML>
<HEAD>
<TITLE>Check Box Layout</TITLE>
</HEAD>
<BODY>
<H1 ALIGN=CENTER>Check Box Layout</H1>
<P>You can create different flows of text using
TABLES. These tables have a border width of 1 so
you can see where the tables are. You can remove
the border by setting a border width of 0 or
omitting the BORDER attribute.</P>
<P>Here is a table used to align check box
labels:</P>
```

```
<TABLE BORDER=1 CELLSPACING=0 CELLPADDING=0>
<TR VALIGN=top>
<TD>
<FORM NAME="form1">
<INPUT TYPE="checkbox"
 NAME="checkbox1"
CHECKED>
</FORM>
</TD>

<TD>
<P>Check box
</TD>
</TR>

<TR VALIGN=top>
<TD>
<FORM NAME="form2">
<INPUT TYPE="checkbox"
 NAME="checkbox1"
 CHECKED>
</FORM>
</TD>

<TD>
<P>Check box
</TD>
</TR>
</TABLE>

<P>In the following example, a table is used to
separate a document into one section with
controls and one section with text.</P>

<TABLE WIDTH="100%" BORDER=1
CELLSPACING=0 CELLPADDING=10>
<TR>
<TD>
<FORM NAME="form3">
<INPUT TYPE="checkbox"
 NAME="checkbox1"
 CHECKED>
Check box<BR>
```

```
<INPUT TYPE="checkbox"
 NAME="checkbox2"
 CHECKED>
Check box<BR>
</FORM>
</TD>

<TD>
<P>To the left is a FORM containing two
check boxes. More text is needed, so: It was a
dark and stormy night. All of the beagles were
safely in their kennels. The bats flew around the
tower, squeaking frantically.</P>

<P>Dosolina stood at the open window wistfully
gazing out over the moors, her long dark tresses
blowing wildly as the wind gusted. Piotor was
long overdue. There were evil things afoot in the
night, and she feared greatly for his safety.</P>
</TD>
</TR>

<TR>
<TD>
<FORM NAME="form4">
<INPUT TYPE="checkbox"
 NAME="checkbox1"
 CHECKED>Check box<BR>
<INPUT TYPE="checkbox"
 NAME="checkbox2"
 CHECKED>Check box<BR>
<INPUT TYPE="checkbox"
 NAME="checkbox3"
 CHECKED>Check box<BR>
</FORM>
</TD>

<TD>
<P>To the left is a FORM containing three
check boxes</P>

<P>There was something unnatural about the light
flickering through the clouds. The beagles bugled
their howls, protesting their captivity.</P>
```

```
</TD>
</TR>
</TABLE>
</DL>

</BODY>
</HTML>
```

Figure 20–6 shows the result of loading the `checkboxTable.html` script.

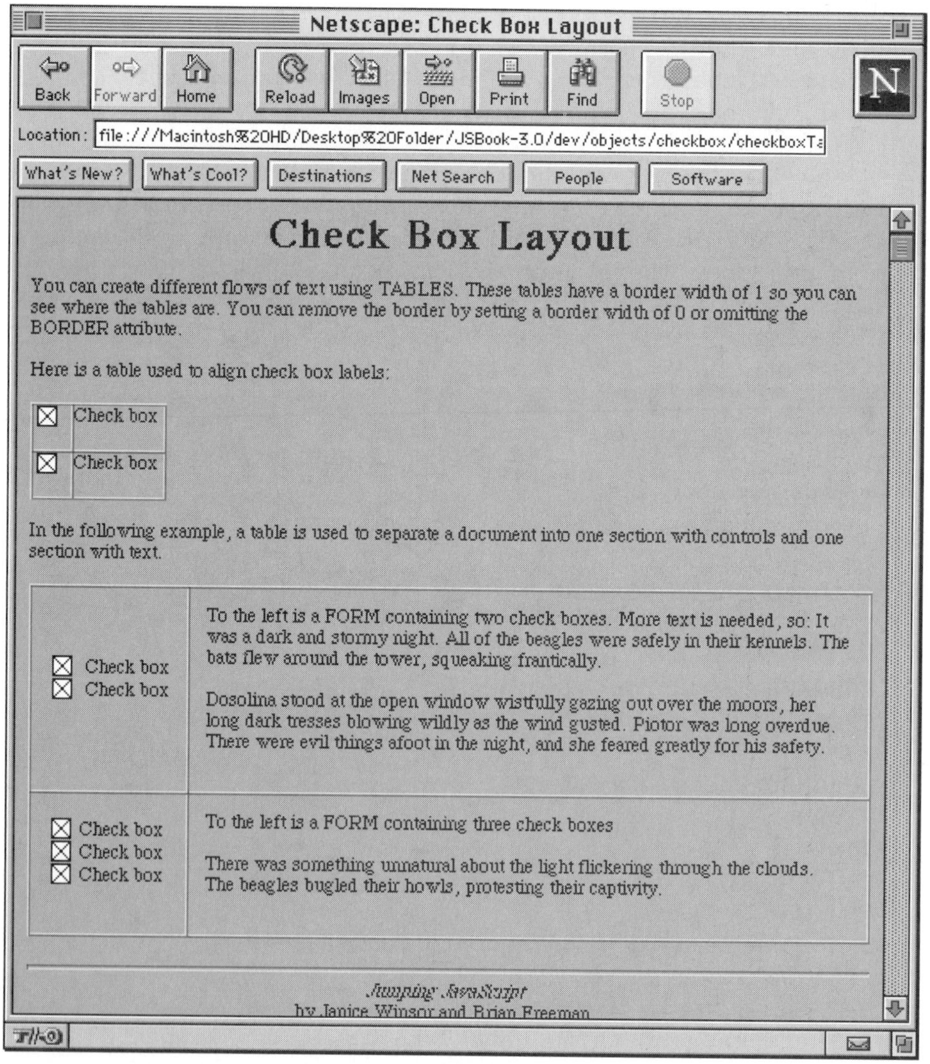

Figure 20–6 Check boxes with table formatting

You may need to experiment with alignment in a table matrix to get the baseline of the text box and the baseline of the text to line up properly. Notice in the script example, that the check boxes in the first table align the text with the top of the cell through the use of the `VALIGN` attribute for the table row:

```
<TR VALIGN=top>
```

Be sure to always verify your formatting and alignment to create a professional-looking page. The following code extract shows a table with no borders and with well-aligned labels:

```
<TABLE BORDER=0 CELLSPACING=0 CELLPADDING=0>
<TR VALIGN=top>
<TD>
<FORM NAME="form1">
<INPUT TYPE="checkbox"
 NAME="checkbox1"
CHECKED>
</FORM>
</TD>

<TD>
<P>Check box
</TD>
</TR>

<TR VALIGN=top>
<TD>
<FORM NAME="form2">
<INPUT TYPE="checkbox"
 NAME="checkbox1"
 CHECKED>
</FORM>
</TD>

<TD>
<P>Check box
</TD>
</TR>
</TABLE>
```

Figure 20–7 shows the results of this formatting.

Here is a table used to align check box labels:

☒ Check box

☒ Check box

Figure 20–7 Check box table with no borders and good alignment

The checkbox Object

Once you have created one or more check boxes, you use the properties, methods, and event handlers for the `checkbox` object, listed in alphabetical order in Table 20-1, to extract information about the state of the check boxes.

Table 20-1 Properties, Methods, and Event Handlers for the checkbox Object

Properties	Methods	Event Handlers
`checked`	`click()`	`onBlur*`
`defaultChecked`	`eval()*`	`onClick`
`form*`	`toString()*`	`onFocus*`
`name`	`valueOf()*`	
`type*`		
`value`		

* New in the Navigator 3.0 release.

You access `checkbox` object properties or methods by using the following syntax:

```
[window.]document.formName.boxName.property |
method([parameters])
[window.]document.formName.elements[index].property |
method([parameters])
[window.]document.forms[index].boxName.property |
method([parameters])
[window.]document.forms[index].elements[index].property |
method([parameters])
```

Getting checkbox Object Names

Names of `checkbox` objects are important in identifying individual check boxes within your JavaScript program as well as in submitting information to CGI scripts on a server.

Property	Value	Gettable	Settable
name	string	Yes	No

Getting checkbox Object Values

You can use the `value` property to extract the value of a `checkbox` object.

Property	Value	Gettable	Settable
value	string	Yes	No

The value of a `checkbox` object is different from the checked or unchecked state that you assign to the check box when you create it. The value can be a string of text that you want to associate with the box. For example, the label you assign to a check box may not be phrased in a way that is useful in your script. However, if you place the alternative wording in the `VALUE` attribute of the `<INPUT>` definition, you can extract that string by using the `value` property.

If you do not assign a string to the `VALUE` attribute, the `value` property always returns the string `"on."` If you submit the results of your script to a CGI program, the value is included as part of the submission when the box is checked. If the box is not checked, nothing is submitted.

You can use the value property to initiate an action when the box is checked or when data from your document is submitted to a CGI program.

Example of Using Check Box Values

The `checkboxValue.html` script below uses the `value` property to extract the values for each check box.

```
<!--
          checkboxValues.html
-->

<HTML>
<HEAD>
<TITLE>Checkbox Value</TITLE>
<SCRIPT LANGUAGE="JavaScript">
<!-- HIDE FROM OLD BROWSERS

function displayValue() {
  var msg_str = ""

  for (var f=0; f < document.forms.length; f++) {
    var theform = document.forms[f]

    if (theform != document.btnForm) {
     for (var e=0; e < theform.length; e++) {
   msg_str += "\n" + theform.elements[e].name
   msg_str += " = " + theform.elements[e].value
      }
    }
  }
  alert(msg_str)
}

// STOP HIDING -->
</SCRIPT>
</HEAD>

<BODY>
<P>This example shows check boxes using the value
property. The parking and credit card check boxes
have the default values of "on" and "off". The price
check boxes set VALUE to strings representing the
price.</P>
```

```
<TABLE WIDTH="100%"
  CELLSPACING=0 CELLPADDING=5>
  <TR>
    <TD ALIGN=left><B>Parking</B></TD>
    <TD ALIGN=left><B>Credit Cards</B></TD>
    <TD ALIGN=left><B>Price</B></TD>
  </TR>
  <TR>
    <TD ALIGN=left>
      <FORM NAME="parkingForm">
      <INPUT TYPE="checkbox"
        NAME="freeParking" VALUE="off"
        onClick="(this.checked) ? this.value='on':
            this.value='off'"
      > Free<BR>
      <INPUT TYPE="checkbox"
        NAME="payParking" VALUE="off"
        onClick="(this.checked) ? this.value='on':
            this.value='off'"
      > Pay
      </FORM>
    </TD>
    <TD ALIGN=left>
      <FORM NAME="cCardForm">
      <INPUT TYPE="checkbox"
        NAME="amexCC" VALUE="off"
        onClick="(this.checked) ? this.value='on':
            this.value='off'"
      > AMEX<BR>
      <INPUT TYPE="checkbox"
        NAME="discoverCC" VALUE="off"
        onClick="(this.checked) ? this.value='on':
            this.value='off'"
      > Discover<BR>
      <INPUT TYPE="checkbox"
        NAME="mcCC" VALUE="off"
        onClick="(this.checked) ? this.value='on':
            this.value='off'"
      > M/C<BR>
      <INPUT TYPE="checkbox"
        NAME="visaCC" VALUE="off"
        onClick="(this.checked) ? this.value='on':
            this.value='off'"
      > Visa
```

```
      </FORM>
    </TD>
    <TD ALIGN=left>
      <FORM NAME="priceForm">
      <INPUT TYPE="checkbox"
        NAME="price_10" VALUE="10"
        onClick="(this.checked) ? this.value='on':
            this.value='off'"
      >$10<BR>
      <INPUT TYPE="checkbox"
        NAME="price_15" VALUE="15"
        onClick="(this.checked) ? this.value='on':
            this.value='off'"
      >$15<BR>
      <INPUT TYPE="checkbox"
        NAME="price_20" VALUE="20"
        onClick="(this.checked) ? this.value='on':
            this.value='off'"
      >$20<BR>
      <INPUT TYPE="checkbox"
        NAME="price_over_20" VALUE="over_20"
        onClick="(this.checked) ? this.value='on':
            this.value='off'"
      >over $20
      </FORM>
    </TD>
  </TR>
</TABLE>

<CENTER>
<FORM NAME="btnForm">
<INPUT TYPE="button" NAME="displayBtn"
  VALUE="Display Values"
  onClick="displayValue()">
</FORM>
</CENTER>

</BODY>
</HTML>
```

Figure 20–8 shows the result of loading the `checkboxValues.html` script.

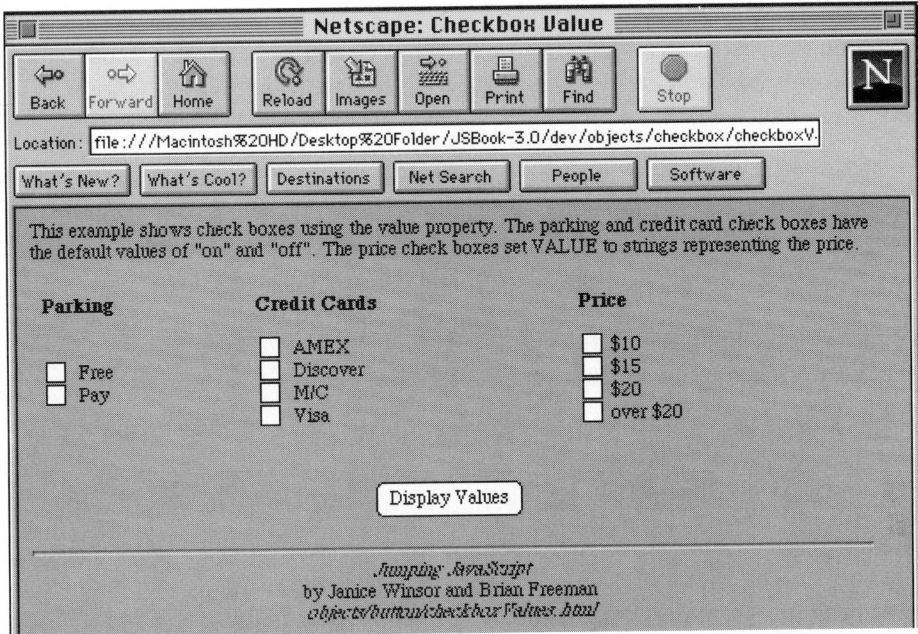

Figure 20–8 Result of loading the `checkboxValues.html` script

After you click on some (or all) of the check boxes, click on the Display Values button to see the values for each of the check boxes, In the example shown in Figure 20–9, the Free Parking, Visa, $10, and $15 check boxes were checked.

```
JavaScript Alert:

freeParking = off
payParking = off
amexCC = off
discoverCC = off
mcCC = off
visaCC = off
price_10 = 10
price_15 = 15
price_20 = 20
price_over_20 = over_20

                         OK
```

Figure 20–9 Check box values

Getting and Setting Check Marks

When you want to determine the value for a `checkbox` object, you use the `checked` property. You can also use this property to change the setting for a check box.

Property	Value	Gettable	Settable
checked	Boolean	Yes	Yes

The value returned by the `checked` property is `true` if the box contains a check. If the box does not contain a check mark, the value returned is `false`.

To change the value of a check box, you assign a value of `true` to the `checked` property, using the following syntax:

```
document.forms[0].boxName.checked = true | false
```

You might want to change the value for a `checkbox` object if users take an action elsewhere in the script that is linked to the check box. For example, while filling out a form, users might provide information in one form that is also related to a set of check boxes elsewhere on the page. If the information is entered in one place, you can use the `checked` property to change the state of the related check box.

Example of Using the checked Property

The `checkboxChecked.html` script below uses the `checked` property to evaluate the checked condition of each box. It is also used to set that value to both `true` and `false`.

```
<!--
         checkboxChecked.html
-->

<HTML>
<HEAD>
<TITLE>Checkbox Checked</TITLE>
<SCRIPT LANGUAGE="JavaScript">
<!-- HIDE FROM OLD BROWSERS

function displayChecked(theform) {
  var msg_str = ""

  for (var e=0; e < theform.length; e++) {
    msg_str += "\n" + theform.elements[e].name
```

```
    msg_str += " = "
    if (theform.elements[e].checked == true) {
      msg_str += "checked"
    }
    else {
      msg_str += "not checked"
    }
  }
  alert(msg_str)
}

function checkEm(theform, state) {
  for (var e=0; e < theform.length; e++) {
    theform.elements[e].checked = state
  }
}

// STOP HIDING -->
</SCRIPT>
</HEAD>

<BODY>
<P>This example plays around with the checked
property. The function checkEm is simply setting
the checked property to either true or false.

<FORM NAME="cCardForm">
<INPUT TYPE="checkbox" NAME="amexCC"
  CHECKED> AMEX<BR>
<INPUT TYPE="checkbox" NAME="discoverCC"
  > Discover<BR>
<INPUT TYPE="checkbox" NAME="mcCC"
  > M/C<BR>
<INPUT TYPE="checkbox" NAME="visaCC"
  > Visa
</FORM>

<CENTER>
<FORM NAME="btnForm">
<INPUT TYPE="button" NAME="displayBtn"
  VALUE="Display Checked"
  onClick="displayChecked(cCardForm)">
<INPUT TYPE="button" NAME="checkEmBtn"
  VALUE="Check Them"
```

```
    onClick="checkEm(cCardForm, true)">
  <INPUT TYPE="button" NAME="unCheckEmBtn"
    VALUE="UnCheck Them"
    onClick="checkEm(cCardForm, false)">
  </FORM>
  </CENTER>


  </BODY>
  </HTML>
```

Figure 20–10 shows the result of loading the `checkboxChecked.html` script.

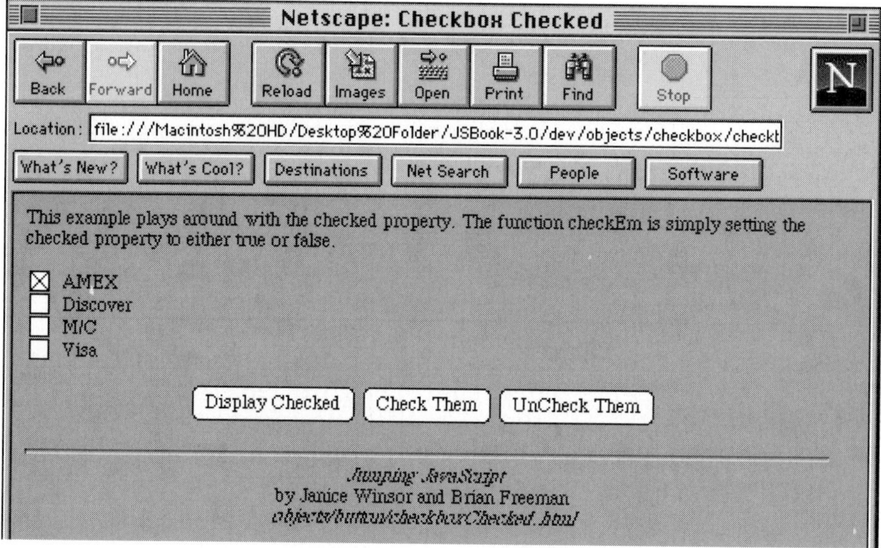

Figure 20–10 Result of loading the `checkboxChecked.html` script

Clicking on the Display Checked button displays an alert that shows the checked values for each check box, as shown in Figure 20–11.

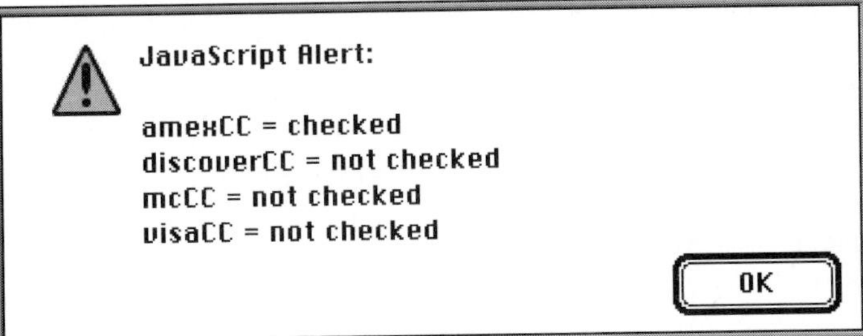

Figure 20–11 Viewing the checked status

When you click on the Check Them button, the script checks all of the check boxes. When you click on the UnCheck Them button, the script removes the check from each box.

Getting a Default Value for a checkbox Object

When you want to determine the default value for a `checkbox` object, you use the `checkbox.defaultChecked` property.

Property	Value	Gettable	Settable
defaultChecked	Boolean	Yes	No

The value returned by the `defaultChecked` property is `true` if you added the `CHECKED` attribute to the `<INPUT>` definition. Otherwise, the value returned is `false`.

You can also use this property to examine the check boxes in your script to see if they have been changed. The following `checkboxDefaultChecked.html` script shows how to reset all check boxes by setting `checked` to the value of `defaultChecked`.

```
<!--
      checkboxDefaultChecked.html
-->

<HTML>
<HEAD>
<TITLE>Checkbox Default Checked</TITLE>
<SCRIPT LANGUAGE="JavaScript">
<!-- HIDE FROM OLD BROWSERS
```

```
function displayChecked(theform) {
  var msg_str = ""

  for (var e=0; e < theform.length; e++) {
    msg_str += "\n" + theform.elements[e].name
    msg_str += " = "
    if (theform.elements[e].checked == true) {
      msg_str += "checked"
    }
    else {
      msg_str += "not checked"
    }
  }
  alert(msg_str)
}

function checkEm(theform, state) {
  for (var e=0; e < theform.length; e++) {
    theform.elements[e].checked = state
  }
}

function defaultCheck(theform) {
  for (var e=0; e < theform.length; e++) {
    theform.elements[e].checked =
      theform.elements[e].defaultChecked
  }
}
// STOP HIDING -->
</SCRIPT>
</HEAD>

<BODY>
<P>This example enables you to reset a set of
check boxes back to the value of their
defaultChecked property.
```

```
<FORM NAME="priceForm">
<INPUT TYPE="checkbox" NAME="price_10"
  CHECKED>$10<BR>
<INPUT TYPE="checkbox" NAME="price_15">$15<BR>
<INPUT TYPE="checkbox" NAME="price_20">$20<BR>
<INPUT TYPE="checkbox" NAME="price_over_20"
  >over $20
</FORM>

<CENTER>
<FORM NAME="btnForm">
<INPUT TYPE="button" NAME="displayBtn"
  VALUE="Display Checked"
  onClick="displayChecked(priceForm)">
<INPUT TYPE="button" NAME="checkEmBtn"
  VALUE="Check Them"
  onClick="checkEm(priceForm, true)">
<INPUT TYPE="button" NAME="unCheckEmBtn"
  VALUE="UnCheck Them"
  onClick="checkEm(priceForm, false)">
<INPUT TYPE="button" NAME="defaultBtn"
  VALUE="Defaults"
  onClick="defaultCheck(priceForm)">
</FORM>
</CENTER>

</BODY>
</HTML>
```

Figure 20–12 shows the result of loading the `checkboxDefaultChecked.html` script.

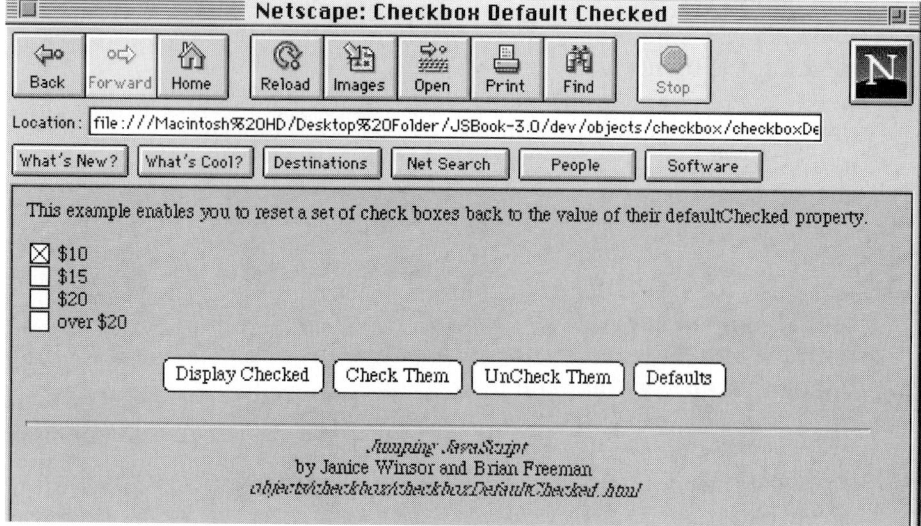

Figure 20–12 Result of loading the `checkboxDefaultChecked.html` script

The `checkboxDefaultChecked.html` script is a modification of the `checkboxChecked.html` script. The modification removes the alerts when you click on the Check Them and UnCheck Them button and adds a Defaults button that returns the check boxes to their default state.

Determining the Type of a Form Object

The `type` property has been added to the available properties for all form elements in the Navigator 3.0 release. This property enables you to test in your scripts to determine the type of any or all of the elements you have created in a form.

Property	Value	Gettable	Settable
type	string	Yes	No

The `type` property extracts the type of an object that you created with the `TYPE` attribute as part of the `<INPUT>`, `<SELECT>`, or `<TEXTAREA>` tags.

Example of checkbox.type

The following `checkboxType.html` script uses a loop to cycle through all of the elements in the form and print the type of each one. The function `displayType()` queries each form element for its type, constructing a string along the way. It displays the resulting string in an alert. You can use this function to display the type of the elements in any form. For more information about creating loops, see Chapter 27, "Creating Loops."

```
<!--
       checkboxType.html
-->

<HTML>
<HEAD>
<TITLE>Checkbox Activities</TITLE>
<SCRIPT LANGUAGE="JavaScript">
<!-- HIDE FROM OLD BROWSERS

function displayType(theform) {
  var msg_str = ""

  for (var e=0; e < theform.length; e++) {
    msg_str += "\n" + theform.elements[e].name
    msg_str += " = " + theform.elements[e].type
  }
  alert(msg_str)
}

// STOP HIDING -->
</SCRIPT>
</HEAD>

<BODY>
<P>A series of activities you can choose using
check boxes:

<FORM NAME="activityForm">
<B>Activities:</B><BR>
<INPUT TYPE="checkbox" NAME="walk"
  VALUE="walking">Walking<BR>
<INPUT TYPE="checkbox" NAME="hike"
  VALUE="hiking">Hiking<BR>
<INPUT TYPE="checkbox" NAME="run"
  VALUE="running">Running<BR>
```

```
<INPUT TYPE="checkbox" NAME="cycle"
  VALUE="cycling">Cycling<BR>
<INPUT TYPE="checkbox" NAME="swim"
  VALUE="swimming">Swimming<BR>
<INPUT TYPE="checkbox" NAME="whale"
  VALUE="whale">Whale Watching<BR>
<INPUT TYPE="checkbox" NAME="bird"
  VALUE="bird">Bird Watching
</FORM>

<CENTER>
<FORM NAME="btnForm">
<INPUT TYPE="button" NAME="displayBtn"
  VALUE="Display type Property"
  onClick="displayType(activityForm)">
</FORM>

</BODY>
</HTML>
```

Figure 20–13 shows the result of loading the `checkboxType.html` script.

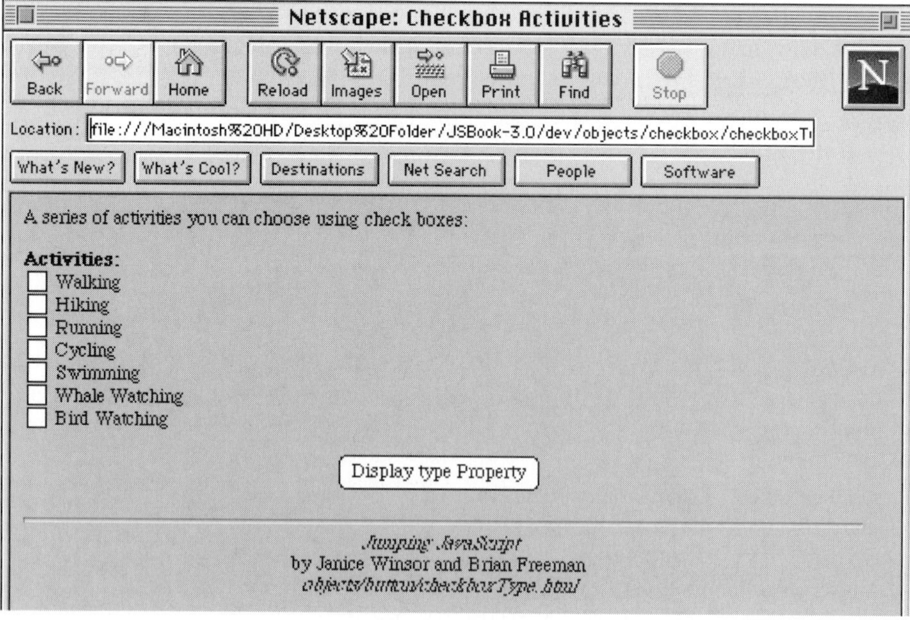

Figure 20–13 Result of loading the `checkboxType.html` script

When you click on the Display type Property button, an alert is displayed, as shown in Figure 20–14, listing the type of all of the elements in the form.

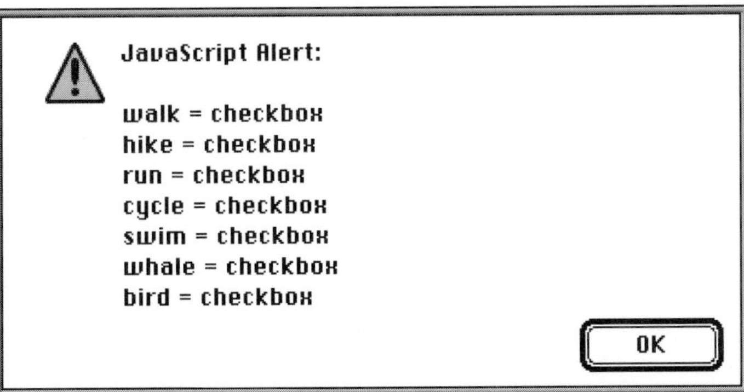

Figure 20–14 Alert showing the type of elements in the form

Clicking on a Check Box

You can use the `click()` method to programmatically click on a check box.

Method

click()

Returns

Nothing

Note – The `click()` method does not work in the Navigator 2.0 releases. If you decide you want to use this method in your scripts, be aware that it may not work on certain versions of Navigator.

Example of Using the click() Method

The `checkboxClick.html` script shown below uses the `click()` method to add functionality to the `checkboxChecked.html` script `clickEm()` does the work.

```
<!--
          checkboxClick.html
-->

<HTML>
<HEAD>
<TITLE>Checkbox Click</TITLE>
<SCRIPT LANGUAGE="JavaScript">
<!-- HIDE FROM OLD BROWSERS

function displayChecked(theform) {
  var msg_str = ""

  for (var e=0; e < theform.length; e++) {
    msg_str += "\n" + theform.elements[e].name
    msg_str += " = "
    if (theform.elements[e].checked == true) {
      msg_str += "checked"
    }
    else {
      msg_str += "not checked"
    }
  }
  alert(msg_str)
}

function checkEm(theform, state) {
  for (var e=0; e < theform.length; e++) {
    theform.elements[e].checked = state
  }
}

function defaultCheck(theform) {
  for (var e=0; e < theform.length; e++) {
    theform.elements[e].checked =
      theform.elements[e].defaultChecked
  }
}

function clickEm(theform) {
  for (var e=0; e < theform.length; e++) {
    theform.elements[e].click()
  }
}
```

```
// STOP HIDING -->
</SCRIPT>
</HEAD>

<BODY>
<P>This example adds to <A
HREF="defaultChecked.html">defaultChecked.html</A>'s
concept by using the click method.

<FORM NAME="cuisineForm">
<INPUT TYPE="checkbox" NAME="amerCAChkbox"
  VALUE="american_californian"> American/Californian<BR>
<INPUT TYPE="checkbox" NAME="asianCAChkbox"
  VALUE="asian_californian"> Asian/Californian<BR>
<INPUT TYPE="checkbox" NAME="bistroChkbox"
  VALUE="bistro"> Bistro<BR>
<INPUT TYPE="checkbox" NAME="cajunCaribChkbox"
  VALUE="cajun_caribbean"> Cajun/Caribbean<BR>
<INPUT TYPE="checkbox" NAME="chineseChkbox"
  VALUE="chinese"> Chinese<BR>
<INPUT TYPE="checkbox" NAME="frContChkbox"
  VALUE="french_continental"> French-Continental<BR>
<INPUT TYPE="checkbox" NAME="germanChkbox"
  VALUE="german"> German<BR>
<INPUT TYPE="checkbox" NAME="greekChkbox"
  VALUE="greek"> Greek<BR>
<INPUT TYPE="checkbox" NAME="indianChkbox"
  VALUE="indian"> Indian<BR>
<INPUT TYPE="checkbox" NAME="italianChkbox"
  VALUE="italian"> Italian<BR>
<INPUT TYPE="checkbox" NAME="japaneseChkbox"
  VALUE="japanese"> Japanese<BR>
<INPUT TYPE="checkbox" NAME="mexicanChkbox"
  VALUE="mexican"> Mexican<BR>
<INPUT TYPE="checkbox" NAME="middleEastChkbox"
  VALUE="middle_eastern"> Middle Eastern<BR>
<INPUT TYPE="checkbox" NAME="seafoodChkbox"
  VALUE="seafood"> Seafood<BR>
<INPUT TYPE="checkbox" NAME="thaiChkbox"
  VALUE="thai"> Thai<BR>
<INPUT TYPE="checkbox" NAME="vietChkbox"
  VALUE="vietnamese"> Vietnamese<BR>
</FORM>
```

```
<CENTER>
<FORM NAME="btnForm">
<INPUT TYPE="button" NAME="displayBtn"
  VALUE="Display Checked"
  onClick="displayChecked(cuisineForm)">
<INPUT TYPE="button" NAME="checkEmBtn"
  VALUE="Check Them"
  onClick="checkEm(cuisineForm, true)">
<INPUT TYPE="button" NAME="unCheckEmBtn"
  VALUE="UnCheck Them"
  onClick="checkEm(cuisineForm, false)">
<INPUT TYPE="button" NAME="clickEmBtn"
  VALUE="click() Them"
  onClick="clickEm(cuisineForm)">
<INPUT TYPE="button" NAME="defaultBtn"
  VALUE="Defaults"
  onClick="defaultCheck(cuisineForm)">
</FORM>
</CENTER>

</BODY>
</HTML>
```

Figure 20–15 shows the result of loading the `checkboxClick.html` script.

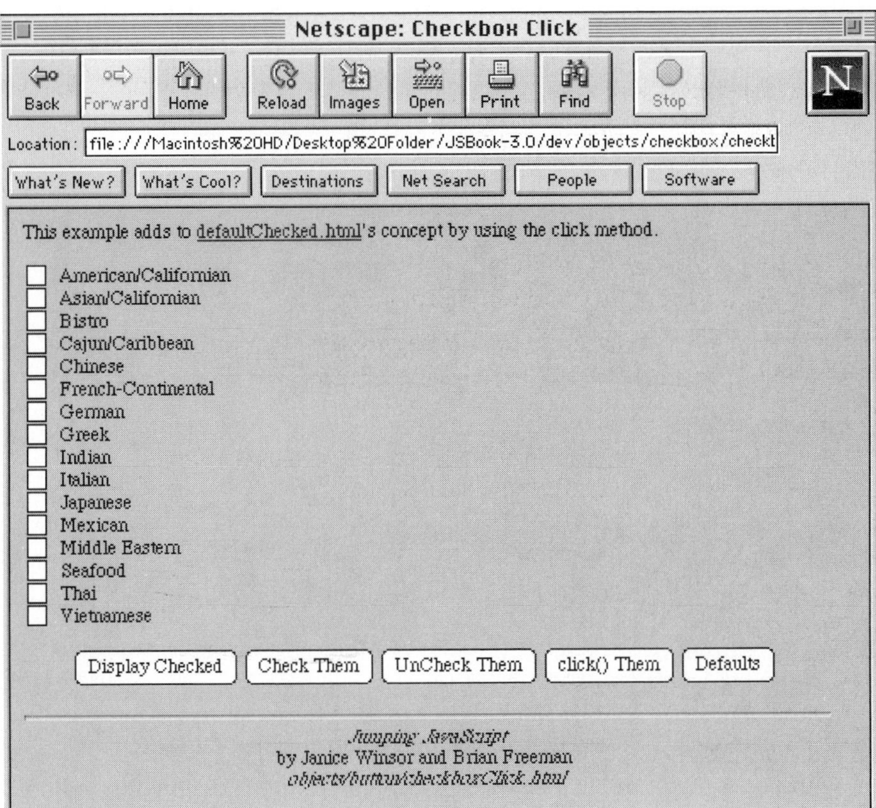

Figure 20–15 Result of loading the `checkboxClick.html` script

Click on the Display Checked button to see the state of each check box. Click on the Check Them button to check all of the boxes. Click on the UnCheck Them button to remove the checks from each box. Click on the click() Them button to have the script check the check boxes. Click on the Defaults button to return the check boxes to their default state.

Performing Script Actions onClick

The `checkbox` object has an `onClick` event handler. This event handler is provided so that you can execute some JavaScript code when users click on a check box. Because the check box is a toggle user-interface element, you should be careful about the amount of work you perform in the event handler when users click on a check box. Usually, you should just record and use the information provided by the user actions when clicking on these elements.

Event Handler

onClick

Syntax

<FORM>

<INPUT TYPE = "checkbox"

NAME = "*Box Name*"

VALUE = "*checkboxValue*"

(CHECKED)

onClick = "*JavaScript code*"

checkboxLabel

</FORM>

Example of onClick Event Handler for the checkbox Object

The following `checkboxOnClick.html` script has an `onClick` event handler that displays an alert dialog containing its value when clicked. The alert is used as a debugging tool in this example to verify that the `onClick` event handler works properly.

```
<!--
   checkboxOnClick.html
-->

<HTML>
<HEAD>
<TITLE>Checkbox onClick Event Handler</TITLE>
</HEAD>

<BODY>

<P>Below is a form that contains a single
check box. The check box has an onClick event handler
registered that displays an alert dialog
containing its value when clicked.</P>
```

```
<FORM>
<INPUT
 TYPE="checkbox"
 NAME="myCheckbox"
 CHECKED
 onClick="(this.checked) ?
           this.value='on' :
           this.value='off' ;
         alert(this.value)"
>
Click on the Box
</FORM>
</BODY>
</HTML>
```

Figure 20–16 shows the result of loading the `checkboxOnClick.html` script and clicking on the check box.

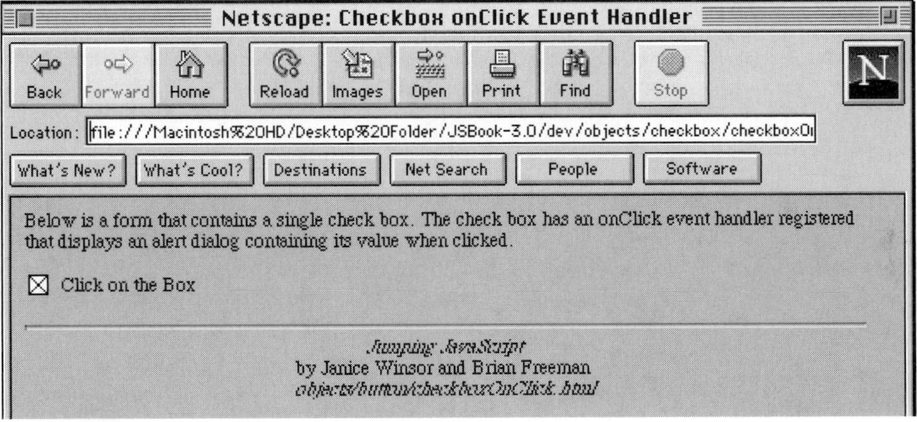

Figure 20–16 Result of loading the `checkboxOnClick.html` script

Example of a Restaurant Review Form

The `restaurant.html` script below combines text fields, check boxes, and a `submit` object to create a restaurant review form. This script combines many of the form elements into one example.

```
<!--
        restaurant.html
-->

<HTML>
<HEAD>
<TITLE>Checkbox Restaurant</TITLE>
<SCRIPT LANGUAGE="JavaScript">
<!-- HIDE FROM OLD BROWSERS

//
// is the string a number?
//
function isANum(str) {
  for (var i=0; i < str.length; i++) {
    var ch = str.substring(i, i+1)
    if (ch < "0" || ch > "9") {
      return false
    }
  }
  return true
}

//
// is the string a zip code?
// Accepted formats are:
//   99999
//   999999999
//   99999 9999
//   99999-9999
//
function isAZip(str) {
  if (str.length == 5 ||
      str.length == 9 ||
      str.length == 10) {

    // the first two cases are all numeric
    if (str.length == 5 || str.length == 9) {
      return isANum(str)
```

```
      }

      // the last two, are somewhat similar, so
      // just loop through and find out if the dash
      // or space is in the right spot.
      for (var i=0; i < str.length; i++) {
        var chr = str.charAt(i)
        if (chr < "0" || chr > "9") {
          if (i != 5 && (chr == "-"||chr == " ")) {
            return false
          }
        }
      }
      return true
    }
    else {
      return false
    }
  }

  //
  // verify the zip code is valid; if not, tell the
  // users and make them reenter.
  //
  function verifyZip(form) {
    if (!isAZip(form.zipField.value)) {
      alert("Please enter a zip of the form 99999-9999")
      form.zipField.focus()
      form.zipField.select()
    }
  }
  // STOP HIDING -->
  </SCRIPT>
  </HEAD>

  <BODY
   onLoad="document.addressForm.nameField.focus()">

  <H1 ALIGN=center>Restaurant Review Form</h1>

  <TABLE WIDTH="100%" CELLPADDING=5>
    <TR>
      <TH>Location
      <TH>Cuisine
```

```
</TR>
<TR>
  <TD>
    <FORM NAME="addressForm">
    <P><B>Name:</B><BR>
    <INPUT TYPE="text" NAME="nameField"
     VALUE="" SIZE=50
     onFocus="this.select()"></P>
    <P><B>Address:</B><BR>
    <INPUT TYPE="text" NAME="addressField"
     VALUE="" SIZE=50
     onFocus="this.select()"></P>
    <TABLE CELLSPACING=0 CELLPADDING=0>
      </TR>
      <TR>
        <TD><B>City:</B></TD>
        <TD><B>State:</B></TD>
        <TD><B>Zip:</B></TD>
      </TR>
      <TR>
        <TD>
        <INPUT TYPE="text" NAME="cityField"
         VALUE="" SIZE=32
         onFocus="this.select()">
        </TD>
        <TD>
        <INPUT TYPE="text" NAME="stateField"
         VALUE="CA" SIZE=2
         onFocus="this.select()"
         onChange="this.value=
           this.value.toUpperCase()">
        </TD>
        <TD>
        <INPUT TYPE="text" NAME="zipField"
         VALUE="99999-9999" SIZE=10
         onFocus="this.select()"
         onChange="verifyZip(this.form)">
        </TD>
      </TR>
    </TABLE>
    <P><B>Phone:</B><BR>
    <INPUT TYPE="text" NAME="phoneField"
     VALUE="(000) 000-0000" SIZE=14
     onFocus="this.select()"></P>
```

```
<TABLE WIDTH="100%"
  CELLSPACING=0 CELLPADDING=0>
  <TR>
    <TD ALIGN=left><B>Parking</B></TD>
    <TD ALIGN=left><B>Credit Cards</B></TD>
    <TD ALIGN=left><B>Price</B></TD>
  </TR>
  <TR>
    <TD ALIGN=left>
      <FORM NAME="parkingForm">
      <INPUT TYPE="checkbox"
        NAME="freeParking"> Free<BR>
      <INPUT TYPE="checkbox"
        NAME="payParking"> Pay
      </FORM>
    </TD>
    <TD ALIGN=left>
      <FORM NAME="cCardForm">
      <INPUT TYPE="checkbox"
        NAME="amexCC"> AMEX<BR>
      <INPUT TYPE="checkbox"
        NAME="discoverCC"> Discover<BR>
      <INPUT TYPE="checkbox"
        NAME="mcCC"> M/C<BR>
      <INPUT TYPE="checkbox"
        NAME="visaCC"> Visa
      </FORM>
    </TD>
    <TD ALIGN=left>
      <FORM NAME="priceForm">
      <INPUT TYPE="checkbox"
        NAME="price_10"
        VALUE="10">$10<BR>
      <INPUT TYPE="checkbox"
        NAME="price_15"
        VALUE="15">$15<BR>
      <INPUT TYPE="checkbox"
        NAME="price_20"
        VALUE="20">$20<BR>
      <INPUT TYPE="checkbox"
        NAME="price_over_20"
        VALUE="over_20">over $20
      </FORM>
    </TD>
```

```
    </TR>
  </TABLE>
  </FORM>
</TD>
<TD>
  <FORM NAME="cuisineForm">
   <INPUT TYPE="checkbox"
     NAME="chkbox"
     VALUE="american_californian">
   American/Californian<BR>
   <INPUT TYPE="checkbox"
     NAME="chkbox"
     VALUE="asian_californian">
   Asian/Californian<BR>
   <INPUT TYPE="checkbox"
     NAME="chkbox"
     VALUE="bistro">
   Bistro<BR>
   <INPUT TYPE="checkbox"
     NAME="chkbox"
     VALUE="cajun_caribbean">
   Cajun/Caribbean<BR>
   <INPUT TYPE="checkbox"
     NAME="chkbox"
     VALUE="chinese">
   Chinese<BR>
   <INPUT TYPE="checkbox"
     NAME="chkbox"
     VALUE="french_continental">
   French-Continental<BR>
   <INPUT TYPE="checkbox"
     NAME="chkbox"
     VALUE="german">
   German<BR>
   <INPUT TYPE="checkbox"
     NAME="chkbox"
     VALUE="greek">
   Greek<BR>
   <INPUT TYPE="checkbox"
     NAME="chkbox"
     VALUE="indian">
   Indian<BR>
   <INPUT TYPE="checkbox"
     NAME="chkbox"
```

```
          VALUE="italian">
        Italian<BR>
        <INPUT TYPE="checkbox"
          NAME="chkbox"
          VALUE="japanese">
        Japanese<BR>
        <INPUT TYPE="checkbox"
          NAME="chkbox"
          VALUE="mexican">
        Mexican<BR>
        <INPUT TYPE="checkbox"
          NAME="chkbox"
          VALUE="middle_eastern">
        Middle Eastern<BR>
        <INPUT TYPE="checkbox"
          NAME="chkbox"
          VALUE="seafood">
        Seafood<BR>
        <INPUT TYPE="checkbox"
          NAME="chkbox"
          VALUE="thai">
        Thai<BR>
        <INPUT TYPE="checkbox"
          NAME="chkbox"
          VALUE="vietnamese">
        Vietnamese<BR>
        </FORM>
      </TD>
    </TR>
  </TABLE>
  <CENTER>
    <FORM NAME="commentsForm">
    <P><B>Comments</B><BR>
    <TEXTAREA NAME="commentsField"
      ROWS="10" COLS="60" WRAP="physical"
    ></TEXTAREA>
    <P><BR>
    <INPUT TYPE="submit" NAME="submitBtn"
      VALUE="Submit"
    ></P>
    </FORM>
  </CENTER>
  </BODY>
  </HTML>
```

Figure 20–17 shows the result of loading the `restaurant.html` script.

Netscape: Checkbox Restaurant

Back Forward Home Reload Images Open Print Find Stop

Location: file:///Macintosh%20HD/Desktop%20Folder/JSBook-3.0/dev/objects/checkbox/restau

What's New? What's Cool? Destinations Net Search People Software

Restaurant Review Form

Location

Name:

Address:

City: State: Zip:

CA 99999-9999

Phone:

(000) 000-0000

Parking

Free
Pay

Credit Cards

AMEX
Discover
M/C
Visa

Price

$10
$15
$20
over $20

Cuisine

American/Californian
Asian/Californian
Bistro
Cajun/Caribbean
Chinese
French-Continental
German
Greek
Indian
Italian
Japanese
Mexican
Middle Eastern
Seafood
Thai
Vietnamese

Comments

Figure 20–17 Result of loading the `restaurant.html` script

When the form is complete, clicking on the Submit button at the bottom of the form could send the results to a server. We've omitted the `ACTION` attribute on the form for this example.

CHAPTER 21

- Defining Radio Buttons
- Radio Button Locations
- Using the hidden Object to Store Radio Button Values
- The radio Object
- Getting radio Object Names
- Getting radio Object Values
- Counting the Number of Radio Buttons in a Set
- Determining Which Radio Button Is Checked
- Getting a Default Value for a radio Object
- Clicking on a Radio Button
- Performing Script Actions on Click

Using Radio Buttons and Hidden Objects

Radio buttons enable you to provide a graphical way for users to make a mutually exclusive choice from two or more items in a list. These controls are like the push-buttons on a car radio that enable you to push a button to listen to one of a set of preselected stations. When the center of the radio button is black or pushed in, the label text is true. When the center of the radio button is empty, the label text is false. Each radio button in a grouping is interrelated with the other radio buttons. If you want to provide a set of unrelated Yes/No elements, use a group of check boxes. For information about how to use check boxes, see Chapter 20, "Using Check Boxes."

Defining Radio Buttons

You define radio buttons with the `<FORM></FORM>` and `<INPUT>` HTML tags. The visual design of the radio buttons that are created depends on the operating system the particular browser runs on. Figure 21–1 shows an example of radio buttons for the Macintosh system.

Gender: ○ Male ◉ Female

Figure 21–1 Radio button style for the Macintosh system

The only part of the radio button that you can control is its label and the default state. The JavaScript language controls the rest of the visual elements of radio buttons. The color and diameter of the radio buttons are automatically created. In addition, each operating system controls the feedback (checked or blank) when the user clicks on a radio button. You cannot control any of these elements in a JavaScript program.

HTML Brushup — Creating Radio Buttons

You create a radio button by using the <FORM></FORM> HTML tags and specifying the parts of the radio buttons by using the <INPUT> tag with NAME and VALUE attributes, as shown below. If you want the default state of the radio button to be checked, you include the CHECKED attribute:

<FORM>

<INPUT TYPE = "radio"

NAME = "*radioGroupName*"

VALUE = "*radioValue*"

(CHECKED)

onClick = "*JavaScript code*"

radioButtonLabel

</FORM>

The <FORM></FORM> HTML tags also have NAME, TARGET, ACTION, METHOD, and ENCTYPE attributes that you must set if you create a form that sends input to a Web server. For more information about creating forms that interact with the server, see Chapter 24, "Using Forms to Send Data to a Server."

The name that you specify is an internal name for the group of radio buttons. You specify the label for each radiio button and a title for the group of radio buttons outside of the `<INPUT>` tag. Radio object names must be a contiguous string of numbers and characters with no spaces.

The value that you specify is an internal value that indicates to the script what value has been chosen when the user clicks on an individual radio button.

Example of Creating Radio Buttons

The following `radio.html` script shows how to create a single radio button using the `CHECKED` attribute. This example shows that you can initiate scripting actions when users click on a radio button. When you have just one radio button, you can never turn it off after users click on it.

```
<!--
          radio.html
-->

<HTML>
<HEAD>
<TITLE>A Single Radio Buttons</TITLE>
</HEAD>

<BODY>

<P>The form below contains a single radio
button. An onClick event handler is registered on
the button to display its value. Because of
the way the radio button is defined, notice that you
can never turn it off.</P>

<FORM>
<INPUT
 TYPE="radio"
 NAME="myRadio"
 VALUE="on"
 CHECKED
 onClick="alert(this.value)"
>
Click On Me.
</FORM>

</BODY>
</HTML>
```

Figure 21–2 shows the result of loading the `radio.html` script.

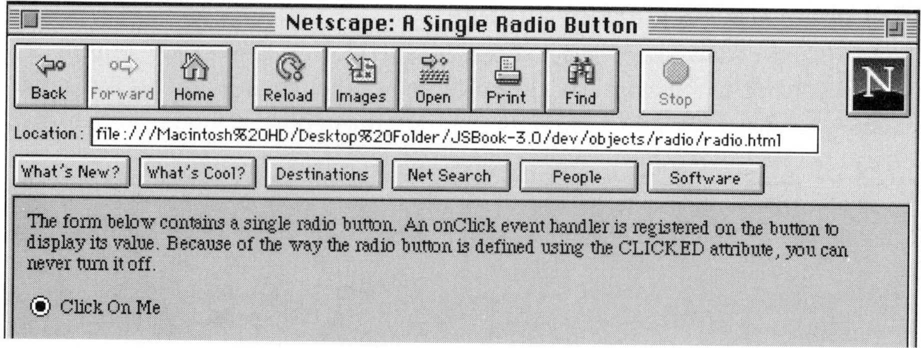

Figure 21–2 Result of loading the `radio.html` script

UI Guideline – When creating radio buttons, be sure to use them to enable users to choose one item from a group of radio buttons. Do not use radio buttons to initiate processes. When choosing labels for radio buttons, keep the label short and easy to read. Consider formatting all radio buttons labels in the same way. Use initial capital letters for the label. Users should be able to tell at a glance what kind of setting they are choosing or what kind of information you expect a Yes or No answer to.

Always position labels in the same way, either to the left or to the right of the radio buttons. Because you cannot depend on consistent alignment, consider putting the radio buttons on the left and the label on the right so that the radio buttons are always aligned with one another. Remember when designing groups of radio buttons that different operating systems may display radio buttons in a different way than you expect. If you put the label on the left, follow it with a colon.

Radio buttons are most effective when used as a group. Always provide a title for a group of radio buttons. Always position the title in the same place. If you have a small group of radio buttons that fit horizontally on a line, put the title at the left margin. If you have a vertical group of radio buttons, put the title above the group of radio buttons and left-align it. Use initial capital letters, a bold font, and follow the title with a colon.

Radio Button Locations

The default location for radio buttons depends on how they are defined in HTML. Figure 21–3 shows the location and spacing for a set of horizontal radio buttons followed by a label.

Gender: Male Female

Figure 21–3 Default checkbox alignment

If you want to display the radio buttons vertically, you can position the title above the group. The following code extract shows a vertical set of radio buttons with a title on top.

```
<FORM NAME="genderForm">
<B>Gender:</B><BR>
<INPUT
 TYPE="hidden"
 NAME="answer"
 VALUE="gender-m">
<INPUT
 TYPE="radio"
 NAME="genderRadio"
 VALUE="gender-m"
 CHECKED
 onClick="genderForm.answer.value='gender-m';
         alert(genderForm.answer.value)"
> Male<BR>
<INPUT
 TYPE="radio"
 NAME="genderRadio"
 VALUE="gender-f"
 onClick="genderForm.answer.value='gender-f';
         alert(genderForm.answer.value)"
> Female<BR>
</FORM>
```

Figure 21–4 shows the results of this code sample on a Macintosh computer.

Figure 21–4 Vertical list of radio buttons and title

For alternative formatting locations, you can use the following HTML tags:

- <CENTER></CENTER> to center a group of radio buttons.
- <DIV ALIGN=RIGHT | LEFT | CENTER> to position a group of radio buttons at the right, left, or center of the page.
- If you present a matrix of radio buttons, you can format them with the <TABLE></TABLE> HTML tags.

The following code extract shows an example of a right-aligned group of vertical radio buttons.

```
<DIV ALIGN=RIGHT>
<FORM NAME="genderForm">
<B>Gender:</B><BR>
 Male
<INPUT
 TYPE="hidden"
 NAME="answer"
 VALUE="gender-m">
<INPUT
 TYPE="radio"
 NAME="genderRadio"
 VALUE="gender-m"
 CHECKED
 onClick="genderForm.answer.value='gender-m';
         alert(genderForm.answer.value)"
><BR>
 Female
<INPUT
 TYPE="radio"
 NAME="genderRadio"
 VALUE="gender-f"
 onClick="genderForm.answer.value='gender-f';
         alert(genderForm.answer.value)"
><BR>
</FORM>
</DIV>
```

Figure 21–5 shows the results of loading this code.

Figure 21–5 Right-aligned radio button and label (Macintosh)

Using the hidden Object to Store Radio Button Values

Within a form, you can create a `hidden` object to store data that is not visible to the users of your Web page. The properties for the `hidden` object are the same as the properties for the `text` object, as listed in Table 21-1. The `hidden` object has no event handlers.

Table 21-1 Properties and Methods for the hidden Object

Properties	Methods	Event Handlers
`form*`	`eval()*`	None
`name`	`toString()*`	
`type*`	`valueOf()*`	
`value`		

* New in the Navigator 3.0 release.

You use the `form`, `name`, and `value` properties in the same way as you do for the `text` object except that these properties are read-only. For more information, see Chapter 16, "Adding Text Fields to a Document."

If you write a complex, multiscreen script that collects user data to be submitted to a CGI script, you may find the `hidden` object to be useful.

In the `hidden.html` script shown below, we use the `hidden` object to store the default value for a set of radio buttons and change that value when the user clicks on a different radio button.

HTML Brushup — Creating Hidden Objects

You create a hidden object by using the <FORM></FORM> HTML tags and specifying the <INPUT> type as "hidden" with NAME and VALUE attributes, as shown below:

<FORM>

<INPUT TYPE = "hidden"

NAME = "*fieldNane*"

VALUE = "*contents*"

</FORM>

The hidden object stores values only for the current loading of the script. If the user reloads the script, any values stored in the hidden object string are erased. If you want more permanent storage, use the document.cookie property described in Chapter 35, "Controlling Script Input and Output with the cookie Property."

Example of Using the hidden Object with Radio Buttons

The following hidden.html script shows how the hidden object is used to store the value for a set of two radio buttons and how to extract that value and display it in an alert dialog.

```
<!--
          hidden.html
-->

<HTML>
<HEAD>
<TITLE>Hidden</TITLE>
</HEAD>

<BODY>

<P>The form below contains two radio buttons and
a hidden object to store the value. The onClick
event handler registered on these radio buttons
displays the hidden object's value. Notice that
clicking on one turns off the other.</P>

<FORM NAME="genderForm">
<B>Gender:</B>
<INPUT
 TYPE="hidden"
 NAME="answer"
 VALUE="gender-m">
<INPUT
 TYPE="radio"
 NAME="genderRadio"
 VALUE="gender-m"
 CHECKED
 onClick="genderForm.answer.value='gender-m';
        alert(genderForm.answer.value)"
> Male
```

```
<INPUT
 TYPE="radio"
 NAME="genderRadio"
 VALUE="gender-f"
 onClick="genderForm.answer.value='gender-f';
         alert(genderForm.answer.value)"
> Female
</FORM>

</BODY>
</HTML>
```

Figure 21–6 shows the results of loading the `hidden.html` script.

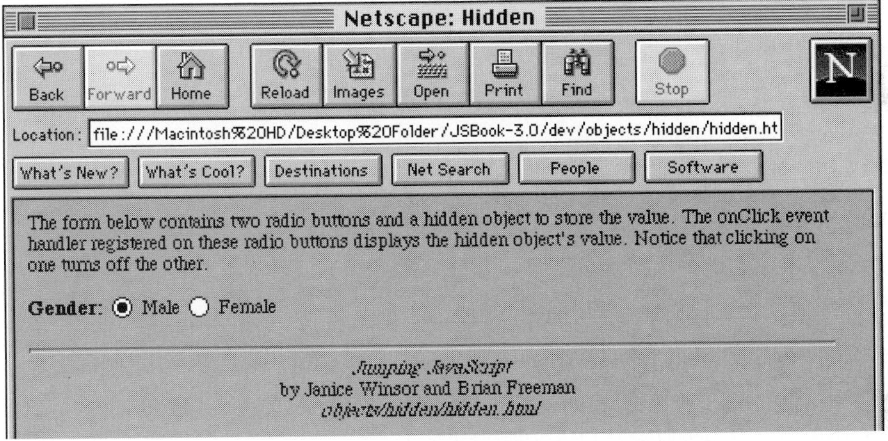

Figure 21–6 Results of loading the `hidden.html` script

When you click on the Female radio button, an alert is displayed, showing the value for that radio button, as shown in Figure 21–7.

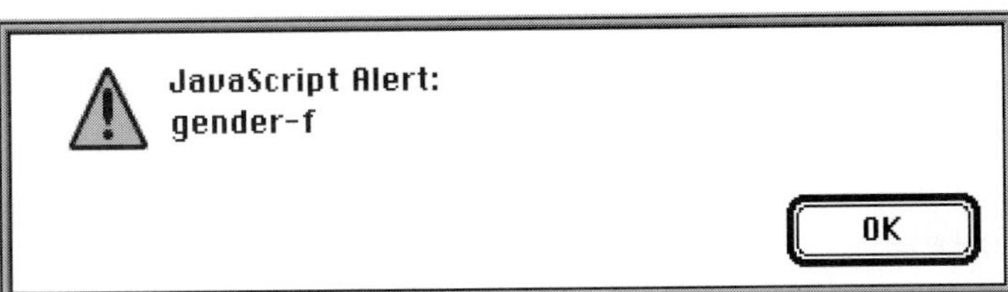

Figure 21–7 Radio button alert

The radio Object

Once you have created one or more radio buttons, you use the properties, methods, and event handlers for the `radio` object, listed in alphabetical order in Table 21-2, to extract information about the state of the radio buttons.

Table 21-2 **Properties, Methods, and Event Handlers for the radio Object**

Properties	Methods	Event Handlers
`checked`	`blur()*`	`onBlur*`
`defaultChecked`	`click()`	`onClick`
`form*`	`eval()*`	`onFocus*`
`length`	`focus()*`	
`name`	`toString()*`	
`type*`	`valueOf()*`	
`value`		

* New in Navigator 3.0.

You access `radio` object properties or methods by using the following syntax:

```
[window.]document.formName.radioGroupName[index].
property | method([parameters])
```

```
[window.]document.forms[index].radioGroupName.property |
method([parameters])
```

Getting radio Object Names

The `radio` object names are different from names of other objects because they do not identify an individual user interface element. Instead, they identify a group of related radio buttons within your JavaScript program.

Property	Value	Gettable	Settable
name	string	Yes	No

The JavaScript language uses an array to reference information about an individual radio button within the group. Any time you reference the `checked`, `defaultChecked`, `index`, or `value` property, you must specify the radio button in the group according to its order in the array. The array is determined by the order of the individual buttons in the HTML document. The syntax for an array is:

```
radioGroupName[index]
```

The following excerpt from the `radioLength.html` script uses the `name` property and the location in the array as part of the loop definition. The name of each radio button in this script is `activityChoice`. The variable `i` is used to represent the index number.

```
function whichRadio() {
  for (var i=0; i < 7; i++) {
    if (document.activityForm.activityChoice[i].checked)
      return i
  }
  return "None"
}
```

See "Example of Using the radio.length Property" on page 656 for the complete script.

Getting radio Object Values

You can use the `radio.value` property to extract the value of a radio button object.

Property	Value	Gettable	Settable
value	string	Yes	No

The value of a `radio` object is different from the checked or unchecked state that you assign to the radio button when you create it. The value can be a string of text that you want to associate with the box. For example, the label you assign to a radio button may not be phrased in a way that is useful in your script. However, if you place the alternative wording in the `VALUE` attribute of the `<INPUT>` definition, you can extract that string by using the `value` property.

"Example of Using the hidden Object with Radio Buttons" on page 652 shows an example of extracting and using the `value` property.

Counting the Number of Radio Buttons in a Set

You can use the `length` property to count the number of individual radio buttons in a set.

Property	Value	Gettable	Settable
length	integer	Yes	No

You can use the `length` property to find out the maximum range of values to use in a repeat loop that cycles through all of the buttons in a group. Using the `length` property instead of using a fixed value makes the loop construction easier to maintain, especially if you change the number of buttons in the group while you are designing your page.

Example of Using the radio.length Property

The `radioLength.html` script below shows you how to determine which radio button is set. It also shows how to use the `length` property to find the total number of radio buttons in a set. It contains two functions, The first function, `whichRadio()`, specifies the literal number of radio buttons in the set. The second function, `whichRadioSet()`, uses the `length` property to specify the number of radio buttons in the set. The second function is the preferred way to provide your script with maximum flexibility.

```
<!--
       radioLength.html
-->

<HTML>
<HEAD>
<TITLE>Radio Length</TITLE>
<SCRIPT LANGUAGE="JavaScript">
<!-- HIDE FROM OLD BROWSERS

//
// determine which radio button is set.
//
function whichRadio() {
  for (var i=0; i < 7; i++) {
    if (document.activityForm.activityChoice[i].checked)
      return i
  }
  return "None"
```

```
}

//
// determine which radio button is set.
//
function whichRadioSet(radioBtn) {
  for (var i=0; i < radioBtn.length; i++) {
    if (radioBtn[i].checked)
      return i
  }
  return "None"
}

// STOP HIDING -->
</SCRIPT>
</HEAD>

<BODY>
<P>This example uses the radio object's length
property. The Display Length button at the bottom
displays an alert dialog with value of
activityChoice.length. Clicking on Which Activity
loops through the activities to determine which
radio button is set. Clicking on Which Radio Btn
is set calls whichRadioSet(), which loops through
the radio buttons until it finds the one that is
checked. The index of the set radio button is
returned and displayed in an alert dialog.

<FORM NAME="activityForm">
<B>Activities:</B><BR>
<INPUT TYPE="radio" NAME="activityChoice"
  VALUE="walking">Walking<BR>
<INPUT TYPE="radio" NAME="activityChoice"
  VALUE="hiking">Hiking<BR>
<INPUT TYPE="radio" NAME="activityChoice"
  VALUE="running">Running<BR>
<INPUT TYPE="radio" NAME="activityChoice"
  VALUE="cycling">Cycling<BR>
<INPUT TYPE="radio" NAME="activityChoice"
  VALUE="swimming">Swimming<BR>
<INPUT TYPE="radio" NAME="activityChoice"
  VALUE="whale">Whale Watching<BR>
<INPUT TYPE="radio" NAME="activityChoice"
```

```
   VALUE="bird">Bird Watching
</FORM>

<CENTER>
<FORM NAME="btnForm">
<INPUT TYPE="button" NAME="displayBtn"
  VALUE="Display Length"
  onClick=
    "alert(activityForm.activityChoice.length)">
<INPUT TYPE="button" NAME="whichBtn"
  VALUE="Which Activity?"
  onClick="alert(whichRadio())">
<INPUT TYPE="button" NAME="whichBtn"
  VALUE="Which Radio Btn is set?"
  onClick="alert(
    whichRadioSet(activityForm.activityChoice))">
</FORM>
</CENTER>

</BODY>
</HTML>
```

Figure 21–8 shows the result of loading the `radioLength.html` script.

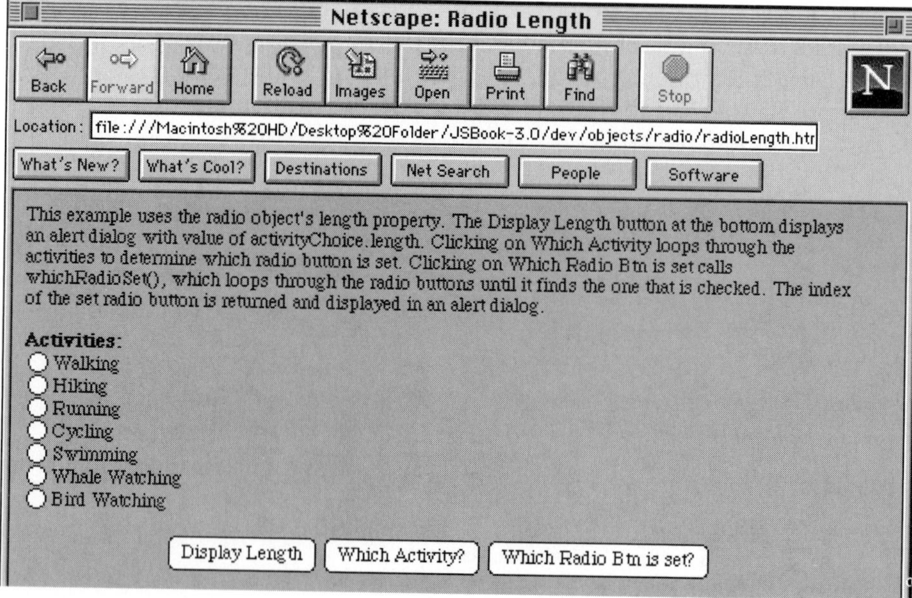

Figure 21–8 Result of loading the `radioLength.html` script

When you click on the Display Length button, the `length` property counts the number of items in the set and displays an alert, as shown in Figure 21–9.

Figure 21–9 Length alert

When you click on either the Which Activity? or Which Radio Button? button with no items checked, an alert is displayed, telling you that no items are checked, as shown in Figure 21–10.

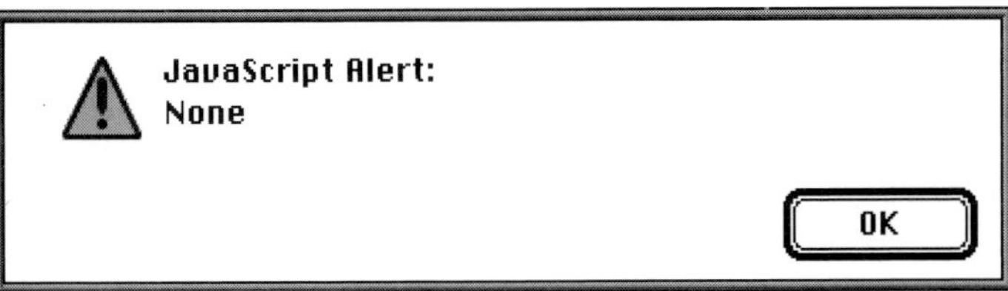

Figure 21–10 When no items are checked

When you click on one of the radio buttons in the list and then click on either the Which Activity? or Which Radio Button? button, an alert is displayed, showing you the number of the item in the list, as shown in Figure 21–11.

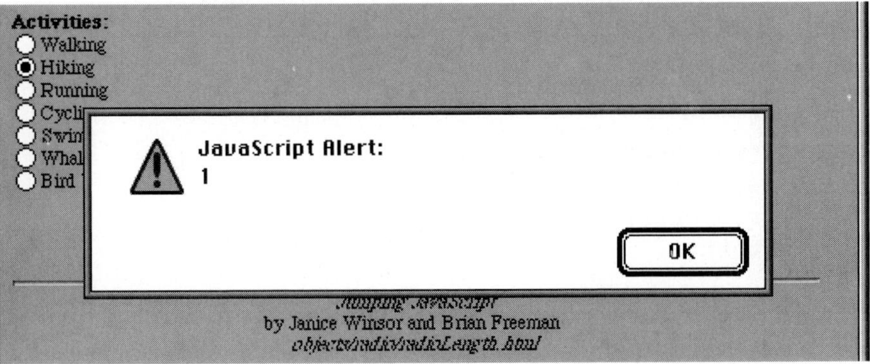

Figure 21–11 Finding the number of the checked radio box

As usual with the JavaScript language, the numbering sequence starts with zero (`0`). As you can see, the second item in the list is checked in the example shown in Figure 21–11, and the alert shows that the number is 1, which is the

second number in a sequence that starts with 0. A Navigator 2.0 bug counts upward from the bottom of the list, not down from the top, so running this script on Navigator 2.0 returns a 5.

Note – Many of the current JavaScript books describe an `index` property for the `radio` object that provides a simple way to find the number on the list. The `radio.index` property does not exist.

Determining Which Radio Button Is Checked

When you want to find out which radio button in the set is checked, you use the `radio.checked` property.

Property	Value	Gettable	Settable
checked	Boolean	Yes	No

The value returned by the `checked` property is `true` if the radio button is on. If the radio button is off, the value returned is `false`.

You must construct a repeat loop to cycle through the buttons in a group and examine the `checked` property to determine which radio button is on.

The `radioLength.html` script also uses the `checked` property as part of the `whichRadioSet()` function shown below. As usual, the variable `i` is used to represent the index number.

```
function whichRadioSet(radioBtn) {
  for (var i=0; i < radioBtn.length; i++) {
    if (radioBtn[i].checked)
      return i
  }
  return "None"
}
```

For the complete `radioLength.html` script, see "Example of Using the radio.length Property" on page 656

Getting a Default Value for a radio Object

When you want to determine the default value for a `radio` object, you use the `defaultChecked` property. The `radio` object should have only one element within a form checked by default. You use this property to find which radio button in a set was originally checked in the script and to reset each of the radio buttons to its initial value.

Property	Value	Gettable	Settable
defaultChecked	Boolean	Yes	No

To check for default value, you can use a loop to check all of the radio buttons in the array, as shown in the `radioDefaultChecked.html` script below.

```
<!--
       radioDefaultChecked.html
-->

<HTML>
<HEAD>
<TITLE>Radio Default Checked</TITLE>
<SCRIPT LANGUAGE="JavaScript">
<!-- HIDE FROM OLD BROWSERS

//
// reset all the radio buttons to their
// defaultChecked value.
//
function resetRadio(radioBtn) {
  for (var i=0; i < radioBtn.length; i++) {
    radioBtn[i].checked =
      radioBtn[i].defaultChecked
  }
}

// STOP HIDING -->
</SCRIPT>
</HEAD>

<BODY>
<P>Clicking on the Defaults button calls the function
resetRadio that loops through all the buttons,
```

```
setting them back to their defaultChecked value.

<FORM NAME="activityForm">
<B>Activities:</B><BR>
<INPUT TYPE="radio" NAME="activityChoice"
  VALUE="walking">Walking<BR>
<INPUT TYPE="radio" NAME="activityChoice"
  VALUE="hiking">Hiking<BR>
<INPUT TYPE="radio" NAME="activityChoice"
  VALUE="running">Running<BR>
<INPUT TYPE="radio" NAME="activityChoice"
  VALUE="cycling">Cycling<BR>
<INPUT TYPE="radio" NAME="activityChoice"
  VALUE="swimming">Swimming<BR>
<INPUT TYPE="radio" NAME="activityChoice"
  VALUE="whale">Whale Watching<BR>
<INPUT TYPE="radio" NAME="activityChoice"
  VALUE="bird">Bird Watching
</FORM>

<CENTER>
<FORM NAME="btnForm">
<INPUT TYPE="button" NAME="defaultBtn"
  VALUE="Defaults"
  onClick="resetRadio(activityForm.activityChoice)">
</FORM>
</CENTER>

</BODY>
</HTML>
```

Figure 21–12 shows the result of loading the `radioDefaultChecked.html` script.

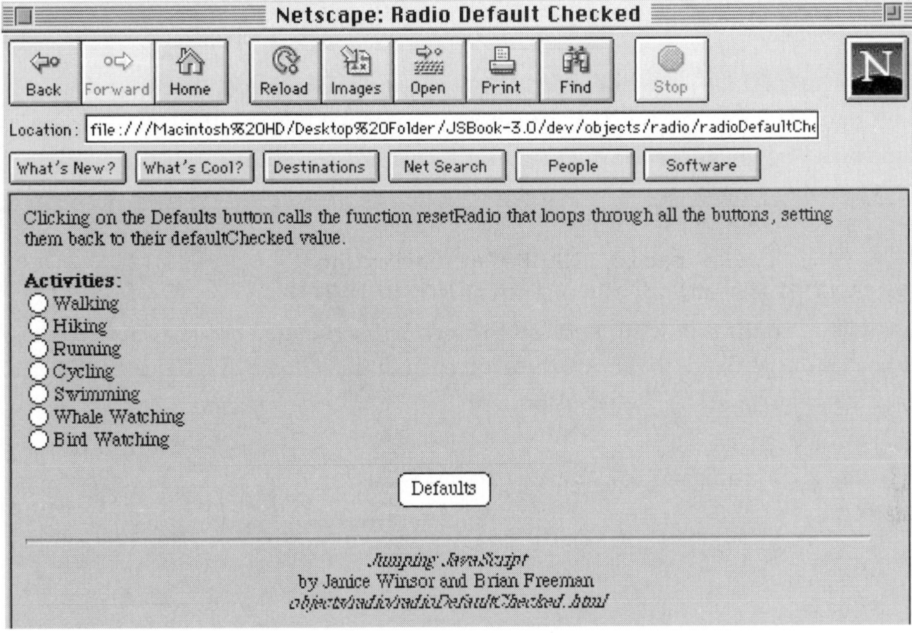

Figure 21–12 Result of loading the `radioDefaultChecked.html` script

When you click on any radio button and then click on the Defaults button, the script cycles through the radio buttons and resets each one to its default checked state.

Clicking on a Radio Button

When you want to have your script click on a radio button, you use the `click()` method.

Methods

click()

Returns

Nothing

Note – The `click()` method does not work on the Macintosh and Windows 95 Navigator 2.02 and on the Macintosh Navigator 3.0 release. It does work on Windows 95 Navigator 3.0.

Example of a Script Clicking on a Radio Button

When you run the following `radioClick.html` script on a browser in which the `click()` bug is fixed, the script clicks on each of the items in the list in turn when you click on the click() Them button.

```
<!--
        radioClick.html
-->

<HTML>
<HEAD>
<TITLE>Radio Click</TITLE>
<SCRIPT LANGUAGE="JavaScript">
<!-- HIDE FROM OLD BROWSERS
var last = 0

function clickEm(theRadio) {
  theRadio[last].click()
  if (last >= theRadio.length -1) {
    last = 0
  }
  else {
    last += 1
  }
  timeout()
}

//
//
//
function timeout() {
  alertID=

setTimeout("clickEm(document.activityForm.activityChoice)
", 1000)
```

```
}
// STOP HIDING -->
</SCRIPT>
</HEAD>

<BODY>
<P>This example shows a person who can't decide.

<P>Really, it shows the radio object's click()
method. When you click on the button, a timeout
is set that clicks a radio button. Then it
repeats...

<FORM NAME="activityForm">
<B>Activities:</B><BR>
<INPUT TYPE="radio" NAME="activityChoice"
  VALUE="walking">Walking<BR>
<INPUT TYPE="radio" NAME="activityChoice"
  VALUE="hiking">Hiking<BR>
<INPUT TYPE="radio" NAME="activityChoice"
  VALUE="running">Running<BR>
<INPUT TYPE="radio" NAME="activityChoice"
  VALUE="cycling">Cycling<BR>
<INPUT TYPE="radio" NAME="activityChoice"
  VALUE="swimming">Swimming<BR>
<INPUT TYPE="radio" NAME="activityChoice"
  VALUE="whale">Whale Watching<BR>
<INPUT TYPE="radio" NAME="activityChoice"
  VALUE="bird">Bird Watching
</FORM>

<CENTER>
<FORM NAME="btnForm">
<INPUT TYPE="button" NAME="clickEmBtn"
  VALUE="click() Them" onClick="timeout()">
</FORM>
</CENTER>

</BODY>
</HTML>
```

Figure 21–13 shows the result of loading the `radioClick.html` script.

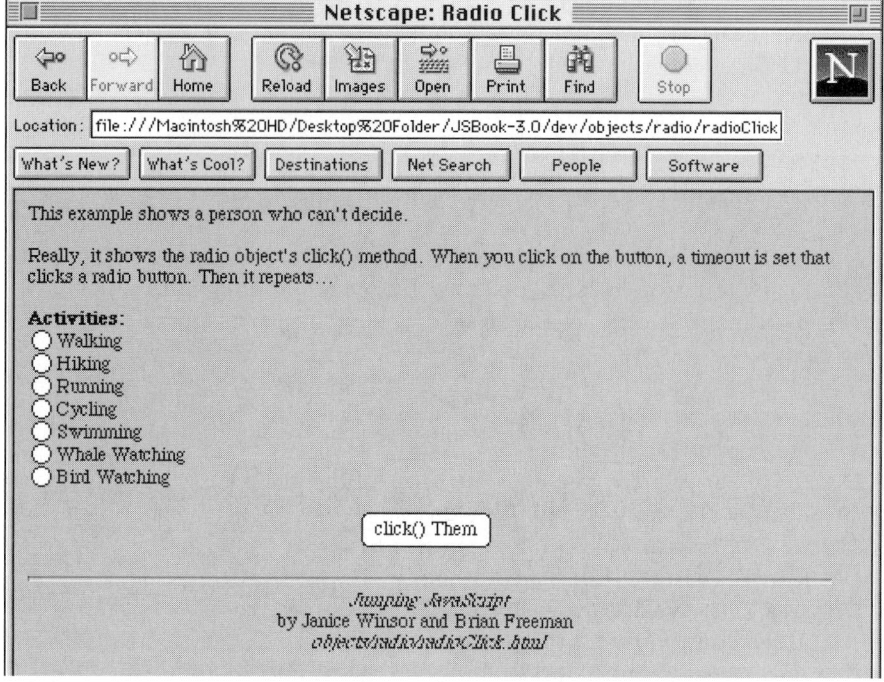

Figure 21–13 Result of `radioClick.html` script

When you click on the click() Them button (if you have a version of the browser where the `click()` method works), the script cycles through the set of radio buttons, clicking each one in turn.

Performing Script Actions on Click

The radio object has an `onClick` event handler. This event handler is provided so that you can perform a script action when users click on a radio button. Because the radio button is an exclusive setting, you should be careful about performing

scripting actions when users click on a radio button. Usually, you should just record and use the information provided by the user actions when clicking on these elements.

Event Handler

onClick

Syntax

<FORM>

<INPUT TYPE = "radio"

NAME = "*radioGroupName*"

VALUE = "*radioValue*"

(CHECKED)

onClick = "*JavaScript code*"

radioButtonLabel

</FORM>

"Example of Using the hidden Object with Radio Buttons" on page 652 shows an example of an `onClick` event handler.

CHAPTER 22

- Defining Selection Lists
- Selection List Locations
- The select Object
- Getting select Object Names
- Counting the Number of Options in a Selection List
- Determining Which Options Are Selected
- Initiating an Action when an Option Is Changed
- Changing the Blur and Focus of a Selection List
- Referencing Individual Options
- Getting a Default Value for an Option
- Getting and Setting the Selected Value for an Option
- Getting and Setting the Text String for an Option
- Getting and Setting the Value for an Option
- Getting the Index Value for an Option
- Referencing Individual Options

Using Selection Lists

Selection lists provide a graphical way for users to choose items from a list. You can define selection lists that enable users to choose any number of items from the list. If you do not define a multiple selection list, then users can choose only choose one item (mutually exclusive) like a radio button. Selection list controls can emulate scrolling lists or pull-down menus, depending on how you choose to implement them. Because of their flexibility, selection lists are a bit more complex than the other user interface elements.

Defining Selection Lists

You defined selection lists with the `<FORM></FORM>` and `<SELECT></SELECT>` HTML tags. The visual design of the selection lists that are created depends on the operating system the particular browser runs on, as well as on the way you configure the list. The only part of the selection list itself that you can control is its label and the default state. The JavaScript language controls the rest of the visual elements of selection lists. The color and diameter of the selection lists are automatically created. In addition, each operating system controls the feedback (selected or unselected) when the user chooses an item from a selection list. You cannot control any of these elements in a JavaScript program.

HTML Brushup — Creating Selection Lists

You create a selection list by using the <FORM></FORM> HTML tags and specifying the parts of the selection lists, using the <SELECT></SELECT> and <OPTION> tags:

```
<FORM>
<SELECT
    NAME = "listName"
    SIZE = "number"
    (MULTIPLE)
    (onBlur = "JavaScript code")
    (onChange = "JavaScript code")
    (onFocus = "JavaScript code")>
        <OPTION
        (SELECTED)
        (VALUE="string")>
        listItem
</SELECT>
</FORM>
```

The indenting in this syntax example is not required by the HTML interpreter, but it does help to show the levels of hierarchy and the relationship of the elements to one another.

The <FORM></FORM> HTML tags also have NAME, TARGET, ACTION, METHOD, and ENCTYPE attributes that you must set if you create a form that sends input to a Web server. For more information about creating forms that interact with the server, see Chapter 24, "Using Forms to Send Data to a Server."

Refer to the HTML Brushup box for the syntax for defining selection lists. The `NAME` attribute that you specify is an internal name for the selection list. You specify the title for the selection list outside of the `<SELECT></SELECT>` tags, and the label for the options in the list outside of the `<OPTION>` tag.

The `MULTIPLE` attribute controls the number of options that users can select at one time. If the `MULTIPLE` attribute is not set, users can choose only one item from the list, just like a group of radio buttons.

You use the `SIZE` attribute to specify the number of options visible at the top level of the list. If you do not specify a size or if `SIZE=1`, the `SELECTED` item in the list is displayed in a rectangle, and when users press on the rectangle, a menu pulls down to display all of the options in the selection list. If you specify a `SIZE` greater than 1 or if `MULTIPLE` is set, the select object displays a list box that contains the number of lines you specify. If `SIZE=1` and `MULTIPLE` is not set, you get the selected list item in the box and the rest are available on a pull-down menu. If the size of the select object is less than the number of items in the list, scrollbars are added to the list.

UI Guideline – When creating selection lists, be sure to use them to enable users to choose one or more item from a list. When choosing labels for selection lists, keep the label short and easy to read. Consider formatting all selection list labels in the same way. Use initial capital letters for the label. Users should be able to tell at a glance what kind of setting they are choosing or what kind of information you expect a Yes or No answer to.

Always position titles in the same way, usually above or to the left of the selection list. Use a bold font, initial capital letters, and follow the title with a colon. Remember when designing groups of selection lists that different operating systems may display selection lists in a different way than you expect.

Keep names for options in the selection list simple and easy to read at a glance. Use initial capital letters, and align the text in the same way, usually at the left.

Because of the amount of space required to display a scrollbar, set the size of a selection list so that at least four options are visible.

Creating a Default Selection List

The following `selectDefault.html` script shows a selection list that is created when you do not specify any attributes except `NAME`.

```
<!--
        selectDefault.html
-->

<HTML>
<HEAD>
<TITLE>Select</TITLE>
</HEAD>

<BODY>

<P>This example shows a selection list created using
only the NAME attribute. As you can see,
when you do not specify the SIZE attribute, the
selection list is displayed as a pull-down menu.

<FORM NAME="activityForm">
<P>
<B>Desired intensity:</B><BR>
<SELECT NAME="intensitySelection">
 <OPTION> Low
 <OPTION SELECTED> Medium
 <OPTION> High
</SELECT>
<P>
</FORM>

</BODY>
</HTML>
```

Figure 22–1 shows the results of loading the `selectDefault.html` script.

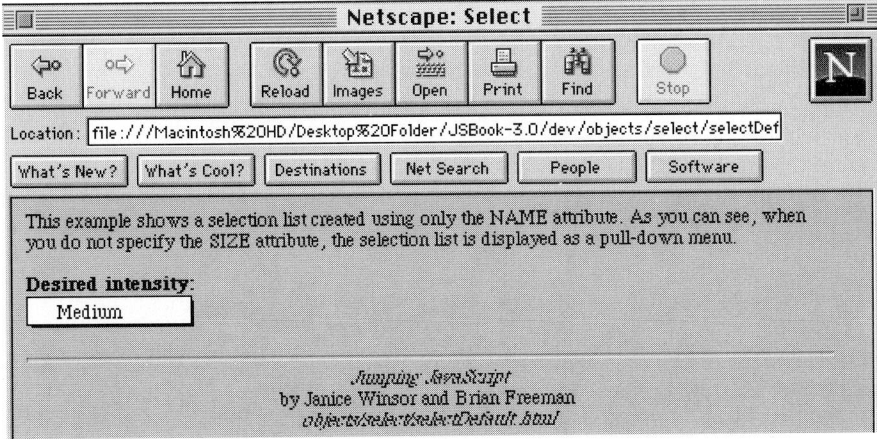

Figure 22–1 Result of `selectDefault.html` script

When a user presses on the Medium rectangle, a pull-down menu is displayed, as shown in Figure 22–2. Notice that the menu uses the default fonts for the operating system platform, not those specified by Navigator.

Figure 22–2 Selection list menu

Showing All of the Options in a Selection List

The following `selectShowAll.html` script is the same as the `selectDefault.html` script except that the `SIZE` attribute is set to 3.

```
<!--
   selectShowAll.html
-->

<HTML>
<HEAD>
<TITLE>Select Show All</TITLE>
</HEAD>

<BODY>

<P>This example shows a selection list created using
the NAME and SIZE attributes.
```

```
<FORM NAME="activityForm">
<P>
<B>Desired intensity:</B><BR>
<SELECT NAME="intensitySelection" SIZE=3>
 <OPTION> Low
 <OPTION SELECTED> Medium
 <OPTION> High
</SELECT>
<P>
</SELECT>
</FORM>

// STOP HIDING -->
</SCRIPT>
</CENTER>
</BODY>
</HTML>
```

Figure 22–3 shows the results of loading the `selectShowAll.html` script.

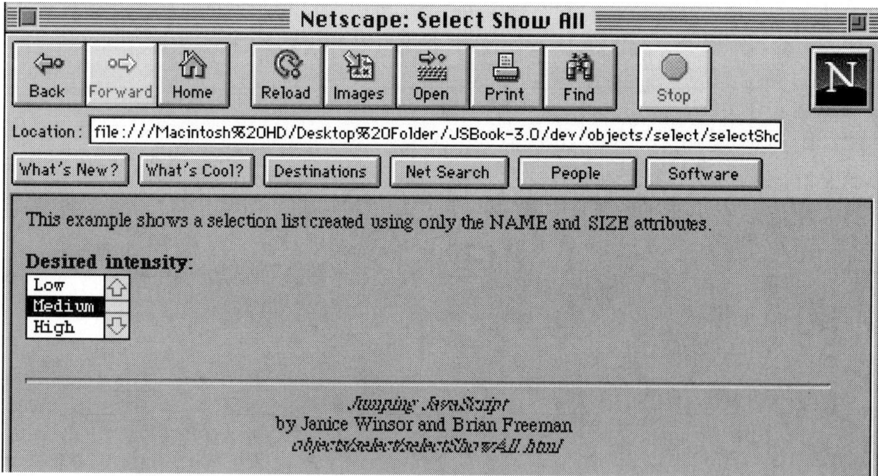

Figure 22–3 Results of `selectShowAll.html` script

Creating a Multiple-Selection List

The following `selectMultiple.html` script creates a selection list from which users can choose one or more options. Users can choose the first item from the list by clicking the mouse button, and additional options by holding down a modifier key (Shift, Control, or Command, depending on the operating system) while clicking on additional options.

```
<!--
          selectMultiple.html
-->

<HTML>
<HEAD>
<TITLE>Select Multiple</TITLE>
</HEAD>

<BODY>

<P>This example uses the MULTIPLE
attribute to create a scrolling list and SIZE to
show more than one line at a time.

<P>
<HR>

<FORM NAME="activityForm">
<P><B>Choose an activity:</B><BR>
<SELECT NAME="activitySelection" SIZE=4 MULTIPLE>
 <OPTION> Walking
 <OPTION SELECTED> Hiking
 <OPTION> Running
 <OPTION> Cycling
 <OPTION> Swimming
 <OPTION> Whale Watching
</SELECT>
</FORM>

</BODY>
</HTML>
```

Figure 22–4 shows the results of loading the `selectMultiple.html` script.

Figure 22–4 Result of `selectMultiple.html` script

You choose a single item by clicking with the mouse button. You choose additional options from the list by pressing a control key while clicking the mouse button. On a Macintosh system, you press the Command (Apple) key while you click the mouse button. On a Windows 95 or an X system, you press Control while you click the mouse button.

Note – In the Navigator 3.0 release, when `SIZE` is set to two or more and you click on an option in the list, the selection list border also highlights.

Selection List Locations

The location for selection lists depends on the HTML. You can use the following HTML tags for formatting:

- `<CENTER></CENTER>` to center a group of selection lists
- `<DIV ALIGN=RIGHT | LEFT | CENTER>` to position a group of selection lists at the right, left, or center of the page
- `<TABLE></TABLE>` HTML tags to format a matrix of selection lists

The select Object

Once you have created one or more selection lists, you use the properties and event handlers for the `select` object listed in alphabetical order in Table 22-1 to extract information about the state of the selection lists.

Table 22-1 Properties and Event Handler for the select Object

Properties	Methods	Event Handlers
`form*`	`blur()*`	`onBlur*`
`length`	`eval()*`	`onChange`
`name`	`focus()*`	`onFocus*`
`options[]`	`toString()*`	
`options[i].defaultSelected`	`valueOf()*`	
`options[i].index`		
`options[i].selected`		
`options[i].text`		
`options[i].value`		
`selectedIndex`		
`type*`		

* New in the Navigator 3.0 release.

You access `select` object properties or methods by using the following syntax:

```
[window.]document.formName.listName.property
[window.]document.forms[index].listName.property
[window.]document.formName.listName.options[index].
property
[window.]document.forms[index].listName.options[index].
property
```

Because many of these properties work together, we'll first introduce several of the properties before showing an example of how to use them in a script.

Getting select Object Names

The `select` object returns the string you assign to the `NAME` attribute of the `<SELECT>` tag. The name refers to the entire selection list, not to individual options within the list.

Property	Value	Gettable	Settable
name	string	Yes	No

You access the `name` property by using the following syntax:

```
listName = document.forms[index].elements[index].name
```

Counting the Number of Options in a Selection List

You use the `length` property to count the number of individual selection lists in a set.

Property	Value	Gettable	Settable
length	integer	Yes	No

Determining Which Options Are Selected

When you want to find out which option in a selection list is selected, you use the `selectedIndex` property.

Property	Value	Gettable	Settable
selectedIndex	Integer	Yes	Yes

When the user clicks on an option in a selection list, the `selectedIndex` property changes to a number that represents the place of the option in the list. As usual with the JavaScript language, the numbering sequence starts with zero (`0`).

The `selectedIndex` property is an index into the options array for the selected item in the list. Use it to directly reference the properties of the selected list item.

Note that the `selectedIndex` property is read-only in Navigator 2.0 and read/write in Navigator 3.0. If the `select` object has the multiple attribute set, it specifies the first selected item or -1 if none are selected. If you have created a

multiple selection list, you need to create a loop to cycle through the list to determine which of the options are selected by using the `options[i].selected` property.

Initiating an Action when an Option Is Changed

The `select` object has an `onChange` event handler. This event handler is provided so that you can perform a script action when users click on an option in a selection list. Usually, you should just record and use the information provided by the user actions when clicking on these elements.

Event Handler

onChange

Syntax

onChange = "*JavaScript code*"

Example of the onChange Event Handler

The following `selectValueChange.html` script extends the `selectValue.html` example to add an `onChange` event handler so that when the user enters the name of a restaurant and then selects that option again, the value of the item is automatically entered in the text field. This functionality makes it easier for a user to edit an existing item without having to retype it.

```
<!--
       selectValueChange.html
-->

<HTML>
<HEAD>
<TITLE>select.options[].value</TITLE>
<SCRIPT LANGUAGE="JavaScript">
<!-- HIDE FROM OLD BROWSERS

// store the text entered in the Input field
var newText = ""

// store the user's response
function setResponse(str) {
  newText = str
}
```

```
// get the user's response
function getResponse() {
  return newText
}

// select the next element for the user
function selectNextItem(sel) {
  if ((sel.selectedIndex + 1) >= sel.length) {
    sel.options[0].selected = true
  } else {
    sel.options[sel.selectedIndex + 1].selected =
      true
  }
}

// change the list option to the user's response
// and store the response in the value property
function updateListItem(sel) {
  // set the text
  sel.options[sel.selectedIndex].text =
    (sel.selectedIndex + 1) + ". " + getResponse()
  sel.options[sel.selectedIndex].value =
    getResponse()

  selectNextItem(sel) // advance for the user
}

// clear the selected list element
function clearListItem(sel) {
  sel.options[sel.selectedIndex].text =
    (sel.selectedIndex + 1) + ". " +
    "*******************"
  sel.options[sel.selectedIndex].value = ""

  selectNextItem(sel) // advance for the user
}

// set the text field's value to that of the
// selected element
function setTextToSelItem(txt, sel) {
  if (sel.options[sel.selectedIndex].value) {
    txt.value =
      sel.options[sel.selectedIndex].value
```

```
    }
    else {
      txt.value = ""
    }
  }

  // STOP HIDING -->
  </SCRIPT>
  </HEAD>

  <BODY>

  <P>This example extends the
  <A HREF="selectValue.html">selectValue.html</A>
  script to make the Input field's value match the
  value of the currently selected item in the
  select object.

  <P>The additional code is an onChange event
  handler for the select object,
  setTxtToSelItem(). It sets a text field's value
  to the value of the selected select object
  element. Calls to setTxtToSelItem() are also
  added to the onClick event handlers for the
  buttons to complete the desired effect.

  <H1> Q: What are your five favorite restaurants?</H1>

  <P>Directions: Click on the list item you want to change,
  then type your answer in the Input field and
  click on the Update Selected Item button.</P>

  <FORM NAME="aForm" WIDTH="100%">
  <B>Restaurants:</B><BR>
  <SELECT NAME="aList" SIZE=5
   onChange="setTextToSelItem(aForm.inField, this)">
   <OPTION SELECTED> 1. *******************
   <OPTION> 2. *******************
   <OPTION> 3. *******************
   <OPTION> 4. *******************
   <OPTION> 5. *******************
  </SELECT>
  <P>
  <P><B>Input</B>:<BR>
```

```
<INPUT TYPE="Text" NAME="inField" SIZE=15
  VALUE="" onChange="setResponse(this.value)"
  onFocus="this.select()">
<BR>
<INPUT TYPE="button" NAME="updateBtn"
  VALUE="Update Selected Item"
  onClick="updateListItem(aForm.aList);
    setTextToSelItem(aForm.inField, aForm.aList)">
<BR>
<INPUT TYPE="button" NAME="clearBtn"
  VALUE="Clear Selected Item"
  onClick="aForm.inField.value='';
    clearListItem(aForm.aList);
    setTextToSelItem(aForm.inField, aForm.aList)">
<BR>
<INPUT TYPE="submit" NAME="submitBtn"
  VALUE="Submit"
</FORM>

</BODY>
</HTML>
```

Figure 22–5 shows the page after the user has entered some restaurant names and then selected one of them.

Netscape: Select Value with onChange

Back Forward Home Reload Images Open Print Find Stop

Location: file:///Macintosh%20HD/Desktop%20Folder/JSBook-3.0/dev/objects/select/selectVal

What's New? What's Cool? Destinations Net Search People Software

This example extends the selectValue.html script to make the Input field's value match the value of the currently selected item in the select object.

The additional code is an onChange event handler for the select object, setTxtToSelItem(). It sets a text field's value to the value of the selected select object element. Calls to setTxtToSelItem() are also added to the onClick event handlers for the buttons to complete the desired effect.

Q: What are your five favorite restaurants?

Directions: Click on the list item you want to change, then type your answer in the Input field and click on the Update Selected Item button.

Restaurants:

1. Gaylord's
2. Hunan Homes
3. Armadillo Willys
4. Stars
5. ********************

Input:

Hunan Homes

Update Selected Item

Clear Selected Item

Submit

Jumping JavaScript
by Janice Winsor and Brian Freeman
objects/select/selectValueChange.html

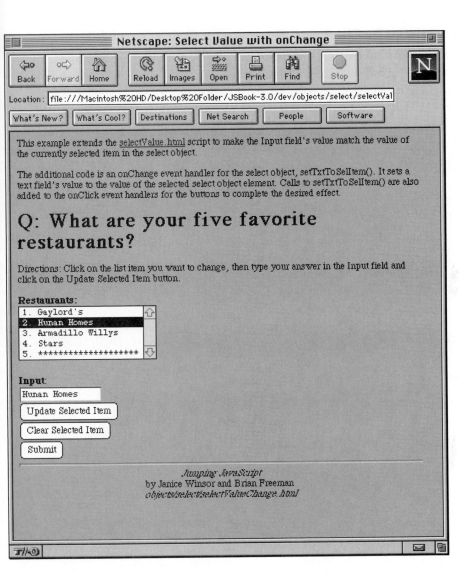

Figure 22–5 Result of loading the `selectValueChange.html` script

Changing the Blur and Focus of a Selection List

The Navigator 3.0 release provides `blur()` and `focus()` methods, and corresponding `onBlur` and `onFocus` event handlers. These methods and event handlers work in the same way as `blur()` and `focus()` and `onBlur` and `onFocus` work for other objects. For examples, see Chapter 16, "Adding Text Fields to a Document."

Methods

blur()

focus()

Syntax

select.blur()

select.focus()

Returns

Nothing

Event Handler

onBlur

onFocus

Syntax

```
<FORM>
<SELECT
  NAME = "listName"
  SIZE = "number"
  (MULTIPLE)
  (onBlur = "JavaScript code")
  (onChange = "JavaScript code")
  (onFocus = "JavaScript code")>
    <OPTION
    (SELECTED)
    (VALUE="string")>
    listItem
</SELECT>
</FORM>
```

Referencing Individual Options

The `options[]` property is an array of option objects. Each element in this array describes one of the options displayed in the `select` object.

Property	Value	Gettable	Settable
options()	array of options	Yes	No

This property is a building block used to reference individual options in a list. You use the `options[]` property to get to them:

```
options[i].defaultSelected
options[i].index
options[i].text
options[i].value
```

Getting a Default Value for an Option

When you want to determine the default value for a `select` object, you use the `options[n].defaultSelected` property to determine if this option is selected by default.

Property	Value	Gettable	Settable
options(*n*).defaultSelected	Boolean	Yes	No

Example of Using a Loop to Evaluate Values and Reset Defaults

The `selectLength.html` script below uses the `name`, `length`, `options[n].selected`, and `options[n].defaultSelected` properties to reset the selection list to its default values.

```
<!--
       selectLength.html
-->

<HTML>
<HEAD>
<TITLE>Select Length</TITLE>
<SCRIPT LANGUAGE="JavaScript">
<!-- HIDE FROM OLD BROWSERS

//
// restore selection list options back to
// their default values.
//
function defaultSelect(selObj) {
  for (var i=0; i < selObj.length; i++) {
    if (selObj.options[i].defaultSelected)
      selObj.options[i].selected = true
    else
      selObj.options[i].selected = false
  }
```

```
}
// STOP HIDING -->
</SCRIPT>
</HEAD>

<BODY>

<P>This example of a selection list uses the
length property to determine how many items are
in the options array and set them back to their
default value, that is, their defaultSelected value.

<FORM NAME="activityForm">
<B>Choose an activity:</B><BR>
<SELECT NAME="activitySel" SIZE=4>
 <OPTION> Walking
 <OPTION SELECTED> Hiking
 <OPTION> Running
 <OPTION> Cycling
</SELECT>
</FORM>

<CENTER>
<FORM NAME="btnForm">
<INPUT TYPE="button" NAME="Btn"
  VALUE="Defaults"
  onClick="defaultSelect(activityForm.activitySel)">
</FORM>
</CENTER>

</BODY>
</HTML>
```

Figure 22–6 shows the result of loading the `selectLength.html` script.

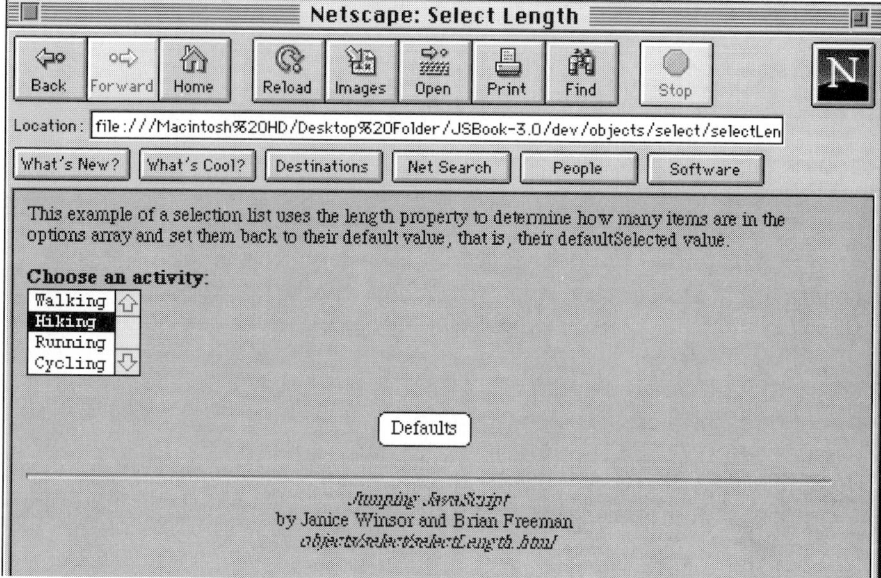

Figure 22–6 Result of `selectLength.html` script

Clicking on the Defaults button resets the selected option in the selection list to its default value.

Analysis of selectLength.html Script

Let's look at some of the elements of the `selectLength.html` script. The `defaultSelect()` function is shown below:

```
function defaultSelect(selObj) {
  for (var i=0; i < selObj.length; i++) {
    if (selObj.options[i].defaultSelected)
      selObj.options[i].selected = true
    else
      selObj.options[i].selected = false
  }
}
```

This function creates a loop to reset the default values on each option within a `select` object. The argument `selObj` specifies the `select` object to act on. A `for` loop is used to cycle through all the options of `selObj`. The variable `i` is used as an index into the options array of `selObj`. Its values range from 0 to the total number of `selObj` options: `selObj.length`. Finally, if the indexed

option's `defaultSelected` property is `true`, the option is selected. If `defaultSelected` is `false`, the option is unselected. This function is called when the button is clicked, with the following statement:

```
onClick="defaultSelect(activityForm.activitySel)">
```

When the user clicks on the Defaults button, the `onClick` event handler that is registered on the button is executed. It calls the function `defaultSelect()` passing in the `activitySel select` object contained in `activityForm`.

Getting and Setting the Selected Value for an Option

When you want to determine whether an option in a selection list is selected or select/deselect an option, use the `options[n].selected` property.

Property	Value	Gettable	Settable
options(*n*).selected	Boolean	Yes	Yes

You use the `selected` property to determine or set the state of an option. Also note that when you set `selected` to `true`, the `onChange` event handler is not invoked.

Example of Evaluating Selections

The `selectSelected.html` script below uses the `options[n].selected` property and a loop to determine how many options in the list are selected.

```
<!--
          selectSelected.html
-->

<HTML>
<HEAD>
<TITLE>Select Selected</TITLE>
<SCRIPT LANGUAGE="JavaScript">
<!-- HIDE FROM OLD BROWSERS

//
// how many select options are selected
//
function numSelected(selObj) {
   var num_selected=0

   for (i=0; i < selObj.options.length; i++) {
      if (selObj.options[i].selected)
```

```
            num_selected++
      }
      return num_selected
}

function displayNumSelected(selObj) {
   var msg_str = ""

   msg_str += "There are "
   msg_str += numSelected(selObj)
   msg_str += " option(s) selected."

   alert(unescape(msg_str))
}

// STOP HIDING -->
</SCRIPT>
</HEAD>

<BODY>

<P>This select object tells you how many options
are selected in a scrolling list.

<FORM NAME="activityForm">
<B>Choose an activity:</B><BR>
<SELECT NAME="activitySel" SIZE=4 MULTIPLE>
 <OPTION> Walking
 <OPTION SELECTED> Hiking
 <OPTION> Running
 <OPTION> Cycling
</SELECT>
</FORM>

<CENTER>
<FORM NAME="btnForm">
<INPUT TYPE="button" NAME="Btn"
   VALUE="How Many Selected?"
   onClick=
     "displayNumSelected(activityForm.activitySel)">
</FORM>
</CENTER>
</BODY>
</HTML>
```

Figure 22–7 shows the result of loading the `selectSelected.html` script and highlighting a second option in the list.

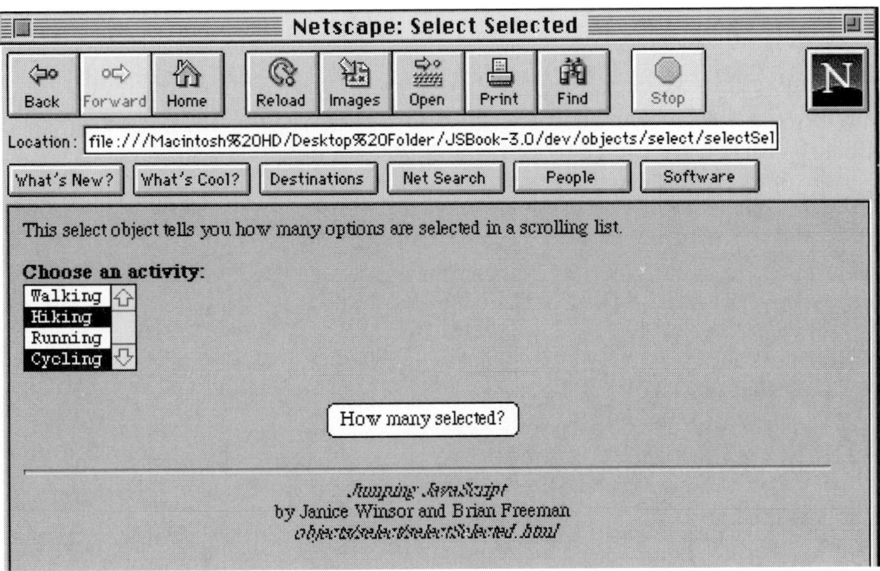

Figure 22–7 Result of `selectSelected.html` script

Clicking on the How many selected? button displays an alert dialog showing how many options in the list are selected, as shown in Figure 22–8.

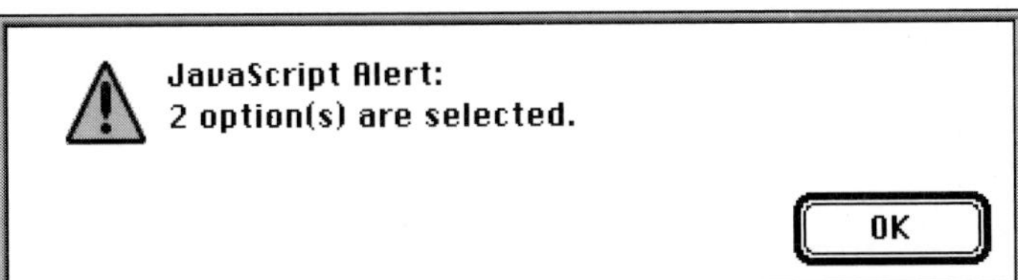

Figure 22–8 Number of selected options

Getting and Setting the Text String for an Option

When you want to extract or set the text string for an option, use the `options[n].text` property.

Property	Value	Gettable	Settable
options(*n*).text	String	Yes	Yes

The value returned by the text property is the text you define after the <OPTION> tag. If you want to provide more information than the label for the option, you can assign a VALUE attribute to the <OPTION> tag and use the options[n].value property to extract and set that value.

Example of Setting and Extracting Text Strings for an Option

The following selectText.html script uses the options[*n*].text property to extract the text string for each option and assign a new value for it.

```
<!--
        selectText.html
-->

<HTML>
<HEAD>
<TITLE>Select Text</TITLE>
<SCRIPT LANGUAGE="JavaScript">
<!-- HIDE FROM OLD BROWSERS
// stores the text entered in the Input field
var newText = ""

// store the user's response
function setResponse(str) {
  newText = str
}

// get the user's response
function getResponse() {
  return newText
}

// select the next element for the user
function selectNextItem(sel) {
  if ((sel.selectedIndex + 1) >= sel.length) {
    sel.options[0].selected = true
  } else {
    sel.options[sel.selectedIndex + 1].selected =
      true
  }
}

// change the list element to the user's response
function updateListItem(sel) {
  // set the text
```

```
    sel.options[sel.selectedIndex].text =
      (sel.selectedIndex + 1) + ". " + getResponse()
    selectNextItem(sel)
  }

  // clear the selected list option
  function clearListItem(sel) {
    sel.options[sel.selectedIndex].text =
      (sel.selectedIndex + 1) + ". " +
      "********************"
    selectNextItem(sel)
  }

  // STOP HIDING -->
  </SCRIPT>
  </HEAD>

  <BODY>

  <P>This example uses the elements of a selection
  list to store a user's responses. It changes the
  text property of the selected option in the
  selection list to the value in the response field
  when a user clicks on the Update Selected Item
  button.  Clicking on the Clear Selected Item
  button returns the element to its default value.

  <H1>Q: What are your five favorite
  restaurants?</H1>

  <P>Directions: Click on the list item you want to
  change, then type your answer in the Input field
  and click on the Update Selected Item button.</P>

  <FORM NAME="aForm" WIDTH="100%">
  <B>Restaurants:</B><BR>
  <SELECT NAME="aList" SIZE=5>
   <OPTION SELECTED> 1. ********************
   <OPTION> 2. ********************
   <OPTION> 3. ********************
   <OPTION> 4. ********************
   <OPTION> 5. ********************
  </SELECT>
  <P>
```

```
<P><B>Input</B>:<BR>
<INPUT TYPE="Text" NAME="inField" SIZE=15
  VALUE="" onChange="setResponse(this.value)"
  onFocus="this.select()">
<BR>
<INPUT TYPE="button" NAME="updateBtn"
  VALUE="Update Selected Item"
  onClick="updateListItem(aForm.aList)">
<BR>
<INPUT TYPE="button" NAME="clearBtn"
  VALUE="Clear Selected Item"
  onClick="aForm.inField.value='';
    clearListItem(aForm.aList)">
</FORM>

</BODY>
</HTML>
```

Figure 22–9 shows the result of loading the `selectText.html` script.

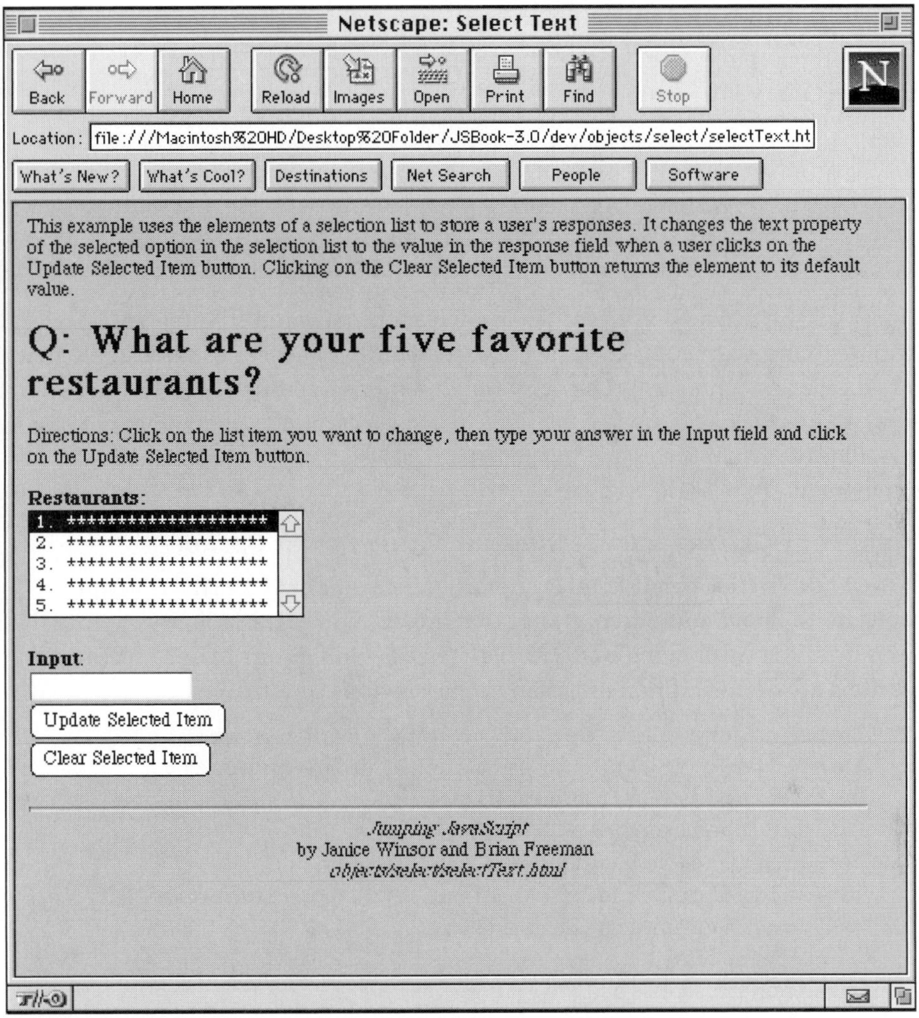

Netscape: Select Text

Back Forward Home Reload Images Open Print Find Stop

Location: file:///Macintosh%20HD/Desktop%20Folder/JSBook-3.0/dev/objects/select/selectText.ht

What's New? What's Cool? Destinations Net Search People Software

This example uses the elements of a selection list to store a user's responses. It changes the text property of the selected option in the selection list to the value in the response field when a user clicks on the Update Selected Item button. Clicking on the Clear Selected Item button returns the element to its default value.

Q: What are your five favorite restaurants?

Directions: Click on the list item you want to change, then type your answer in the Input field and click on the Update Selected Item button.

Restaurants:

1. ********************
2. ********************
3. ********************
4. ********************
5. ********************

Input:

Update Selected Item

Clear Selected Item

Jumping JavaScript
by Janice Winsor and Brian Freeman
objects/select/selectText.html

Figure 22–9 Result of `selectText.html` script

This form enables users to specify their own five favorite restaurants by highlighting an item, typing the name of the restaurant into the Input field, and clicking on the Update Selected Item button. Users can also clear a selected item or highlight an item and change it.

Getting and Setting the Value for an Option

When you want to extract and set the value for an option, use the `options[n].value` property.

Property	Value	Gettable	Settable
options(*n*).value	String	Yes	Yes

Before you can use this property, you define an initial value with the `VALUE` attribute to the `<OPTION>` tag when you created the selection list. It is likely that you will find assigning a `VALUE` attribute to options in the selection list quite useful. In this way, you can keep the text in the selection list short and easy to scan and still provide a more expanded value for each option that you can use elsewhere in your script.

Example of Getting and Setting the Value for an Option

The `selectValue.html` script is similar to the `selectText.html` script shown in the previous section, except that it uses the `value` property to store the user's input. The following `updateListItem()` and `clearListItem()` functions are defined differently than in the previous script:

```
// change the list option to the user's response
// and store the response in the value property
function updateListItem(sel) {
  // set the text
  sel.options[sel.selectedIndex].text =
    (sel.selectedIndex + 1) + ".  " + getResponse()
  sel.options[sel.selectedIndex].value =
    getResponse()
  selectNextItem(sel)
}

// clear the selected list element
function clearListItem(sel) {
  sel.options[sel.selectedIndex].text =
    (sel.selectedIndex + 1) + ".  " +
    "********************"
  sel.options[sel.selectedIndex].value = ""
  selectNextItem(sel)
}
```

The other new functionality is the Submit button included at the end of the script:

```
<INPUT TYPE="submit" NAME="submitBtn"
  VALUE="Submit"
```

Figure 22–10 shows the result of loading the `selectValue.html` script.

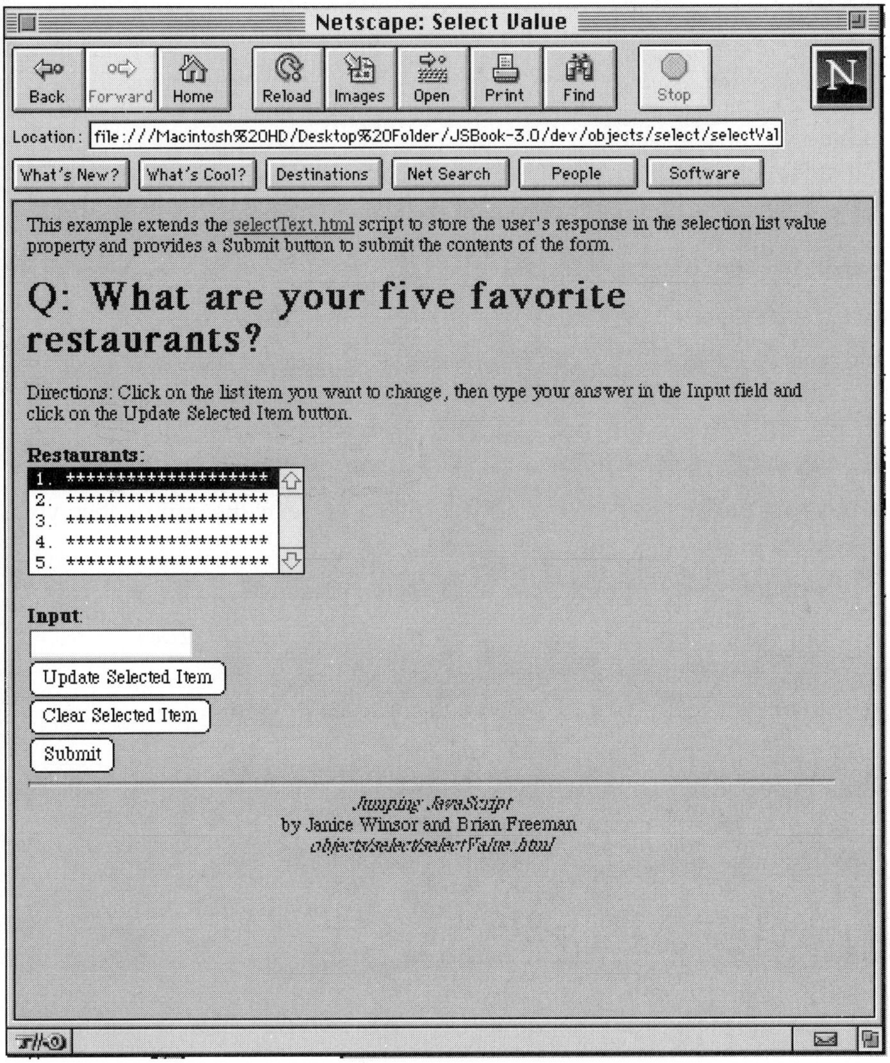

Figure 22–10 Result of `selectValue.html` script

Getting the Index Value for an Option

When you want to extract the index value for an option, use the `options[n].index` property.

Property	Value	Gettable	Settable
options(*n*).index	Integer	Yes	No

This property is provided for completeness. Because you cannot access an option without already knowing its index, you'll probably find that you don't need to use this property. The first option object in the array is at index 0, and has an `index` property set to 0. The second is 1, and so on.

Dynamically Adding Options to a Selection List

The Navigator 3.0 release provides an `Option()` constructor that you can use to enable users to dynamically add options to an existing selection list. Any options that are created with the `Option()` constructor have the same properties as any other option in the selection list.

To use the `Option()` constructor in a script, first you create the option, then you add the option to an existing `select` object.

Use the following syntax to create an option to add to an existing `select` object:

```
optionName = new Option([optionText, optionValue,
defaultSelected, selected])
```

where *`optionName`* is the name of a new object or the property of an existing object.

The following `addListItem()` function adds a new option to the `select` object: `sel` is an argument of `addListItem`.

```
function addListItem(sel) {
  if (sel) {
    var txt = (sel.length + 1) + ". " +
      "********************"

    sel.options[sel.length] =
      new Option(txt, "", false, false)
```

After you have created the option, you add it to an existing `select` object by using the following syntax:

selectName.options[*index*.length] = *optionName*

where *selectName* is the name of the selection list.

The following example adds the option to the `aList select` object in the `aForm` form when the user clicks on the Add button.

```
<INPUT TYPE="button" NAME="addBtn"
  VALUE="Add Item"
  onClick="addListItem(aForm.aList)">
```

Example of Using the Option() Constructor

The following `selectOption.html` script extends the `selectChange.html` script to add a new option to the selection list when the user clicks on the Add button. To make it easier to see the additional options, the size of the list has been changed from 5 to 10.

```
<!--
       SelectOption.html
-->

<HTML>
<HEAD>
<TITLE>Select Option</TITLE>
<SCRIPT LANGUAGE="JavaScript">
<!-- HIDE FROM OLD BROWSERS

// store the text entered in the Input field
var newText = ""

// store the user's response
function setResponse(str) {
  newText = str
}

// get the user's response
function getResponse() {
  return newText
}

// select the next element for the user
function selectNextItem(sel) {
  if ((sel.selectedIndex + 1) >= sel.length) {
    sel.options[0].selected = true
  } else {
    sel.options[sel.selectedIndex + 1].selected =
```

```
        true
    }
}

// change the list option to the user's response
// and store the response in the value property
function updateListItem(sel) {
  // set the text
  sel.options[sel.selectedIndex].text =
    (sel.selectedIndex + 1) + ". " + getResponse()
  sel.options[sel.selectedIndex].value =
    getResponse()

  selectNextItem(sel) // advance for the user
}

// clear the selected list element
function clearListItem(sel) {
  sel.options[sel.selectedIndex].text =
    (sel.selectedIndex + 1) + ". " +
    "********************"
  sel.options[sel.selectedIndex].value = ""

  selectNextItem(sel) // advance for the user
}

// add a list element to the end of the list
function addListItem(sel) {
  if (sel) {
    var txt = (sel.length + 1) + ". " +
      "********************"

    // create new option at the end
    sel.options[sel.length] =
      new Option(txt, "", false, false)

    // Workaround for bug
    //
    // The option we just added with selected
    // equal to false IS selected. Force the
    // selection back to the element that Navigator
    // thinks is selected.
    //
    // Occurs on: Navigtor 3.0b6, Solaris 2.4
```

```
    //            Navigtor 3.0b7, Mac
    //            Navigtor 3.0b7, Win95
    //
    // Verify on FCS
    if(navigator.appVersion.indexOf("(X11") != -1
    || navigator.appVersion.indexOf("(Mac") != -1
    || navigator.appVersion.indexOf("(Win") != -1)
    {
      sel.options[sel.selectedIndex].selected=true
    }

    // refresh the page (required)
    history.go(0)
  }
}

// set the text field's value to that of the
// selected element
function setTextToSelItem(txt, sel) {
  if (sel.options[sel.selectedIndex].value) {
    txt.value =
      sel.options[sel.selectedIndex].value
  }
  else {
    txt.value = ""
  }
}

// STOP HIDING -->
</SCRIPT>
</HEAD>

<BODY>

<P>This example extends the
<A HREF="selectValueChange.html">
selectValueChange.html</A> script to allow the
user to create new items for the selection
list.</P>

<P>An additional button is added that calls the
new function addListItem. addListItem adds an
element to the select object and sets defaults for its
text and value properties.</P>
```

```
<H1>Q: What are your five favorite
restaurants?</H1>

<P>Directions: Click on the list item you want to
change, then type your answer in the Input field
and click on the Update Selected Item button.</P>

<FORM NAME="aForm" WIDTH="100%">
<B>Restaurants:</B><BR>
<SELECT NAME="aList" SIZE=5
 onChange="setTextToSelItem(aForm.inField, this)">
 <OPTION SELECTED> 1. ********************
 <OPTION> 2. ********************
 <OPTION> 3. ********************
 <OPTION> 4. ********************
 <OPTION> 5. ********************
</SELECT>
<P>
<P><B>Input</B>:<BR>
<INPUT TYPE="Text" NAME="inField" SIZE=15
  VALUE="" onChange="setResponse(this.value)"
  onFocus="this.select()">
<BR>
<INPUT TYPE="button" NAME="updateBtn"
  VALUE="Update Selected Item"
  onClick="updateListItem(aForm.aList);
    setTextToSelItem(aForm.inField, aForm.aList)">
<BR>
<INPUT TYPE="button" NAME="clearBtn"
  VALUE="Clear Selected Item"
  onClick="aForm.inField.value='';
    clearListItem(aForm.aList);
    setTextToSelItem(aForm.inField, aForm.aList)">
<BR>
<INPUT TYPE="button" NAME="addBtn"
  VALUE="Add Item"
  onClick="addListItem(aForm.aList)">
<BR>
<INPUT TYPE="submit" NAME="submitBtn"
  VALUE="Submit"
</FORM>
</BODY>
</HTML>
```

Figure 22–11 shows the result of loading the `selectOption.html` script.

Netscape: Select Option

Back | Forward | Home | Reload | Images | Open | Print | Find | Stop

Location: file:///Macintosh%20HD/Desktop%20Folder/JSBook-3.0/dev/objects/select/selectOption.h

What's New? | What's Cool? | Destinations | Net Search | People | Software

This example extends the selectValueChange.html script to allow the user to create new items for the selection list.

An additional button is added that calls the new function addListItem. addListItem adds an element to the select object and sets defaults for its text and value properties.

Q: What are your five favorite restaurants?

Directions: Click on the list item you want to change, then type your answer in the Input field and click on the Update Selected Item button.

Restaurants:

1. ********************
2. ********************
3. ********************
4. ********************
5. ********************

Input:

Update Selected Item

Clear Selected Item

Add Item

Submit

Jumping JavaScript
by Janice Winsor and Brian Freeman
objects/select/selectOption.html

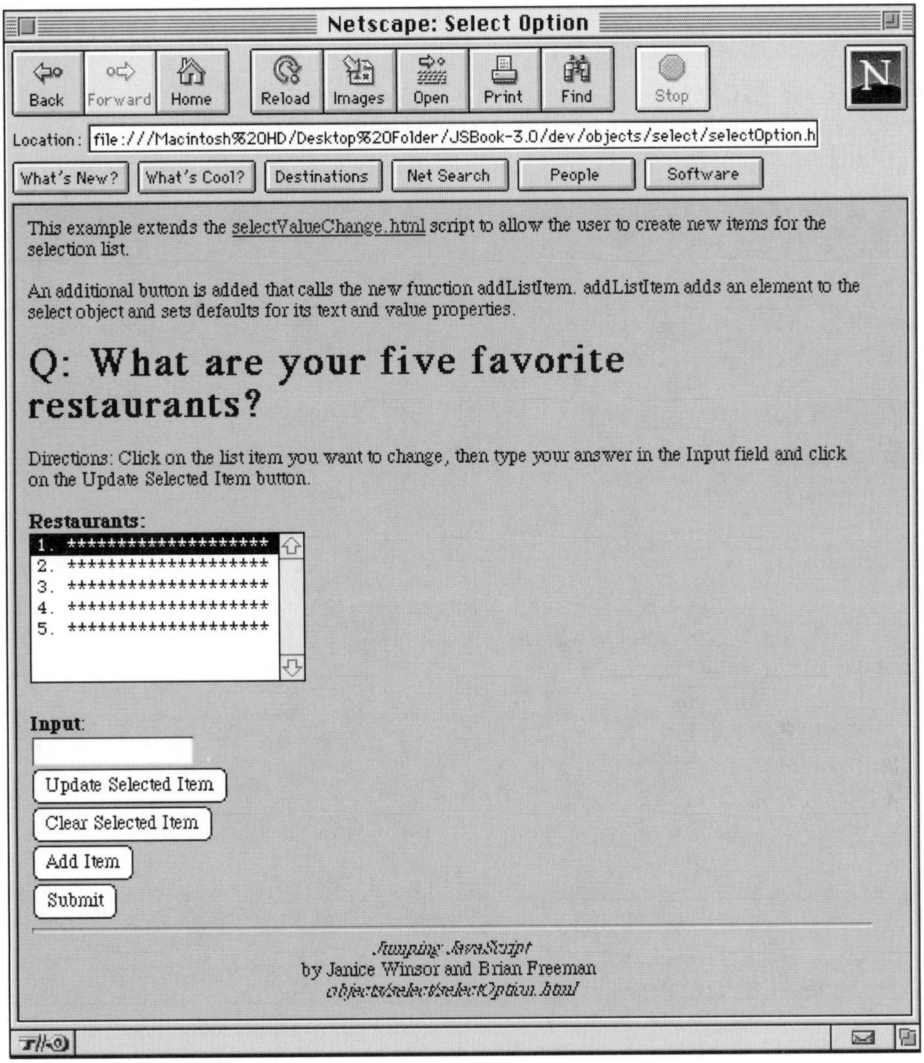

Figure 22–11 Result of `selectOption.html` script

Clicking on the Add Item button adds another item to the list. The script puts no limit on the number of options that you can add. Figure 22–12 shows the list with one option added. After users add options, they can edit the text by using the Input text field and the Update Selected Item and Clear Selected Item buttons.

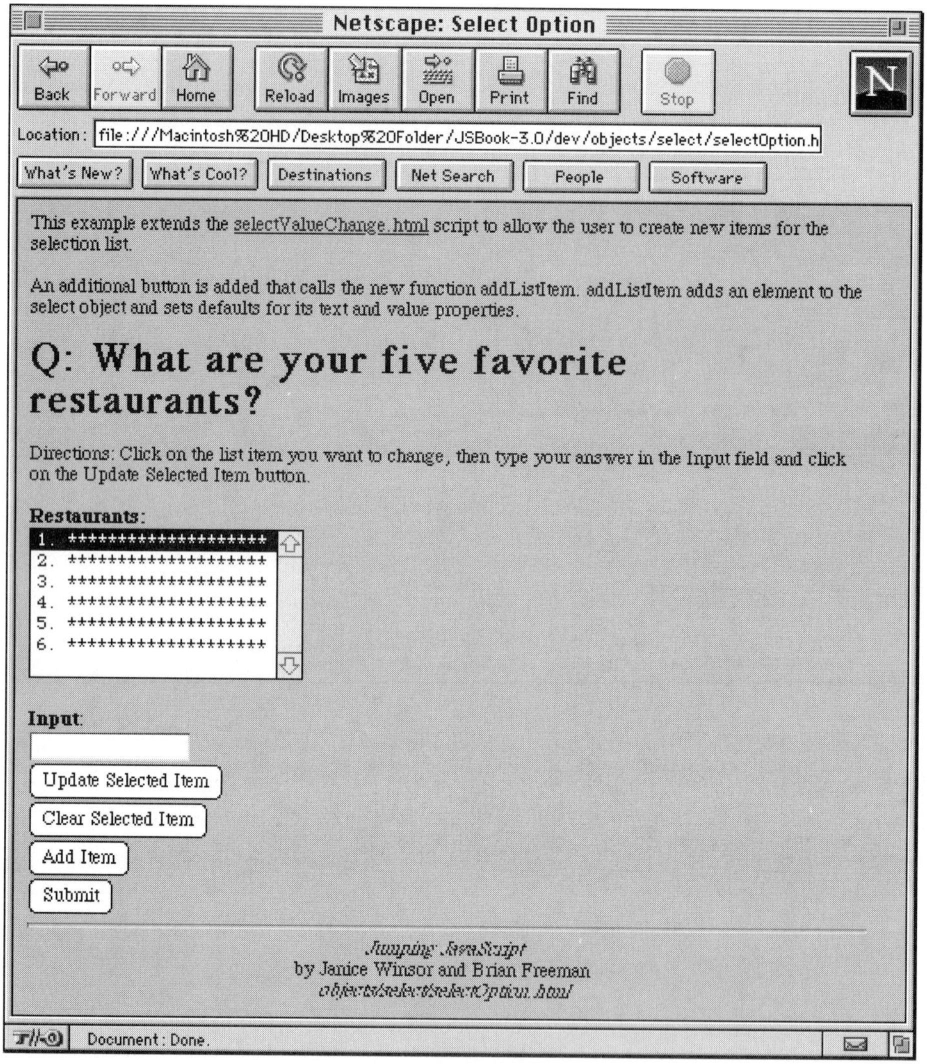

Figure 22–12 Adding an option to the list

CHAPTER 23

- Creating a fileUpload Object
- Displaying Properties of the fileUpload Object
- Determining the Name of the fileUpload Object
- Determining the Value of the fileUpload Object
- Displaying the Type of a Form
- Controlling Keyboard Focus
- Handling Events when the Keyboard Focus Changes

Including Files in an Upload

The Navigator 3.0 release provides a new `fileUpload` object. You can use this object to enable users to specify which file on their system they want to upload to a server as part of a form.

Using the `fileUpload` object is similar to adding an attachment to an e-mail message. With this object, the user can specify a single file that is attached to a form to be uploaded to a server. For security reasons, only the user can specify that a file be attached to a form for uploading. The JavaScript language cannot access files without user input or enter text into the input file in any way. All of the properties are read-only. This implementation prevents the creating of scripts that could potentially upload files from a client system without the user's knowledge.

The properties, methods, and event handlers for the `fileUpload` object are listed in alphabetical order in Table 23-1.

Table 23-1 Properties, Methods, and Event Handlers for the fileUpload Object

Properties	Methods	Event Handlers
`form`	`blur()`	`onBlur`
`name`	`eval()`	`onChange`
`type`	`focus()`	`onFocus`
`value`	`toString()`	
	`valueOf()`	

Creating a fileUpload Object

To create a `fileUpload` object, you create a form and specify `TYPE=file` for the `INPUT` attribute. Refer to the HTML Brushup box for a of review the syntax and attributes of the `<FORM></FORM>` tags that create the `fileUpload` object. When you specify `TYPE=file`, the JavaScript language creates the `fileUpload` object, and a field and a browser button are displayed when the page is loaded. You use the `SIZE` attribute to define the length of the field, and the `MAXLENGTH` attribute to specify the maximum number of characters that the field can accept. Usually, you should use a `MAXLENGTH` of 256 characters.

The `fileUpload` object must use the `"multipart/form-data"` encoding and the `POST` method on the form that contains it. For security reasons, the `fileUpload` object does not recognize the HTML value attribute.

Example of Creating a fileUpload Object

The following `fileUpload.html` script creates a `fileUpload` object. This script specifies a dummy URL as the location to receive the uploaded file and displays an alert when you click on the Submit button.

HTML Brushup — fileUpload Object

You create a fileUpload object by using the following syntax:

<FORM

<INPUT

NAME = "*name*"

TYPE = "file"

MAXLENGTH = "*numberOfCharacters*"

(TARGET = "*windowName*")

ACTION = "*serverURL*"

METHOD = "POST"

ENCTYPE = "multipart/form-data"

(onBlur = "*JavaScript code*")

(onFocus = "*JavaScript code*")

(onChange = "*JavaScript code*")>

</FORM>

```
<!--
                  fileUpload.html
-->

<HTML>
<HEAD>
<TITLE>fileUpload</TITLE>
</HEAD>

<BODY>

<P>When you enter a file name into the fileUpload
field and click on the Submit button, Navigator
submits the contents of the file along with the form.
The fileUpload object requires that the form containing
it is encoded as "multipart/form-data" and uses
the post method.</P>

<P>For security reasons, all of the fileUpload's
properties are read-only. Thus, the object does
```

```
not recognize the HTML value attribute.</P>

<P>You access to the fileUpload object through:
<DL>
<DT>form.<I>name</I>
<DT>form.elements[<I>i</I>]
<DT>form.elements[<I>name</I>]
</DL>

<FORM NAME="myForm"
    METHOD="POST"
    ENCtype="multipart/form-data"
    ACTION="a_url_goes_here"
    onSubmit="alert('Thanks!'); return false">
<B>Click on the Browse button and choose a file:</B><BR>
<INPUT TYPE="file"
    NAME="fileObj"
    SIZE=30
   MAXLENGTH=256>
<BR>
<INPUT TYPE="submit"
    NAME="submitBtn"
    VALUE="Submit">
</FORM>

</BODY>
</HTML>
```

Notice that the text field and Browse button are not specifically created in the form; they are part of the `fileUpload` object:

```
<INPUT TYPE="file"
    NAME="fileObj"
    SIZE=30
   MAXLENGTH=256>
```

For information about the `submit` object, see "submit and reset Objects" on page 598.

Figure 23–1 shows the result of loading the `fileUpload.html` script.

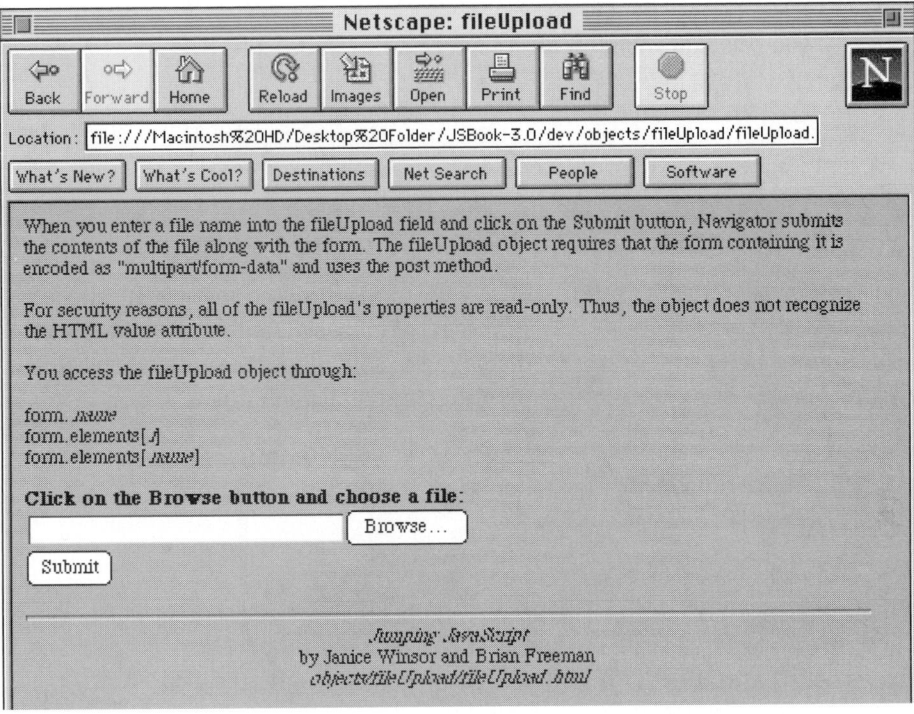

Figure 23–1 Result of loading the `fileUpload.html` script

Notice that you cannot type directly into the text field. To enter the name of a file, you click on the Browse button; the browser for your platform is displayed. Figure 23–2 shows the Macintosh browser.

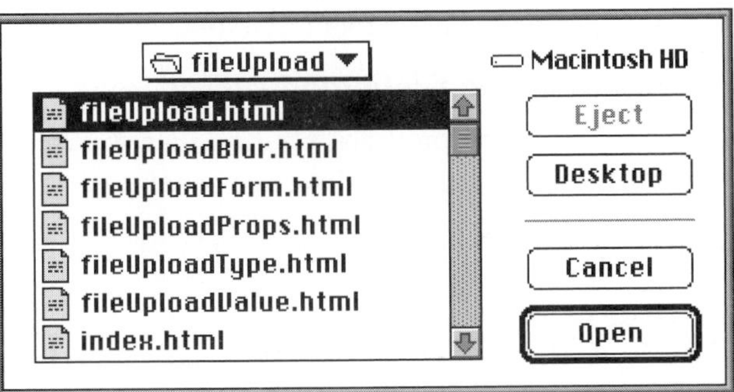

Figure 23–2 Clicking on the Browse button displays the browser for your computer

If you click on a file that is of a type that cannot be attached, an alert is displayed, as shown in Figure 23–3.

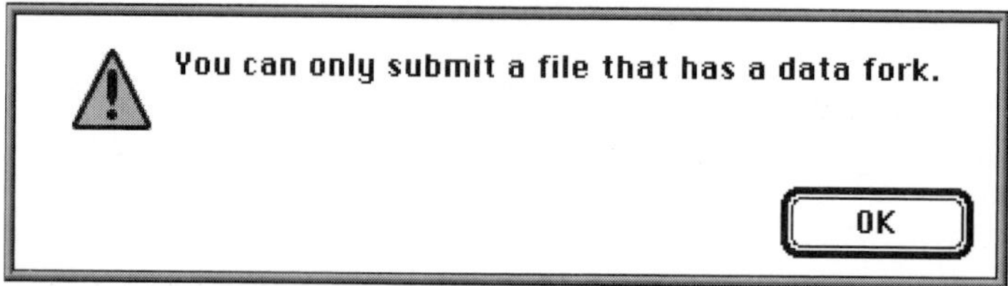

Figure 23–3 Incorrect file type for the `fileUpload` object

When you click on the Submit button, the form is submitted to the URL specified by the `ACTION` attribute of the `<FORM>` tag. In this script, the `ACTION` attribute has a dummy URL, and an alert is displayed to show that the `submit` object is working, as shown in Figure 23–4. Nothing is actually submitted.

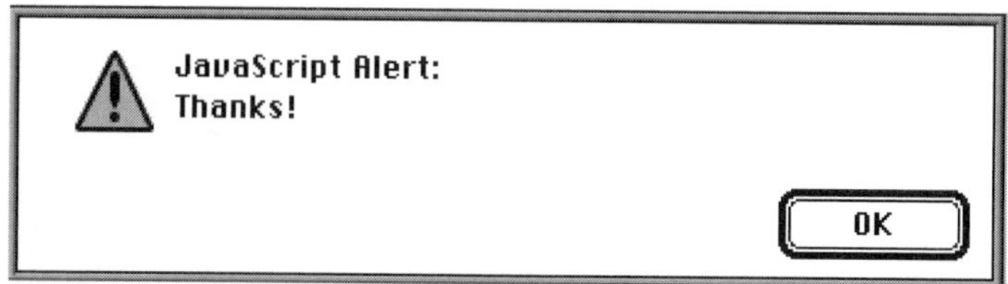

Figure 23–4 An alert is displayed when you submit the form

If the script had a proper server URL, the file would be uploaded to the server along with the values for any input elements in the form.

Displaying Properties of the fileUpload Object

For security, all of the properties of the `fileUpload` object are read-only. You can extract their values in a script, but you cannot change them dynamically.

Example of Displaying Properties of the fileUpload Object

The following `fileUploadProps.html` script provides a button that you can click on to display the properties for the `fileUpload` object in a separate window.

```
<!--
              fileUploadProps.html

    Display all the fileUpload properties in a
    window when the button is clicked.
-->

<HTML>
<HEAD>
```

```
<TITLE>fileUpload Properties</TITLE>

<!-- Include for displayPropsWin() -->
<SCRIPT SRC="../../debug/getProps.js"></SCRIPT>
<!--
    Include displayPropsWin(), which displays
    the properties of a given object in a new
    window.
-->
<SCRIPT SRC="../../debug/displayPropsWin.js">
</SCRIPT>
</HEAD>
<BODY>

<P>Click on the button below to display the
fileUpload object's properties.</P>

<CENTER>
<FORM NAME="myForm"
    METHOD="POST"
   ENCtype="multipart/form-data"
   ACTION="a_url_goes_here"
  onSubmit="alert('Thanks!'); return false">

<B>Enter the name of your file here:</B><BR>
<INPUT TYPE="file"
       NAME="fileObj"
       SIZE=30
  MAXLENGTH=256>
<P>
<INPUT TYPE="button"
       NAME="fileProps"
      VALUE="fileUpload Properties"
    onClick="displayPropsWin(myForm.fileObj,
            'myForm.fileObj')">
<BR>
<INPUT TYPE="submit"
       NAME="submitBtn"
      VALUE="Submit">
</FORM>
</CENTER>

</BODY>
</HTML>
```

Figure 23–5 shows the result of loading the `fileUploadProps.html` script.

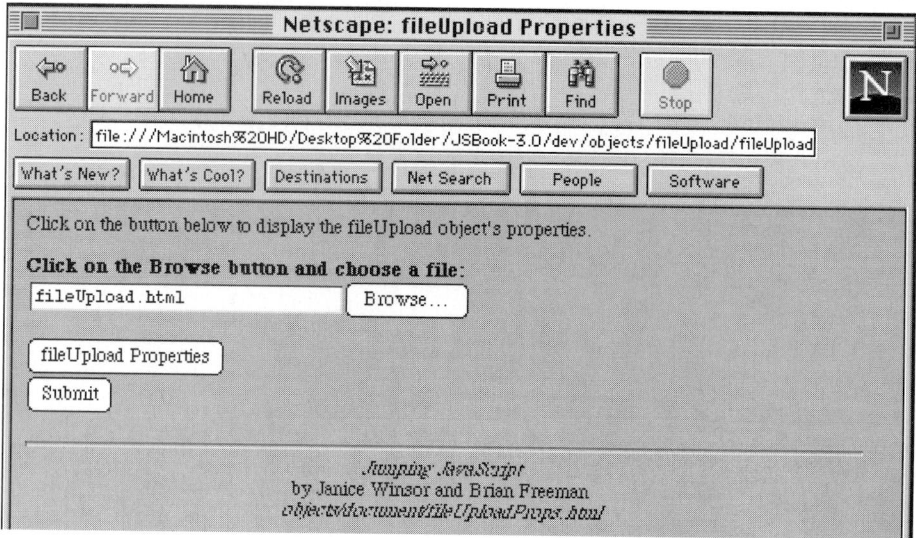

Figure 23–5 Result of loading the `fileUploadProps.html` script

To see the properties for the file that will be uploaded, click on the Browse button and choose a file to upload before you click on the fileUpload Properties button. Figure 23–6 shows the properties window when a file has been chosen for uploading.

Netscape: myForm.fileObj's Properties

```
The properties of the object myForm.fileObj are:
        myForm.fileObj.type = file
        myForm.fileObj.name = fileObj
        myForm.fileObj.form = [object Form]
        myForm.fileObj.value = /Macintosh HD/Desktop
Folder/JSBook-3.0/dev/objects/fileUpload/fileUpload.html
        myForm.fileObj.defaultValue =
        myForm.fileObj.length = null
        myForm.fileObj.options = null
        myForm.fileObj.selectedIndex = null
        myForm.fileObj.checked = null
        myForm.fileObj.defaultChecked = null
        myForm.fileObj.type = file
        myForm.fileObj.name = fileObj
        myForm.fileObj.form = [object Form]
        myForm.fileObj.value = /Macintosh HD/Desktop
Folder/JSBook-3.0/dev/objects/fileUpload/fileUpload.html
        myForm.fileObj.defaultValue =
        myForm.fileObj.length = null
        myForm.fileObj.options = null
        myForm.fileObj.selectedIndex = null
        myForm.fileObj.checked = null
        myForm.fileObj.defaultChecked = null
```

Figure 23–6 `fileUpload` properties

Determining the Name of the fileUpload Object

You can use the `name` property to determine the name of the form. It is read-only so you cannot change it.

Property	Value	Gettable	Settable
name	string	Yes	No

Example of Determining the Name of the fileUpload Object

The following `fileUploadForm.html` script contains an `onClick` event handler that displays an alert containing the name of the form when you choose a file to upload.

```
<!--
                fileUploadForm.html
-->

<HTML>
<HEAD>
<TITLE>fileUpload Form Property</TITLE>
```

```
<SCRIPT LANGUAGE="JavaScript">
<!-- HIDE FROM OLD BROWSERS

// display the name of the form containing the
// fileUpload object.
function displayFormName(fileObj) {
  alert("The form containing " + fileObj.name +
    " is " + fileObj.form.name)
}

// STOP HIDING -->
</SCRIPT></HEAD>

<BODY>

<P>The fileUpload object's form property provides
a read-only reference to the Form object that
contains it.</P>

<P>In this example, an onChange event handler is
used to display an alert dialog informing you of
the file object's name.</P>

<FORM NAME="myForm"
    METHOD="POST"
   ENCtype="multipart/form-data"
    ACTION="a_url_goes_here"
  onSubmit="alert('Thanks!'); return false">
<B>Click on the Browse button and choose a file:</B><BR>
<INPUT TYPE="file"
       NAME="fileObj"
       SIZE=30
  MAXLENGTH=256
   onChange="displayFormName(this)">
<BR>
<INPUT TYPE="submit"
       NAME="submitBtn"
      VALUE="Submit">
</FORM>

</BODY>
</HTML>
```

Figure 23–7 shows the result of loading the `fileUploadForm.html` script after choosing a file from the browser.

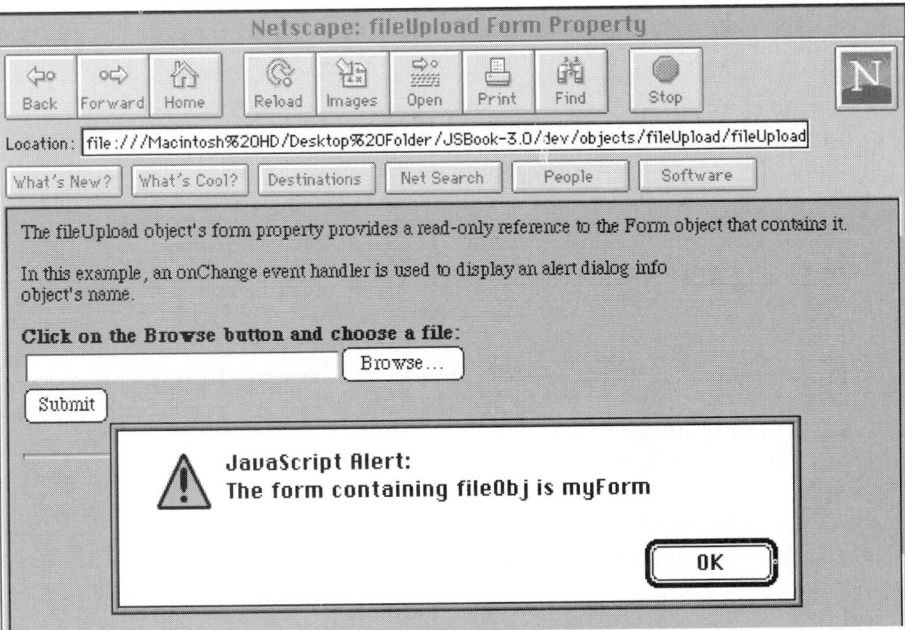

Figure 23–7 Result of loading the `fileUploadForm.html` script

Determining the Value of the fileUpload Object

You use the `value` property to determine the value contained in the input field of the `fileUpload` object. This value is the name of the file that the user wants to include in the upload and the value sent to the server when the form is submitted from a Navigator 3.0 browser. In the Navigator 2.0 release, this field is always blank. You cannot set this property in a script.

Property	Value	Gettable	Settable
value	string	Yes	No

Example of Determining the Value of the fileUpload Object

The following `fileUploadValue.html` script has a Display value Property button. When you click on this button, an alert is displayed that shows the path and file name of the file in the text field.

```
<!--
               fileUploadValue.html
-->

<HTML>
<HEAD>
<TITLE>fileUpload Value Property</TITLE>
<SCRIPT LANGUAGE="JavaScript">
<!-- HIDE FROM OLD BROWSERS

// display the value of the fileUpload object
function displayValue(theObj) {
  var msg_str = ""

  msg_str += "\n" + theObj.name + "'s value"
  msg_str += " = " + theObj.value
  alert(msg_str)
}

// STOP HIDING -->
</SCRIPT></HEAD>

<BODY>

<P>The value property is a read-only string
containing what is in the input field. value is
also sent to the server when the form is
submitted. On Navigator 2.0, this field is always
blank; on 3.0, any file name the user specifies
can be read, but the property is not guaranteed
to be set.</P>

<FORM NAME="myForm"
    METHOD="POST"
   ENCvalue="multipart/form-data"
    ACTION="a_url_goes_here"
  onSubmit="alert('Thanks!'); return false">
<B>Click on the Browse button and choose a file:</B><BR>
<INPUT TYPE="file"
       NAME="fileObj"
       SIZE=30
  MAXLENGTH=256>
<P>
<INPUT TYPE="button"
```

```
        NAME="displayBtn"
       VALUE="Display value Property"
     onClick="displayValue(myForm.fileObj)">
<P>
<INPUT TYPE="submit"
        NAME="submitBtn"
       VALUE="Submit">
</FORM>

</BODY>
</HTML>
```

If you click on the Display value Property button without first choosing a file from the browser, the alert displays no value for the property. Figure 23–8 shows the result of loading the `fileUploadValue.html` script after choosing a file from the browser.

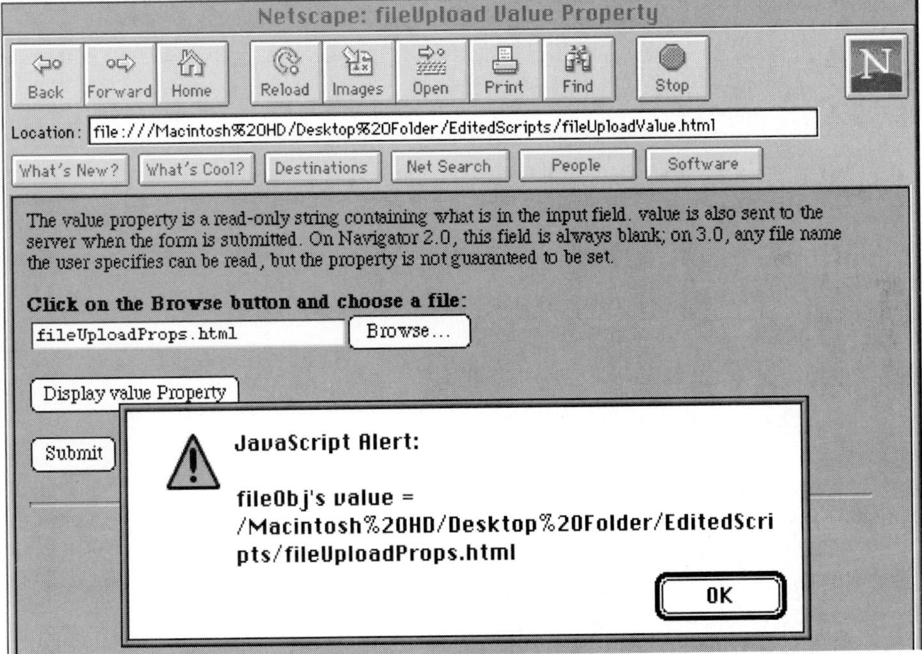

Figure 23–8 Result of loading the `fileUploadValue.html` script and clicking on the Display value Property button

Displaying the Type of a Form

You use the `type` property to display the type for a `form` object. The type for the `fileUpload` object is `"file"`. The `type` property is useful for finding the `fileUpload` objects in a complex form. You cannot set this property.

Property	Value	Gettable	Settable
type	string	Yes	No

Example of Displaying the Type of a fileUpload

The following `fileUploadType.html` script contains a Display type Property button that you can click on to display the type of the `fileUpload`.

```
<!--
                fileUploadType.html
-->

<HTML>
<HEAD>
<TITLE>fileUpload Type Property</TITLE>
<SCRIPT LANGUAGE="JavaScript">
<!-- HIDE FROM OLD BROWSERS

function displayType(theObj) {
  var msg_str = ""

  msg_str += "\n" + theObj.name + "'s type"
  msg_str += " = " + theObj.type
  alert(msg_str)
}

// STOP HIDING -->
</SCRIPT></HEAD>

<BODY>

<P>The type property is a read-only string that
specifies the kind of form element for the
fileUpload object. For the fileUpload object,
the type is "file".</P>
```

```
<CENTER>
<FORM NAME="myForm"
    METHOD="POST"
   ENCtype="multipart/form-data"
    ACTION="a_url_goes_here"
  onSubmit="alert('Thanks!'); return false">
<B>Click on the Browse button and choose a file:</B><BR>
<INPUT TYPE="file"
       NAME="fileObj"
       SIZE=30
  MAXLENGTH=256>
<P>
<INPUT TYPE="button"
       NAME="displayBtn"
      VALUE="Display type Property"
    onClick="displayType(myForm.fileObj)">
<P>
<INPUT TYPE="submit"
       NAME="submitBtn"
      VALUE="Submit">
</FORM>
</CENTER>

</BODY>
</HTML>
```

Figure 23–9 shows the result of loading the `fileUploadType.html` script.

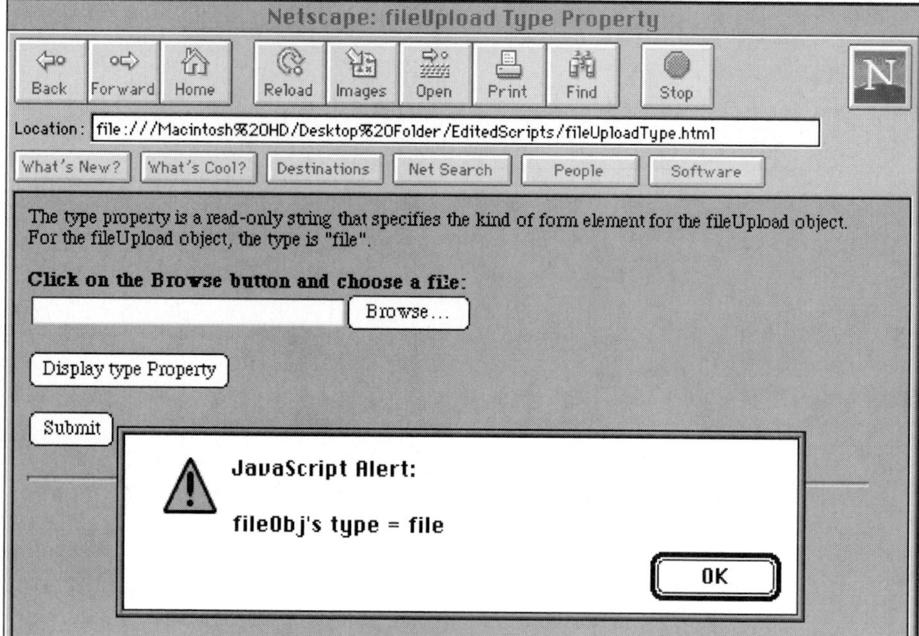

Figure 23–9 Result of loading the `fileUploadType.html` script

Controlling Keyboard Focus

You can use the `blur()` and `focus()` methods to remove the keyboard focus from the `fileUpload` object or to set the keyboard focus to the `fileUpload` object. When the `fileUpload` object has the focus, all keystrokes are automatically entered into this object.

Methods

blur()

focus()

Syntax

fileUpload.blur()

fileUpload.focus()

Returns

Nothing

Example of Controlling Keyboard Focus

The following `fileUploadBlur.html` script removes keyboard focus from the `fileUpload` object. Using the `blur()` method in this way ensures that any uncommitted user edits are saved before the contents are submitted.

```
<!--
               fileUploadBlur.html
-->

<HTML>
<HEAD>
<TITLE>fileUpload Blur Method</TITLE>
</HEAD>

<BODY>

<P>The blur method removes keyboard focus from
the fileUpload object. When you call blur() in your form's
onSubmit event handler, any uncommitted user edits are
set before the contents are submitted.</P>

<FORM NAME="myForm"
    METHOD="POST"
  ENCvalue="multipart/form-data"
    ACTION="a_url_goes_here"
  onSubmit="this.fileObj.blur(); return false">
```

```
<B>Click on the Browse button and choose a file:</B><BR>
<INPUT TYPE="file"
       NAME="fileObj"
       SIZE=30
  MAXLENGTH=256>
<BR>
<INPUT TYPE="submit"
       NAME="submitBtn"
      VALUE="Submit">
</FORM>

</BODY>
</HTML>
```

Figure 23–10 shows the result of loading the `fileUploadBlur.html` script.

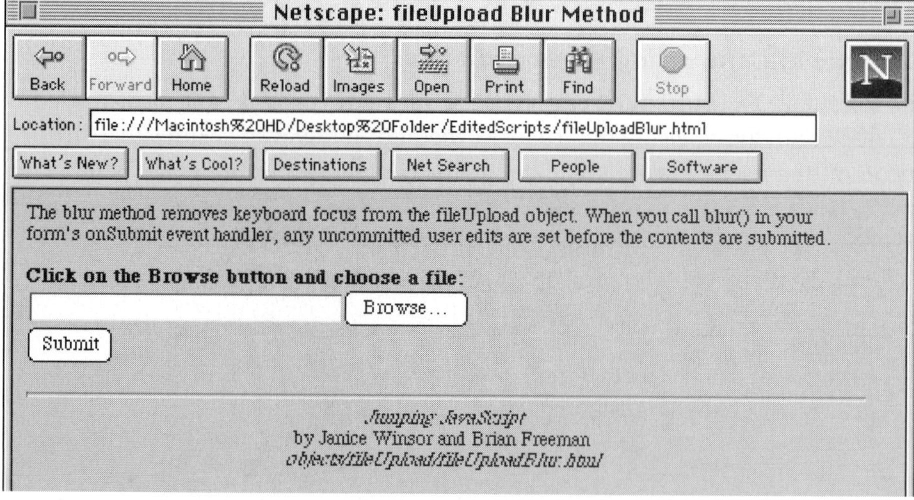

Figure 23–10 Result of loading the `fileUploadBlur.html` script

Handling Events when the Keyboard Focus Changes

You use the event handlers of the `fileUpload` object to initiate actions when the object has or loses the keyboard focus (`onFocus`, `onBlur`), and when the object is changed (`onChange`).

Event Handler

onBlur

onChange

onFocus

Syntax

```
<FORM>
<INPUT
   NAME = "name"
   TYPE = "file"
   MAXLENGTH = "numberOfCharacters"
    (TARGET = "windowName")
   ACTION = "serverURL"
    METHOD = "POST"
    ENCTYPE = "multipart/form-data"
    (onBlur = "JavaScript code")
    (onFocus = "JavaScript code")
    (onChange = "JavaScript code")>
</FORM>
```

CHAPTER 24

- Overview of How a Form Is Submitted
- Determining the Number of Input Elements in a Form
- Specifying Where to Send Your Forms Data
- Specifying How Data Is Transmitted
- Specifying the Window or Frame That Receives Server Output
- Encoding Form Data with a MIME Type
- Submitting a Form
- Resetting a Form to Its Default Values
- Controlling Actions when Users Submit a Form
- Controlling Events When Users Reset a Form
- Summary of New Terms and Concepts

Using Forms to Send Data to a Server

The `form` object is at the heart of the Web. The `form` object bridges the gap between the client and server and enables information to flow freely back and forth between these two systems.

Forms and their elements provide a way for users to interact with your JavaScript programs and to submit user data to a Web server. You define a form by using the `<FORM></FORM>` HTML tags, and you work with the elements of the form in scripts, by using their properties, methods, and event handlers. Writing the HTML code to create forms is easy. Writing the scripts that interpret the data that users enter into the forms is a bit more complicated.

You've already learned how to use the `<FORM></FORM>` HTML tags to create user interface elements in your documents. This chapter discusses the attributes of the `<FORM></FORM>` HTML tags that you use to submit forms to a Web server and describes the methods, properties, and event handlers of the JavaScript `form` object.

Before you can submit forms, you need to have a server capable of accepting data from your forms. The most common way to communicate data from your forms is to Web servers that support the common gateway interface (CGI). Typically, CGI programs or scripts are written in the Perl language. Other technologies such as LiveWire provide CGI functionality along with other benefits and features. Describing CGI scripts and LiveWire is beyond the scope of this book. We recommend the following books if you are interested in more information:

- *CGI Developer's Resource: Web Programming in Tcl and Perl*, J.M. Ivler, 1997, Prentice Hall Professional Technical Reference
- *CGI Programming on the World Wide Web*, Shishir Gundavaram, 1996, O'Reilly & Associates
- *Programming Perl*, 2nd Edition, Larry Wall, Tom Christiansen, and Randal L. Schwartz, 1996, O'Reilly & Associates

Before we introduce the JavaScript `forms` object, refer to the HTML Brushup box to review the syntax and attributes of the `<FORM></FORM>` tags.

HTML Brushup

You create a form by using the following syntax:

<FORM

(NAME = "*formName*")

(TARGET = "*windowName*")

(ACTION = "*serverURL*")

(METHOD = "GET | POST")

(ENCTYPE = "*MIMEType*")

(onReset = "*JavaScript code*")

(onSubmit = "*JavaScript code*") >

</FORM>

The way you define a form depends on how you plan to use the information from the elements of the form. If you never plan to send data to a server from the form, you do not need to use the `ACTION`, `TARGET`, or `METHOD` attributes described in Table 24-1. On the other hand, if your Web page sends information or queries back to the server, you need to specify values for these attributes.

Table 24-1 <FORM> Attributes

Attribute	Description
`NAME = "`*`formName`*`"`	The name of the form.
`TARGET = "`*`windowName`*`"`	Name of the window in which to display responses to the form. You can use the special names of `_top`, `_parent`, `_self`, and `_blank` as arguments for this attribute.
`ACTION = "`*`serverURL`*`"`	The URL where you want to submit the form data.
`ENCTYPE = "`*`MIMEType`*`"`	Use this attribute to specify the MIME encoding of the data being sent to the server. Typically if `METHOD="POST"`, the default `ENCTYPE` is `"application/x-www-form-urlencoded"`. If the form contains a `fileUpload` object, use `"multipart/form-data"`.
`METHOD = GET | POST`	How to submit form data. GET is the default and it is the usual method.

Overview of How a Form Is Submitted

When you submit a form and receive information back from the server, the exchange between each client request and server response has three parts:

- A request and response line
- An (optional) header that specifies the type of browser on the client system, and the document formats that the browser knows about
- An (optional) entity body that specifies the way that information is sent and received

Suppose the client computer has a form that a user has filled out. You need to submit information from that form to the server. On the server, a CGI or LiveWire script takes the input from all of the fields in the form, parses it all, and processes it. Usually, the server sends some information back to the client to acknowledge receipt of the data or to display the result of a query.

The properties, methods, and event handlers for the `form` object are listed in alphabetical order in Table 24-2.

Table 24-2 Properties, Methods, and Event Handlers for the form Object

Properties	Methods	Event Handlers
`action`	`eval()*`	`onReset*`
`elements[]`	`reset()*`	`onSubmit`
`encoding`	`submit()`	
`method`	`toString()*`	
`name`	`valueOf()*`	
`target`		

* New in Navigator 3.0.

Forms are the way you enable the user to enter information that can be sent back to the server. How the server uses the information depends on the programs running on the server. If the server is at your site and under your control, the sky's the limit. However, if you rely on an Internet service provider to store your HTML files, you are limited to a set of programs that are available to all customers of that service.

You use the `form` object properties to specify the information to be transmitted between the client and server.

When you write a JavaScript program to submit a form, you ordinarily would use an `onSubmit` event handler in your script to catch the data just before it is sent to the server. At this time, you can use the `elements` property to walk through all of the input elements in the form, validate those elements, and change any values before the form is submitted. You can check any required fields for values. If a required field has no value, you can display an alert that asks the user to fill in the essential information and return the form to them so they can fill in the data before the form is submitted.

You use the `action` property to point to where to send the data that is in the form. You use the `encoding` property to specify how to send the data from the client browser to the server, and you use the `target` property to specify where you want any data that is returned from the server to be displayed.

Regardless of your Internet server status, you can use JavaScript programs to preprocess information and format it on the client system before you send it to the server.

Example of Displaying Form Properties in a Window

The following `formProps.html` script displays the properties for the `form` object in a separate window when you click on the Form Properties button.

```
<!--
                formProps.html

    Display all the form properties in a window.
-->

<HTML>
<HEAD>
<TITLE>Form Properties</TITLE>

<!-- Include for displayPropsWin() -->
<SCRIPT SRC="../../debug/getProps.js"></SCRIPT>
<!--
    Include displayPropsWin(), which displays
    the properties of a given object in a new
    window.
-->
<SCRIPT SRC="../../debug/displayPropsWin.js">
</SCRIPT>
</HEAD>
<BODY>

<P>Click on Form Properties to display the Form
object's properties.</P>

<CENTER>
<FORM NAME="myForm" METHOD="POST"
   ENCtype="application/x-www-form-urlencoded"
   ACTION="/a_url_goes_here"
  onSubmit="alert('Thanks!'); return false">
<P>
<INPUT TYPE="button" NAME="formPropsBtn"
      VALUE="Form Properties"
    onClick="displayPropsWin(myForm, 'myForm')">
<BR>
<INPUT TYPE="submit"
```

```
         NAME="submitBtn"
        VALUE="Submit">
</FORM>
</CENTER>

</BODY>
</HTML>
```

Figure 24–1 shows the result of loading the `formProps.html` script.

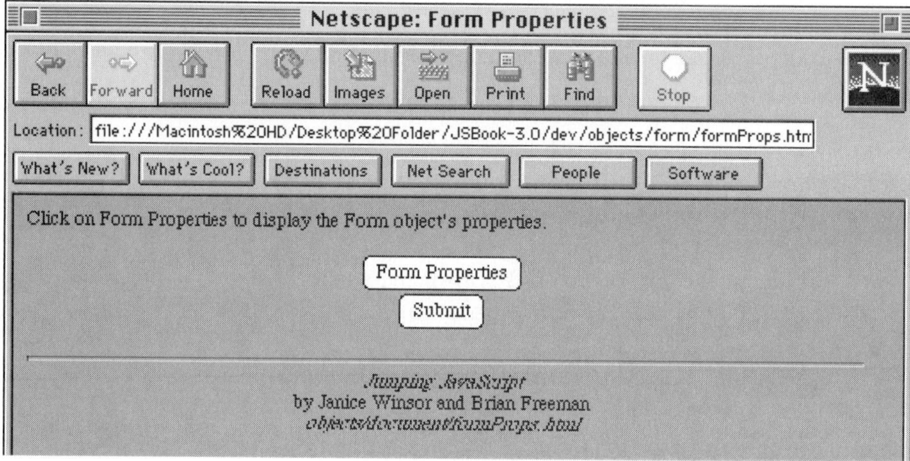

Figure 24–1 Result of loading the `formProps.html` script

When you click on the Form Properties button, a new window opens, containing a list of the properties for the form, as shown in Figure 24–2.

Netscape: myForm's Properties

The properties of the object myForm are:
myForm.formPropsBtn =
myForm.submitBtn =
myForm.length = 2
myForm.name = myForm
myForm.elements = [object Form]
myForm.method = post
myForm.action = file:///a_url_goes_here
myForm.encoding = application/x-www-form-urlencoded
myForm.target =

Figure 24–2 Properties for the `form` object

Determining the Number of Input Elements in a Form

When you have a form that accepts user input, you need to cycle through the input elements in the array and extract the values that the user has entered. To do this, you use the `elements` property of the `form` object. The `elements` property is an array that contains a list of all of the input elements between the `<FORM></FORM>` tags. The `elements` array is a collection of all of the input elements that you have included in the form.

Property	Value	Gettable	Settable
elements	array of subobjects	Yes	No

As with other arrays, you can use the `elements.length` property to determine how many elements you have in your array.

You can reference the element of a form by using the following syntax:

```
formName.propertyName
formName.methodName(parameters)
forms[index].propertyName
forms[index].methodName(parameters)
```

Example of Determining the Number of Input Elements in a Form

The following `form.html` script creates a form and shows you a number of ways to reference its properties.

```
<!--
           form.html

    This example creates a form and shows how to
    reference its properties and methods in a
    couple of ways.
-->

<HTML>
<HEAD>
<TITLE>Form</TITLE>
</HEAD>

<BODY>

<P>Below is a form defined with all of the
possible attributes. When you click one of the
buttons in the form, an alert dialog displays
```

```
the property named in the button.</P>

<FORM
  NAME="nowhereForm"
  TARGET="_self"
  ACTION="http://url.to.the.server"
  METHOD="GET"
  ENCTYPE="application/x-www-form-urlencoded"
  onSubmit="return"
>
<INPUT TYPE="button" NAME="actionBtn"
 VALUE="action"
 onClick="alert(nowhereForm.action)">

<INPUT TYPE="button" NAME="elementsBtn"
 VALUE="elements"
 onClick="alert(nowhereForm.elements)">

<INPUT TYPE="button" NAME="encodingBtn"
 VALUE="encoding"
 onClick="alert(nowhereForm.encoding)">

<INPUT TYPE="button" NAME="lengthBtn"
 VALUE="length"
 onClick="alert(nowhereForm.length)">

<INPUT TYPE="button" NAME="methodBtn"
 VALUE="method"
 onClick="alert(nowhereForm.method)">

<INPUT TYPE="button" NAME="targetBtn"
 VALUE="target"
 onClick="alert(nowhereForm.target)">
</FORM>

<P>Several ways to access a form are:</P>
<OL>
<LI><I>formName</I>.<I>propertyName</I>
<LI><I>formName</I>.<I>methodName</I>
(<I>parameters</I>)
<LI>forms[<I>index</I>].<I>propertyName</I>
<LI>forms[<I>index</I>].<I>methodName</I>
(<I>parameters</I>)
</OL>
```

```
<I>formName</I> is the value of the NAME
attribute of a form object. In this case it is
"nowhereForm".<BR>
<I>propertyName</I> is one of the properties.<BR>
<I>methodName</I> is one of the methods.<BR>
<I>index</I> is an integer representing a
form object.

<P>For example:</P>

<SCRIPT LANGUAGE="JavaScript">
<!-- HIDE FROM OLD BROWSERS
var mstr = "<OL>"

mstr+="<LI>document.nowhereForm.action = " +
       document.nowhereForm.action
mstr+="<LI>document.nowhereForm.submit()"
mstr+="<LI>document.forms[0].action = " +
       document.forms[0].action
mstr+="<LI>document.forms[0].submit()"
mstr+="</OL>"

document.open()
document.write(mstr)
document.close()

// STOP HIDING -->
</SCRIPT>

</BODY>
</HTML>
```

Figure 24–3 shows the result of loading the `form.html` script.

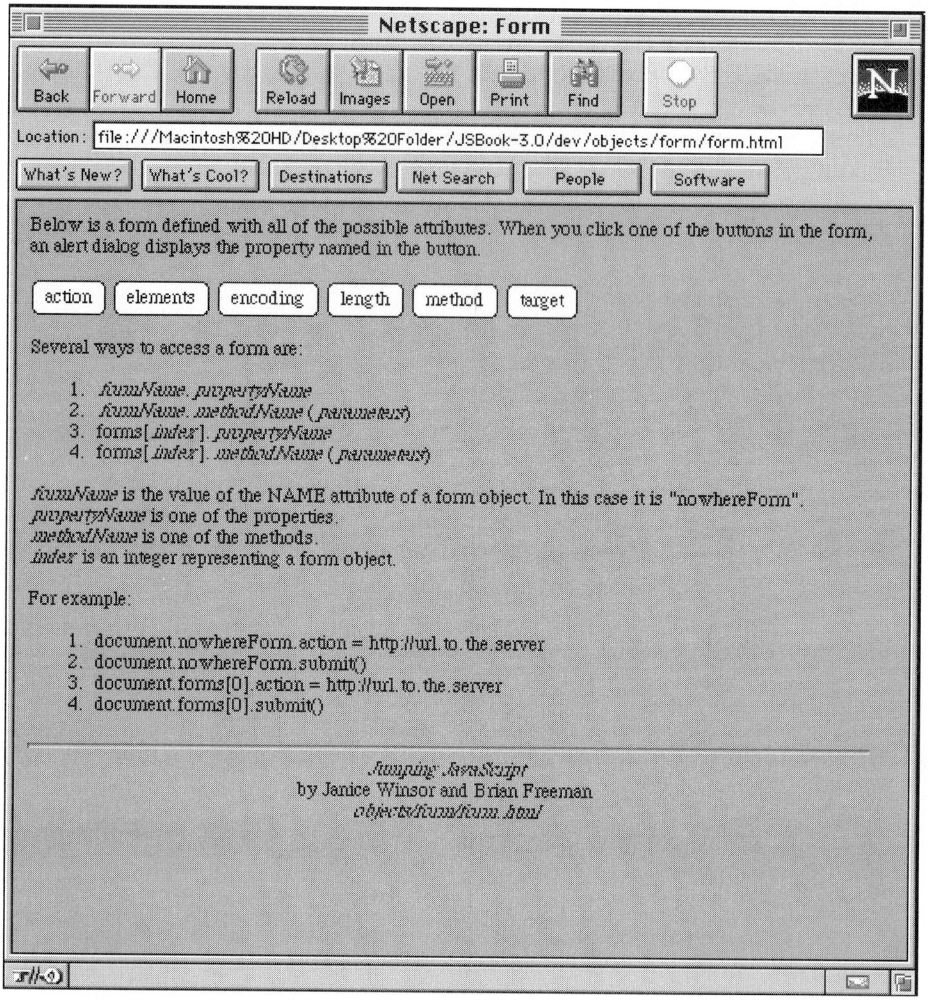

Netscape: Form

Back Forward Home Reload Images Open Print Find Stop

Location: file:///Macintosh%20HD/Desktop%20Folder/JSBook-3.0/dev/objects/form/form.html

What's New? What's Cool? Destinations Net Search People Software

Below is a form defined with all of the possible attributes. When you click one of the buttons in the form, an alert dialog displays the property named in the button.

action elements encoding length method target

Several ways to access a form are:

1. *formName.propertyName*
2. *formName.methodName* (*parameters*)
3. forms[*index*].*propertyName*
4. forms[*index*].*methodName* (*parameters*)

formName is the value of the NAME attribute of a form object. In this case it is "nowhereForm".
propertyName is one of the properties.
methodName is one of the methods.
index is an integer representing a form object.

For example:

1. document.nowhereForm.action = http://url.to.the.server
2. document.nowhereForm.submit()
3. document.forms[0].action = http://url.to.the.server
4. document.forms[0].submit()

Jumping JavaScript
by Janice Winsor and Brian Freeman
objects/form/form.html

Figure 24–3 Result of loading the `form.html` script

Each of the buttons represents one of the `form` properties. Clicking on each button displays an alert containing the value of the property named on the button. The alert shown in Figure 24–4 shows that the `action` property value is `http://url.to.the.server`.

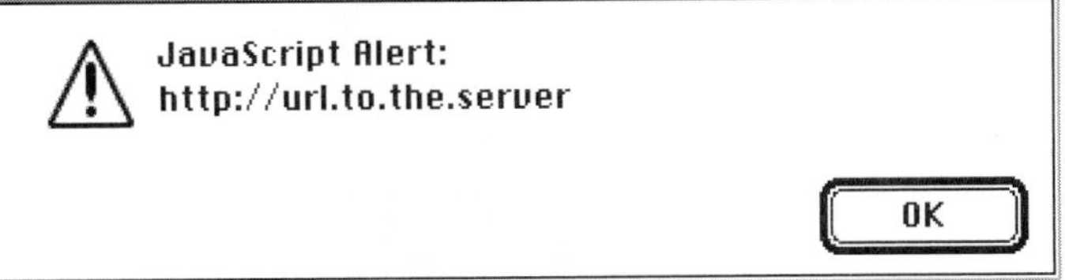

Figure 24–4 Form action property alert

The alert shown in Figure 24–5 shows that the `elements` property value is `[object Form]`.

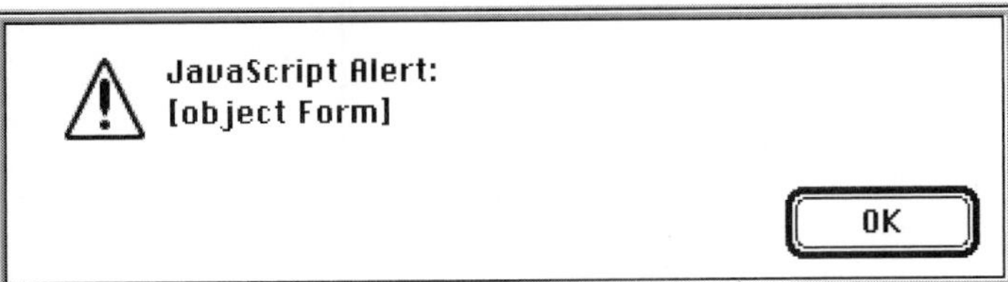

Figure 24–5 Form elements property alert

The alert shown in Figure 24–6 shows that the `encoding` property value is `application/x-www-form-urlencoded`.

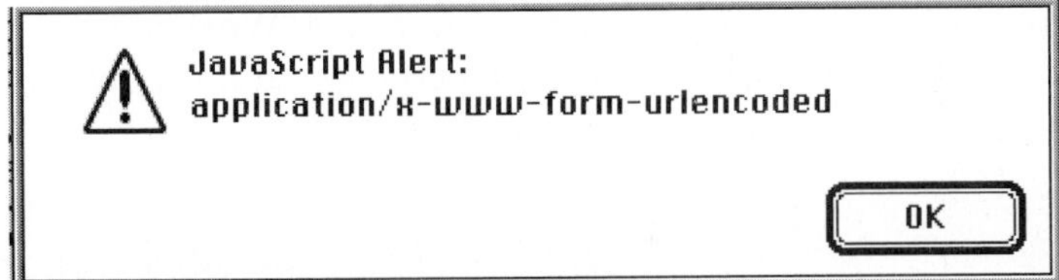

Figure 24–6 Form encoding property alert

The alert shown in Figure 24–7 shows that the `length` property value is `6`.

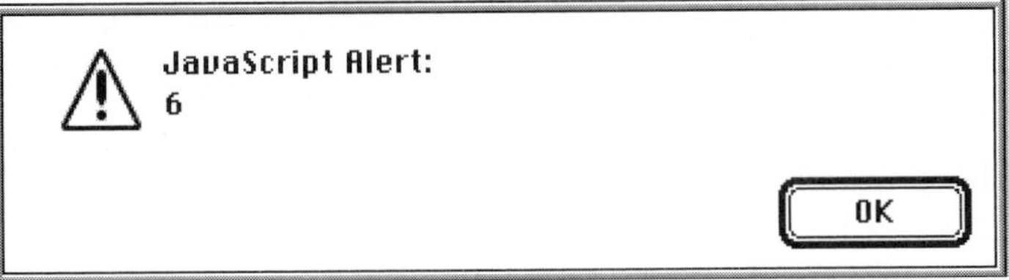

Figure 24–7 Form length property alert

The alert shown in Figure 24–8 shows that the `method` property value is `get`.

JavaScript Alert:
get
OK

Figure 24–8 Form method property alert

The alert shown in Figure 24–9 shows that the `target` property value is `_self`.

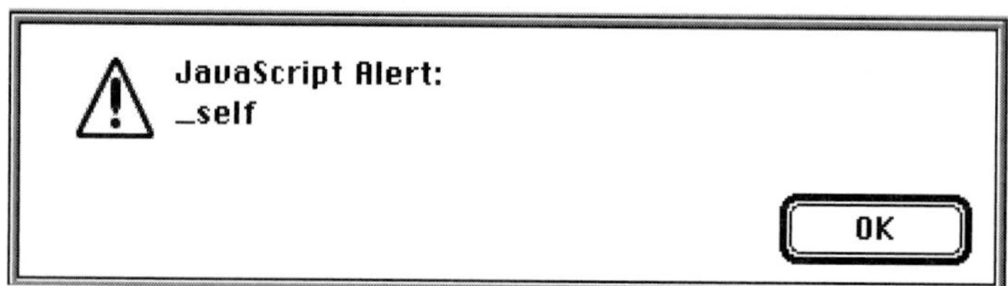

Figure 24–9 Form target property alert

Specifying Where to Send Your Forms Data

When you submit data from a form, you need to specify where that data goes. You use the `action` property of the `form` object to specify where to send the data. In other words, the `action` property answers the question "What do you want to do with the data in the form?" The `action` property is your link between the client form and the service being provided by the server.

Property	Value	Gettable	Settable
action	URL	Yes	Yes

The URL value is not limited to the `http` protocol. You can use any available URL protocol as part of the value for the `action` property, for example: `mailto`, `ftp`, `http`. The way the data is submitted depends on the URL that you specify. For example, if you specify the `mailto` protocol, a mail window opens.

Let's take a look at a classic search example. Suppose you have a form with one text field in it and a Submit button. The form is designed to search a database, using the keyword the user types into the text field. When the user clicks on the Submit button, the value for the `action` property specifies the URL to receive the data from the form. The URL has a CGI script that receives a keyword, such as JavaScript, and reads it in. The script interfaces with the database on the server

and asks "How many instances of JavaScript do I have?" The script finds the references, creates a page, and sends the page back to the client system that initiated the search request.

Example of Specifying Where to Send Your Forms Data

The following `formAction.html` script defines a `ccUser()` function that asks if users want a copy of their data e-mailed back to them. The function uses the `action` property and the `submit()` method. The form uses an `onSubmit` event handler to call the function. Because this script does not submit actual data to a server, you'll receive an error alert from Navigator. You'll also receive other alerts along the way, depending on how your Networking Preferences are set and whether you have data tainting enabled.

```
<!--
                   formAction.html
-->

<HTML>
<HEAD>
<TITLE>Form Action Property</TITLE>
<SCRIPT LANGUAGE="JavaScript">
<!-- HIDE FROM OLD BROWSERS

// An onSubmit event handler asks users
// if they would like a copy of the data they are
// submitting.
function ccUser(aForm) {

  // normally the URL that processes the form
  // data would be assigned here. Fake it. An
  // error dialog is displayed instead.
  aForm.action = "/Ignore this error."
  aForm.submit()

  // ask if the user wants a copy
  mstr  = "\nWould you like a copy of the data you "
  mstr += "submitted to be sent to your e-mail address?\n"

  if (confirm(mstr)) {
    // yes, submit the form.

    // change the action to the mailto protocol
    // and add the user's e-mail address
    aForm.action = "mailto:" + aForm.emailAddr.value
```

```
    aForm.submit()
  }
}

// STOP HIDING -->
</SCRIPT>
</HEAD>

<BODY>

<P>This example of the Form object's action
property enables users to send a copy of the
data that is submitted in the form to their e-mail
address. The action property's value is set in
the ccUser() onSubmit event handler. If users
elect to send themselves a copy, the action
property is changed to the mailto protocol and
the form is resubmitted.</P>

<P>Because we don't actually have a server here,
we use a bogus URL for the first form
submission. This bogus URL generates an error dialog
from Navigator, but you can just click on OK and
ignore it.</P>

<P>Depending on your Network Preferences, you may
also receive another dialog informing you of the
e-mail submission.</P>

<FORM NAME="theForm"
    ACTION="replaced_in_ccUser"
    METHOD="POST"
  onSubmit="ccUser(this)">

<B>First Name: </B><BR>
<INPUT TYPE="text"
 NAME="firstName" VALUE="" SIZE=25>

<BR><B>Last Name: </B><BR>
<INPUT TYPE="text" NAME="lastName" VALUE=""
 SIZE=25>

<BR><B>E-Mail Address: </B><BR>
<INPUT TYPE="text" NAME="emailAddr" VALUE=""
```

```
 SIZE=25>

<BR>
<INPUT TYPE="submit" NAME="submitBtn"
 VALUE="Submit">
</FORM>

</BODY>
</HTML>
```

Figure 24–10 shows the result of loading the `formAction.html` script.

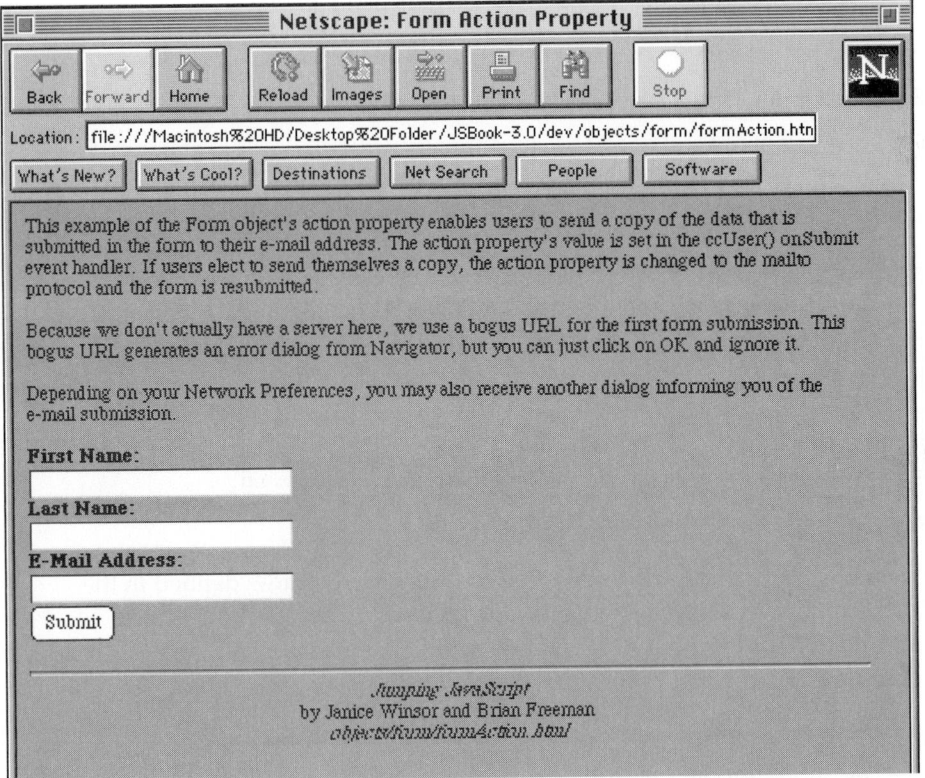

Figure 24–10 Result of loading the `formAction.html` script

When you type your name and e-mail address into the text fields and click on the Submit button, the browser displays an alert warning you that the information you transmit is not secure, as shown in Figure 24–11.

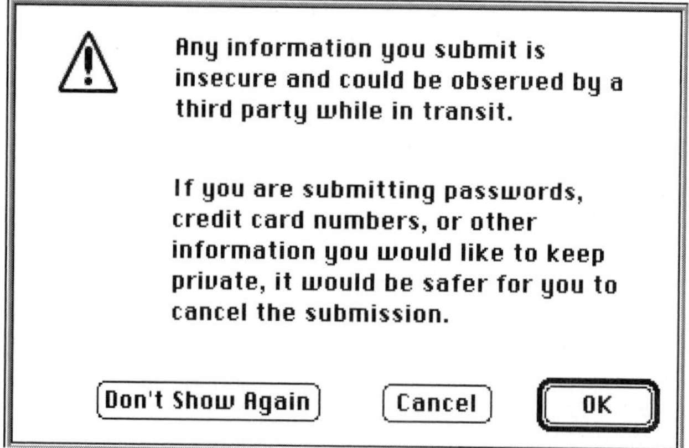

Figure 24–11 Insecure transmission alert

When you click on the OK button, the browser displays another alert, as shown in Figure 24–12. This alert is displayed because the `formAction.html` script uses a dummy URL.

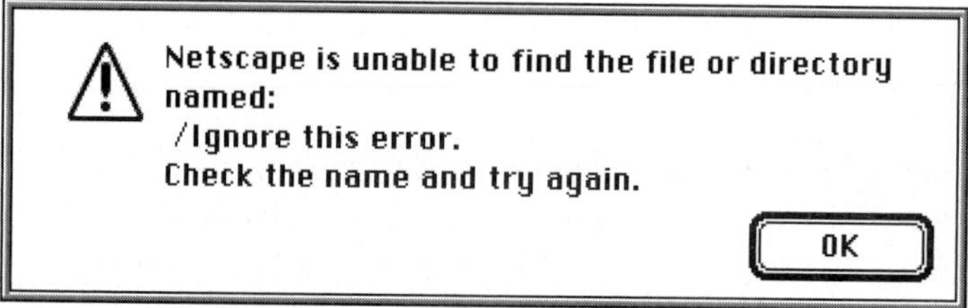

Figure 24–12 Dummy URL alert

When you click on the OK button, the confirmation window defined in the `formAction.html` script is displayed, as shown in Figure 24–13. This confirmation window asks users if they want an e-mail copy of the data that is submitted.

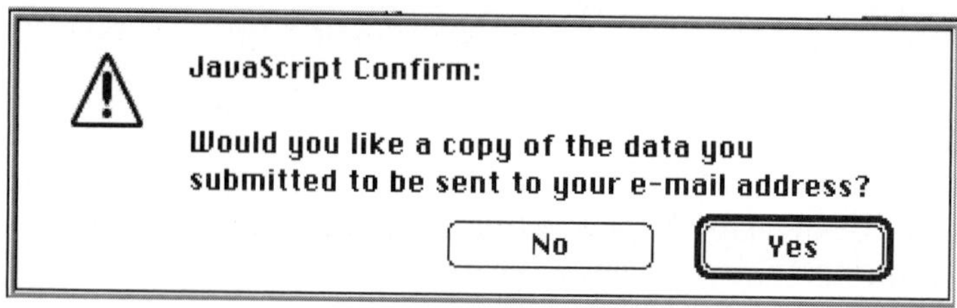

Figure 24–13 E-mail confirmation window

When you click on the Yes button, the e-mail protocol is called and the browser displays another alert, shown in Figure 24–14. This alert contains another warning about security and privacy.

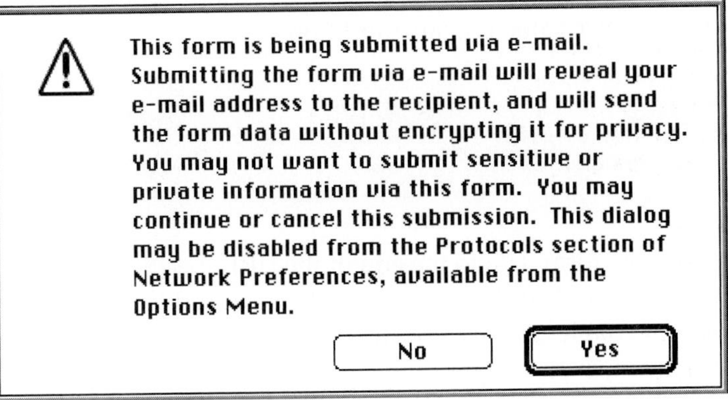

This form is being submitted via e-mail. Submitting the form via e-mail will reveal your e-mail address to the recipient, and will send the form data without encrypting it for privacy. You may not want to submit sensitive or private information via this form. You may continue or cancel this submission. This dialog may be disabled from the Protocols section of Network Preferences, available from the Options Menu.
No
Yes

Figure 24–14 Security and privacy e-mail alert

When you click on the Yes button, the form is submitted along with the request to e-mail the contents back to the user. The return values are included in an attachment, as shown in Figure 24–15.

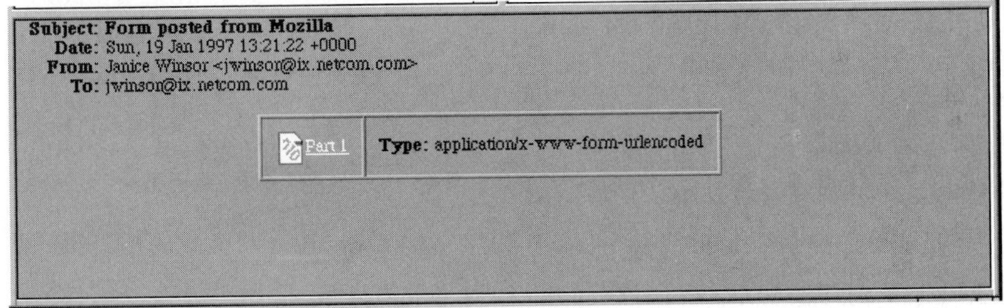

Figure 24–15 E-mail received from an `email` form submission

When you double-click on the attachment, the information is displayed in the main browser window. Figure 24–16 shows the information that was returned from this example.

```
firstName=Janice&lastName=Winsor&emailAddr=jwinsor@ix.netcom.com&submitBtn=Submit
```

Figure 24–16 Contents of the attachment

Specifying How Data Is Transmitted

You use the `method` property to specify the technique for submitting the form. You can choose one of two values for the `method` property: `GET` or `POST`. This value specifies how HTML and CGI work together. The `GET` value for the method property is the oldest. The `POST` value is a later addition.

Property	Value	Gettable	Settable
method	GET or POST	Yes	Yes

The `GET` method appends the form data to the end of the URL specified by `ACTION` and sends it to the server. At the server, the data is typically available through the environment variable `QUERY_STRING`. For example, you can use a `GET` method to perform a search and request the output of a program.

The `POST` method sends the form input as a data body to the server. The data is then available on standard input (`stdin`) to the CGI program and the environment variable `CONTENT_LENGTH` specifies the size in number of bytes. For example, you would use the `POST` method to send the contents of a file or submit a newsgroup posting.

The `GET` and `POST` values seem quite similar, and in fact, there is quite a bit of overlap between the two. The difference is in how the data is passed to the CGI. If you really want to research the difference, we suggest that you go to different Web sites that have forms and view the source to see whether they're using `GET` or `POST` to submit data from a specific form.

Example of a Form That Uses GET

The Lycos search page, shown in Figure 24–17, uses `method="GET"` to submit its data. To see the HTML for this page, go to the Lycos page and choose Document Source from the View menu in the browser.

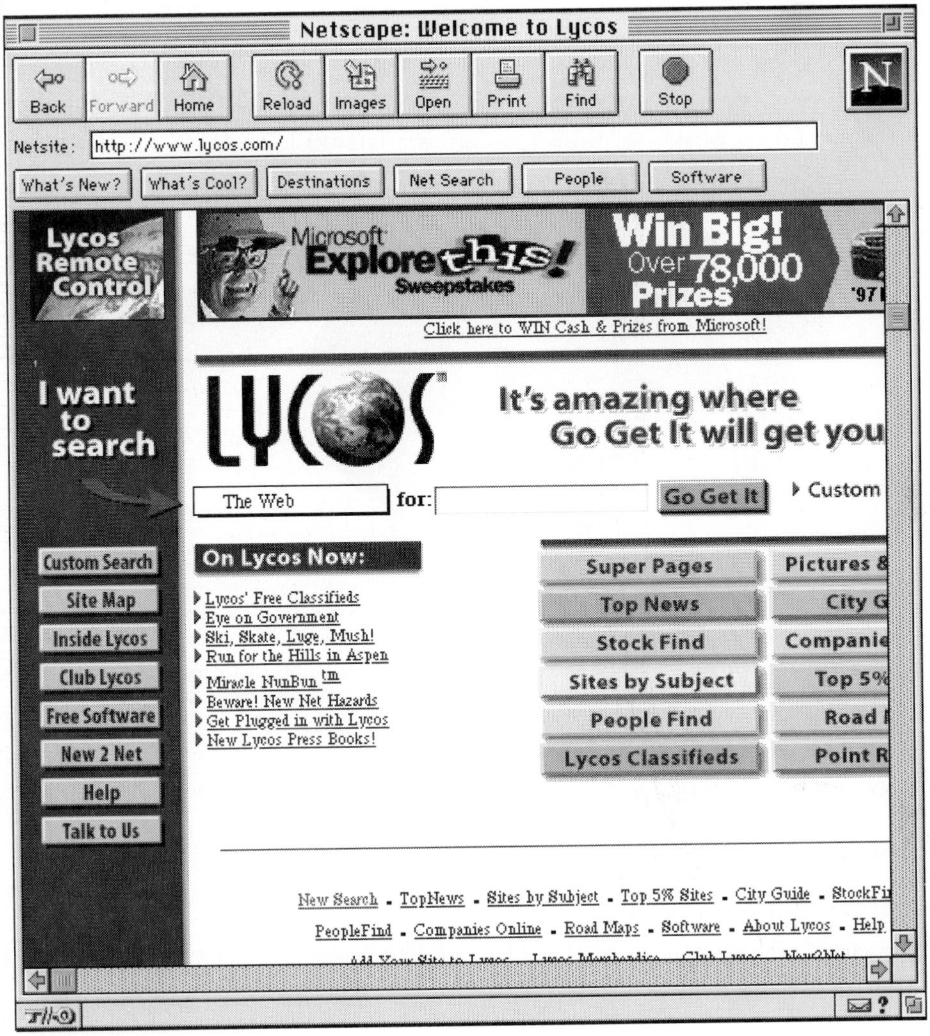

Figure 24–17 Lycos home page uses `method="GET"`

Example of a Form That Uses POST

The Java Store, shown in Figure 24–18, uses `method="POST"` to submit its data. To see the HTML for this page, go to `http://www.sun.com` and choose Java, then Java Store, and click on an item to get to the page with a form. Then choose Document Source from the View menu in the browser.

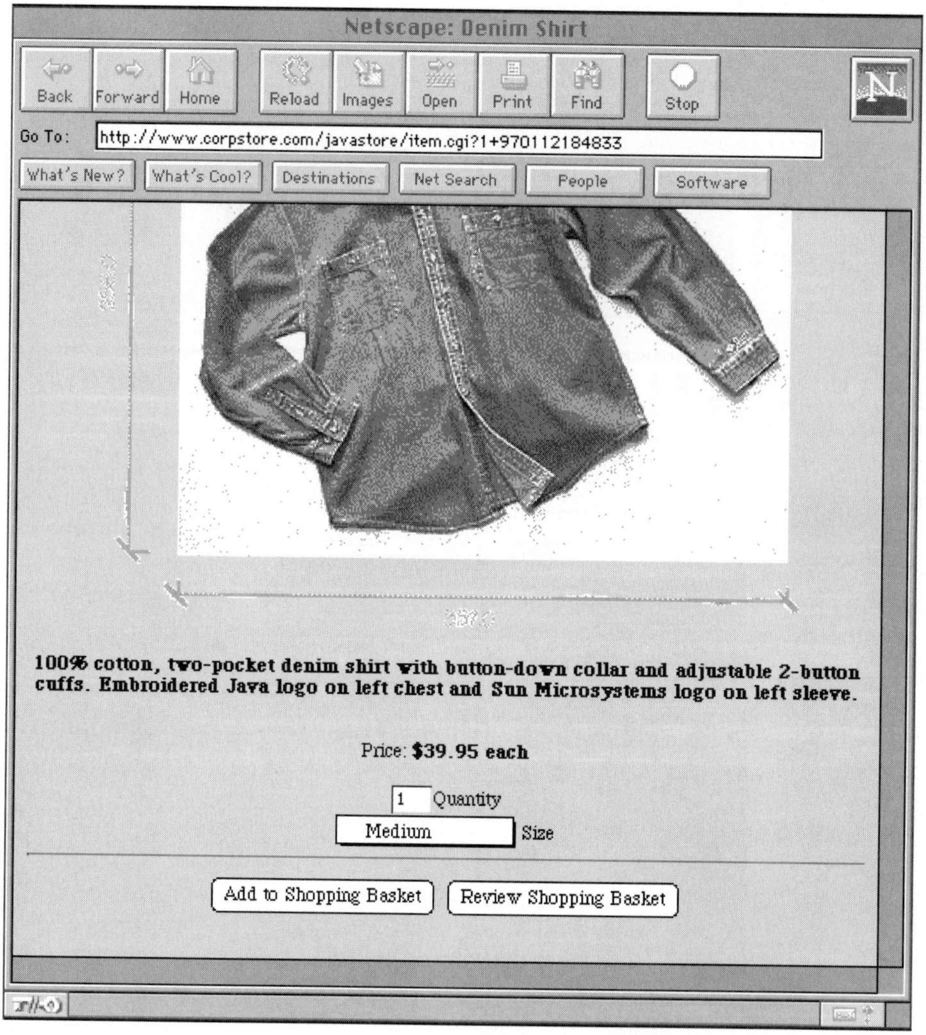

Figure 24–18 Java Store page uses method="POST"

Specifying the Window or Frame That Receives Server Output

The `target` property tells the CGI script where to display the results of submitting the form.

Property	Value	Gettable	Settable
target	windowNameString	Yes	Yes

You can use `_top`, `_parent`, `_self`, and `_blank` as values for the `target` property, or you can use a specific window or frame name. If you specify no `target` property, `_self` is the default value that is used for the `target` property. The values `_top` and `_parent` specify location within a hierarchy of frames. `_blank` enables you to open a new window, using the current window size to specify the width and height of the new window. The window is not actually blank, because when it opens, it contains the results of the form submitted to the CGI script.

Example of Specifying a Window or Frame to Receive Server Output

The following `formTarget.html` script specifies that search results are to be displayed in a separate window named `targetWindow`.

```
<!--
        formTarget.html
-->

<HTML>
<HEAD>
<TITLE>Form Target</TITLE>
<SCRIPT LANGUAGE="JavaScript">
<!-- HIDE FROM OLD BROWSERS

function formAction() {
  var actionStr = "http://altavista.digital.com"
  actionStr += "/cgi-bin/query?"
  actionStr += "pg=aq&what=web&fmt=.&"
  actionStr += "q=%22JavaScript+Books%22&r=&d0=&d1="

  document.theForm.action = actionStr
  document.theForm.submit()
}
```

```
// STOP HIDING -->
</SCRIPT>
</HEAD>
<BODY>

<P>This example uses a link to call the Form
object's onSubmit event handler. The results of
the submission are displayed in a new target
window named "targetWindow".</P>

<FORM NAME="theForm" METHOD="GET"
 TARGET="targetWindow"
 onSubmit="formAction()">
</FORM>

<P><A HREF="#" onClick="document.theForm.onsubmit()"
 onMouseOver="window.status='Submit';return true"
 onMouseOut="">Search</A> AltaVista for
 JavaScript Books.</P>

</BODY>
</HTML>
```

Figure 24–19 shows the result of loading the `formTarget.html` script.

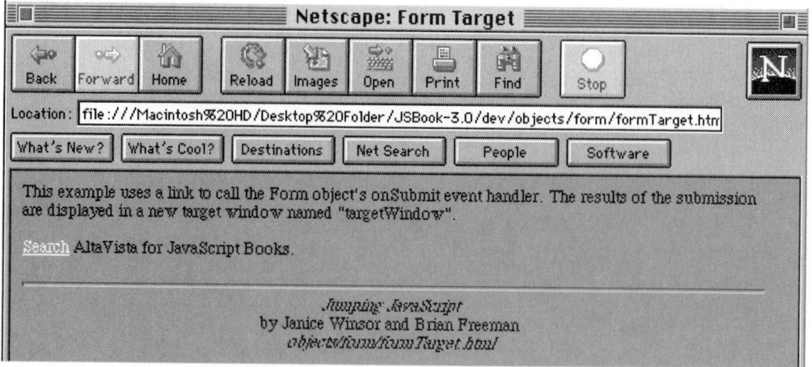

Figure 24–19 Result of loading the `formTarget.html` script

Clicking on the Search link calls the `formAction()` function, which loads the URL and submits the request. The results of the search are displayed in the targetWindow, as shown in Figure 24–20.

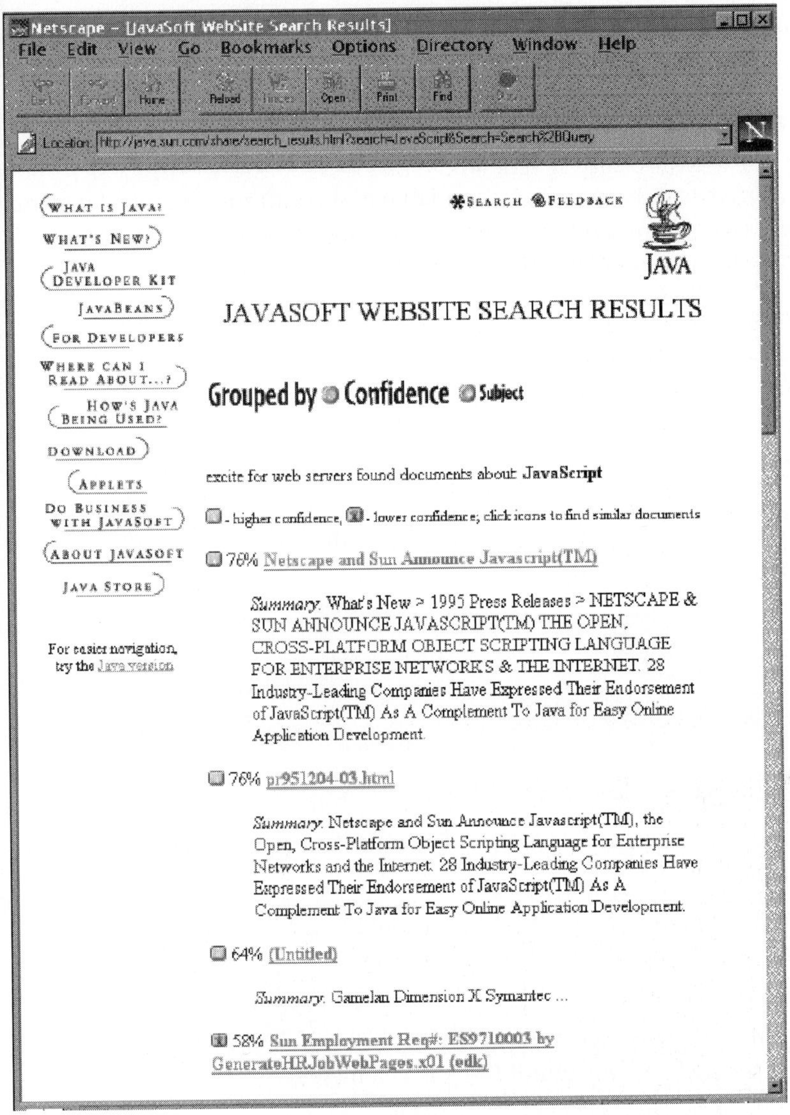

Figure 24–20 Search results displayed in targetWindow

Note – Because the `formTarget.html` script does not work on the Macintosh version of Navigator 3.01, the screen shots show a mixture of Macintosh and Windows 95 browsers. Also note that the `formTarget.html` script depends on the `java.sun.com` site remaining available and continuing to use the same search engine. We recommend that you do not create your scripts with this kind of built-in dependency.

Encoding Form Data with a MIME Type

You use the `encoding` property to specify the *MIME* type. MIME stands for multipurpose Internet mail extension. It was designed as a way to send attachments to e-mail messages on the Internet. See the box for a brief description of MIME types.

Property	Value	Gettable	Settable
encoding	MIMETypeString	Yes	Yes

The encoding property supports two MIME type strings:

- The default is `application/x-www-form-urlencoded` if you do not specify a MIME type.
- Use `multipart/form-data` if the form contains a `fileUpload` object.

Submitting a Form

The `submit()` method provides a way to submit a form. It emulates the `submit` object that the user clicks on to submit the form elements.

Method
submit()

Returns
Nothing

MIME Types

MIME types are a string that represents the type of data you have. The string uses the format:

type/subtype

For example, if you have a MIME type of `application/pdf`, then you know that the file that is being sent is a PDF (PostScript® Display Format) document. Within the MIME type string, you can use asterisks (`*`) to represent wildcard characters. A MIME type of `*/*` means that all types and subtypes are supported. A MIME type of `text/*` means a text type that supports all subtypes. A MIME type of `text/html` means an HTML file.

The available MIME types are:

- application
- text
- image
- audio
- message
- multipart
- video

For a complete list of MIME types and subtypes, see Appendix C, "JavaScript Quick Reference."

Another way to specify the type of data is to use standard file name extensions to help identify the type of the file. Some common examples are: .ps for a PostScript file, .pdf for a PostScript Display Format file, .txt for a text file, .html (or .htm) for an HTML file, and .rtf for a Rich Text Format file.

You can use the onSubmit event handler to call a function that verifies or validates the data *after* the user clicks on a Submit button and *before* you send the data off to the server.

For examples of scripts that use the submit() method, see "Example of Specifying Where to Send Your Forms Data" on page 739 and "Example of Specifying a Window or Frame to Receive Server Output" on page 747.

Resetting a Form to Its Default Values

The Navigator 3.0 release provides a reset() method for the form object. This method is the same as the reset object. It enables you to reset a form to its default settings automatically without any user action.

Method

reset()

Returns

Nothing

It's good practice to return a form to its default values after the contents have been submitted.

Example of Resetting a Form to Its Default Values

The following formReset.html script provides Submit and Reset links at the bottom of the page that enable users to either submit the form or reset the form to its default values.

```
<!--
        formReset.html
-->

<HTML>
<HEAD>
<TITLE>Form Reset</TITLE>
</HEAD>
<BODY>

<P>This example of the Form object's reset
method uses the links at the bottom of the
document to reset and submit the form.</P>
```

```
<FORM NAME="theForm" ACTION="/a_url_goes_here"
    METHOD="GET">
<B>First Name: </B><BR>
<INPUT TYPE="text"
 NAME="firstName" VALUE="" SIZE=25>
<BR><B>Last Name: </B><BR>
<INPUT TYPE="text" NAME="lastName" VALUE=""
 SIZE=25>
<BR><B>E-Mail Address: </B><BR>
<INPUT TYPE="text" NAME="emailAddr" VALUE=""
 SIZE=25>
<BR><B>First Born:) </B><BR>
<INPUT TYPE="text" NAME="firstBorn" VALUE=""
 SIZE=25>
</FORM>

<P><A HREF="#" onClick="theForm.submit()"
onMouseOver="window.status='Submit';return true"
onMouseOut=""> Submit</A> the form.</P>

<P><A HREF="#" onClick="theForm.reset()"
onMouseOver="window.status='Reset';return true"
onMouseOut=""> Reset</A> the form.</P>

</BODY>
</HTML>
```

Figure 24–21 shows the result of loading the `formReset.html` script.

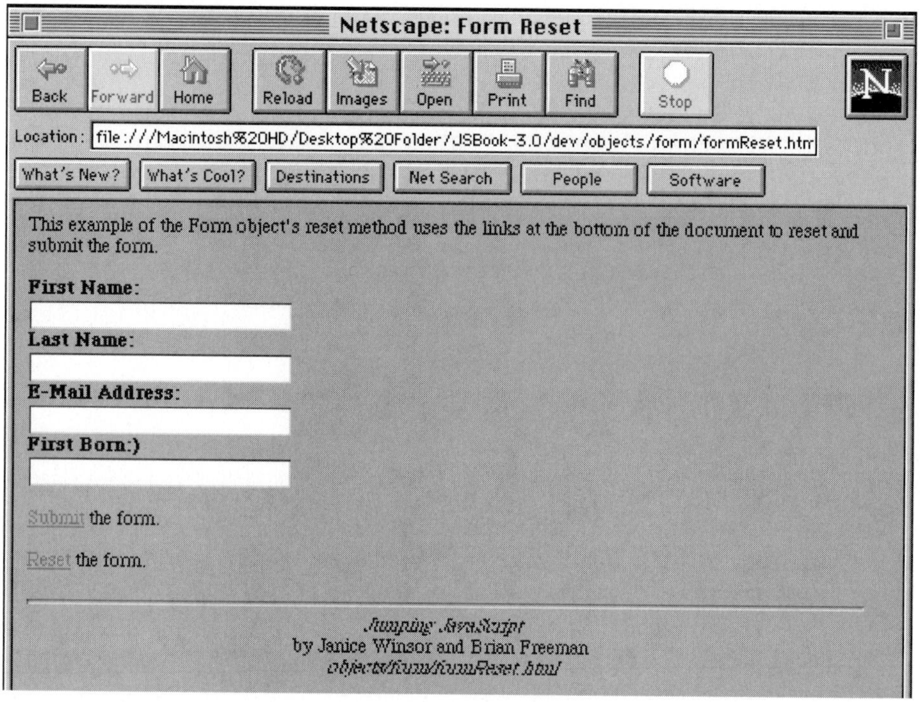

Netscape: Form Reset

Back Forward Home Reload Images Open Print Find Stop

Location: file:///Macintosh%20HD/Desktop%20Folder/JSBook-3.0/dev/objects/form/formReset.htm

What's New? What's Cool? Destinations Net Search People Software

This example of the Form object's reset method uses the links at the bottom of the document to reset and submit the form.

First Name:

Last Name:

E-Mail Address:

First Born:)

Submit the form.

Reset the form.

Jumping JavaScript
by Janice Winsor and Brian Freeman
objects/form/formReset.html

Figure 24–21 Result of loading the `formReset.html` script

Clicking on the Submit link submits the form. Clicking on the Reset link resets the elements of the form to their default values.

Controlling Actions when Users Submit a Form

You can use the `onSubmit` event handler to intercept the data from a form before it is submitted.

Event Handler

onSubmit

Syntax

<FORM
    (NAME = "*formName*")
    (TARGET = "*windowName*")
    (ACTION = "*serverURL*")
    (METHOD = "GET | POST")
    (ENCTYPE = "*MIMEType*")
    (onReset = "*JavaScript code*")
    (onSubmit = "*JavaScript code*") >
</FORM>

The value returned from an `onSubmit` event handler determines if the form is actually submitted. If a value of `true` is returned, the data is sent. If a value of `false` is returned, the data is not sent.

For an example of using the `onSubmit` event handler, see "Example of Specifying Where to Send Your Forms Data" on page 739.

Controlling Events When Users Reset a Form

The Navigator 3.0 release provides an `onReset` event handler for the `form` object. You can use this event handler to notify users that they may lose data if they reset the form.

Event Handler

onReset

Syntax

<FORM

(NAME = "*formName*")

(TARGET = "*windowName*")

(ACTION = "*serverURL*")

(METHOD = "GET | POST")

(ENCTYPE = "*MIMEType*")

(onReset = "*JavaScript code*")

(onSubmit = "*JavaScript code*") >

</FORM>

Example of Controlling Events When Users Reset a Form

The following `formOnReset.html` script uses the `onReset` event handler to display an alert when users click on the Reset button.

```
<!--
                formOnReset.html
-->

<HTML>
<HEAD>
<TITLE>Form onReset</TITLE>
<SCRIPT LANGUAGE="JavaScript">
<!-- HIDE FROM OLD BROWSERS

function confirmReset() {
  var mstr = "\n"
  mstr += "You will lose anything you've entered "
  mstr += "into the form.\nAre you sure you want "
```

```
    mstr += "to reset the form?"

    if (confirm(mstr)) {
      document.theForm.reset()
    }
  }

// STOP HIDING -->
</SCRIPT>
</HEAD>
<BODY>

<P>This example of the form object's onReset
event handler asks for user confirmation before
the form is actually reset.</P>

<FORM NAME="theForm" ACTION="/a_url_goes_here"
    METHOD="GET" onReset="confirmReset()"
  onSubmit="alert('Thanks.');return false">
<B>First Name: </B><BR>
<INPUT TYPE="text"
 NAME="firstName" VALUE="" SIZE=25>
<BR><B>Last Name: </B><BR>
<INPUT TYPE="text" NAME="lastName" VALUE=""
 SIZE=25>
<BR><B>E-Mail Address: </B><BR>
<INPUT TYPE="text" NAME="emailAddr" VALUE=""
 SIZE=25>
<BR>
<INPUT TYPE="submit" NAME="submitBtn"
 VALUE="Submit" SIZE=25>
<INPUT TYPE="reset" NAME="resetBtn"
 VALUE="Reset" SIZE=25>
</FORM>

</BODY>
</HTML>
```

Figure 24–22 shows the result of loading the `formOnReset.html` script.

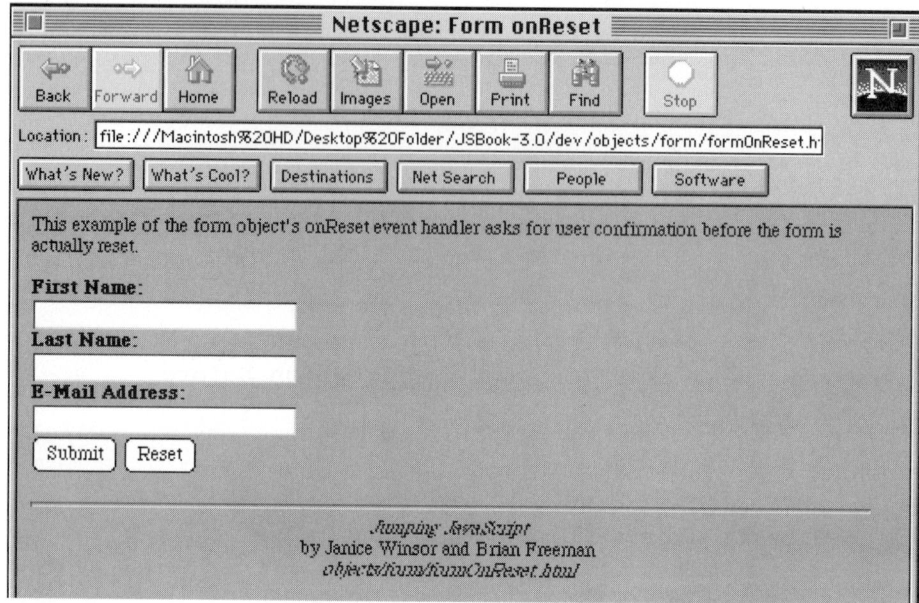

Figure 24–22 Result of loading the `formOnReset.html` script

When you click on the Reset button, a confirmation window is displayed, as shown in Figure 24–23, asking if you are sure you want to reset the form.

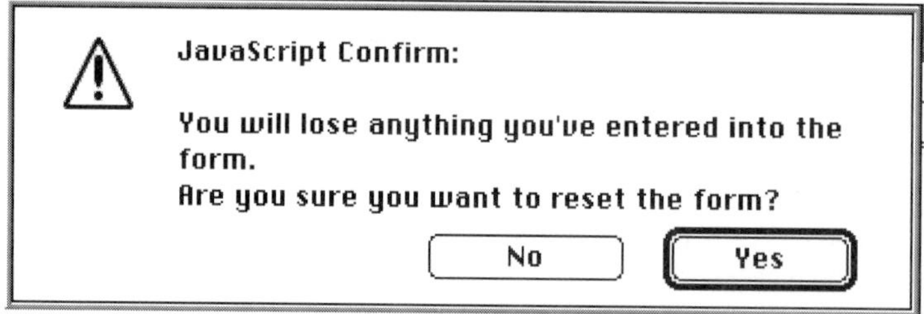

Figure 24–23 Reset confirmation window

Summary of New Terms and Concepts

The new terms and concepts introduced in this chapter are listed in alphabetical order in Table 24-3. The terms and concepts are also included in the glossary at the end of the book.

Table 24-3 Summary of New Terms and Concepts

Term/Concept	Description
CGI script	Common gateway interface scripts that are used to process data and interface with databases on a Web server
MIME types	Multipurpose Internet mail extension types provide a way to send attachments to e-mail messages on the Internet.

Controlling Your Scripts

CHAPTER 25

- Mathematical Operators
- Assignment Operators
- Comparison Operators
- Unary Operators
- Binary (or Bitwise) Operators
- Operator Precedence
- Summary of New Terms and Concepts

Understanding Operators

The JavaScript language provides many operators that you can use on values to compare, contrast, and calculate values. The values that operators use to compute the result are called operands. Operators combine variables and literals into expressions.

We introduced the concept of operators in Chapter 3, "Introducing General Scripting Concepts." Now it's time to take an in-depth look at all of the operators so that you know what they are and how to use them to perform more complex scripting actions.

You use operators to tell the interpreter what action you want the JavaScript language to perform on elements of your scripts. We've divided these operators into five groups, described in Table 25-1.

Table 25-1 **Groups of JavaScript Operators**

Group	Description
Mathematical	Perform mathematical calculations on two or more operands, adding, subtracting, multiplying, or dividing.
Unary	Perform operations on a single value.
Assignment	Assign the value of the right-hand operand into the variable name on the left side of the assignment operator.

Table 25-1 **Groups of JavaScript Operators (Continued)**

Group	Description
Comparison	Compare the value of two operands and determine if the operands are the same or different. If the same, return a value of `true`, if different, return a value of `false`.
Bitwise	Perform arithmetic or column-shifting actions on the binary (base-2) representations of two operands.

The JavaScript language allows for both *binary* and *unary* operators. A binary operator requires two operands, one before the operator and one after, using the following syntax:

```
operand1 operator operand2
```

For example:

```
7 + 3
x * y
```

A unary operator requires a single operand, which can be either before or after the operator:

```
operator operand
```

or

```
operand operator
```

For example:

```
x++
```

means use the value contained in x, then increment, while

```
++x
```

means increment the value of x, then use it.

The position of the operator determines when the operation takes place. If the operator is before the operand, the value is returned after the operation is performed. If the operator follows the operand, the value of `x` is returned and then the operation is performed.

Mathematical Operators

You're probably already familiar with the mathematical operators listed in Table 25-2.

Table 25-2 Mathematical Operators

Operator	Operation
+	Addition
-	Subtraction
*	Multiplication
/	Division
%	Modulus (return the remainder of a division)

When you use any of these operators, the values that these operators use to compute the result are called operands. In the following statement:

```
2 + 4
```

The 2 and 4 are operands, and the + is the operator. This example uses literal numbers for values. In scripts, it's much more common to use operands that are variables. For example:

```
total = price * discount
```

When the values are numeric, the JavaScript language adds the numbers and returns a single numeric value.

You can, however, use the plus sign (+) to join (or concatenate) two or more strings. The plus sign, which acts as a *string concatenation operator,* combines the exact value of the strings. It does not know about words and spaces. When you join phrases by using this operator, be sure to add a space character, either as part of the individual strings or as a separate space. You can add the space as a literal string, as shown in the following example:

```
firstName = Fred
lastName = Spirit
fullName = firstName + "  " + LastName
```

The `fullName` variable returns the value:

```
Fred Spirit
```

You can also use a similar construction to include values returned by a script in a more user-friendly output format.

Assignment Operators

You use assignment operators, listed in Table 25-3, to specify a value for a variable. The equal sign (=) is the most common assignment operator. You can, however, assign values that are not equal. Assignment operators also provide you with a shortcut syntax that makes your statements more compact and understandable.

Table 25-3 **Assignment Operators**

Operator	Operation
=	Equals
+=	Add by value
-=	Subtract by value
*=	Multiply by value
/=	Divide by value
%=	Modulo by value
<<=	Left shift by value
>>=	Right shift by value
>>>=	Zero fill by value
&=	Bitwise AND by value
^=	Bitwise OR by value
|=	Bitwise XOR by value

You can use assignment operators for strings as well as for mathematical expressions. The following statements use the += operator to combine a message string with the output of the `document.title` property.

```
// document.title
mstr += "document.title = "
mstr += "\"" + document.title + "\"<P>"
```

Comparison Operators

Any time you compare two values in a script, the JavaScript language returns a Boolean literal of either `true` or `false`. The six comparison operators are listed in Table 25-4.

Table 25-4 Comparison Operators

Operator	Operation
==	Equals
!=	Not equal to
>	Greater than
>=	Greater than or equal to
<	Less than
<=	Less than or equal to

You can use the comparison operators to compare mathematical values, strings, and values returned by evaluating expressions. When you compare strings, the JavaScript language converts each character to its ASCII value. Because the JavaScript language is case sensitive, two strings with different capitalization are not equal to one another. When you are validating data in a form, you can use comparison operators to test to see if the string has a value.

For example, the following statements use the Boolean not equal to (`!=`) to test for the version of the browser:

```
var newWin = window.open(myURL,'myWin')
if (navigator.appVersion.indexOf("(X11") != -1 ||
   navigator.appVersion.indexOf("(Mac") != -1)
       newWin = window.open(myURL,'myWin')
```

When you compare string values that contain numbers to real numbers, the JavaScript language assumes that you want to compare numeric values. To be absolutely certain that a string that contains a number is treated as a number, you can use the `parseInt()` or `parseFloat()` functions to convert the string to a numeric value for comparison. The following example extracts the height of an image and uses the `parseInt()` function to convert that string to a number:

```
function getImageHeight(num) {
  var    dim = ""
  var height = ""
```

```
    dim    = getImageDimension(num)
    height = dim.substring(
                 dim.indexOf('x') + 1,
                 dim.length)
    return parseInt(height, 0)
}
```

Unary Operators

You use unary operators, described in Table 25-5, to perform operations on a single numerical operand. These unary operators operate directly on the operand. You can position the operator either before or after the operand in most cases, and the position determines when the operator is evaluated.

Table 25-5 Unary Operators

Operator	Operation
-	Unary negation
~	Bitwise complement
++	Increment
--	Decrement

Unary negation changes the sign of a number. Bitwise complement changes each bit of the variable to a 1 if it is a 0, and to 0 if it is a 1. Increment increases the value of the variable by 1, and decrement decreases the value of a variable by 1.

You can increment or decrement either before or after the statement. The position of the operator determines the order in which the operation is performed. If you put the operator before the statement, the operation is performed before the statement. For example:

```
A = 1
B = ++A
```

The result of this operation is:

```
A = 2
B = 2
```

because A is incremented first and then the value is assigned.

If you put the operator after the statement, the statement is performed and then the operation.

```
A = 1
B = A++
```

The result of this operation is:

```
A = 2
B = 1
```

because the value is assigned before A is incremented.

Binary (or Bitwise) Operators

You use binary operators, also sometimes called bitwise operators, to perform an operation on two operands. Unlike the unary operators, the binary operators do not change the value of the operand. Instead, the return a value that must be assigned to a variable.

Binary operators are an advanced topic, and unless you are dealing with external processes on CGI scripts or connecting to Java applets, you're not likely to need to use them. Table 25-6 lists the binary operators.

Table 25-6 Binary Operators

Operator	Operation
&	Bitwise AND
|	Bitwise OR
^	Bitwise XOR
<<	Left shift
>>	Right shift
>>>	Zero fill right shift

Numerical operands can be decimal, octal, or hexadecimal numbers. When the operator has an operand, that value is converted to a 32-bit binary number. For the `&`, `|`, and `^` operations, the individual bits of one operand are compared with the other operand. The resulting value that is returned for each bit depends on the operator. The shift operators operate on a single operand.

Operator Precedence

When the interpreter evaluates operators, the JavaScript language evaluates those expressions in a specific order. This operator precedence determines which operators precede which other operators. Because the interpreter cannot evaluate all of the expressions at the same time, it needs to know where to start. The JavaScript language assigns each operator a different priority. It is important for you to understand these priority assignments because you may not get the result you want from your script if your understanding of how the operators are evaluated is not the same as what actually happens.

You can use parentheses to override operator precedence.

Table 25-7 shows the operator precedence used by the JavaScript language, with 1 being the highest precedence and 14 the lowest. Those operators at precedence level 1 are evaluted first.

Table 25-7 **JavaScript Operator Precedence**

Precedence Level	Description	Operator
1	Nested parentheses are evaluated from innermost to outermost.	`()`
	Array index value	`[]`

2	Negation and increment	`!`
		`~`
		`-`
		`++`
		`--`

3	Multiplication, division, modulo	`*`
		`/`
		`%`

4	Addition and subtraction	`+` `-`

5	Bitwise shifts	`<<`
		`>>`
		`>>>`

Table 25-7 JavaScript Operator Precedence (Continued)

<table>
<tr><th>Precedence Level</th><th>Description</th><th>Operator</th></tr>
<tr><td>6</td><td>Comparison operators</td><td><
<=
>
>=</td></tr>
<tr><td>7</td><td>Equality</td><td>==
!=</td></tr>
<tr><td>8</td><td>Bitwise XOR</td><td>^</td></tr>
<tr><td>9</td><td>Bitwise OR</td><td>|</td></tr>
<tr><td>10</td><td>Logical AND</td><td>&&</td></tr>
<tr><td>11</td><td>Logical OR</td><td>||</td></tr>
<tr><td>12</td><td>Conditional expression</td><td>?:</td></tr>
<tr><td>13</td><td>Assignment operators</td><td>=
+=
-+
*=
/=
%=
<<=
>>=
>>>=
&=
^=
|=</td></tr>
<tr><td>14</td><td>comma</td><td>,</td></tr>
</table>

An expression that contains operators at the same level is evaluated from left to right. Notice that mathematical and string concatenation operations are performed before any comparison operators. This operator precedence fully evaluates all expressions that act as operands before the comparison is performed.

For example:

```
1 + 1 * 2
```

evaluates to three because the multiplication is performed before the addition.

```
1 + (1 * 2)
```

evaluates to 3 because the statement in parentheses is evaluated before the addition is performed.

```
(1 + 1) * 2
```

evaluates to 4 because the statement in parentheses is evaluated before the multiplication is performed.

The following statement:

```
1 + 1 * 2 == 4 / 2 + 1
```

evaluates to `true` because the statements on either side of the == sign both evaluate to three.

With nested parentheses, the following statement:

```
(1 + (1 * 2)) == ((4 / 2) + 1)
```

evaluates to `true` because the statements on either side of the == sign both still evaluate to 3.

Summary of New Terms and Concepts

The new terms and concepts introduced in this chapter are listed in alphabetical order in Table 25-8. The terms and concepts are also included in the glossary at the end of the book.

Table 25-8 New Terms and Concepts

Term/Concept	Description
binary operator	An operator that requires two operands, one before the operator and one after it.
unary operator	An operator that requires a single operand, which can be either before or after the operator.

773

CHAPTER 26

- Boolean Operators
- Testing for a Single Condition
- Testing for Multiple Conditions
- Nesting if ... else Statements
- Conditional Operator
- Summary of New Terms and Concepts

Testing for Conditions

When writing scripts, you frequently want to test for conditions. The simplest test is to determine whether a condition is true or false. If the expression is true, execute any subsequent commands; if not, continue with the script.

The JavaScript language provides the following statements that you can use to test for conditions:

```
if
if ... else
variable = (condition) ? value1 : value2
```

You use the `if` statement to test for a single conditions, and the other two statements to test for two or more conditions.

Boolean Operators

You use the Boolean operators listed in Table 26-1 to test whether conditions are true or false.

Table 26-1 **Boolean Operators**

Operator	Operation
`&&`	AND
`||`	OR
`!`	NOT

You put the NOT (`!`) operator in front of any Boolean value to switch it back to the opposite value.

You use the AND (`&&`) operator to join two Boolean values together to evaluate whether the statement is true or false based on the combined results. Table 26-2 helps you to understand the values returned by the AND (`&&`) operator.

Table 26-2 **And Operator Return Values**

Left Operand	AND Operator	Right Operand	Return Value
true	`&&`	true	`true`
true	`&&`	false	`false`
false	`&&`	true	`false`
false	`&&`	false	`false`

By definition of AND (`&&`), both sides of the statement must be true to return `true`. If `A` has a value of false, you do not need to test the value of `B` because you know that the whole statement is already false. If `A` is true, then you need to test to see if `B` is also true to know if the whole statement is true. If you want to test a variable where a string can have a value of either `null` or an empty string, you should test for `null` before you test for the empty string.

```
inputString is != null && inputString != ""
```

You should first test for:

```
variable != null
```

before you test to see whether the variable has a value.

The case is reversed for an OR (||) statement. It evaluates the left operator only if the right operator is false. If you have variables `A` or `B`, and `A` is true, you do not need to test `B`, because by definition of OR, one or the other has to be true for the whole statement to be true.

Testing for a Single Condition

When you want to test for a single condition, you use the `if` statement. The syntax for this statement is:

```
if (condition) {
    statements
}
```

If the condition is met, the statements between the curly braces are executed. If the statement is not true, the script continues with the next statement following the closing brace of the `if` statement.

For example, the following function contains two `if` statements. The first `if` statement tests to see if the first function called is not `setDefaultStatus()` and returns a value of `false`. The second `if` statement tests to see if the next function called is not `setStatus()` and returns a value of `false`.

```
function homeStatus(win) {
  var default_str = "Click on the link to go home."
  var status_str  = "Hey, this isn't our home page!"

  if (!setDefaultStatus(win, default_str))
    return false
  if (!setStatus(win, status_str))
    return false
  return true
}
```

See "Example of status and defaultStatus Properties" on page 107 for the complete example.

Testing for Multiple Conditions

Many times in a script you need to test for more than one condition. The answer is not a simple yes or no, true or false. For multiple conditions, you can use the `if ... else` statement. The syntax for this statement is:

```
if (condition) {
    statements
} else {
    statements
}
```

With this construction, if the first condition is true, the statements between the first set of curly braces are executed. If the first condition is false, then the script provides a set of statements to execute a particular action before continuing with the rest of the script.

For example, the following function contains an `if ... else` statement that cycles through an array of available images.

```
function loadImage() {
  // adjust currentImage so it cycles through the
  // available images.
  if (currentImage < my_images.length -1) {
    currentImage++
  } else {
    currentImage = 0
  }
```

See "Using the onLoad Event Handler to Create a Slide Show" on page 357 for the complete script.

Nesting if ... else Statements

When you have a particularly complex decision process to handle in a script, you can use a set of *nested* `if ... else` statements. What this means is that inside one `if ... else` statement, you include one or more additional `if ... else` statements. It's common programming practice when nesting `if ... else` statements to use spaces or tabs to show the relative position of the nested statements in the operational hierarchy.

The following example shows nested `if ... else` statements to cycle through an array.

```
if (index <= 0) {
   index = 0
} else {
   if (index >= (arrayName.length -1)) {
        index = 0
   } else {
        index ++
   }
}
```

Conditional Operator

The JavaScript language provides a special type of operator that you can use in place of the `if ... else` statement if you want to assign one of two values to a variable, depending on the outcome of some condition. The syntax for the conditional expression is:

```
variable = (condition) ? value1 : value2
```

If the result of the conditional statement is `true`, the JavaScript language assigns *`value1`* to the variable. Otherwise, it assigns *`value2`* to the variable. The first expression must return a Boolean (`true` or `false`) value or an error occurs.

The conditional operator `?:` uses the Boolean value of one expression to decide which of two other expressions should be evaluated. This expression is a shorthand way of doing an `if...else` statement and making assignments to the same variable.

When you run the script, the first expression is evaluated and returns a Boolean value, either `true` or `false`. The result is then used to choose either the second or the third operand expression.

For example:

```
A?B:C
```

If `A` is true, `B` is evaluated. If `A` is false, then `C` is evaluated.

The rule is:

- If the first expression is evaluated as `true`, then the second operand expression is evaluated.
- If the first expression is evaluated as `false`, then the third operand expression is evaluated.

Suppose you have an array and you have an index value that you want to keep within the range of zero to `arrayName.length -1`. You are stepping through the array. You want to increment your index value, and when you reach the end of your array, you want to go back to zero.

Instead of writing:

```
if (index <= 0) {
   index = 0
} else {
   if (index >= (arrayName.length -1)) {
        index = 0
   } else {
        index ++
   }
}
```

you can accomplish the same result with the following line of code:

```
(index <= 0) ? index = 0 :
 ((index >= (arrayName.length -1)) ? index = 0 : index ++)
```

Summary of New Terms and Concepts

The new terms and concepts introduced in this chapter are listed in alphabetical order in Table 26-3. The terms and concepts are also included in the glossary at the end of the book.

Table 26-3 Summary of New Terms and Concepts

Term/Concept	Description
nested statements	A set of statements that include one or more additional statements. For example, you can use nested `if ... else` statements to handle complex decision processes.

781

CHAPTER 27

- Repeat Loops (for, for ... in)
- Repeatedly Executing a Group of Commands (while)
- Summary of New Terms and Concepts
- Referencing a Specific Object in a Loop (with)
- Controlling Loop Execution (continue)
- Breaking Out of a Loop (break)
- Summary of New Terms and Concepts

Creating Loops

You can use *loops* to control the flow of execution in a script. A loop is an iterative mechanism that repeats a sequence of instructions until a predetermined condition is satisfied. You can also use loops to create counters or to cycle through the properties for an object. The JavaScript language provides the following statements to create and control loops:

```
for
for ... in
continue
while
break
with
```

Repeat Loops (for, for ... in)

You use a `for` loop when you want to cycle through every entry in an array or every item of a form. The syntax of the `for` loop, shown below, is the same as that used in the C programming language:

```
for ( (initial expression) ; (condition) ; (update expression)) {
   statements
}
```

For example, the following `createImgs()` function uses a `for` loop to create an array of images from the data in the `image_info` array.

```
// Create the imgs array from the data in the
// image_info array.
//
function createImgs() {

  // loop through the image_info array.
  for (var i=0; i < amt_images; i++) {
    // create the image object and load it.
    imgs[i]          = new Image(
                           getImageWidth(i),
                           getImageHeight(i))
    imgs[i].lowsrc = getImageLowsrc(i)
    imgs[i].src      = getImageSrc(i)
  }
}
```

For the complete script, see "Example of Prestaging Big Images with Low-Resolution Files" on page 332.

Repeatedly Executing a Group of Commands (while)

Use `while` loops to repeatedly execute a group of commands within the body of a loop until the test condition in the expression is no longer true. In other words, the `while` loop says, "While the expression is true, execute these commands." The `while` loop assumes that at some point your script will reach a condition that will exit the repeat loop. The syntax for a `while` loop is:

```
while (condition) {
    statements
}
```

The *`condition`* variable is the same kind of condition you use in `if` statements and in the middle parameter of the `for` loop. Use a `while` loop when some condition in your code evaluates to `true` before the interpreter reaches the `while` loop.

For example, the following `while.html` script is a slightly different implementation of the `continue.html` script. It opens a confirmation window and creates a counter. The number of times you click on the Yes button is counted. When you click on the No button, an alert is displayed, showing the number of times you repeated the loop.

```
<!--
                   while.html

    This example shows the use of the while
    statement.
-->

<HTML>
<HEAD>
<TITLE>While Statement</TITLE>
</HEAD>
<BODY>

<SCRIPT LANGUAGE="JavaScript">
<!-- HIDE FROM OLD BROWSERS

var count = 0

while(confirm("Loop Again?")) {
  count++
}

alert("Wow, " + count + " times!")

// STOP HIDING -->
</SCRIPT>

</BODY>
</HTML>
```

When you load the `while.html` script, the same confirmation window is displayed as for the `continue.html` script. When you click on the Yes button, another confirmation window is displayed. This loop is repeated until you click on the No button. When you click on the No button, an alert is displayed, as shown in Figure 27–1. The counter is used to store and return, as part of the alert message, the number of times you repeated the loop.

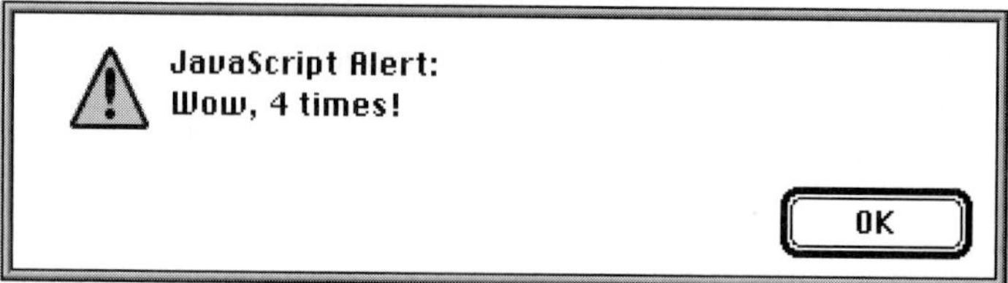

Figure 27–1 Alert that concludes the `while` loop

Looping Through Properties (for var in object)

The JavaScript language provides a variation of the `for` loop called a `for ... in` loop that extracts the names and values of any object property that is currently in browser memory. The syntax for a `for ... in` loop is:

```
for (var in object) {
    statements
}
```

The *`object`* variable is not the string name of an object, but the object itself.

For example, the `getProps.js` script contains a `getProps()` function that uses a `for (var in object)` loop to cycle through the properties of a given object and returns the value in the format specified by the `getProps()` function, as shown below. This generic script for returning the value of JavaScript object properties is included in examples throughout this book.

```
/*
** getProps
*/

// Get the properties for the given object
//
// Arguments:
//    obj      - obtain properties from this
//               object
//    obj_name - a string representing the
//               object name
//    html     - generate html output?
//
// Return Value
//    string of the form:
```

```
//      object_name.property = "value"
//      object_name.property = "value"
//      ...
//
//
function getProps(obj, obj_name, html) {
  var rvalue = ""

  rvalue += newline(html)
  rvalue += "The properties of the object "
  rvalue += obj_name + " are:"
  rvalue += newline(html)

  for (var i in obj) {
    rvalue += indent(html)
    rvalue += obj_name + "." + i
    rvalue += " = " + obj[i]
    rvalue += newline(html)
  }
  rvalue += newline(html)

  return unescape(rvalue)
}
```

For the complete `getProps.js` script, see "Looking at Object Properties" on page 77.

Referencing a Specific Object in a Loop (with)

A `with` statement lets you specify which object your script is referencing so that you do not need to provide complete object references within the statement. The syntax for the `with` statement is:

```
with (object) {
  statements
}
```

The *`object`* variable is any valid object currently in the browser memory.

The following `with.html` script encloses a series of document method calls in a `with` statement.

```
<!--
           with.html

    This example shows how to use the with
    statement.
-->

<HTML>
<HEAD>
<TITLE>with example</TITLE>
</HEAD>

<BODY>
<SCRIPT LANGUAGE="JavaScript">
<!-- HIDE FROM OLD BROWSERS

with( window.document ) {
  open()
  writeln("This is a test of the with statement")
  writeln("...")
  writeln("this is ONLY a test.<BR>")
  writeln("In the case of a real use, put")
  writeln("a different message here!")
  close()
}

// STOP HIDING -->
</SCRIPT>


</BODY>
</HTML>
```

Figure 27–2 shows the result of loading the `with.html` script.

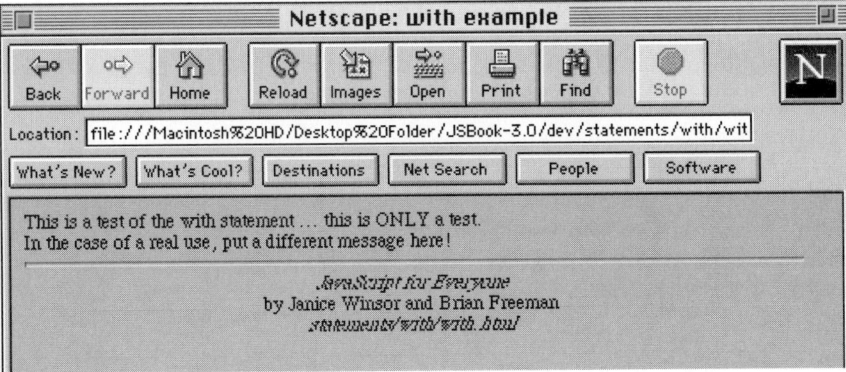

Figure 27–2 Result of loading the `with.html` script

Controlling Loop Execution (continue)

You can use the `continue` statement to skip execution of a nested statement for just one condition.

The following `continue.html` script opens a confirmation window and creates a counter. The number of times you click on the Yes button is counted. When you click on the No button, a break statement stops the loop and displays an alert showing the number of times you repeated the loop.

```
<!--
                    continue.html

    This example shows the use of the continue
    statement.
-->

<HTML>
<HEAD>
<TITLE>Continue Statement</TITLE>
</HEAD>
<BODY>

<SCRIPT LANGUAGE="JavaScript">
<!-- HIDE FROM OLD BROWSERS

var count = 0

while(true) {
  if (confirm("Loop again?")){
```

```
      continue
    } else {
      break
    }
    count++
  }

  alert("Wow, " + count + " times!")

  // STOP HIDING -->
  </SCRIPT>

  </BODY>
  </HTML>
```

Figure 27–3 shows the confirmation window that is displayed when you load the `continue.html` script.

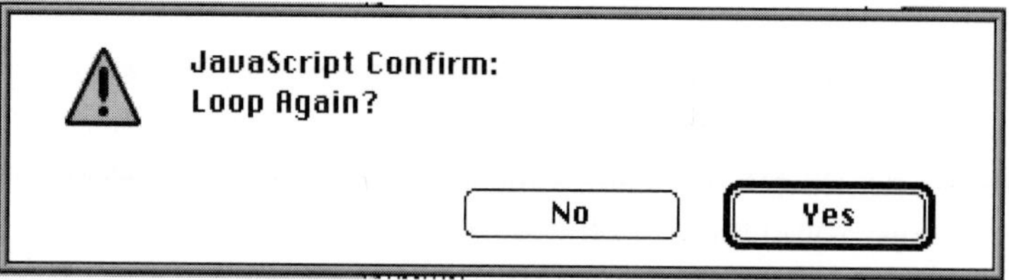

Figure 27–3 Confirmation window for `continue.html` script

Figure 27–4 shows the alert that is displayed when you click on the No button in the confirmation window. Notice that, because the `continue` statement jumps outside of the loop, the counter is never incremented.

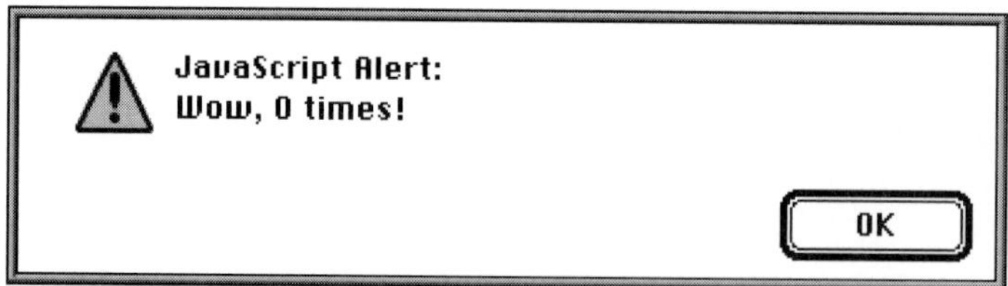

Figure 27–4 Alert that concludes the continue loop

Breaking Out of a Loop (break)

You use the `break` statement to break out of a loop that you've created by using either the `continue` or the `while` statement. For an example of using the break statement, see the `continue.html` script in "Controlling Loop Execution (continue)" on page 789.

Summary of New Terms and Concepts

The new terms and concepts introduced in this chapter are listed in alphabetical order in Table 27-1. The terms and concepts are also included in the glossary at the end of the book.

Table 27-1 **Summary of New Terms and Concepts**

Term/Concept	Description
loop	An iterative script mechanism that repeats a sequence of instructions until a predetermined condition is satisfied.

PART SIX

Using System Objects

CHAPTER 28

- Defining a String
- Combining String Literals and Variables
- String Formatting Escape Characters
- Converting Numbers to Strings
- Converting Strings to Numbers
- Evaluating Text Expressions
- Escaping and Unescaping ASCII Characters
- Introducing the String Object
- Finding the Number of Characters in a String
- Creating Custom String Functions
- Converting a String into an Anchor or a Link
- Using String Object Methods to Format Text
- Converting Case
- Searching for Part of a String
- Getting a Substring
- Getting the nth Character in a String
- Splitting a String into an Array
- Splitting a String into an Array

Working with Strings and String Objects

Working with strings and `String` objects is one of the basics of writing scripts. Whenever you have strings stored in objects or variables, you often need to join strings together (concatenate them), extract segments of strings, delete parts of strings, and replace one part of a string with some other string.

Defining a String

You define a string in one of two ways:

- By creating a string data type
- By creating a `String` object

The Navigator 2.0 release does not distinguish between these two ways of creating a string. In the Navigator 3.0 release, you can programmatically tell them apart by using the `typeOf()` method. A string returns a type of `"string"` and a `String` object returns `"object"`.

Creating a String Data Type

You create a string data type by including one or more ASCII text characters within single or double quotes. For example, the following two statements are treated in the same way by the JavaScript language:

```
var aStr    = "This is a string"
var aStr    = 'This is a string'
```

If you include the string within another string, you can enclose a string with single quotes inside of double quotes, or you can enclose a string with double quotes inside of single quotes, as long as the quotation marks match up in pairs. For example, the following two statements are treated in the same way by the JavaScript language:

```
onClick="displayString('blink')"> blink<BR>
onClick='displayString("blink")'> blink<BR>
```

It's a good idea to use a consistent quotation format for your scripts. Decide on one style and use it consistently in your scripts.

Every quoted string value can be used as a `string` object.

Note – In the Navigator 2.0 release, you had to add an empty string ("") to the end of a statement containing a string value if you wanted to pass that value to another window. This problem was fixed in the Navigator 3.0 release.

Creating a String Object

The JavaScript language automatically converts string literals (the text between the quotation marks) to a `String` object when necessary. It does not, however, automatically convert all string literals to `String` objects.

If you want to specifically create a `String` object, you can do so by using the `new` keyword:

```
var variableName = new String("string text")
```

An example of when you might want to specifically create `string` objects would be when you are writing a text-editor script that does heavy-duty string manipulation on user input.

Note – When you use the `new` keyword to create a `String` object, capitalize the word `String`. In this chapter we follow the common practice of referring to the `String` object in text by using an initial capital letter.

The Navigator 3.0 release provides a `prototype` property that you can use to write your own functions for any objects that can be created with the `new` keyword, such as `String`, `Date`, and user-defined objects. For more information on the `prototype` property, see "Creating Custom String Functions" on page 809.

Example of the Difference Between a String Data Type and a String Object

The following `string.html` script creates a string data type and a `String` object and shows how the value returned by each string differs.

```
<!--
         string.html
-->

<HTML>
<HEAD>
<TITLE>String</TITLE>
</HEAD>
<BODY>

<P>The String object provides methods for
operating on the basic JavaScript string data type.</P>

<P>The string data type and the String object are
not the same. Although the Navigator 2.0 release
treated them in the same way, in the Navigator 3.0
and later releases, the string data type and the String
object are treated differently. In Navigator 3.0, you can
use the <B>typeof</B> operator to tell the difference.
A string has the type "string" and a String object
has the type "object". In this example, a string
and a String object are created and the type for
each is displayed.</P>

<SCRIPT LANGUAGE="JavaScript">
<!-- HIDE FROM OLD BROWSERS

  var aStr    = "This is a string"
  var aStrObj = new String(aStr + " object")

  with (document) {
    open()
    write("aStr's type = " + typeof(aStr))
```

```
    write("<BR>")
    write("aStrObj's type = " + typeof(aStrObj))
    write("<BR>")
    close()
  }

// STOP HIDING -->
</SCRIPT>

<P>Because JavaScript language converts
string data types to strings when needed, you can
use them almost interchangeably.</P>

</BODY>
</HTML>
```

Figure 28–1 shows the result of loading the `string.html` script.

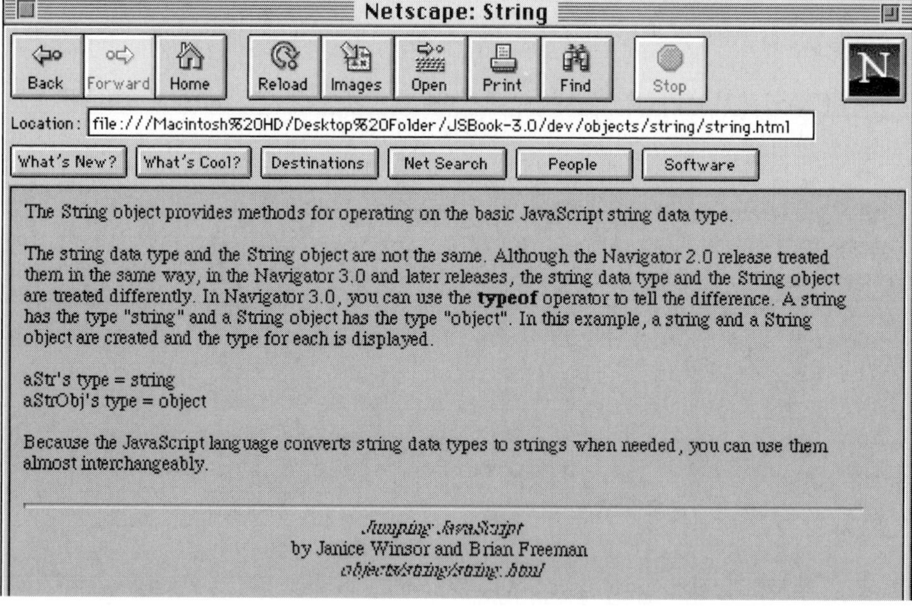

Figure 28–1 Result of loading the `string.html` script

Combining String Literals and Variables

You can combine strings by using the += assignment operator. This assignment operator appends the right-hand side of the equation to the left-hand side. The following statements combine into one sentence that is displayed in a confirmation window:

```
// ask if the user wants a copy
mstr  = "\nWould you like a copy of the data "
mstr += "you submitted to be sent to your "
mstr += "e-mail address?\n"
```

The `\n` characters are escape characters that put a line feed (new line) at the beginning and the end of the sentence. For a complete list of escape characters that you can use in string formatting, see Table 28-1 on 800.

It's a good idea to break up a long text string in this way to keep the elements short enough to fit on one line. Using this style makes your scripts easier to read and maintain.

You can also use the += assignment operator to create a string that is a combination of literal string and variable values that are extracted by the script.

You've already seen many examples of this combination of string literals and variables in previous chapters. The following statements combine literal string and variables to create an output message:

```
var mstr = "<BR>"  // message string

mstr += "<P>The location of this document"
mstr += ", \"" + document.title + "\", is "
mstr += "\"" + document.URL + "\"</P>"
mstr += "<P>The referring document is "
mstr += "\"" + document.referrer + "\"</P>"
```

As you can see from the above example, you can include HTML formatting commands as part of the quoted message strings. The example uses the escape characters `\"` to put quotation marks into the formatted message string.

String Formatting Escape Characters

When you want to include a character that the JavaScript language interprets as part of a command, you put a backslash (\) in front of the character. This syntax is called escaping a character. The backslash tells the JavaScript interpreter to treat the character immediately following the backslash as an ASCII character and not as part of a command. In addition, some ASCII characters are interpreted as

special formatting characters when preceded by a backslash. Table 28-1 lists the escape characters you can use in string formatting. This table is also included in Appendix C, "JavaScript Quick Reference."

Table 28-1 Escape Characters Used in String Formatting

Escape Sequence	Description	Character/ Abbreviation
`\b`	Backspace	BS
`\t`	Horizontal tab	HT
`\n`	Line feed	LF
`\f`	Form feed	FF
`\r`	Carriage return	CR
`\"`	Double quote	"
`\'`	Single quote	'
`\\`	Backslash	\
\ *OctalDigit*	Octal Escape	One of 0 1 2 3 4 5 6 7
\ *OctalDigit OctalDigit*	Octal Escape	One of 0 1 2 3 4 5 6 7
\ ZeroToThree *OctalDigit OctalDigit*	ZeroToThree Escape	One of 0 1 2 3
\ *xHexDigit HexDigit*	Hexadecimal Escape	One of 0 1 2 3 4 5 6 7 8 9 a b c d e f A B C D E F

Converting Numbers to Strings

Just as you may need to convert a string into a number to perform calcuations on the value, so you also may need to convert a number into a string.

To convert a number into a string, the Navigator 3.0 release provides the built-in `toString()` function. You can specify the base number, called the *radix*, to be used in the conversion. If you do not specify a base number, the `toString()` function uses base 10 for decimal numbers. You specify the radix as a value in parentheses following the function. The radix is an integer between 2 and 16.

For example, you can create a new number that is base 10 and convert it to hexadecimal and binary by the following statements:

```
var n = new Number(10)
document.write("Number in hex = " n.toString(16) ",
in bin = "n.toString(2))
```

Converting Strings to Numbers

Although the JavaScript language is a dynamically typed language, at times you will need to convert a number that is represented as a string into a number so that you can perform arithmetic operations on it. The JavaScript language has two built-in functions that you can use to do this conversion:

- `parseInt(string, [radix])`
- `parseFloat(string)`

The word parse means to analyze a series of words and statements to determine their collective meaning. In the context of these functions, the parsing involves analyzing the value enclosed in the parentheses and converting it either to an integer or to a floating-point number.

The `parseInt()` function takes an optional integer argument that represents the radix of the number to be parsed. When the `parseInt()` function encounters a character that is not a valid numeral for the specified radix, the function returns `NaN`. `NaN` is a reserved value that stands for "Not a Number."

All the following statements return a value of 10:

```
parseInt("A", 16)
parseInt("12", 8)
parseInt("1010", 2)

var intStr = "22"
parseInt(intStr, 4)
```

All the following statements return a value of 3.14:

```
parseFloat("3.14")
parseFloat("314e-2")
parseFloat("0.0314E+2")

var x = "3.14"
parseFloat(x)
```

The Navigator 3.0 release provides a built-in `isNaN()` function that you can use to test to see if the value returned is `NaN`. The `isNaN()` function returns a value of `true` when the expression tested is `NaN`. It returns a value of `false` when the expression tested is a legal number, a string, or any other type.

The following statements show how you can use the `isNaN()` function:

```
var intVariable = parseInt(intString)

if isNaN(intVariable) {
  // intVariable is not a number
} else {
  // intVariable is a number
}
```

Evaluating Text Expressions

Sometimes you may find your script returns a string value that contains an expression that must be evaluated before any further action can be taken. Suppose that a user enters an arithmetic expression into a text field. Your script extracts the value of that text field as a string. If a numerical calculation is required, the JavaScript language cannot perform a calculation on a string.

You can use the built-in `eval()` function to enclose any possible expressions before returning a value. The `eval()` function has been enhanced in the Navigator 3.0 release to be a method of every object. In the Navigator 2.0 release, the `eval()` function operated as though it was a method of the `window` object.

To test the `eval()` function, from the File menu of the browser, choose Open Location, type **`javaScript:`** into the Open window, and click on the Open button.

You can evaluate single expressions by typing them into the text field. The result of the evaluation is displayed in the top frame. For example, typing `eval("2 + 2")` and pressing Return displays `4` in the top frame as the result of the evaluation.

Escaping and Unescaping ASCII Characters

Spaces, punctuation, and accented characters that are not ASCII letters or numbers can be represented in the form `%`*`xx`*, where *`xx`* is two hexadecimal digits that represent the ISO-8859-1 encoding of the character. For example, the Macintosh system represents spaces in file names as `%20`, which is the ISO-8859-1 encoding for a space.

You can decode an encoded string by using the built-in `unescape()` function, and you can encode a string for transmission by using the built-in `escape()` function. A common use of the `escape()` function is to encode values that are stored in a cookie.

Introducing the String Object

The JavaScript language has a `string` object, with its own properties and methods that you can use to work with strings. All properties and methods for the `String` object, listed in alphabetical order in Table 28-2, work both on strings that are created as string data types and strings created as `String` objects, except for the `prototype` property, which applies only to explicitly created `String` objects.

Table 28-2 **Properties and Methods for the String Object**

Properties	Methods	Event Handlers
`length`	`anchor()`	None
`prototype*`	`big()`	
	`blink()`	
	`bold()`	
	`charAt()`	
	`eval()*`	
	`fixed()`	
	`fontcolor()`	
	`fontsize()`	
	`indexOf()`	
	`italics()`	
	`lastIndexOf()`	
	`link()`	
	`small()`	
	`split()*`	
	`strike()`	
	`sub()`	
	`substring()`	

Table 28-2 Properties and Methods for the String Object (Continued)

Properties	Methods	Event Handlers
	`sup()`	
	`toLowerCase()`	
	`toString()*`	
	`toUpperCase()`	
	`valueOf()*`	

* New in Navigator 3.0.

String properties and methods use the same syntax as for other object properties and methods:

```
stringObject.property
stringObject.method()
```

The *`stringObject`* part of the syntax can be a quoted string or an expression that evaluates to a string, including variables containing strings or other object properties. String methods do not change the string itself. Instead, the method returns a value that you can use either to assign to a variable or as a parameter to another method or function call.

Finding the Number of Characters in a String

As wioth arrays, you use the `length` property to find how many characters are in the string. The `length` property counts all of the characters in the string, including spaces and punctuation characters. Any escape sequences, such as `\n` or `\"` that are embedded in a quoted string count as a single character. For example, the `length` property evaluates the following string as 19 characters:

```
var myString = "It\'s a cloudy day.\n"
```

Property	Value	Gettable	Settable
length	integer	Yes	No

Example of Finding the Number of Characters in a String

The following `stringLength.html` script creates the frameset to contain the rest of the example provided in `stringLengthBody.html`. The `stringLength.html` script also references the `blank.html` script, which is used as a placeholder for the resulting string, and the `footer.html` script, which displays standard footer information.

```
<!--
                stringLength.html
    This FRAMESET defines the page for the
    stringLength example. The FRAMESET
    comprises the following documents:
    stringLengthBody.html, which contains the
    example code; blank.html, which is a
    placeholder for the resulting string; and
    footer.html, which contains our standard footer
    information.
-->
<HTML>
<HEAD>
<TITLE>String Length</TITLE>
</HEAD>
<FRAMESET ROWS="70%,20%,10%" BORDER=1>
  <BASE TARGET="results">
  <FRAME SRC="stringLengthBody.html" NAME="body">
  <FRAME SRC="blank.html" NAME="results">
  <FRAME SRC="footer.html" NAME="footer">
</FRAMESET>
<NOFRAMES>
<P>For viewing this page, a browser that supports frames
is required.</P>
</NOFRAMES>
</HTML>
```

The following `stringLengthBody.html` script contains the string functions.

```
<!--
              stringLengthBody.html
    This file contains the body frame of the
    stringLength example.
-->
<HTML>
<HEAD>
<SCRIPT LANGUAGE="JavaScript">
<!-- HIDE FROM OLD BROWSERS
```

```
//
function getLength(theText) {
  var aStr = new String(theText.value)
  var mStr = new String()

  mStr += "The string is "
  mStr += aStr.length + " characters "
  mStr += "in length."

  with (window.top.frames[1].document) {
    open()
    write("<HTML>")
    write("<BODY>")
    write("<P>")
    write(mStr)
    write("</P>")
    write("</BODY>")
    write("</HTML>")
    close()
  }
}

// STOP HIDING -->
</SCRIPT>
</HEAD>
<BODY>

<P>Each String object has a length property that
tells you the number of characters in the
string. For any string, <B>str</B>, the index of
the last character is <B>str.length - 1</B>.

<FORM>
Enter a String:<BR>
<INPUT TYPE="text" NAME="txtField" VALUE=""
 SIZE=40><BR>
<INPUT TYPE="button" NAME="lengthBtn"
 VALUE="Get Length"
 onClick="getLength(this.form.txtField)">
</FORM>
</BODY>
</HTML>
```

The following `blank.html` script contains the HTML that is used to display the length of the string you type into the text field.

```
<!--
            blank.html
-->
<HTML>
<BODY>
</BODY>
</HTML>
```

Figure 28–2 shows the result of loading the `stringLength.html` script.

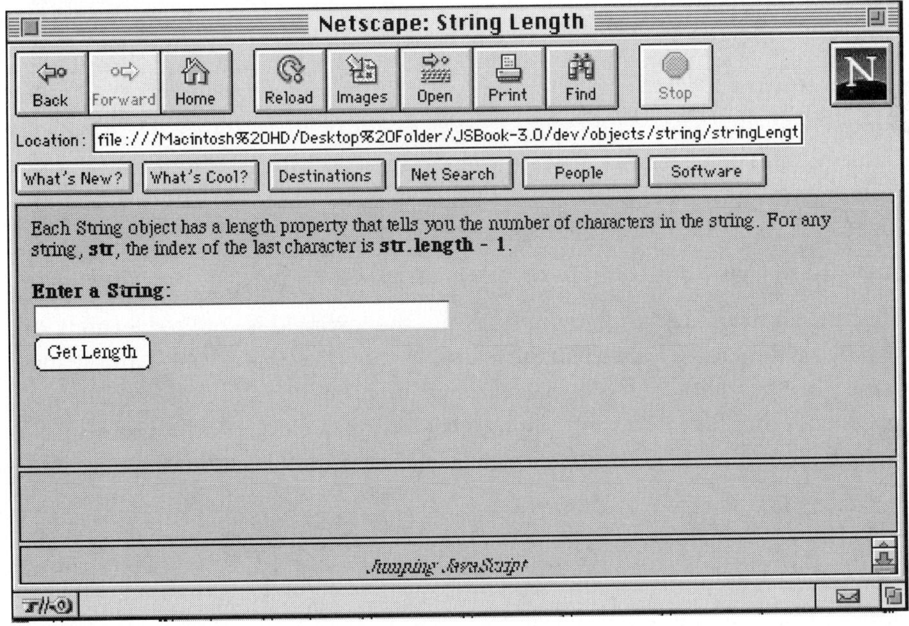

Figure 28–2 Result of loading the `stringLength.html` script

You can type a string into the text field. The text field is 40 characters wide. If you type more than 40 characters, the text field scrolls. When you click on the Get Length button, the length of the string is displayed in the middle frame of the window, as shown in Figure 28–3.

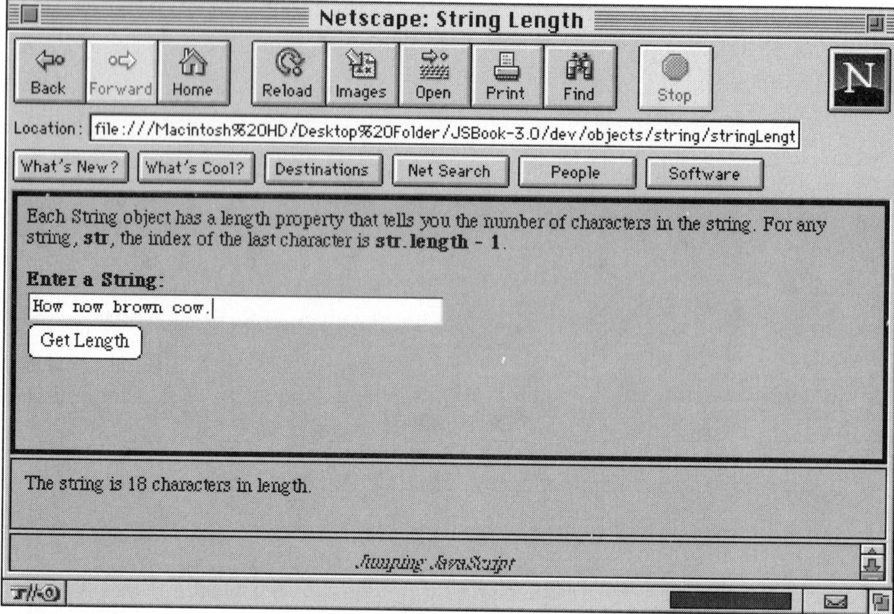

Figure 28–3 Viewing the length of a string

In this script, any character that you type into the text field is counted, even if it is an escaped character sequence. In the example shown in Figure 28–4, the string contains six characters and three backslashes which escape the characters that follow them. The `string.length` property returns a value of 9 for this string. However, if you evaluated the same string in a script as the statement:

```
var myString = "\"Yes\"\n"
```

the `string.length` property would return a value of `6`.

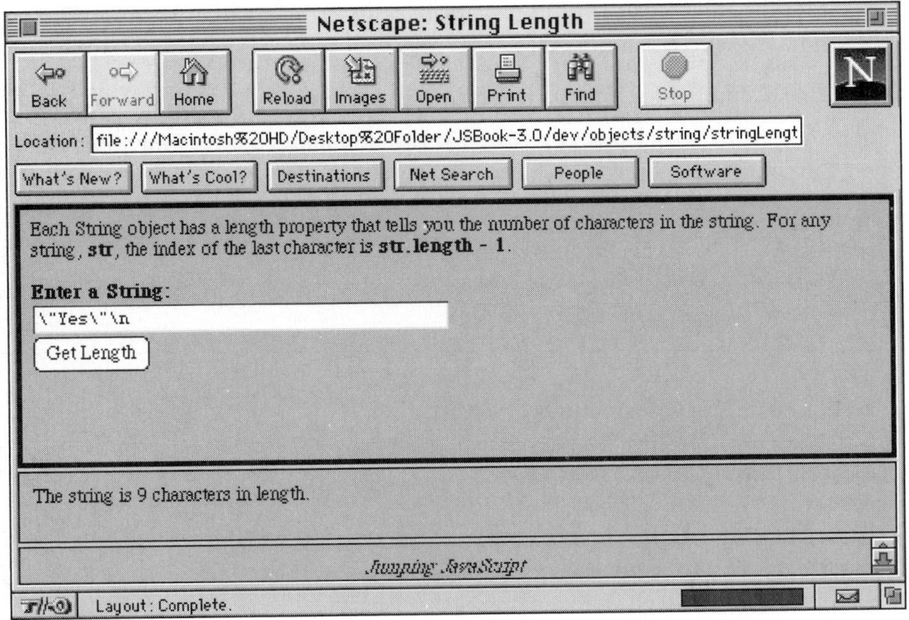

Figure 28–4 Length of string with escape characters

To fix the `stringLength.html` script so that it evaluates the escape characters in the string by using the `eval()` function, change the first line of the `getLength()` function to the following statement:

```
var aStr = new String(eval(theText.value))
```

With the `eval()` function in the script, you can type

```
"\"Yes\"\n"
```

into the text field, and the script evaluates the length as 6 characters.

Creating Custom String Functions

The Navigator 3.0 release provides a `prototype` property that you can use to add properties and methods to any object that can be created with the `new` keyword, such as `String`, `Date`, and user-defined objects.

Property	Value	Gettable	Settable
prototype	string	Yes	Yes

In the Navigator 3.0 release, prototypes apply only to the current window. They cannot be shared across windows.

Example of Creating a Custom String Function

The following `stringPrototype.html` script creates a custom function that changes the first character in a string to an uppercase character.

```
<!--
              stringPrototype.html
-->

<HTML>
<HEAD>
<TITLE>String Prototype</TITLE>
<SCRIPT LANGUAGE="JavaScript">
<!-- HIDE FROM OLD BROWSERS

// A String object prototype function that
// capitalizes the first character of the
// string.
function capitalizeString() {
  var returnStr = new String()

  returnStr += this.charAt(0).toUpperCase()
  returnStr += this.substring(1, this.length)

  return returnStr
}

// STOP HIDING -->
</SCRIPT>
</HEAD>
<BODY>

<P>You can add a prototype function, such as
Date, String, and user-defined objects, to any object
created with new.</P>

<P>So, let's create a prototype that capitalizes
the first character of a string for you.</P>

<PRE>
// A String object prototype function that
// capitalizes the first character of the
```

```
// string.
function capitalizeString() {
  var returnStr = new String()

  returnStr += this.charAt(0).toUpperCase()
  returnStr += this.substring(1, this.length)

  return returnStr
}
</PRE>

<P>To add the prototype function to a String
object, first create a string with the new
operator and then assign the prototype a
name:</P>

<PRE>
  var aSentence = new String("this is a test")

  // add the capitalization prototype to String
  String.prototype.cap = capitalizeString
</PRE>

<P>Then, you can use the function by simply
calling the name you assigned, like so:<P>

<PRE>
  write(aSentence.cap())
</PRE>

<P>Just to prove it works:</P>

<SCRIPT LANGUAGE="JavaScript">
<!-- HIDE FROM OLD BROWSERS
  var aSentence = new String("this is a test")

  // add the capitalization prototype to String
  String.prototype.cap = capitalizeString

  with (document) {
    open()
    write("<P>The original string's value is:")
    write("<BR>" + aSentence.valueOf() + "</P>")
    write("<P>And a call to the prototype returns:")
```

```
    write("<BR>" + aSentence.cap() + "</P>")
    close()
  }
// STOP HIDING -->
</SCRIPT>
</BODY>
</HTML>
```

Figure 28–5 shows the result of loading the `stringPrototype.html` script.

Netscape: String Prototype

Back Forward Home Reload Images Open Print Find Stop

Location: file:///Macintosh%20HD/Desktop%20Folder/JSBook-3.0/dev/objects/string/stringPrototy

What's New? What's Cool? Destinations Net Search People Software

You can add a prototype function, such as Date, String, and user-defined objects, to any object created with new.

So, let's create a prototype that capitalizes the first character of a string for you.

```
// A String object prototype function that
// capitalizes the first character of the
// string.
function capitalizeString() {
  var returnStr = new String()

  returnStr += this.charAt(0).toUpperCase()
  returnStr += this.substring(1, this.length)

  return returnStr
}
```

To add the prototype function to a String object, first create a string with the new operator and then assign the prototype a name:

```
  var aSentence = new String("this is a test")

  // add the capitalization prototype to String
  String.prototype.cap = capitalizeString
```

Then, you can use the function by simply calling the name you assigned, like so:

```
  write(aSentence.cap())
```

Just to prove it works:

The original string's value is:
this is a test

And a call to the prototype returns:
This is a test

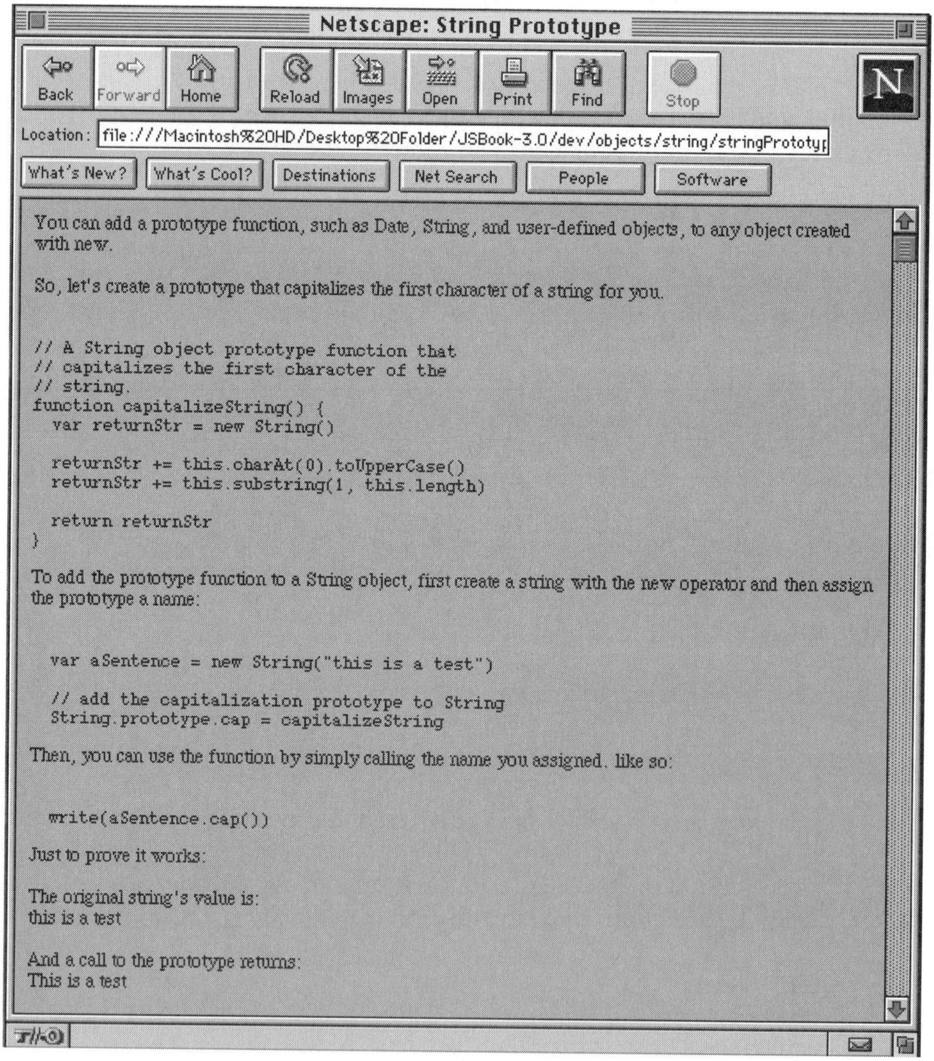

Figure 28–5 Result of loading the `stringPrototype.html` script

Converting a String into an Anchor or a Link

You can use the `anchor()` and `link()` methods to convert a string into an anchor or a link.

> **Methods**
>
> anchor("*anchorName*")
>
> link(*URL*)
>
> **Return**
>
> The string converted to the appropriate anchor or link

The `anchor("anchorName")` method returns a copy of the string in the following format:

```
<A NAME="anchorName">StringText</A>
```

The name that is assigned to the anchor is the name that you specify in parentheses as the argument to the anchor method.

The `link()` method is similar to the `anchor()` method. Instead of specifying an anchor name as the argument to the `link()` method, you specify a URL. The method returns a copy of the string in the following format:

```
<A HREF="URL">StringText</A>
```

Example of Converting a String into an Anchor and a Link

The following `stringLinks.html` script creates an anchor and a link.

```
<!--
                  stringLinks.html
-->

<HTML>
<HEAD>
<TITLE>String Links</TITLE>
</HEAD>
<BODY>

<P>The String object has two methods for dealing
with links: anchor() and link().
</P>
```

```
<P>The anchor method returns a string enclosed in
&lt;A NAME="anchor_name"&gt; and &lt;/A&gt;. The
following link is created with the anchor
method.</P>

<SCRIPT LANGUAGE="JavaScript">
<!-- HIDE FROM OLD BROWSERS

  var str = new String("An anchor for the link.")

  with (document) {
    open()
    write(str.anchor("an_anchor"))
    close()
  }

// STOP HIDING -->
</SCRIPT>

<P>The link method returns a string enclosed in
&lt;A HREF="url"&gt; and &lt;/A&gt;. The
following link is created with the link method
and simply goes to the anchor above.</P>

<SCRIPT LANGUAGE="JavaScript">
<!-- HIDE FROM OLD BROWSERS

  var str = new String("A link to the anchor.")

  with (document) {
    open()
    write(str.link("#an_anchor"))
    close()
  }

// STOP HIDING -->
</SCRIPT>

</BODY>
</HTML>
```

Figure 28–6 shows the result of loading the `stringLinks.html` script.

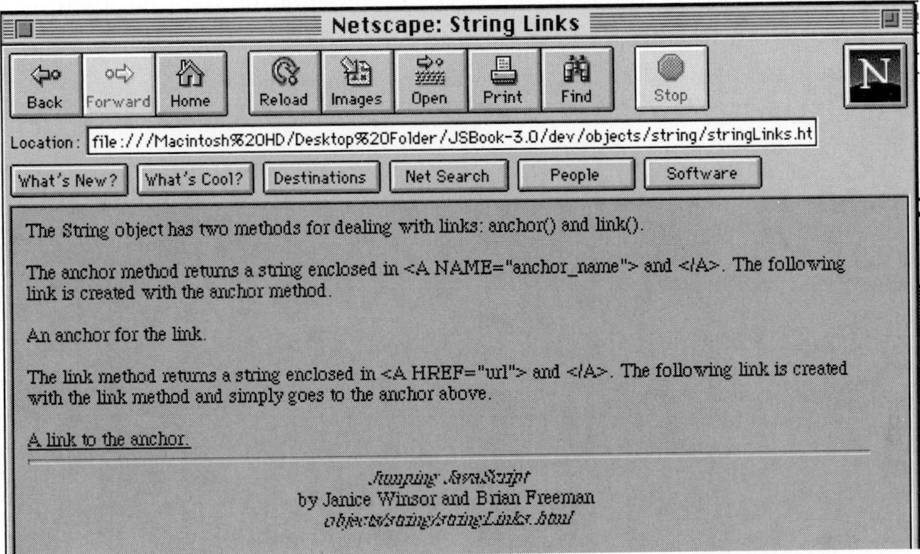

Figure 28–6 Result of loading the `stringLinks.html` script

Using String Object Methods to Format Text

The `String` object text formatting methods return the string value enclosed within the HTML tags that provide the appropriate formatting.

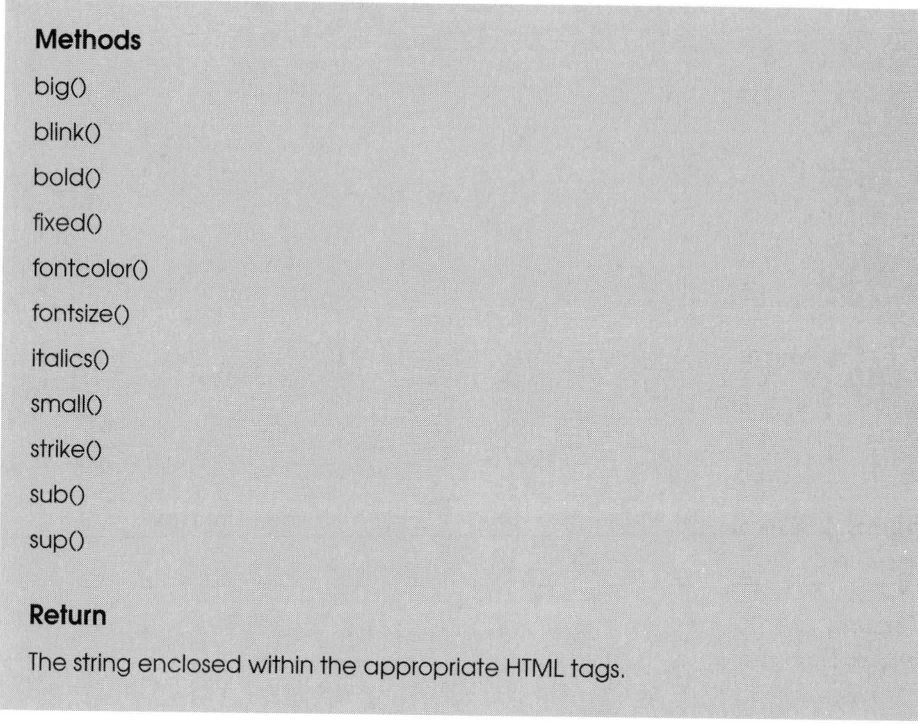

Methods

big()

blink()

bold()

fixed()

fontcolor()

fontsize()

italics()

small()

strike()

sub()

sup()

Return

The string enclosed within the appropriate HTML tags.

Table 28-3 lists the HTML tags that are used with each of the string text formatting methods.

Table 28-3 HTML Tags for String Object Text Formatting Methods

Method	HTML Tags	Description
`big()`	`<BIG></BIG>`	Bigger font
`blink()`	`<BLINK></BLINK>`	Blinking font
`bold()`	`<B></B>`	Bold font
`fixed()`	`<TT></TT>`	Fixed-width teletype font
`fontcolor()`	`<FONT COLOR="color"></FONT>`	Font color

Table 28-3 HTML Tags for String Object Text Formatting Methods (Continued)

Method	HTML Tags	Description
`fontsize()`	<FONT SIZE="size"></FONT>	Font point size
`italics()`	<I></I>	Italic font
`small()`	<SMALL></SMALL>	Smaller font
`strike()`	<STRIKE></STRIKE>	Horizontal strikeout line through font.
`sub()`		Subscript font position
`sup()`		Superscript font position

Example Using String Object Methods to Format Text

The following `stringAttributes.html` script defines the frameset and loads the `stringAttributesBody.html` script and two other formatting scripts.

```
<!--
              stringAttributes.html

    This FRAMESET defines the page for the
    stringAttributes example. The FRAMESET
    comprises the following documents:
    stringAttributesBody.html, which contains the
    example code; blank.html, which is a
    placeholder for the resulting string; and
    footer.html, which contains our standard footer
    information.
-->

<HTML>
<HEAD>
<TITLE>String Attributes</TITLE>
</HEAD>
<FRAMESET ROWS="70%,20%,10%" BORDER=1>
  <BASE TARGET="results">
  <FRAME SRC="stringAttributesBody.html" NAME="body">
  <FRAME SRC="blank.html" NAME="results">
  <FRAME SRC="footer.html" NAME="footer">
</FRAMESET>
```

```
<NOFRAMES>
<P>For viewing this page, a browser that supports frames
is required.</P>
</NOFRAMES>
</HTML>
```

The following `stringAttributesBody.html` script uses all of the text formatting methods except `fontColor()` and `fontSize()`.

```
<!--
            stringAttributesBody.html

    This file contains the body frame of the
    stringAttributes example.
-->

<HTML>
<HEAD>
<SCRIPT LANGUAGE="JavaScript">
<!-- HIDE FROM OLD BROWSERS


function displayString(attr) {
  var theForm = document.forms[0]
  var aStr = theForm.txtField.value

  with (window.top.frames[1].document) {
    open()
    write("<HTML>")
    write("<BODY>")
    write("<P>")
    if (attr == "big") {
      write(aStr.big())
    } else
    if (attr == "blink") {
      write(aStr.blink())
    } else
    if (attr == "bold") {
      write(aStr.bold())
    } else
    if (attr == "fixed") {
      write(aStr.fixed())
    } else
    if (attr == "italics") {
      write(aStr.italics())
```

```
    } else
    if (attr == "small") {
      write(aStr.small())
    } else
    if (attr == "strike") {
      write(aStr.strike())
    } else
    if (attr == "sub") {
      write(aStr.sub())
    } else
    if (attr == "sup") {
      write(aStr.sup())
    }
    write("</P>")
    write("</BODY>")
    write("</HTML>")
    close()
  }
}

// STOP HIDING -->
</SCRIPT>
</HEAD>
<BODY>


<FORM>
<P><B>Enter a String:</B><BR>
<INPUT TYPE="text" NAME="txtField" VALUE=""
 SIZE=60></P>

<P>Tag to wrap the string in:<BR>
<INPUT TYPE="radio" NAME="aRadio"
 onClick="displayString('big')"> big<BR>
<INPUT TYPE="radio" NAME="aRadio"
 onClick="displayString('blink')"> blink<BR>
<INPUT TYPE="radio" NAME="aRadio"
 onClick="displayString('bold')"> bold<BR>
<INPUT TYPE="radio" NAME="aRadio"
 onClick="displayString('fixed')"> fixed<BR>
<INPUT TYPE="radio" NAME="aRadio"
 onClick="displayString('italics')"> italics<BR>
<INPUT TYPE="radio" NAME="aRadio"
 onClick="displayString('small')"> small<BR>
```

```
<INPUT TYPE="radio" NAME="aRadio"
 onClick="displayString('strike')"> strike<BR>
<INPUT TYPE="radio" NAME="aRadio"
 onClick="displayString('sub')"> sub<BR>
<INPUT TYPE="radio" NAME="aRadio"
 onClick="displayString('sup')"> sup<BR>
</P>
</FORM>
</BODY>
</HTML>
```

Figure 28–7 shows the result of loading the `stringAttributes.html` script.

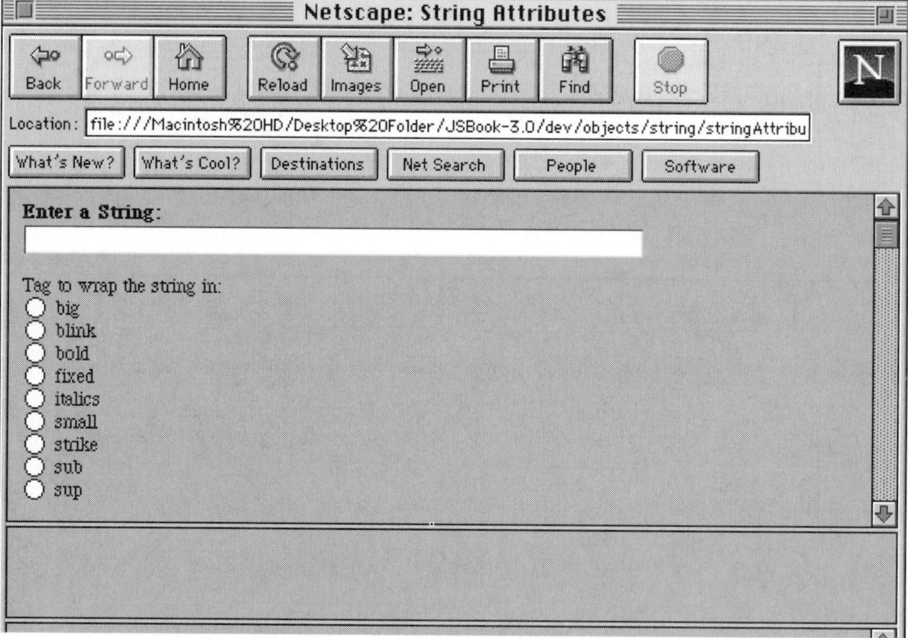

Figure 28–7 Result of loading the `stringAttributes.html` script

Figure 28–8 shows the result of each of the methods shown in Figure 28–7

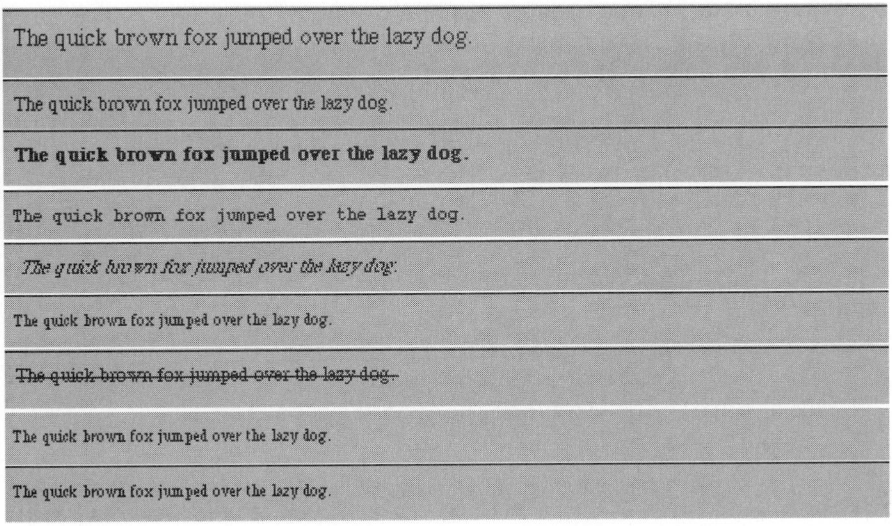

The quick brown fox jumped over the lazy dog.

The quick brown fox jumped over the lazy dog.

The quick brown fox jumped over the lazy dog.

`The quick brown fox jumped over the lazy dog.`

The quick brown fox jumped over the lazy dog.

The quick brown fox jumped over the lazy dog.

~~The quick brown fox jumped over the lazy dog.~~

The quick brown fox jumped over the lazy dog.

The quick brown fox jumped over the lazy dog.

Figure 28–8 Result of loading the `big()`, `blink()`, `bold()`, `fixed()`, `italics()`, `small()`, `strike()`, `sub()`, and `sup()` methods

Example of Changing Font Size and Color

The following `stringFonts.html` script creates the frameset for an example that uses the `fontColor()` and `fontSize()` methods.

```
<!--
                stringFonts.html

    This FRAMESET defines the page for the
    stringFonts example. The FRAMESET
    comprises the following documents:
    stringFontsBody.html, which contains the
    example code; blank.html, which is a
    placeholder for the resulting string; and
    footer.html, which contains our standard footer
    information.
-->

<HTML>
<HEAD>
<TITLE>String Font Methods</TITLE>
</HEAD>
<FRAMESET ROWS="70%,20%,10%" BORDER=1>
  <BASE TARGET="results">
  <FRAME SRC="stringFontsBody.html" NAME="body">
```

```
    <FRAME SRC="blank.html" NAME="results">
    <FRAME SRC="footer.html" NAME="footer">
  </FRAMESET>
  <NOFRAMES>
  <P>For viewing this page, a browser that supports
  frames is required.</P>
  </NOFRAMES>
  </HTML>
```

The following `stringFontBody.html` script enables users to change font color and point size.

```
<!--
               stringFontsBody.html
    This file contains the body frame of the
    stringFonts example.
-->
<HTML>
<HEAD>
<SCRIPT LANGUAGE="JavaScript">
<!-- HIDE FROM OLD BROWSERS

var theString = new String()
var theColor  = new String("black")
var theSign   = new String("")

function displayString() {
  var theForm = document.forms[0]
  var theSize = theSign

  theSize += theForm.sizeSel.selectedIndex + 1

  with (window.top.frames[1].document) {
    open()
    write("<HTML>")
    write("<BODY>")
    write("<P>")
    write(
      theString.fontcolor(theColor).fontsize(theSize))
    write("</P>")
    write("</BODY>")
    write("</HTML>")
    close()
  }
}
```

```
// STOP HIDING -->
</SCRIPT>
</HEAD>
<BODY>

<FORM>
<P>Enter a String:<BR>
<INPUT TYPE="text" NAME="txtField" VALUE=""
 SIZE=60 onChange="theString=this.value"></P>

<P>Font Color:<BR>
<INPUT TYPE="radio" NAME="colorRadio"
 onClick="theColor='red'"> red<BR>
<INPUT TYPE="radio" NAME="colorRadio"
 onClick="theColor='green'"> green<BR>
<INPUT TYPE="radio" NAME="colorRadio"
 onClick="theColor='blue'"> blue
</P>

<P>Increase/Decrease Font Size:<BR>
<INPUT TYPE="radio" NAME="sizeRadio"
 onClick="theSign='+'"> increase<BR>
<INPUT TYPE="radio" NAME="sizeRadio"
 onClick="theSign='-'"> decrease<BR>

<P>Font Size:<BR>
<SELECT NAME="sizeSel" SIZE=7>
 <OPTION> 1
 <OPTION> 2
 <OPTION> 3
 <OPTION> 4
 <OPTION> 5
 <OPTION> 6
 <OPTION> 7
</SELECT>
</P>

<INPUT TYPE="button" NAME="displayBtn"
 VALUE="Display String" onClick="displayString()">
</P>
</FORM>
</BODY>
</HTML>
```

Figure 28–9 shows the result of loading the `stringFonts.html` script.

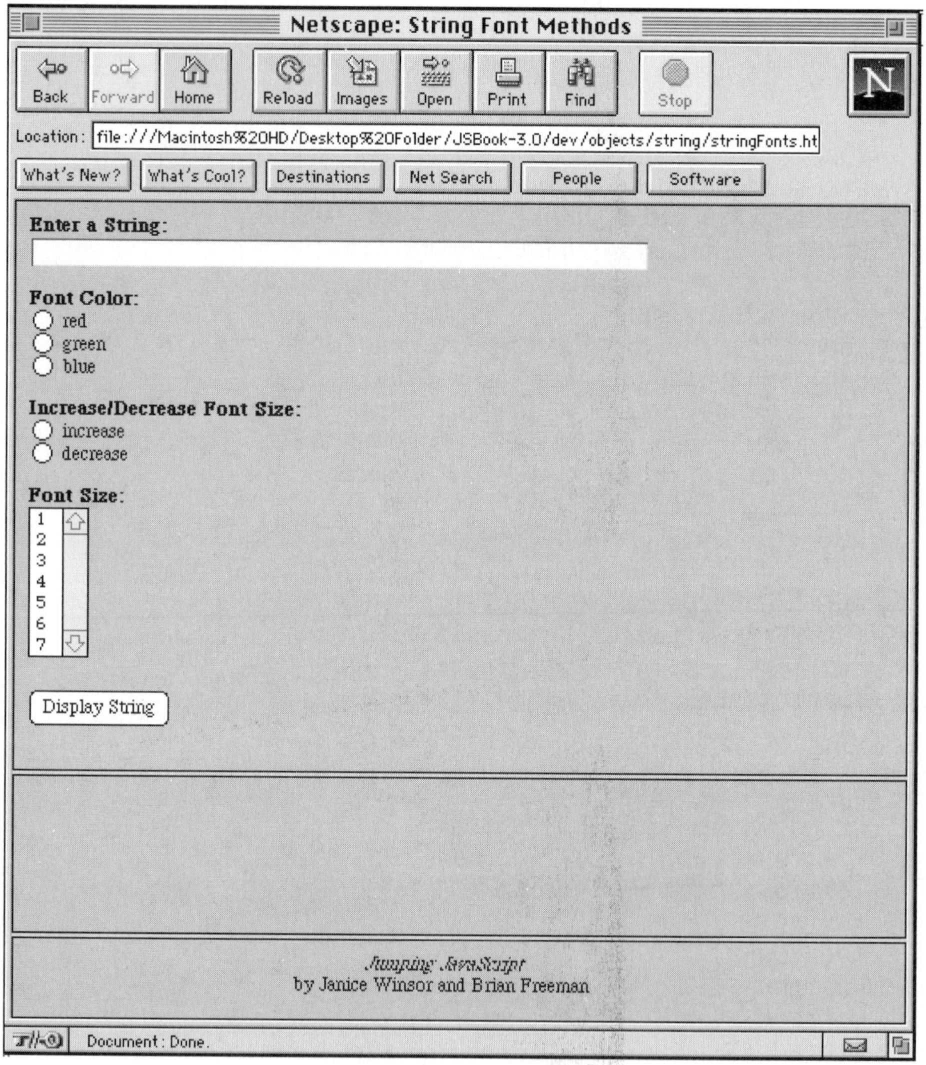

Figure 28–9 Result of loading the `stringFonts.html` script

Type a string into the text field, and choose a color and font size. Clicking on the increase or decrease radio button makes the chosen font size bigger or smaller. Figure 28–10 shows a blue string, with increase and point size at the seventh option. Note that the numbers 1 through 7 do not correspond to actual point sizes but instead represent a scale from small to large.

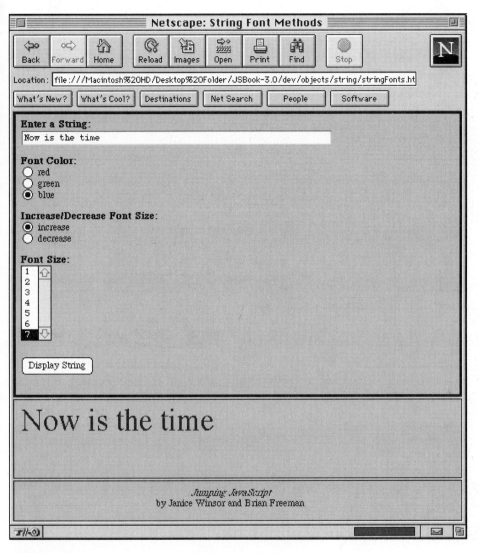

Figure 28–10 Changing font color and point size

Converting Case

You can use the `toLowerCase()` and `toUpperCase()` methods to convert all of the characters in the string to the same case. Because the JavaScript language and most operating systems are case sensitive, you may find it useful to convert input and output strings to a consistent case before you compare them.

Method

string.toLowerCase()

string.toUpperCase()

Returns

The string converted to the appropriate case, depending on the method used

For an example of using the `toUpperCase()` method, see "Example of Creating a Custom String Function" on page 810.

Searching for Part of a String

You can use the `indexOf()` method to return the position of the first character in the search string. The `indexOf()` method searches from the beginning of the string or from the *`startIndex`* that you specify. Indexing of the string starts at 0 and goes to `stringName.length -1`, indexing from left to right.

Method

indexOf(*searchString*, (, *startIndex*))

Returns

Index value of the character within the *string* where the *searchString* begins

Because the `indexOf()` method considers the text in the string to be an array, it starts the counting sequence at `0`. If the method does not find a match in the string, it returns a value of `-1`. If the string you're searching is empty, the `indexOf()` method returns an empty string.

```
if (str.length > 0) {
   if (str.indexOf(searchString, startIndex) != -1){
        Do what you want here
   }
}
```

The `lastIndexOf()` method is similar to the `indexOf()` method, except that this method starts its search for a match from the end of the string and searches backward toward the beginning of the string.

Method

string.lastIndexOf(*searchString*, (, *startIndex*))

Returns

Index value of the last character within the *string* where the *searchString* begins

The `lastIndexOf()` method starts the counting sequence at `0` from the back of the string. This method can be useful when you are searching for a specific file type suffix.

Example of Searching for Part of a String with the indexOf() Method

The following extract from the `imageLowsrc.html` script uses the `indexOf()` method to extract the number of the image from the array. It also uses the `indexOf()` and `substring` methods to extract the height and width dimensions from the array definition and the `parseInt()` function to convert the string to a number.

```
// Obtain the src value for the indicated
// image.
//
function getImageSrc(num) {
  var rstr = ""
  var name = ""

  name = image_info[num].substring(
           0,
           image_info[num].indexOf(' '))

  rstr = image_path + name + ".jpg"

  return rstr
}
```

```
// Obtain the lowsrc value for the
// indicated image.
//
function getImageLowsrc(num) {
  var rstr = ""
  var name = ""

  name = image_info[num].substring(
           0,
           image_info[num].indexOf(' '))

  rstr = image_path + name + ".gif"

  return rstr
}

// Obtain the dimension of the indicated image.
//
function getImageDimension(num) {
  var rstr = ""

  rstr = image_info[num].substring(
           image_info[num].indexOf(' ') + 1,
           image_info[num].length)

  return rstr
}

// Obtain the width of the indicated image.
//
function getImageWidth(num) {
  var   dim = ""
  var width = ""

  dim   = getImageDimension(num)
  width = dim.substring(0, dim.indexOf('x'))

  return parseInt(width, 0)
}

// Obtain the height of the indicated image.
//
function getImageHeight(num) {
```

```
    var    dim = ""
    var height = ""

    dim    = getImageDimension(num)
    height = dim.substring(
                 dim.indexOf('x') + 1,
                 dim.length)
    return parseInt(height, 0)
  }
```

For the complete example, see Chapter 9, "Working with Images."

Example of Searching for Part of a String with the lastIndexOf() Method

The following extract from the `AyersRock.html` script uses the `lastIndexOf()` method to extract the size of the image. This script also uses the `indexOf()` and `substring()` methods.

```
  function displayImage(image_num, image_path) {
    var          rstr = ""
    var    image_file = ""
    var    image_name = ""
    var     image_dim = ""
    var   image_width = ""
    var image_height = ""

    image_file   = img[image_num].substring(0,
  img[image_num].indexOf(' '))
    image_name   = image_file.substring(0,
  image_file.lastIndexOf('.'))
    image_dim    =
  img[image_num].substring(img[image_num].indexOf(' ') + 1,
  img[image_num].length)
    image_width  = image_dim.substring(0,
  image_dim.indexOf('x'))
    image_height =
  image_dim.substring(image_dim.indexOf('x') + 1,
  image_dim.length)

    rstr += "<TABLE BORDER=4><CAPTION> [ " + image_dim + " ] "
    rstr += image_file + " </CAPTION>\n"
    rstr += "<TR><TD><IMG SRC='" + image_path + image_file +
  "' "
    rstr += "NAME='" + image_name + "' "
    rstr += "WIDTH=" + image_width + " "
```

```
    rstr += "HEIGHT=" + image_height
    rstr += "></TD></TR>\n"
    rstr += "</TABLE><BR><BR>\n"

    return rstr
 }
```

For the complete example, see Chapter 9, "Working with Images."

Getting a Substring

A *substring* is a contiguous set of characters that are contained within a string. Using the `substring()` method, you can extract a subset of a string. The parameters that you use for the `substring()` method are the ***indexA*** value, which specifies the beginning character of the substring, and ***indexB***, which specifies the beginning character of the substring that follows.

Method

substring(*indexA*,*indexB*)

Returns

indexA is any integer from 0 to *strName*.length -1.

indexB is any integer from 0 to *strName*.length.

For ***indexA*** < ***indexB***, substring is the subset starting at ***indexA*** and ending at the character before ***indexB***.

For ***indexA*** > ***indexB***, substring is the subset starting at the character before ***indexB*** and ending with the character at ***indexA***.

For ***indexA*** = ***indexB***, substring is an empty string.

indexA and ***indexB*** can be reversed somewhat, giving you slightly different results.

For examples of the `substring()` method, see "Example of Searching for Part of a String with the indexOf() Method" on page 827 and "Example of Searching for Part of a String with the lastIndexOf() Method" on page 829.

Getting the nth Character in a String

The `charAt()` method returns one character at the location that corresponds to the index value you specify as the parameter for the `charAt()` method. The first character in the string is at `0` index value.

> **Methods**
>
> *string*.charAt(*index*)
>
> **Returns**
>
> The character in the *string* at the *index* count

Example of Getting the nth Character in a String

The following extract from the `textValueVerify.html` script uses the `charAt()` method to check for a dash at the 6th character of the zip code field.

```
function isAZip(str) {
  if (str.length == 5 ||
      str.length == 9 ||
      str.length == 10) {

    // the first two cases are all numeric
    if (str.length == 5 || str.length == 9) {
      return isANum(str)
    }

    // the last two are somewhat similar, so
    // just loop through and find out if the dash or
    // space is in the right spot.
    for (var i=0; i < str.length; i++) {
      var chr = str.charAt(i)
      if (chr < "0" || chr > "9") {
   if (i != 5 && (chr == "-" || chr == " ")) {
     return false
   }
      }
    }
    return true
  }
  else {
    return false
```

```
    }
  }
```

For the complete example, see Chapter 16, "Adding Text Fields to a Document."

Splitting a String into an Array

The Navigator 3.0 release provides a new `split()` method for the `String` object. You can use the `split()` method to divide a string into an array. You specify the delimiter character as the parameter to the `split()` method.

Methods

string.split("*delimiterCharacter*")

Returns

An array of items separated by the *delimiterCharacter*

You can use the `split()` method to split up a string into words for sorting by using `split(" ")`, to separate a comma-delimited list by using `split(",")`, to separate a string by sentences or at a decimal point by using `split(".")`, and to separate a string by lines by using `split("\n")`. This list of examples is representative, not complete. You can use any delimiter character as a parameter.

The following `stringSplit.html` script creates the frameset for this example. It loads the `stringSplitBody.html` script and two other scripts.

```
<!--
                stringSplit.html

    This FRAMESET defines the page for the
    stringSplit example. The FRAMESET
    comprises the following documents:
    stringSplitBody.html, which contains the
    example code' blank.html, which is a
    placeholder for the resulting string; and
    footer.html, which contains our standard footer
    information.
-->

<HTML>
<HEAD>
<TITLE>String Split Method</TITLE>
</HEAD>
```

```
<FRAMESET ROWS="70%,20%,10%" BORDER=1>
  <BASE TARGET="results">
  <FRAME SRC="stringSplitBody.html" NAME="body">
  <FRAME SRC="blank.html" NAME="results">
  <FRAME SRC="footer.html" NAME="footer">
</FRAMESET>
<NOFRAMES>
<P>For viewing this page, a browser that
supports frames is required.</P>
</NOFRAMES>
</HTML>
```

The following `stringSplitBody.html` script contains a text area and a Sort button. You can sort the default text that is displayed in the text area, or you can type in your own text and then click on the Sort button. This script uses a space as the delimiter character for the `split()` method. It also uses the `sort()` method of the `Array` property to perform the sorting. For more information about the `Array` property, see Chapter 29, "Working with Arrays."

```
<!--
              stringSplitBody.html

    This file contains the body frame of the
    stringSplit example.
-->

<HTML>
<HEAD>
<SCRIPT LANGUAGE="JavaScript">
<!-- HIDE FROM OLD BROWSERS

function sortString() {
  var theForm  = document.forms[0]
  var theStr   = new String(theForm.textField.value)
  var strArray = theStr.split(" ")

  strArray.sort()

  resultsStr = new String("")
  for (var i=0; i < strArray.length; i++) {
    resultsStr += strArray[i] + "<BR>"
  }

  with (window.top.frames[1].document) {
    open()
```

```
        write("<HTML>")
        write("<BODY>")
        write("<P>")
        write(resultsStr)
        write("</P>")
        write("</BODY>")
        write("</HTML>")
        close()
    }
}

// STOP HIDING -->
</SCRIPT>
</HEAD>
<BODY>

<P>When you click on the Sort button, the String
object's split method separates the string
entered into the text area. The resulting array
is sorted and then displayed to you in the lower
frame. Notice that the words</P>

routine. this

<P>are not split because they are separated
by a new line and not by a space, which
is the delimiter in this script.</P>

<FORM>
<P><B>Enter some text to sort:</B><BR>
<TEXTAREA NAME="textField" ROWS=10 COLS=78
 WRAP="physical">
this is a test of the emergency sorting routine.
this is only a test.
</TEXTAREA>
</P>

<INPUT TYPE="button" NAME="sortBtn"
 VALUE="Sort" onClick="sortString()">
</P>
</FORM>
</BODY>
</HTML>
```

Figure 28–11 shows the result of loading the `stringSplit.html` script.

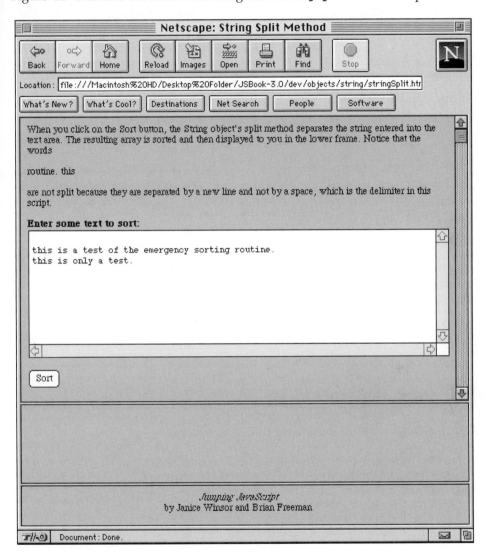

Figure 28–11 Result of loading the `stringSplit.html` script

When you click on the Sort button, the string is split into sections and sorted. The result of the sort is shown in Figure 28–12.

```
this
a
a
emergency
is
is
of
```

Figure 28–12 Split and sorted string

Note – The result of the sort is incorrect in Figure 28–12. It should start with `a`, `a`, not with the word `this`. On the Macintosh PowerPC™ platform, the `Array.sort()` method is buggy. It does not work properly and forced the system to reboot more often than it worked.

The script did, however, keep together the words `routine. this` because they are separated by a new line characer and not a space, as shown in Figure 28–13.

```
of
only
routine. this
sorting
test
test.
the
```

Figure 28–13 Part of the string that was not split

Summary of New Terms and Concepts

The new terms and concepts introduced in this chapter are listed in alphabetical order in Table 28-4. The terms and concepts are also included in the glossary at the end of the book.

Table 28-4 Summary of New Terms and Concepts

Term/Concept	Description
radix	The value of the base number in a numbering system. In the decimal system, the radix is 10; in the binary system, the radix is 2; in the octal system, the radix is 8; in the hexadecimal system, the radix is 16.
substring	A contiguous part of a string contained within another string.

CHAPTER 29

- Constructing an Array
- Determining the Length of an Array
- Extracting String Data from an Array
- Reversing the Order of Data in an Array
- Sorting Items in an Array
- Creating Your Own Properties for an Array Object
- Summary of New Terms and Concepts

Working with Arrays

An *array* is a collection of individual data items that are organized so that the entire collection can be treated as a single piece of data. Individual elements of the array have similar data types and can be addressed one by one or as a group. JavaScript arrays are simply an ordered list of related items. You've already done quite a bit of work with JavaScript arrays. You've seen how to use arrays to cycle through the elements of a form and the links, applets, and plug-ins in a document.

NEW IN 3.0

The Navigator 3.0 release provides an `Array` object with the properties and methods listed in Table 29-1. The `Array` object has no event handlers. The `Array` object provides an `Array()` constructor that you can use to build your own arrays.

Table 29-1 **Properties and Methods for the Array Object**

Properties	Methods	Event Handlers
`length`	`eval()*`	None
`prototype`	`join()`	
	`reverse()`	

Table 29-1 Properties and Methods for the Array Object

Properties	Methods	Event Handlers
	`sort()`	
	`toString()*`	
	`valueOf()*`	

Constructing an Array

You create a new `Array` object by using the `new` keyword, as shown in the following example:

```
anArray = new Array()
```

A new, empty `Array` object has a `length` property of zero. There are no elements in the array.

You can initialize the number of entries for an array by specifying a numeric value as a parameter to the constructor. When you specify the number of entries for an array, the entries are preloaded with null values. Specifying the number of items in a array does not limit or restrict your ability to dynamically adjust the number of items in an array. The `length` property automatically adjusts to reflect the new count. The following example initializes an array with ten entries with index values from 0 to 9:

```
anArray = new Array(10)
```

When you have used either one of these constructions, you create an array with no values. To enter data into the array, you simply create a series of assignment statements, one for each element of the array.

The following example initializes an array with seven entries and assigns a value to each of the array entries:

```
var marineMammalsArray = new Array(7)

marineMammalsArray[0] = "whale"
marineMammalsArray[1] = "dolphin"
marineMammalsArray[2] = "porpoise"
marineMammalsArray[3] = "manatee"
marineMammalsArray[4] = "dugong"
marineMammalsArray[5] = "seal"
marineMammalsArray[6] = "sea lion"
```

You can initialize the array to the elements by specifying them as a comma-separated list of parameters to the constructor. This construction is called a *dense array,* and you create it by using the following syntax:

```
anArray = new Array("element", "element", etc.)
```

The following example creates a dense array of marine mammals:

```
marineMammalsArray = new Array("whale", "dolphin",
"porpoise", "manatee", "dugong", "seal", "sea lion")
```

A JavaScript arrays are associative; they are a one-dimensional array of pairsYou access the left member by a numeric index and the right member with a string index equal to the value of the left member. For example:

```
anArray[0] = "left"
anArray["left"] = "right"
```

You can create multidimensional arrays by assigning another array to an array element. The following example creates a 2 by 10 array:

```
var anArray = new Array(2)
anArray[0] = new Array(10)
anArray[1] = new Array(10)
```

Example of Creating New Array Objects

The following `array.html` script shows how to create new `Array` objects.

```
<!--
          array.html
-->
<HTML>
<HEAD>
<TITLE>Array</TITLE>
</HEAD>
<BODY>
<P>You create an array with the new operator.</P>
<DL>
  <DT>new Array()
  <DD>with no arguments
  <DT>new Array(size)
  <DD>size = the number of elements desired
  <DT>new Array(element, element, etc.)
  <DD>initialize to the given elements
</DL>

<P>It is important to note that JavaScript's
arrays are associative; they are a
```

```
one-dimensional array of pairs. You access the
left member by a numeric index and the right
member with a string index equal to the value of
the left member. For example:<P>

<DL>
  <DT>anArray[0] = "left"
  <DT>anArray["left"] = "right"
</DL>

<P>You create multidimensional arrays by
assigning another array to an existing array element.
The following example creates a 2 by 10 array:

<PRE>
var anArray = new Array(2)
anArray[0] = new Array(10)
anArray[1] = new Array(10)
</PRE>

<P>Here is another 2 by 10 array:</P>

<SCRIPT LANGUAGE="JavaScript">
<!-- HIDE FROM OLD BROWSERS
var anArray = new Array(2)

for (var i=0; i < 2; i++) {
  anArray[i] = new Array(10)
  for (var j=0; j < 10; j++) {
    anArray[i][j] = i + "," + j
  }
}

for (var i=0; i < 2; i++) {
  for (var j=0; j < 10; j++) {
    document.write(
      "anArray[" + i + "][" + j + "] = " +
      anArray[i][j] + "<BR>")
  }
}
// STOP HIDING -->
</SCRIPT>
</BODY>
</HTML>
```

Figure 29–1 shows the result of loading the `array.html` script.

Netscape: Array

Back Forward Home Reload Images Open Print Find Stop

Location: file:///Macintosh%20HD/Desktop%20Folder/JSBook-3.0/dev/objects/Array/array.html

What's New? What's Cool? Destinations Net Search People Software

You create an array with the new operator.

new Array()
    with no arguments
new Array(size)
    size = the number of elements desired
new Array(element, element, etc.)
    initialize to the given elements

It is important to note that JavaScript's arrays are associative; they are a one-dimensional array of pairs. You access the left member by a numeric index and the right member with a string index equal to the value of the left member. For example:

anArray[0] = "left"
anArray["left"] = "right"

You create multidimensional arrays by assigning another array to an existing array element. The following example creates a 2 by 10 array:

```
var anArray = new Array(2)
anArray[0] = new Array(10)
anArray[1] = new Array(10)
```

Here is another 2 by 10 array:

anArray[0][0] = 0,0
anArray[0][1] = 0,1
anArray[0][2] = 0,2
anArray[0][3] = 0,3
anArray[0][4] = 0,4
anArray[0][5] = 0,5
anArray[0][6] = 0,6
anArray[0][7] = 0,7
anArray[0][8] = 0,8
anArray[0][9] = 0,9
anArray[1][0] = 1,0

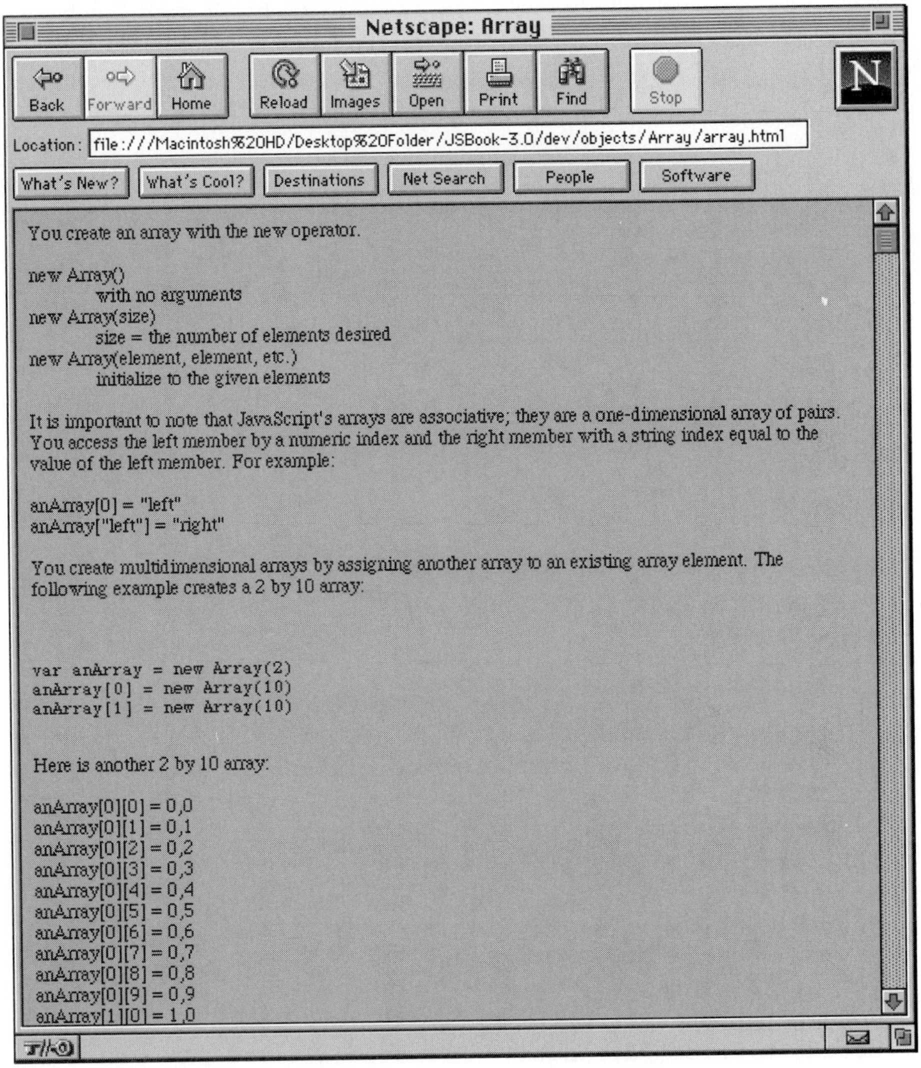

Figure 29–1 Result of loading the `array.html` script

Determining the Length of an Array

Use the `length` property to find the number of elements in the array. When you initialize an empty array, the value for the `length` property is zero. When the array contains elements that are not contiguous, the `length` property specifies a number one larger than the last element in the array.

Property	Value	Gettable	Settable
length	number	Yes	Yes

The following `arrayLength.html` script uses the `length` property with several different arrays.

```
<!--
                arrayLength.html
-->

<HTML>
<HEAD>
<TITLE>Array Length Property</TITLE>
</HEAD>
<BODY>

<P>The array length property is a read/write
integer specifying the number of elements in the
array. When the array doesn't contain contiguous
elements, length specifies a number one larger
than the last element in the array.</P>

<SCRIPT LANGUAGE="JavaScript">
<!-- HIDE FROM OLD BROWSERS
var a = new Array()
document.write("var a = new Array()<BR>")
document.write("a.length = " + a.length + "<BR>")

var b = new Array(20)
document.write("<BR>var b = new Array(20)<BR>")
document.write("b.length = " + b.length + "<BR>")
```

```
var c = new Array("alpha", "bravo")
document.write('<BR>var c = new Array("alpha",
"bravo")<BR>')
document.write("c.length = " + c.length + "<BR>")

c[3] = "delta"
document.write('c[3] = "delta"<BR>')
document.write("c.length = " + c.length + "<BR>")

c[19] = "tango"
document.write('c[19] = "tango"<BR>')
document.write("c.length = " + c.length + "<BR>")

c[25] = "zulu"
document.write('c[25] = "zulu"<BR>')
document.write("c.length = " + c.length + "<BR>")

// STOP HIDING -->
</SCRIPT>

</BODY>
</HTML>
```

Figure 29–2 shows the result of loading the `arrayLength.html` script.

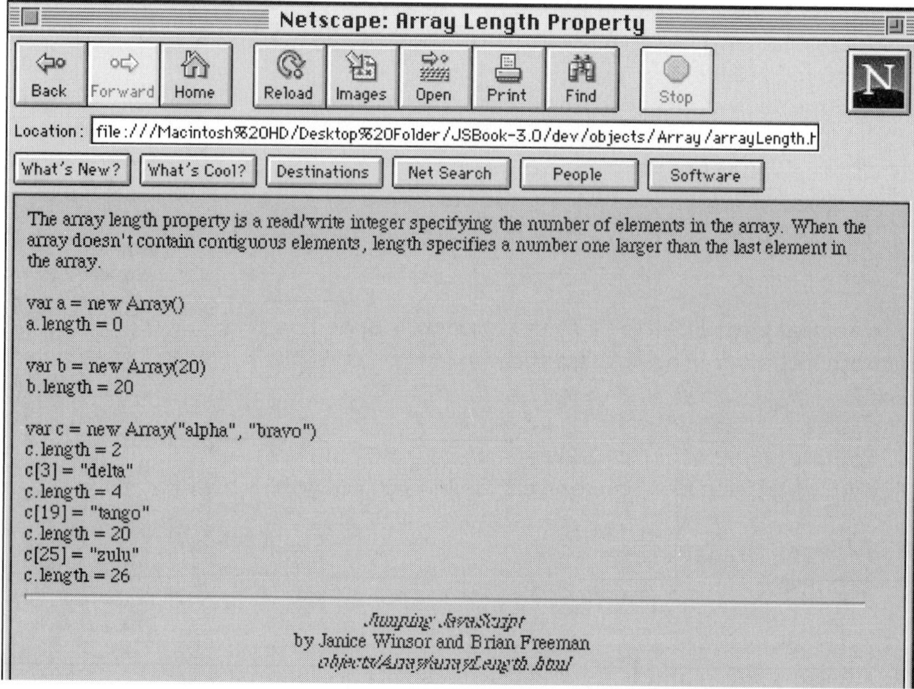

Figure 29–2 Result of loading the `arrayLength.html` script

Extracting String Data from an Array

When you want to extract the data from an array to use as a string, you can use the `join()` method to specify the character or set of characters you want to use as a delimiter between entries.

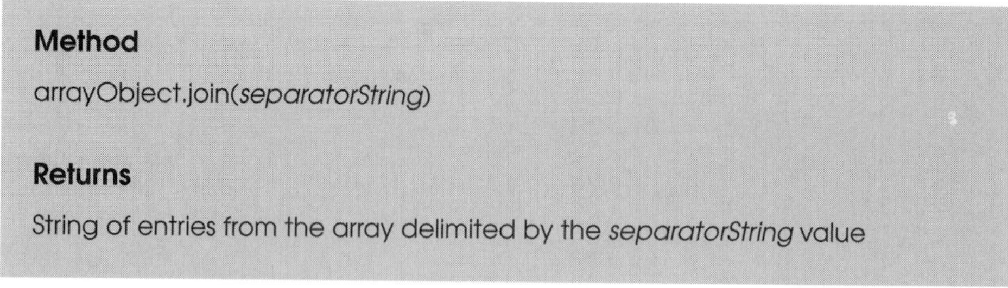

Method

arrayObject.join(*separatorString*)

Returns

String of entries from the array delimited by the *separatorString* value

The following `arrayJoin.html` script uses the `split()` method to split a comma-separated string into an array and then uses the `join()` method to join the elements back together, using a colon (`:`) as the new separator.

```
<!--
         arrayJoin.html
-->

<HTML>
<HEAD>
<TITLE>Array Join</TITLE>
</HEAD>
<BODY>

<P>This example splits a string into an array and
then joins it back together with a different
separator.</P>

<SCRIPT LANGUAGE="JavaScript">
<!-- HIDE FROM OLD BROWSERS
  var str = new String("1,2,3,4,5,6,7,8,9")
  var a   = str.split(',')
  var b   = a.join(':')

  with (document) {
    write("<P>The original string is = " + str)
    write("</P>")

    write("<P>The array a's elements are:<BR>")
    for (var i = 0; i < a.length; i++) {
      write("a[" + i + "] = " + a[i] + "<BR>")
    }
    write("</P>")

    write("<P>The joined array b = " + b + "</P>")
  }

// STOP HIDING -->
</SCRIPT>

</BODY>
</HTML>
```

Figure 29–3 shows the result of loading the `arrayJoin.html` script.

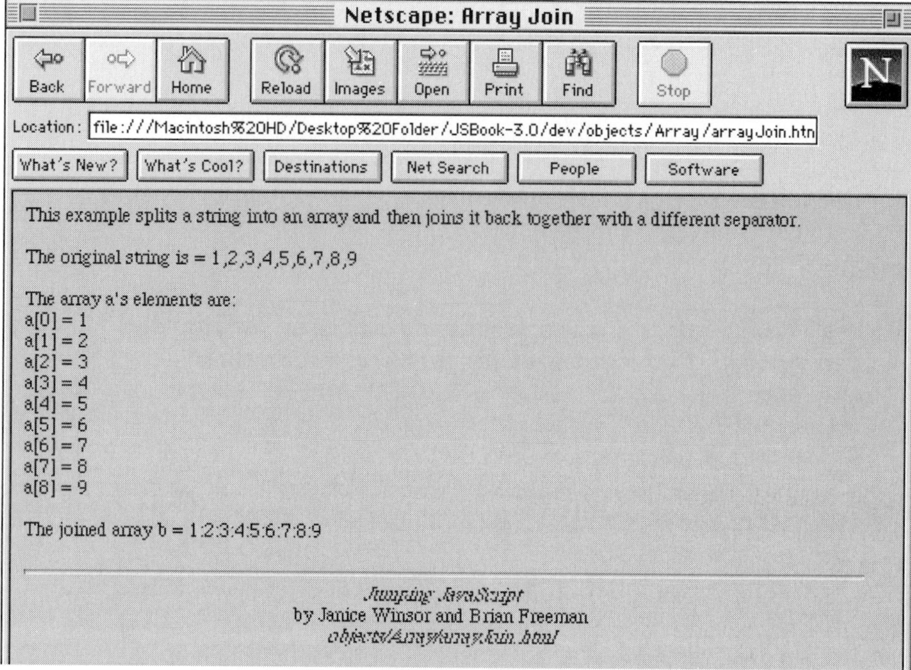

Netscape: Array Join
Back
Forward
Home
Reload
Images
Open
Print
Find
Stop
Location: file:///Macintosh%20HD/Desktop%20Folder/JSBook-3.0/dev/objects/Array/arrayJoin.htm
What's New?
What's Cool?
Destinations
Net Search
People
Software
This example splits a string into an array and then joins it back together with a different separator.
The original string is = 1,2,3,4,5,6,7,8,9
The array a's elements are:
a[0] = 1
a[1] = 2
a[2] = 3
a[3] = 4
a[4] = 5
a[5] = 6
a[6] = 7
a[7] = 8
a[8] = 9
The joined array b = 1:2:3:4:5:6:7:8:9
Jumping JavaScript
by Janice Winsor and Brian Freeman
objects/Array/arrayJoin.html

Figure 29–3 Result of loading the `arrayJoin.html` script

Reversing the Order of Data in an Array

You can use the `reverse()` method to reverse the order of the data in the array. When you use the `reverse()` method, it restructures the original array so that the last element in the array becomes the first element.

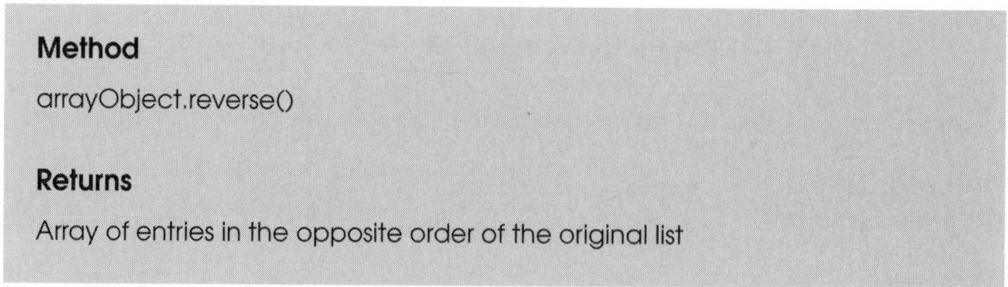

Method

arrayObject.reverse()

Returns

Array of entries in the opposite order of the original list

Example of Reversing the Order of Data in an Array

The following `arrayReverse.html` script creates an array of numbers and then reverses the order.

```
<!--
                arrayReverse.html
-->
<HTML>
<HEAD>
<TITLE>Array Reverse</TITLE>
</HEAD>
<BODY>
<P>This example creates an array assigning the
index value to each element, calls reverse, and
then displays the contents of the array.</P>

<P>Here it is:</P>

<SCRIPT LANGUAGE="JavaScript">
<!-- HIDE FROM OLD BROWSERS
  var anArray = new Array(10)

  // initialize the array to the index value
  for (var i = 0; i < anArray.length; i++) {
    anArray[i] = i
  }

  with (document) {
    write("<P>The array anArray's elements are:<BR>")
    for (var i = 0; i < anArray.length; i++) {
      write("anArray[" + i + "] = " + anArray[i] + "<BR>")
    }
    write("</P>")

    write("<P>Reverse!</P>")
    anArray.reverse()

    write("<P>The array anArray's elements are:<BR>")
    for (var i = 0; i < anArray.length; i++) {
      write("anArray[" + i + "] = " + anArray[i] + "<BR>")
    }
    write("</P>")
  }

// STOP HIDING -->
</SCRIPT>
</BODY>
</HTML>
```

Figure 29–4 shows the result of loading the `arrayReverse.html` script.

Netscape: Array Reverse

Back Forward Home Reload Images Open Print Find Stop

Location: file:///Macintosh%20HD/Desktop%20Folder/JSBook-3.0/dev/objects/Array/arrayReverse

What's New? What's Cool? Destinations Net Search People Software

This example creates an array assigning the index value to each element, calls reverse, and then displays the contents of the array.

Here it is:

The array anArray's elements are:
anArray[0] = 0
anArray[1] = 1
anArray[2] = 2
anArray[3] = 3
anArray[4] = 4
anArray[5] = 5
anArray[6] = 6
anArray[7] = 7
anArray[8] = 8
anArray[9] = 9

Reverse!

The array anArray's elements are:
anArray[0] = 9
anArray[1] = 8
anArray[2] = 7
anArray[3] = 6
anArray[4] = 5
anArray[5] = 4
anArray[6] = 3
anArray[7] = 2
anArray[8] = 1
anArray[9] = 0

Jumping JavaScript
by Janice Winsor and Brian Freeman
objects/Array/arrayReverse.html

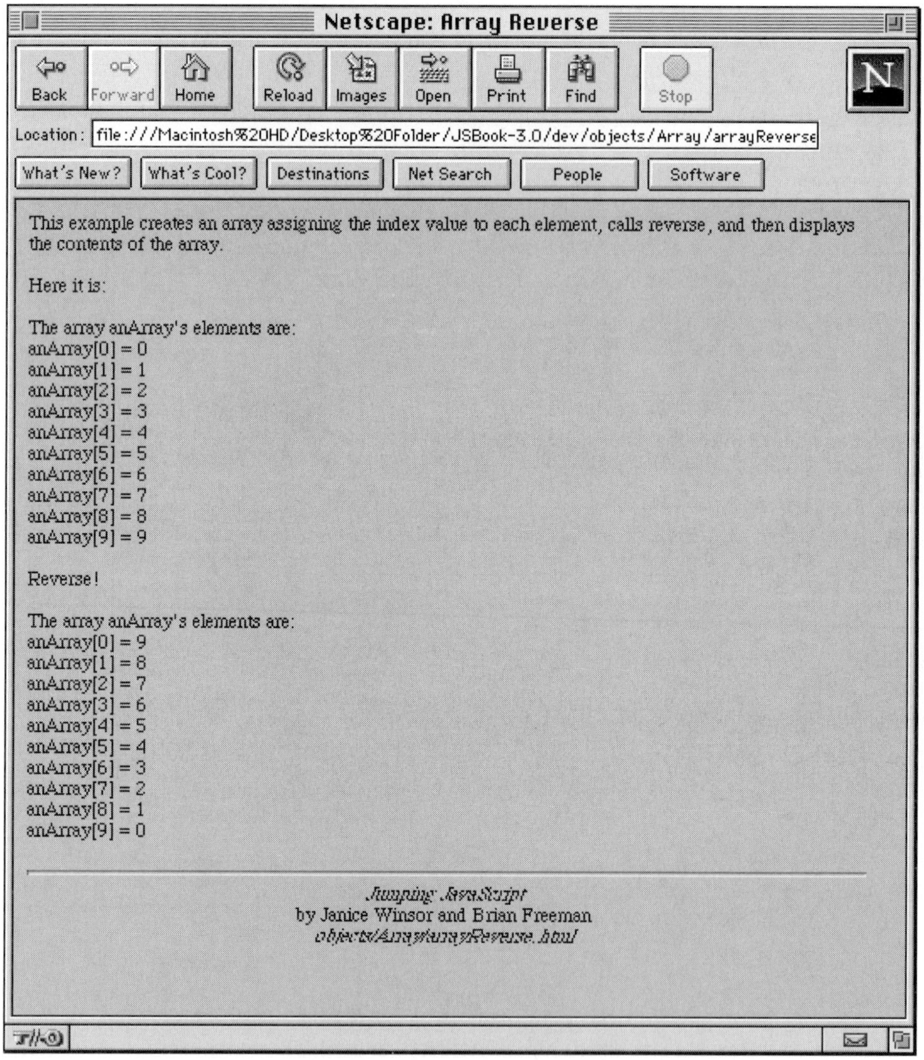

Figure 29–4 Result of loading the `arrayReverse.html` script

Sorting Items in an Array

The `sort()` method enables you to do sophisticated sorting on the values in an array. This method changes the sort order of the original array; it does not return a copy. If you want to retain the original array, make a copy of it before you sort it or reload the document to restore an array to its original order. Performing repeated sorts on JavaScript arrays is not cumulative.

Note – The `sort()` method does not work in the Macintosh version of Navigator 3.0. In some cases, the method fails by doing nothing. In other cases, it forces a restart of the computer.

Method

sort((*compareFunction*))

Returns

Array of entries in the order determined by the *compareFunction* algorithm. If *compareFunction* is not provided, the sort is alphabetical.

When you use the `sort()` method with no arguments, the JavaScript language converts the array values to strings and sorts them by using the ASCII collating sequence. Numbers are sorted by their string values, not by their numeric values. If you sort a string of numbers from 1 to 20, the sort order is:

1
10
11
12
13
14
15
16
17
18
19

2
20
3
4
5
6
7
8
9

To enhance the power of the `sort()` function, you can supply a comparison function that compares two values and returns a number indicating their relative order. The comparison function must have two arguments, `a` and `b`. The way you specify the return values determines how the `sort()` method determines the final sort sequence. Table 29-2 lists the return values for the comparison function.

Table 29-2 Return Values for the sort() Method Comparison Function

Return Value	Description
`< 0`	Sort value `b` above value `a`
`0`	Do not change the order of `a` and `b`
`> 0`	Sort value `a` above value `b`

Example of Sorting an Array

The following `arraySort.html` script sorts the array alphabetically and then in reverse alphabetical order.

```
<!--
                arraySort.html
-->

<HTML>
<HEAD>
<TITLE>Array Sort</TITLE>
<SCRIPT LANGUAGE="JavaScript">
<!-- HIDE FROM OLD BROWSERS

var anArray = new Array("Alpha", "Bravo",
  "Charlie", "Delta", "Echo", "Foxtrot",
  "Golf", "Hotel", "India", "Juliet",
  "Kilo", "Lima", "Mike", "November",
  "Oscar", "Papa", "Quebec", "Romeo",
  "Sierra", "Tango", "Uniform", "Victor",
  "Whiskey", "X-ray", "Yankee", "Zulu")


function sort_alpha(a, b) {
  if ( a <= b ) {
    return -1
  } else {
    return 1
  }
}

function sort_reverse(a, b) {
  if ( a >= b ) {
    return -1
  } else {
    return 1
  }
}

// STOP HIDING -->
</SCRIPT>
</HEAD>
<BODY>

<P>This example sorts an array with the sort
method's optional order function. If you do not
specify an order function, the list is sorted
alphabetically.</P>
```

```
<SCRIPT LANGUAGE="JavaScript">
<!-- HIDE FROM OLD BROWSERS

document.write("<P>The original array:<BR>")
for (var i = 0; i < anArray.length; i++) {
  document.write(anArray[i] + "<BR>")
}

anArray.sort(sort_reverse)
document.write("<P>Sorted by sort_reverse:<BR>")
for (var i = 0; i < anArray.length; i++) {
  document.write(anArray[i] + "<BR>")
}

anArray.sort(sort_alpha)
document.write("<P>Sorted by sort_alpha:<BR>")
for (var i = 0; i < anArray.length; i++) {
  document.write(anArray[i] + "<BR>")
}

// STOP HIDING -->
</SCRIPT>

</BODY>
</HTML>
```

Figure 29–5 shows the result of loading the `arraySort.html` script.

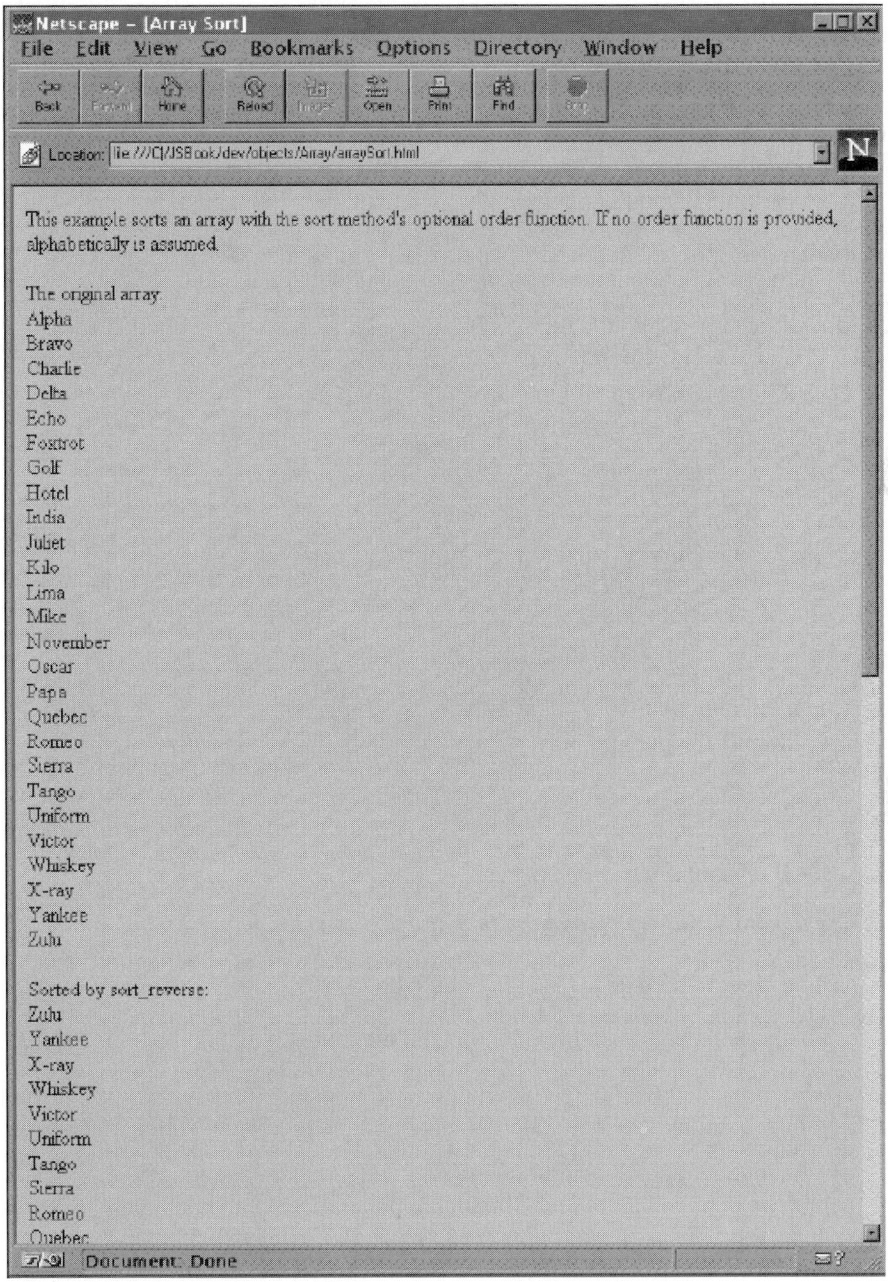

Netscape – [Array Sort]

File Edit View Go Bookmarks Options Directory Window Help

Back Forward Home Reload Images Open Print Find Stop

Location: file:///C|/JSBook/dev/objects/Array/arraySort.html

This example sorts an array with the sort method's optional order function. If no order function is provided, alphabetically is assumed.

The original array:
Alpha
Bravo
Charlie
Delta
Echo
Foxtrot
Golf
Hotel
India
Juliet
Kilo
Lima
Mike
November
Oscar
Papa
Quebec
Romeo
Sierra
Tango
Uniform
Victor
Whiskey
X-ray
Yankee
Zulu

Sorted by sort_reverse:
Zulu
Yankee
X-ray
Whiskey
Victor
Uniform
Tango
Sierra
Romeo
Quebec

Document: Done

Figure 29–5 Result of loading the `arraySort.html` script

The window already contains the complete result of the sorting actions specified in the `arraySort.html` script. Scrolling down the page, Figure 29–6 shows the complete array list sorted in reverse.

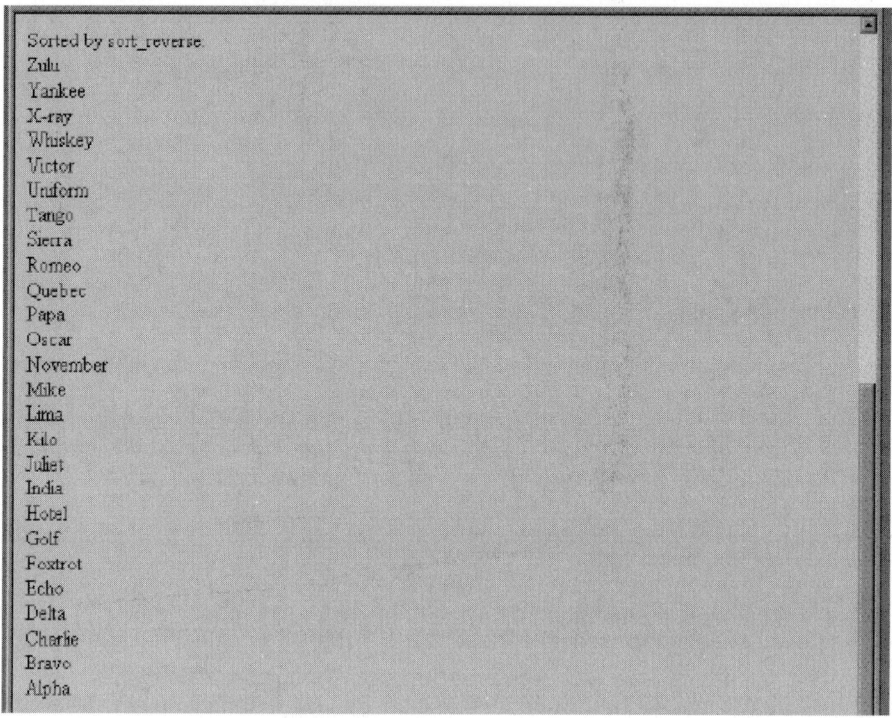

Figure 29–6 Array sorted in reverse

Figure 29–7 shows the array list re-sorted into the original sequence.

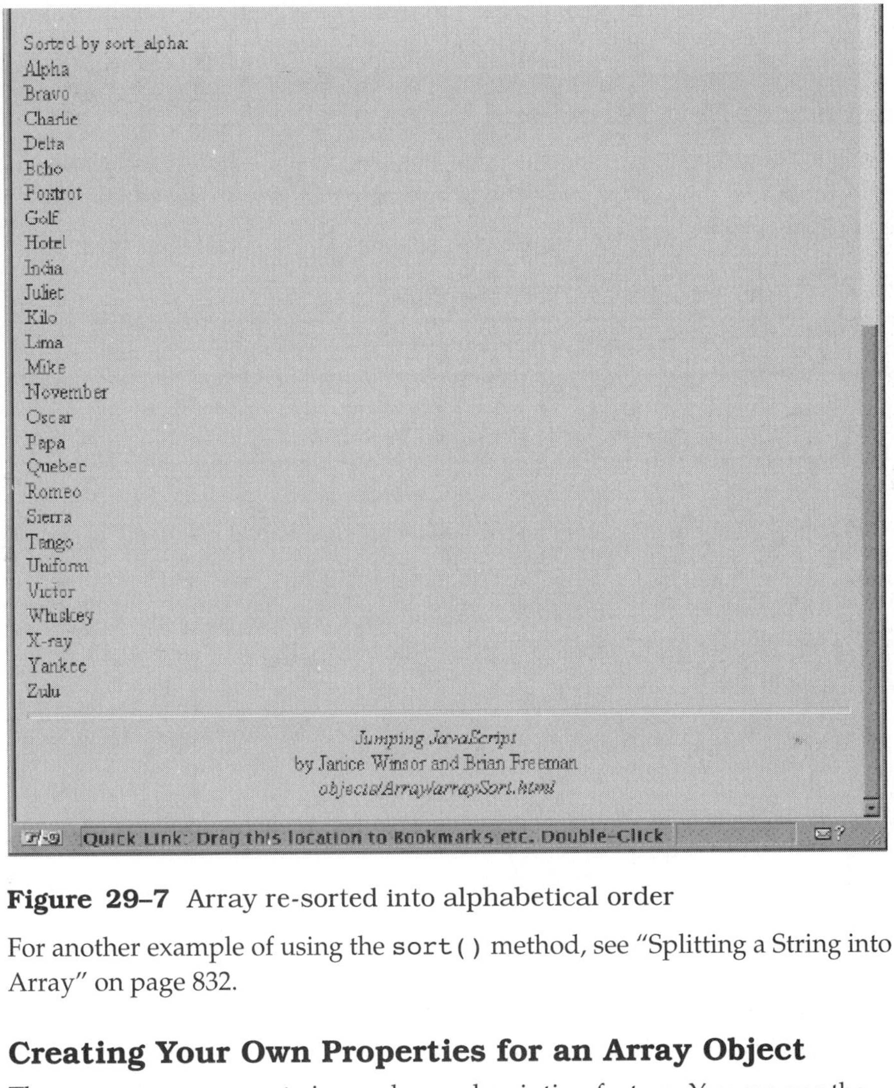

Sorted by sort_alpha:
Alpha
Bravo
Charlie
Delta
Echo
Foxtrot
Golf
Hotel
India
Juliet
Kilo
Lima
Mike
November
Oscar
Papa
Quebec
Romeo
Sierra
Tango
Uniform
Victor
Whiskey
X-ray
Yankee
Zulu

Jumping JavaScript
by Janice Winsor and Brian Freeman
objects/Array/arraySort.html

Quick Link: Drag this location to Bookmarks etc. Double-Click

Figure 29–7 Array re-sorted into alphabetical order

For another example of using the `sort()` method, see "Splitting a String into an Array" on page 832.

Creating Your Own Properties for an Array Object

The `prototype` property is an advanced scripting feature. You can use the `prototype` property to create your own properties or methods that apply to all of the objects you create with the `new` keyword.

Property	Value	Gettable	Settable
prototype	string	Yes	No

For an example of using the `prototype` property, see “Creating Custom String Functions” on page 809 and Chapter 34, "Creating Your Own JavaScript Objects."

Summary of New Terms and Concepts

The new terms and concepts introduced in this chapter are listed in alphabetical order in Table 29-3. The terms and concepts are also included in the glossary at the end of the book.

Table 29-3 Summary of New Terms and Concepts

Term/Concept	Description
dense array	An array with a fixed set of values that you define as parameters to the `Array()` constructor.

859

CHAPTER 30

- Creating a Date Object
- Parsing Date Strings
- Getting and Setting Date and Time Elements
- Getting the Time Zone Offset
- Obtaining a Date String in GMT Format
- Obtaining a Date String in the Current Locale
- Universal Coordinated Time
- Creating Your Own Properties for a Date Object
- Summary of New Terms and Concepts

Using the Date Object

The `Date` object is a JavaScript object that is not created by an HTML definition. Instead, when you want to perform calculations or display date and time values in your scripts, you create a new `Date` object. Once created, the `Date` object provides a collection of methods that enable you to manipulate and display the date in several different formats.

How the `Date` object represents its value is noteworthy and you should understand its limitations. Like dates in the Java language, the JavaScript language stores dates internally as the number of milliseconds (thousandths of a second) since midnight Greenwich mean time (GMT) on January 1, 1970. You cannot store any date before January 1, 1970.

January 1, 1970 at midnight GMT is significant because this date is considered the beginning of UNIX time and it defines a date, time, and global position. From this reference point, the `Date` object performs conversions for you into different time zones around the world.

The methods of the `Date` object enable you to get and set every aspect of date and time that you can imagine, as well as some that you might not have thought of. For example, you can get the local time offset from GMT, parse a string that contains a date into the object, and format the date into *universal coordinated time* (UTC). Note that the acronym does not match the word order of the English definition because the standard that defines UTC originated in France.

The Date object provides a set of methods, listed in alphabetical order in Table 30-1, that you can use to both get and to set parts of date and time strings.

Table 30-1 Properties and Methods for the Date Object

Properties	Methods	Event Handlers
prototype*	eval()*	None
	get/setDate()	
	getDay()	
	get/setHours()	
	get/setMinutes()	
	get/setMonth()	
	get/setSeconds()	
	get/setTime()	
	get/setYear()	
	getTimezoneOffset()	
	parse()	
	toGMTString()	
	toLocaleString()*	
	toString()*	
	UTC()	
	valueOf()*	

* New in Navigator 3.0.

As you can see from the list of methods in Table 30-1, the Date object also contains information about time.

Note – A word of caution. Be careful with the arguments to the methods of the `Date` object. Some of them start counting at `0` instead of `1`. So, January is `0`, February is `1`, and so on. The day and date methods also can be confusing. The `get/setDate` methods return and set the day of the month. `getDay` returns the day of the week the date falls on, but there is no corresponding `setDay` method.

Creating a Date Object

You create a new `Date` object by using the `new` keyword, as shown in the following example:

```
DateVariable = new Date(dateFormat)
```

The following examples create a new date in millisecond format:

```
var msDate = new Date(822204900000)
```

Example of Creating a Date Object

The following `date.html` script creates several `Date` objects by using several different forms of the `Date` constructor.

```
<!--
                    date.html
-->

<HTML>
<HEAD>
<TITLE>Date</TITLE>
</HEAD>
<BODY>

<P>The Date Object is a built-in JavaScript
object; there is no HTML equivalent for
it. With no arguments, Date() creates a new Date
object set to the current date and time.</P>

<SCRIPT LANGUAGE="JavaScript">
<!-- HIDE FROM OLD BROWSERS
  var theDate = new Date()
```

```
  document.write("<P>The current date is: " +
    theDate.toLocaleString() + "</P>")

  document.write("<P>The current date relative to GMT is:
" +
    theDate.toGMTString() + "</P>")

// STOP HIDING -->
</SCRIPT>

<P>You create a new Date object with several
different variations of the Date constructor.</P>

<DL>
  <DT>new Date(milliseconds)
  <DD>milliseconds between date and 12AM 1/1/70
  <DT>new Date(date_string)
  <DD>date_string = month_name dd, yy [hh:mm[:ss]]
  <DT>new Date(year, month, day)
  <DD>year is minus 1900, month 0-11, day 1-31
  <DT>new Date(year, month, day, hours, minutes,
  seconds)
  <DD>24-hour clock
</UL>

<P>The following:</P>
<PRE>
  var msDate  = new Date(822204900000)
  var strDate = new Date("January 20, 96 22:15:00")
  var ymdDate = new Date(96, 01, 20)
  var hrDate  = new Date(96, 01, 20, 22, 15, 00)
</PRE>

<P>yields:</P>
<SCRIPT LANGUAGE="JavaScript">
<!-- HIDE FROM OLD BROWSERS
  var msDate  = new Date(822204900000)
  var strDate = new Date("January 20, 96 22:15:00")
  var ymdDate = new Date(96, 01, 20)
  var hrDate  = new Date(96, 01, 20, 22, 15, 00)

  var dstr = ""

  dstr += "<P>msDate = " + msDate + "<BR>"
```

```
    dstr += "strDate = " + strDate + "<BR>"
    dstr += "ymdDate = " + ymdDate + "<BR>"
    dstr += "hrDate = " + hrDate + "</P>"

    document.write(dstr)
  // STOP HIDING -->
  </SCRIPT>

  </BODY>
  </HTML>
```

Figure 30–1 shows the result of loading the `date.html` script.

Netscape: Date

Back Forward Home Reload Images Open Print Find Stop

Location: file:///Macintosh%20HD/Desktop%20Folder/JSBook-3.0/dev/objects/Date/date.html

What's New? What's Cool? Destinations Net Search People Software

The Date Object is a built-in JavaScript object; there is no HTML equivalent for it. With no arguments, Date() creates a new Date object set to the current date and time.

The current date is: Feb 8 15:32:45 1997

The current date relative to GMT is: Sat, 08 Feb 1997 23:32:45 GMT

You create a new Date object with several different variations of the Date constructor.

new Date(milliseconds)
    milliseconds between date and 12AM 1/1/70
new Date(date_string)
    date_string = month_name dd, yy [hh:mm[:ss]]
new Date(year, month, day)
    year is minus 1900, month 0-11, day 1-31
new Date(year, month, day, hours, minutes, seconds)
    24-hour clock

The following:

```
  var msDate  = new Date(822204900000)
  var strDate = new Date("January 20, 96 22:15:00")
  var ymdDate = new Date(96, 01, 20)
  var hrDate  = new Date(96, 01, 20, 22, 15, 00)
```

yields:

msDate = Sat Jan 20 22:15:00 1996
strDate = Sat Jan 20 22:15:00 1996
ymdDate = Tue Feb 20 00:00:00 1996
hrDate = Tue Feb 20 22:15:00 1996

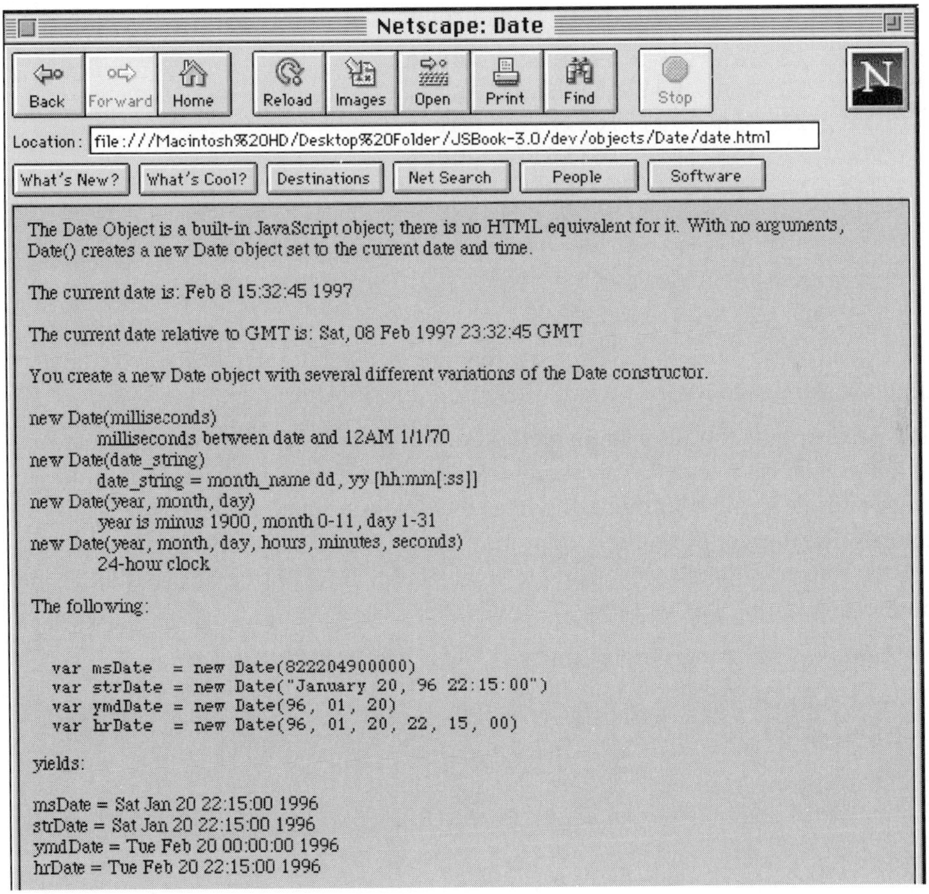

Figure 30–1 Result of loading the `date.html` script

Parsing Date Strings

You can use the `parse()` method to parse a date/time string from a variety of formats. The `parse()` method recognizes the Internet Engineering Task Force (IETF) standard date format that is used in e-mail and other Internet communications. The IETF standard date format looks like the following:

```
Sun, 2 Feb 1997 13:58:02 -0400
```

Note that `-0400` means four hours east of the Greenwich meridian. `+0400` would be four hours west of the Greenwich meridian.

The `parse()` method also recognizes partial dates of IETF format, the GMT time zone, and all the U.S. standard time zone abbreviations. The `parse()` method can interpret any of the following date formats:

```
Mon, 13 Jan 1997 15:18:54 -0800
Mon, 13 Jan 1997 15:18:54 PST
Tue, 21 Jan 1997 16:16:22 GMT
Tue, 21 Jan 1997 16:16:22 -0000
Sat Jan 20 22:15:00 PST 1996
Tue Feb 20 00:00:00 MST 1996
01/21/97 08:16:22
13 Jan 1997 15:18:54 PST
13 Jan 1997 15:18:54
```

It can also parse dates in IETF format that are missing the day of the week, the time zone, the seconds, or the complete time specification.

The `parse()` method is a static method of the `Date` object. You do not create a new `Date` object to use it. You always use it as `Date.parse()`. This method takes a single string argument. It parses the date contained in this string and returns the number of milliseconds since Jan 1, 1970 00:00:00, local time. You can use the return value directly, use it to create a new Date object, or use it to set the date in an existing `Date` object. For example:

```
MyDate.setTime(Date.parse("Apr 19, 1997:))
```

Method

Date.parse("*dateString*")

Returns

Converts string date to milliseconds since Jan 1, 1970 00:00:00, local time

Example of Parsing a Date

The following `dateParse.html` script provides a text field in which you can type a date in one of the formats shown on the page. When you click on the `parse()` button, the date is parsed and the result is displayed in an alert.

```
<!--
                    dateParse.html
-->

<HTML>
<HEAD>
<TITLE>Date Parse</TITLE>
<SCRIPT LANGUAGE="JavaScript">
<!-- HIDE FROM OLD BROWSERS

var theDate = new Date()

function displayDate() {
  alert(theDate)
}

function parseDate() {
  var theForm = document.aForm

  theDate.setTime(Date.parse(theForm.dateTxt.value))
  displayDate()
}

// STOP HIDING -->
</SCRIPT>
</HEAD>
<BODY>

<P>Date.parse() is a function attached to the
Date object that parses a date/time string and
returns the number of milliseconds between the
specified date/time and 12 A.M. Jan 1, 1970 GMT. It
is important to recognize that it is not a method
of the Date object and you always call it by
referencing the Date object, not an instance of
the date object. In other words, you call it with
Date.parse().</P>

<P>Date.parse() understands the IETF date format
```

```
used in e-mail, partial dates of this format, the
GMT time zone, and all the U.S. standard time zone
abbreviations.</P>

<P>For example:<BR>
<DL>
  <DT>Mon, 13 Jan 1997 15:18:54 -0800
  <DT>Mon, 13 Jan 1997 15:18:54 PST
  <DT>Tue, 21 Jan 1997 16:16:22 GMT
  <DT>Tue, 21 Jan 1997 16:16:22 -0000
  <DT>Sat Jan 20 22:15:00 PST 1996
  <DT>Tue Feb 20 00:00:00 MST 1996
  <DT>01/21/97 08:16:22
  <DT>13 Jan 1997 15:18:54 PST
  <DT>13 Jan 1997 15:18:54
</DL>

<FORM NAME="aForm">
<P>
<B>Enter a date:</B><BR>
<INPUT TYPE="text" NAME="dateTxt" VALUE="" SIZE=40>
</P>

<P>
<INPUT TYPE="button" NAME="parseBtn"
 VALUE="parse()" onClick="parseDate()">
</P>
</FORM>

</BODY>
</HTML>
```

Figure 30–2 shows the result of loading the `dateParse.html` script.

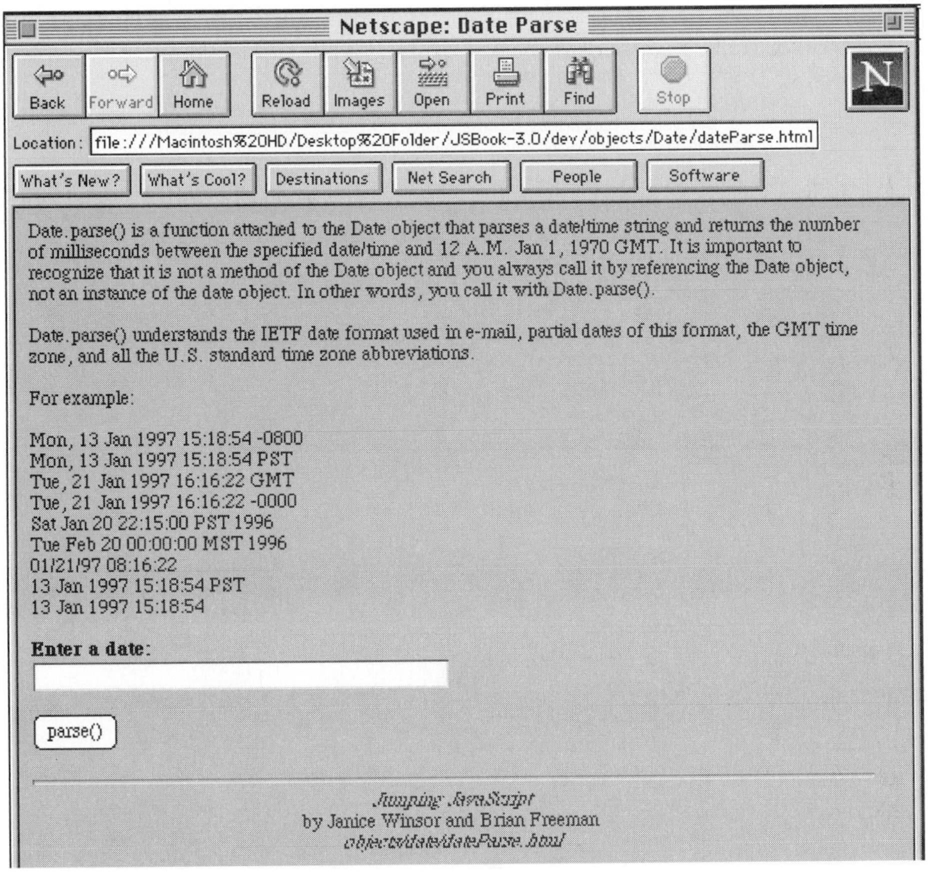

Figure 30–2 Result of loading the `dateParse.html` script

Type a date into the text field and then click on the `parse()` button. Regardless of the date format you use, the output is formatted in the following way, as shown in Figure 30–3:

```
Sat Feb 08 00:00:00 1997
```

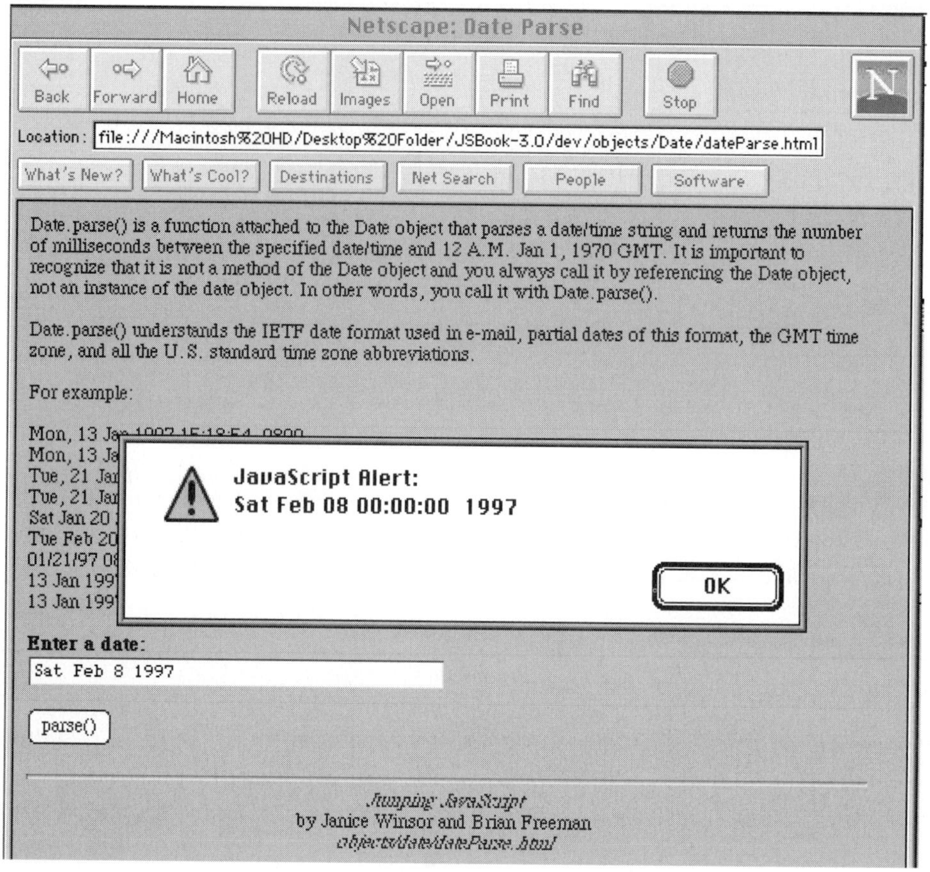

Figure 30–3 Parsed date

Getting and Setting Date and Time Elements

You use the methods in this section to get and set the time, year, month, date, hours, minutes, and seconds components of a date and time string and to get the day of the week. For an example of how to use the methods described in this section, see "Example of Getting and Setting Date and Time Elements" on page 874.

Getting and Setting the Date of the Month

Use the `getDate()` and `setDate()` methods to obtain and specify the day of the month value for a `Date` object. The values range from 1 to 31.

Method

getDate()

setDate(*1-31*)

Returns/Uses

Date (day) within the month

Getting and Setting the Month

Use the `getMonth()` and `setMonth()` methods to obtain and specify the month value of a date. The month value is a number between 0 and 11 that represents the month of the year. January is represented by 0 and December by 11.

Method

getMonth()

setMonth(*0-11*)

Returns/Uses

Month within the year. January = 0

Getting the Day of the Week

Use the `getDay()` method to return the numbered day of the week. Return values are between 0 (Sunday) and 6 (Saturday). Note that there is not a corresponding `setDay()` method for the `Date` object.

Method

getDay()

Returns

Date (day) within the month

Getting and Setting the Year

Use the `getYear()` and `setYear()` methods to obtain and specify the year value of a date. The year value is the year minus 1900. For example, if the date represents a date in 1997, then the value returned is `97`.

Method

getYear()

setYear(*70-...*)

Returns/Uses

Specified year minus 1900

Getting and Setting the Time

Use the `getTime()` and `setTime()` methods to obtain and specify the value of a `Date` object. `getTime()` returns the number of milliseconds between midnight (GMT) on 1/1/1970 and the date and time specified.

Method

getTime()

setTime(*0-...*)

Returns/Uses

Milliseconds since 1/1/70 00:00:00 GMT

Getting and Setting the Hour

Use the `getHours()` and `setHours()` methods to obtain and specify the hour of the day in 24-hour time for a `Date` object. The hour is represented in military time from 0 (midnight) to 23 (11 p.m.).

Method

getHours()

setHours(*0-23*)

Returns/Uses

Hour of the day in 24-hour time starting at 0

Getting and Setting the Minute

Use the `getMinutes()` and `setMinutes()` methods to obtain and specify the number of minutes for a `Date` object. Values are from 0 to 59.

Method

getMinutes()

setMinutes(*0-59*)

Returns/Uses

Minute of the specified hour, starting at 0

Getting and Setting the Second

Use the `getSeconds()` and `setSeconds()` methods to obtain and specify the number of seconds for a `Date` object. Values are from 0 to 59.

Method

getSeconds()

setSeconds(*0-59*)

Returns/Uses

Second of the specified minute, starting at 0

Example of Getting and Setting Date and Time Elements

The following `dateGetSet.html` script uses all of the date and time elements to both get and set the date and time.

```
<!--
                    dateGetSet.html
-->

<HTML>
<HEAD>
<TITLE>Date Get & Set Methods</TITLE>
<SCRIPT LANGUAGE="JavaScript">
<!-- HIDE FROM OLD BROWSERS

var theDate = new Date()

// STOP HIDING -->
</SCRIPT>
</HEAD>

<BODY>

<FORM NAME="aForm">
<P>
<INPUT TYPE="button" NAME="getDateBtn"
 VALUE="getDate()"
 onClick="alert(theDate.getDate())">
<B>Set the day of the month:</B>
<INPUT TYPE="text" NAME="setDateTxt" VALUE=""
SIZE=2>
<INPUT TYPE="button" NAME="setDateBtn"
VALUE="setDate()"
onClick="theDate.setDate(this.form.setDateTxt.value)">
</P>

<P>
<INPUT TYPE="button" NAME="getDayBtn"
VALUE="getDay()"
onClick="alert(theDate.getDay())">
</P>

<P>
<INPUT TYPE="button" NAME="getHoursBtn"
VALUE="getHours()"
```

```
onClick="alert(theDate.getHours())">
<B>Set the hour:</B>
<INPUT TYPE="text" NAME="setHourTxt" VALUE=""
SIZE=2>
<INPUT TYPE="button" NAME="setHoursBtn"
VALUE="setHours()"
onClick="theDate.setHours(this.form.setHourTxt.value)">
</P>

<P>
<INPUT TYPE="button" NAME="getMinutesBtn"
VALUE="getMinutes()"
onClick="alert(theDate.getMinutes())">
<B>Set the minutes:</B>
<INPUT TYPE="text" NAME="setMinTxt" VALUE=""
SIZE=2>
<INPUT TYPE="button" NAME="setMinutesBtn"
VALUE="setMinutes()"
onClick="theDate.setMinutes(this.form.setMinTxt.value)">
</P>

<P>
<INPUT TYPE="button" NAME="getMonthBtn"
VALUE="getMonth()"
onClick="alert(theDate.getMonth())">
<B>Set the month:</B>
<INPUT TYPE="text" NAME="setMonTxt" VALUE=""
SIZE=2>
<INPUT TYPE="button" NAME="setMonthBtn"
VALUE="setMonth()"
onClick="theDate.setMonth(this.form.setMonTxt.value)">
</P>

<P>
<INPUT TYPE="button" NAME="getSecondsBtn"
VALUE="getSeconds()"
onClick="alert(theDate.getSeconds())">
<B>Set the seconds:</B>
<INPUT TYPE="text" NAME="setSecTxt" VALUE=""
SIZE=2>
<INPUT TYPE="button" NAME="setSecondsBtn"
VALUE="setSeconds()"
onClick="theDate.setSeconds(this.form.setSecTxt.value)">
</P>
```

```
<P>
<INPUT TYPE="button" NAME="getTimeBtn"
VALUE="getTime()"
onClick="alert(theDate.getTime())">
<B>Set the time in milliseconds:</B>
<INPUT TYPE="text" NAME="setTimeTxt" VALUE=""
SIZE=20>
<INPUT TYPE="button" NAME="setTimeBtn"
VALUE="setTime()"
onClick="theDate.setTime(this.form.setTimeTxt.value)">
</P>

<P>
<INPUT TYPE="button" NAME="getYearBtn"
VALUE="getYear()"
onClick="alert(theDate.getYear())">
<B>Set the year:</B>
<INPUT TYPE="text" NAME="setYearTxt" VALUE=""
SIZE=2>
<INPUT TYPE="button" NAME="setYearBtn"
VALUE="setYear()"
onClick="theDate.setYear(this.form.setYearTxt.value)">
</P>

<P>
<INPUT TYPE="button" NAME="getTimezoneOffsetBtn"
VALUE="getTimezoneOffset()"
onClick="alert(theDate.getTimezoneOffset())">
</P>
</FORM>

</BODY>
</HTML>
```

Figure 30–4 shows the result of loading the `dateGetSet.html` script.

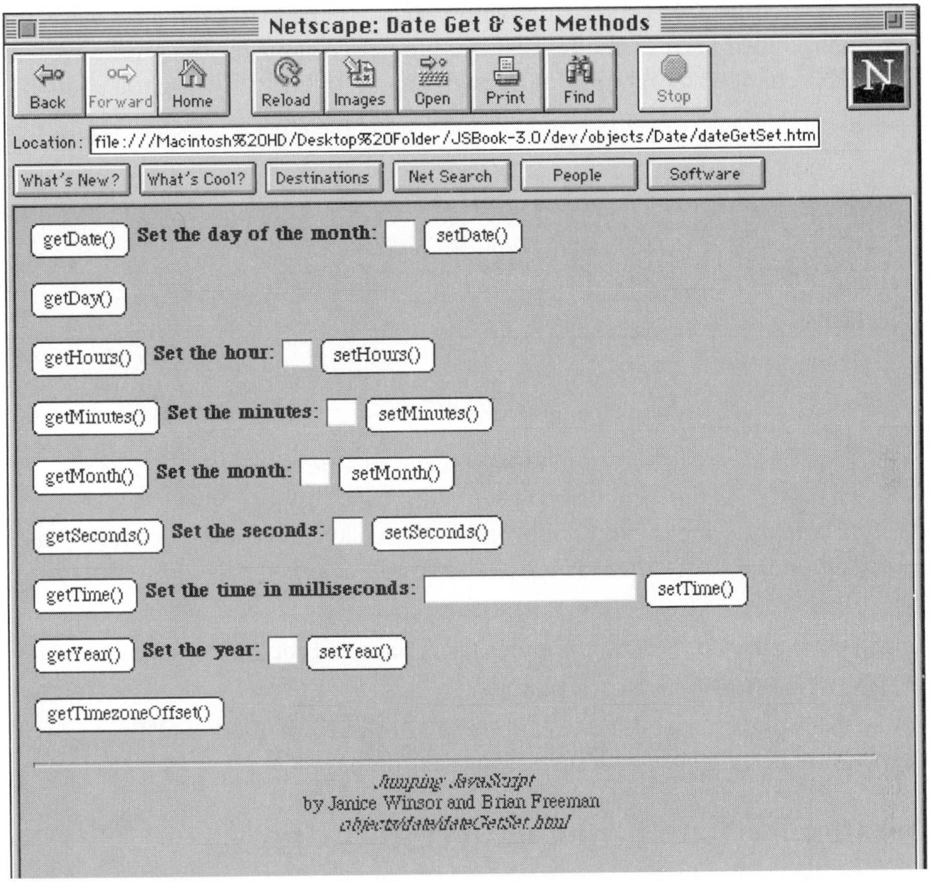

Figure 30–4 Result of loading the `dateGetSet.html` script

Type a value into each text field. Clicking on one of the Set buttons registers the value from the text field. Clicking on one of the Get buttons displays an alert showing the value as interpreted by the `Date` object. Clicking on the `getTimezoneOffset()` button displays the number of minutes the time zone is offset from GMT. The `getTimezoneOffset()` method returns a value of 1440 for a Macintosh computer in Half Moon Bay, California, with the time zone set to Abu Dhabi. With the time zone set correctly it returns a value of 480.

Getting the Time Zone Offset

The `getTimezoneOffset()` method is not new in Navigator 3.0. However, the Navigator 3.0 release has made a substantive change in the way it generates time zone offsets. In the Navigator 2.0 release, for time zones west of GMT, the `getTimezoneOffset()` method returned negative values because the actual time is earlier than GMT the farther west you go. In the Navigator 3.0 release, the `getTimezoneOffset()` method returns a positive value for time zones west of GMT. This change was made to be consistent with the way Java returns these values.

> **Method**
>
> getTimezoneOffset(*0-...*)
>
> **Returns**
>
> Minutes offset from GMT

The `getTimezoneOffset()` method returns a value of minutes difference between GMT and the local time zone. On the West Coast of North America, Pacific Standard Time is eight hours earlier than GMT. So, for a script run on a computer on the West Coast, the `getTimezoneOffset()` method returns a value of 480.

Chances are good that many computer users have not set their system clocks to the proper time zone.

For an example of using the `getTimezoneOffset()` method, see "Example of Getting and Setting Date and Time Elements" on page 874.

Obtaining a Date String in GMT Format

You can use the `toGMTString()` method to convert a date to a GMT time zone string. The format of the string that is returned depends on the user's computer platform, but it usually has a format similar to the IETF standard date format:

```
Mon, 03 Feb 1997 13:58:02 GMT
```

> **Method**
>
> toGMTString()
>
> **Returns**
>
> Date string formatted using the Internet GMT conventions

For an example of using the `toGMTString()` method, see "Example of Creating a Date Object" on page 863.

Obtaining a Date String in the Current Locale

You can use the `toLocaleString()` method to convert a date to a string using the conventions of the current locale. This method also uses conventions for date and time formatting in the current locale. Locales are typically associated with countries or regions, for example, `En_US`, `fr`, `jp`. Use this method to show dates in the format users are accustomed to.

Note – Because of the inconsistency of date and time formatting worldwide, you should avoid using this method to format any date string that must be passed to a CGI script or used for further calculations.

The format of the string that is returned depends on the user's locale. In the United States, the `toLocaleString()` method returns dates in the following format:

```
Feb 2 19:35:26 1997
```

Method

toLocaleString()

Returns

Date string in the locale the user's computer is set to

For an example of using the `toLocaleString()` method, see "Example of Creating a Date Object" on page 863.

Universal Coordinated Time

The `Date.UTC()` method is a static method of the `Date` object. You do not create a new `Date` object to use it. You use this method as `Date.UTC()`. It takes a comma-separated list of values as parameters, and displays the date in the following format:

```
Sat Feb 01 20:45:12 1997
```

Method

Date.UTC(*date values*)

Returns

The number of milliseconds since 1/1/70 UTC

You provide the parameters in the sequence `yy`, `mm`, `dd` [`hh`, `mm`, `ss`].

```
yy = year after 1900
mm = 0-11
dd = 1-31
hh = 0-23
mm = 0-59
ss = 0-59
```

Example of Using the Date.UTC() Method

The following `dateUTC.html` script enables you to enter date and time elements into text fields and display the formatted output as an alert.

```
<!--
                  dateUTC.html
-->

<HTML>
<HEAD>
<TITLE>Date UTC</TITLE>
<SCRIPT LANGUAGE="JavaScript">
<!-- HIDE FROM OLD BROWSERS

var theDate = new Date()

function displayDate() {
  alert(theDate)
}
```

```
function UTCDate() {
  var theForm = document.aForm

  theDate.setTime(
    Date.UTC(
      theForm.yrsTxt.value,
      theForm.monTxt.value,
      theForm.dayTxt.value,
      theForm.hrsTxt.value,
      theForm.minTxt.value,
      theForm.secTxt.value
      )
    )
  displayDate()
}

// STOP HIDING -->
</SCRIPT>
</HEAD>
<BODY>

<P>Date.UTC() is a function attached to the Date
object that parses a time string in Universal
Coordinated Time format and returns the number of
milliseconds between the specified date/time and
12 A.M. Jan 1, 1970. It's always in the GMT time
zone. It is important to recognize that it is not
a method of the Date object and you always call
it by referencing the Date object, not an
instance of the date object. In other words, you
call it with Date.UTC().</P>

<FORM NAME="aForm">
<P>
<B>Enter a UTC time:</B><BR>
year
<INPUT TYPE="text" NAME="yrsTxt" VALUE="" SIZE=2>
month
<INPUT TYPE="text" NAME="monTxt" VALUE="" SIZE=2>
day
```

```
<INPUT TYPE="text" NAME="dayTxt" VALUE="" SIZE=2>
hours
<INPUT TYPE="text" NAME="hrsTxt" VALUE="" SIZE=2>
minutes
<INPUT TYPE="text" NAME="minTxt" VALUE="" SIZE=2>
seconds
<INPUT TYPE="text" NAME="secTxt" VALUE="" SIZE=2>
</P>

<P>
<INPUT TYPE="button" NAME="UTCBtn"
 VALUE="UTC()" onClick="UTCDate()">
</P>
</FORM>

</BODY>
</HTML>
```

Figure 30–5 shows the result of loading the `dateUTC.html` script, entering date and time information, and clicking on the `UTC()` button.

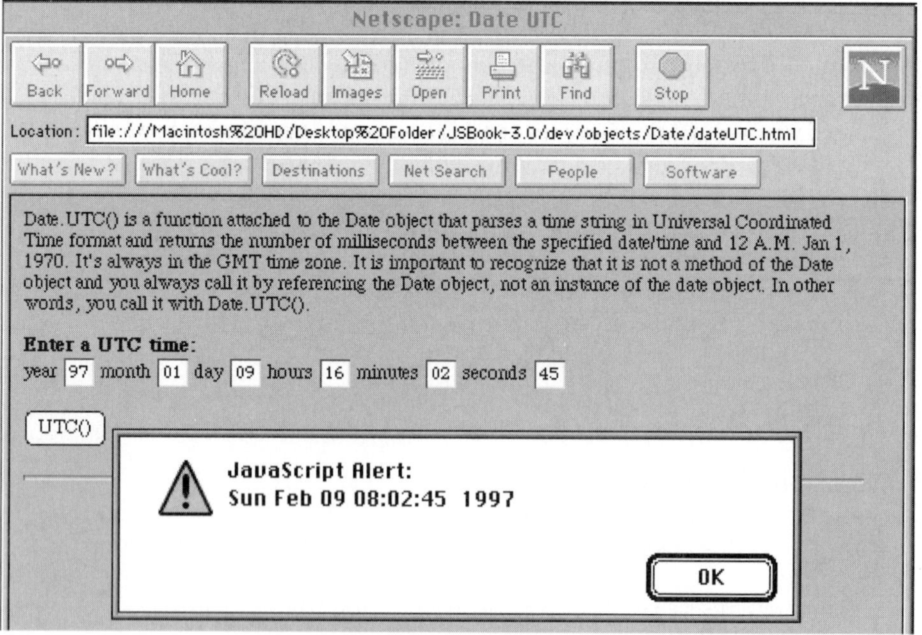

Figure 30–5 Result of loading the `dateUTC.html` script

Creating Your Own Properties for a Date Object

The Navigator 3.0 release provides a `prototype` property for the `Date` object that enables you to apply new properties and methods to every `Date` object. The `prototype` property is an advanced scripting feature. You can use the `prototype` property to create your own properties or methods that apply to all of the objects you create using the `new` keyword.

Property	Value	Gettable	Settable
prototype	string	Yes	Yes

For an example of using the `prototype` property, see "Creating Custom String Functions" on page 809 and Chapter 34, "Creating Your Own JavaScript Objects."

Summary of New Terms and Concepts

The new terms and concepts introduced in this chapter are listed in alphabetical order in Table 30-2. The terms and concepts are also included in the glossary at the end of the book.

Table 30-2 Summary of New Terms and Concepts

Term/Concept	Description
universal coordinated time	UTC is the specified date represented as an integer that represents number of milliseconds since midnight Greenwich mean time (GMT) on January 1, 1970, and the specified date.

CHAPTER 31

- Using Constants
- Comparing Values
- Rounding Numbers
- Generating Random Numbers
- Calculating Square Roots
- Using Trigonometric Methods
- Changing the Power of a Number
- Calculating Natural Logarithms
- Computing Ex
- Summary of New Terms and Concepts

Doing Math

The built-in `Math` object provides a set of read-only constants and methods that you can use to perform advanced mathematical calculations. For example, the constant `PI` has the value of pi. You reference them by using the same dot syntax that you use for other JavaScript objects. For example, to reference `PI`, you use the syntax:

```
Math.PI
```

Note that you always use an initial capital when referencing the `Math` object. Because Math is simply a container or placeholder object, you do not need to use the `new` statement to create a copy of the `Math` object.

The `Math` object provides standard mathematical constants and functions that include trigonometric, logarithmic, and exponential functions. Table 31-1 alphabetically lists the properties and methods of the `Math` object. The `Math` object has no event handlers.

Table 31-1 Properties and Methods for the Math Object

Properties	Methods	Event Handlers
E	abs()	None
LN2	acos()	
LN10	asin()	
LOG2E	atan()	
LOG10E	atan2()	
PI	ceil()	
SQRT1_2	cos()	
SQRT2	eval()*	
	exp()	
	floor()	
	log()	
	max()	
	min()	
	pow()	
	random()	
	round()	
	sin()	
	sqrt()	
	tan()	
	toString()*	
	valueOf()*	

* New in Navigator 3.0.

You can use the `with` statement in combination with the `Math` object to declare a function as being `with(Math)`. In this way, you can refer to the properties and methods of the `Math` object without using the `Math` object name as a prefix to every call. The following function uses the `with` statement in this way:

```
function doIt() {
 var choice = 0

 with (Math) {
  for (var i = 0; i < document.images.length; i++) {
   choice = ceil((random() * 100) % 7)
   document.images[i].src = colors[choice].src
  }
 }
 setTimeout("doIt()", 1000)
}
```

For a complete example of the script, see "Example of Generating Random Numbers" on page 901.

Using Constants

All of the properties of the `Math` object are constants that are used in calculations.

Property	Value	Description
E	2.718281828459045091	Euler's constant
LN2	0.6931471805599452862	Natural log of 2
LN10	2.302585092994045901	Natural log of 10
LOG2E	1.442695040888963387	Log base-2 of E
LOG10E	0.4342944819032518167	Log base-10 of E
PI	3.145926535897931 16	π
SQRT1_2	0.7071067811865475727	Square root of 0.5
SQRT2	1.414213562373095145	Square root of 2

You can use any of these properties in your regular arithmetic expressions. For example, the following statement returns the circumference of a circle whose diameter is the variable d:

```
circumference = d * Math.PI
```

Example of Using Constants

The following `mathConstants.html` script displays all of the properties of the `Math` object.

```
<!--
                  mathConstants.html

    This example displays all of the Math
    object's constants.
-->

<HTML>
<HEAD>
<TITLE>Math Constants</TITLE>
</HEAD>
<BODY>

<P>The Math object's constants and their values
are:</P>

<SCRIPT LANGUAGE="JavaScript">
<!-- HIDE FROM OLD BROWSERS
var mStr = ""

mStr += "<CENTER>"
mStr += "<TABLE COLS=2 WIDTH=300>\n"
mStr += "<TR>\n"
mStr += "  <TD>Math.E</TD>\n"
mStr += "  <TD>" + Math.E + "</TD>\n"
mStr += "</TR>\n"
mStr += "<TR>\n"
mStr += "  <TD>Math.LN10</TD>\n"
mStr += "  <TD>" + Math.LN10 + "</TD>\n"
mStr += "</TR>\n"
mStr += "<TR>\n"
mStr += "  <TD>Math.LN2</TD>\n"
mStr += "  <TD>" + Math.LN2 + "</TD>\n"
mStr += "</TR>\n"
mStr += "<TR>\n"
mStr += "  <TD>Math.LOG10E</TD>\n"
mStr += "  <TD>" + Math.LOG10E + "</TD>\n"
mStr += "</TR>\n"
mStr += "<TR>\n"
mStr += "  <TD>Math.LOG2E</TD>\n"
```

```
mStr += "   <TD>" + Math.LOG2E + "</TD>\n"
mStr += "</TR>\n"
mStr += "<TR>\n"
mStr += "   <TD>Math.PI</TD>\n"
mStr += "   <TD>" + Math.PI + "</TD>\n"
mStr += "</TR>\n"
mStr += "<TR>\n"
mStr += "   <TD>Math.SQRT1_2</TD>\n"
mStr += "   <TD>" + Math.SQRT1_2 + "</TD>\n"
mStr += "</TR>\n"
mStr += "<TR>\n"
mStr += "   <TD>Math.SQRT2</TD>\n"
mStr += "   <TD>" + Math.SQRT2 + "</TD>\n"
mStr += "</TR>\n"
mStr += "</TABLE>\n"
mStr += "</CENTER>"

document.open()
document.write(mStr)
document.close()

// STOP HIDING -->
</SCRIPT>


</BODY>
</HTML>
```

Figure 31–1 shows the result of loading the `mathConstants.html` script.

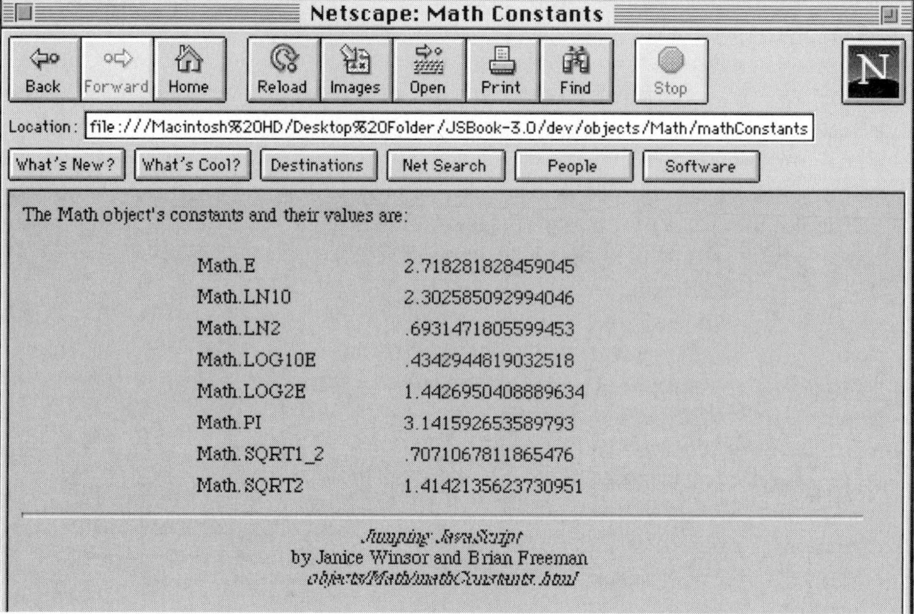

Figure 31–1 Result of loading the `mathConstants.html` script

Comparing Values

You can use the `max()` and `min()` to compare two numbers and determine which is the greater or lesser value.

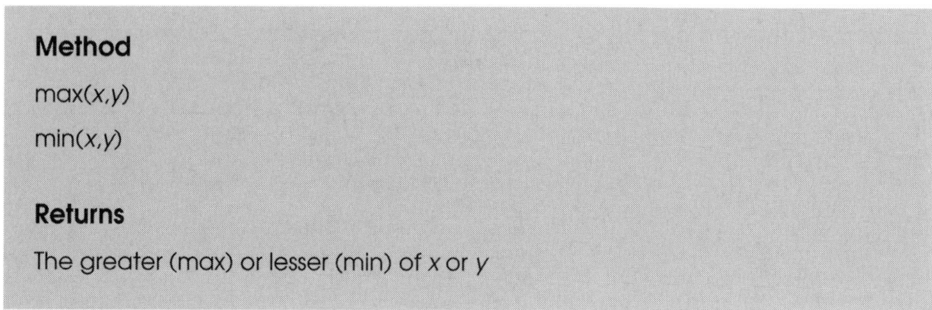

Method

max(*x*,*y*)

min(*x*,*y*)

Returns

The greater (max) or lesser (min) of *x* or *y*

Example of Finding the Largest Value

The following `mathMax.html` script provides a text field in which you can enter numbers separated by spaces and a button that you can click on to find the maximum. The script uses the `max()` method to find the largest number.

```
<!--
                  mathMax.html
-->

<HTML>
<HEAD>
<TITLE>Math Max</TITLE>
<SCRIPT LANGUAGE="JavaScript">
<!-- HIDE FROM OLD BROWSERS

// Find the largest value entered.
//
function maximum(values) {
  var vArray = values.split(" ")
  var largest = null

  // Convert all the strings to numbers.
  for (var i = 0; i < vArray.length; i++) {
    vArray[i] = parseInt(vArray[i])
  }

  // Find the largest.
  for (i = 0; i < vArray.length; i++) {
    if ((typeof(vArray[i]) == "number")
      && (! isNaN(vArray[i]))) {
      if (largest == null) {
        largest = vArray[i]
      } else {
        largest = Math.max(largest, vArray[i])
      }
    }
  }
  if (largest == null) {
    alert("No numbers were entered.")
  } else {
    alert("The largest value entered is: " +
          largest)
  }
}
// STOP HIDING -->
</SCRIPT>
</HEAD>
```

```
<BODY>
<P>This example uses Math.max() to find the
largest number entered in the field below.</P>

<FORM NAME="inputForm">
<P><B>Enter numbers separated by spaces:</B><BR>
<INPUT TYPE="text" NAME="values" SIZE=40
 onChange="maximum(this.value)"><BR><BR>
<INPUT TYPE="button" VALUE="Find Maximum"
 onClick="maximum(this.form.values.value)">
</P></FORM>

</BODY>
</HTML>
```

Figure 31–2 shows the result of loading the `mathMax.html` script.

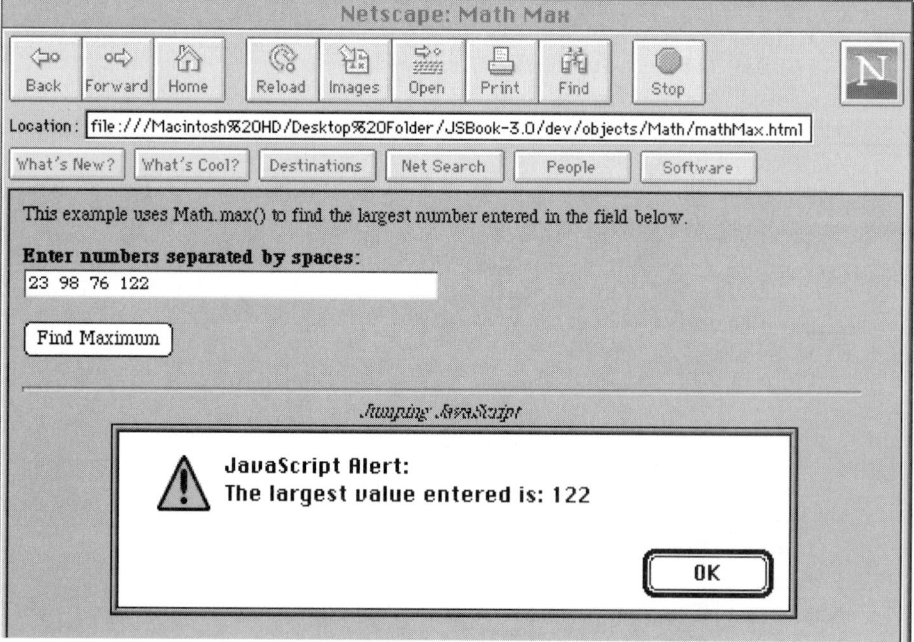

Figure 31–2 Result of loading the `mathMax.html` script

Example of Finding the Smallest Value

The following `mathMin.html` script uses the `min()` method to find the smallest number entered in a text field.

```
<!--
                    mathMin.html
-->

<HTML>
<HEAD>
<TITLE>Math Min</TITLE>
<SCRIPT LANGUAGE="JavaScript">
<!-- HIDE FROM OLD BROWSERS

// Find the smallest value entered.
//
function minimum(values) {
  var vArray = values.split(" ")
  var smallest = null

  // Convert all the strings to numbers.
  for (var i = 0; i < vArray.length; i++) {
    vArray[i] = parseInt(vArray[i])
  }

  // Find the smallest.
  for (i = 0; i < vArray.length; i++) {
    if ((typeof(vArray[i]) == "number")
      && (! isNaN(vArray[i]))) {
      if (smallest == null) {
        smallest = vArray[i]
      } else {
        smallest = Math.min(smallest, vArray[i])
      }
    }
  }
  if (smallest == null) {
    alert("No numbers were entered.")
  } else {
    alert("The smallest value entered is: " +
          smallest)
  }
}
```

```
// STOP HIDING -->
</SCRIPT>
</HEAD>

<BODY>
<P>This example uses Math.min() to find the
smallest number entered in the field below.</P>

<FORM NAME="inputForm">
<P><B>Enter numbers separated by spaces:</B><BR>
<INPUT TYPE="text" NAME="values" SIZE=40
 onChange="minimum(this.value)"><BR><BR>
<INPUT TYPE="button" VALUE="Find Minimum"
 onClick="minimum(this.form.values.value)">
</P></FORM>

</BODY>
</HTML>
```

Figure 31–3 shows the result of loading the `mathMin.html` script.

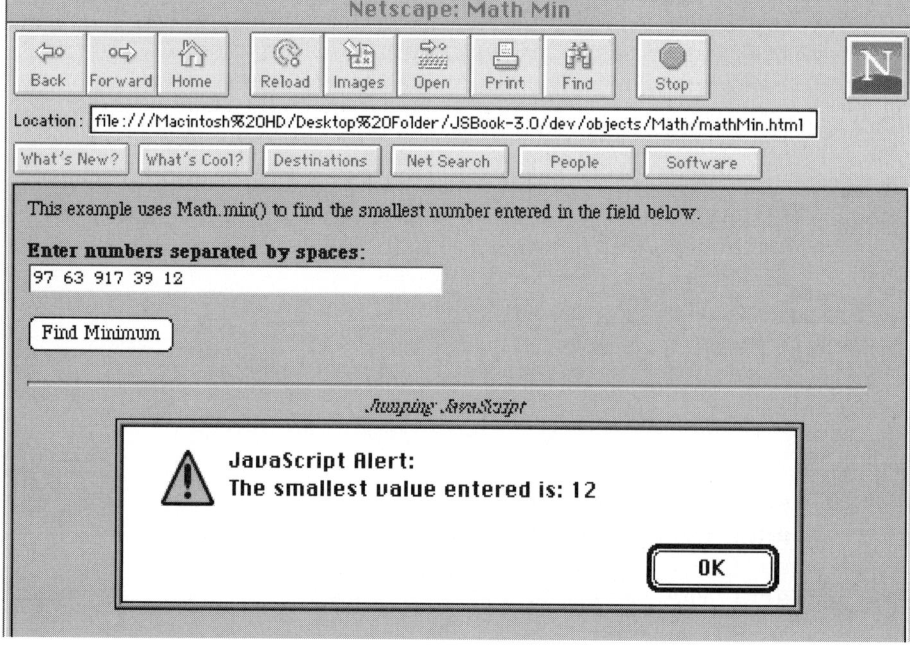

Figure 31–3 Result of loading the `mathMin.html` script

Rounding Numbers

The `Math` object has four methods that you can use to round numbers:

- `abs()`
- `ceil()`
- `floor()`
- `round()`

Returning an Absolute Value

The `abs()` method returns the *absolute value* of a number. The absolute value is a number without its sign. For example, the absolute value of both -47 and +47 is simply 47.

Method

abs(*x*)

Returns

Absolute value of *x*

The following `mathAbs.html` script creates a text field and a Compute button. When you enter either a positive or negative number in the text field and click on the Compute button, the absolute value of the number is returned.

```
<!--
                    mathAbs.html
-->

<HTML>
<HEAD>
<TITLE>Math Absolute Value</TITLE>
</HEAD>
<BODY>

<P>Enter a positive or negative number in the
field below and click on Compute to have
Math.abs() calculate the absolute value of your
number.</P>
```

```
<FORM>
<P><B>Enter a number:</B><BR>
<INPUT TYPE="text" NAME="x" VALUE="" SIZE=20
onChange="this.value=Math.abs(eval(this.value))">
</P><P>
<INPUT TYPE="button" NAME="btn" VALUE="Compute">
</P>
</FORM>

</BODY>
</HTML>
```

Figure 31–4 shows the result of loading the `mathAbs.html` script and typing a negative number in the text field.

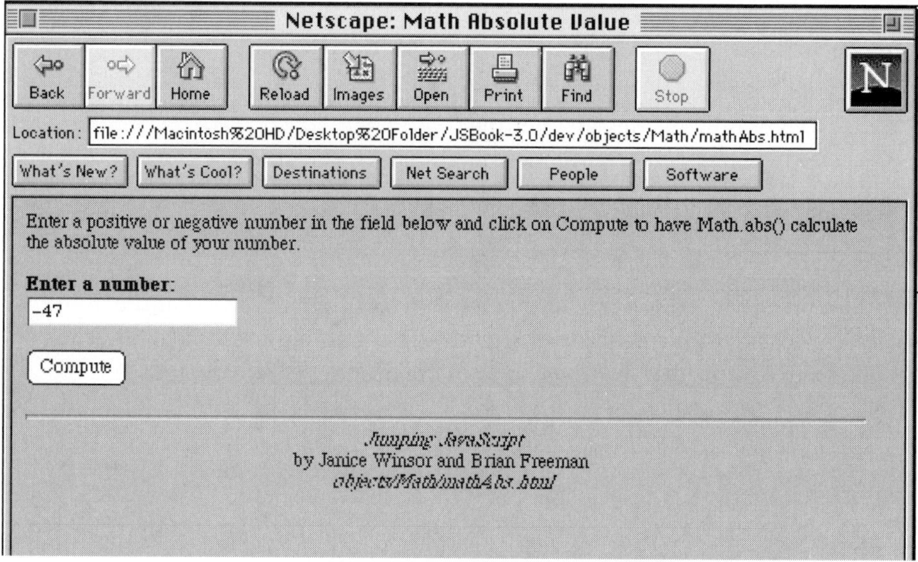

Figure 31–4 Result of loading the `mathAbs.html` script

Clicking on the Compute button returns the absolute value of the number in the text field. Figure 31–5 shows the result of clicking on the Compute button.

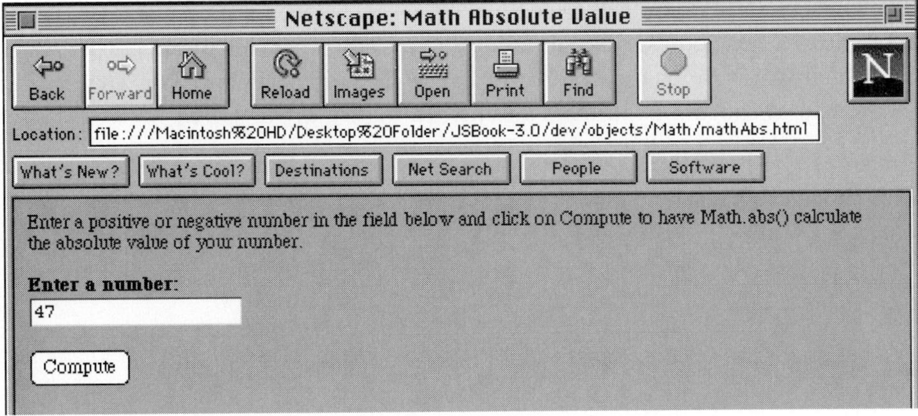

Figure 31–5 Result of clicking on the Compute button

Note – If you type a positive number with a plus sign (+47) in the text field, you'll get an error message. A number without a sign is assumed to be a positive number, and the `abs()` method does not know how to interpret the plus sign.

Rounding a Number Up

The `ceil()` method rounds anumber up to the next closest integer. In other words, it always rounds the number up to the next whole number. This method does not round negative numbers to greater negative numbers. It rounds them up to zero.

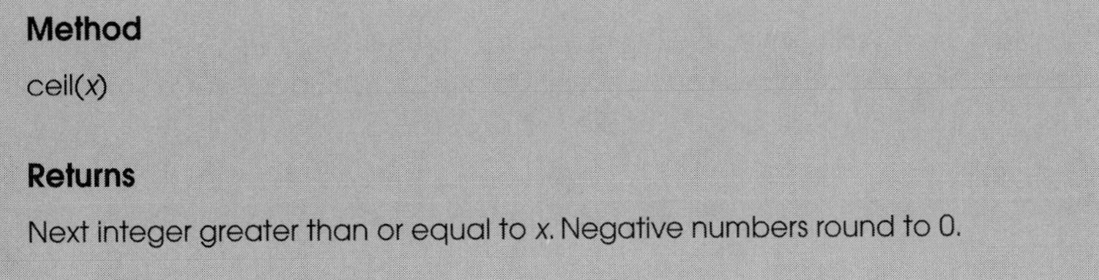

Method

ceil(*x*)

Returns

Next integer greater than or equal to *x*. Negative numbers round to 0.

For an example of using the `ceil()` method, see "Calculating the Angle of Polar Coordinates" on page 917.

Rounding a Number Down

The `floor()` method rounds a number down to the next closest integer. In other words, it always rounds the number down to the next whole number. This method rounds negative numbers downward to be more negative.

Method

floor(*x*)

Returns

Next integer less than or equal to *x*

For an example of using the `floor()` method, see "Calculating the Sine" on page 922.

Rounding Numbers

The `round()` method rounds the value up or down to the nearest integer. In the Navigator 2.0 release, this method did not correctly round very large numbers. The `round()` method differs from the `ceil()` and `floor()` methods in that it rounds up when the value is equal to or greater than half the number, and down when the value is less than half the number.

Method

round(*x*)

Returns

N+1 when *x* is equal to or greater than half the number; otherwise N

The following `mathRound.html` script creates a timer that displays the number of minutes and seconds that you have spent on the page. It uses the `round()` method to adjust the timer to the nearest integer value.

```
<!--
                        mathRound.html
-->

<HTML>
<HEAD>
<TITLE>Math Round</TITLE>
```

```
<SCRIPT LANGUAGE="JavaScript">
<!-- HIDE FROM OLD BROWSERS

// A global variable that stores when timing
// began. It is initialized in initTimer().
var startTime = null

// Initialize the timer and set a timeout to
// display the time spent on the page in a
// second.
//
function initTimer() {
  var startDate = new Date()

  startTime = startDate.getTime()
  setTimeout("displayTime()", 0)
}

// Get the difference in time from the start of
// the timer to now.
//
// The return value is in seconds.
//
function getTimeDelta() {
  var rval = 0      // the return value
  var currentDate = new Date()

  rval = (currentDate.getTime() - startTime)/1000

  return(rval)
}

// Format the time difference for display. If
// either the minutes or seconds are less than
// nine, a zero is prepended to the string.
//
// A string formatted like "00:00" is returned.
//
function formatDelta() {
  var totalSeconds = Math.round(getTimeDelta())

  // Calculate the minutes and seconds.
  var minutes = Math.round((totalSeconds-30)/60)
  var seconds = totalSeconds % 60
```

```
  // Prepend the "0" if necessary.
  var rtnMinutes =
    ((minutes > 9) ? minutes : "0" + minutes)
  var rtnSeconds =
    ((seconds > 9) ? seconds : "0" + seconds)

  // return the formatted string
  return( rtnMinutes + ":" + rtnSeconds )
}

// Display the time spent on this page in the
// form and set a timer to call this function in
// another second.
//
function displayTime() {
  document.timeForm.duration.value = formatDelta()
  setTimeout('displayTime()', 1000)
}

// STOP HIDING -->
</SCRIPT>
</HEAD>
<BODY onLoad="setTimeout('initTimer()', 0)">

<P>This example displays the amount of time you
spend on this page in minutes and seconds. It
uses Math.round() in the calculations for minutes
and seconds to adjust the timer to the nearest
integer value.</P>

<P>The time you've spent on this page is:</P>

<CENTER><FORM NAME="timeForm">
<INPUT TYPE="text" NAME="duration" VALUE="00:00"
SIZE=5></FORM></CENTER>

</BODY>
</HTML>
```

Figure 31–6 shows the result of loading the `mathRound.html` script.

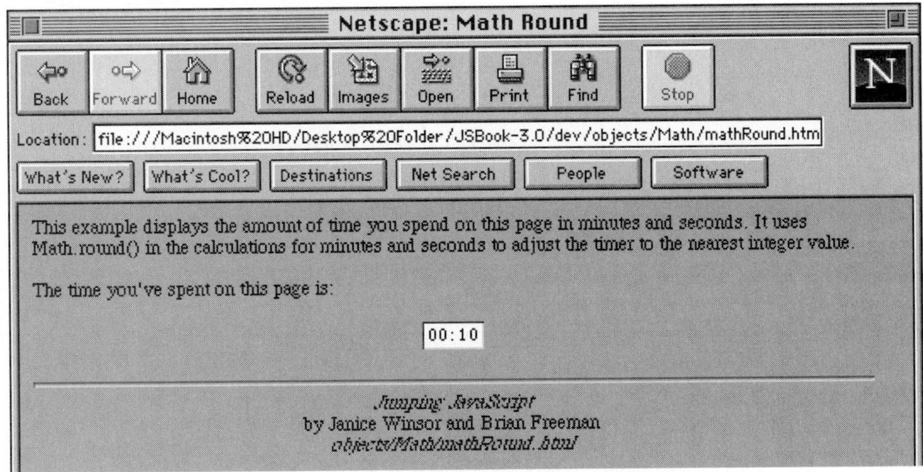

Figure 31–6 Result of loading the `mathRound.html` script

Generating Random Numbers

The `random()` method generates a pseudorandom number between 0.0 and 1.0. In the Navigator 2.0 release, this method worked only on UNIX platforms.

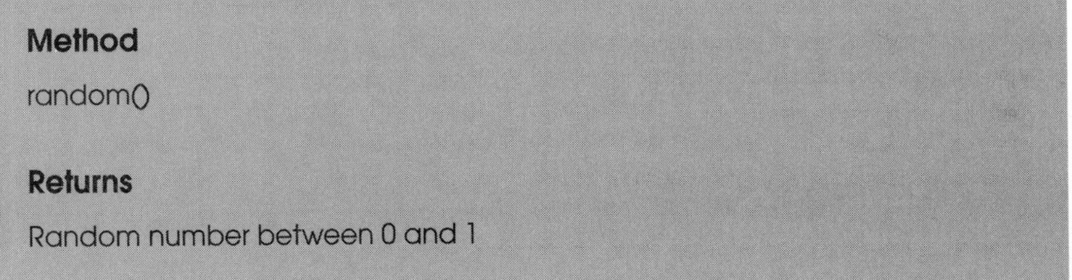

Method

random()

Returns

Random number between 0 and 1

Example of Generating Random Numbers

The following `mathRandom.html` script uses the `random()` method to randomly choose the color of the bar, change it, and then randomly permute the order of colors that are displayed.

```
<!--
                        mathRandom.html
-->

<HTML>
<HEAD>
<TITLE>Math Random</TITLE>
<SCRIPT LANGUAGE="JavaScript">
```

```
<!-- HIDE FROM OLD BROWSERS
var colors = new Array(8)

colors[0] = new Image(1, 100)
colors[0].src = "../../icons/black_dot.gif"
colors[1] = new Image(1, 100)
colors[1].src = "../../icons/blue_dot.gif"
colors[2] = new Image(1, 100)
colors[2].src = "../../icons/green_dot.gif"
colors[3] = new Image(1, 100)
colors[3].src = "../../icons/pink_dot.gif"
colors[4] = new Image(1, 100)
colors[4].src = "../../icons/purple_dot.gif"
colors[5] = new Image(1, 100)
colors[5].src = "../../icons/red_dot.gif"
colors[6] = new Image(1, 100)
colors[6].src = "../../icons/white_dot.gif"
colors[7] = new Image(1, 100)
colors[7].src = "../../icons/yellow_dot.gif"

// Randomly select the color of the bar,
// change it, and then do it all again after a
// second.
//
function doIt() {
 var choice = 0

 with (Math) {
  for (var i = 0; i < document.images.length; i++) {
   choice = ceil((random() * 100) % 7)
   document.images[i].src = colors[choice].src
  }
 }
 setTimeout("doIt()", 1000)
}

// STOP HIDING -->
</SCRIPT>
</HEAD>
<BODY onLoad="doIt()">

<P>Math.random() is used to select the color of the
bars below and to permute the colors randomly</P>
```

```
<TABLE COLS=32 WIDTH='100%' BORDER=0
  CELLSPACING=0 CELLPADDING=0>
  <TR>
    <TD VALIGN=bottom>
      <IMG WIDTH=1 HEIGHT=100
SRC=../../icons/black_dot.gif>
    </TD>
    <TD VALIGN=bottom>
     <IMG WIDTH=1 HEIGHT=100 SRC=../../icons/blue_dot.gif>
    </TD>
    <TD VALIGN=bottom>
      <IMG WIDTH=1 HEIGHT=100
SRC=../../icons/green_dot.gif>
    </TD>
    <TD VALIGN=bottom>
     <IMG WIDTH=1 HEIGHT=100 SRC=../../icons/pink_dot.gif>
    </TD>
    <TD VALIGN=bottom>
      <IMG WIDTH=1 HEIGHT=100
SRC=../../icons/purple_dot.gif>
    </TD>
    <TD VALIGN=bottom>
     <IMG WIDTH=1 HEIGHT=100 SRC=../../icons/red_dot.gif>
    </TD>
    <TD VALIGN=bottom>
      <IMG WIDTH=1 HEIGHT=100
SRC=../../icons/white_dot.gif>
    </TD>
    <TD VALIGN=bottom>
      <IMG WIDTH=1 HEIGHT=100
SRC=../../icons/yellow_dot.gif>
    </TD>
    <TD VALIGN=bottom>
      <IMG WIDTH=1 HEIGHT=100
SRC=../../icons/black_dot.gif>
    </TD>
    <TD VALIGN=bottom>
     <IMG WIDTH=1 HEIGHT=100 SRC=../../icons/blue_dot.gif>
    </TD>
    <TD VALIGN=bottom>
      <IMG WIDTH=1 HEIGHT=100
SRC=../../icons/green_dot.gif>
    </TD>
    <TD VALIGN=bottom>
```

```
 <IMG WIDTH=1 HEIGHT=100 SRC=../../icons/pink_dot.gif>
</TD>
<TD VALIGN=bottom>
  <IMG WIDTH=1 HEIGHT=100
SRC=../../icons/purple_dot.gif>
</TD>
<TD VALIGN=bottom>
 <IMG WIDTH=1 HEIGHT=100 SRC=../../icons/red_dot.gif>
</TD>
<TD VALIGN=bottom>
  <IMG WIDTH=1 HEIGHT=100
SRC=../../icons/white_dot.gif>
</TD>
<TD VALIGN=bottom>
  <IMG WIDTH=1 HEIGHT=100
SRC=../../icons/yellow_dot.gif>
</TD>
<TD VALIGN=bottom>
  <IMG WIDTH=1 HEIGHT=100
SRC=../../icons/black_dot.gif>
</TD>
<TD VALIGN=bottom>
 <IMG WIDTH=1 HEIGHT=100 SRC=../../icons/blue_dot.gif>
</TD>
<TD VALIGN=bottom>
  <IMG WIDTH=1 HEIGHT=100
SRC=../../icons/green_dot.gif>
</TD>
<TD VALIGN=bottom>
 <IMG WIDTH=1 HEIGHT=100 SRC=../../icons/pink_dot.gif>
</TD>
<TD VALIGN=bottom>
  <IMG WIDTH=1 HEIGHT=100
SRC=../../icons/purple_dot.gif>
</TD>
<TD VALIGN=bottom>
 <IMG WIDTH=1 HEIGHT=100 SRC=../../icons/red_dot.gif>
</TD>
<TD VALIGN=bottom>
  <IMG WIDTH=1 HEIGHT=100
SRC=../../icons/white_dot.gif>
</TD>
<TD VALIGN=bottom>
  <IMG WIDTH=1 HEIGHT=100
```

```
SRC=../../icons/yellow_dot.gif>
    </TD>
    <TD VALIGN=bottom>
      <IMG WIDTH=1 HEIGHT=100
SRC=../../icons/black_dot.gif>
    </TD>
    <TD VALIGN=bottom>
     <IMG WIDTH=1 HEIGHT=100 SRC=../../icons/blue_dot.gif>
    </TD>
    <TD VALIGN=bottom>
      <IMG WIDTH=1 HEIGHT=100
SRC=../../icons/green_dot.gif>
    </TD>
    <TD VALIGN=bottom>
     <IMG WIDTH=1 HEIGHT=100 SRC=../../icons/pink_dot.gif>
    </TD>
    <TD VALIGN=bottom>
      <IMG WIDTH=1 HEIGHT=100
SRC=../../icons/purple_dot.gif>
    </TD>
    <TD VALIGN=bottom>
     <IMG WIDTH=1 HEIGHT=100 SRC=../../icons/red_dot.gif>
    </TD>
    <TD VALIGN=bottom>
      <IMG WIDTH=1 HEIGHT=100
SRC=../../icons/white_dot.gif>
    </TD>
    <TD VALIGN=bottom>
      <IMG WIDTH=1 HEIGHT=100
SRC=../../icons/yellow_dot.gif>
    </TD>
  </TR>
</TABLE>

</BODY>
</HTML>
```

Figure 31–7 shows the result of loading the `mathRandom.html` script.

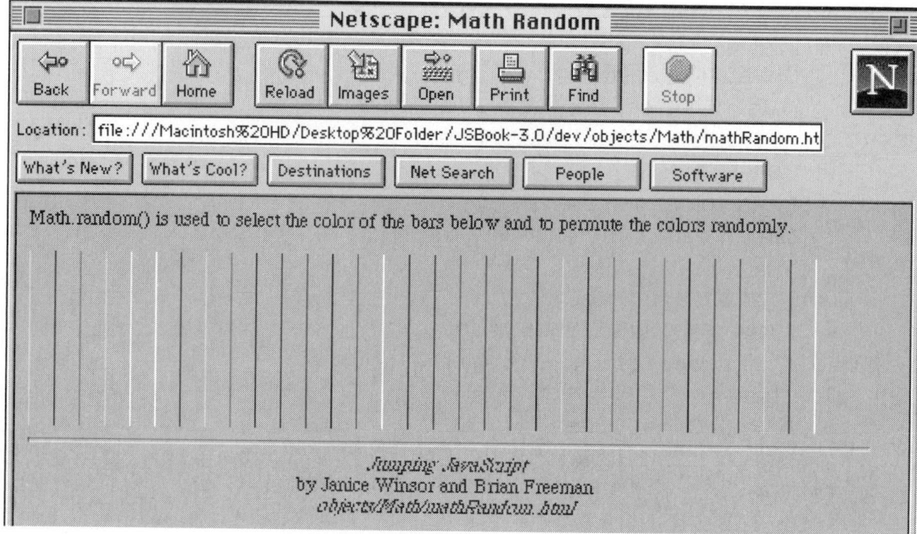

Figure 31–7 Result of loading the `mathRandom.html` script

Calculating Square Roots

The `sqrt()` method returns the square root of a number.

Method

sqrt(*x*)

Returns

Square root of *x*

Example of Calculating Square Roots

The following `mathSqrt.html` script calculates a result and displays a graph of the first quadrant that results from the calculation.

```
<!--
                    mathSqrt.html
-->

<HTML>
<HEAD>
<TITLE>Math Square Root</TITLE>
</HEAD>
```

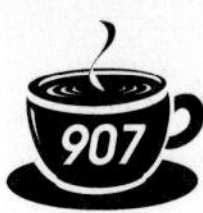


```
<BODY>

<P>This example uses Math.sqrt() to graph the
first quadrant of the function:</P>
<DD>y = f(x) = b * sqrt(1 - pow(x, 2) / pow(a, 2))

<SCRIPT LANGUAGE="JavaScript">
<!-- HIDE FROM OLD BROWSERS
var mStr = ""

mStr += "<TABLE COLS=181 WIDTH='100%' BORDER=0"
mStr += "CELLSPACING=0 CELLPADDING=0>"
mStr += "<TR>"

var a = 9
var b = 400

for (var x = 0; x < a; x += 0.05) {
  var y = 0

  with (Math) {
    y = b * sqrt(1 - (pow(x, 2)/pow(a, 2)))
  }
  mStr += "<TD VALIGN=bottom>"
  mStr += "<IMG WIDTH=1 HEIGHT="
  mStr += y + " SRC=../../icons/red_dot.gif>"
  mStr += "</TD>"
}
mStr += "</TR>"
mStr += "</TABLE>"

document.open()
document.write(mStr)
document.close()

// STOP HIDING -->
</SCRIPT>

</BODY>
</HTML>
```

Figure 31–8 shows the result of loading the `mathSqrt.html` script.

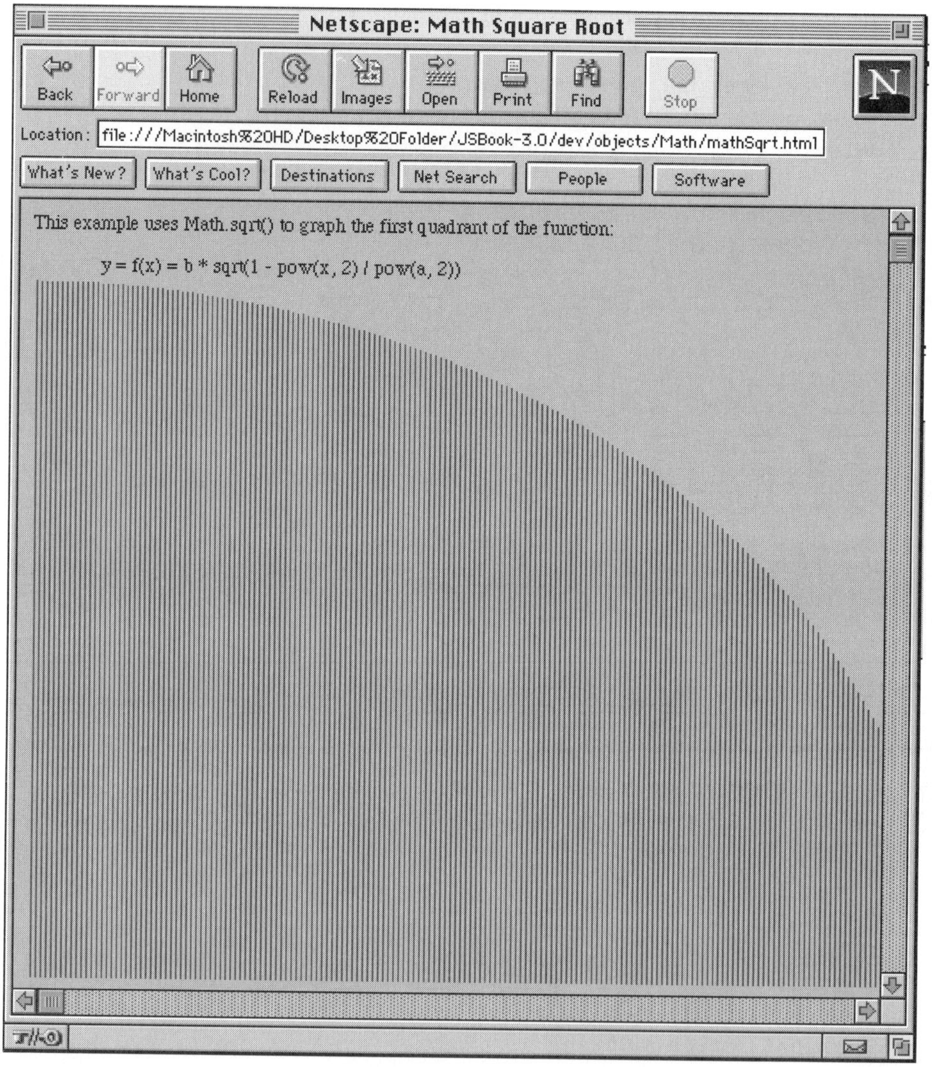

Figure 31–8 Result of loading the `mathSqrt.html` script

Using Trigonometric Methods

The `Math` object provides the six trigonometric functions as methods:

- `acos` (arc cosine)
- `asin` (arc sine)
- `atan` (arc tangent)

- atan2 (arc tangent) (new in Navigator 3.0)
- cos (cosine)
- sin (sine)
- tan (tangent)

Note – All trigonometric methods of the Math object take arguments in radians. A *radian* is a unit of plane angular measurement that is equal to the angle at the center of a circle subtended by an arc equal in length to the radius.

Finding the Arc Cosine

The acos() method returns the arc cosine in radians.

Method

acos(*x*)

Returns

Arc cosine of *x* in radians. The return value is between 0 and pi radians.

The following mathAcos.html script uses the acos() method to calculate the arc cosine from -1.0 to 1.0 and display the results as a graph.

```
<!--
                    mathAcos.html
-->

<HTML>
<HEAD>
<TITLE>Math Arc Cosine</TITLE>
</HEAD>
<BODY>

<P>This example calculates the arc cosine from
-1.0 to 1.0, incrementing by 0.01 after each
calculation. The result is scaled by 100 before
it is displayed in the graph.</P>
```

```
<SCRIPT LANGUAGE="JavaScript">
<!-- HIDE FROM OLD BROWSERS
var mStr = ""

mStr += "<TABLE COLS=200 WIDTH='100%' BORDER=0"
mStr += "CELLSPACING=0 CELLPADDING=0>"
mStr += "<TR>"

for (var i = -1.0; i <= 1.0; i+=.01) {
  var barHeight = Math.acos(i) * 100

  mStr += "<TD VALIGN=bottom>"
  mStr += "<IMG WIDTH=1 HEIGHT="
  mStr += Math.floor(barHeight) + " SRC="
  mStr += "../../icons/black_dot.gif>"
  mStr += "</TD>"
}
mStr += "</TR>"
mStr += "</TABLE>"

document.open()
document.write(mStr)
document.close()

// STOP HIDING -->
</SCRIPT>

</BODY>
</HTML>
```

Figure 31–9 shows the result of loading the `mathAcos.html` script.

Netscape: Math Arc Cosine

Location: file:///Macintosh%20HD/Desktop%20Folder/JSBook-3.0/dev/objects/Math/mathAcos.html

This example calculates the arc cosine from -1.0 to 1.0, incrementing by 0.01 after each calculation. The result is scaled by 100 before it is displayed in the graph.

Jumping JavaScript
by Janice Winsor and Brian Freeman
objects/Math/mathAcos.html

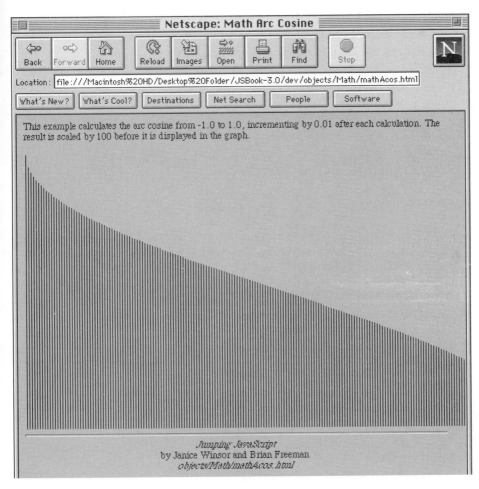

Figure 31–9 Result of loading the `mathAcos.html` script

Calculating the Arc Sine

The `asin()` method returns the arc sine in radians.

> **Method**
>
> asin(*x*)
>
> **Returns**
>
> Arc sine of *x* in radians. The return value is between -π/2 or π/2 radians.

The following `mathAsin.html` script calculates the arc sine from -1.0 to 1.0 and displays the result in a graph. Notice that this script uses the `floor()` and `abs()` methods to limit the height of the top of the graph.

```
<!--
                    mathAsin.html
-->

<HTML>
<HEAD>
<TITLE>Math Arc Sine</TITLE>
</HEAD>
<BODY>

<P>This example calculates the arc sine from
-1.0 to 1.0, incrementing by 0.025 after each
calculation. The result is scaled by 100 before
it is displayed in the graph.</P>

<SCRIPT LANGUAGE="JavaScript">
<!-- HIDE FROM OLD BROWSERS
var axis = Math.floor(Math.asin(1.0) * 100)
var mStr  = ""

mStr += "<TABLE COLS=80 WIDTH='100%' BORDER=0"
mStr += "CELLSPACING=0 CELLPADDING=0>"
mStr += "<TR>"

for (var i = -1.0; i < 0.0; i+=0.025) {
  var barHeight = Math.asin(i) * 100

  mStr += "<TD VALIGN=top>"
  mStr += "<TABLE ROWS=2 BORDER=0 CELLSPACING=0"
  mStr += "CELLPADDING=0><TR><TD>"
  mStr += "<IMG WIDTH=4 HEIGHT=" + axis + " "
  mStr += "SRC=../../icons/white_dot.gif>"
  mStr += "</TD></TR><TR><TD><IMG WIDTH=4 HEIGHT="
  mStr += Math.floor(Math.abs(barHeight))
  mStr += " SRC=../../icons/black_dot.gif>"
  mStr += "</TD></TR></TABLE></TD>"
}

for (var i = 0.0; i <= 1.0; i+=0.025) {
  var barHeight = Math.asin(i) * 100
```

```
    mStr += "<TD VALIGN=bottom>"
    mStr += "<TABLE ROWS=2 BORDER=0 CELLSPACING=0"
    mStr += "CELLPADDING=0><TR><TD>"
    mStr += "<IMG WIDTH=4 HEIGHT="
    mStr += Math.floor(barHeight) + " SRC="
    mStr += "../../icons/black_dot.gif>"
    mStr += "</TD></TR><TR><TD><IMG WIDTH=4 HEIGHT="
    mStr += axis + " SRC=../../icons/white_dot.gif>"
    mStr += "</TD></TR></TABLE></TD>"
  }
  mStr += "</TR>"
  mStr += "</TABLE>"

  document.open()
  document.write(mStr)
  document.close()

  // STOP HIDING -->
  </SCRIPT>

  </BODY>
  </HTML>
```

Figure 31–10 shows the result of loading the `mathAsin.html` script.

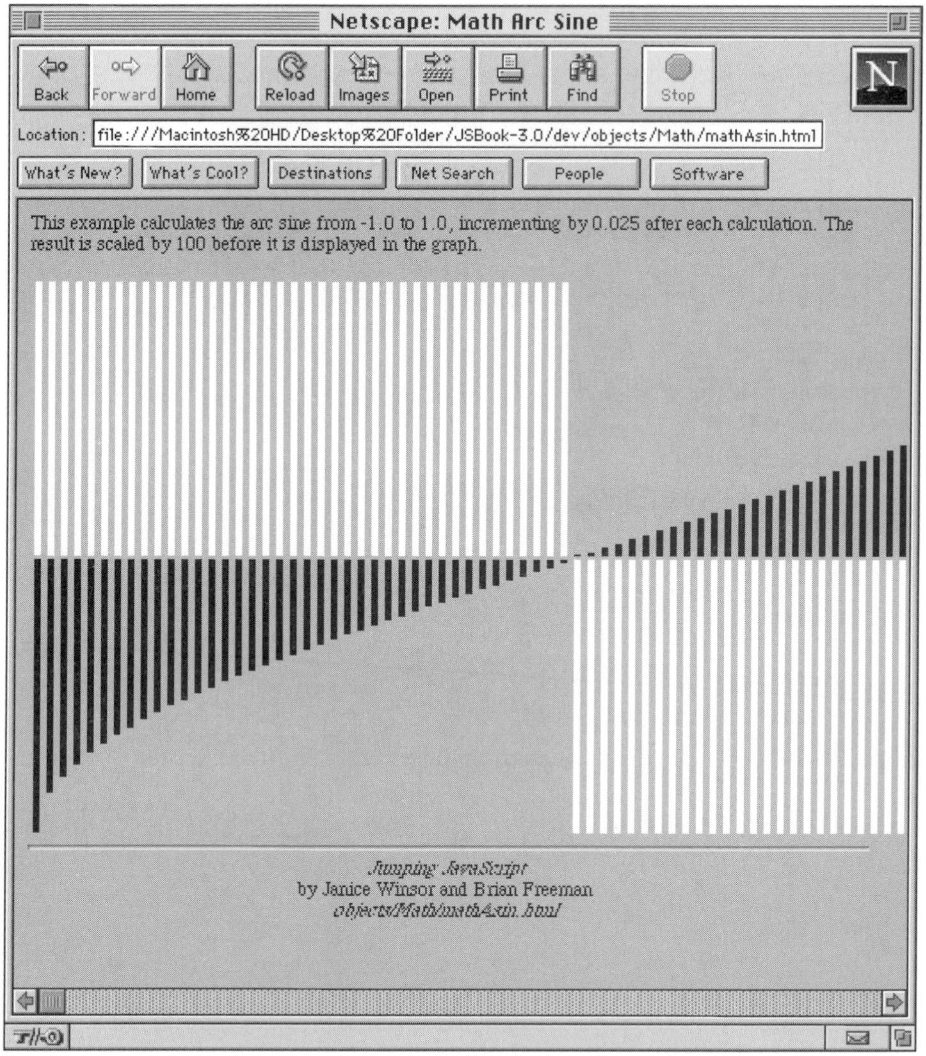

Figure 31–10 Result of loading the `mathAsin.html` script

Calculating the Arc Tangent

The `atan()` method returns the arc tangent of the value in radians.

Method

atan(*x*)

Returns

Arc tangent of *x* in radians. The return value is between $-\pi/2$ and $\pi/2$ radians.

The following `mathAtan.html` script calculates the arc tangent from 0.0 to $\pi/2$ and displays the results in a graph.

```
<!--
                    mathAtan.html
-->

<HTML>
<HEAD>
<TITLE>Math Arc Tangent</TITLE>
</HEAD>
<BODY>

<P>This example calculates the arc tangent from
0.0 to PI/2, incrementing by 0.01 after each
calculation. The result is scaled by 100 before
it is displayed in the graph.</P>

<SCRIPT LANGUAGE="JavaScript">
<!-- HIDE FROM OLD BROWSERS
var mStr = ""

mStr += "<TABLE COLS=158 WIDTH='100%' BORDER=0"
mStr += "CELLSPACING=0 CELLPADDING=0>"
mStr += "<TR>"

for (var i = 0.0; i <= (Math.PI/2); i+=.01) {
  var barHeight = Math.atan(i) * 100

  mStr += "<TD VALIGN=bottom>"
  mStr += "<IMG WIDTH=1 HEIGHT="
  mStr += Math.floor(barHeight) + " SRC="
```

```
    mStr += "../../icons/purple_dot.gif>"
    mStr += "</TD>"
  }
  mStr += "</TR>"
  mStr += "</TABLE>"

  document.open()
  document.write(mStr)
  document.close()

  // STOP HIDING -->
  </SCRIPT>

  </BODY>
  </HTML>
```

Figure 31–11 shows the result of loading the `mathAtan.html` script.

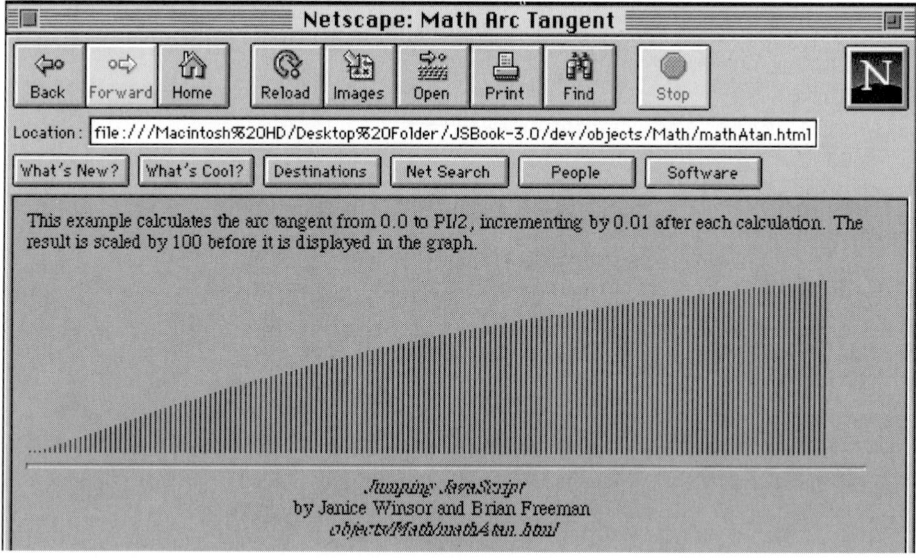

Figure 31–11 Result of loading the `mathAtan.html` script

Calculating the Angle of Polar Coordinates

The Navigator 3.0 release provides an `atan2()` method that returns the angle in radians from the x axis to a point (*x*, *y*). *x* is a number representing the cartesian x coordinate; *y* is a number representing the cartesian y coordinate.

Method

atan2(*x*,*y*)

Returns

The counterclockwise angle between the positive X axis and the point (*x*,*y*)

The following `mathAtan2.html` script calculates `atan2()` from (0,PI/4) to (PI/4,0) and displays the results as a graph.

```
<!--
                  mathAtan2.html
-->

<HTML>
<HEAD>
<TITLE>Math atan2</TITLE>
</HEAD>
<BODY>

<P>This example calculates atan2 from (0,PI/4) to
(PI/4, 0). The result, theta, is scaled by
400 before it is displayed.</P>

<SCRIPT LANGUAGE="JavaScript">
<!-- HIDE FROM OLD BROWSERS
var mStr = ""

mStr += "<TABLE ROWS=256 HEIGHT='100%' BORDER=0"
mStr += "CELLSPACING=0 CELLPADDING=0>"

for (var x = 0.0; x <= (Math.PI/4); x += 0.05) {
  for (var y = (Math.PI/4); y >= 0.0; y -= 0.05) {
    var barHeight = Math.atan2(x, y) * 400

    mStr += "<TR><TD>"
    mStr += "<IMG HEIGHT=1 WIDTH="
```

```
        with (Math) {
         mStr += ceil(abs(barHeight)) + " SRC="
        }
        mStr += "../../icons/black_dot.gif>"
        mStr += "</TD></TR>"
      }
    }
    mStr += "</TABLE>"

    document.open()
    document.write(mStr)
    document.close()

    // STOP HIDING -->
    </SCRIPT>

    </BODY>
    </HTML>
```

Figure 31–12 shows the result of loading the `mathAtan2.html` script.

Netscape: Math atan2

Back Forward Home Reload Images Open Print Find Stop

Location: file:///Macintosh%20HD/Desktop%20Folder/JSBook-3.0/dev/objects/Math/mathAtan2.htm

What's New? What's Cool? Destinations Net Search People Software

This example calculates atan2 from (0,PI/4) to (PI/4, 0). The result, theta, is scaled by 400 before it is displayed.

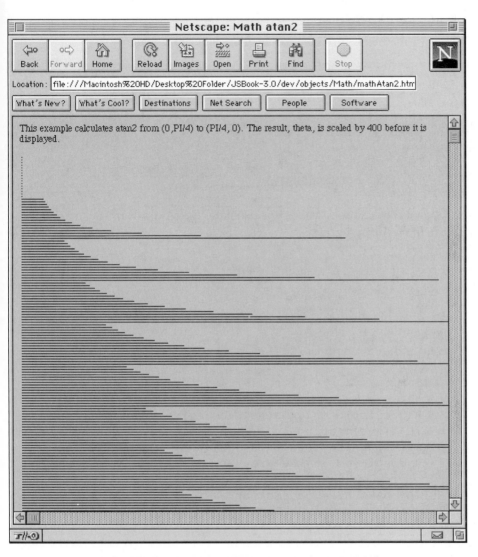

Figure 31–12 Result of loading the `mathAtan2.html` script

Calculating the Cosine

The `cos()` method returns the cosine of the value in radians.

Method

cos(*x*)

Returns

Cosine of *x* in radians. The return value is between -1.0 and 1.0 radians.

The following `mathCos.html` script calculates the cosine from -1.0 to 1.0 and displays the result as a graph.

```
<!--
                    mathCos.html
-->

<HTML>
<HEAD>
<TITLE>Math Cosine</TITLE>
</HEAD>
<BODY>

<P>This example calculates the cosine from -1.0
to 1.0, incrementing by 0.01 after each
calculation. The result is scaled by 100 before
it is displayed in the graph.</P>

<SCRIPT LANGUAGE="JavaScript">
<!-- HIDE FROM OLD BROWSERS
var mStr = ""

mStr += "<TABLE COLS=200 WIDTH='100%' BORDER=0"
mStr += "CELLSPACING=0 CELLPADDING=0>"
mStr += "<TR>"

for (var i = -1.0; i <= 1.0; i+=.01) {
  var barHeight = Math.cos(i) * 100

  mStr += "<TD VALIGN=bottom>"
  mStr += "<IMG WIDTH=1 HEIGHT="
  mStr += Math.floor(barHeight) + " SRC="
```

```
      mStr += "../../icons/black_dot.gif>"
      mStr += "</TD>"
   }
   mStr += "</TR>"
   mStr += "</TABLE>"

   document.open()
   document.write(mStr)
   document.close()

   // STOP HIDING -->
   </SCRIPT>

   </BODY>
   </HTML>
```

Figure 31–13 shows the result of loading the `mathCos.html` script.

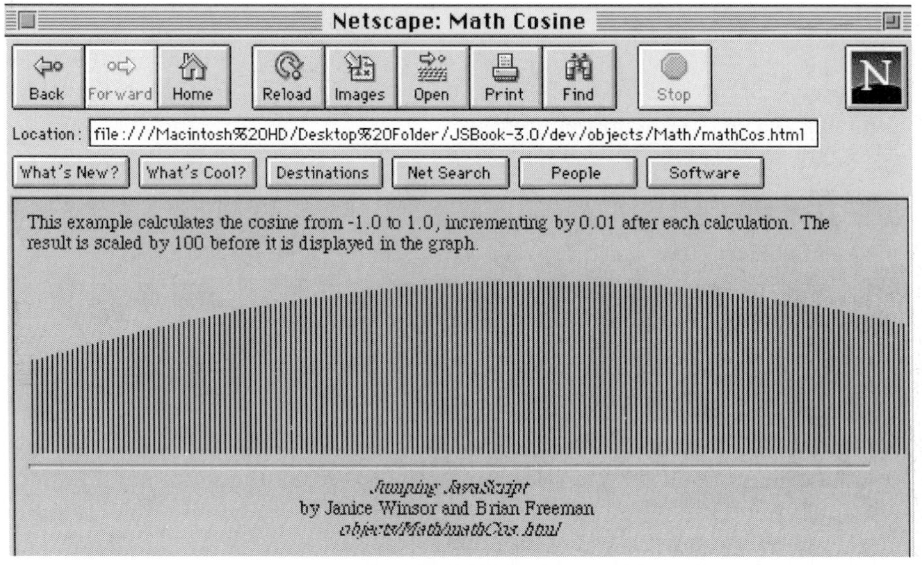

Figure 31–13 Result of loading the `mathCos.html` script

Calculating the Sine

The `sin()` method returns the sine of the value in radians.

Method

sin(*x*)

Returns

Sine of *x* in radians

The following `mathSin.html` script calculates the sine from -1.0 to 1.0 and displays the result as a graph.

```
<!--
                  mathSin.html
-->

<HTML>
<HEAD>
<TITLE>Math Sine</TITLE>
</HEAD>
<BODY>

<P>This example calculates the sine from -1.0 to
1.0, incrementing by 0.025 after each calculation.
The result is scaled by 100 before it is
displayed in the graph.</P>

<SCRIPT LANGUAGE="JavaScript">
<!-- HIDE FROM OLD BROWSERS
var axis = Math.floor(Math.sin(1.0) * 100)
var mStr  = ""

mStr += "<TABLE COLS=80 WIDTH='100%' BORDER=0"
mStr += "CELLSPACING=0 CELLPADDING=0>"
mStr += "<TR>"

for (var i = -1.0; i < 0.0; i+=0.025) {
  var barHeight = Math.sin(i) * 100

  mStr += "<TD VALIGN=top>"
  mStr += "<TABLE ROWS=2 BORDER=0 CELLSPACING=0"
```

```
    mStr += "CELLPADDING=0><TR><TD>"
    mStr += "<IMG WIDTH=4 HEIGHT=" + axis + " "
    mStr += "SRC=../../icons/white_dot.gif>"
    mStr += "</TD></TR><TR><TD><IMG WIDTH=4 HEIGHT="
    mStr += Math.floor(Math.abs(barHeight))
    mStr += " SRC=../../icons/black_dot.gif>"
    mStr += "</TD></TR></TABLE></TD>"
  }

  for (var i = 0.0; i <= 1.0; i+=0.025) {
    var barHeight = Math.sin(i) * 100

    mStr += "<TD VALIGN=bottom>"
    mStr += "<TABLE ROWS=2 BORDER=0 CELLSPACING=0"
    mStr += "CELLPADDING=0><TR><TD>"
    mStr += "<IMG WIDTH=4 HEIGHT="
    mStr += Math.floor(barHeight) + " SRC="
    mStr += "../../icons/black_dot.gif>"
    mStr += "</TD></TR><TR><TD><IMG WIDTH=4 HEIGHT="
    mStr += axis + " SRC=../../icons/white_dot.gif>"
    mStr += "</TD></TR></TABLE></TD>"
  }
  mStr += "</TR>"
  mStr += "</TABLE>"

  document.open()
  document.write(mStr)
  document.close()

  // STOP HIDING -->
  </SCRIPT>

  </BODY>
  </HTML>
```

Figure 31–14 shows the result of loading the `mathSin.html` script.

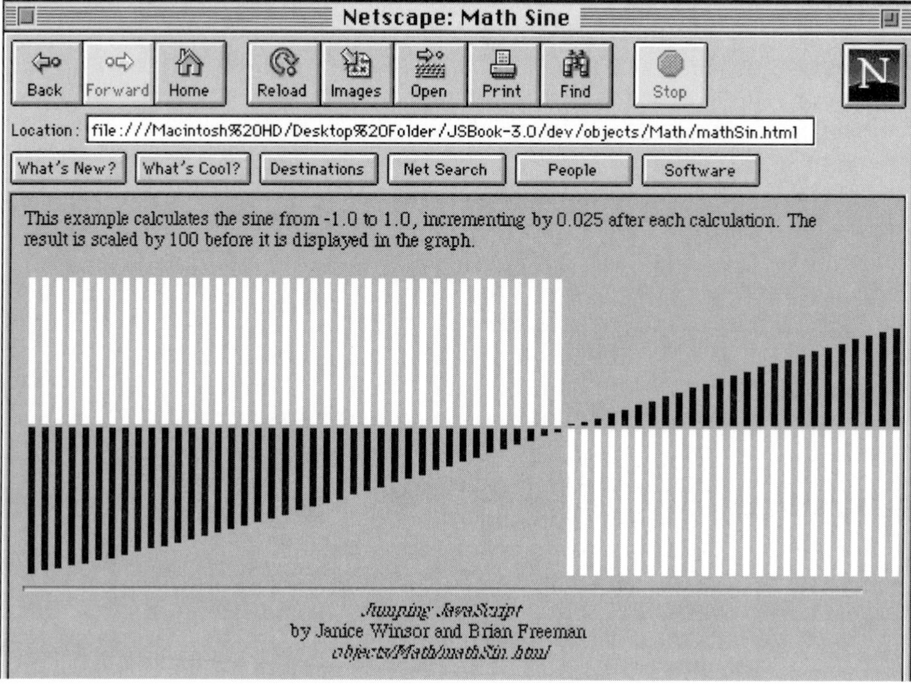

Figure 31–14 Result of loading the `mathSin.html` script

Calculating the Tangent

The `tan()` method returns the tangent of the value in radians.

Method

tan(*x*)

Returns

Tangent of *x* in radians

The following `mathTan.html` script calculates the tangent from 0.0 to PI/2 and displays the results as a graph.

```
<!--
                    mathTan.html
-->

<HTML>
<HEAD>
<TITLE>Math Tangent</TITLE>
</HEAD>
<BODY>

<P>This example calculates the tangent from 0.0
to PI/2, incrementing by 0.025 after each
calculation. The result is scaled by 10 before
it is displayed in the graph.</P>

<SCRIPT LANGUAGE="JavaScript">
<!-- HIDE FROM OLD BROWSERS
var mStr = ""

mStr += "<TABLE COLS=63 WIDTH='100%' BORDER=0"
mStr += "CELLSPACING=0 CELLPADDING=0>"
mStr += "<TR>"

for (var i = 0.0; i < (Math.PI/2); i += 0.025) {
  var barHeight = Math.tan(i) * 10

  mStr += "<TD VALIGN=bottom>"
  mStr += "<IMG WIDTH=2 HEIGHT="
  mStr += Math.floor(barHeight) + " SRC="
  mStr += "../../icons/blue_dot.gif>"
  mStr += "</TD>"
}
mStr += "</TR>"
mStr += "</TABLE>"

document.open()
document.write(mStr)
document.close()

// STOP HIDING -->
</SCRIPT>

</BODY>
</HTML>
```

Figure 31–15 shows the result of loading the `mathTan.html` script.

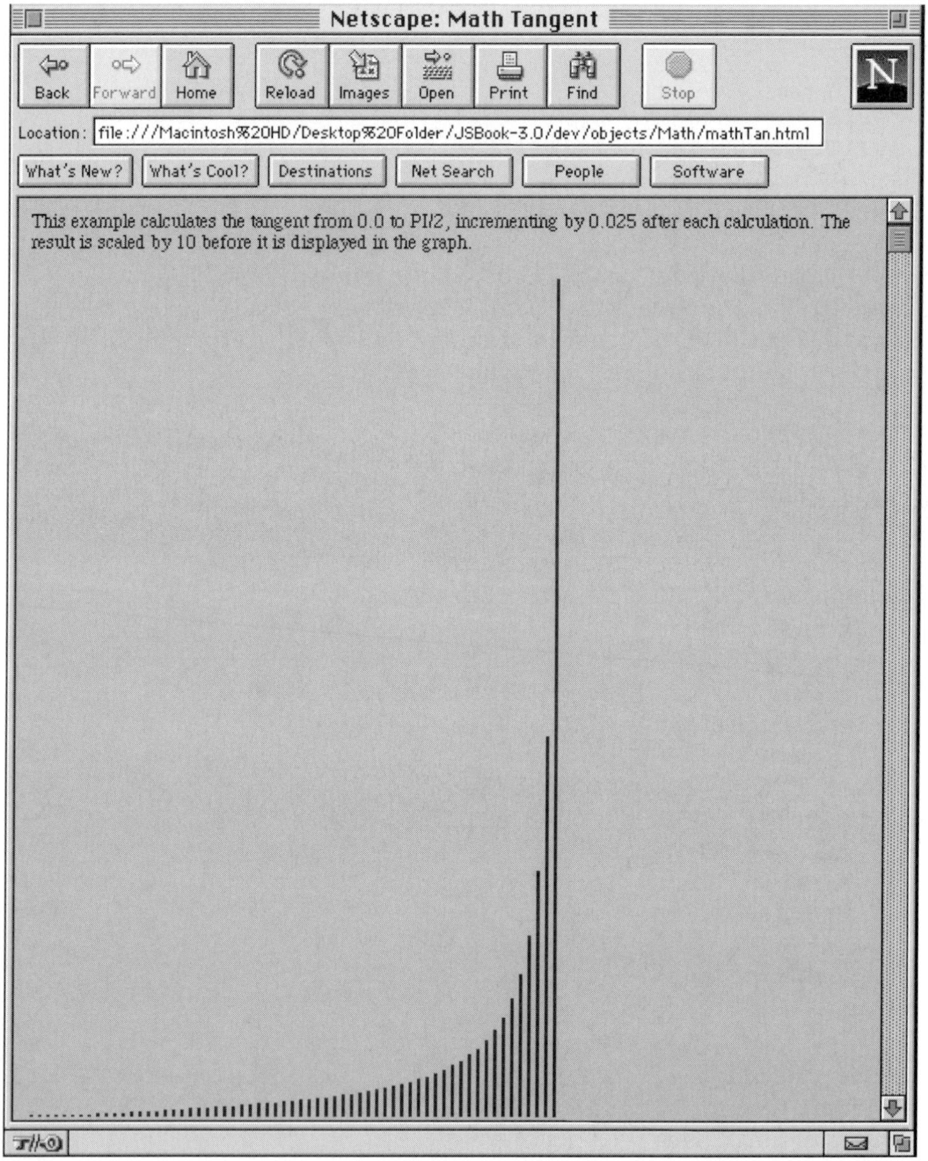

Figure 31–15 Result of loading the `mathTan.html` script

Changing the Power of a Number

The `pow()` method raises the first argument to the power of its second argument and returns the result.

Method

pow(*x*,*y*)

Returns

x to the *y* power

Example of Changing the Power of a Number

The following `mathPow.html` script uses the `pow()` method to raise the numbers from 0 through 25 to the power of 2 and displays the results as a graph.

```
<!--
                    mathPow.html
-->

<HTML>
<HEAD>
<TITLE>Math pow()</TITLE>
</HEAD>
<BODY>

<P>This example raises the numbers from 0
through 25 to the power of 2 with Math.pow().
</P>

<SCRIPT LANGUAGE="JavaScript">
<!-- HIDE FROM OLD BROWSERS
var mStr = ""

mStr += "<TABLE COLS=25 WIDTH='100%' BORDER=0"
mStr += "CELLSPACING=0 CELLPADDING=0>"
mStr += "<TR>"

for (var i = 0; i <= 25; i++) {
  var barHeight = Math.pow(i, 2)

  mStr += "<TD VALIGN=bottom>"
  mStr += "<IMG WIDTH=10 HEIGHT="
```

```
    mStr += barHeight + " SRC="
    mStr += "../../icons/pink_dot.gif>"
    mStr += "</TD>"
  }
  mStr += "</TR>"
  mStr += "</TABLE>"

  document.open()
  document.write(mStr)
  document.close()

  // STOP HIDING -->
  </SCRIPT>

  </BODY>
  </HTML>
```

Figure 31–16 shows the result of loading the `mathPow.html` script.

Netscape: Math pow()

Back Forward Home Reload Images Open Print Find Stop

Location: file:///Macintosh%20HD/Desktop%20Folder/JSBook-3.0/dev/objects/Math/mathPow.html

What's New? What's Cool? Destinations Net Search People Software

This example raises the numbers from 0 through 25 to the power of 2 with Math.pow().

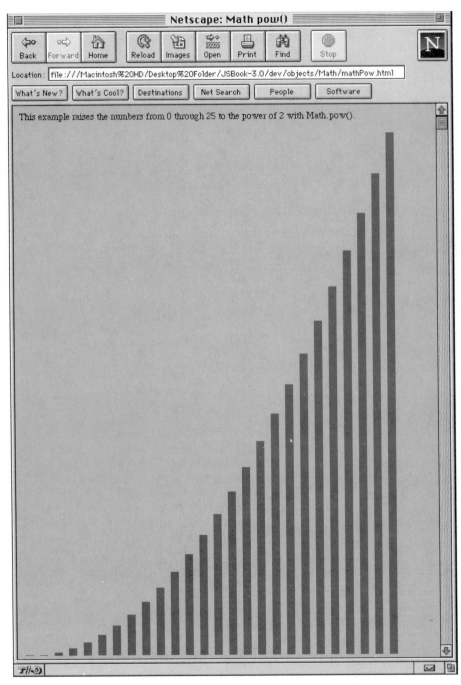

Figure 31–16 Result of loading the `mathPow.html` script

Calculating Natural Logarithms

The `log()` method returns the natural logarithm of a number.

Method

log(*x*)

Returns

Natural logarithm (base e) of *x* where *x* is ≥ 0

Example of Calculating Natural Logarithms

The following `mathLog.html` script calculates the natural logarithm from 0 to 100 and displays the results as a graph.

```
<!--
                   mathLog.html
-->

<HTML>
<HEAD>
<TITLE>Math Natural Logarithm</TITLE>
</HEAD>
<BODY>

<P>This example calculates the natural logarithm
from 0 to 100, incrementing by 1 after each
calculation. The result is scaled by 10 before
it is displayed in the graph.</P>

<SCRIPT LANGUAGE="JavaScript">
<!-- HIDE FROM OLD BROWSERS
var mStr = ""

mStr += "<TABLE COLS=100 WIDTH='100%' BORDER=0"
mStr += "CELLSPACING=0 CELLPADDING=0>"
mStr += "<TR>"

for (var i = 0; i <= 100; i++) {
  var barHeight = Math.log(i) * 10

  mStr += "<TD VALIGN=bottom>"
  mStr += "<IMG WIDTH=4 HEIGHT="
```

```
    mStr += Math.floor(barHeight) + " SRC="
    mStr += "../../icons/purple_dot.gif>"
    mStr += "</TD>"
  }
  mStr += "</TR>"
  mStr += "</TABLE>"

  document.open()
  document.write(mStr)
  document.close()

  // STOP HIDING -->
  </SCRIPT>

  </BODY>
  </HTML>
```

Figure 31–17 shows the result of loading the `mathLog.html` script.

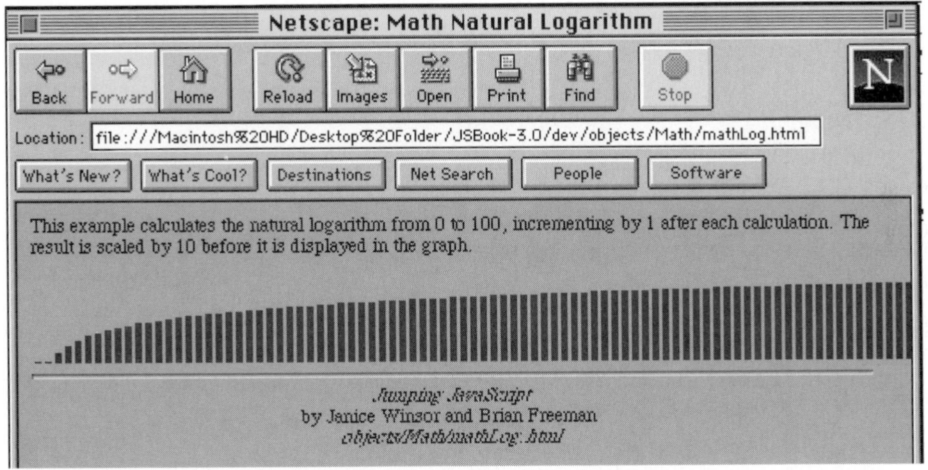

Figure 31–17 Result of loading the `mathLog.html` script

Computing E^x

The `exp()` method raises e, Euler's constant and the base of the natural logarithms, to the power of *x*. The natural log value is approximately 2.71828.

Method

exp(*x*)

Returns

Euler's constant to the power of *x*

Example of Computing E^x

The following `mathExp.html` script calculates the exponential function from 0.0 to 1 and displays the results as a graph.

```
<!--
                    mathExp.html
-->

<HTML>
<HEAD>
<TITLE>Math Exponential Function</TITLE>
</HEAD>
<BODY>

<P>This example calculates the exponential function
from 0.0 to 1, incrementing by 0.01 after each
calculation. The result is scaled by 100 before
it is displayed.</P>

<SCRIPT LANGUAGE="JavaScript">
<!-- HIDE FROM OLD BROWSERS
var mStr = ""

mStr += "<TABLE COLS=100 WIDTH='100%' BORDER=0"
mStr += "CELLSPACING=0 CELLPADDING=0>"
mStr += "<TR>"

for (var i = 0.0; i < 1; i += 0.01) {
  var barHeight = Math.exp(i) * 100
```

```
    mStr += "<TD VALIGN=bottom>"
    mStr += "<IMG WIDTH=4 HEIGHT="
    mStr += barHeight + " SRC="
    mStr += "../../icons/yellow_dot.gif>"
    mStr += "</TD>"
  }
  mStr += "</TR>"
  mStr += "</TABLE>"

  document.open()
  document.write(mStr)
  document.close()

  // STOP HIDING -->
  </SCRIPT>

  </BODY>
  </HTML>
```

Figure 31–18 shows the result of loading the `mathExp.html` script.

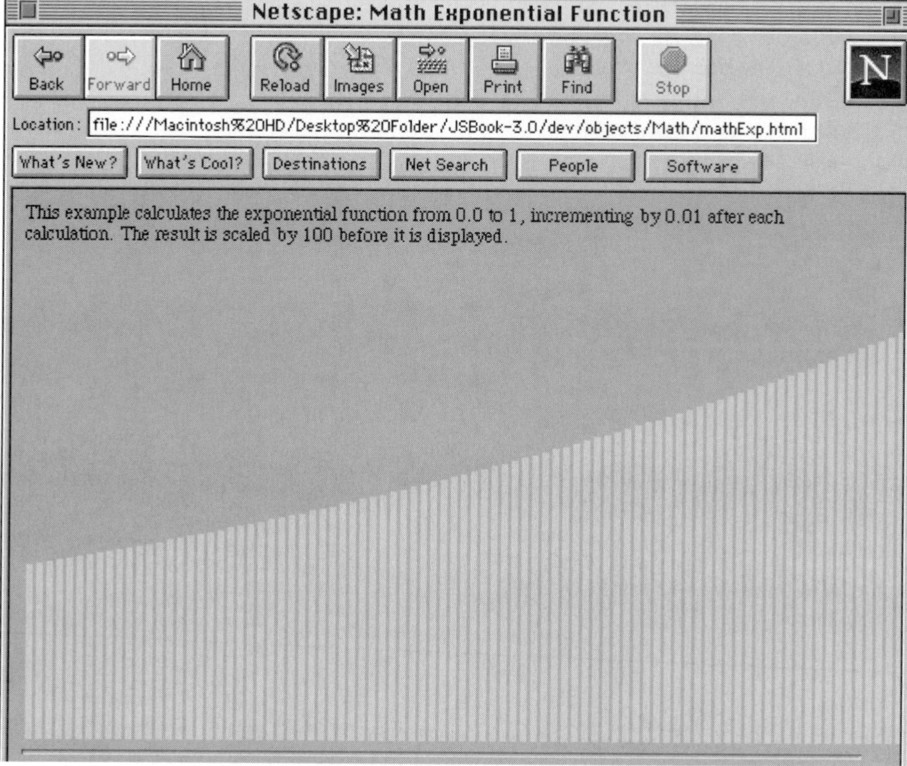

Figure 31–18 Result of loading the `mathExp.html` script

Summary of New Terms and Concepts

The new terms and concepts introduced in this chapter are listed in alphabetical order in Table 31-2. The terms and concepts are also included in the glossary at the end of the book.

Table 31-2 Summary of New Terms and Concepts

Term/Concept	Description
absolute value	The value of a number without its sign. For example, the absolute value of both -47 and +47 is simply 47.
radian	A unit of plane angular measurement that is equal to the angle at the center of a circle subtended by an arc equal in length to the radius. All trigonometric methods of the `Math` object take arguments in radians.

935

CHAPTER 32

- Displaying navigator Properties
- Identifying the Browser Software
- Identifying the Platform and Version of the Browser
- Identifying the HTTP User-Agent Value
- Testing Whether Java Is Enabled
- Testing Whether Data Tainting Is Enabled
- The plugin and mimeType Properties

Using the navigator Object

The `navigator` object contains properties and methods that describe the browser that is used as part of browsers published by Netscape. Other browsers may not be able to use information returned by the `navigator` object, although Microsoft Internet Explorer does support this object.

You can use the properties of the `navigator` object to perform platform-specific customization such as checking Navigator version and platform the user of your script is running. You can also test to see if the browser is Java enabled, if data tainting is enabled, and determine which MIME types are available to the browser on the client computer.

The properties and methods for the `navigator` object are listed in alphabetical order in Table 32-1. The `navigator` object has no event handlers.

Table 32-1 Properties and Methods for the navigator Object

Properties	Methods	Event Handlers
appCodeName	eval()*	None
appName	javaEnabled()	
appVersion	taintEnabled()*	

Table 32-1 Properties and Methods for the navigator Object (Continued)

Properties	Methods	Event Handlers
`mimeTypes[]*`	`toString()*`	
`plugins[]*`	`valueOf()*`	
`userAgent`		

* New in Navigator 3.0 release.

Displaying navigator Properties

The properties of the `navigator` object display information about the browser that is running a script on the user's computer.

Property	Value	Gettable	Settable
appCodeName	string	Yes	No
appName	string	Yes	No
appVersion	string	Yes	No
mimeTypes*	array	Yes	No
plugins*	array	Yes	No
userAgent	string	Yes	No

* New in Navigator 3.0.

The `appCodeName` property returns the internal code name of the browser. The `appName` property returns the official name of the browser. The `appVersion` property returns information about the platform of the browser and the country for which the browser is released. The `userAgent` property returns the string the browser passes to the server in the user-agent HTTP header. The `mimeTypes` and `plugins` properties return arrays of the MIME types and plug-ins available to the browser.

The following `navigator.html` displays the properties for the `navigator` object.

```
<!--
         navigator.html
-->

<HTML>
<HEAD>
<TITLE>Navigator</TITLE>
</HEAD>
<BODY>

<P>The navigator object contains properties and
methods that describe the Web browser in
use. When queried, these properties and methods
can be used to perform platform-specific
customizations in your code.</P>

<P>The properties and their values for the browser
you are using are:</P>

<SCRIPT LANGUAGE="JavaScript">
<!-- HIDE FROM OLD BROWSERS
var mstr = "<DL>"

for (var i in navigator) {
  mstr += "<DT>"
  mstr += "navigator." + i
  mstr += " = " + navigator[i]
  mstr += "</DT>"
}
mstr += "</DL>"

document.open()
document.write(unescape(mstr))
document.close()

// STOP HIDING -->
</SCRIPT>

</BODY>
</HTML>
```

Figure 32–1 shows the result of loading the `navigator.html` script on a Macintosh computer.

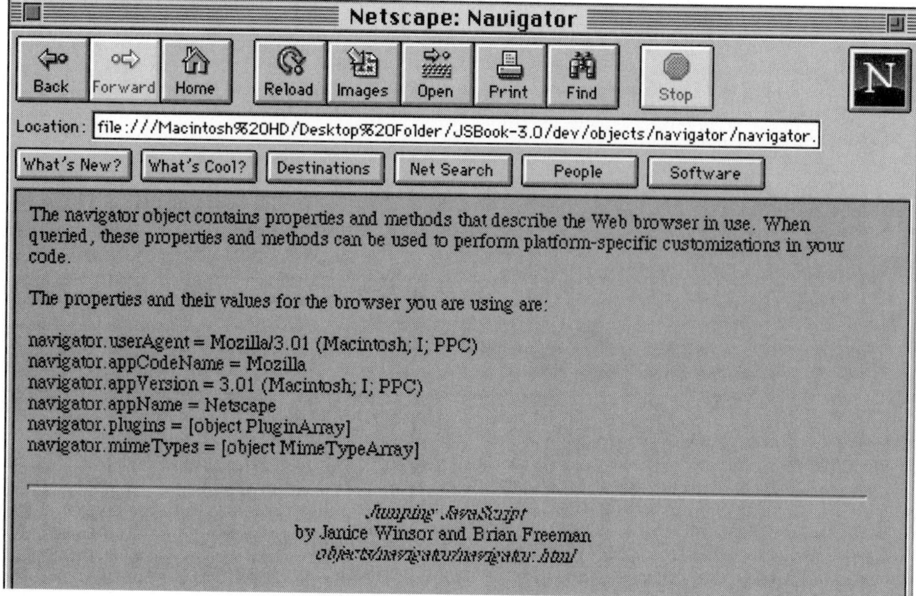

Figure 32–1 Result of loading the `navigator.html` script on a Macintosh computer

Identifying the Browser Software

You can use the `appName` and `appCodeName` properties to identify the browser software that is available to the user. These properties return the string specified in the browser.

The `appName` property returns the string `Netscape` for Navigator releases. The property returns the string `Microsoft Internet Explorer` for Microsoft Internet Explorer 3.0.

The `appCodeName` property returns the string `Mozilla` for Navigator releases. The property also returns the string `Mozilla` for Microsoft Internet Explorer 3.0.

The `appVersion` property described in "Identifying the Platform and Version of the Browser" on page 944, identifies the browser software version and the platform that is available to the user.

Example of Identifying the Browser Software by Name

The following `navigatorAppName.html` script tests to see if the script is loaded on Microsoft Internet Explorer. If so, it displays a message; if not, it displays the properties for Netscape Navigator.

```
<!--
              navigatorAppName.html
-->

<HTML>
<HEAD>
<TITLE>Navigator appName</TITLE>
</HEAD>
<BODY>

<P>If you've tried <A HREF="navigator.html">
navigator.html</A> on Internet Explorer, you
would have noticed that none of the properties
printed out. To correct that, we can use the
appName property to make the code more specific
to Netscape Navigator.</P>

<P>The value of navigator.appName for this
browser is:
<SCRIPT LANGUAGE="JavaScript">
<!-- HIDE FROM OLD BROWSERS

document.open()
document.write( " " + navigator.appName + ".")
document.close()

// STOP HIDING -->
</SCRIPT>

<P>The properties and their values for the browser
you are using are:</P>

<SCRIPT LANGUAGE="JavaScript">
<!-- HIDE FROM OLD BROWSERS
var mstr = ""

if (navigator.appName ==
    "Microsoft Internet Explorer") {
  mstr += "Microsoft Internet Explorer doesn't "
  mstr += "like the other code for some reason."
} else {
  mstr = "<DL>"
  for (var i in navigator) {
    mstr += "<DT>"
```

```
        mstr += "navigator." + i
        mstr += " = " + navigator[i]
        mstr += "</DT>"
      }
    mstr += "</DL>"
  }
document.open()
document.write(unescape(mstr))
document.close()

// STOP HIDING -->
</SCRIPT>

</BODY>
</HTML>
```

Figure 32–2 shows the result of loading the `navigatorAppName.html` script.

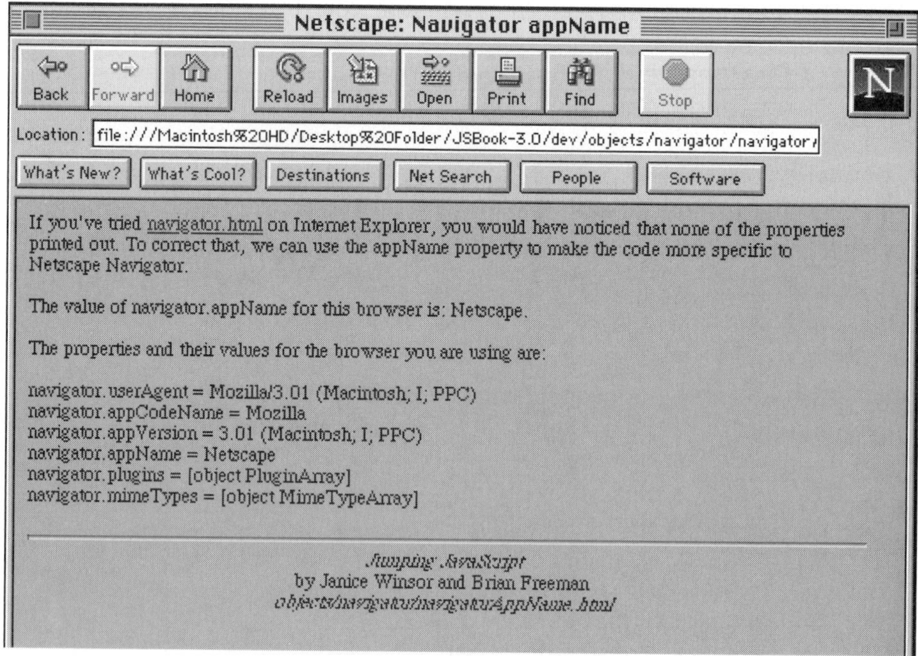

Figure 32–2 Result of loading the `navigatorAppName.html` script

Example of Identifying the Browser Software by Code Name

The following `navigatorAppCodeName.html` script tests to see if the `appCodeName` property returns a value of `Mozilla`. If so, one message is displayed; if not, another message is displayed.

```
<!--
            navigatorAppCodeName.html

    This example tests the navigator object's
    appCodeName property to determine if the user
    is running Mozilla. If so, a different
    message is displayed.
-->

<HTML>
<HEAD>
<TITLE>Navigator appCodeName</TITLE>
</HEAD>
<BODY>

<SCRIPT LANGUAGE="JavaScript">
<!-- HIDE FROM OLD BROWSERS
var mstr = ""

if (navigator.appCodeName == "Mozilla") {
  // Mozilla specific code.
  mstr += "<P>You're using Mozilla. "
  mstr += "So, you're running either Navigator "
  mstr += "or Internet Explorer.</P>"
} else {
  // non Navigator code
  mstr += "<P>You are using " +
    navigator.appCodeName + ".</P>"
}
document.open()
document.write(mstr)
document.close()

// STOP HIDING -->
</SCRIPT>

</BODY>
</HTML>
```

Figure 32–3 shows the result of loading the `navigatorAppCodeName.html` script.

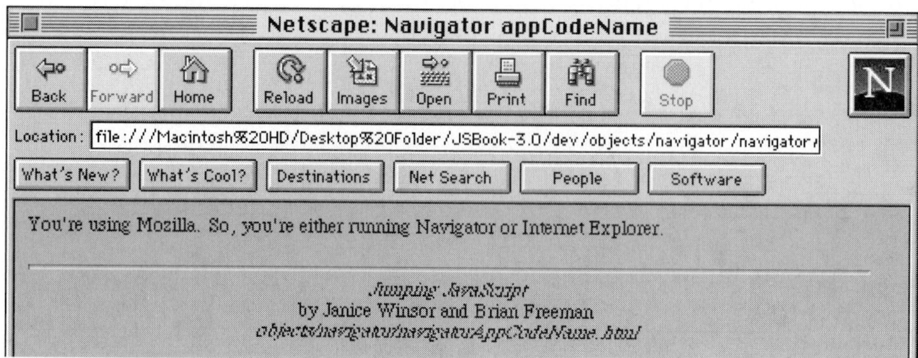

Figure 32–3 Result of loading the `navigatorAppCodeName.html` script

Identifying the Platform and Version of the Browser

With the `appVersion` property, you can determine what platform and version of the browser are available to the user. With these properties you can test for conditions and perform different scripting actions depending on which platform and which version of the browser are available.

For Navigator 2.0 and 3.0 releases, the property uses the following format:

```
version (platform; encryption[; detail])
```

Version numbers indicate the version number of the release, for example, `2.0` and `3.01`.

The *`platform`* is an abbreviation for the platform. Table 32-2 lists some of the possible values.

Table 32-2 Values for platform

Value	Description
`Win16`	16-bit version of Windows
`Win95`	Windows 95
`X11`	UNIX platform running the X Window System
`Macintosh`	Macintosh platform

The encryption is either `U` for a domestic U.S. release of Navigator with strong encryption or `I` for an international release with weaker encryption capabilities, which complies with U.S. government export control laws on cryptographic technologies.

`detail` may provide additional information about the platform; for example, a Macintosh Power PC platform returns the additional detail `PPC`.

Example of Identifying the Platform and Version of the Browser

The following `navigatorAppVersion.html` script shows how you can test for the version of the browser and perform a scripting action based on the value that is returned.

```
<!--
            navigatorAppVersion.html
-->
<HTML>
<HEAD>
<TITLE>Navigator appVersion</TITLE>
<SCRIPT LANGUAGE="JavaScript">
<!-- HIDE FROM OLD BROWSERS

//  windowOpen() is a workaround for the window
//  object's open() bug. On the Mac and X11
//  platforms, Navigator 2.0 requires a second
//  open() call to actually create the window.
//
//  The workaround checks to see which browser
//  you are on and issues the second open() call
//  if necessary.
//
function windowOpen(url, name, wopts) {
  var newWin = window.open(url, name, wopts)

  if (navigator.appVersion.indexOf("2.0")  != -1
   || navigator.appVersion.indexOf("(X11") != -1
   || navigator.appVersion.indexOf("(Mac") != -1)
  {
    newWin = window.open(url, name, wopts)
  }
  return newWin
}

// STOP HIDING -->
```

```
</SCRIPT>
</HEAD>
<BODY>

<P>navigator.appVersion is a read-only property
that specifies the version information for the
browser. For this browser, appVersion is:

<SCRIPT LANGUAGE="JavaScript">
<!-- HIDE FROM OLD BROWSERS

document.open()
document.write(" " + navigator.appVersion + ".")
document.close()

// STOP HIDING -->
</SCRIPT>
</P>

<P>Use it to test for and direct version-specific
code. This example provides a workaround for the
Navigator 2.0 window open bug.<P>

<FORM>
<INPUT TYPE="button" VALUE="Open a Window"
onClick="windowOpen('index.html', '', '')">
</FORM>

</BODY>
</HTML>
```

Figure 32–4 shows the result of loading the `navigatorAppVersion.html` script.

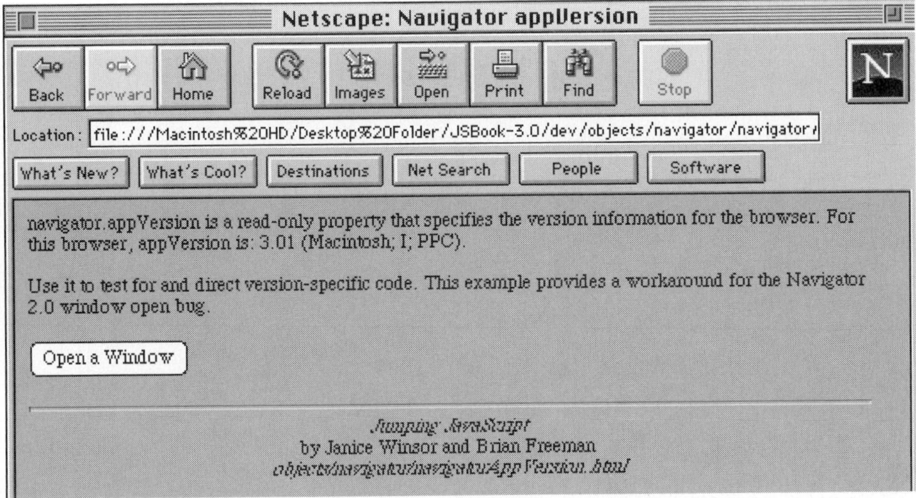

Figure 32–4 Result of loading the `navigatorAppVersion.html` script

When you click on the Open a Window button, a window is opened. If you are running the script on Navigator 2.0, the workaround is used to call the `window.open()` method a second time. The window that is opened displays information about the `navigator` object, as shown in Figure 32–5.

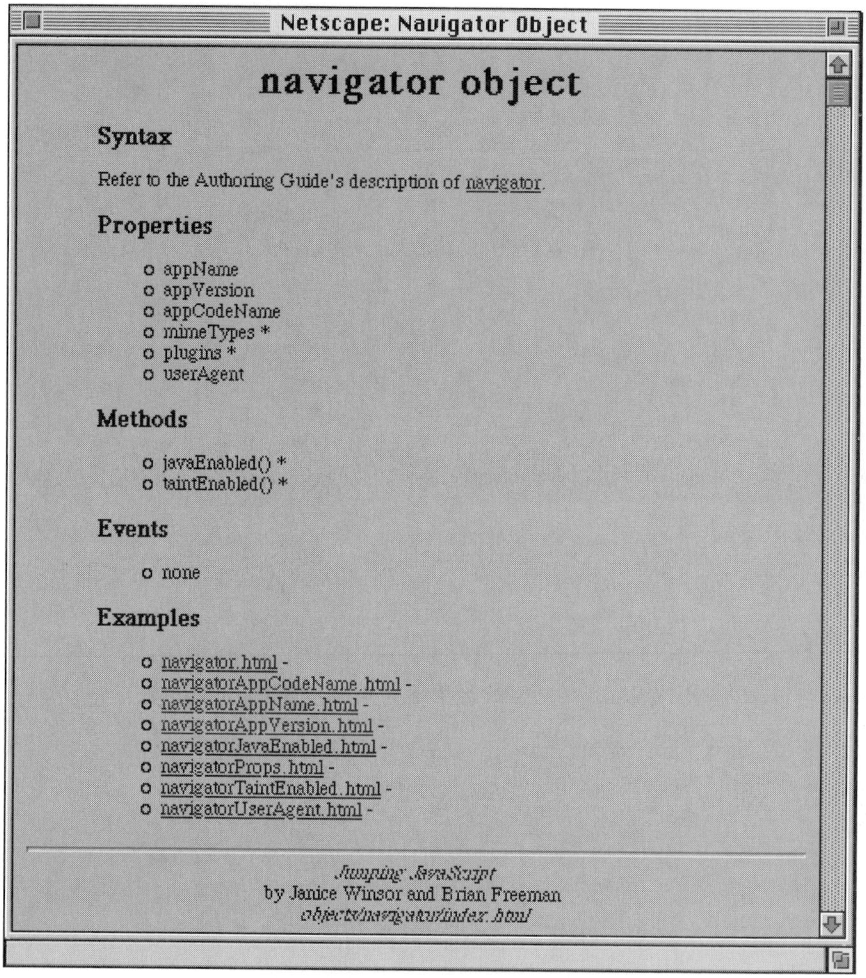

Netscape: Navigator Object

navigator object

Syntax

Refer to the Authoring Guide's description of navigator.

Properties

- appName
- appVersion
- appCodeName
- mimeTypes *
- plugins *
- userAgent

Methods

- javaEnabled() *
- taintEnabled() *

Events

- none

Examples

- navigator.html -
- navigatorAppCodeName.html -
- navigatorAppName.html -
- navigatorAppVersion.html -
- navigatorJavaEnabled.html -
- navigatorProps.html -
- navigatorTaintEnabled.html -
- navigatorUserAgent.html -

Jumping JavaScript
by Janice Winsor and Brian Freeman
objects/navigator/index.html

Figure 32–5 Window with information about the `navigator` object

Identifying the HTTP User-Agent Value

You can use the `userAgent` property to examine the read-only string that the browser uses to identify the user-agent header in HTTP requests. The `userAgent` property combines the value of `appCodeName` property, a slash (`/`), and the value of the `appVersion` property:

```
appCodeName/version (platform; encryption[; detail])
```

Here are some examples:

```
Mozilla/3.01 (Macintosh; I; PPC)
Mozilla/3.01Gold (Win95; I)
Mozilla/2.02 (X11; I; SunOS 5.5 sun4m)
```

You can use the `indexOf()` method of the `String` object to extract information from the `userAgent` property value.

Example of Identifying the HTTP User Agent Value

The following `navigatorUserAgent.html` script displays the `userAgent` value for the current browser and provides two links to additional information about browsers and user agents.

```
<!--
             navigatorUserAgent.html
-->
<HTML>
<HEAD>
<TITLE>Navigator userAgent</TITLE>
</HEAD>
<BODY>

<P>navigator.userAgent is a read-only string that
contains the complete HTTP user-agent header for
the browser. For Netscape Navigator 2.0 and 3.0,
this property is the value of appCodeName followed
by a slash and then the value of appVersion.</P>

<P>The value for the browser you are using is:

<SCRIPT LANGUAGE="JavaScript">
<!-- HIDE FROM OLD BROWSERS

document.open()
document.write(" " + navigator.userAgent + ".")
document.close()

// STOP HIDING -->
</SCRIPT>

<P><A HREF="http://browserwatch.iworld.com/">
BrowserWatch</A> contains an extensive list of
all the different browsers. Check out the <A
HREF="http://browserwatch.iworld.com/stats.html">
```

```
stats</A> pages where the browsers are sorted by
user agent.</P>

</BODY>
</HTML>
```

Figure 32–6 shows the result of loading the `navigatorUserAgent.html` script.

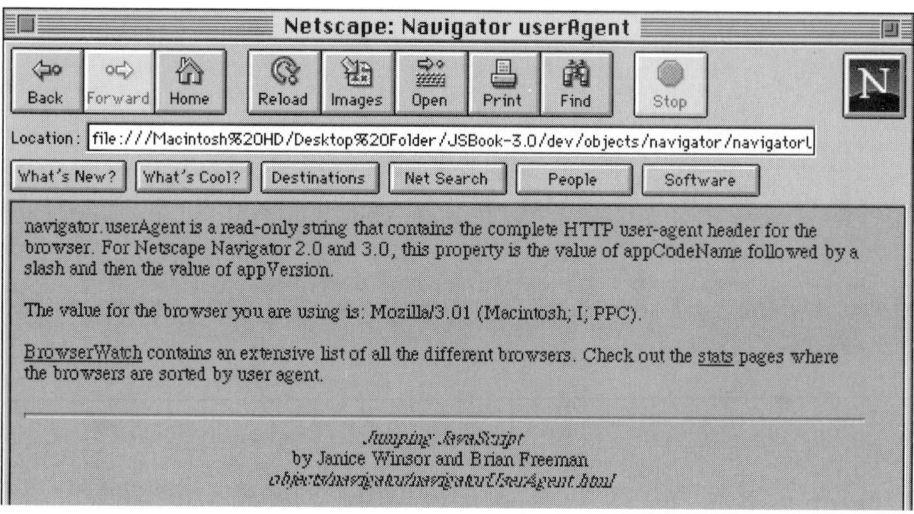

Figure 32–6 Result of loading the `navigatorUserAgent.html` script

Testing Whether Java Is Enabled

The Navigator 3.0 release provides a `navigator.javaEnabled()` method that you can use to determine whether the current browser supports and has Java enabled. A Java-enabled browser can display and run Java applets. When Java is not available, you can use the JavaScript language to provide an alternative action. Netscape ships Navigator releases with Java enabled; however, users can easily disable Java.

Method

javaEnabled()

Returns

Boolean (true or false)

Example of Testing Whether Java Is Enabled

The following `navigatorJavaEnabled.html` script provides a button that you can use to test whether Java is supported and enabled on the current browser.

```
<!--
            navigatorJavaEnabled.html
-->
<HTML>
<HEAD>
<TITLE>Navigator javaEnabled</TITLE>
<SCRIPT LANGUAGE="JavaScript">
<!-- HIDE FROM OLD BROWSERS

// Test if Java is enabled.
function isJavaEnabled() {

  if (navigator.javaEnabled()) {
    alert("Yes")
  } else {
    alert("No")
  }
}

// STOP HIDING -->
</SCRIPT>
</HEAD>
<BODY>

<P>navigator.javaEnabled() tests to see if Java
is supported and enabled in the current browser.
To test it now, click on the Is Java Enabled button.</P>

<FORM>
<INPUT TYPE="button" VALUE="Is Java Enabled"
onClick="isJavaEnabled()">
</FORM>

</BODY>
</HTML>
```

Figure 32–7 shows the result of loading the `navigatorJavaEnabled.html` script.

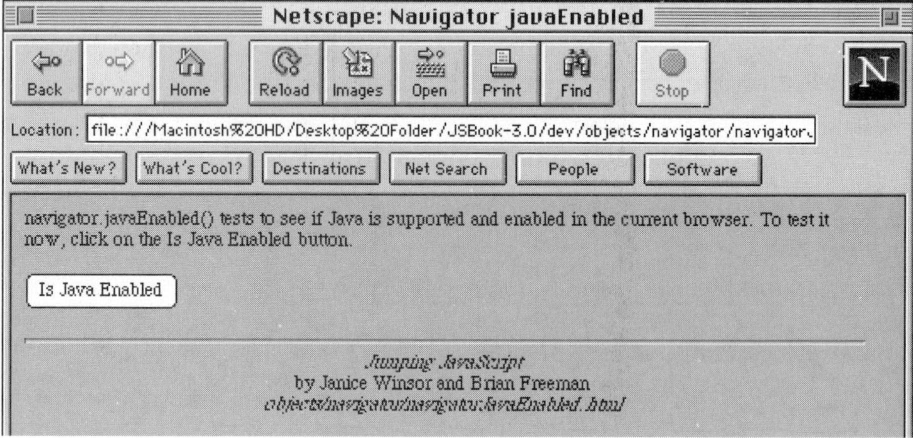

Figure 32–7 Result of loading the `navigatorJavaEnabled.html` script

When you click on the Is Java Enabled button, an alert is displayed. In the example shown in Figure 32–8, Java is enabled.

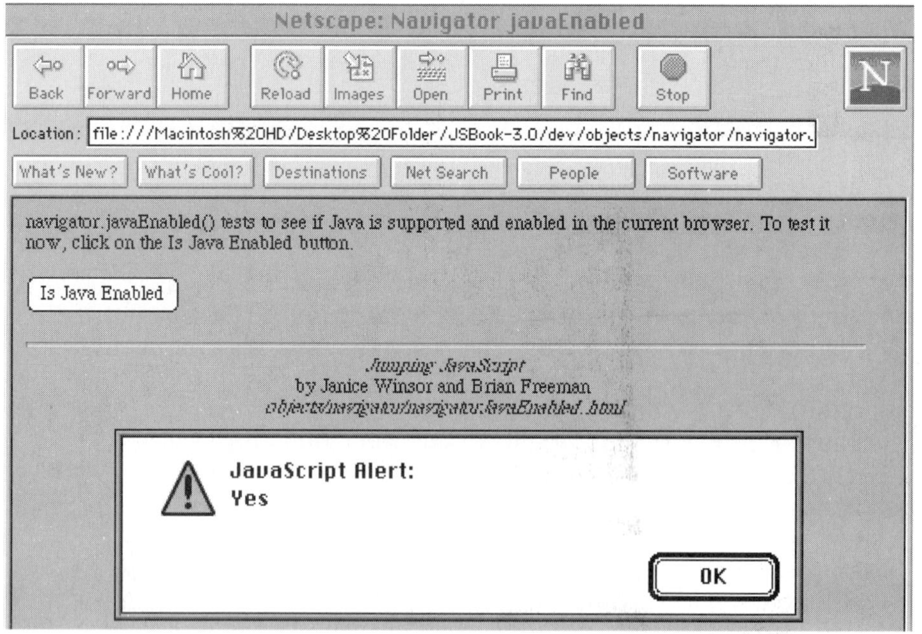

Figure 32–8 Java enabled alert

Testing Whether Data Tainting Is Enabled

The Navigator 3.0 release provides a `navigator.taintEnabled()` method that you can use to determine whether the current browser suports and has enabled data tainting. Data tainting is a security model that is available with Navigator 3.0 and later releases. When data tainting is not enabled, some property values cannot be returned. When data tainting is enabled, your script is restricted on the kinds of data it can send to a server when submitting a form. For more information on data tainting, see Chapter 36, "Controlling Data Tainting."

Method

taintEnabled()

Returns

Boolean (true or false)

Example of Testing Whether Data Tainting Is Enabled

The following `navigatorTaintEnabled.html` script provides a button that you can use to test whether data tainting is enabled on the current browser.

```
<!--
           navigatorTaintEnabled.html
-->
<HTML>
<HEAD>
<TITLE>Navigator taintEnabled</TITLE>
<SCRIPT LANGUAGE="JavaScript">
<!-- HIDE FROM OLD BROWSERS

// Test if data tainting is enabled.
function isTaintEnabled() {

  if (navigator.taintEnabled()) {
    alert("Yes")
  } else {
    alert("No")
  }
}

// STOP HIDING -->
</SCRIPT>
```

```
</HEAD>
<BODY>

<P>navigator.taintEnabled() tests to see if data
tainting is supported and enabled in the current
browser.  To test it now, click on the Is Taint
Enabled button.</P>

<FORM>
<INPUT TYPE="button" VALUE="Is Taint Enabled"
onClick="isTaintEnabled()">
</FORM>

</BODY>
</HTML>
```

Figure 32–9 shows the result of loading the `navigatorTaintEnabled.html` script.

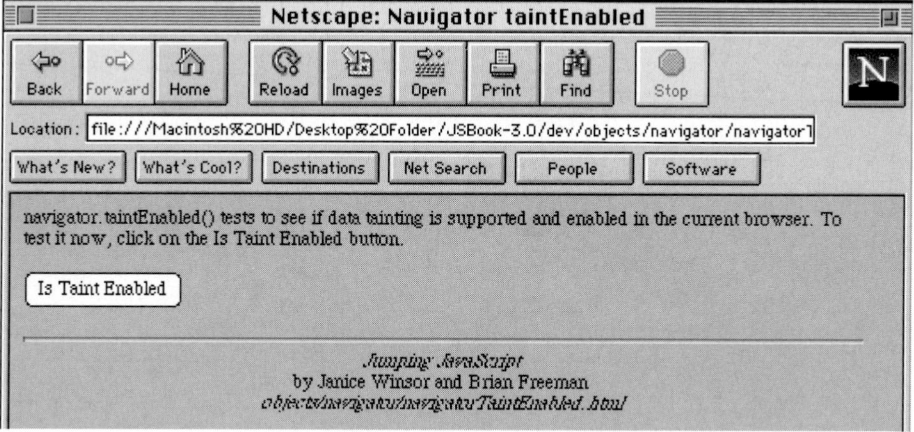

Figure 32–9 Result of loading the `navigatorTaintEnabled.html` script

When you click on the Is Taint Enabled button, an alert is displayed. In the example shown in Figure 32–10, data tainting is enabled.

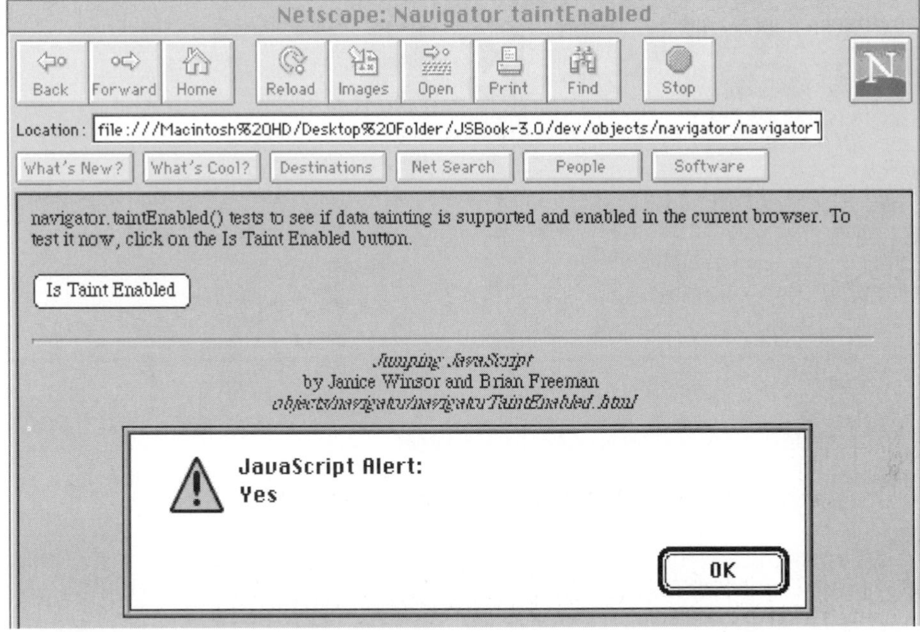

Figure 32–10 Data tainting enabled alert

The plugin and mimeType Properties

The `plugin` and `mimeType` objects that are properties of the `navigator` object are discussed in separate chapters. For information about the plugin object, see Chapter 11, "Using the plugin Object." For information about the `mimeType` object, see Chapter 33, "Specifying MIME Types."

CHAPTER 33

- The mimeType Object
- Accessing a Description of a MIME Type
- Determining the Plug-in That Handles the MIME Type
- Determining the Type of a MIME Type
- Determining MIME Type Suffixes
- Summary of New Terms and Concepts

Specifying MIME Types

The Navigator 3.0 release provides a `mimeType` object. MIME stands for multipurpose Internet mail extension. It was designed as a way to send attachments to e-mail messages on the Internet. MIME types are a string that represents the type or format of data you have. The string uses the format:

NEW IN 3.0

```
type/subtype
```

For example, if you have a MIME type of `application/pdf`, then you know that the file is a PDF (PostScript Display Format) document. Within the MIME type string, you can use asterisks (`*`) to represent wildcard characters. A MIME type of `*/*` means that all types and subtypes are supported. A MIME type of `text/*` means a text type that supports all subtypes. A MIME type of `text/html` means an HTML file.

Some of the available MIME types are:

- application
- text
- image
- audio
- message
- multipart
- video

For a list of MIME types and subtypes, see Appendix C, "JavaScript Quick Reference."

The mimeType Object

The `mimeType` object has four properties, no methods, and no event handlers. Table 33-1 lists the properties for the `mimeType` object in alphabetical order.

Table 33-1 **Properties for the mimeType Object**

Properties	Methods	Event Handlers
`description`	`eval()*`	None
`enabledPlugin`	`toString()*`	
`type`	`valueOf()*`	
`suffixes`		

* New in Navigator 3.0.

When a server sends information to a browser, it usually sends a header that contains the MIME type as part of its description of the document. If a file does not specify the MIME type, the browser uses the `text/plain` MIME type as the default.

When a file is loaded from the `file:` protocol, the browser looks at the *extension* of the file name to determine the type of the file. A file extension is the period and set of characters at the end of the file name. For example, `.rtf`, `.pdf`, and `.jpeg` are extensions that specify rich text format, PostScript display format, and JPEG file types, respectively.

With the `mimeType` object, you can determine whether the browser on the client computer has a particular MIME type available to it and whether the corresponding plug-in is installed and enabled. Because MIME types and plug-ins are closely related, you usually use the `mimeType` and `plugin` objects together in the same script. For more information about the `plugin` object, see Chapter 11, "Using the plugin Object."

The following `mimeType.html` script shows how to access MIME types by accessing the `navigator.mimeTypes[]` array.

```
<!--
                 mimeType.html
-->

<HTML>
<HEAD>
<TITLE>MimeType</TITLE>

<!-- Includes -->
<SCRIPT SRC="../../debug/documentUtils.js"></SCRIPT>
<SCRIPT SRC="../../debug/windowOpen.js"></SCRIPT>
<SCRIPT SRC="../../debug/generateWindow.js"></SCRIPT>

<!-- local functions -->
<SCRIPT LANGUAGE="JavaScript">
<!-- HIDE FROM OLD BROWSERS

// Display the properties of the mimeType objects.
//
// Description:
//   A function suitable for use as the 'fcn'
//   argument of generateWindow(). See the file
//   generateWindow.js for more information on
//   generateWindow().
//
// Arguments:
//   args - an array with three elements in the
//          following order:
//      obj      - the object to obtain properties from
//      obj_name - a string representing the object
//      html     - generate html output
//
// Return Value
//    string of the form:
//      object_name.property = "value"
//      object_name.property = "value"
//      ...
//
function displayMimeTypeProperties(args) {
  var rvalue = ""

  // convert args array elements to more usable
  // variable names
  var      obj = args[0]
```

```
  var obj_name = args[1]
  var     html = args[2]

  // make sure we have the correct number of arguments
  if (args.length != 3) {
    return null
  }

  rvalue += newline(html)
  rvalue += "The properties of the object "
  rvalue += obj_name + " are:"
  rvalue += newline(html)

  rvalue += obj_name + " = " + obj
  rvalue += newline(html)
  rvalue += obj_name + ".length = " + obj.length
  rvalue += newline(html)

  // loop through all the object's properties
  for (var i = 0; i < obj.length; i++) {
    var mimeType = obj[i]
    rvalue += obj_name + "[" + i + "] = " + mimeType
    rvalue += newline(html)

    // loop through all the mimeType's properties
    for (var j in mimeType) {
      rvalue += obj_name + "[" + i + "]." + j
      rvalue += " = " + mimeType[j]
      rvalue += newline(html)
    }
  }
  return unescape(rvalue)
}

// display all the properties of the
// navigator.mimeTypes array.
//
function mimeTypeProps() {

  // load an array with the arguments for
  // displayProperties().
  // The order of the arguments is:
  //   obj
  //   obj_name
```

```
  //   html
  //
  var displayPropsArgs = new Array(3)
  displayPropsArgs[0] = navigator.mimeTypes
  displayPropsArgs[1] = "navigator.mimeTypes"
  displayPropsArgs[2] = true

  // generateWindow() creates a window and calls
  // the function passed as the 5th argument. The
  // last argument, an array, holds any arguments
  // you want to pass to the function.
  //
  // In this case displayProperties() is the
  // function and displayPropsArgs[] is the
  // argument array I want to pass to
  // displayProperties().
  //
  generateWindow("mimeTypePropsWin",
"navigator.mimeTypes",
                 500, 500, displayMimeTypeProperties,
                 displayPropsArgs)
}
// STOP HIDING -->
</SCRIPT>
</HEAD>
<BODY>

<P>The mimeType object represents a MIME data type
supported by the browser through either a helper
application or a plug-in. You access the
mimeType objects with the navigator.mimeTypes
array.</P>

<P>For example:</P>
<DL>
  <DD>navigator.mimeTypes[i]
  <DD>navigator.mimeTypes["name"]
  <DD>navigator.mimeTypes.length
</DL>

<P>Click on the MIME Types button to see which
MIME types are supported by this client.</P>

<CENTER><FORM>
```

```
<INPUT TYPE="button" NAME="mimeTypePropsBtn"
  VALUE="MIME Types" onClick="mimeTypeProps()">
</FORM></CENTER>

</BODY>
</HTML>
```

Figure 33–1 shows the result of loading the `mimeType.html` script.

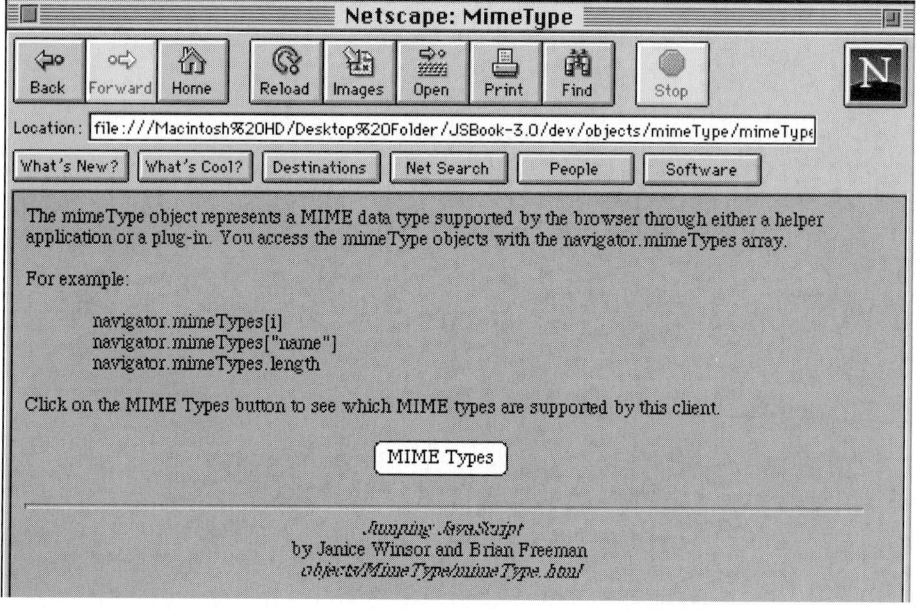

Figure 33–1 Result of loading the `mimeType.html` script

Clicking on the MIME Types button displays a list of the MIME types available on the client computer. Figure 33–2 shows the beginning of a lengthy list of available MIME types.

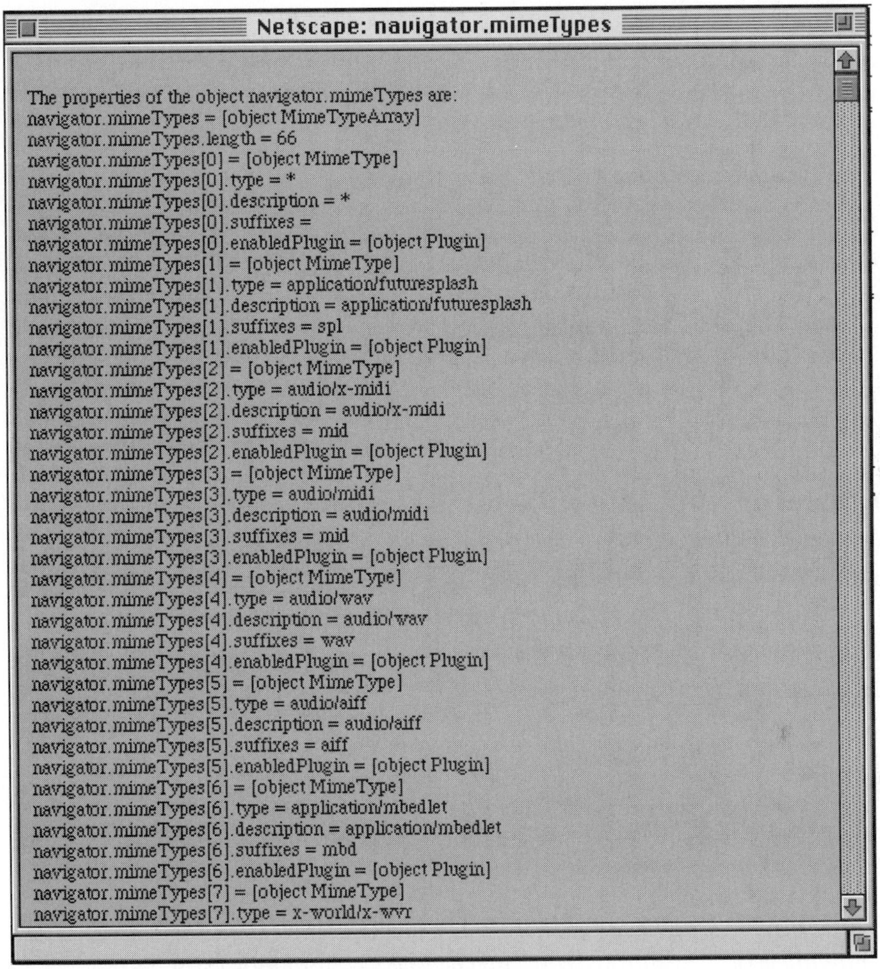

Netscape: navigator.mimeTypes

```
The properties of the object navigator.mimeTypes are:
navigator.mimeTypes = [object MimeTypeArray]
navigator.mimeTypes.length = 66
navigator.mimeTypes[0] = [object MimeType]
navigator.mimeTypes[0].type = *
navigator.mimeTypes[0].description = *
navigator.mimeTypes[0].suffixes =
navigator.mimeTypes[0].enabledPlugin = [object Plugin]
navigator.mimeTypes[1] = [object MimeType]
navigator.mimeTypes[1].type = application/futuresplash
navigator.mimeTypes[1].description = application/futuresplash
navigator.mimeTypes[1].suffixes = spl
navigator.mimeTypes[1].enabledPlugin = [object Plugin]
navigator.mimeTypes[2] = [object MimeType]
navigator.mimeTypes[2].type = audio/x-midi
navigator.mimeTypes[2].description = audio/x-midi
navigator.mimeTypes[2].suffixes = mid
navigator.mimeTypes[2].enabledPlugin = [object Plugin]
navigator.mimeTypes[3] = [object MimeType]
navigator.mimeTypes[3].type = audio/midi
navigator.mimeTypes[3].description = audio/midi
navigator.mimeTypes[3].suffixes = mid
navigator.mimeTypes[3].enabledPlugin = [object Plugin]
navigator.mimeTypes[4] = [object MimeType]
navigator.mimeTypes[4].type = audio/wav
navigator.mimeTypes[4].description = audio/wav
navigator.mimeTypes[4].suffixes = wav
navigator.mimeTypes[4].enabledPlugin = [object Plugin]
navigator.mimeTypes[5] = [object MimeType]
navigator.mimeTypes[5].type = audio/aiff
navigator.mimeTypes[5].description = audio/aiff
navigator.mimeTypes[5].suffixes = aiff
navigator.mimeTypes[5].enabledPlugin = [object Plugin]
navigator.mimeTypes[6] = [object MimeType]
navigator.mimeTypes[6].type = application/mbedlet
navigator.mimeTypes[6].description = application/mbedlet
navigator.mimeTypes[6].suffixes = mbd
navigator.mimeTypes[6].enabledPlugin = [object Plugin]
navigator.mimeTypes[7] = [object MimeType]
navigator.mimeTypes[7].type = x-world/x-wvr
```

Figure 33–2 List of available MIME types

Accessing a Description of a MIME Type

The `description` property is a read-only property that returns a human-readable description of the contents and encoding described by the `mimeType` object. You use the following syntax for this property:

```
mimeType.description
```

Property	Value	Gettable	Settable
description	string	Yes	No

For an example of using the `description` property, see "Example of Determining MIME Type Suffixes" on page 969.

Determining the Plug-in That Handles the MIME Type

The `enabledPlugin` property is a read-only property that returns a reference to a `plugin` object that supports this MIME type. If no plug-in supports the MIME type, the `enabledPlugin` property returns a value of `null`. You use the following syntax for this property:

```
mimeType.enabledPlugin
```

Property	Value	Gettable	Settable
enabledPlugin	string	Yes	No

Example of Determing the Plug-in That Handles the MIME Type

The following `mimeTypeEnabledPlugin.html` script loops through the `mimeType` array and determines which of the available MIME types are supported by plug-ins.

```
<!--
          mimeTypeEnabledPlugin.html
-->
<HTML>
<HEAD>
<TITLE>MimeType enabledPlugin</TITLE>
</HEAD>
<BODY>

<P>The mimeType.enabledPlugin property is a
```

```
reference to the plugin object that supports the
MIME type in question. The property value is null
if no installed or enabled plug-in supports the
MIME type.</P>

<P>For the MIME types supported by this browser,
the following are supported by plugin objects:</P>

<SCRIPT LANGUAGE="JavaScript">
<!-- HIDE FROM OLD BROWSERS
var mstr = "<BR>"

mstr += "<OL>\n"

// Loop through all the mimeTypes printing only
// those that are supported by plugin objects.
for (var i = 0; i < navigator.mimeTypes.length; i++) {
  if (navigator.mimeTypes[i].enabledPlugin != null) {
    mstr += "<LI>"
    mstr += navigator.mimeTypes[i].type
    mstr += "</LI>\n"
  }
}

mstr += "</OL>\n"

document.open()
document.write(mstr)
document.close()

// STOP HIDING -->
</SCRIPT>

</BODY>
</HTML>
```

Figure 33–3 shows the result of loading the `mimeTypeEnabledPlugin.html` script.

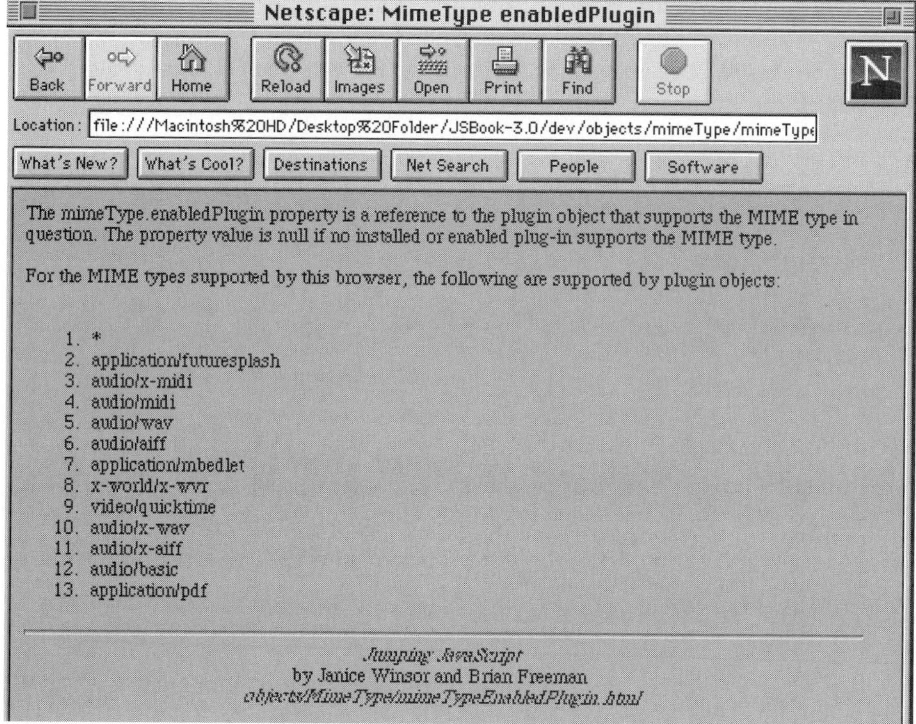

Figure 33–3 Result of loading the `mimeTypeEnabledPlugin.html` script

Determining the Type of a MIME Type

The `type` property is a read-only property that returns the combination of type and subtype for the MIME type, for example, `text/html` or `image/jpeg`.

Property	Value	Gettable	Settable
type	string	Yes	No

Example of Determining the Type of a MIME Type

The following `mimeTypeType.html` script creates a list of the available MIME types by looping through the `mimeType` array.

```
<!--
                mimeTypeType.html
-->
<HTML>
<HEAD>
<TITLE>MimeType Type</TITLE>
</HEAD>
<BODY>

<P>The mimeType.type property is a read-only
string that contains the name of the MIME
data type. It can also be used as an index into
the navigator.mimeTypes[] array.</P>

<P>The names of the MIME types supported by this
browser are:</P>

<SCRIPT LANGUAGE="JavaScript">
<!-- HIDE FROM OLD BROWSERS
var mstr = "<BR>"

mstr += "<OL>\n"

// Loop through all the mimeTypes, printing the
// type property.
for (var i = 0; i < navigator.mimeTypes.length; i++) {
  mstr += "<LI>"
  mstr += navigator.mimeTypes[i].type
  mstr += "</LI>\n"
}

mstr += "</OL>\n"

document.open()
document.write(mstr)
document.close()

// STOP HIDING -->
</SCRIPT>

</BODY>
</HTML>
```

Figure 33–4 shows the result of loading the `mimeTypeType.html` script.

Netscape: MimeType Type

Back Forward Home Reload Images Open Print Find Stop

Location: file:///Macintosh%20HD/Desktop%20Folder/JSBook-3.0/dev/objects/mimeType/mimeTyp

What's New? What's Cool? Destinations Net Search People Software

The mimeType.type property is a read-only string that contains the name of the MIME data type. It can also be used as an index into the navigator.mimeTypes[] array.

The names of the MIME types supported by this browser are:

1. *
2. application/futuresplash
3. audio/x-midi
4. audio/midi
5. audio/wav
6. audio/aiff
7. application/mbedlet
8. x-world/x-wvr
9. application/aiff
10. application/x-netscape-autoconfigure-dialer
11. application/x-compressed
12. application/x-macbinary
13. image/pict
14. application/x-scriptx-title
15. application/x-scriptx-lib
16. application/x-gzip
17. application/x-compress
18. application/x-ns-proxy-autoconfig
19. application/x-javascript
20. application/x-perl
21. application/x-tcl
22. application/x-sh
23. application/x-csh
24. application/postscript
25. application/octet-stream
26. application/x-cpio
27. application/x-gtar
28. application/x-tar
29. application/x-shar
30. application/x-zip-compressed
31. application/x-stuffit
32. application/mac-binhex40

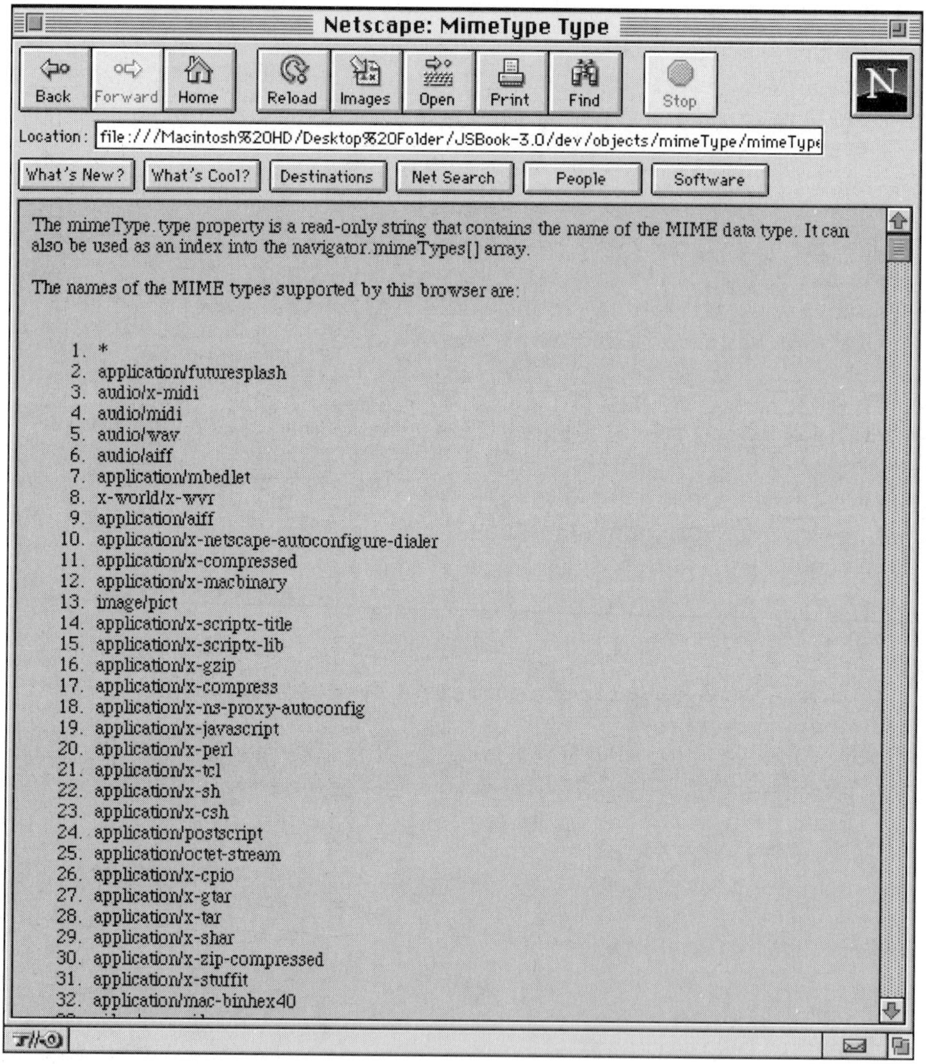

Figure 33–4 Result of loading the `mimeTypeType.html` script

Determining MIME Type Suffixes

The `suffixes` property is a read-only property that returns a comma-separated list of file name extensions (without the period) that are used with files of the specified MIME type. For example, the suffixes for the MIME type `text/html` are `html` and `htm`.

Property	Value	Gettable	Settable
suffixes	string	Yes	No

Example of Determining MIME Type Suffixes

The following `mimeTypeSuffixes.html` script provides a text field that you can use to enter a suffix. When you press Return or click on the Find button, an alert is displayed that uses the `description` property to display a description of the MIME type for that suffix.

```
<!--
              mimeTypeSuffixes.html
-->
<HTML>
<HEAD>
<TITLE>MimeType Suffixes</TITLE>
<SCRIPT LANGUAGE="JavaScript">
<!-- HIDE FROM OLD BROWSERS


// Test to see if there is a handler for the
// given suffix.
//
// The index of the mimeType object in the
// mimeTypes array is returned if a handler is
// found. Otherwise, -1 is returned.
//
function isSuffixHandler(suffix) {
  var rvalue = -1

  for (var i=0; i<navigator.mimeTypes.length; i++) {
    var suffixes = navigator.mimeTypes[i].suffixes

    if (suffixes.indexOf(suffix) != -1) {
      rvalue = i
      break
```

```
    }
  }
  return rvalue
}

// Display the description of the mimeType object
// that handles the suffix.
//
function findHandler(suffix) {
  var index = isSuffixHandler(suffix)

  if (index < 0) {
    alert("No handler for " + suffix +
      " was found.")
  } else {
    alert(suffix + " is an extension for " +
      navigator.mimeTypes[index].description + ".")
  }
}
// STOP HIDING -->
</SCRIPT>
</HEAD>
<BODY>

<P>The mimeType object's suffixes property is a
read-only, comma-separated list of common
file name extensions for the MIME type. For
example:</P>
<DL>
  <DD>aif
  <DD>aiff
  <DD>wav
  <DD>mid
  <DD>midi
  <DD>html
  <DD>htm
  <DD>txt
</DL>

<P>In the text field, enter the name of a suffix
you want to search for. When you press Return or
click on the Find button, the description of the
MIME type for the suffix is displayed.</P>
```

```
<FORM>
<P><B>Enter a suffix:</B><BR>
<INPUT TYPE="text" NAME="sField" VALUE=""
SIZE=20 onChange="findHandler(this.value)">
<P>
<INPUT TYPE="button" VALUE="Find"
onClick="findHandler(this.form.sField.value)">
</FORM>

</BODY>
</HTML>
```

Figure 33–5 shows the result of loading the `mimeTypeSuffixes.html` script.

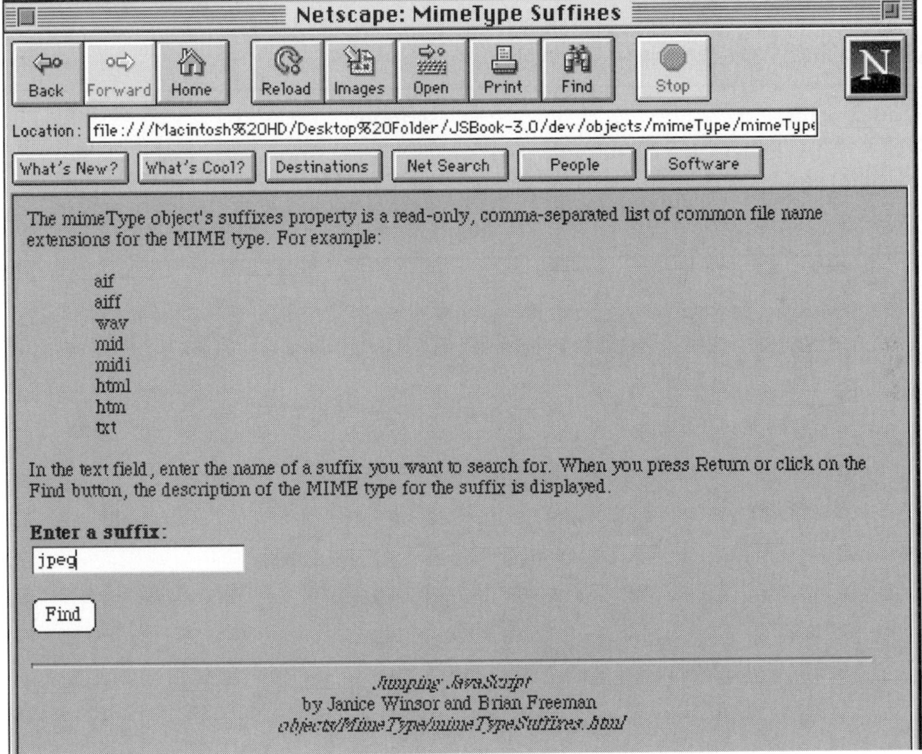

Figure 33–5 Result of loading the `mimeTypeSuffixes.html` script

Type a suffix in the text field and either press Return or click on the Find button. An alert is displayed, showing the description for the suffix in the text field, as shown in Figure 33–6.

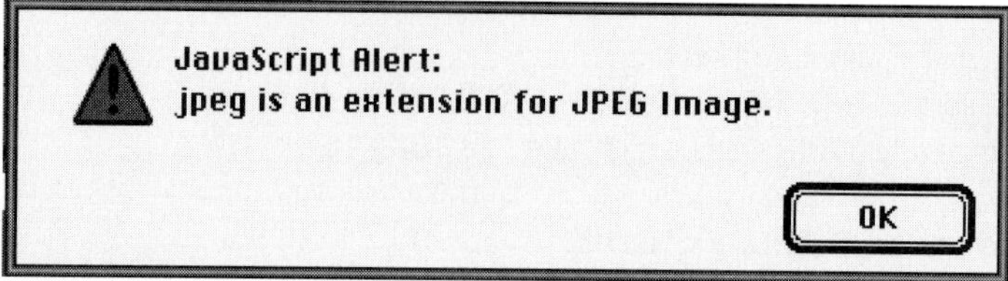

Figure 33–6 MIME type description alert

Summary of New Terms and Concepts

The new terms and concepts introduced in this chapter are listed in alphabetical order in Table 33-2. The terms and concepts are also included in the glossary at the end of the book.

Table 33-2 New Terms and Concepts

Term/Concept	Description
extension	The period and the characters that follow the period at the end of the file name and specify the file type. Also called a suffix.

PART SEVEN

Advanced JavaScript

CHAPTER 34

- Using the function Object
- Creating Custom Object Functions
- Creating an Instance of a Custom Object
- Accessing Custom Object Properties and Methods
- Creating a Custom Name Object
- Displaying Property Values for a Custom Object
- Creating a Prototype Method for a Custom Object
- Combining Custom Objects

Creating Your Own JavaScript Objects

By now you should be quite familiar with using the JavaScript built-in objects, properties, methods, and event handlers. In addition to providing you with a rich set of built-in objects, the JavaScript language also enables you to create your own objects with their own properties and methods.

The framework provides constructor functions, prototype objects, and the `new` operator. The constructor functions enable you to define new objects. Prototype objects enable you to attach shared properties to all objects created by a constructor. The `new` operator enables you to create instances of objects.

Using the function Object

Creating a new object is as simple as defining a function. As you know, functions are self-contained mini-scripts that you can use to organize blocks of code that recur several times within a script. By creating a function, you can use a single command to trigger complex actions without needing to repeat the code a number of times within the script.

To use functions, first you declare the function by using the `function` keyword in the following syntax:

```
function functionName(arguments) {
...
}
```

After you have created the function, you call it, using the following syntax, from the place in the script where you want the function code to execute:

```
functionName()
```

The built-in `function` object has three properties, listed in Table 34-1, that you can use to control and enhance your custom objects. It has no methods or event handlers.

Table 34-1 Properties for the function Object

Properties	Methods	Event Handlers
`caller`	None	None
`arguments[]`		
`prototype*`		

* New in Navigator 3.0.

Determining Who Called a Function

The `caller` property returns a description of the function that called the current function. If the current function was called from the top level of a script, then the return value is `null`. The property is available only within a function body.

Property	Value	Gettable	Settable
caller	string	Yes	No

The following `functionCaller.html` script defines two functions, `foo()` and `bar()`. (When programmers are talking about some generic function, they frequently use these two names.) The `foo()` function calls `bar()`. The `bar()` function displays an alert by using the `caller` property, which displays the description of the function.

```
<!--
                    functionCaller.html
-->
<HTML>
<HEAD>
<TITLE>Function Caller</TITLE>
<SCRIPT LANGUAGE="JavaScript">
<!-- HIDE FROM OLD BROWSERS
```

```
function foo() {
  bar()
}

function bar() {
  alert(bar.caller)
}

// STOP HIDING -->
</SCRIPT>
</HEAD>
<BODY>

<P>The function bar() tells you who called it in an
alert dialog. If you call foo(), it calls bar()
for you.</P>

<CENTER><FORM>
<INPUT TYPE="button" NAME="fooBtn"
 VALUE="Have foo() call bar()" onClick="foo()">
<BR><BR>
<INPUT TYPE="button" NAME="barBtn"
 VALUE="Call bar()" onClick="bar()">
</FORM></CENTER>

</BODY>
</HTML>
```

Figure 34–1 shows the result of loading the `functionCaller.html` script.

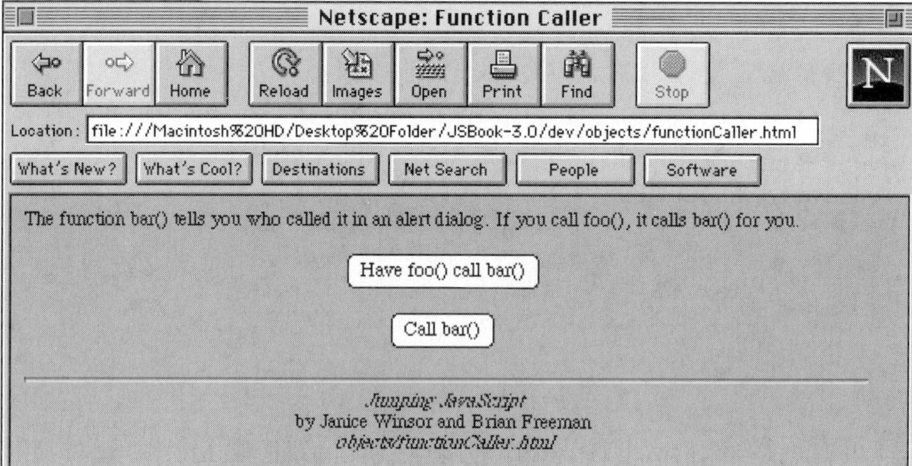

Figure 34–1 Result of loading the `functionCaller.html` script

When you click on the Have foo() call bar() button, an alert is displayed, showing the description of the `foo()` function, as shown in Figure 34–2. The `foo()` function is the one that called the `bar()` function, which uses the `caller` property to identify its caller.

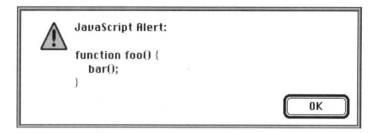

Figure 34–2 Description of the `foo()` function

When you click on the Call bar() button, an alert is displayed, showing the description of the `bar()` function, as shown in Figure 34–3. Because the `bar()` function calls itself, the alert shows its description.

JavaScript Alert:

```
function onclick() {
   bar();
}
```

OK

Figure 34–3 Description of the `bar()` function

Determining the Arguments Passed to a Function

You can use the `arguments[]` property to pass a varying number of arguments to a function. Because `arguments[]` is an array, you can use its `length` property to determine the number of arguments passed to the function. You extract the value of the argument by indexing into the `arguments[]` array.

Property	Value	Gettable	Settable
arguments()	string	Yes	No

The following `functionArguments.html` script provides buttons that you can click on to display the number of arguments and the values for those arguments for three examples.

```
<!--
                  functionArguments.html
-->
<HTML>
<HEAD>
<TITLE>Function Arguments</TITLE>
<SCRIPT LANGUAGE="JavaScript">
<!-- HIDE FROM OLD BROWSERS

// Display the arguments used in the call to this.
// function.
//
function args() {
  var mstr = "\n"

  mstr += "The function args has "
  mstr += args.arguments.length + " argument"
  if (args.arguments.length > 0) {
```

```
    // One or more arguments
    if ( args.arguments.length == 1 ) {
      // Only one.
      mstr += ".\n\nAnd it is:\n"
    } else {
      // More than one, make sentence plural.
      mstr += "s.\n\nAnd they are:\n"
    }
    // Add all the arguments.
    for (var i=0; i < args.arguments.length; i++) {
      mstr += "   " + args.arguments[i] + "\n"
    }
  } else {
    // Zero arguments. Add the period onto the
    // sentence and end.
    mstr += "."
  }
  alert(unescape(mstr))
}

// Call args() with one argument
//
function oneArg() {
  args("One")
}

// Call args() with two arguments
//
function twoArgs() {
  args("One", "Two")
}

// Call args() with three arguments
//
function threeArgs() {
  args("One", "Two", "Three")
}

// STOP HIDING -->
</SCRIPT>
</HEAD>
<BODY>

<P>This example displays the number of and the
```

```
actual arguments used to call the args()
function. </P>

<CENTER>
<FORM>
<INPUT TYPE="button" onClick="oneArg()"
VALUE="Call args() with one argument">
<BR><BR>
<INPUT TYPE="button" onClick="twoArgs()"
VALUE="Call args() with two arguments">
<BR><BR>
<INPUT TYPE="button" onClick="threeArgs()"
VALUE="Call args() with three arguments">
</FORM>
</CENTER>

</BODY>
</HTML>
```

Figure 34–4 shows the result of loading the `functionArguments.html` script.

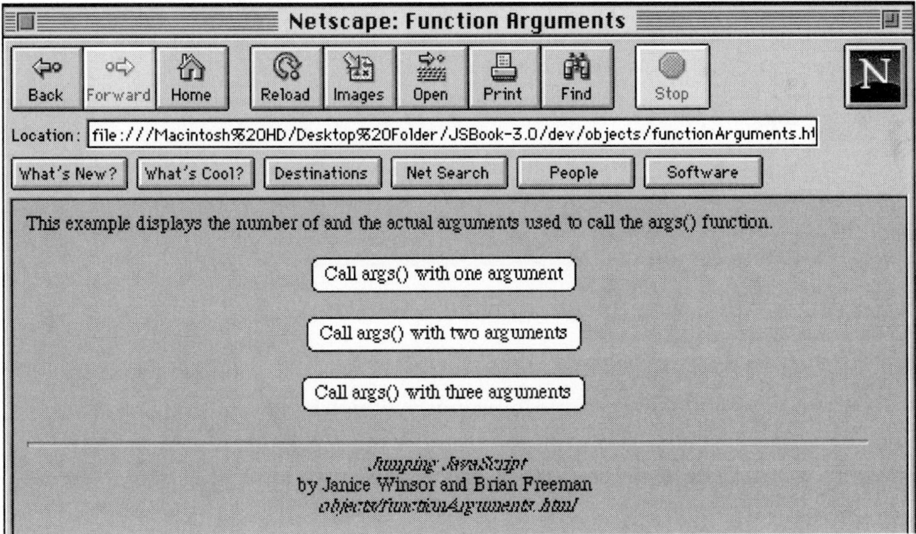

Figure 34–4 Result of loading the `functionArguments.html` script

Clicking on each of the buttons displays an alert with the number of arguments and the value for those arguments. Figure 34–5 shows the alerts for each of the three buttons.

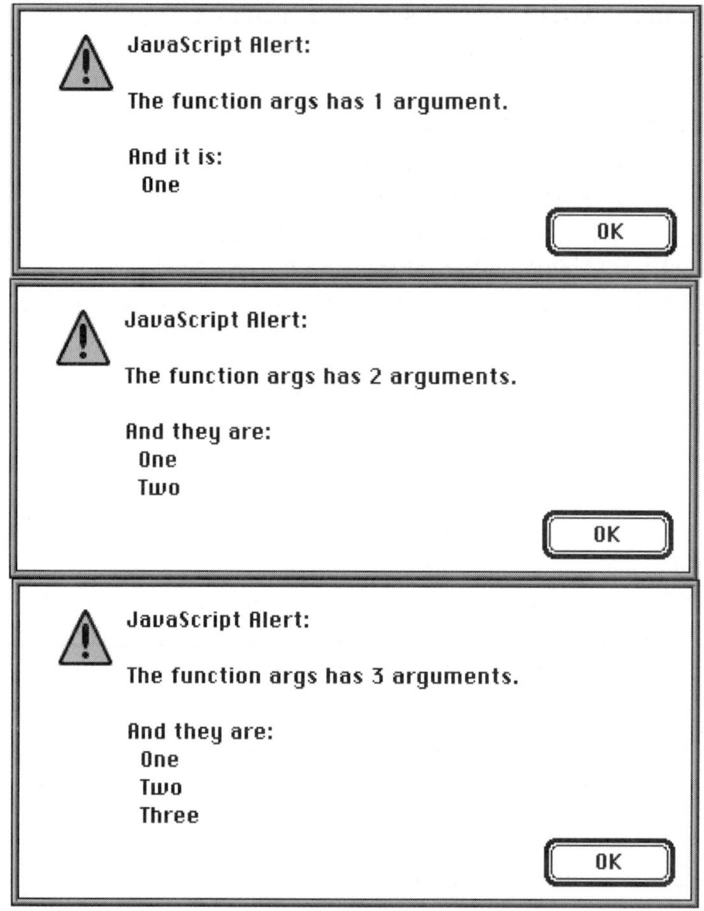

Figure 34–5 Alerts for the `arguments` property

NEW IN 3.0

Creating Prototype Methods for a Function

Navigator 3.0 provides a `prototype` property, which is actually a property of the `function` object. You've seen examples of this property in this chapter and elsewhere in this book for objects such as `String` and `Array` that you can create with the `new` statement.

Property	Value	Gettable	Settable
prototype	string	Yes	Yes

For an example of creating a `prototype` function for a custom object, see "Creating a Prototype Method for a Custom Object" on page 991.

Creating Custom Object Functions

Functions that define objects are called constructors. The function is like the Platonic ideal. It's the concept of the object. When you use the function constructor, you create an instance of the object. Instance is an object-oriented term that means "one of those objects with a certain specific set of properties." Or, to carry out the Platonic metaphor, the instance of the horse is the shadow on the wall of the cave that carries the generic concept of horse and makes it real.

Before we create a new object, let's consider the Platonic ideal of a horse. It's a large mammal with four legs, a head, a tail, a color, a size, a breed, and a personality. Generally, you would assume that any horse would be a mammal and have four legs, a head, and a tail, so you do not need to create properties that reflect these properties that are (we hope) shared by all horses. Alternatively, you could create a mammal object and make it a property of Horse.

The properties that can differ from horse to horse are the color, size, breed, and personality. These are properties that distinguish one horse from another and make each horse unique. If you wrote a constructor to define the concept of a horse, it could look like this:

```
function Horse (color, size, breed, personality) {
   this.color = color
   this.size = size
   this.breed = breed
   this.personality = personality
}
```

In this particular example, the names of the properties are the same as the parameters that you specified for the `Horse` constructor, although they do not need to be the same. You could abbreviate the parameters or specify a different property name. For example, you could define the properties as:

```
this.color = theColor
```

Creating an Instance of a Custom Object

After you have defined the constructor for the `Horse` object, you can create a specific instance of the `Horse` object by using the `new` statement:

```
aHorse = new Horse("bay", "14 hands", "quarter horse",
"gentle")
```

Accessing Custom Object Properties and Methods

Once you have created an instance of the object, you can reference its properties in the same way as you reference the properties of any other JavaScript object. For example, to determine the size of `aHorse`, you would refer to the object in this way:

```
aHorse.size
```

Creating a Custom Name Object

The following `object.html` script creates a custom `Name` object with three properties and one method. Adding a method to a custom object is as simple as writing a function and including the function name as part of the custom object function definition.

```
<!--
                  object.html
-->
<HTML>
<HEAD>
<TITLE>Object</TITLE>
<SCRIPT LANGUAGE="JavaScript">
<!-- HIDE FROM OLD BROWSERS

// Display method for the Name object.
//
function displayName() {
  alert(this.firstName + " " +
        this.middleInitial + " " +
        this.lastName)
}

// Name Object
//
function Name(first, mi, last) {
  // properties
  this.firstName     = first
```

```
  this.lastName      = last
  this.middleInitial = mi

  // methods
  this.display       = displayName
}

// global variable that stores name input from the form
var aName = new Name("Brian", "K.", "Freeman")

// STOP HIDING -->
</SCRIPT>
</HEAD>
<BODY>

<P>This example creates a user-defined object
called Name by defining a constructor function
for the object. Within Name's constructor
function, properties and methods are assigned to
the object with the this keyword.</P>

<P>The name object is defined with three
properties:
<DL>
<DD>firstName
<DD>middleInitial
<DD>lastName
</DL>

<P>and one method:
<DL>
<DD>display()
</DL>

<P>The following FORM enables you to manipulate
the properties and methods of this object. I've
initialized the object with my name to get you
started.</P>

<FORM>
<B>Name:</B><BR>
<INPUT TYPE="text" NAME="fname" SIZE=40 VALUE="Brian"
onChange="aName.firstName=this.value"><BR>
<B>Middle Initial:</B><BR>
```

```
<INPUT TYPE="text" NAME="mi" SIZE=2 VALUE="K."
onChange="aName.middleInitial=this.value"><BR>
<B>Last Name:</B><BR>
<INPUT TYPE="text" NAME="lname" SIZE=40 VALUE="Freeman"
onChange="aName.lastName=this.value"><BR><BR>
<INPUT TYPE="button" NAME="display" VALUE="display"
onClick="aName.display()">
</FORM>

</BODY>
</HTML>
```

Figure 34–6 shows the result of loading the `object.html` script. Notice that the default values defined for the instance of `aName` are specified by the script and displayed in the text field.

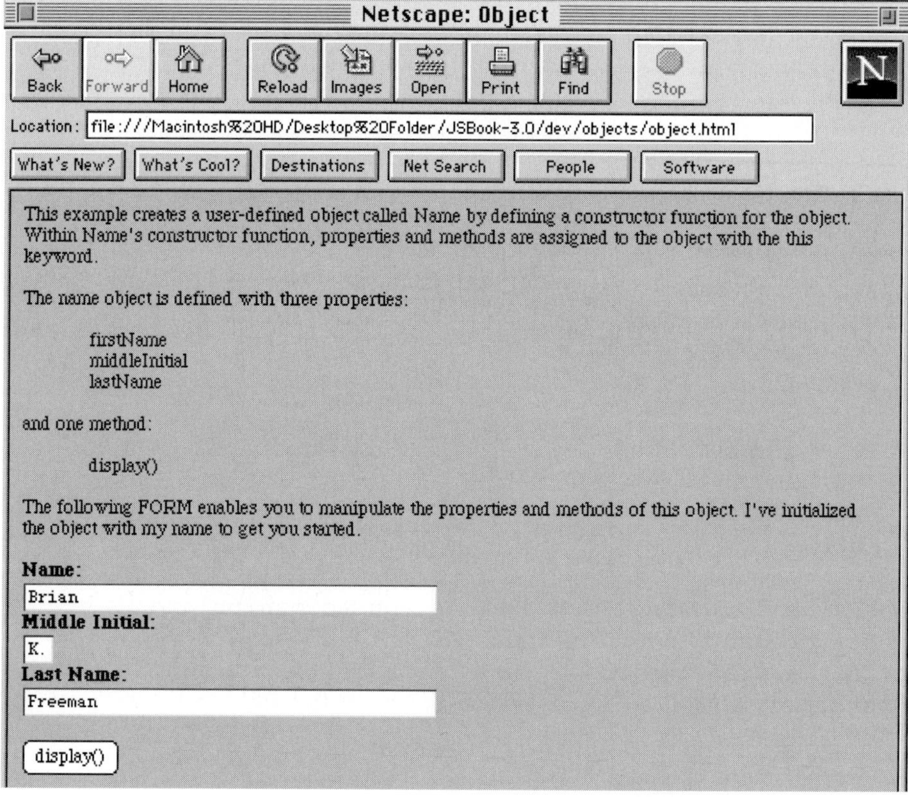

Figure 34–6 Result of loading the `object.html` script

When you click on the display() button, the `display()` method defined in the script displays an alert, shown in Figure 34–7, containing the values for the three properties of the `Name` object.

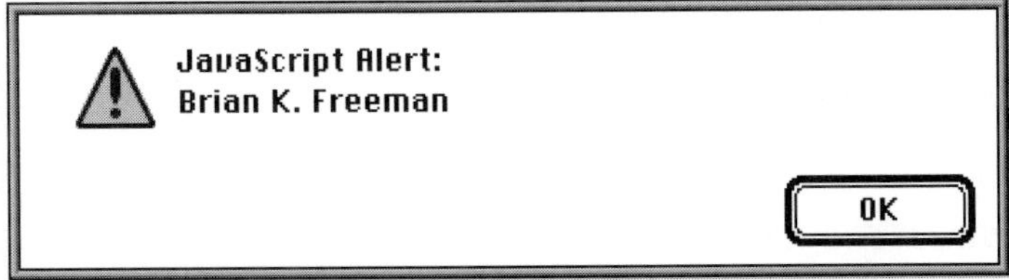

Figure 34–7 Property values of the `Name` object

When using an object constructor, you do not need to provide all the arguments. If you define a constructor to take three arguments and the calling statement specifies only two, JavaScript returns a `null` value for the third argument.

When you type a first and last name with no middle initial and click on the display() button, the alert that is displayed ignores the missing property value and displays the `firstName` and `lastName` values, as shown in Figure 34–8.

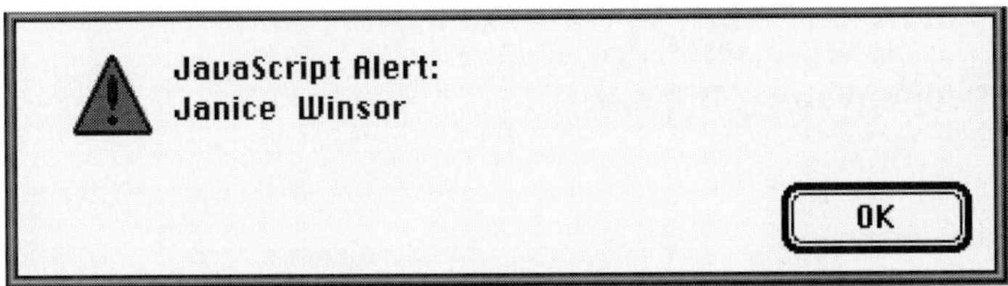

Figure 34–8 Alert with invisible `null` property value

In fact, the alert does contain an extra space between the first and last name because of the way the message string is formatted in the script.

Displaying Property Values for a Custom Object

You can add a method to a custom object to extract and display the values for each property in a custom object. The following `objectForIn.html` script expands the `object.html` script by adding a `properties()` method that defines a `for ... in` loop to cycle through the object and determine the values for each property.

```
<!--
                objectForIn.html
-->
<HTML>
<HEAD>
<TITLE>Object For...In</TITLE>
<SCRIPT LANGUAGE="JavaScript">
<!-- HIDE FROM OLD BROWSERS

// Display method for the Name object.
//
function displayName() {
  alert(this.firstName + " " +
        this.middleInitial + " " +
        this.lastName)
}

// Properties method for the Name object.
//
// Loop through the properties, constructing a
// list of the properties and their values.
//
function nameProperties(objName) {
  var rvalue = "\n"

  for (var i in this) {
    rvalue += objName + "." + i
    rvalue += " = " + this[i] + "\n"
  }
  rvalue += "\n"

  return rvalue
}

// Name Object
//
function Name(first, mi, last) {
  // properties
  this.firstName     = first
  this.lastName      = last
  this.middleInitial = mi

  // methods
  this.display       = displayName
```

```
  this.properties    = nameProperties
}

// global variable that stores name input from the form
var aName = new Name("Brian", "K.", "Freeman")

// STOP HIDING -->
</SCRIPT>
</HEAD>
<BODY>

<P>This example adds the properties method to the
Name object started in <A HREF="object.html">
object.html</A>. properties() uses the for...in
statement to cycle through the Name object's
properties and construct a string containing
their name and values.</P>

<P>The name object is defined with three
properties:
<DL>
<DD>firstName
<DD>middleInitial
<DD>lastName
</DL>

<P>and two methods:
<DL>
<DD>display()
<DD>properties()
</DL>

<P>Manipulate the Name object with the FORM
below. I've initialized the object with my name to
get you started.</P>

<FORM>
<B>Name:</B><BR>
<INPUT TYPE="text" NAME="fname" SIZE=40 VALUE="Brian"
onChange="aName.firstName=this.value"><BR>
<B>Middle Initial:</B><BR>
<INPUT TYPE="text" NAME="mi" SIZE=2 VALUE="K."
onChange="aName.middleInitial=this.value"><BR>
<B>Last Name:</B><BR>
```

```
<INPUT TYPE="text" NAME="lname" SIZE=40 VALUE="Freeman"
onChange="aName.lastName=this.value"><BR><BR>
<INPUT TYPE="button" NAME="display" VALUE="display()"
onClick="aName.display()"><BR>
<INPUT TYPE="button" NAME="displayProps"
VALUE="properties()"
onClick="alert(aName.properties('aName'))">
</FORM>

</BODY>
</HTML>
```

Figure 34–9 shows the result of loading the `objectForIn.html` script.

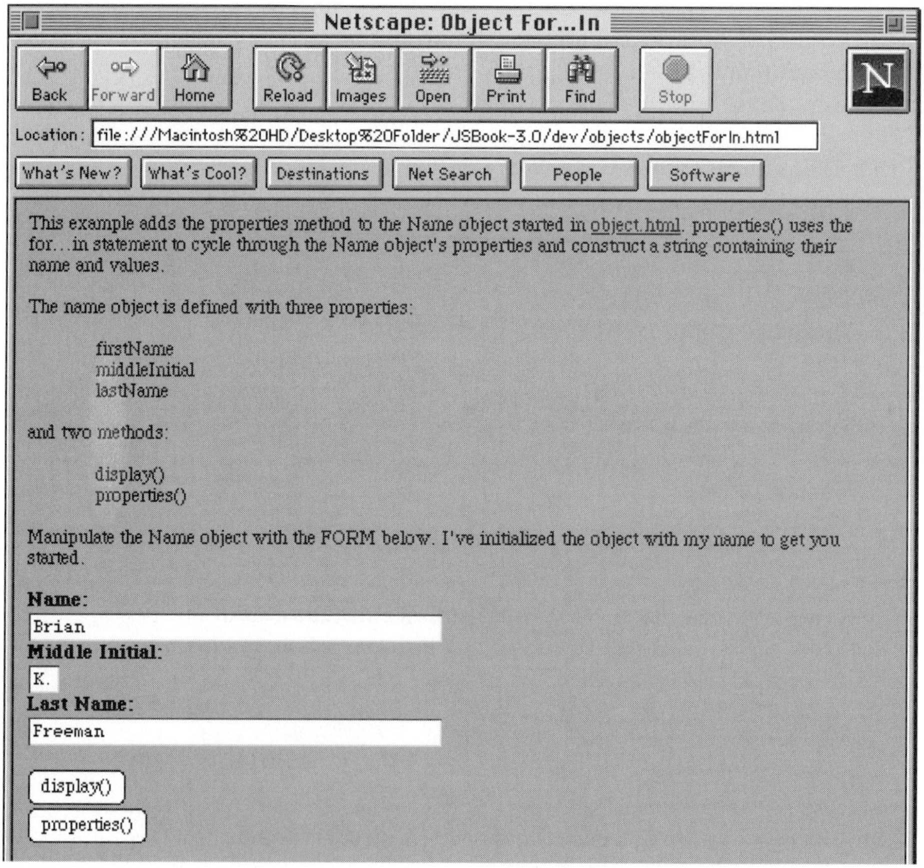

Figure 34–9 Result of loading the `objectForIn.html` script

Clicking on the properties() button displays an alert showing the values for the properties of the `Name` object, as shown in Figure 34–10.

```
JavaScript Alert:

aName.firstName = Brian
aName.lastName = Freeman
aName.middleInitial = K.
aName.display =
function displayName() {
   alert(this.firstName + " " + this.middleInitial +
" " + this.lastName);
}

aName.properties =
function nameProperties(objName) {
   var rvalue = "\n";
   for (var i in this) {
      rvalue += objName + "." + i;
      rvalue += " = " + this[i] + "\n";
   }
   rvalue += "\n";
   return rvalue;
}

OK
```

Figure 34–10 Properties of the `Name` object

Creating a Prototype Method for a Custom Object

One of the powers of creating custom objects is that you can define `prototype` methods that apply to all instances of an object you crate with the new operator. You can create a `prototype` function with the new operator, as shown in the following example:

```
Name.prototype.toString = new Function(
"return this.firstName + ' ' + this.middleInitial + ' ' +
this.lastName")
```

This new function adds a `toString()` method to the `Name` object. Similar to the `toString()` methods found on built-in objects, this function converts the property values to a formatted string, enabling you to use the name of a `Name` object in a `document.alert()` or `document.write()` call. Note that you need to create an instance of the object before you define the `prototype` function.

```
<!--
              objectPrototype.html
-->
<HTML>
<HEAD>
<TITLE>Object Prototype</TITLE>
<SCRIPT LANGUAGE="JavaScript">
<!-- HIDE FROM OLD BROWSERS

// Display method for the Name object.
//
function displayName() {
  alert(this.firstName + " " +
        this.middleInitial + " " +
        this.lastName)
}

// Properties method for the Name object.
//
// Loop through the properties, constructing a
// list of the properties and their values.
//
function nameProperties(objName) {
  var rvalue = "\n"

  for (var i in this) {
    rvalue += objName + "." + i
    rvalue += " = " + this[i] + "\n"
  }
  rvalue += "\n"

  return rvalue
}

// Name Object
//
function Name(first, mi, last) {
  // properties
  this.firstName     = first
  this.lastName      = last
  this.middleInitial = mi

  // methods
  this.display       = displayName
```

```
  this.properties    = nameProperties
}

// A global variable that stores name input from
// the form.
var aName = new Name("Brian", "K.", "Freeman")

// Add a toString method to Name object.
Name.prototype.toString      = new Function(
    "return this.firstName + ' ' + this.middleInitial + '
' + this.lastName")

// STOP HIDING -->
</SCRIPT>
</HEAD>
<BODY>

<P>This example adds another method to the Name
object by using an object prototype. In this
case, the toString method is added. toString()
converts the object to a string, making the Name
object similar to JavaScript's built-in objects.
It enables you to simply use the object's instance
name in a document.alert() or document.write()
call.</P>

<P>Note: Before you can add the prototype, you must
create, with the new statement, one object of the
type to which you are adding the prototype.
For example, moving the lines:</P>

<PRE>
// Add a toString method to Name object.
Name.prototype.toString      = new Function(
    "return this.firstName + ' ' + this.middleInitial + '
' + this.lastName")
</PRE>

<P>above the lines:</P>

<PRE>
// A global variable that stores name input from
// the form.
var aName = new Name("Brian", "K.", "Freeman")
```

```
</PRE>

<P>results in the JavaScript error:
Function.prototype has no property named
'toString'.</P>


<P>Alternatively, adding toString into the object
constructor, like so:</P>

<PRE>
// Name Object
//
function Name(first, mi, last) {
  // properties
  this.firstName     = first
  this.lastName      = last
  this.middleInitial = mi

  // methods
  this.display       = displayName
  this.properties    = nameProperties
  this.toString      = new Function(
    "return this.firstName + ' ' + this.middleInitial + '
' + this.lastName")
}
</PRE>

<P>accomplishes the same thing.</P>

<P>If you don't want to modify the object, using
an object prototype is a slick way of adding the
needed functionality on-the-fly.</P>

<P>The name object now has three properties:
<DL>
<DD>firstName
<DD>middleInitial
<DD>lastName
</DL>

<P>and three methods:</P>
```

```
<DL>
<DD>display()
<DD>properties()
<DD>toString()
</DL>

<P>Manipulate the Name object with the FORM
below. I've initialized the object with my name to
get you started.</P>

<FORM>
<B>Name:</B><BR>
<INPUT TYPE="text" NAME="fname" SIZE=40 VALUE="Brian"
onChange="aName.firstName=this.value"><BR>
<B>Middle Initial:</B><BR>
<INPUT TYPE="text" NAME="mi" SIZE=2 VALUE="K."
onChange="aName.middleInitial=this.value"><BR>
<B>Last Name:</B><BR>
<INPUT TYPE="text" NAME="lname" SIZE=40 VALUE="Freeman"
onChange="aName.lastName=this.value"><BR><BR>
<INPUT TYPE="button" NAME="display" VALUE="display()"
onClick="aName.display()"><BR>
<INPUT TYPE="button" NAME="props"
VALUE="properties()"
onClick="alert(aName.properties('aName'))"><BR>
<INPUT TYPE="button" NAME="tostring"
VALUE="toString()"
onClick="alert(aName.toString())"><BR>
<INPUT TYPE="button" NAME="variable"
VALUE="alert(aName)"
onClick="alert(aName)">
</FORM>

</BODY>
</HTML>
```

Figure 34–11 shows the result of loading the `objectPrototype.html` script.

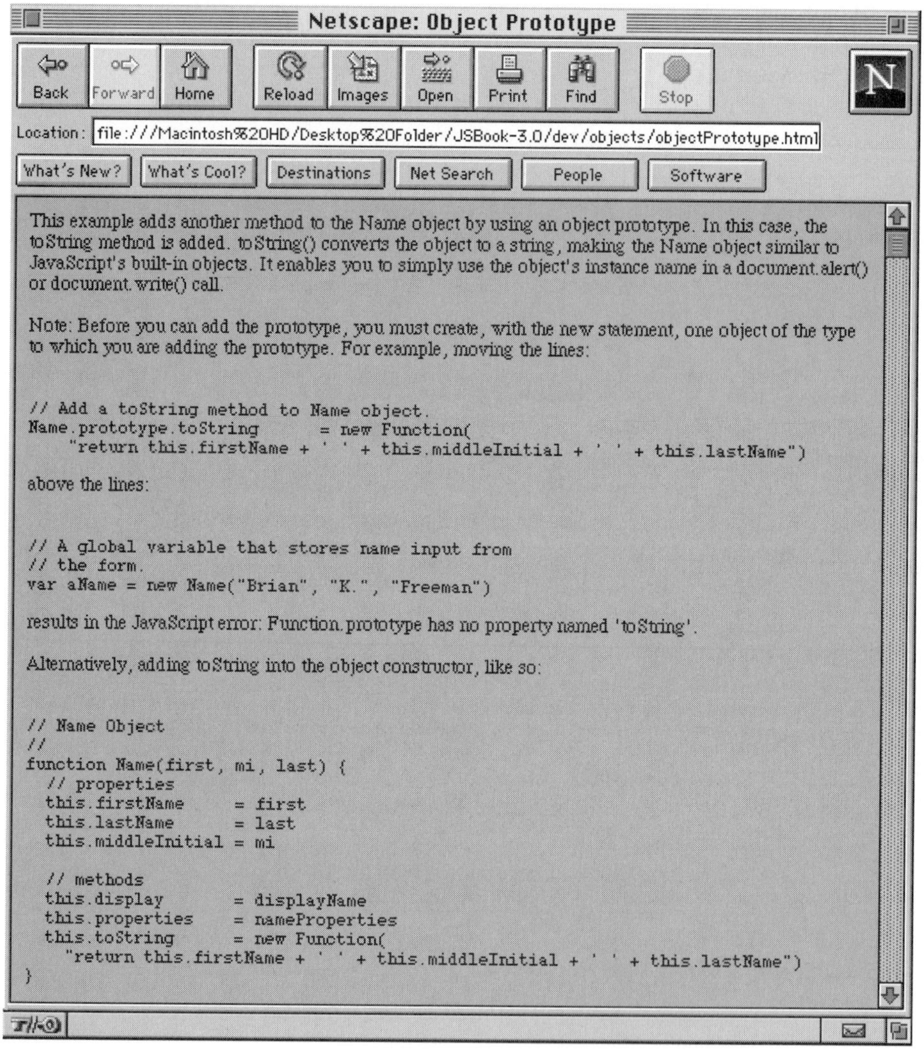

Netscape: Object Prototype

Back | Forward | Home | Reload | Images | Open | Print | Find | Stop

Location: file:///Macintosh%20HD/Desktop%20Folder/JSBook-3.0/dev/objects/objectPrototype.html

What's New? | What's Cool? | Destinations | Net Search | People | Software

This example adds another method to the Name object by using an object prototype. In this case, the toString method is added. toString() converts the object to a string, making the Name object similar to JavaScript's built-in objects. It enables you to simply use the object's instance name in a document.alert() or document.write() call.

Note: Before you can add the prototype, you must create, with the new statement, one object of the type to which you are adding the prototype. For example, moving the lines:

```
// Add a toString method to Name object.
Name.prototype.toString      = new Function(
    "return this.firstName + ' ' + this.middleInitial + ' ' + this.lastName")
```

above the lines:

```
// A global variable that stores name input from
// the form.
var aName = new Name("Brian", "K.", "Freeman")
```

results in the JavaScript error: Function.prototype has no property named 'toString'.

Alternatively, adding toString into the object constructor, like so:

```
// Name Object
//
function Name(first, mi, last) {
  // properties
  this.firstName     = first
  this.lastName      = last
  this.middleInitial = mi

  // methods
  this.display       = displayName
  this.properties    = nameProperties
  this.toString      = new Function(
    "return this.firstName + ' ' + this.middleInitial + ' ' + this.lastName")
}
```

Figure 34–11 Result of loading the `objectPrototype.html` script

Figure 34–12 shows the second screen of the `objectPrototype.html` script.

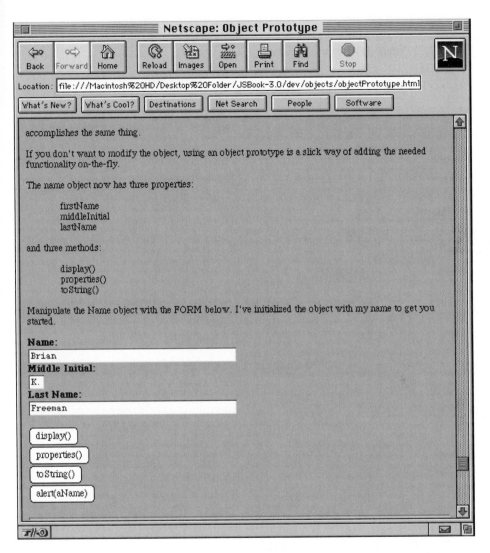

Figure 34–12 Second screen of the `objectPrototype.html` script

Because the `toString()` function prototype was added to the example, clicking on the display(), toString(), and alert(aName) buttons displays the same thing in the alert, shown in Figure 34–13.

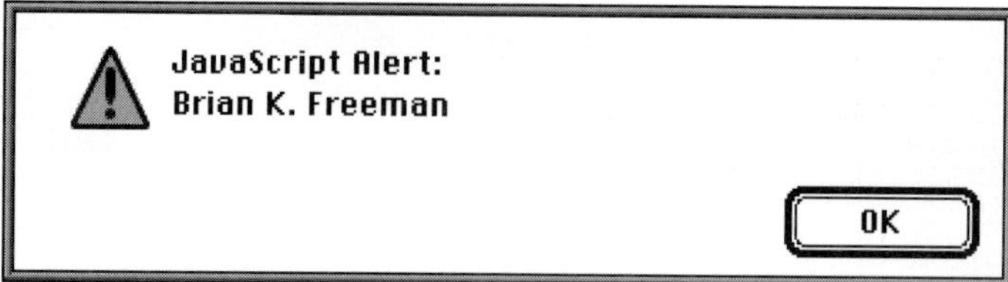

Figure 34–13 Alert name string

The action the script takes depends on which button is clicked on. The display() button uses the `display()` method to create the string. The `toString()` `onClick` event handler calls the object's `toString()` method:

```
onClick="alert(aName.toString())">
```

The `alert()` `onClick` event handler simply uses the identifier name of the object:

```
onClick="alert(aName)"
```

Note that the JavaScript language automatically calls the `toString()` method. So, we've successfully provided `toString()` functionality for our new `Name` object.

Combining Custom Objects

A custom object can use another custom object as a property, effectively enabling you to create objects within objects. The following `userAddress.html` script creates a `Person` object, a `Name` object, and an `Address` object. The `Person` object calls the `Name` and `Address` objects as properties.

```
<!--
                userAddress.html
-->
<HTML>
<HEAD>
<TITLE>User Address</TITLE>
<SCRIPT LANGUAGE="JavaScript">
<!-- HIDE FROM OLD BROWSERS

// formatProps method.
//
// Loop through the properties, constructing a
// list of the properties and their values.
//
function formatProps(objName) {
  var rvalue = "\n"
```

```
    for (var i in this) {
      rvalue += objName + "." + i
      rvalue += " = " + this[i] + "\n"
    }
    rvalue += "\n"

    return rvalue
  }


  //
  // Name Object Definition
  //

  // Display method for the Name object.
  //
  function displayName() {
    alert(this.firstName + " " + this.middleInitial
          + " " + this.lastName)
  }

  // Name object constructor.
  //
  function Name(first, mi, last) {
    // properties
    this.firstName     = first
    this.lastName      = last
    this.middleInitial = mi
    this.type          = "Name"

    // methods
    this.display       = displayName
    this.properties    = formatProps
    this.toString      = new Function(
      "return this.firstName + ' ' + this.middleInitial + '
' + this.lastName")
  }


  //
  // Address Object Definition
  //
```

```
// Display method for the Address object.
//
function displayAddress() {
  alert(this.street1 + "\n" + this.street2 + "\n" +
        this.city + "\n" + this.state + "\n" +
        this.zip)
}

// Address object constructor.
//
function Address(street1, street2, city, state, zip) {
  // properties
  this.city           = city
  this.state          = state
  this.street1        = street1
  this.street2        = street2
  this.type           = "Address"
  this.zip            = zip

  // methods
  this.display        = displayAddress
  this.properties     = formatProps
  this.toString       = new Function(
    "return this.street1 + '\\n' + this.street2 + '\\n' +
this.city + '\\n' + this.state + '\\n' + this.zip")
}


//
// Person Object Definition
//

// Display method for the Person object.
//
function displayPerson() {
  alert(this.name.toString() + "\n" +
        this.address.toString() + "\n" +
        this.phone + "\n" + this.email)
}

// Person object constructor.
//
function Person(name, address, phone, email) {
  // properties
```

```
  if (address == null || address == "" || address ==
"undefined") {
    this.address     = new Address()
  } else {
    this.address     = address
  }
  this.email         = email
  if (name == null || name == "" || name == "undefined") {
    this.name        = new Name()
  } else {
    this.name        = name
  }
  this.phone         = phone
  this.type          = "Person"

  // methods
  this.display       = displayPerson
  this.properties    = formatProps
  this.toString      = new Function(
    "return this.name.toString() + '\\n' +
this.address.toString() + ' \\n' + this.phone + '\\n' +
this.email")
}

//
// Stores the data for the form.
//
var thePerson = new Person()

// STOP HIDING -->
</SCRIPT>
</HEAD>
<BODY>

<P>This example creates a Person object. It is a
user-defined object that stores the data
associated in the form below.  Its properties
are name, address, phone, and email. The methods
are display and properties.  display() posts an
alert dialog containing the values of the
properties, and properties() returns a formatted
string containing all of the object's
properties.</P>
```

```
<P>One property, type, and one method, toString,
are also defined. type gives an easy way to
determine the type of the object. It is defined
as the string "Person". toString() converts the
object to a string. One thing toString enables you
to do is to obtain the value of a Person object
instance by simply using the instance
variable. For example:</P>

<CODE>
var thePerson = new Person()
alert(thePerson)
</CODE>

<P>The name and address properties are also
user-defined objects. Name is an instance of
the Name object, and address is an instance of
the Address object. You can provide instances of
the Name and Address objects when creating a
Person object in the following way:</P>

<CODE>
var aName     = new Name("Brian", "K.", "Freeman")
var anAddress = new Address("Attention: Brian", "1234 A
Street", "Silicon Valley", "CA", "00000-000")
var aPerson   = new Person(aName, anAddress, "(123) 123-
1234", "bkf@sgi.com")
</CODE>

<P>Or leave them blank and they will be created
for you.</P>

<CODE>
var thePerson = new Person()
</CODE>

<P>If you want to initialize the phone and email
properties but have name and address created for
you, you need to leave placeholders for the
parameters:</P>

<CODE>
var thePerson = new Person("", "", "(123) 123-1234",
"nobody@somewhere.com")
```

```
</CODE>

<P>Or:</P>

<CODE>
var thePerson = new Person(null, null, "(123) 123-1234",
"nobody@somewhere.com")
</CODE>

<P>When you click on the Send button, the
onSubmit callback calls the Person Object's
display method.</P>

<FORM onSubmit="thePerson.display(); return false;">
<TABLE COLS=3 BORDER=0 CELLSPACING=0
 CELLPADDING=4>
<TR>
  <TD ALIGN=left><B>First Name:</B></TD>
  <TD ALIGN=left><B>MI:</B></TD>
  <TD ALIGN=left><B>Last Name:</B></TD>
</TR>
<TR>
  <TD><INPUT
   TYPE="text"
   NAME="firstName"
   VALUE=""
   SIZE=25
   onChange="thePerson.name.firstName=this.value"
   onFocus="this.select()"></TD>
  <TD> <INPUT
   TYPE="text"
   NAME="middleInitial"
   VALUE=""
   SIZE=2
   onChange="thePerson.name.middleInitial=this.value"
   onFocus="this.select()"></TD>
  <TD><INPUT
   TYPE="text"
   NAME="lastName"
   VALUE=""
   SIZE=30
   onChange="thePerson.name.lastName=this.value"
   onFocus="this.select()"></TD>
</TR>
```

```
</TABLE>

<TABLE COLS=3 BORDER=0 CELLSPACING=0
 CELLPADDING=4>
<TR>
  <TD ALIGN=left><B>Street Address: </B><BR></TD>
</TR>
 <TD><INPUT
 TYPE="text"
 NAME="street1"
 VALUE=""
 SIZE=64
 onChange="thePerson.address.street1=this.value"
 onFocus="this.select()"><BR></TD>
</TR>
 <TD><INPUT
 TYPE="text"
 NAME="street2"
 VALUE=""
 SIZE=64
 onChange="thePerson.address.street2=this.value"
 onFocus="this.select()"></TD>
</TR>
</TABLE>

<TABLE COLS=3 BORDER=0 CELLSPACING=0
 CELLPADDING=4>
<TR>
  <TD ALIGN=left><B>City:</B></TD>
  <TD ALIGN=left><B>State:</B></TD>
  <TD ALIGN=left><B>Zip:</B></TD>
</TR>
<TR>
  <TD><INPUT
   TYPE="text"
   NAME="city"
   VALUE=""
   SIZE=43
   onChange="thePerson.address.city=this.value"
   onFocus="this.select()"></TD>
  <TD><INPUT
   TYPE="text"
   NAME="state"
   VALUE=""
```

```
    SIZE=2
    onChange="thePerson.address.state=this.value"
    onFocus="this.select()"></TD>
   <TD><INPUT
    TYPE="text"
    NAME="zip"
    VALUE=""
    SIZE=10
    onChange="thePerson.address.zip=this.value"
    onFocus="this.select()"></TD>
</TR>
</TABLE>

<TABLE COLS=2 BORDER=0 CELLSPACING=0
 CELLPADDING=4>
<TR>
  <TD ALIGN=left><B>Phone:</B></TD>
  <TD ALIGN=left><B>E-Mail:</B></TD>
</TR>
<TR>
  <TD><INPUT
   TYPE="text"
   NAME="phone"
   VALUE=""
   SIZE=15
   onChange="thePerson.phone=this.value"
   onFocus="this.select()"></TD>
  <TD><INPUT
   TYPE="text"
   NAME="email"
   VALUE=""
   SIZE=45
   onChange="thePerson.email=this.value"
   onFocus="this.select()"></TD>
</TR>
</TABLE>
<INPUT TYPE="submit" VALUE="Send">
</FORM>

</BODY>
</HTML>
```

Figure 34–14 shows the result of loading the `userAddress.html` script.

Netscape: User Address

Back | Forward | Home | Reload | Images | Open | Print | Find | Stop

Location: file:///Macintosh%20HD/Desktop%20Folder/JSBook-3.0/dev/objects/Person/userAddress.

What's New? | What's Cool? | Destinations | Net Search | People | Software

This example creates a Person object. It is a user-defined object that stores the data associated in the form below. Its properties are name, address, phone, and email. The methods are display and properties. display() posts an alert dialog containing the values of the properties, and properties() returns a formatted string containing all of the object's properties.

One property, type, and one method, toString, are also defined. type gives an easy way to determine the type of the object. It is defined as the string "Person". toString() converts the object to a string. One thing toString enables you to do is to obtain the value of a Person object instance by simply using the instance variable. For example:

```
var thePerson = new Person() alert(thePerson)
```

The name and address properties are also user-defined objects. Name is an instance of the Name object, and address is an instance of the Address object. You can provide instances of the Name and Address objects when creating a Person object in the following way:

```
var aName = new Name("Brian", "K.", "Freeman") var anAddress = new
Address("Attention: Brian", "1234 A Street", "Silicon Valley", "CA", "00000-000")
var aPerson = new Person(aName, anAddress, "(123) 123-1234", "bkf@sgi.com")
```

Or leave them blank and they will be created for you.

```
var thePerson = new Person()
```

If you want to initialize the phone and email properties but have name and address created for you, you need to leave placeholders for the parameters:

```
var thePerson = new Person("", "", "(123) 123-1234", "nobody@somewhere.com")
```

Or:

```
var thePerson = new Person(null, null, "(123) 123-1234", "nobody@somewhere.com")
```

When you click on the Send button, the onSubmit callback calls the Person Object's display method.

First Name: **MI:** **Last Name:**

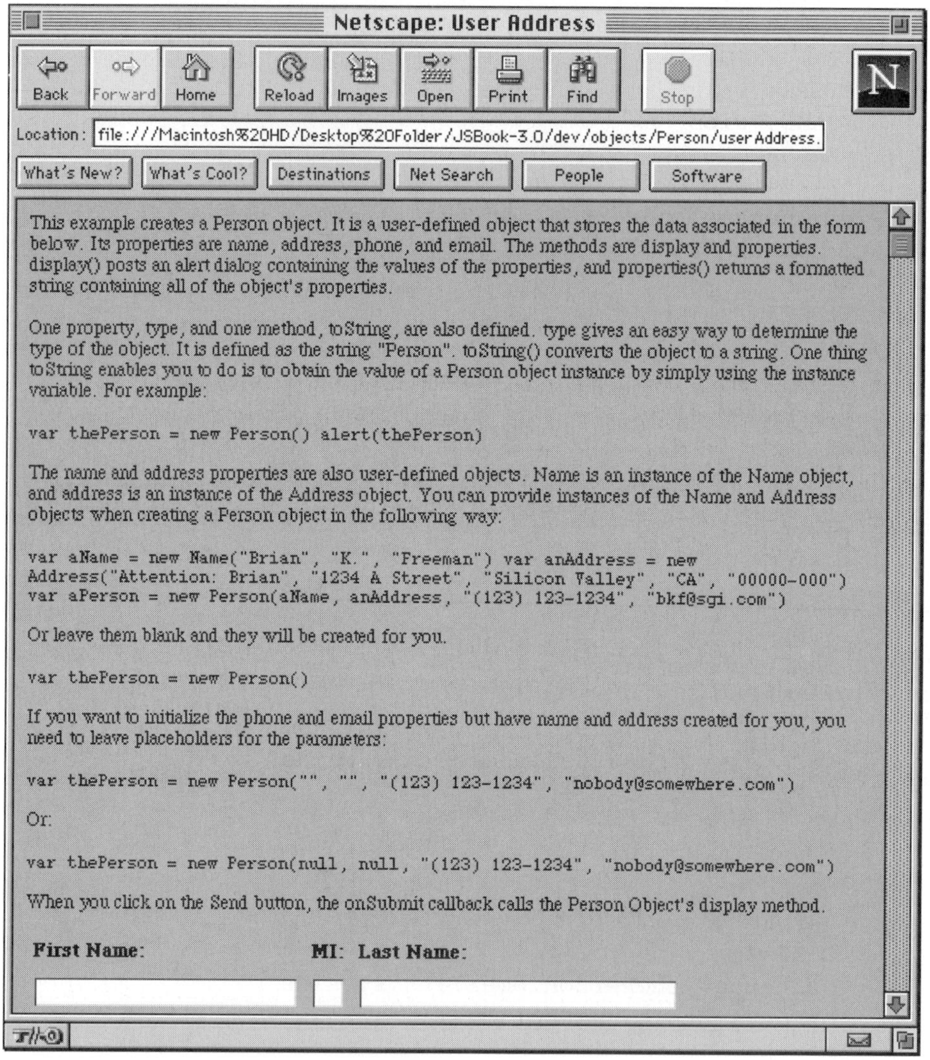

Figure 34–14 Result of loading the `userAddress.html` script

Figure 34–15 shows the second screen of the `userAddress.html` script.

Netscape: User Address

Back | Forward | Home | Reload | Images | Open | Print | Find | Stop

Location: file:///Macintosh%20HD/Desktop%20Folder/JSBook-3.0/dev/objects/Person/userAddress.

What's New? | What's Cool? | Destinations | Net Search | People | Software

```
var thePerson = new Person()
```

If you want to initialize the phone and email properties but have name and address created for you, you need to leave placeholders for the parameters:

```
var thePerson = new Person("", "", "(123) 123-1234", "nobody@somewhere.com")
```

Or:

```
var thePerson = new Person(null, null, "(123) 123-1234", "nobody@somewhere.com")
```

When you click on the Send button, the onSubmit callback calls the Person Object's display method.

First Name: **MI:** **Last Name:**

Street Address:

City: **State:** **Zip:**

Phone: **E-Mail:**

Send

Jumping JavaScript
by Janice Winsor and Brian Freeman
objects/Person/userAddress.html

Figure 34–15 Second screen of the `userAddress.html` script

When you fill in the form and click on the Send button, the `onClick` event handler displays an alert, as shown in Figure 34–16, that contains the values that would be submitted to the server if one were available. Notice that if you do not specify a value for the field, the string `undefined` is displayed as the value.

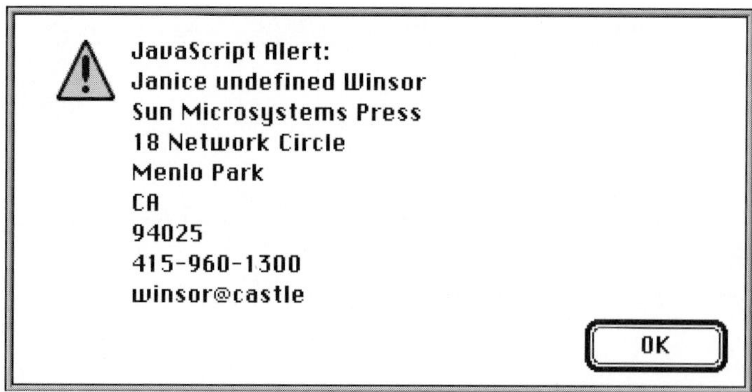

Figure 34–16 Alert containing `Person` object values

1009

CHAPTER 35

- Location of the Cookie File
- Limitations of the cookie Property
- Security Issues and Cookies
- Accessing Cookies from JavaScript
- Accessing Public-Domain Cookie Functions
- Creating a Basic Cookie Name
- Creating a Cookie with a Path Name
- Setting an Expiration Date for a Cookie
- Deleting a Cookie
- Setting a Cookie Domain
- Creating a Secure Cookie
- A Complex Cookie Example
- Summary of New Terms and Concepts

Controlling Script Input and Output with the cookie Property

When you ask users to fill in information, JavaScript stores that information on the client system as an entry in a text file that is located in the Netscape directory. Typically, this file is used by server-side CGI scripts to store information on the client computer. Cookie data is automatically transmitted between the browser and the Web server when appropriate. You can use the `document.cookie` property to access information that is stored in a cookie file.

The cookie specification titled "Persistent Client State HTTP Cookies," available at `http://home.netscape.com/newsref/std/cookie_spec.html`, contains Netscape's definition of the `cookie` property. It introduces cookies in the following way:

> Cookies are a general mechanism which server side connections (such as CGI scripts) can use to both store and retrieve information on the client side of the connection. The addition of a simple, persistent, client-side state significantly extends the capabilities of Web-based client/server applications.

CGI scripts typically use the cookie to store the user name and password. The CGI script instructs the browser to encrypt the password and write the information back to a cookie file on your client system.

The Overview from the cookie specification explains:

> A server, when returning an HTTP object to a client, may also send a piece of state information which the client will store. Included in that state object is a description of the range of URLs for which that state is valid. Any future HTTP requests made by the client which fall in that range will include a transmittal of the current value of the state object from the client back to the server. The state object is called a cookie, for no compelling reason.
>
> This simple mechanism provides a powerful new tool which enables a host of new types of applications to be written for web-based environments. Shopping applications can now store information about the currently selected items, for fee services can send back registration information and free the client from retyping a user-id on next connection, sites can store per-user preferences on the client, and have the client supply those preferences every time that site is connected to.

The rest of the specification defines cookie behavior mostly from the server's perspective.

Location of the Cookie File

The cookie mechanism isolates CGI script access to one special text file that is located in a specific place in your file system.

On Windows and UNIX platforms of Navigator, the cookie file is located in the Navigator directory and is named `cookies.txt`. On Macintosh platforms, the `MagicCookie` file is located in the `System:Preferences:Netscape` folder. The cookie file is a text file but, because the file type is not TEXT, Macintosh users cannot open the file directly. If you double-click on the `MagicCookie` file with the Netscape browser running, the file opens in the browser window, as shown in Figure 35–1.

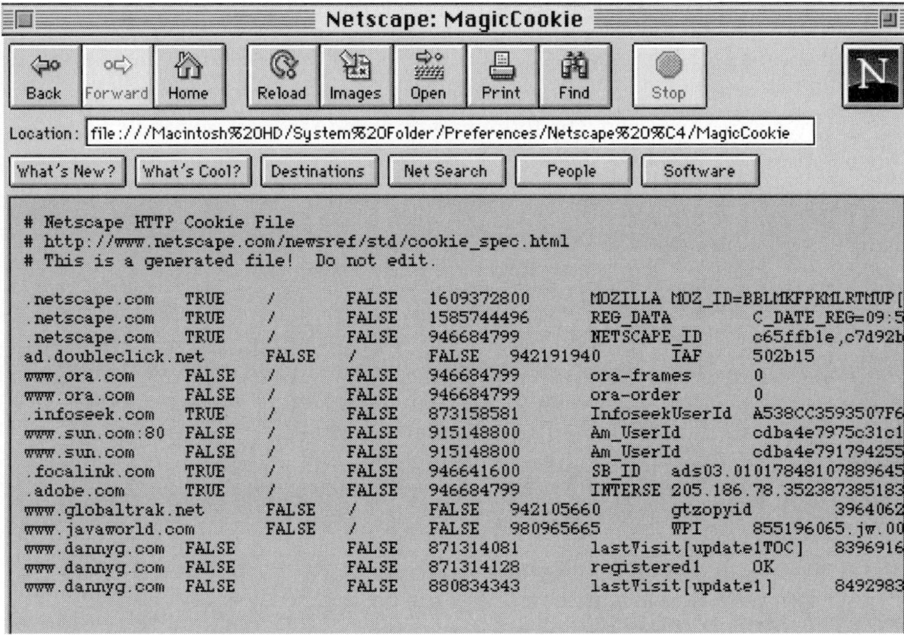

Figure 35–1 Macintosh `MagicCookie` file

The cookie has the following internal information in addition to its string contents:

- Domain name of the server that created the cookie
- Name of the cookie entry
- Expiration date
- Path name of URLs that can access the cookie

Limitations of the cookie Property

The `cookie` property has the following limitations:

- The Netscape environment can create a total of only 300 cookies.
- Each cookie is limited to 4 Kbytes in size, effectively limiting the file to about 1.2 Mbytes.
- A single site can have only 30 cookie entries.
- Sites can access cookie entries only within the same domain.

Security Issues and Cookies

Although server access to a user's computer is restricted to a single file in a single location, some people are concerned that access to cookie information is a potential invasion of privacy. The following quotation is from an article titled "Cyber-Snooping," by Steve Ulfelder, in the *San Francisco Examiner*, Sunday, October 20, 1996:

> "For every web access," Winkler [Ira Winkler, directory of technology at the National Computer Security Association in Carlisle, Pennsylvania says] "There's an access log." Less well-known, and more strenuously objected to by privacy advocates, is Client-Side Persistent information, better known as "cookies." Cookies are bits of data that a Web server stores on your hard drive when you visit a site. The server can read this data on subsequent visits to the site. One of the major uses of cookies is to track users' surfing habits. (Netscape Communications Corp.'s Navigator 3.0 allows you to set a preference that alerts you when you encounter a cookie.)
>
> Of course, information-gathering itself—for business, government or prurient reasons—is hardly new. But the growing ease of on-line snoopery has led to a new batch of questions on what should be publicly available.

Accessing Cookies from JavaScript

The JavaScript language enables you to access the cookie file on the client system with the `document.cookie` property. The JavaScript language can only read to or write from the browser's cookie file.

Property	Value	Gettable	Settable
cookie	string	Yes	Yes

When you assign values to a cookie, you use a simple JavaScript assignment operator. The following syntax shows the required and optional (in brackets) attributes that you can write to a cookie file. Note that you must separate each name/value pair with a semicolon and include the entire statement in quotation marks:

```
document.cookie = "cookieName=cookieValue
[; path=pathName]
[; expires=timeInGMTString]
[; domain=domainName]
[; secure]
```

The following sections look at each of the attributes individually.

To read Danny Goodman's explanation of cookies, visit the URL `http://developer.netscape.com/news/viewsource/archive/goodman_cookies.html`.

Accessing Public-Domain Cookie Functions

When using cookies, you do not need to figure it all out on your own. Public domain functions are available on the Web. For example, Bill Dortch of hIdaho, `bdortch@hidaho.com`, has written a set of cookies functions that he has released to the public domain. See `http://www.hidaho.com/cookies/cookie.txt` and `http://www.hidaho.com/cookies/cookie.html` to access these functions. We have used several of these public-domain functions in the examples in this chapter. Each such function is identified in the script comments as provided by Bill Dortch.

For a complete list of Bill's cookie functions, see "A Complex Cookie Example" on page 1028.

Creating a Basic Cookie Name

Each cookie you create must have a name and string value, even if the value is an empty string. For example, to create a basic cookie with a name of `myCookie` and a value of `ChocolateChip`, the statement is:

```
document.cookie="myCookie=ChocolateChip"
```

The following `name.html` script creates a cookie and uses the `document.cookie` property to read the values back to make sure that the cookie was set properly. If the current domain has no existing cookie with the name you use, then it creates the entry for you. If a cookie with that name already exists, then Navigator replaces the old data with the new data.

```
<!--
                    name.html
-->
<HTML>
<HEAD>
<TITLE>A Basic Cookie</TITLE>
</HEAD>
<BODY>

<P>The simplest form of a cookie sets the
document.cookie property to a name/value pair,
like so:</P>
```

```
<PRE>
document.cookie="theCookieName=theCookieValue"
</PRE>

<P>Every cookie must have a name and value, even
if the value is an empty string. The remaining
fields are optional and are defaulted if not
present.</P>

<P>So, let's create the following cookie:</P>

<PRE>
document.cookie="myCookie=ChocolateChip"
</PRE>

<SCRIPT LANGUAGE="JavaScript">
<!-- HIDE FROM OLD BROWSERS

document.cookie="myCookie=ChocolateChip"

// STOP HIDING -->
</SCRIPT>

<P>and read it back, just to make sure it was
set:</P>

<SCRIPT LANGUAGE="JavaScript">
<!-- HIDE FROM OLD BROWSERS

document.open()
document.write("document.cookie = ")
document.write(document.cookie)
document.close()

// STOP HIDING -->
</SCRIPT>

</BODY>
</HTML>
```

Figure 35–2 shows the result of loading the `name.html` script.

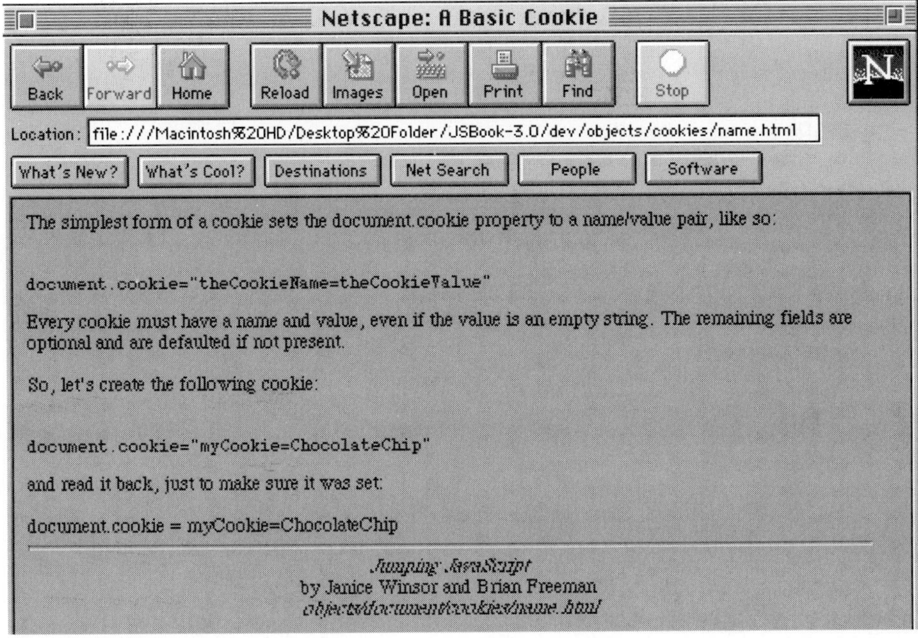

Figure 35–2 Result of loading the `name.html` script

Note – By their nature, cookies persist. If you have created any cookies in the current directory, your page may show existing cookie values along with the new value created by the `name.html` script.

Creating a Cookie with a Path Name

Use the optional `path` attribute if you want to set a specific path to contain the cookie file. If you do not specify a path, the default is to put the cookie in the current directory. For this attribute, the path value `"/"` specifies the current directory.

The following `path.html` script creates a cookie, using the default path, and checks to make sure that the cookie is accessible to another script in the same directory.

```
<!--
        path.html
-->
<HTML>
<HEAD>
<TITLE>Cookie Path</TITLE>
<SCRIPT LANGUAGE="JavaScript">
<!-- HIDE FROM OLD BROWSERS

document.cookie="myCookie=sugar"

// STOP HIDING -->
</SCRIPT>
</HEAD>
<BODY>

<P>A cookie can store an optional path name
capable of accessing the cookie. Stored in the
"path" field, it allows multiple documents to
share the same cookie data. If omitted, path is
set as "/", indicating the current directory.

<P>So, let's create a cookie and see if another
document can access it.</P>

<P>This document creates myCookie, and <A
HREF="path2.html">path2.html</A> should be able
to read it.

</BODY>
</HTML>
```

Figure 35–3 shows the result of loading the `path.html` script.

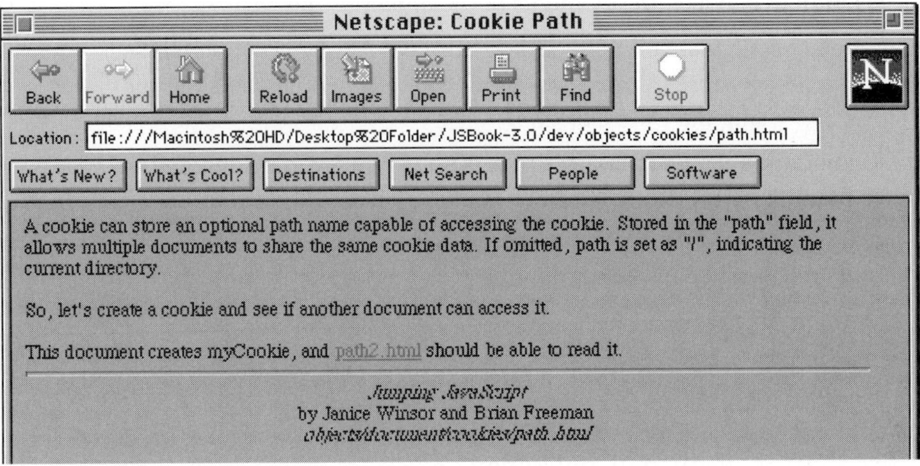

Figure 35–3 Result of loading the `path.html` script

Clicking on the path2.html link verifies that another script in the same directory can access the cookie. The cookie name and value are displayed in the `path2.html` page, as shown in Figure 35–4.

Figure 35–4 Result of clicking on the path2.html link

Setting an Expiration Date for a Cookie

The optional `expires` attribute specifies a date string that defines the end of the valid lifetime of that cookie. When the expiration date is reached, the cookie is no longer stored or given out.

The date string must be provided in Greenwich mean time and is formatted as:

```
Wdy, DD-Mon-YYYY HH:MM:SS GMT
```

The separators between the elements of the date must be dashes.

If you do not specify an expiration date, the cookie expires when the user's session ends. For more information about formatting dates in GMT, see Chapter 30, "Using the Date Object."

The following `expires.html` script sets an expiration date one hour from now. Notice that this script uses one of Bill Dortch's public-domain cookie functions.

```
<!--
        expires.html
-->
<HTML>
<HEAD>
<TITLE>Cookie Expires</TITLE>
<SCRIPT LANGUAGE="JavaScript">
<!-- HIDE FROM OLD BROWSERS

//  Cookie Functions - "Night of the Living Cookie"
//  Version (25-Jul-96)
//
//  Written by:  Bill Dortch, hIdaho Design
//  <bdortch@hidaho.com>
//  The following functions are released
//  to the public domain.

//
//  Function to correct for 2.x Mac date bug.
//  Call this function to fix a date object
//  prior to passing it to SetCookie.
//  IMPORTANT:  This function should only be
//  called *once* for any given date object!
//  See example at the end of this document.
//
function FixCookieDate (date) {
  var base = new Date(0);
 var skew = base.getTime(); // dawn of (Unix) time - should
be 0
  if (skew > 0)  // Except on the Mac - ahead of its time
    date.setTime (date.getTime() - skew);
}
// STOP HIDING -->
</SCRIPT>
</HEAD>
<BODY>
```

```
<P>You can provide an optional expiration date
for your cookie. It is stored in the "expires"
field, and the value must be a GMT date string.
When provided, Navigator writes the expiration date
to the cookie file and remembers it even if you quit.
Omitting it tells Navigator the cookie is temporary.

<P>Be careful with the date. The Mac 2.x version
of Navigator had a bug. See the function
FixCookieDate for a workaround.</P>

<P>To set a cookie that expires 1 hour from now,
use the following:</P>

<PRE>
  var expire = new Date()
  FixCookieDate(expire)
  var oneHour = expire.getTime() + (60 * 60 * 1000)
  expire.setTime(oneHour)

  document.cookie = "theCookie=value; expires=" +
    expire.toGMTString()
</PRE>

<P>Here we set the cookie and print out the value
of document.cookie.</P>

<SCRIPT LANGUAGE="JavaScript">
<!-- HIDE FROM OLD BROWSERS
  var expire = new Date()
  FixCookieDate(expire)
  var oneHour = expire.getTime() + (60 * 60 * 1000)
  expire.setTime(oneHour)

  document.cookie = "theCookie=value; expires=" +
    expire.toGMTString()

  document.open()
  document.write(document.cookie)
  document.close()
// STOP HIDING -->
</SCRIPT>
</BODY>
</HTML>
```

Figure 35–5 shows the result of loading the `expires.html` script.

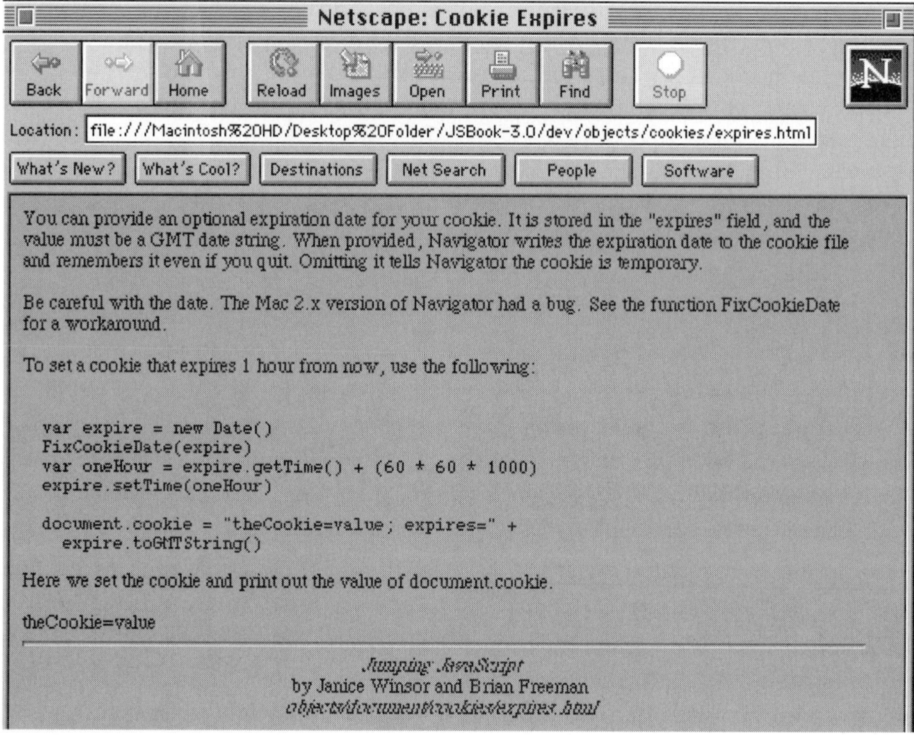

Figure 35–5 Result of loading the `expires.html` script

Deleting a Cookie

You can use the `expires` attribute to delete a client-side cookie by setting the `expires` attribute to an earlier time. The following `delete.html` script creates a cookie and provides buttons that you can use to set, display, and delete the cookie. In a classic bit of overkill, the delete button sets the time way back to the beginning of computer time: 01-Jan-70.

```
<!--
        delete.html
-->
<HTML>
<HEAD>
<TITLE>Deleting a Cookie</TITLE>
<SCRIPT LANGUAGE="JavaScript">
<!-- HIDE FROM OLD BROWSERS
```

```
//  Cookie Functions - "Night of the Living Cookie"
//  Version (25-Jul-96)
//
//  Written by:  Bill Dortch, hIdaho Design //
<bdortch@hidaho.com>
//  The following functions are released to
//  the public domain.
//
//  Function to correct for 2.x Mac date bug.
//  Call this function to fix a date object
//  prior to passing it to SetCookie.
//  IMPORTANT:  This function should only be
//  called *once* for any given date object!
//  See example at the end of this document.
//
function FixCookieDate (date) {
  var base = new Date(0);
  var skew = base.getTime(); // dawn of (Unix) time -
   should be 0
  if (skew > 0)  // Except on the Mac - ahead of its time
    date.setTime (date.getTime() - skew);
}

// Display document.cookie.
//
function displayCookie() {
  alert(document.cookie)
}

// Create the cookie gotaGo.
function setIt() {
  var expire = new Date()
  FixCookieDate(expire)
  var oneHour = expire.getTime() + (60 * 60 * 1000)
  expire.setTime(oneHour)

  document.cookie = "gotaGo=value; expires=" +
    expire.toGMTString()
}

// Delete the cookie gotaGo.
//
function deleteIt() {
  document.cookie = "gotaGo=value;
```

```
   expires=Thu, 01-Jan-70 00:00:01 GMT"
}

// STOP HIDING -->
</SCRIPT>
</HEAD>
<BODY onLoad="setIt()" onUnload="deleteIt()">

<P>You can delete a cookie that has not reached
its expiration date by resetting the cookie's
expiration date to a time in the past.</P>

<P>Here we create the cookie gotaGo that expires
in one hour:</P>

<PRE>
  var expire = new Date()
  FixCookieDate(expire)
  var oneHour = expire.getTime() + (60 * 60 * 1000)
  expire.setTime(oneHour)

  document.cookie = "gotaGo=value; expires=" +
    expire.toGMTString()
</PRE>

<P>To see that it is set, click on the Display button.
To delete it, click on the Delete button; the following
statement is executed:

<PRE>
  document.cookie = "gotaGo=value; expires=Thu, 01-Jan-70
00:00:01 GMT"
</PRE>

<FORM>
<INPUT TYPE="button" VALUE="Set"
onClick="setIt()">
<INPUT TYPE="button" VALUE="Display"
onClick="displayCookie()">
<INPUT TYPE="button" VALUE="Delete"
onClick="deleteIt()">
</FORM>
</BODY>
</HTML>
```

Figure 35–6 shows the result of loading the `delete.html` script.

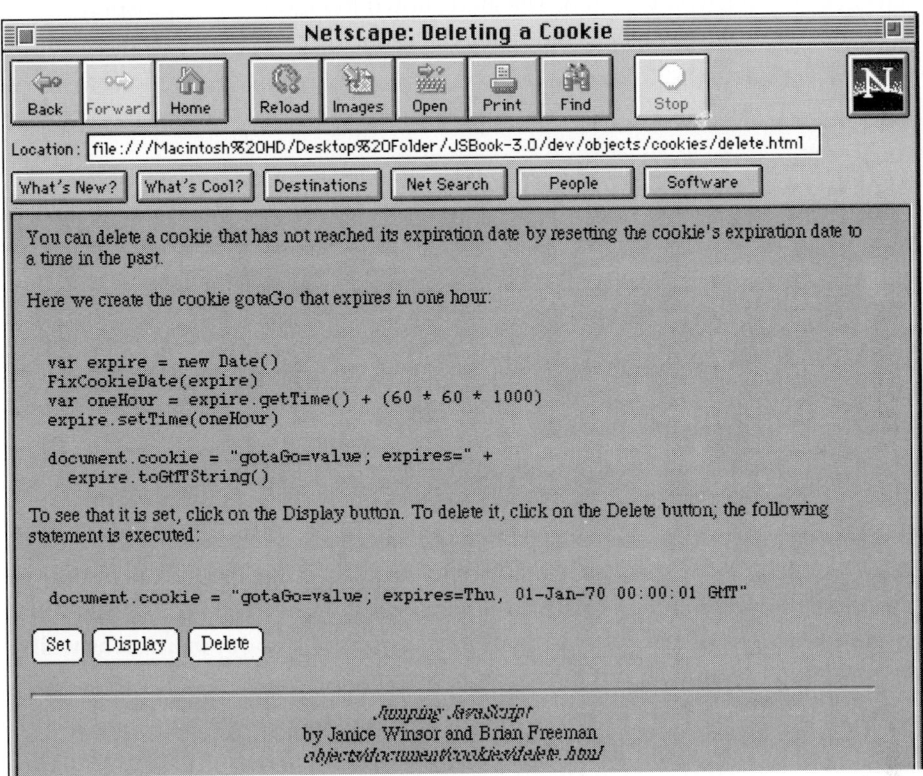

Figure 35–6 Result of loading the `delete.html` script

Click on the Set button to set the time, then click on the Display button. An alert is displayed, as shown in Figure 35–7, showing the value for the `gotaGo` cookie. Notice that the `sugar` cookie in that directory is still there.

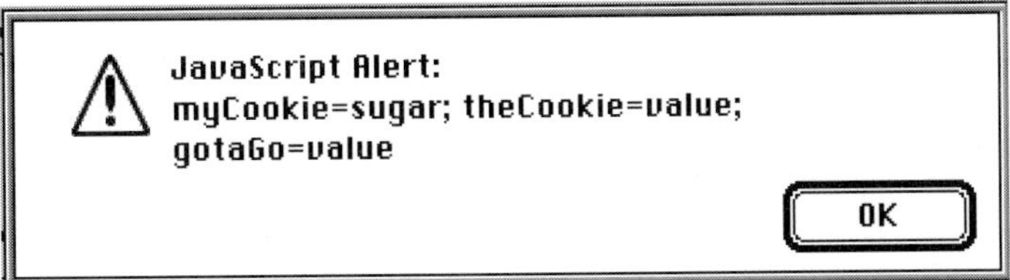

Figure 35–7 Alert showing the `gotaGo` cookie

Click on the Delete button to delete the cookie by setting the date to 01-Jan-70. Then click on the Display button. The alert shown in Figure 35–8 is displayed. Notice that the `sugar` cookie is not deleted, but the `gotaGo` cookie is no longer there.

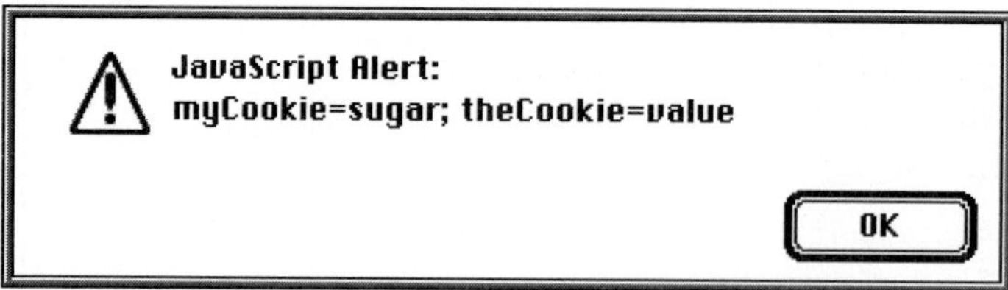

Figure 35–8 Deleted `gotaGo` cookie

Setting a Cookie Domain

The optional `domain` attribute enables you to specify a domain for the cookie. If you do not specify a domain, the default value is the host name of the server. If you do specify a domain, the JavaScript language does something called *tail matching*, which means that domain attribute is matched against the tail of the fully qualified domain name of the host. For example, a domain attribute of `frogtown.com` would match host names of `bigpond.frogtown.com` as well as `croak.smallpond.frogtown.com`.

Only hosts within the specified domain can set a cookie for a domain, and domains must have at least two dots in them to prevent domains of the form: `.com`, `.edu`, and `va.us`. Any domain that falls within one of the seven special, top-level domains—`com`, `edu`, `net`, `org`, `gov`, `mil`, and `int`—requires only two dots.

The following `domain.html` script describes the domain attribute but does not specify one because we don't have access to an example domain.

```
<!--
        domain.html
-->
<HTML>
<HEAD>
<TITLE>Cookie Domain</TITLE>
</HEAD>
<BODY>

<P>A cookie's domain is an optional field that
stores the domain of the server that created the
cookie. It works with the path field to
```

```
synchronize cookie data with a document and enable
sharing of that data across documents. Navigator
automatically supplies the domain of the current
document.

<P>You can provide an entire URL to the domain,
including the protocol in the domain field.
Note that the URL must have at least two dots in
the setting. Like:</P>

<DL>
  <DT>.sun.com
  <DT>.sgi.com
  <DT>.netscape.com
</DL>

<P>If you were to create a cookie sharable
across all of sun's domain, you would use the
following:<P>

<PRE>
document.cookie="userName=Brian; domain=.sun.com"
</PRE>

</BODY>
</HTML>
```

Figure 35–9 shows the result of loading the `domain.html` script.

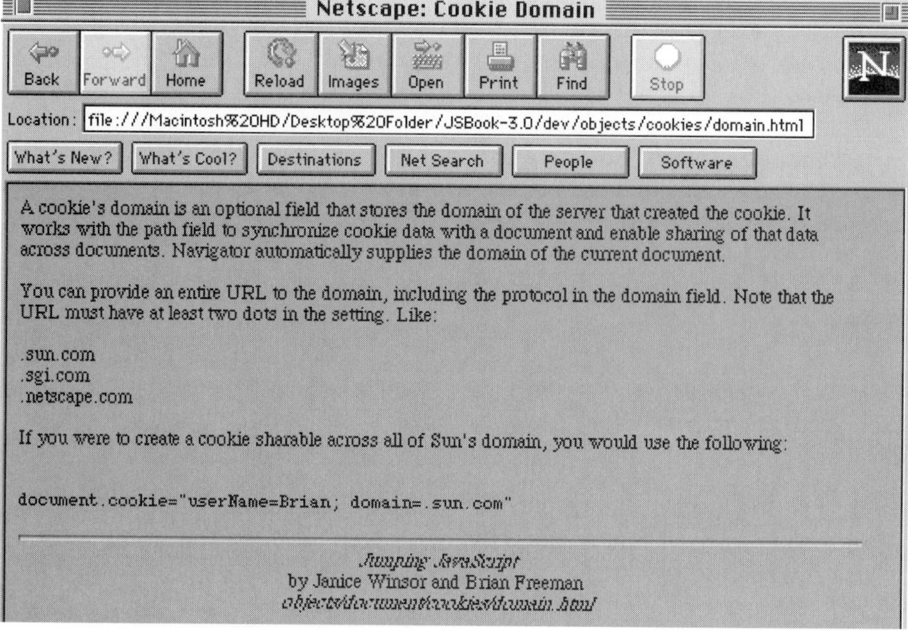

Figure 35–9 Result of loading the `domain.html` script

Creating a Secure Cookie

The optional `secure` attribute has no value. If a cookie is marked `secure`, it is transmitted only if the communications channel with the host is a secure one. Currently, this means that secure cookies are sent only to HTTPS (HTTP over SSL) servers. If you do not specify the `secure` attribute, a cookie is considered safe to be sent over unsecured channels. Generally, you omit the `secure` attribute when you create a client-side cookie.

The following statement creates a secure cookie:

```
document.cookie="userName=Brian; domain=.sun.com; secure"
```

A Complex Cookie Example

The following `todo.html` script creates a cookie to store a list of to-do items. This script also includes all of Bill Dortch's public-domain cookie functions and uses some of them in the script.

```
<!--
        todo.html
-->
<HTML>
<HEAD>
<TITLE>A Cookie To Do List</TITLE>
<SCRIPT LANGUAGE="JavaScript">
<!-- HIDE FROM OLD BROWSERS

//
//  Cookie Functions - "Night of the Living Cookie"
//  Version (25-Jul-96)
//
//  Written by:  Bill Dortch, hIdaho Design
//  <bdortch@hidaho.com>
//
//  The following functions are released to the
//  public domain.
//
//  This version takes a more aggressive approach
//  to deleting cookies.  Previous versions set
//  the expiration date to one millisecond prior
//  to the current time; however, this method did
//  not work in Netscape 2.02 (though it does in
//  earlier and later versions), resulting in
//  "zombie" cookies that would not die.
//  DeleteCookie now sets the expiration date to
//  the earliest usable date (one second into
//  1970), and sets the cookie's value to null
//  for good measure.
//
//  Also, this version adds optional path and
//  domain parameters to the DeleteCookie
//  function.  If you specify a path and/or
//  domain when creating (setting) a cookie**,
//  you must specify the same path/domain when
//  deleting it, or deletion will not occur.
//
//  The FixCookieDate function must now be called
//  explicitly to correct for the 2.x Mac date
//  bug.  This function should be called *once*
//  after a Date object is created and before it
//  is passed (as an expiration date) to
//  SetCookie.  Because the Mac date bug affects
```

```
//  all dates, not just those passed to
//  SetCookie, you might want to make it a habit
//  to call FixCookieDate any time you create a
//  new Date object:
//
//    var theDate = new Date();
//    FixCookieDate (theDate);
//
//  Calling FixCookieDate has no effect on
//  platforms other than the Mac, so there is no
//  need to determine the user's platform prior
//  to calling it.
//
//  This version also incorporates several minor
//  coding improvements.
//
//  **Note that it is possible to set multiple
//  cookies with the same name but different
//  (nested) paths.  For example:
//
//    SetCookie ("color","red",null,"/outer");
//    SetCookie ("color","blue",null,"/outer/inner");
//
//  However, GetCookie cannot distinguish between
//  these and will return the first cookie that
//  matches a given name.  It is therefore
//  recommended that you *not* use the same name
//  for cookies with different paths.  (Bear in
//  mind that there is *always* a path associated
//  with a cookie; if you don't explicitly
//  specify one, the path of the setting document
//  is used.)
//
//  Revision History:
//
//    "Toss Your Cookies" Version (22-Mar-96)
//      - Added FixCookieDate() function to
//        correct for Mac date bug
//
//    "Second Helping" Version (21-Jan-96)
//      - Added path, domain and secure
//        parameters to SetCookie
//      - Replaced home-rolled encode/decode
//        functions with Netscape's new (then)
```

```
//        escape and unescape functions
//
//    "Free Cookies" Version (December 95)
//
//
//  For information on the significance of cookie
//  parameters, and on cookies in general,
//  please refer to the official cookie spec, at:
//
//  http://www.netscape.com/newsref/std/cookie_spec.html
//
//*************************************************
//
// "Internal" function to return the decoded
//  value of a cookie
//
function getCookieVal (offset) {
  var endstr =
    document.cookie.indexOf (";", offset);
  if (endstr == -1)
    endstr = document.cookie.length;
  return unescape(document.cookie.substring(offset,
endstr));
}
//
//  Function to correct for 2.x Mac date bug.
//  Call this function to fix a date object prior
//  to passing it to SetCookie.  IMPORTANT: This
//  function should only be called *once* for any
//  given date object!  See example at the end of
//  this document.
//
function FixCookieDate (date) {
  var base = new Date(0);
  var skew = base.getTime(); // dawn of (Unix)
                             //  time-should be 0
  if (skew > 0)
    // Except on the Mac - ahead of its time
    date.setTime (date.getTime() - skew);
}
//
//  Function to return the value of the cookie
//  specified by "name".
//
```

```
//     name - String object containing the cookie
//            name.
//     returns - String object containing the
//            cookie value, or null if the cookie
//            does not exist.
//
function GetCookie (name) {
  var arg = name + "=";
  var alen = arg.length;
  var clen = document.cookie.length;
  var i = 0;
  while (i < clen) {
    var j = i + alen;
    if (document.cookie.substring(i, j) == arg)
      return getCookieVal (j);
    i = document.cookie.indexOf(" ", i) + 1;
    if (i == 0) break;
  }
  return null;
}
//
//  Function to create or update a cookie.
//     name - String object containing the cookie
//            name.
//     value - String object containing the cookie
//            value.  May contain any valid string
//            characters.
//     [expires] - Date object containing the
//            expiration data of the cookie.  If
//            omitted or null, expires the cookie
//            at the end of the current session.
//     [path] - String object indicating the path
//            for which the cookie is valid. If
//            omitted or null, uses the path of
//            the calling document.
//     [domain] - String object indicating the
//            domain for which the cookie is
//            valid.  If omitted or null, uses the
//            domain of the calling document.
//     [secure] - Boolean (true/false) value
//            indicating whether cookie
//            transmission requires a secure
//            channel (HTTPS).
//
```

```
//  The first two parameters are required.  The
//  others, if supplied, must be passed in the
//  order listed above.  To omit an unused
//  optional field, use null as a place holder.
//  For example, to call SetCookie using name,
//  value and path, you would code:
//
//      SetCookie ("myCookieName",
//                 "myCookieValue", null, "/");
//
//  Note that trailing omitted parameters do not
//  require a placeholder.
//
//  To set a secure cookie for path "/myPath",
//  that expires after the current session, you
//  might code:
//
//      SetCookie (myCookieVar, cookieValueVar,
//                 null, "/myPath", null, true);
//
function SetCookie (name, value, expires, path,
                    domain, secure) {
  document.cookie =
    name + "=" + escape (value) +
   ((expires) ? "; expires=" + expires.toGMTString() : "")
+
    ((path) ? "; path=" + path : "") +
    ((domain) ? "; domain=" + domain : "") +
    ((secure) ? "; secure" : "");
}

//  Function to delete a cookie. (Sets expiration
//  date to start of epoch)
//    name -   String object containing the
//             cookie name
//    path -   String object containing the path
//             of the cookie to delete.  This
//             MUST be the same as the path used
//             to create the cookie, or
//             null/omitted if no path was
//             specified when creating the
//             cookie.
//    domain - String object containing the
//             domain of the cookie to delete.
```

```
//                This MUST be the same as the
//                domain used to create the cookie,
//                or null/omitted if no domain was
//                specified when creating the
//                cookie.
//
function DeleteCookie (name,path,domain) {
  if (GetCookie(name)) {
    document.cookie = name + "=" +
      ((path) ? "; path=" + path : "") +
      ((domain) ? "; domain=" + domain : "") +
      "; expires=Thu, 01-Jan-70 00:00:01 GMT";
  }
}


//
// Local variables and functions
//


// global variable to count the number of to do
// cookies set.
var numberOfCookies = 0

// A document onLoad event handler to obtain the
// number of cookies in the to do list and load
// the selection list with their values.
//
function getNumberOfCookies() {
  numberOfCookies = GetCookie("todoNumber")

  // Load the selection list if necessary.
  if (numberOfCookies > 0 ) {
    var select = document.todoForm.items.options

    for (var i = 0; i <= numberOfCookies; i++) {
      var value = GetCookie("todo" + i)
      select[select.length] =
        new Option(unescape(value),"",false,false)
    }
  }
}
```

```
// Add a to do item to the list.
//
function addToDoCookie(theForm) {
  if (theForm.item.value.length <= 0) {
    alert("Please enter a new item.")
    return false
  } else {
    var expdate = new Date();
    var select  = document.todoForm.items.options

    // Fix the date and set the cookies to expire
    // 24 hours from now.
    FixCookieDate(expdate)
    expdate.setTime(expdate.getTime() +
      (24 * 60 * 60 * 1000))

    // Set the cookies
    SetCookie("todo" + numberOfCookies,
              theForm.item.value, expdate)
    SetCookie("todoNumber",numberOfCookies,expdate)
    numberOfCookies++

    // Add the item to the selection list
    select[select.length] =
      new Option(theForm.item.value,"",false,false)
    return true
  }
}

// STOP HIDING -->
</SCRIPT>
</HEAD>
<BODY onLoad="getNumberOfCookies()">

<P>This example constructs a to-do list with Bill
Dortch's cookie functions. For each to-do list
item you add, a new cookie is created, named
"todoN", where N is the total number of to do
cookies set. The number of cookies is stored in
the cookie "todoNumber".</P>

<P>Deleting to-do items is the next logical
progression of this example; because the
selection list needed options defined to give it
```

```
width, I didn't tackle it. Maybe there will be
time in the next revision or some kind reader
will work it out. If so, we'll definitely pass it
on.</P>

<P>Then again, it kind of looks like one of my
lists. Never shrinking ;-)</P>

<FORM NAME="todoForm"
 onSubmit="addToDoCookie(this); return false">
<P><B>To Do Items:</B><BR>
<SELECT NAME="items" SIZE=10>
  <OPTION> Read the rest of the Cookies chapter.
  <OPTION> Experiment with Bill Dortch's functions.
  <OPTION> Come up with an example of my own.
</SELECT>

<P><B>New Item:</B><BR>
<INPUT TYPE="text" NAME="item" SIZE=40 VALUE="">
</P>
<INPUT TYPE="submit" VALUE="Add To Do Item">
</FORM>

</BODY>
</HTML>
```

Figure 35–10 shows the result of loading the `todo.html` script.

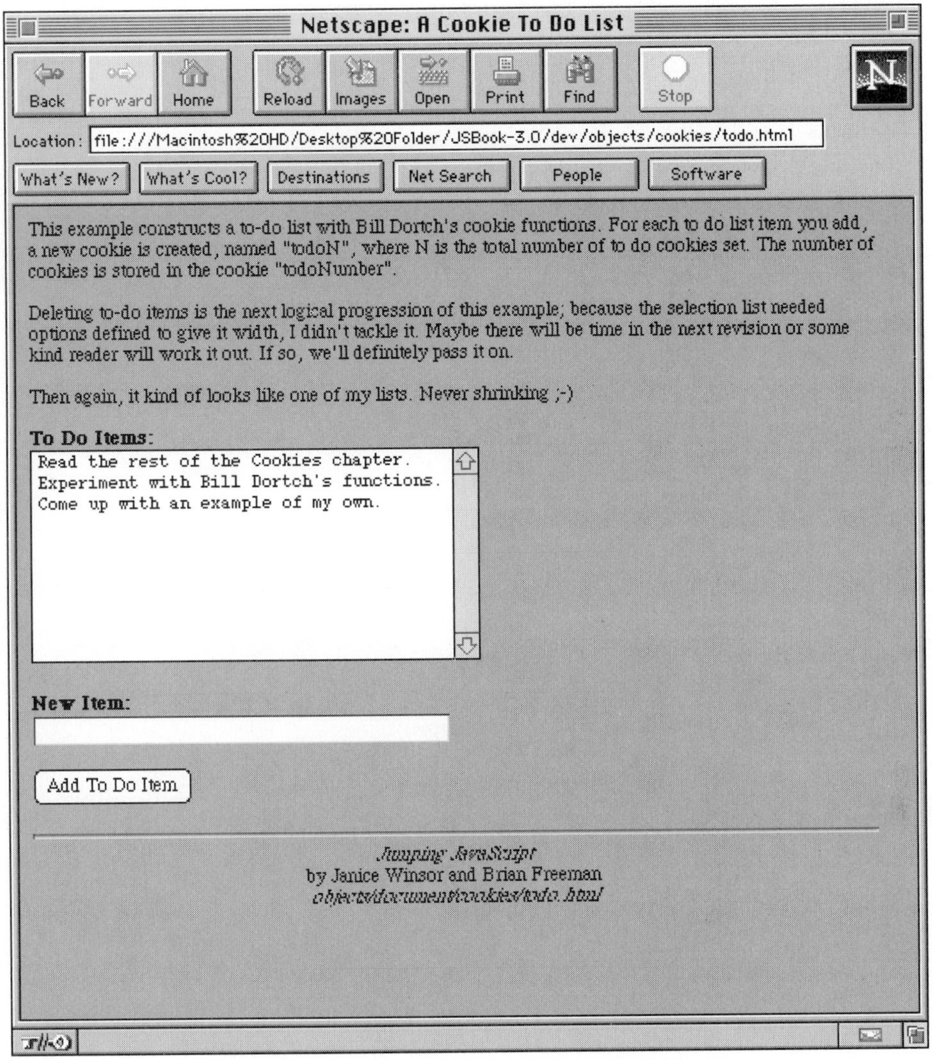

Netscape: A Cookie To Do List

Back Forward Home Reload Images Open Print Find Stop

Location: file:///Macintosh%20HD/Desktop%20Folder/JSBook-3.0/dev/objects/cookies/todo.html

What's New? What's Cool? Destinations Net Search People Software

This example constructs a to-do list with Bill Dortch's cookie functions. For each to do list item you add, a new cookie is created, named "todoN", where N is the total number of to do cookies set. The number of cookies is stored in the cookie "todoNumber".

Deleting to-do items is the next logical progression of this example; because the selection list needed options defined to give it width, I didn't tackle it. Maybe there will be time in the next revision or some kind reader will work it out. If so, we'll definitely pass it on.

Then again, it kind of looks like one of my lists. Never shrinking ;-)

To Do Items:

Read the rest of the Cookies chapter.
Experiment with Bill Dortch's functions.
Come up with an example of my own.

New Item:

Add To Do Item

Jumping JavaScript
by Janice Winsor and Brian Freeman
objects/document/cookies/todo.html

Figure 35–10 Result of loading the `todo.html` script

To add a new item to the to-do list, type it into the text field and click on the Add To Do Item button, as shown in Figure 35–11.

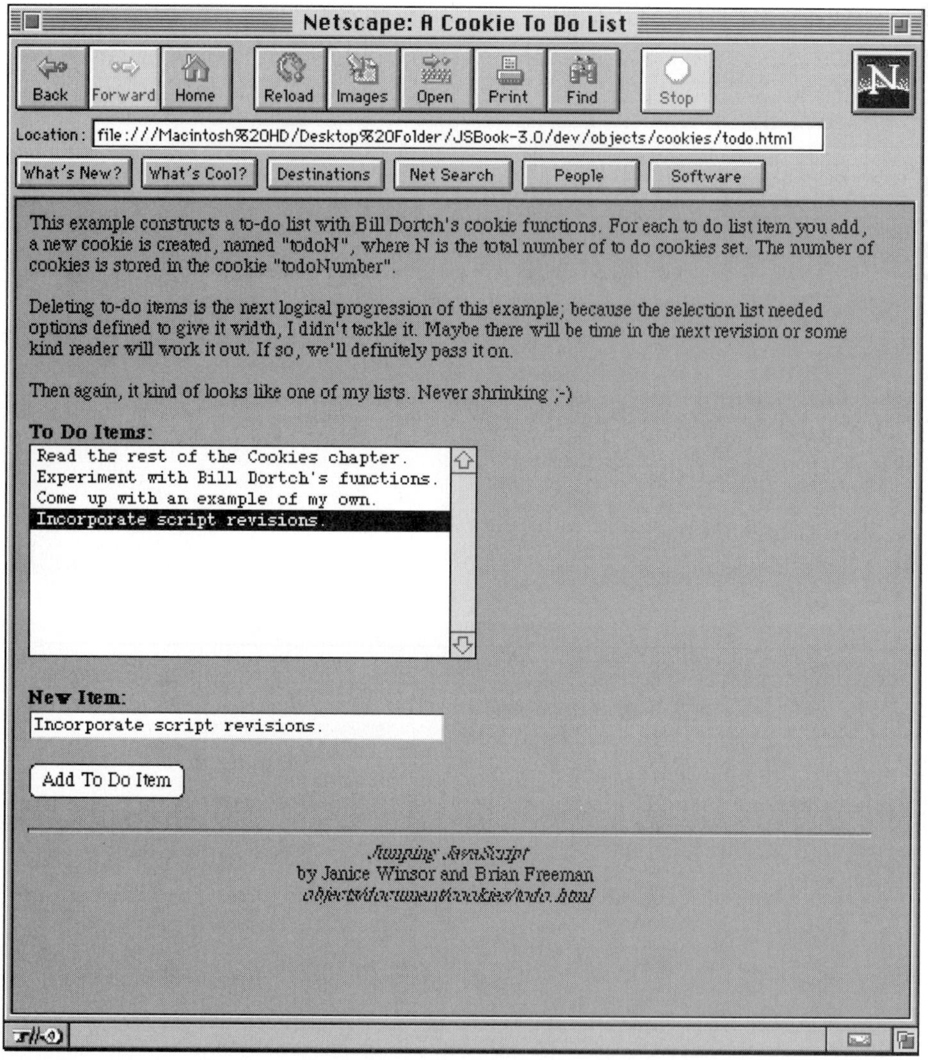

Figure 35–11 New item added to the to-do list

Summary of New Terms and Concepts

The new terms and concepts introduced in this chapter are listed in alphabetical order in Table 35-1. The terms and concepts are also included in the glossary at the end of the book.

Table 35-1 New Terms and Concepts

Term/Concept	Description
tail matching	The way a cookie domain is matched—starting from the end of the fully qualified domain name of the host and working backward.

CHAPTER 36

- Enabling Data Tainting on Your Platform
- Accessing Windows with Tainted Data
- Tainting Data
- Untainting Data
- Summary of New Terms and Concepts

Controlling Data Tainting

The Navigator 3.0 release implements a new security model that is based on a concept known as *data tainting*. This concept is borrowed from the Perl programming language. A script author can mark as tainted any element that contains property values or data that should be secure and private. This tainting enables the JavaScript language to keep close tabs on data that is supposed to be private to the client and to distinguish it from data that is not private.

Tainting is contagious in that any values derived in any way from tainted data are also tainted. If you add a tainted string to an untainted string, the resulting string is tainted. If you pass a tainted value to a function, the return value of the function is tainted. If that value is used in the result, then any substring is also tainted. If a script examines a tainted value, then the script itself becomes tainted.

By default, the properties for the objects listed in Table 36-1 are tainted.

Table 36-1 **Properties That Are Tainted by Default**

Object	Tainted Properties
`checkbox`	`checked, defaultChecked, defaultValue, name, selectedIndex, value`
`document`	`cookie, domain, forms, lastModified, links, referrer,, title, URL`

Table 36-1 **Properties That Are Tainted by Default (Continued)**

Object	Tainted Properties
`form`	`action`
`history`	`current, next, previous, toString`
`link`	`hash, host, hostname, href, pathname, port, protocol, search, toString`
`location`	`hash, host, hostname, href, pathname, port, protocol, search, toString`
`radio`	`checked, defaultChecked, defaultValue, name, selectedIndex, value`
`select.option`	`defaultSelected, selected, text, value`
`text, textarea, password`	`name toString, value`
`window`	`defaultStatus, status`

You control data tainting by using the following two JavaScript built-in functions:

- `taint()`
- `untaint()`

Data tainting is implemented for any Navigator 3.*x* browser. Data tainting has two components:

- Whether tainting is enabled on the user's computer
- How tainting is controlled from the author's scripts

The following list describes how data tainting behaves for users with data tainting not enabled, which is the default:

- The properties in Table 36-1 are tainted by default.
- In scripts, user can see only objects and properties that come from their own server.
- Scripts cannot send the values to other servers by URL or by posting a form without the user's knowledge and permission.

- If a script taints a property or a custom object, then it is added to the list of properties or objects that scripts cannot send to other servers by URL or by posting a form without the user's knowledge and permission.
- If a script untaints a property or a custom object, then the script can send the value returned from the `untaint()` function to other servers by URL or by posting a form without the user's knowledge or permission.

Users can enable data tainting on their platform by following the instructions in "Enabling Data Tainting on Your Platform" on page 1044. When data tainting is enabled, data tainting behaves in the same way as when data tainting is not enabled, except for the following:

- Users can see objects and properties that come from other servers. Scripts on the user's system still cannot capture those values or submit them to other servers by URL or by posting a form without the user's knowledge or permission.
- Every time users access a site that contains sensitive or private information, a confirmation window that is generated by the browser is displayed. Figure 36–1 shows the Macintosh version of this confirmation window.

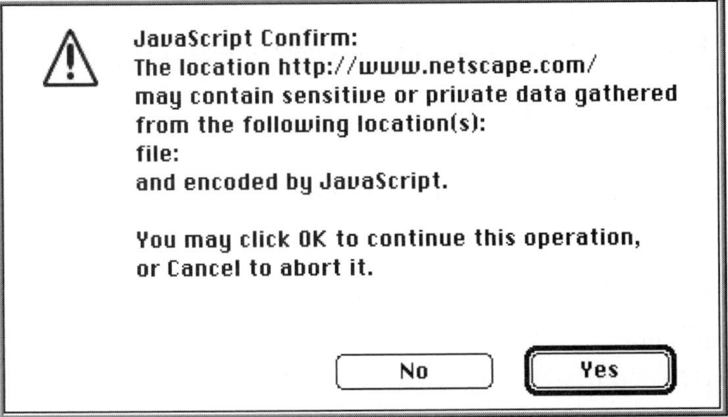

Figure 36–1 Data tainting confirmation window

Notice that in the Macintosh version of this confirmation, the wording of the text does not match the names on the buttons. The text says you may click OK to continue the operation or Cancel to abort it. However, the buttons are titled No and Yes. You can click on the Yes button to continue or on the No button to cancel the operation. On Windows 95 and X-11 platforms, the buttons are named OK and Cancel.

Enabling Data Tainting on Your Platform

When data tainting is enabled, properties from another window are available to other windows and the browser displays an alert informing users that they are accessing a window that contains restricted information. Scripts cannot pass these tainted values on to a server with the user's permission.

When data tainting is disabled, no script can access any properties of a window on another server.

When You Should Enable Data Tainting

You should enable data tainting when you want to display values for any of the properties that are tainted by default from scripts on other servers. For example, in the analyzer scripts for the `location` object, you must enable data tainting before you can see the values returned by the `location` object properties.

The following instructions describe how to enable data tainting for your platform. You enable data tainting by setting the `NS_ENABLE_TAINT` environment variable.

UNIX Systems

On UNIX systems, use the `setenv` command if you are running `csh`.

1. Exit your current Navigator.
2. In a shell, type `setenv NS_ENABLE_TAINT true` and press Return.
3. Restart Navigator from the same shell.

Windows Systems

On Windows systems, use the `set` command.

1. Exit your current Navigator.
2. Add `SET NS_ENABLE_TAINT=TRUE` to your `autoexec.bat` file.
3. Restart your computer.
4. Restart Navigator.

Macintosh Systems

On Macintosh systems, sad to say, enabling data tainting is very complex and not at all intuitive. It also requires an application, ResEdit, that is not part of the Navigator software and is not standard on Macintosh systems. ResEdit stands for resource editor. Be sure you use the following procedure exactly.

1. Use `ftp` to download the ResEdit software from the following site:

   `ftp://ftpdev.info.apple.com/Developer_Services/`
   `Tool_Chest/Developer_Utilities/ResEdit_22.1.3/`
   `ResEdit_2.1.3.sea.hqx`

2. Drag the `ResEdit_2.1.3.sea.hqx` file onto Stuffit Expander. A `ResEdit_2.1.3.sea` file is created in the same folder that contains the `ResEdit_2.1.3.sea.hqx` file.

3. Double-click on the `ResEdit_2.1.3.sea` icon. The file is expanded, and a ResEdit_2.1.3 folder is created in the same folder that contains the `ResEdit_2.1.3.sea` file.

4. If you are running Navigator, quit the application.

5. Open the `ResEdit 2.1.3` folder and double-click on `ResEdit`. A startup window is displayed, as shown in Figure 36–2.

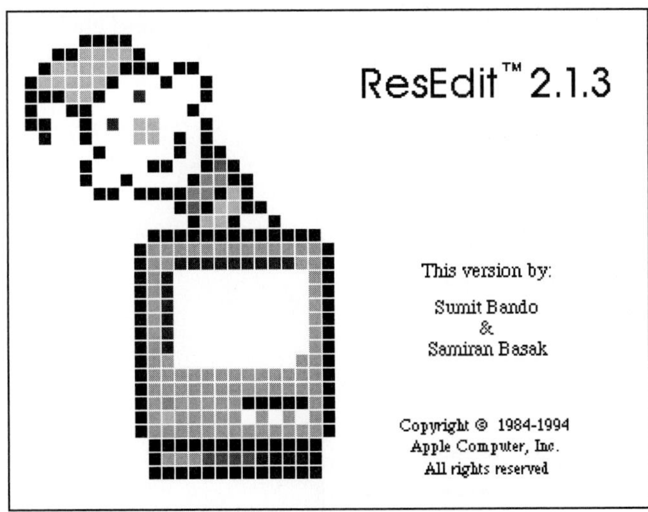

ResEdit™ 2.1.3
This version by:
Sumit Bando
&
Samiran Basak
Copyright © 1984-1994
Apple Computer, Inc.
All rights reserved

Figure 36–2 ResEdit startup window

6. Press any key to dismiss this window and display a finder window. The finder window is displayed, as shown in Figure 36–3.

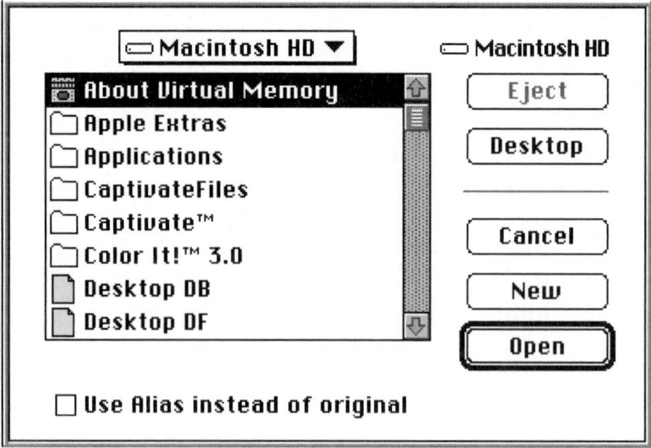

Figure 36–3 ResEdit finder window

7. Open your Navigator folder, highlight the Navigator program, and click in the Use Alias instead of original checkbox at the bottom of the window, as shown in Figure 36–4.

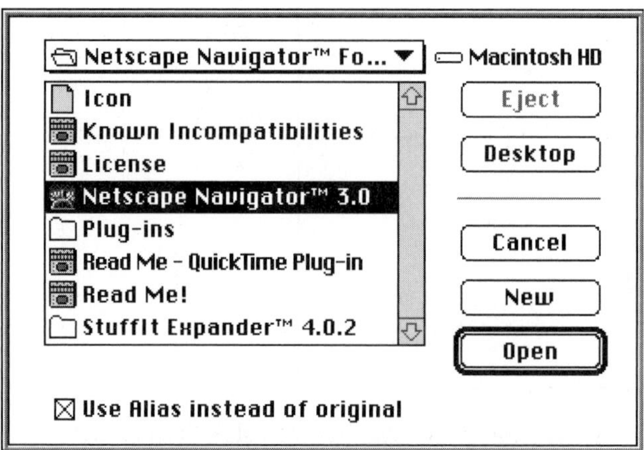

Figure 36–4 Highlighted Navigator program

8. Click on the Open button. A window opens, showing icons for Netscape resources, as shown in Figure 36–5.

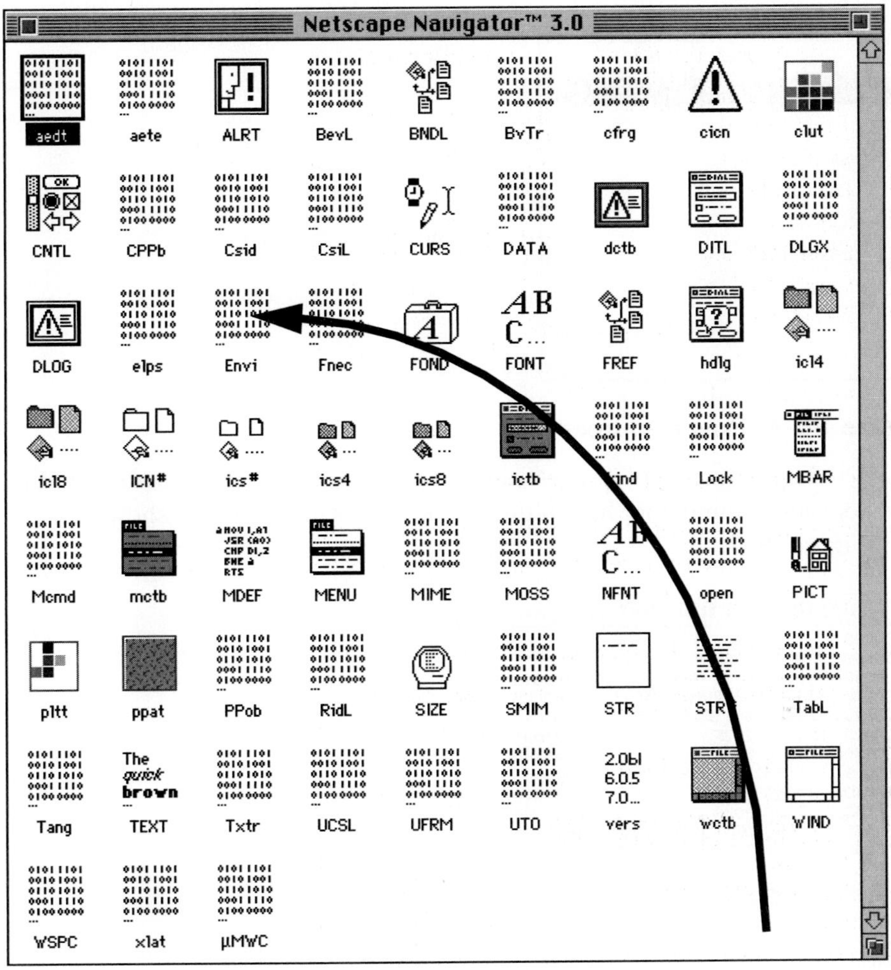

Figure 36–5 Netscape resources

9. Locate the `Envi` icon, as shown by the arrow, and double-click on it. A window opens, showing an ID of 128, as shown in Figure 36–6.

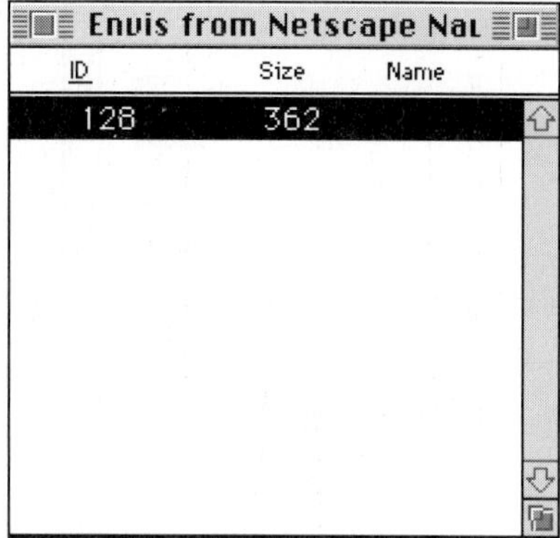

Figure 36–6 Envi resources

10. Double-click on the 128. A window opens showing a list of resources with a location column, four hex columns, and an ASCII column, as shown in Figure 36–7.

```
Envi ID = 128 from Netscape Nav
000000    434F 4E53 4F4C 455F   CONSOLE_
000008    4C4F 475F 4E41 4D45   LOG_NAME
000010    3D43 6F6E 736F 6C65   =Console
000018    204C 6F67 0D43 4C41    Log□CLA
000020    5353 5041 5448 3D2F   SSPATH=/
000028    7573 722F 6C6F 6361   usr/loca
000030    6C2F 6E65 7473 6361   l/netsca
000038    7065 2F6A 6176 612F   pe/java/
000040    4C69 622F 6A61 7661   Lib/java
000048    5F33 303A 2F75 7372   _30:/usr
000050    2F6C 6F63 616C 2F6E   /local/n
000058    6574 7363 6170 652F   etscape/
000060    6A61 7661 2F4C 6962   java/Lib
000068    2F6A 6176 6163 2E7A   /javac.z
```

Figure 36–7 128 resource data

11. From the Find menu, choose Find ASCII. A find window is displayed.
12. Type `NS_ENABLE_TAINT` in the find window, as shown in Figure 36–8.

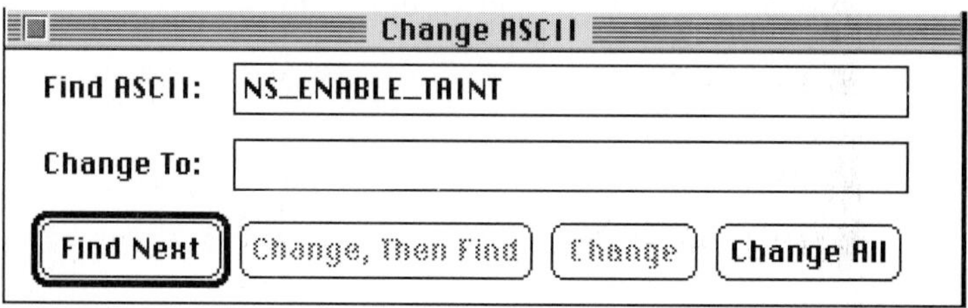

Figure 36–8 Find window

13. Click on the Find Next button. The text in the Envi ID 128 window is highlighted, as shown in Figure 36–9.

```
Envi ID = 128 from Netscape Navi
0000D0   615F 3330 313A 2F75   a_301:/u
0000D8   7372 2F6C 6F63 616C   sr/local
0000E0   2F6E 6574 7363 6170   /netscap
0000E8   652F 6A61 7661 2F4E   e/java/N
0000F0   5350 525F 4C4F 475F   SPR_LOG_
0000F8   4D4F 4455 4C45 533D   MODULES=
000100   5448 5245 4144 3D30   THREAD=0
000108   2C4D 4F4E 4954 4F52   ,MONITOR
000110   3D30 2C53 4348 4544   =0,SCHED
000118   3D30 2C43 4C4F 434B   =0,CLOCK
000120   3D30 2C47 433D 302C   =0,GC=0,
000128   494F 3D30 2C4E 4554   IO=0,NET
000130   4C49 423D 302C 4E53   LIB=0,NS
000138   4A41 5641 3D30 2C4D   JAVA=0,M
000140   4554 484F 4453 3D30   ETHODS=0
000148   2C0D 4E53 5F45 4E41   ,□NS_ENA
000150   424C 455F 4D4F 4A41   BLE_MOJA
000158   3D31 0D2F 2F4E 535F   =1□//NS_
000160   454E 4142 4C45 5F54   ENABLE_T
000168   4149 4E54 3D31 0D     AINT=1□
```

Figure 36–9 Highlighted `NS_ENABLE_TAINT` environment variable

14. Position the cursor after the // and before the NS in the window.

15. Backspace twice to remove the // from in front of `NS_ENABLE_TAINT`. Be sure to leave the =10 at the front of the line.

16. Choose Save from the File menu.

17. Close all of the ResEdit windows, and then quit the ResEdit application.

18. Start Netscape 3.0. Data tainting is now enabled on your system.

Accessing Windows with Tainted Data

When data tainting is enabled, you can access information from a page that contains tainted data.

Note – All of the examples in this chapter are computer-specific. You will need access to two servers and will have to modify the scripts to reflect your own environment before you can run them.

The following set of scripts shows an example of accessing a Web page with tainted data and reading that data with data tainting enabled and then with it disabled. The following `index.html` script defines the frameset to contain the example.

```
<!--
         dataTainting/basics/index.html

    This FRAMESET defines the page for the basic
    data tainting example. The FRAMESET comprises
    the following documents: hasProperty.html,
    which contains a property to read; and
    readsProperty.html, which contains code to
    access the property in hasProperty.html.
-->
<HTML>
<HEAD>
<TITLE>A Basic Data Tainting Example</TITLE>
</HEAD>
<FRAMESET ROWS="50%,50%" BORDER=1>
  <FRAME SRC="hasProperty.html" NAME="has">
  <FRAME
SRC="http://sampras/~bkf/jsbook/dataTainting/basics/reads
Property.html" NAME="reads">
</FRAMESET>
<NOFRAMES>
<P>For viewing this page, a browser that supports
frames is required.</P>
</NOFRAMES>
</HTML>
```

The following `hasProperty.html` script is loaded into the top frame.

```
<!--
                hasProperty.html
-->
<HTML>
<TITLE>From bungi</TITLE>
<BODY>

<P>This window contains the document
hasProperty.html that is retrieved from the
server bungi.corp.sgi.com. The value of its
location.href property is:</P>
```

```
<SCRIPT LANGUAGE="JavaScript">
<!-- HIDE FROM OLD BROWSERS

document.open()
document.write("<P>" + location.href + "</P>")
document.close()

// STOP HIDING -->
</SCRIPT>

</BODY>
</HTML>
```

The following `readsProperty.html` script is loaded into the bottom frame.

```
<!--
                readsProperty.html
-->
<HTML>
<TITLE>From sampras</TITLE>
<BODY>

<P>This window contains readsProperty.html, which
was retrieved from sampras.corp.sgi.com. With data
tainting enabled, the script can read a property of
hasProperty.html's window.

The value of hasProperty.html's location.href
property is:</P>

<SCRIPT LANGUAGE="JavaScript">
<!-- HIDE FROM OLD BROWSERS

document.open()
document.write("<P>" + parent.has.location.href + "</P>")
document.close()

// STOP HIDING -->
</SCRIPT>

</BODY>
</HTML>
```

Figure 36–10 shows the JavaScript error message that is displayed when data tainting is not enabled between scripts and you load the `index.html` script.

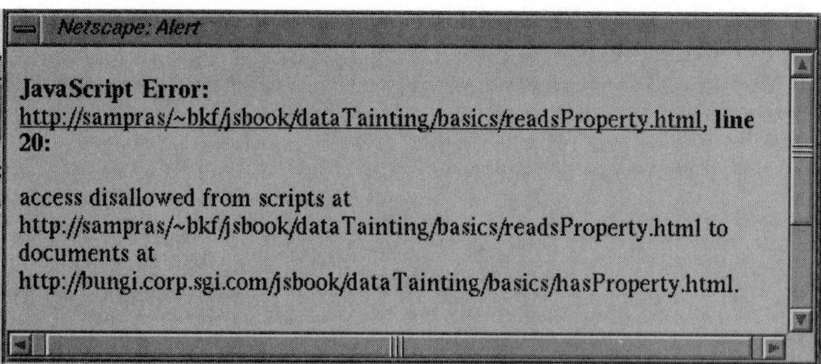

Figure 36–10 JavaScript error message when data tainting is not enabled

When you scroll to the bottom of the alert and click on the OK button, the window shown in Figure 36–11 is displayed. Notice that the bottom frame does not return a value for the `location.href` property.

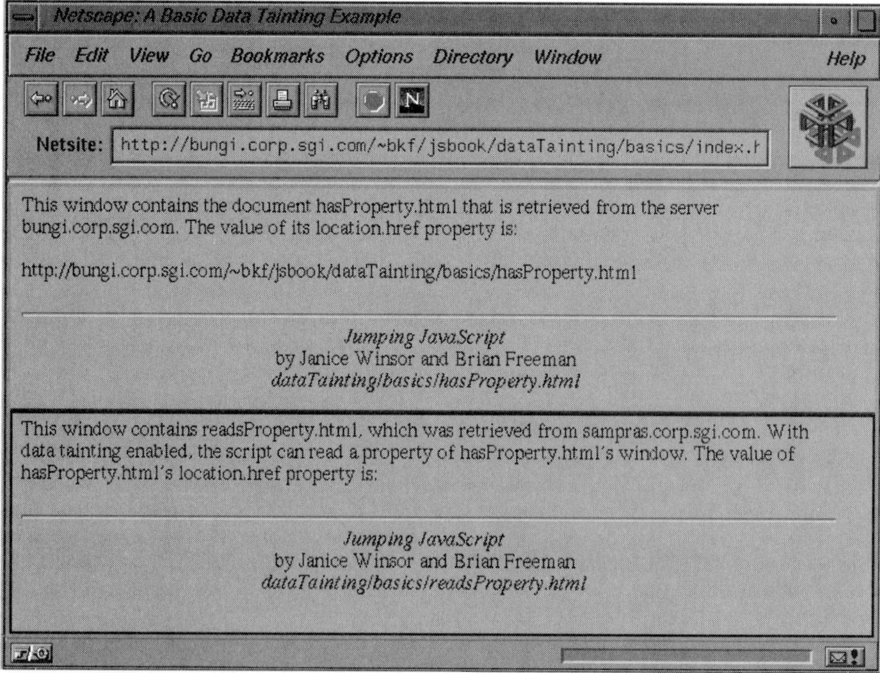

Figure 36–11 Result of loading the `index.html` script with data tainting not enabled

After data tainting is enabled and the `index.html` script is reloaded, a confirmation window is displayed, as shown in Figure 36–12, warning you that the page you are loading contains sensitive or private data.

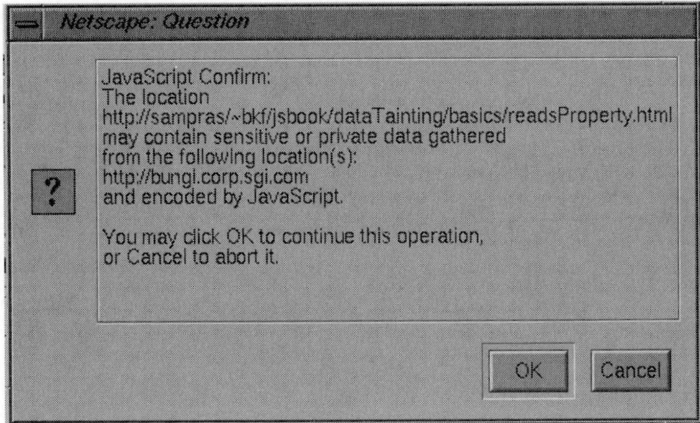

Figure 36–12 Data tainting alert for X-11 platform

When you click on the OK button, the `index.html` script is loaded. Notice that the `location.href` property from the other server is now displayed in the bottom frame, as shown in Figure 36–13.

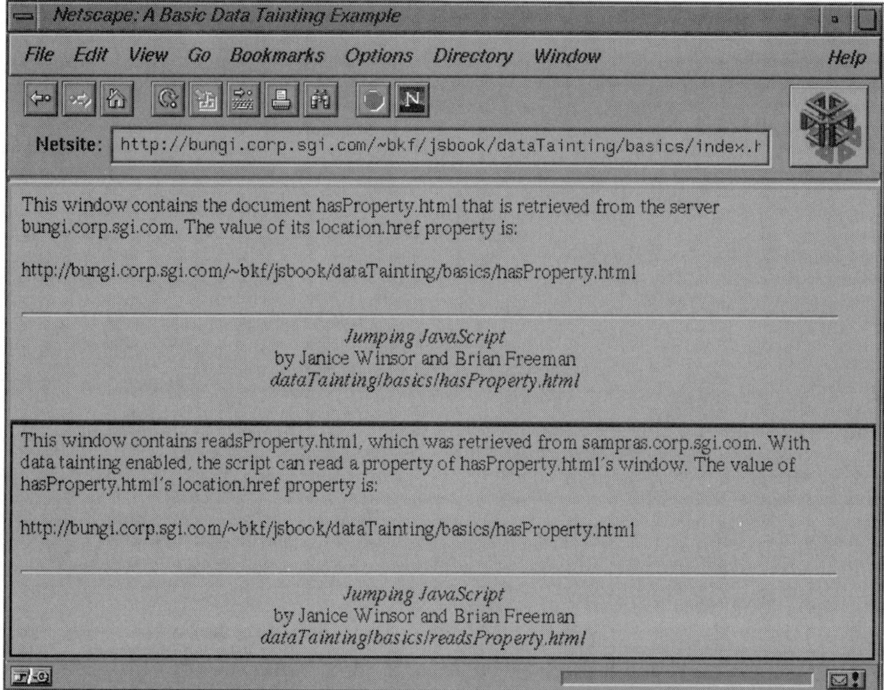

Figure 36–13 Result of loading the `index.html` script with data tainting enabled

Tainting Data

Table 36-1 on page 1041 contains a list of elements that are tainted by default. You can use the built-in `taint()` function to taint any additional script elements, such as custom objects and functions that you use to control sensitive information about a document. The `taint()` function assigns a mark, called a *taint code*, to the value and returns a marked reference to the data. It does not change the data element itself.

Example of Tainting Data

The following set of scripts shows an example of tainting a `document.URL` property and storing it in a variable. The following `index.html` script defines the frameset to contain the example.

```
<!--
         dataTainting/taint/index.html

     This FRAMESET defines the page for the taint
     data tainting example. The FRAMESET comprises
     the following documents: hasProperty.html,
     which contains a property to read; and
     readsProperty.html, which contains code to
     access the property in hasProperty.html.
-->
<HTML>
<HEAD>
<TITLE>taint()</TITLE>
</HEAD>
<FRAMESET ROWS="50%,50%" BORDER=1>
  <FRAME SRC="taintsProperty.html" NAME="taints">
  <FRAME
SRC="http://sampras/~bkf/jsbook/dataTainting/taint/readsP
roperty.html" NAME="reads">
</FRAMESET>
<NOFRAMES>
<P>For viewing this page, a browser that supports
frames is required.</P>
</NOFRAMES>
</HTML>
```

The following `taintsProperty.html` script taints the `document.URL` property and stores the value in the `taintedURL` variable.

```
<!--
         taintsProperty.html
-->
<HTML>
<HEAD>
<SCRIPT LANGUAGE="JavaScript">
<!-- HIDE FROM OLD BROWSERS
taint()
taintedURL=taint(document.URL)

// STOP HIDING -->
```

```
</SCRIPT>
</HEAD>
<BODY>

<P>This window calls taint() on the document.URL
property and stores it in the variable
taintedURL. Now, taintedURL cannot be sent to
another server without the user's permission.</P>

<P>The value of taintedURL is:</P>

<SCRIPT LANGUAGE="JavaScript">
<!-- HIDE FROM OLD BROWSERS

document.open()
document.write("<P>" + document.URL + "</P>")
document.close()

// STOP HIDING -->
</SCRIPT>

</BODY>
</HTML>
```

The following `readsProperty.html` script reads the value from the `taintedURL` variable and displays it. When you click on the Send button, an alert is displayed, asking you to confirm that it is OK to submit tainted data.

```
<!--
                readsProperty.html
-->
<HTML>
<HEAD>
<SCRIPT LANGUAGE="JavaScript">
<!-- HIDE FROM OLD BROWSERS

function sendData(theForm) {
  theForm.textF.value += parent.taints.tainedURL
  return true
}

// STOP HIDING -->
</SCRIPT>
</HEAD>
<BODY>
```

```
<P>This window reads the property taintedURL from
taintsProperty.html and displays it for you
below. But when data tainting is enabled and you
click on the Send button below, a dialog asks you
to confirm the submission.</P>

taintedURL's value is:</P>

<SCRIPT LANGUAGE="JavaScript">
<!-- HIDE FROM OLD BROWSERS

document.open()
document.write("<P>" + parent.taints.taintedURL + "</P>")
document.close()

// STOP HIDING -->
</SCRIPT>

<FORM ACTION="/cgi-bin/xxx.cgi"
 ENCTYPE="application/x-www-form-urlencoded"
 onSubmit="return sendData(this)">
<INPUT TYPE="text" NAME="textF" SIZE=20 VALUE="">
<INPUT TYPE="submit" VALUE="Send">
</FORM>

</BODY>
</HTML>
```

Figure 36–14 shows the result of loading the `index.html` script.

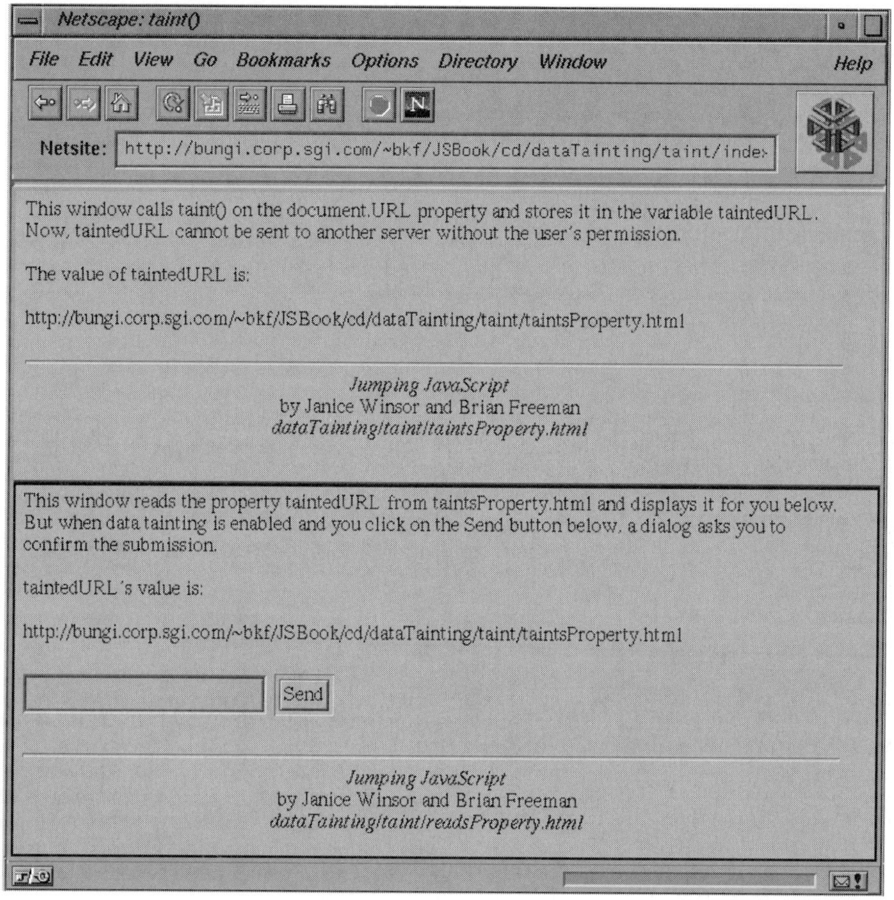

Netscape: taint()

File Edit View Go Bookmarks Options Directory Window Help

Netsite: http://bungi.corp.sgi.com/~bkf/JSBook/cd/dataTainting/taint/inde>

This window calls taint() on the document.URL property and stores it in the variable taintedURL. Now, taintedURL cannot be sent to another server without the user's permission.

The value of taintedURL is:

http://bungi.corp.sgi.com/~bkf/JSBook/cd/dataTainting/taint/taintsProperty.html

Jumping JavaScript
by Janice Winsor and Brian Freeman
dataTainting/taint/taintsProperty.html

This window reads the property taintedURL from taintsProperty.html and displays it for you below. But when data tainting is enabled and you click on the Send button below, a dialog asks you to confirm the submission.

taintedURL's value is:

http://bungi.corp.sgi.com/~bkf/JSBook/cd/dataTainting/taint/taintsProperty.html

Send

Jumping JavaScript
by Janice Winsor and Brian Freeman
dataTainting/taint/readsProperty.html

Figure 36–14 Result of loading the `index.html` script

When you click on the Send button, a confirmation window is displayed, as shown in Figure 36–15. This confirmation window is generated by the browser.

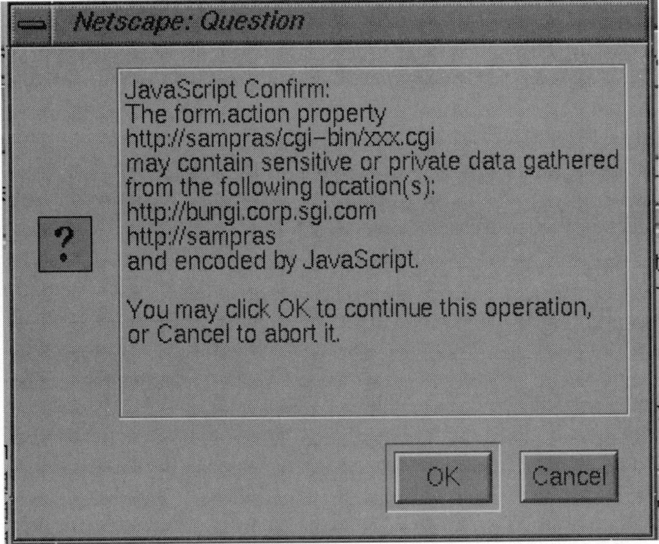

Figure 36–15 Taint alert

Untainting Data

Use the `untaint()` function to clear tainting from data in a script so that it can be sent to another server. A script can untaint only data that originated in that script. Untainted data has a taint code of `identity (null)`. If you untaint a data element from another server's script (or any data that you cannot untaint), `untaint()` returns the data without change or error. You can untaint any properties that are tainted by your script, including those properties that are tainted by default.

The `untaint()` function does not modify the data; instead, it returns an unmarked reference to the value.

The JavaScript language keeps track of tainted data by using a *taint accumulator* for each window. The taint accumulator stores taint codes from the conditional part of `if`, `for`, and `while` statements.

You can remove tainting from the script's window by calling `untaint()` with no arguments.

Example of Untainting a Property

The following set of scripts shows an example of untainting the `window.location.href` property from one document and displaying the property in another.

The following `index.html` script defines the frameset to contain the example.

```
<!--
      dataTainting/untaintCorrect/index.html

    This FRAMESET defines the page for the
    untaint data tainting example. The FRAMESET
    comprises the following documents:
    hasProperty.html, which contains a property
    to read; and postProperty.html, which
    contains a form that posts the read property to
    a server after untainting it.
-->
<HTML>
<HEAD>
<TITLE>An untaint Example</TITLE>
</HEAD>
<FRAMESET ROWS="50%,50%" BORDER=1>
  <FRAME SRC="untaintsProperty.html" NAME="untaints">
  <FRAME
SRC="http://sampras/~bkf/jsbook/dataTainting/untaintCorre
ct/postsProperty.html" NAME="post">
</FRAMESET>
<NOFRAMES>
<P>For viewing this page, a browser that supports
frames is required.</P>
</NOFRAMES>
</HTML>
```

The following `untaintsProperty.html` script that uses the the `untaint()` function is loaded into the top frame.

```
<!--
         untaintsProperty.html
-->
<HTML>
<SCRIPT LANGUAGE="JavaScript">
<!-- HIDE FROM OLD BROWSERS

var untaintedURL = untaint(document.URL)

// STOP HIDING -->
</SCRIPT>
<BODY>
```

```
<P>This window contains the document
untaintsProperty.html. It creates an untainted
property, untaintedURL, that can be read and
posted to other servers with data tainting
enabled. The value of untaintedURL is:</P>

<SCRIPT LANGUAGE="JavaScript">
<!-- HIDE FROM OLD BROWSERS

document.open()
document.write("<P>" + unescape(untaintedURL)
  + "</P>")
document.close()

// STOP HIDING -->
</SCRIPT>

</BODY>
</HTML>
```

The following `postsProperty.html` script is loaded into the bottom frame. This script reads the property from the `untaintsProperty.html` script and displays it in an alert when you click on the Submit button.

```
<!--
       postsProperty.html
-->
<HTML>
<HEAD>
<SCRIPT LANGUAGE="JavaScript">
<!-- HIDE FROM OLD BROWSERS

// Reads untaintedURL from untaintsProperty.html
// and includes it in the FORM submission.
//
function includeAProperty(theForm) {
  theForm.aProperty.value =
    parent.untaints.untaintedURL
  alert(unescape(theForm.aProperty.value))
  return true
}

// STOP HIDING -->
</SCRIPT>
</HEAD>
```

```
<BODY>

<P>This window is postsProperty.html and when you
click on Submit, it obtains the untaintedURL
property of untaintsProperty.html and submits it
along with the FORM below.</P>

<P>The untainted value is displayed in an alert
window before it is actually submitted, so you can
see it's value.</P>

<FORM METHOD="POST" ACTION="/cgi-bin/nada.pl"
  ENCTYPE="application/x-www-form-urlencoded"
  onSubmit="return includeAProperty(this)">
<INPUT TYPE="hidden" NAME="aProperty" VALUE="">
<INPUT TYPE="submit" VALUE="Submit">
</FORM>

</BODY>
</HTML>
```

Figure 36–16 shows the result of loading the `index.html` script.

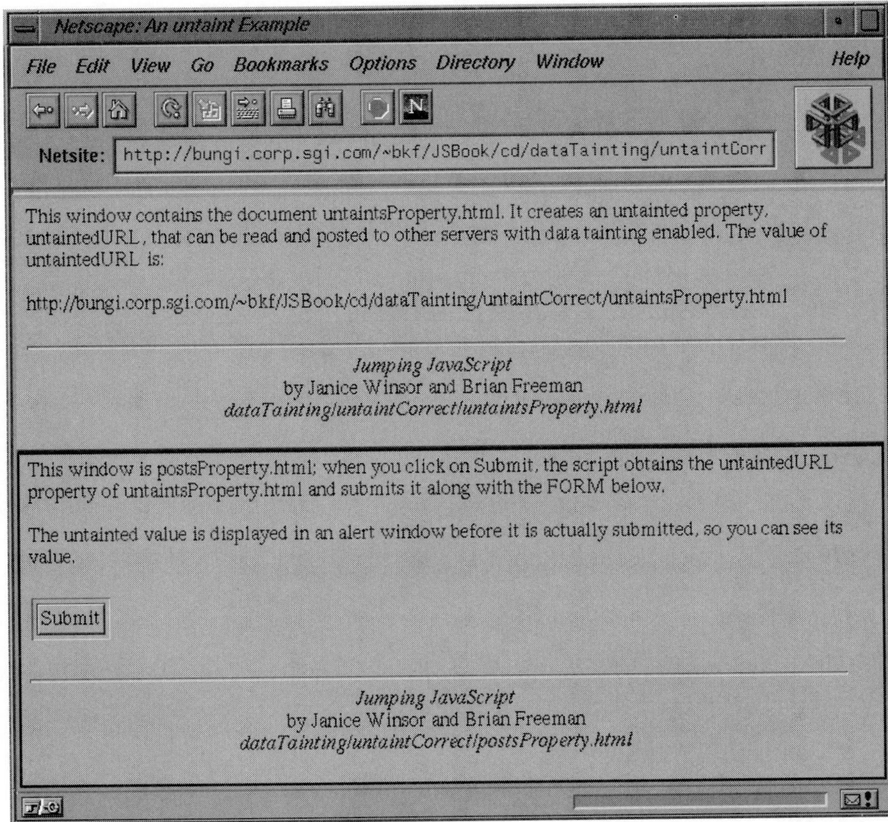

Figure 36–16 Result of loading the `index.html` script

When you click on the Submit button, an alert containing the untainted value is displayed, as shown in Figure 36–17.

Figure 36–17 Alert with untainted value

When you click on the OK button, no data tainting confirmation window is displayed, which indicates that the untainted value is successfully retrieved from one script and transmitted to another one.

Example of Trying to Untaint the Property from Another Script

The following set of scripts shows an example of untainting the `window.location.href` property from another document. Because you can't untaint a property that did not originate in your script, the example does not work. It does not, however, display any error messages or interfere with any other script operation.

The following `index.html` script defines the frameset to contain the example.

```
<!--
         dataTainting/untaint/index.html

    This FRAMESET defines the page for the
    untaint data tainting example. The FRAMESET
    comprises the following documents:
    hasProperty.html, which contains a property
    to read; and postProperty.html, which
    contains a form that posts the read property to
    a server after untainting it.
-->
<HTML>
<HEAD>
<TITLE>An untaint Example</TITLE>
</HEAD>
<FRAMESET ROWS="50%,50%" BORDER=1>
  <FRAME SRC="hasProperty.html" NAME="has">
  <FRAME
SRC="http://sampras/~bkf/jsbook/dataTainting/untaint/
postsProperty.html" NAME="post">
</FRAMESET>
<NOFRAMES>
<P>For viewing this page, a browser that supports
frames is required.</P>
</NOFRAMES>
</HTML>
```

The following `hasProperty.html` script is loaded into the top frame. It displays the value of the `window.location.href` property.

```
<!--
                  hasProperty.html
-->
<HTML>
<BODY>
```

```
<P>This window contains the document
hasProperty.html. The value of its
window.location.href property is:</P>

<SCRIPT LANGUAGE="JavaScript">
<!-- HIDE FROM OLD BROWSERS

document.open()
document.write("<P>" +
   unescape(window.location.href) +
   "</P>")
document.close()

// STOP HIDING -->
</SCRIPT>

</BODY>
</HTML>
```

The following `postsProperty.html` script reads the `window.location.href` property from the `hasProperty.html` script, untaints the property, and includes it in the form for submission.

```
<!--
               postsProperty.html
-->
<HTML>
<HEAD>
<SCRIPT LANGUAGE="JavaScript">
<!-- HIDE FROM OLD BROWSERS

// Reads window.location.href from
// hasProperty.html and includes it in the FORM
// submission.
//
function includeAProperty(theForm) {
  untainted = untaint(parent.has.location.href)

  theForm.aProperty.value = untainted
  alert(unescape(theForm.aProperty.value))
  return true
}

// STOP HIDING -->
</SCRIPT>
```

```
</HEAD>

<BODY>

<P>This window is postsProperty.html; when you
click on Submit, the script obtains the
window.location.href property of hasProperty.html
and submits it along with the FORM below.</P>

<P>The untainted value is displayed in an alert
window before it is actually submitted, so you
can see its value.</P>

<FORM METHOD="POST" ACTION="http://a.server.com"
  ENCTYPE="application/x-www-form-urlencoded"
  onSubmit="return includeAProperty(this)">
<INPUT TYPE="hidden" NAME="aProperty" VALUE="">
<INPUT TYPE="submit" VALUE="Submit">
</FORM>

</BODY>
</HTML>
```

Figure 36–18 shows the result of loading the `index.html` script.

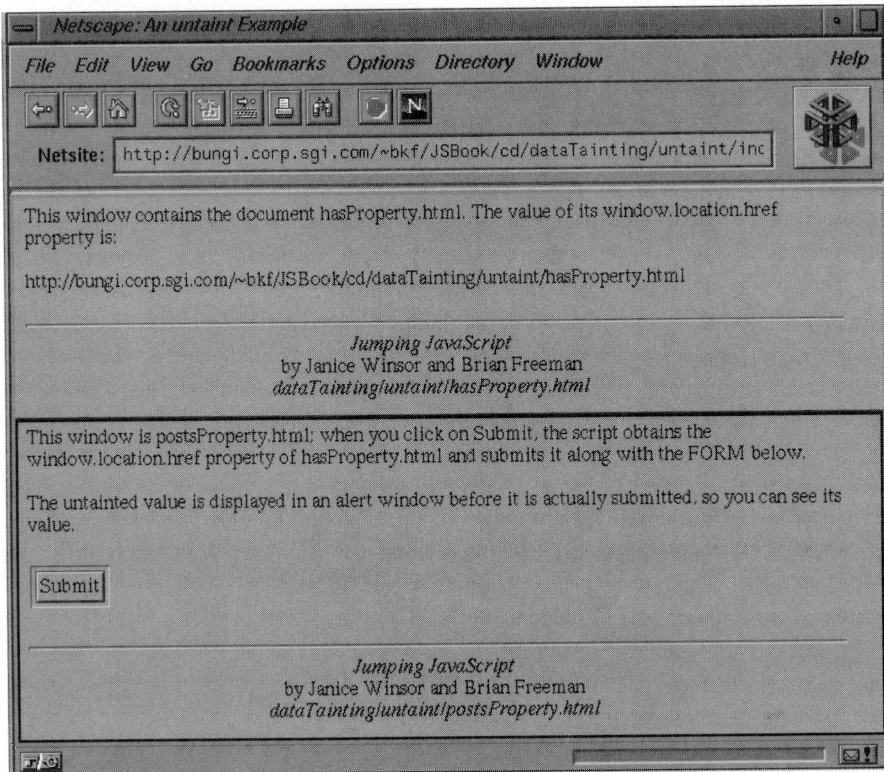

Figure 36–18 Result of loading the `index.html` script

When you click on the Submit button, the script generates an alert, shown in Figure 36–19, containing the value for the untainted property.

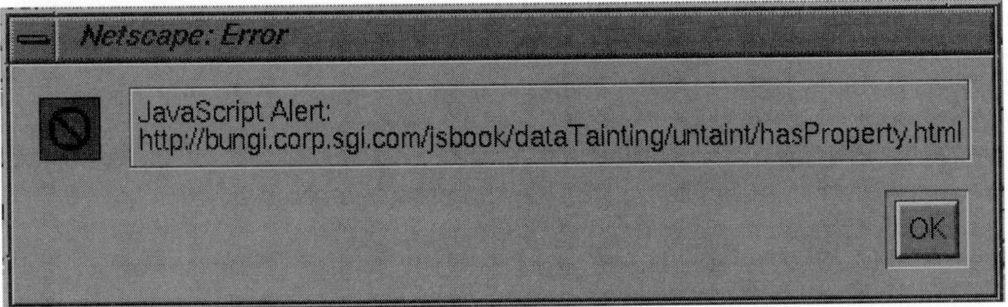

Figure 36–19 Untaint alert

The Confirmation window generated by the browser, shown in Figure 36–20, is displayed on top of the alert. Because this confirmation window is displayed by the browser, you can tell that the script is accessing tainted data; we now know that the script did not successfully untaint the data.

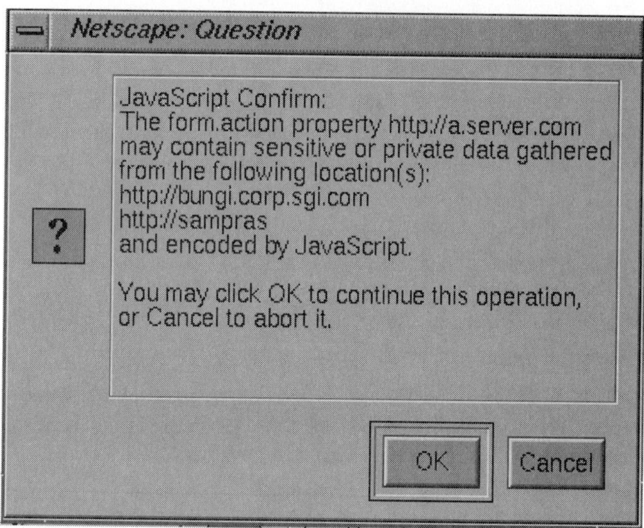

Figure 36–20 Taint confirmation window

Summary of New Terms and Concepts

The new terms and concepts introduced in this chapter are listed in alphabetical order in Table 36-2. The terms and concepts are also included in the glossary at the end of the book.

Table 36-2 Summary of New Terms and Concepts

Term/Concept	Description
taint accumulator	The mechanism that keeps a record of taint values for each individual window.
taint code	The unique mark that is applied to a copy of data that is marked as tainted.

PART EIGHT

Appendixes

APPENDIX A

- What Are Frames?
- Frame Components
- Design your frames so that only the main content window scrolls.

HTML Frames

This appendix provides examples and exercises to illustrate how to format HTML frames. In these examples, each frame is created as its own separate file — for instance, `frdata02.html`. These frame files are fit together by means of a master file — for instance, `frex01.html` — that contains references to each of the separate frame files. To make these frame examples function correctly, you need a frame-capable browser such as Netscape®2.x or equivalent. You also need a simple text editor. You do not need to connect to a server on the Web to try these examples if the files are available on your local system.

What Are Frames?

Frames are like separate panes of a browser window that can be operated independently. You can make each pane of the window fit your own design, so that you can control where data is displayed. You can use frames, for instance, to display a table of contents or glossary as part of your browser window.

Frame Components

You construct frames as containers like others used in HTML documents. A regular HTML document uses HTML tags to identify the start and end of the document, and a title to announce the topic. A frame document does the same. Table A-1 lists the frame tags and attributes used in this appendix.

Table A-1 **HTML Frame Tags Used in This Appendix**

Tag	Attribute	Description
<FRAMESET>		Starts a frameset definition
	ROWS	Defines the width of the window
	COLS	Defines the height of the window
</FRAMESET>		Ends a frameset definition
<FRAME>		Starts a frame definition
	SRC	Defines the source file
	NAME	Names the source file
	MARGINHEIGHT	Defines the vertical margin around the window
	MARGINWIDTH	Defines the horizontal margin around the window
	SCROLLING	Defines whether scrolling should be employed
	TARGET	Identifies the specific window for loading
</FRAME>		Ends a frame definition
<NOFRAMES>		Starts a comment for browsers that do not display frames
</NOFRAMES>		Ends a comment for browsers that do not display frames

You begin a frame declaration with a `<FRAMESET>` tag and end it with a `</FRAMESET>` tag. These tags create a container for the frame. You can divide frames into horizontal rows, using the `ROWS` attribute, and vertical columns by using the `COLS` attribute. The basic markup frame is shown in Table A-2:

Table A-2 **Frame Tags with Column Definitions — frex01.html**

```
<HTML> <HEAD>
<TITLE>Frames Example #1 </TITLE>
</HEAD>
<!-- this is a comment -->
<FRAMESET COLS="100, *">
<FRAME SRC="frdata01.html">
<FRAME SRC="frdata02.html">
```

Table A-2 **Frame Tags with Column Definitions — frex01.html (Continued)**

```
</FRAMESET>
</HTML>
```

Creating Frames

In Table A-2, <FRAMESET=COLS="100,*"> creates two columns, side by side. The value 100, separated by a comma, followed by an asterisk, indicates that FRAMESET is to make the first column 100 pixels wide. The second column uses the rest of the available space. If you specify values in both columns, the results are unpredictable.

1. **From the Navigator File menu, choose Open File.**
2. **Open the file /frex01.html.**

   This step assumes that the file is available on your local system.
3. **View the HTML source with File->View Source.**

   Notice that within the frameset container a single frame is marked by a <FRAME> tag. Because it is not a container, it has no end tag. The line:

   ```
   <FRAME SRC="frdata01.html">
   ```

   means that the source of the input file used to fill the declared space is "fradata01.html".

Figure A-1 shows the result of loading frex01.html in Netscape Navigator.

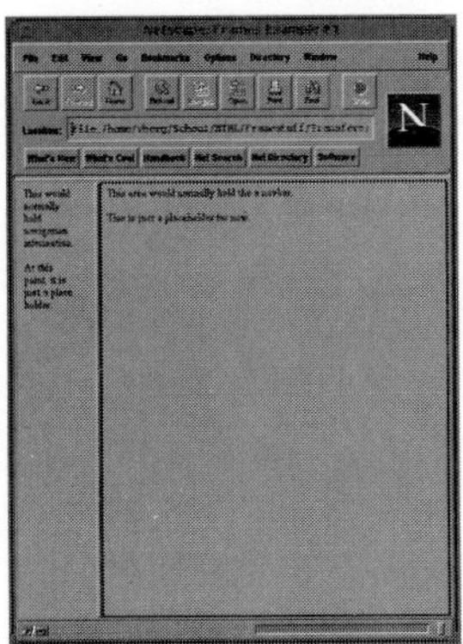

Figure A-1 Two-column frame format

Note – Do not put <FRAMESET> and <FRAME> tags in the head of the document. In addition, you do not use <BODY> tags in the master. You do use <BODY> tags in the document that defines each individual frame.

Changing Frame Column Sizes

In the previous example, you specified the size, in pixels, of one column, and the second column used the remaining space. You can also create columns in specific proportions, using percentages. For example, to divide the vertical space 30/70, you would specify: `COLS="30%,70%"`. If percentage values total more than 100, proportions are scaled.

Table A-3 shows the code for creating two columns, using percentages to scale the size of the panes in the window.

Table A-3 **Adjusted Two Column Frame — frex02.html**

```
<HTML> <HEAD>
<TITLE>Frames Example #1 </TITLE>
</HEAD>
<!-- this is a comment -->
<FRAMESET COLS="30%, 70%">
<FRAME SRC="frdata01.html">
<FRAME SRC="frdata02.html">
</FRAMESET>
</HTML>
```

Figure A-2 shows the result of loading `frex02.html`.

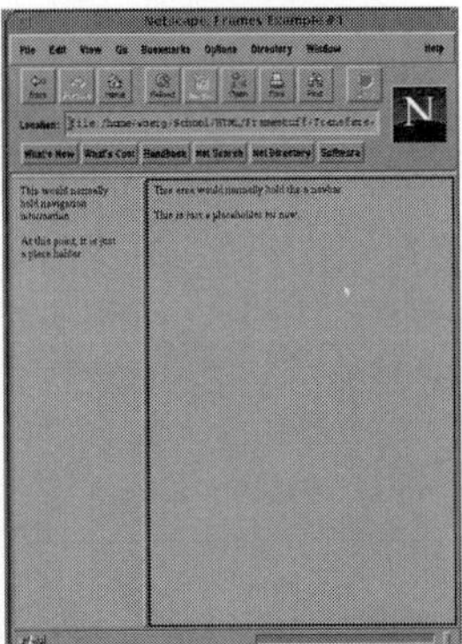

Figure A-2 Frame column sizing with percentages

Creating Vertical Frames

Just as columns can be defined in percentages, so can rows. Table A-4 uses `<ROWS="30%,70%">` to make vertical window panes.

Table A-4 Frame Rows — frex03.html

```
<HTML> <HEAD>
<TITLE>Frames Example #1 </TITLE>
</HEAD>
<!-- this is a comment -->
<FRAMESET ROWS="30%, 70%">
<FRAME SRC="frdata01.html">
<FRAME SRC="frdata02.html">
</FRAMESET>
</HTML>
```

Notice how vertical and horizontal adjustments scale in the result shown in Figure A-3.

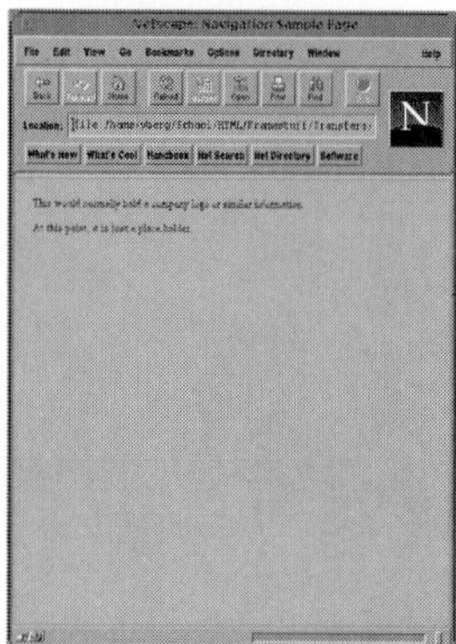

Figure A-3 Vertical frames using percentage

Creating a Compound Frame

When you combine rows and columns in the same frameset container, you can combine them into the same expression.

```
<FRAMESET COLS="200,*"  ROWS="10%,90%">
```

Each window pane has its own frame source file, identified separately as shown in Table A-5.

Table A-5 **Markup for Compound Frame — frex04.htm**

```
<HTML> <HEAD>
<TITLE>Frames Example #1 </TITLE>
</HEAD>
<!-- this is a comment -->
<FRAMESET COLS="200,*" ROWS="10%, 90%">
<FRAME SRC="frdata01.html">
<FRAME SRC="frdata02.html">
<FRAME SRC="frdata03.html">
<FRAME SRC="frdata04.html">
</FRAMESET>
</HTML>
```

1. From the Navigator File menu, choose Open File, and open frex04.html.

2. View the HTML source with File->View Source.

Figure A-4 shows the order in which the source files are displayed. Notice also that when the size of the file exceeds window space, scrollbars are automatically added.

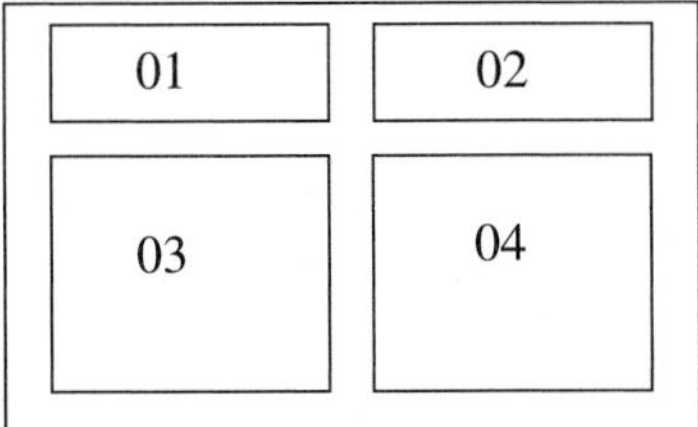

Figure A-4 Ordering of source files for a compound frame - frex04.html

Figure A-5 shows the result of loading `frex04.html`.

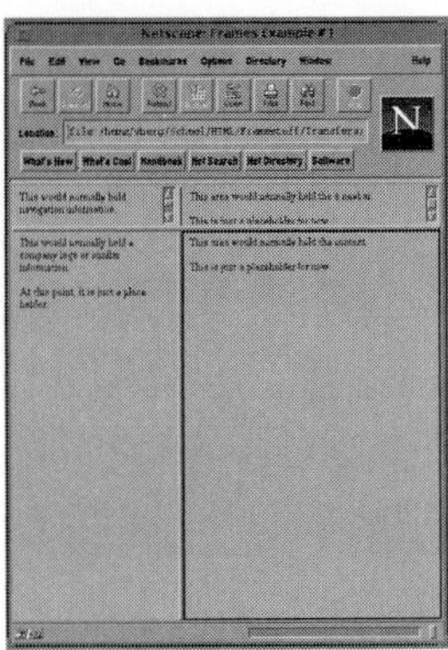

Figure A-5 Compound frame using horizontal and vertical windows

Creating the Nested Frame

To create a more complex window, you can nest a subframe inside a larger space. The file shown in Table A-6 creates three rows, the middle row consisting of two nested frames. The code is read as if the screen is being painted from left to right and top to bottom, the way a TV screen is filled. The code line:

```
<FRAMESET ROWS="100,*,100">
```

produces two, equal, fixed-pixel rows top and bottom, with the third, middle, row filling the remaining space. The code line:

```
<FRAME SRC="frdata01.html">
```

identifies the text to go in the top row.

This statement is followed by:

```
<FRAMESET COLS="30%,70%">
```

to identify the two middle nested panes. The next two code lines identify the data source files that fill those two columns. It is then important to close this part of the `FRAMESET` declaration.

These statements are followed by:

```
<FRAME SRC="frdata04.html">
```

to identify the data source file to fill the bottom row. The final `FRAMESET` declaration is closed. Because `ROWS` and `COLS` are declared separately, you must provide two closing tags, one for each `FRAMESET`.

1. **From the Navigator File menu, choose Open File and load the file frex05.html.**
2. **View the HTML source with File->View Source.**

Table A-6 **Markup for Nested Frame — frex05.html**

```
<HTML> <HEAD>
<TITLE>Frames Example #1 </TITLE>
</HEAD>
<!-- this is a comment -->
<FRAMESET ROWS="100, *, 100">
<FRAME SRC="frdata01.html">
<FRAMESET COLS="30%, 70%">
<FRAME SRC="frdata02.html">
<FRAME SRC="frdata03.html">
</FRAMESET>
<FRAME SRC="frdata04.html">
</FRAMESET>
</HTML>
```

Notice the order of the code lines in the markup identifying the source files and compare them to Figure A-6, which describes the way they appear in the window.

The browser fills the rows with source files in the order in which you declare them, filling from left to right.

```
<FRAME SRC="frdata01.html>
<FRANE SRC="frdata04.html>
```

Because the text overflows the leftmost column, a scrollbar is added.

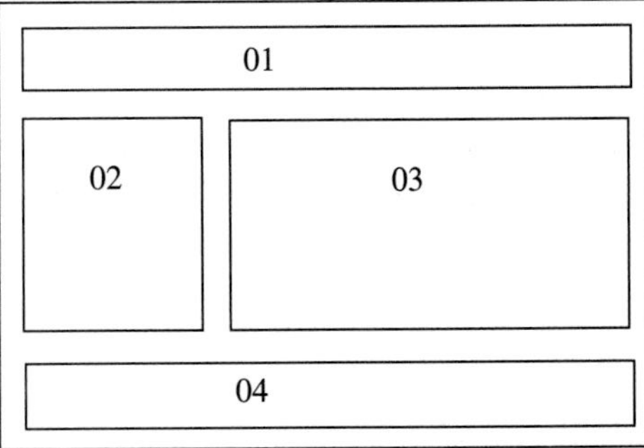

Figure A-6 Ordering of source files in sample nested frame

Figure A-6 identifies where each of the files in the code example shown in Table A-6 appears on the display. Figure A-7 shows the result.

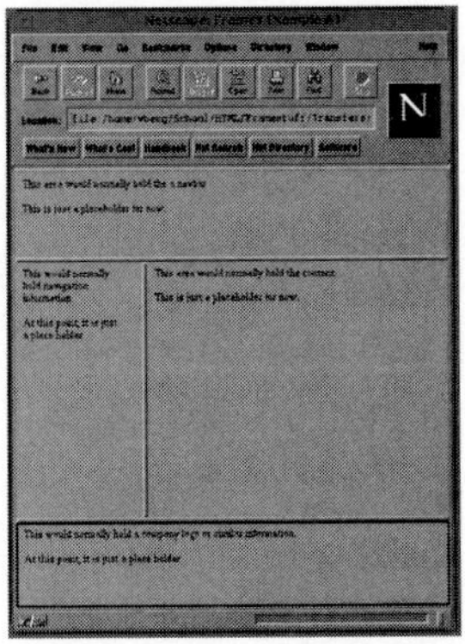

Figure A-7 Compound nested frame

Creating a Named Frame

Here we name a frame, then target a specific window to display the data.

A named frame looks like:

```
<FRAME SRC="frdata05.html" NAME="nav">
<FRAME SRC="frdata04.html" NAME="content">
```

In this case, the name `"nav"` has been assigned to the file `frdata05.html`, and the name `"content"` to the file `frdata04.html`.

The HTML code sample show in Table A-7 uses the named files in the markup.

Table A-7 **Markup for Named Frame — frex06.html**

```
<HTML> <HEAD>
<TITLE>Frames Example #1 </TITLE>
</HEAD>
<!-- this is a comment -->
<FRAMESET COLS="100, *">
<FRAME SRC="frdata05.html" NAME="nav">
<FRAME SRC="frdata04.html" NAME="content">
</FRAMESET>
</HTML>
```

Having named the file, look at the source, `frdata05.html`, shown in Table A-8.

1. **From the Navigator File menu, choose Open File and load the file frdata05.html.**
2. **View the HTML source with File->View Source.**

Table A-8 **Markup for Target Frame — frdata05.html**

```
<HTML> <HEAD>
<TITLE>Navigation Sample Page </TITLE>
</HEAD>
<!-- this is a comment -->
<BODY>
<A HREF="frdata06.html" TARGET="content">This</A>
will load content in the content window.
<P>
</BODY>
</HTML>
```

Having named `frdata04.html` as `"content"`, the line:

```
<A HREF="frdata06.html" TARGET="content">This</A>
```

gives a target where `frdata06.html` should be loaded. Simply put, by adding `TARGET` to the anchor tag, the link is forced to load into the targeted window. In this case, the window has a name. `TARGET` is where the window `NAME` lands.

Figure A-8 shows the way the named files are loaded, with "navbar" loaded into the first column, and "content" loaded into the second. A key word in the first column (05) activates the loading of another file (06) into the content frame (04).

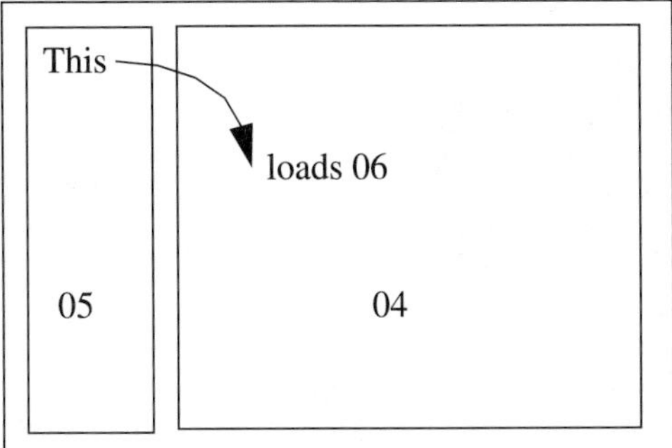

Figure A-8 Loading order of source files in a named frame

You can also use the TARGET attribute with <FORM>, <BASE>, and <AREA> tags. You use <FORM> when you want to display a form in a target window, <BASE> when most links are targeted in the same window, and <AREA> when a shaped area forces the load of clients' link into a target window.

Special Frames

Special frames introduce special ways of using the TARGET attribute. Most TARGET names must begin with an alphabetic character. The exceptions, sometimes called "magic" names are _blank, _self, _parent, and _top.

The attribute _blank replaces the entire visible window with a new window. _self loads into the pane from which the anchor was clicked (the originating window). _parent loads into the immediate FRAMESET parent and defaults to _self if there is no parent. _top loads into the entire screen and defaults to acting like _self if the document is already at the top. This name is useful for breaking out of deep FRAME nesting.

Begin by looking at the frames for named files:

1. **From the Navigator File menu, choose Open File and load the file frex07.html.**

2. **View the HTML source with File->View Source.**

The window panes are filled with named files `nav`, `navbar`, `content`, and `glossary`, identified in Table A-9.

Table A-9 **Special Frames HTML Tags — frex07.html**

```
<HTML> <HEAD>
<TITLE>Frames Example #1 </TITLE>
</HEAD>
<!-- this is a comment -->
<FRAMESET COLS="100, *">
<FRAME SRC="frdata02.html" NAME="nav">
<FRAMESET ROWS="10%, 80%,10%">
<FRAME SRC="frdata03.html" NAME="navbar">
<FRAME SRC="frdata07.html" NAME="content">
<FRAME SRC="frdata02.html" NAME="glossary">
</FRAMESET>
</FRAMESET>
</HTML>
```

Figure A-9 shows the sequence that the browser uses to load the special frames. The numbers refer to the data files that load into them.

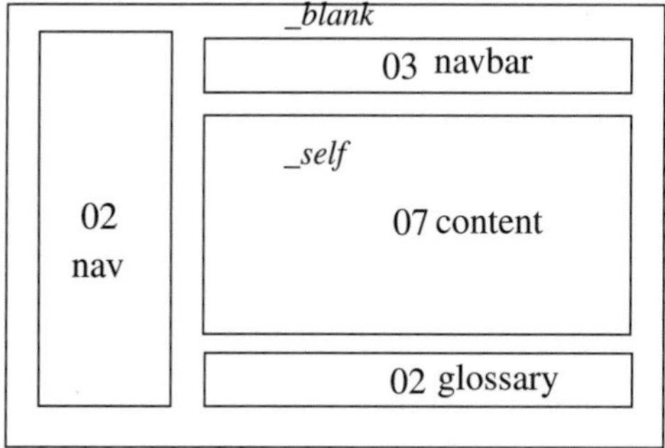

Figure A-9 Ordering of special frames

Table A-10 shows the HTML code for four targeted windows: blank, self, parent, and top, activated by the anchor word >`This`<.

Table A-10 **Special Frames Tags — frdata07.html**

```
<HTML> <HEAD>
<TITLE>Navigation Sample Page </TITLE>
</HEAD>
<!-- this is a comment -->
<BODY>
```

Table A-10 Special Frames Tags — frdata07.html (Continued)

```
<UL>
<LI><A HREF="frdata06.html" TARGET="_blank">This</A>
will load content in a new window.
<LI><A HREF="frdata06.html" TARGET="_self">This</A>
will load content in the same window.
<LI><A HREF="frdata06.html" TARGET="_parent">This</A>
will load content in the parent window.
<LI><A HREF="frdata06.html" TARGET="_top">This</A>
will load content in the topmost window.
</UL>
<P>
</BODY>
</HTML>
```

The result is shown in Figure A-10.

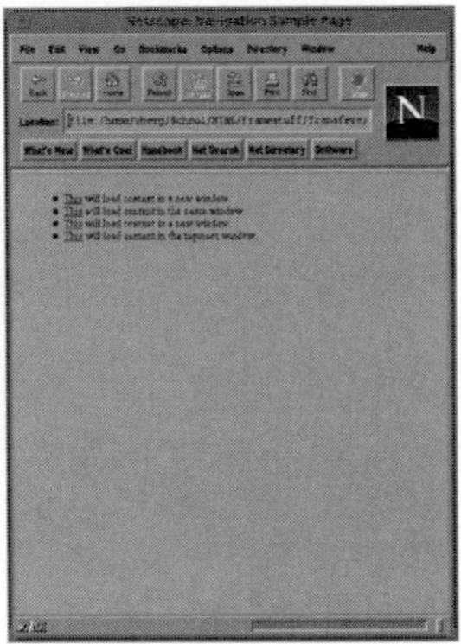

Figure A-10 Special frames example — `frex07.html`

Making a New Browser Window

To create a new browser window, you need to identify a `TARGET="name"` that is not defined in your current `FRAMESET`. Comparing Table A-11 with the previous example, the third `TARGET "_parent"` has been replaced by `"newwindow"`, which the browser doesn't know about, so it spawns a new window.

Table A-11 New Browser Window — frex011.html

```
<HTML> <HEAD>
<TITLE>Navigation Sample Page </TITLE>
</HEAD>
<!-- this is a comment -->
<BODY>
<UL>
<LI><A HREF="frdata06.html" TARGET="_blank">This</A>
will load content in a new window.
<LI><A HREF="frdata06.html" TARGET="_self">This</A>
will load content in the same window.
<LI><A HREF="frdata06.html" TARGET="newwindow">This</A>
will load content in a new browser window.
<LI><A HREF="frdata06.html" TARGET="_top">This</A>
will load content in the topmost window.
</UL>
<P>
</BODY>
</HTML>
```

For No-Frame Clients

Some clients cannot display frames. To accommodate them, put messages in `<NO FRAMES>` tags. Notice the `<NOFRAME>` tags are used at the end of the regular frame tags. It is a good idea to include no-frames html as the lowest common denominator of HTML 2.0.

Table A-12 shows how to add the `NOFRAMES` tag to the previous example so that it can be displayed on a no-frames browser.

Table A-12 No-Frames Tags — frex08.html

```
<HTML> <HEAD>
<TITLE>Frames Example #1 </TITLE>
</HEAD>
<!-- this is a comment -->
```

Table A-12 No-Frames Tags — frex08.html (Continued)

```
<FRAMESET COLS="100, *">
<FRAME SRC="frdata02.html" NAME="nav">
<FRAMESET ROWS="10%, 80%,10%">
<FRAME SRC="frdata03.html" NAME="navbar">
<FRAME SRC="frdata07.html" NAME="content">
<FRAME SRC="frdata02.html" NAME="glossary">
</FRAMESET>
</FRAMESET>
<NOFRAMES>
This message will be displayed on a non-frames browser.
</NOFRAMES>
</HTML>
```

Scrolling

On occasion, you may want to control scrolling. Normally, scrolling automatically occurs if the text to be displayed exceeds the window size chosen. By restraining the scrolling attribute to a frame, you can force the window to confine the image.

Do not force `"no scrolling"` for text frames because it may truncate text, particularly if the user resizes text.

Table A-13 shows the same three rows as in the previous example, with `"no scrolling"` assigned to one of the windows.

Table A-13 No-Scrolling Tags — frex09.html

```
<HTML> <HEAD>
<TITLE>Frames Example #1 </TITLE>
</HEAD>
<!-- this is a comment -->
<FRAMESET COLS="100, *">
<FRAME SRC="frdata02.html" NAME="nav">
<FRAMESET ROWS="10%, 80%,10%">
<FRAME SRC="frdata03.html" NAME="navbar" SCROLLING="no">
<FRAME SRC="frdata07.html" NAME="content" SCROLLING="yes">
<FRAME SRC="frdata02.html" NAME="glossary">
</FRAMESET>
</FRAMESET>
<NOFRAMES>
This message will be displayed on a non-frames browser.
</NOFRAMES>
</HTML>
```

Figure A-11 shows the result.

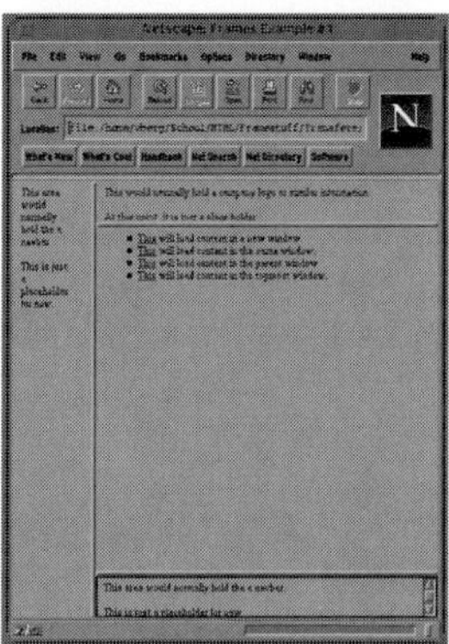

Figure A-11 No-Scrolling Example — `frex09.html`

Establishing Margins

For greater control over where text appears within a pane, you can create margins with the attributes `MARGINWIDTH` and `MARGINHEIGHT`. In the example shown in Table A-14, by specification of `MARGINHEIGHT="30"` attribute, the top margin drops the designated pixel space.

Table A-14 **Margin Tags — frex10.html**

```
<HTML> <HEAD>
<TITLE>Frames Example #1 </TITLE>
</HEAD>
<!-- this is a comment -->
<FRAMESET COLS="100, *">
<FRAME SRC="frdata02.html" NAME="nav">
<FRAMESET ROWS="10%, 80%,10%">
<FRAME SRC="frdata03.html" NAME="navbar">
<FRAME SRC="frdata07.html" NAME="content" MARGINHEIGHT="30"
MARGINWIDTH="20">
<FRAME SRC="frdata02.html" NAME="glossary">
</FRAMESET>
</FRAMESET>
<NOFRAMES>
This message will be displayed on a non-frames browser.
</NOFRAMES>
</HTML>
```

Figure A-12 shows the result.

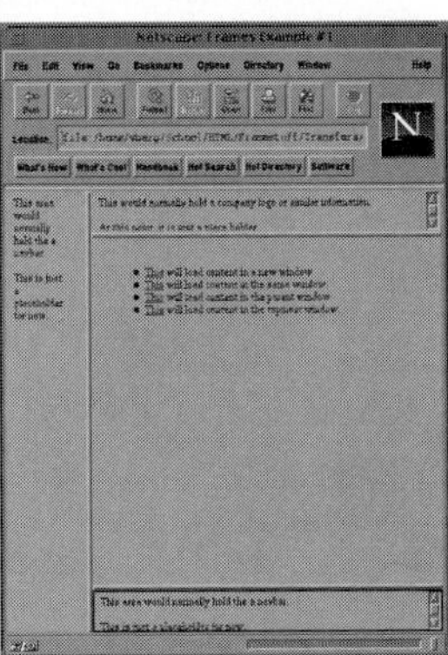

Figure A-12 Frame margin example — `frex10.html`

Design Concerns

In working within frames, use the following guidelines to make your work more visually attractive.

- Make frames large enough to display useful data.
- Keep the total number of frames small.
- Provide reasonable margins around images so scrollbars are not needed.
- Design your frames so that only the main content window scrolls.

APPENDIX B

JavaScript Predefined Colors

This appendix lists in Table B-1 the 140 predefined colors you can use to specify fonts for the `document` object properties `alinkColor`, `bgColor`, `fgColor`, `linkColor`, and `vlinkColor` and for the `fontcolor` method.

You can also use these string literals to set the color in the HTML attributes of these properties, for example:

```
<BODY BGCOLOR="bisque">
```

and to set the `COLOR` attribute of the `FONT` tag, for example:

```
<FONT COLOR="blue">color</font
```

The red, green, and blue values are in hexadecimal.

Table B-1 **JavaScript Predefined Colors and Hexadecimal Values**

Color	Red	Green	Blue
aliceblue	F0	F8	FF
antiquewhite	FA	EB	D7
aqua	00	FF	FF
aquamarine	7F	FF	D4
azure	F0	FF	FF
beige	F5	F5	DC

Table B-1 JavaScript Predefined Colors and Hexadecimal Values (Continued)

Color	Red	Green	Blue
bisque	FF	E4	C4
black	00	00	00
blanchedalmond	FF	EB	CD
blue	00	00	FF
blueviolet	8A	2B	E2
brown	A5	2A	2A
burlywood	DE	B8	87
cadetblue	5F	9E	A0
chartreuse	7F	FF	00
chocolate	D2	69	1E
coral	FF	7F	50
cornflowerblue	64	95	ED
cornsilk	FF	F8	DC
crimson	DC	14	3C
cyan	00	FF	FF
darkblue	00	00	8B
darkcyan	00	8B	8B
darkgoldenrod	B8	86	0B
darkgray	A9	A9	A9
darkgreen	00	64	00
darkkhaki	BD	B7	6B
darkmagenta	8B	00	8B
darkolivegreen	55	6B	2F
darkorange	FF	8C	00
darkorchid	99	32	CC
darkred	8B	00	00
darksalmon	E9	96	7A
darkseagreen	8F	BC	8F
darkslateblue	48	3D	8B
darkslategray	2F	4F	4F
darkturquoise	00	CE	D1
darkviolet	94	00	D3
deeppink	FF	14	93

Table B-1 JavaScript Predefined Colors and Hexadecimal Values (Continued)

Color	Red	Green	Blue
deepskyblue	00	BF	FF
dimgray	69	69	69
dodgerblue	1E	90	FF
firebrick	B2	22	22
floralwhite	FF	FA	F0
forestgreen	22	8B	22
fuchsia	FF	00	FF
gainsboro	DC	DC	DC
ghostwhite	F8	F8	FF
gold	FF	D7	00
goldenrod	DA	A5	20
gray	80	80	80
green	00	80	00
greenyellow	AD	FF	2F
honeydew	F0	FF	F0
hotpink	FF	69	B4
indianred	CD	5C	5C
indigo	4B	00	82
ivory	FF	FF	F0
khaki	F0	E6	8C
lavender	E6	E6	FA
lavenderblush	FF	F0	F5
lawngreen	7C	FC	00
lemonchiffon	FF	FA	CD
lightblue	AD	D8	E6
lightcoral	F0	80	80
lightcyan	E0	FF	FF
lightgoldenrodyellow	FA	FA	D2
lightgreen	90	EE	90
lightgrey	D3	D3	D3
lightpink	FF	B6	C1
lightsalmon	FF	A0	7A
lightseagreen	20	B2	AA

Table B-1 JavaScript Predefined Colors and Hexadecimal Values (Continued)

Color	Red	Green	Blue
lightskyblue	87	CE	FA
lightslategray	77	88	99
lightsteelblue	B0	C4	DE
lightyellow	FF	FF	E0
lime	00	FF	00
limegreen	32	CD	32
linen	FA	F0	E6
magenta	FF	00	FF
maroon	80	00	00
mediumaquamarine	66	CD	AA
mediumblue	00	00	CD
mediumorchid	BA	55	D3
mediumpurple	93	70	DB
mediumseagreen	3C	B3	71
mediumslateblue	7B	68	EE
mediumspringgreen	00	FA	9A
mediumturquoise	48	D1	CC
mediumvioletred	C7	15	85
midnightblue	19	19	70
mintcream	F5	FF	FA
mistyrose	FF	E4	E1
moccasin	FF	E4	B5
navajowhite	FF	DE	AD
navy	00	00	80
oldlace	FD	F5	E6
olive	80	80	00
olivedrab	6B	8E	23
orange	FF	A5	00
orangered	FF	45	00
orchid	DA	70	D6
palegoldenrod	EE	E8	AA
palegreen	98	FB	98
paleturquoise	AF	EE	EE

Table B-1 JavaScript Predefined Colors and Hexadecimal Values (Continued)

Color	Red	Green	Blue
palevioletred	DB	70	93
papayawhip	FF	EF	D5
peachpuff	FF	DA	B9
peru	CD	85	3F
pink	FF	C0	CB
plum	DD	A0	DD
powderblue	B0	E0	E6
purple	80	00	80
red	FF	00	00
rosybrown	BC	8F	8F
royalblue	41	69	E1
saddlebrown	8B	45	13
salmon	FA	80	72
sandybrown	F4	A4	60
seagreen	2E	8B	57
seashell	FF	F5	EE
sienna	A0	52	2D
silver	C0	C0	C0
skyblue	87	CE	EB
slateblue	6A	5A	CD
slategray	70	80	90
snow	FF	FA	FA
springgreen	00	FF	7F
steelblue	46	82	B4
tan	D2	B4	8C
teal	00	80	80
thistle	D8	BF	D8
tomato	FF	63	47
turquoise	40	E0	D0
violet	EE	82	EE
wheat	F5	DE	B3
white	FF	FF	FF

Table B-1 JavaScript Predefined Colors and Hexadecimal Values (Continued)

Color	Red	Green	Blue
whitesmoke	F5	F5	F5
yellow	FF	FF	00
yellowgreen	9A	CD	32

1095

APPENDIX C

- JavaScript Objects
- Control Structures
- Operators
- JavaScript Functions and Methods
- Reserved JavaScript Keywords
- Escape Characters for String Formatting
- HTTP MIME Types

JavaScript Quick Reference

JavaScript Objects

This section provides an alphabetical list of JavaScript objects with HTML (where appropriate) and summary information about each object's properties, methods, and event handlers. An asterisk means "new in Navigator 3.0 release."

Anchor Object

HTML

```
<A
HREF = "URL" | NAME = "destination"
[TARGET = "WindowName"]
>
Text of anchor
</A>
```

applet Object

HTML

```
<APPLET
CODE = "filename.class"
WIDTH= number
HEIGHT = number
MAYSCRIPT
```

```
[CODEBASE = "base directory for the applet"]
[ALT = "alternative character data that is displayed if the
browser cannot run the applet"]
[NAME = "name for the applet instance"]
[ALIGN =
left|right|top|texttop|middle|absmiddle|baseline|bottom|
absbottom]
[VSPACE= number]
[HSPACE = number]>
[ARCHIVE=JavaClass.zip]
<PARAM NAME = "NameOfParameter"  VALUE = "Value">
</APPLET>
```

Properties

All public properties of the Java applet.

Methods

All public methods of the Java applet.

Event Handlers

```
None
```

Area Object

HTML

```
<MAP NAME="areaMapName"
   <AREA
        COORDS="x1,y1,x2,y2,..." | "x-center,y-
center,radius"
        HREF = "URL"
        [NOHREF]
        [SHAPE = "rect" | "poly" | "circle" | "default"]
        [TARGET = "WindowName"]
        [onMouseOver = "JavaScript code"]
        [onMouseOut = "JavaScript code"]
   >
</MAP>
```

Properties

You reference properties of the `Area` object by using the document.`links` array and `location` properties. The `area` object does not have any properties of its own.

Property	Value	Gettable	Settable
links.length	number	Yes	No
links(index).target	string	Yes	Yes
(location object properties)			

Methods

```
eval()*
toString()*
valueOf()*
```

Event Handlers

```
onMouseOut
onMouseOver
```

Array Object*

Properties

Property	Value	Gettable	Settable
length	number	Yes	Yes
prototype*	string	Yes	Yes

Methods

```
eval()*
join()
reverse()
sort()
toString()*
valueOf()*
```

Event Handlers

```
None
```

button Object

HTML

```
<FORM>
<INPUT TYPE = "button"
[NAME = "Button Name"]
VALUE = "Button Text"
onBlur = "JavaScript code"
onClick = "JavaScript code"
onFocus = "JavaScript code">
</FORM>
```

Properties

Property	Value	Gettable	Settable
form*	containing form object	Yes	No
name	string	Yes	No
type*	string	Yes	No
value	string	Yes	No

Methods

```
blur()
click()
eval()*
focus()
toString()*
valueOf()*
```

Event Handlers

```
onBlur
onClick
onFocus
```

checkbox Object

HTML

```
<FORM>
<INPUT TYPE = "checkbox"
NAME = "Box Name"
VALUE = "checkboxValue"
[CHECKED]
onBlur = "JavaScript code"
onClick = "JavaScript code"
onFocus = "JavaScript code"
checkboxLabel>
</FORM>
```

Properties

Property	Value	Gettable	Settable
checked	Boolean	Yes	Yes
defaultChecked	Boolean	Yes	No
form*	containing form object	Yes	No
name	string	Yes	No
type*	string	Yes	No
value	string	Yes	No

Methods

```
blur()
click()
eval()*
focus()
toString()*
valueOf()*
```

Event Handlers

```
onBlur
onClick
onFocus
```

Date Object

Properties

Property	Value	Gettable	Settable
prototype*	string	Yes	Yes

Methods

```
eval()*
get/setDate()
getDay()
get/setHours()
get/setMinutes()
get/setMonth()
get/setSeconds()
get/setTime()
get/setYear()
getTimezoneOffset()
parse("dateString")
toGMTString()
toLocaleString()*
toString()*
UTC(date vals)
valueOf()*
```

Event Handlers

None

document Object

HTML

```
<BODY
[BACKGROUND = "backgroundImage"]
[BGCOLOR = "backgroundColor"]
[FGCOLOR = "foregroundColor"]
TEXT
[LINK = "linkColor"]
[ALINK = "activatedLinkColor"]
[VLINK = "visitedLinkColor"]>
</BODY>
```

Properties

Property	Value	Gettable	Settable
alinkColor	hexadecimal string or predefined JavaScript Color	Yes	No
anchors()	array of anchor objects	Yes	No
applets()*	array	Yes	No
bgColor	hexadecimal string or predefined JavaScript color	Yes	No
cookie	string	Yes	Yes
domain*	string	Yes	Yes
embeds()*	array	Yes	No
fgColor	hexadecimal string or predefined JavaScript Color	Yes	No
forms	array	Yes	No
images*	array	Yes	No
lastModified	date string	Yes	No
linkColor	hexadecimal string or predefined JavaScript color	Yes	No
links	array of link objects	Yes	No
location	string	Yes	No
plugins()*	array of plug-in objects	Yes	No
referrer	string	Yes	No
title	string	Yes	No
URL*	string	Yes	No
vlinkColor	hexadecimal string or predefined JavaScript color	Yes	No

Methods

```
clear()
close()
eval()*
open()
toString()*
valueOf()*
write()
writeln()
```

Event Handlers

None

fileUpload Object*

HTML

```
<FORM
<INPUT
     NAME = "name"
     TYPE = "file"
     [onBlur = "JavaScript code"]
     [onChange = "JavaScript code"]
     [onFocus = "JavaScript code"]>
</FORM>
```

Properties

Property	Value	Gettable	Settable
form*	containing form object	Yes	No
name	string	Yes	No
type*	string	Yes	No
value	string	Yes	No

Methods

```
blur()
eval()*
focus()
toString()*
valueOf()*
```

Event Handlers

```
onBlur
onChange*
onFocus
```

form Object

HTML

```
<FORM
NAME = "formName"
TARGET = "windowName"
ACTION = "serverURL"
METHOD = "GET | POST"
ENCTYPE = "MIMEType"
[onReset = "JavaScript code"]
[onSubmit = "JavaScript code"] >
</FORM>
```

Properties

Property	Value	Gettable	Settable
action	URL	Yes	Yes
elements	array of subobjects	Yes	No
encoding	MIMETypeString	Yes	Yes
length	number	Yes	No
method	GET or POST	Yes	Yes
name	string	Yes	No
target	windowNameString	Yes	Yes

Methods

```
eval()*
reset()*
submit()
toString()*
valueOf()*
```

Event Handlers

```
onReset*
onSubmit
```

function Object*

Properties

Property	Value	Gettable	Settable
caller	string	Yes	No
arguments()	string	Yes	No
prototype	string	Yes	Yes

Methods

```
eval()*
toString()*
valueOf()*
```

Event Handlers

```
None
```

hidden Object

HTML

```
<FORM>
<INPUT TYPE = "hidden"
NAME = "fieldNane"
[VALUE = "contents"]>
</FORM>
```

Properties

Property	Value	Gettable	Settable
form*	containing form object	Yes	No
name	string	Yes	No
type*	string	Yes	No
value	string	Yes	No

Methods

```
eval()*
toString()*
valueOf()*
```

Event Handlers

None

history Object

Properties

Property	Value	Gettable	Settable
current*	URL	Yes	No
length	number	Yes	No
next*	URL	Yes	No
previous*	URL	Yes	No

Methods

```
back()
eval()*
forward()
go()
toString()*
valueOf()*
```

Event Handlers

None

image Object

HTML

```
<IMG
SRC = "ImageURL"
[LOWSRC = "LowResImageURL"]
[NAME = "ImageName"]
[WIDTH = "Pixels" | "PercentValue"]
[HEIGHT = "Pixels" | "PercentValue"]
[HSPACE = "Pixels"]
[VSPACE = "Pixels"]
[BORDER = "Pixels"]
[ALIGN = "left" | "right" | "top" | "absmiddle" |
"absbottom" | "texttop" | "middle" | "baseline" |
"bottom" ]
[ISMAP]
[USEMAP = "#AreaMapName"]
```

```
[onLoad = "JavaScript code"]
[onAbort = "JavaScript code"]
[onError = "JavaScript code"]
>
```

Properties

Property	Value	Gettable	Settable
border	pixels	Yes	No
complete	Boolean	Yes	No
height	pixels	Yes	No
hspace	pixels	Yes	No
lowsrc	URL	Yes	No
name	string	Yes	No
prototype*	string	Yes	Yes
src	URL	Yes	Yes
vspace	pixels	Yes	No
width	pixels	Yes	No

Methods

```
eval()*
toString()*
valueOf()*
```

Event Handlers

```
onAbort
onError
onLoad
```

link Object

HTML

```
<A
HREF = "URL" | [NAME = "destinationTag"]
[TARGET = "WindowName"]
[onClick = "JavaScript code"]
[onMouseOut = "JavaScript code"]
[onMouseOver = "JavaScript code"]
>
Text of anchor
</A>
```

Properties

Property	Value	Gettable	Settable
hash	string	Yes	Yes
host	string	Yes	Yes
hostname	string	Yes	Yes
href	URL	Yes	Yes
length	number	Yes	No
pathname	string	Yes	Yes
port	string	Yes	Yes
protocol	string	Yes	Yes
search	string	Yes	Yes
target	string	Yes	No

Methods

```
eval()*
toString()*
valueOf()*
```

Event Handlers

```
onClick
onMouseOut*
onMouseOver
```

location Object

Properties

Property	Value	Gettable	Settable
hash	string	Yes	Yes
host	string	Yes	Yes
hostname	string	Yes	Yes
href	URL	Yes	Yes
pathname	string	Yes	Yes
port	string	Yes	Yes
protocol	string	Yes	Yes
search	string	Yes	Yes

Methods

```
eval()*
reload()*
replace()*
toString()*
valueOf()*
```

Event Handlers

None

Math Object

Properties

Property	Value	Description
E	2.718281828459045091	Euler's constant
LN2	0.6931471805599452862	Natural log of 2
LN10	2.302585092994045901	Natural log of 10
LOG2E	1.442695040888963387	Log base-2 of E
LOG10E	0.4342944819032518167	Log base-10 of E
PI	3.145926535897931 16	π
SQRT1_2	0.7071067811865475727	Square root of 0.5
SQRT2	1.414213562373095145	Square root of 2

Methods

```
abs()
acos()
asin()
atan()
atan2()*
ceil()
cos()
eval()*
exp()
floor()
log()
max()
min()
pow()
random()
round()
sin()
sqrt()
tan()
toString()*
valueOf()*
```

Event Handlers

None

mimeType Object*

Properties

Property	Value	Gettable	Settable
description	string	Yes	No
enabledPlugin	string	Yes	No
type	string	Yes	No
suffixes	string	Yes	No

Methods

```
eval()*
toString()*
valueOf()*
```

Event Handlers

None

navigator Object

Properties

Property	Value	Gettable	Settable
appCodeName	string	Yes	No
appName	string	Yes	No
appVersion	string	Yes	No
mimeTypes()*	array	Yes	No
plugins()*	array	Yes	No
userAgent	string	Yes	No

Methods

```
eval()*
javaEnabled()*
taintEnabled()*
```

```
toString()*
valueOf()*
```

Event Handlers

```
None
```

password Object

HTML

```
<FORM>
<INPUT TYPE = "password"
NAME = "Field Name"
VALUE = "Contents"
SIZE = "Character Count"
[onBlur = "JavaScript code"]
[onFocus = "JavaScript code"]
[onSelect = "JavaScript code"]>
</FORM>
```

Properties

Property	Value	Gettable	Settable
defaultValue	string	Yes	No
form*	containing form object	Yes	No
name	string	Yes	No
type*	string	Yes	No
value	string	Yes	No

Methods

```
blur()
eval()*
focus()
select()
toString()*
valueOf()*
```

Event Handlers

```
onBlur
onFocus
onSelect
```

plugin Object*

HTML

```
<EMBED
SRC = "Source URL"
WIDTH= number in pixels for the embedded object.
HEIGHT = number in pixels for the embedded object.
attribute_1="..."
attribute_2="..."
attribute_3="...">
characters
</EMBED>
```

Properties

Property	Value	Gettable	Settable
description	string	Yes	No
filename	string	Yes	No
length	integer	Yes	No
name	string	Yes	No

Methods

```
eval()*
refresh()
toString()*
valueOf()*
```

Event Handlers

None

radio Object

HTML

```
<FORM>
<INPUT TYPE = "radio"
NAME = "radioGroupName"
VALUE = "radioValue"
[CHECKED]
[onBlur = "JavaScript code"]
[onClick = "JavaScript code"]
[onFocus = "JavaScript code"]
radioButtonLabel
</FORM>
```

Properties

Property	Value	Gettable	Settable
checked	Boolean	Yes	No
defaultChecked	Boolean	Yes	No
form*	containing form object	Yes	No
length	integer	Yes	No
name	string	Yes	No
type*	string	Yes	No
value	string	Yes	No

Methods

```
blur()
click()
eval()*
focus()
toString()*
valueOf()*
```

Event Handlers

```
onBlur*
onClick
onFocus*
```

reset Object

HTML

```
<FORM>
<INPUT TYPE = "reset"
NAME = "Button Name"
VALUE = "Button Text"
[onBlur = "JavaScript code"]
[onClick = "JavaScript code"]
[onFocus = "JavaScript code"]>
</FORM>
```

Properties

Property	Value	Gettable	Settable
form*	containing form object	Yes	No
name	string	Yes	No
type*	string	Yes	No
value	string	Yes	No

Methods

```
blur()
click()
eval()*
toString()*
valueOf()*
```

Event Handlers

```
onBlur
onClick
onFocus
```

select Object

HTML

```
<FORM>
<SELECT
   NAME = "listName"
   [SIZE = "number"]
   [MULTIPLE]
   [onBlur = "JavaScript code"]
```

```
    [onChange = "JavaScript code"]
    [onFocus = "JavaScript code"]>
        <OPTION
        [SELECTED]
        [VALUE="string"]>
        listItem
</SELECT>
</FORM>
```

Properties

Property	Value	Gettable	Settable
form*	containing form object	Yes	No
length	integer	Yes	No
name	string	Yes	No
options(n)	array	Yes	No
options(*n*).defaultSelected	Boolean	Yes	No
options(*n*).index	integer	Yes	No
options(*n*).selected	Boolean	Yes	Yes
options(*n*).text	string	Yes	Yes
options(*n*).value	string	Yes	Yes
selectedIndex	Integer	Yes	Yes
type*	string	Yes	No

Methods

```
blur()
eval()*
focus()
toString()*
valueOf()*
```

Event Handlers

```
onBlur
onChange
onFocus
```

String Object

Properties

Property	Value	Gettable	Settable
length	integer	Yes	No
prototype*	string	Yes	Yes

Methods

```
anchor()
big()
blink()
bold()
charAt()
eval()*
fixed()
fontcolor()
fontsize()
indexOf()
italics()
lastIndexOf()
link()
small()
split(char)
strike()
sub()
substring()
sup()
toLowerCase()
toString()*
toUpperCase()
valueOf()*
```

Event Handlers

None

submit Object

HTML

```
<FORM>
<INPUT TYPE = "submit"
[NAME = "Button Name"]
```

```
VALUE = "Button Text"
[onBlur = "JavaScript code"]
[onClick = "JavaScript code"]
[onFocus = "JavaScript code"]>
</FORM>
```

Properties

Property	Value	Gettable	Settable
form*	containing form object	Yes	No
name	string	Yes	No
type*	string	Yes	No
value	string	Yes	No

Methods

```
blur()
click()
eval()*
focus()
toString()*
valueOf()*
```

Event Handlers

```
onBlur
onClick
onFocus
```

text Object

HTML

```
<FORM>
<INPUT TYPE = "text"
NAME = "Field Name"
VALUE = "Contents"
SIZE = "Character Count"
[onBlur = "JavaScript code"]
[onChange = "JavaScript code"]
[onFocus = "JavaScript code"]
[onSelect = "JavaScript code"]>
</FORM>
```

Properties

Property	Value	Gettable	Settable
defaultValue	string	Yes	No
form*	containing form object	Yes	No
name	string	Yes	No
type*	string	Yes	No
value	string	Yes	Yes

Methods

```
blur()
eval()*
focus()
select()
toString()*
valueOf()*
```

Event Handlers

```
onBlur
onChange
onFocus
onSelect
```

textarea Object

HTML

```
<FORM>
<TEXTAREA
NAME = "Field Name"
ROWS = "NumberOfRows"
COLS = "NumberOfColumns"
[WRAP = "off" | "virtual" | "physical"]
[onBlur = "JavaScript code"]
[onChange = "JavaScript code"]
[onFocus = "JavaScript code"]
[onSelect = "JavaScript code"]>
defaultText
</TEXTAREA>
</FORM>
```

Properties

Property	Value	Gettable	Settable
defaultValue	string	Yes	No
form*	containing form object	Yes	No
name	string	Yes	No
type*	string	Yes	No
value	string	Yes	No

Methods

```
blur()
eval()*
focus()
select()
toString()*
valueOf()*
```

Event Handlers

```
onBlur
onChange
onFocus
onSelect
```

window Object

HTML

```
<FRAMESET>
   COLS = "NumberOfColumns"
   ROWS = "NumberOfRows"
   [FRAMEBORDER = YES | NO]
   [BORDER = pixelSize]
   [BORDERCOLOR = colorSpecification]
   [onLoad = "JavaScript code"]
   [onUnload = "JavaScript code"]
   [onFocus = "JavaScript code"]
   [onBlur = "JavaScript code"]
       <FRAME
           SRC = "URL"
           NAME = "NameOfFirstFrame"
           [BORDER = pixelSize]
```

```
                [BORDERCOLOR = colorSpecification]>
</FRAMESET>
<BODY
...
[onBlur = "JavaScript code"]
[onFocus = "JavaScript code"]
[onLoad = "JavaScript code"]
[onUnload = "JavaScript code"]>
</BODY>
```

Properties

Property	Value	Gettable	Settable
closed	Boolean	Yes	No
defaultStatus	string	Yes	Yes
document	document object	Yes	No
frames()	array of window objects	Yes	No
history	history object	Yes	No
length	integer	Yes	No
location	location object	Yes	Yes
name	windowName	Yes	No
opener*	window object or null	Yes	No
parent	windowName	Yes	No
self	windowName	Yes	No
status	string	Yes	Yes
top	windowName	Yes	No
window	windowName	Yes	No

Methods

```
alert()
blur()*
clearTimeout()
close()
confirm()
eval()
```

```
focus()*
open()
prompt()
scroll()*
setTimeout()
toString()*
valueOf()*
```

Event Handlers

```
onBlur*
onerror*
onFocus*
onLoad
onUnload
```

Control Structures

```
if (condition) {
   statementsIfTrue
}

if (condition) {
   statementsIfTrue
} else {
   statementsIfFalse
}

variable = condition ? value1 : value2

for ([initial expression]; [condition]; [new expression])
{
   statements
}

for (var in object) {
   statements
}

while (condition) {
   statements
}
```

```
with (object) {
   statements
}
```

Operators

Table C-1 lists the mathematical operators.

Table C-1 Mathematical Operators

Operator	Operation
+	Addition
-	Subtraction
*	Multiplication
/	Division
%	Modulus (return the remainder of a division)

Table C-2 lists the assignment operators.

Table C-2 Assignment Operators

Operator	Operation
=	Equals
+=	Add by value
-=	Subtract by value
*=	Multiply by value
/=	Divide by value
%=	Modulo by value
<<=	Left shift by value
>>=	Right shift by value
>>>=	Zero fill by value

Table C-2 Assignment Operators (Continued)

<table>
<tr><th>Operator</th><th>Operation</th></tr>
<tr><td>&=</td><td>Bitwise AND by value</td></tr>
<tr><td>^=</td><td>Bitwise OR by value</td></tr>
<tr><td>|=</td><td>Bitwise XOR by value</td></tr>
</table>

Table C-3 lists the comparison operators.

Table C-3 Comparison Operators

Operator	Operation
==	Equals
!=	Not equal to
>	Greater than
>=	Greater than or equal to
<	Less than
<=	Less than or equal to

Table C-4 lists the unary operators.

Table C-4 Unary Operators

Operator	Operation
-	Unary negation
~	Bitwise complement
++	Increment
--	Decrement

Table C-5 lists the binary operators.

Table C-5 **Binary Operators**

<table>
<tr><th>Operator</th><th>Operation</th></tr>
<tr><td>&</td><td>Bitwise AND</td></tr>
<tr><td>|</td><td>Bitwise OR</td></tr>
<tr><td>^</td><td>Bitwise XOR</td></tr>
<tr><td><<</td><td>Left shift</td></tr>
<tr><td>>></td><td>Right shift</td></tr>
<tr><td>>>></td><td>Zero fill right shift</td></tr>
</table>

Table C-6 lists the Boolean operators.

Table C-6 **Boolean Operators**

<table>
<tr><th>Operator</th><th>Operation</th></tr>
<tr><td>&&</td><td>AND</td></tr>
<tr><td>||</td><td>OR</td></tr>
<tr><td>!</td><td>NOT</td></tr>
</table>

Table C-7 lists JavaScript operator precedence. 1 is the highest precedence and operators with precedence closest to 1 are evaluated before operators with lower precedence.

Table C-7 **JavaScript Operator Precedence**

Precedence Level	Description	Operator
1	Nested parentheses are evaluated from innermost to outermost.	( )
	Array index value	[ ]
2	Negation and increment	! ~ - ++ --
3	Multiplication, division, modulo	* / %
4	Addition and subtraction	+ -
5	Bitwise shifts	<< >> >>>
6	Comparison operators	< <= > >=
7	Equality	== !=
8	Bitwise XOR	^
9	Bitwise OR	|
10	Logical AND	&&
11	Logical OR	||

Table C-7 JavaScript Operator Precedence (Continued)

<table>
<tr><th>Precedence Level</th><th>Description</th><th>Operator</th></tr>
<tr><td>12</td><td>Conditional expression</td><td>?:</td></tr>
<tr><td>13</td><td>Assignment operators</td><td>=
+=
-+
*=
/=
%=
<<=
>>=
>>>=
&=
^=
|=</td></tr>
<tr><td>14</td><td>comma</td><td>,</td></tr>
</table>

JavaScript Functions and Methods

```
parseInt("string")
parseFloat("string")
object.eval(expression)
taint([object])*
untaint([object])*
isNaN(expression)*
object.toString()*
escape()
unescape()
object.valueOf()*
```

Reserved JavaScript Keywords

Table C-8 lists JavaScript reserved keywords.

Table C-8 Reserved JavaScript Keywords

abstract	else	int	switch
boolean	extends	interface	synchronized
break	false	long	this
byte	final	native	throw
case	finally	new	throws
catch	float	null	transient
char	for	package	true
class	function	private	try
const	goto	protected	typeof
continue	if	public	var
default	implements	return	void
delete	import	short	volatile
do	in	static	while
double	instanceof	super	with

Escape Characters for String Formatting

Table C-9 lists the escape characters for string formatting.

Table C-9 Escape Characters for String Formatting

Escape Sequence	Description	Character/ Abbreviation
`\b`	Backspace	BS
`\t`	Horizontal tab	HT
`\n`	Line feed	LF
`\f`	Form feed	FF
`\r`	Carriage return	CR
`\"`	Double quote	"
`\'`	Single quote	'
`\\`	Backslash	\
`\` *`OctalDigit`*	Octal escape	One of 0 1 2 3 4 5 6 7
`\` *`OctalDigit OctalDigit`*	Octal escape	One of 0 1 2 3 4 5 6 7
`\ ZeroToThree` *`OctalDigit OctalDigit`*	ZeroToThree escape	One of 0 1 2 3
`\` *`xHexDigit HexDigit`*	Hexadecimal escape	One of 0 1 2 3 4 5 6 7 8 9 a b c d e f A B C D E F

HTTP MIME Types

Table C-10 lists commonly used MIME types and the file name suffix that is recognized by most servers.

Table C-10 Commonly Used MIME Types

Type/Subtype	Extension
`application/activemessage`	
`application/andrew-inset`	
`application/applefile`	
`application/atomicmail`	
`application/cals-1840`	
`application/commonground`	
`application/cybercash`	
`application/dca-rft`	
`application/dec-dx`	

Table C-10 Commonly Used MIME Types (Continued)

Type/Subtype	Extension
application/eshop	
application/iges	
application/mac-binhex40	
application/macwriteii	
application/mathematica	
application/msword	
application/news-message-id	
application/news-transmission	
application/octet-stream	bin
application/oda	oda
application/pdf	pdf
application/postscript	ai, eps, ps
application/remote-printing	
application/riscos	
application/rtf	rtf
application/sgml	
application/slate	
application/vnd.framemaker	
application/vnd.koan	
application/vnd.mif	
application/vnd.ms-artgalry	
application/vnd.ms-excel	
application/vnd.ms-powerpoint	
application/vnd.ms-project	
application/vnd.ms-tnef	
application/vnd.ms-works	
application/vnd.music-niff	
application/vnd.svd	
application/vnd.truedoc	
application/wuta	
application/wordperfect5.1	
application/x-bcpio	bcpio
application/x-cpio	cpio

Table C-10 Commonly Used MIME Types (Continued)

Type/Subtype	Extension
application/x-csh	csh
application/x-dvi	dvi
application/x-gtar	gtar
application/x-hdf	hdf
application/x-latex	latex
application/x-mif	mif
application/x-netcdf	nc, cdf
application/x-sh	sh
application/x-shar	shar
application/x-sv4cpio	sv4cpio
application/x-sv4crc	sv4crc
application/x-tar	tar
application/x-tcl	tcl
application/x-tex	tex
application/x-texinfo	texinfo, texi
application/x-troff	t, tr, roff
application/x-troff-man	man
application/x-troff-me	me
application/x-troff-ms	ms
application/x-ustar	ustar
application/x-wais-source	src
application/x400-bp	
application/zip	zip
audio/32kadpcm	
audio/basic	au, snd
audio/x-aiff	aif, aiff, aifc
audio/x-wav	wav
image/cgm	
image/g3fax	
image/gif	gif
image/ief	ief
image/jpeg	jpeg, jpg, jpe
image/naplps	

Table C-10 Commonly Used MIME Types (Continued)

Type/Subtype	Extension
image/tiff	tiff, tif
image/vnd.dwg	
image/vnd.dxf	
image/vnd.svf	
image/x-cmu-raster	ras
image/x-portable-anymap	rpnm
image/x-portable-bitmap	pbm
image/x-portable-graymap	pgm
image/x-portable-pixmal	ppm
image/x-rgb	rgb
image/x-xbitmap	xbm
image/x-xpixmap	xpm
image/x-xwindowdump	xwd
message/external-body	
message/http	
message/news	
message/partial	
message/rfc8222	
multipart/alternative	
multipart/appledouble	
multipart/digest	
multipart/form-data	
multipart/header-set	
multipart/mixed	
multipart/parallel	
multipart/related	
multipart/report	
multipart/voice-message	
text/enriched	
text/html	html, htm
text/plain	txt
text/richtext	rtx
text/sgml	

Table C-10 Commonly Used MIME Types (Continued)

Type/Subtype	Extension
text/tab-separated-values	tsv
text/x-settext	etx
video/mpeg	mpeg, mpg, mpe
video/quicktime	qt, mov
video/vdn.vivo	
video/x-msvideo	qvi
video/x-sgi-movie	movie

Glossary

absolute value The value of a number without its sign. For example, the absolute value of both -47 and +47 is simply 47.

alert window A modal window that displays an information or warning message to users. You create an alert using the `window.alert()` method.

applet A small application written in the Java language that requires a Java-aware browser to execute.

array 1) A collection of individual data items that are organized so that the entire collection can be treated as a single piece of data. Individual elements of the array have similar data types, and may be addressed one by one, or as a group.

2) A list of properties for an object. The properties are listed in numerical order, starting with zero (0). For example, `frame[0]`, `frame[1]`, `frame[2]`.

assign To change the value of an existing variable.

assignment operator A symbol that indicates an action to be performed on one or two values. An assignment operator is one of the following symbols: =, +=, =+, *=, /=, %=, <<=, >>=, >>>=, &=, ^=, or |=. The equal sign is the

most common assignment operator. The equal sign assigns the value on the right side of the equal sign to the variable on the left side of the equal sign.

attribute An HTML structure that sets a particular parameter value for a specific HTML tag. Examples of attributes are the `LANGUAGE` and `SRC` properties that you can assign to the HTML `<SCRIPT>` tag to define the scripting language and identify the location of a JavaScript file that is not embedded in an HTML document.

back-end programs The programs, such as databases, on the server that provide information to CGI scripts.

binary operator An operator that requires two operands, one before the operator and one after it.

blur The action that occurs when the user clicks or moves the pointer away from a window or text object that has focus.

breakpoint A predefined address in a program at which execution is stopped and control is passed to debugging software.

browser An application that downloads HTML files from a Web server and displays the formatted file. Also called a client.

bug Any error in either hardware or software that results in an unexpected result or a computer malfunction.

built-in object An object that the JavaScript language automatically creates that corresponds to HTML definitions for window, document, frame, and form elements. Each built-in object has its own predefined set of properties, methods, and event handlers.

call A programming term that represents a temporary branch in a script to use a different routine, such as a function. After the routine is executed, the main script continues at the next instruction.

CGI script Common gateway interface scripts that are used to process data and interface with databases on a Web server.

change The event that occurs when the user makes any alteration to the contents of a text field and then either tabs or clicks away from the field to blur the focus.

.class files The standard suffix for compiled binary files for a Java applet.

click The action that occurs when users move the mouse pointer onto a button and press and release the mouse button.

click-to-type To set the insert point by a mouse click in an area of the screen that accepts keyboard input.

client-server model The arrangement of computers on the World Wide Web in which some computers (the clients) receive data and information from another computer (the server) that handles requests for information and locates the files.

code The complete set of statements that make up a script.

comments Any annotation in a script that is marked with special characters either at the beginning of a line or at the beginning and end of the annotation. The interpreter skips over any characters marked as comments.

compiled code Any script or program that must be checked and verified by a compiler before it can be run.

concatenate To combine two or more similar elements, such as character strings, to form a new, larger element.

confirmation window A message to users displayed in a transitory window that blocks any user input to the application. Users must click on a button in the confirmation window to dismiss it. You create a confirmation message with the `window.confirm()` method.

cookie An entry in a text file called `cookies.txt` (Windows and UNIX platforms) or `MagicCookie` (Macintosh) that is located in the Netscape directory. Typically, this file is used by server-side CGI scripts to store information on the client computer. The JavaScript language can only read to or write from the browser's cookie file.

data The information that you use as part of a script. Data can also be referred to as a value.

data tainting A security mechanism that marks, or taints, any property values or data that should be secure and private.

data type The numerical, string, boolean, or null type assigned to a piece of data.

declare a variable To assign an identifier to a variable and assign an initial value to it.

debug To diagnose and fix software and hardware problems.

dense array An array with a fixed set of values that you define as parameters to the `Array()` constructor.

device-independent language A language that does not need to be compiled to run on a specific hardware platform. Java is a device-independent language.

disk cache A memory buffer area that contains a large block of information read from or to be written to the disk.

domain A directory structure used for network and e-mail naming. Within the United States, top-level Internet domains include `com` for commercial organizations, `edu` for educational organizations, `gov` for government, `mil` for the military, `net` for networking organizations, and `org` for other organizations. Outside of the United States, top-level Internet domains designate the country. Subdomains designate the organization and the individual system.

dynamically typed language A programming language in which you do not need to specify the type of data when you declare a variable. Instead, the data type is determined at runtime and depends on its context.

e-mail Electronic mail.

escape a character To put a backslash (\) in front of a special character such as a quotation mark (") so that the character is displayed as a part of the output of a script.

escape sequence A backslash (\) and the character that follows it.

event A specific user action, such as `Click` or `MouseOver`, that is recognized by the JavaScript language.

event handler A JavaScript function that responds to a specific event such as a mouse click in a certain location.

expression A combination of variables, literals, functions, objects, and operators that evaluates to a single value.

extension The set of characters following the period at the end of the file name that specify the file type.

focus The event that occurs when the user clicks or moves the pointer in a text object or highlights text. Only one text object can have focus at a time. In the Navigator 3.0 release, focus has been extended to apply to a window or frame.

frame A subwindow within a browser window.

ftp A file transfer protocol used to transfer text or binary files from one computer to another over a network.

function A self-contained script or portion of a script designed to do a specific task and, optionally, to return a value.

gettable A JavaScript property that can be obtained.

gopher A file transfer protocol used to transfer text or binary files from one computer to another over a network. The name originated because you ask the program to "go for" it. Not to be confused with the common garden pest that eats your plants from below ground.

helper application An application that can display special formats; opened when the user clicks on an item in the browser that contains special formatting. Although the helper application is started from a browser, it is not integrated into the browser.

history The list of URL sites a user has visited during the current session.

HTML Hypertext Markup Language is the platform-independent hypermedia markup language used by the World Wide Web.

http Hypertext transfer protocol is used to transfer HTML files over the Internet.

HTTP media types A way to designate the type of attachment for the `http` protocol. HTTP media types are closely related to MIME types, and the terms are frequently used interchangeably.

identifier The name you assign to a variable, function, or object.

initialize To assign a value to a variable or object at the time you declare it.

instance A specific object that is created from HTML code by the browser at runtime.

Internet A network of networks that enables individuals on a computer on one network to share information with individuals on another network that may be right next door or halfway around the world.

interpreted code Any script or program that is read line-by-line at the time it is run.

Java Developer's Kit (JDK) The collection of utilities and libraries available free from Sun Microsystems, Inc. that enable you to compile Java source code, view applets, and understand the Java API.

.java files The standard suffix for source code files for Java applets.

keyword Any of the terms reserved for a special purpose in the JavaScript language. You cannot use keywords as variable names.

layout The way the interpreter transforms the HTML tags and values into a graphical display on your computer screen.

literal An actual numeric, string, Boolean, or null value; for example 76 or "trombones". You must enclose string literals in single or double quotes.

LiveConnect A scripting language that provides two-way communications between JavaScript scripts and Java applets or plug-ins.

loop An iterative script mechanism that repeats a sequence of instructions until a predetermined condition is satisfied.

mathematical operators The +, -, *, /, and % symbols that you use to perform the addition, subtraction, multiplication, division, and modulus mathematical operations in a script.

method An attribute of an object that instructs the object to perform specific tasks. A method is a function that is attached to an object.

MIME types An acronym for multipurpose Internet mail extensions. MIME defines the format of the contents of Internet mail messages and provides a way to include both text and attachments in message bodies.

modal window A transitory window that displays a message to users and blocks any other input to the application. Users cannot perform any other activities in the application until they click on the OK button to close the modal window. See also **alert window, confirmation window**, and **prompt window**.

move pointer To set the insert point by moving the pointer into an area of the screen that accepts keyboard input.

nested statements A set of statements that include one or more additional statements. For example, you can use nested `if ... else` statements to handle complex decision processes.

network A group of computers that are connected electronically so that they can share information with one another.

object A special kind of a variable that provides a way to organize and present data, specify attributes, and provide methods for performing specific tasks.

object-based A programming lnaguage that uses the concepts of objects, methods, and events but does not provide all of the complexity of a true object-oriented programming style.

object-oriented A programming style in which programs are organized as cooperative collections of objects, each of which represents an instance of some class, and whose classes are all members of a hierarchy of classes that are united by inheritance relationships.

operand The variable values that operators act on.

operator A symbol that indicates an action to be performed on one or two values. You can have mathematical operators (addition, subtraction, multiplication, division), logical operators (and, or, and not) and relational operators (equals, less than, and greater than).

operator precedence The hierarchy assigned to JavaScript operators that determine the sequence in which expressions are evaluated.

parse To analyze a series of words and statements to determine their collective meaning.

pass To send data or values to a function or applet.

Perl The scripting language that is used to write most CGI scripts.

pixel A single dot on a display screen. Pixel is a contraction for picture element.

plug-in A helper application that enhances and expands the capability of another application.

precedence The sequence that determines which operators precede, or come before, which other operators when an expression is evaluated.

programming style The specific way you choose to format your scripting code so that it is easy for a person (as opposed to the computer) to read and interpret.

prompt window A modal window that you use to enable users to provide typed input in response to a question.

property A variable of an object. An object has a set of related variables known as properties, and each property is a variable or a function. You refer to a property by using the syntax *`object.property`*, for example, `document.bgColor`.

protocol A formal set of conventions that define the format and control of input and output between devices and programs. Common protocols are TCP/IP, ftp, gopher, http, and e-mail.

radian A unit of plane angular measurement that is equal to the angle at the center of a circle subtended by an arc equal in length to the radius. All trigonometric methods of the `Math` object take arguments in radians.

radix The value of the base number in a numbering system. In the decimal system, the radix is 10; in the binary system, the radix is 2; in the octal system, the radix is 8; in the hexadecimal system, the radix is 16.

reserved word See keyword.

return a value A value retrieved from memory. When you assign a value to a variable, the value is stored in computer memory. When the script asks for the value for a particular variable, the value is retrieved from memory.

root directory The directory at the very top of the file system hierarchy; represented by a slash (/).

route-independent address An e-mail address that uses domain information to locate the recipient without needing to know the specific route that the message takes.

runtime system A system that provides basic language services to a device-independent language that enables the language to run on specific hardware platforms.

<SCRIPT></SCRIPT> tags The HTML tags that you use to define the beginning and end of a portion of JavaScript code.

select The event that occurs when a user highlights text by pressing the mouse button, dragging the pointer, and then releasing the mouse button.

servlet An applet that is sent to the server from the client.

settable A JavaScript property that can be changed.

SMTP Simple mail transport protocol is the most common e-mail protocol used in open systems today.

statement A single unit of programming code that defines and controls the flow of the program.

status bar The region at the bottom of the browser window where you can display `status` and `defaultStatus` messages.

string A series of alphanumeric characters enclosed in quotation marks.

string concatenation operator The plus sign (+) that you can use to combine separate strings to form longer phrases.

strongly typed language A programming language in which variables are assigned a specific data type.

substring A contiguous part of a string contained within another string.

syntax The correct way of writing a statement.

system object An object provided by the JavaScript language that is not created automatically by an HTML tag definition and is not part of the object hierarchy. `Array`, `Date`, `Math`, and `String` are system objects.

tail matching The way a cookie domain is matched — starting from the end of the fully-qualified domain name of the host and working backward.

taint accumulator The mechanism that keeps a record of taint values for each individual window.

taint code The unique mark that is applied to a copy of data that is marked as tainted.

template A structured model to use to determine where to locate pieces of JavaScript code within an HTML file.

timeout JavaScript `window` object methods that enable you to delay the evaluation of an expression for a specific period of time.

transparent Any application or process that is started automatically so that no user action is required. Another use for this term is to describe a system that passes through all data exactly as it is received.

unary operator An operator that requires a single operand, which can be either before or after the operator.

universal coordinated time UTC is the specified date represented as an integer that represents number of milliseconds since midnight Greenwich mean time (GMT) on January 1, 1970, and the specified date.

value Data, either numeric or alphanumeric.

variable An identifier that you use to name specific data elements that you plan to use in a script. The contents of a variable are stored in computer memory during the execution of a script.

Web client The recipient of downloaded information from a server.

Web server A device that is dedicated to serving other nodes attached to the network. Also, an application that enables HTML files to be linked across the network.

white space The spaces, tabs, form feeds, and new lines between characters in a script.

World Wide Web The part of the Internet that uses the http protocol to deliver information. Abbreviated as WWW or the Web. Some anonymous pundit claims that the acronym WWW actually stands for world wide wait.

INDEX

Numerics

A

B

C

D

1151

E

F

1153

1155

K

L

M

N

1161

P

1165

1167

T

1169

U

V